Joseph Foster

Members of Parliament, Scotland, including the minor barons, the

commissioners for the shires, and the commissioners for the burghs,

1357-1882. On the basis of the parliamentary return 1880, with

genealogical and biographical notices

Joseph Foster

Members of Parliament, Scotland, including the minor barons, the commissioners for the shires, and the commissioners for the burghs, 1357-1882. On the basis of the parliamentary return 1880, with genealogical and biographical notices

ISBN/EAN: 9783743346178

Manufactured in Europe, USA, Canada, Australia, Japa

Cover: Foto ©ninafisch / pixelio.de

Manufactured and distributed by brebook publishing software (www.brebook.com)

Joseph Foster

**Members of Parliament, Scotland, including the minor barons, the
commissioners for the shires, and the commissioners for the burghs,
1357-1882. On the basis of the parliamentary return 1880, with
genealogical and biographical notices**

CONTENTS.

PREFACE.

A N historical list of Members of Parliament, alphabetically arranged and systematically annotated, will at once be admitted by all biographers to supply a want that has long been felt, and to deserve a place of the highest rank among the working tools of the historian, the genealogical student, and the journalist. But, dealing as it does with a subject of such widespread and commanding interest, I may naturally expect that it will be widely appreciated beyond the sphere of professional writers, and that it will be valued by the members of every family whose name is to be found in its pages, as being practically the only available record of the parliamentary service of their ancestry and their kindred. Of this work, which I have undertaken to produce, with the assistance of eminent literary friends, the present volume is the first instalment.

It is to be regretted that the errors which so glaringly disfigure the official return of the Irish members, as has been shown (in my *Collectanea*) by Mr. Beaven, have compelled me to postpone for the present that section—in the hope that Government may feel bound to issue a somewhat more correct edition—for the Scottish members are in some respects so unsatisfactory to deal with as to form the least favourable commencement of the series. Scanty, indeed, is the information to be gleaned from the printed works that exist on Scottish genealogy and topography, and its gist has too often to be tediously sought, buried like a kernel in the imposing mass of a crabbed and wordy document. True, there is Wood's

Peerage by Douglas; but I fear I am unaware of any similar work dealing exclusively with Scottish genealogy which is worthy to be classed in the same rank. This is the more remarkable when we remember the advantage enjoyed by genealogists beyond the border in having easy access to the varied and voluminous records of the General Register at Edinburgh. I must, however, always except the Record publications now in progress, *e.g.* the Great Seal Register, the Privy Council Register, the Exchequer Rolls, etc.; but as these principally refer to the fifteenth century, they can only throw light on a small portion of the period embraced in this work. Those great Club Societies, the Roxburgh, the Bannatyne, and the Maitland, who might have edited and printed so much valuable material, have practically missed their mark by catering for the powerful few instead of the majority of the nation. How much more might have been achieved by the publication, on some definite plan, of Wills, Charters, Registers, etc., and, better even than Parish Registers, now-a-days so much the fashion, would be the more important and exclusive yet comprehensive National Registers of the Students of the Learned Professions; and perhaps the various Guild Registers of the kingdom would prove of even greater value. Such work, when once done, would indeed be to genealogists "a joy for ever."

It is partly on this account that I have to acknowledge a greater preponderance of un-identified names in this portion of the work than will occur in those embracing the English and Irish members. But this is also a natural result of the Scottish surnames being comparatively so few. A mere enumeration of the numbers bearing the same surnames would give but a faint idea of the confusion and perplexity involved, as most of them sat in several Parliaments, and often for different districts. Thus, there are not only more than eighty Campbells and more than ninety Stewarts, but there are three or four times as many separate entries of these names, all requiring to be assorted! As if to increase the difficulties inseparable from such a task as this, identification is rendered additionally troublesome, not only by the different territorial or local designations assigned to the same person, but also by the varying combinations (and therefore designations) of the burgh districts. As this peculiarity has evidently proved a source of confusion to former writers, I have printed these districts in detail on p. xvi.

But while entitled to claim, on these weighty grounds, a lenient judgment on the performance of my task, it is gratifying to add that, with the help of my coadjutors, my efforts have in the main been crowned with success. I have already stated that our subject has a widespread and commanding interest, and that, not only because parliamentary service has been the stepping-stone to power and honour for so many of our noble houses, but also because a seat in the House of Commons is the legitimate aspiration of all classes of men, and specially of those whose energy and ability have raised them in the social scale. These will here find their names recorded side by side with those of our historic governing families, enrolled alike in the great Walhalla of the Parliaments of the British Empire.

Nor will the general public fail to discover in these pages names which appeal to all lovers of their country. Here will be found the hero of Corunna, and Abercromby the hero of Aboukir Bay. Here, too, is the gallant Graham, driven by grief to a martial career which led to victory and a peerage, and Simon Fraser, the loyal chieftain, who fought and bled for England to atone for the treason of his house. Here, among authors, are Hume and Macaulay; among Premiers, are Melbourne (Lamb) and Gladstone. Here is the sorely tried Melville, a scion of Dundas of Arniston; and here is Monmouth's evil genius, the fanatical Fletcher of Saltoun.

There are two features which in a marked degree have characterized political life north of the Tweed. The first is the persistence of certain families, where in England there is a continuous rise and fall. The second is the tradition of hereditary feuds, the struggles of rival clans and families, which, even though unconsciously, are perpetuated to this day at the poll. Of the former there will be found some striking instances in the chart pedigrees I have inserted in the text. Thus, the houses of Elliot (Earl of Minto), Grant (Earl of Seafield), Hope, and Anstruther, can actually boast an unbroken descent of seven generations in Parliament, Campbell of Calder (Lord Cawdor), Dundas of Arniston (Lord Melville), and Erskine (Earl of Rosslyn), show six generations, while Dundas (Earl of Zetland), and Foulis, each exhibit five. And as the governing families continued, so also did their politics and their feuds. The Cavaliers who voted in " the drunken parliament " were the sons of the men who had ridden with Montrose, the fathers of the men who rode with Dundee, and whose sons and grandsons, in turn, were ruined in the cause of the Pretender. The Campbells who voted for their chieftain's son at the election of 1878 (p. 50) were the descendants of the men who, centuries before, had followed to the field the " Bourbons of the Highlands " at the fiery cross of the McAllum More.

Scotland has ever had her Montagues and her Capulets. To select from our pages one instance out of many, the representation of Roxburghshire was shared, in the days before the Civil Wars, by the houses of Elliot and of Douglas. In the following century a Douglas sat from 1700 till he was ousted by an Elliot in 1708, who in his turn gave way to a Douglas in 1715. In our own day a Douglas was returned in 1874, but was ousted by an Elliot in 1880 (p. 122). Thus has the unending contest been carried on from generation to generation.

The names of members and other parliamentary information derived from the return are kept totally distinct from the annotations, and appear in a larger and different kind of type.

It is hoped, as this part will be found reliable, that it will prove of considerable value to the historian ; I have also incorporated the members of the Cromwellian parliaments as given in Willis's *Notitia Parliamentaria.* The chart pedigrees, eighty in number, will be of considerable interest to their representatives, and of valuable assistance to the historian, for they exhibit at a glance the parliamentary repre-

[viii]

sentation of the great governing families. It may be as well to repeat that in 1590 the minor barons or lairds reappear in Parliament, and continue to be variously styled small barons, commissioners for the small barons, and commissioners for shires, and also that this latter designation was continued until the Union, prior to which event the representatives of the burghs were styled commissioners for the burghs. These various designations, which are cumbersome and of no very great consequence to the general reader, have not been retained—doubtless the pedant will charge me with perpetrating an anachronism—the parliamentary return has, however, been adhered to in the case of the minor barons, and all persons appear here as M.P.'s, in the same sense in which they appear in the return.

The annotations, which are principally taken from my own Peerage and Baronetage, are chiefly intended to serve as a means of ready identification for the general reader. I am indebted for some valuable information—always most cordially given me—to Thomas Dickson, esq., Curator of the Historical Department, General Register-house, Edinburgh, the responsible compiler of the Scottish parliamentary return, and I am equally grateful to J. T. Clark, esq., of Edinburgh, Advocate's librarian, for the trouble he has taken in supplying me with dates of admissions of advocates and other particulars from his own collections, which have often been of the greatest importance in assisting to identify some of the less prominent individuals.

In marked contrast to the cordial co-operation of these gentlemen is the churlish reception of my work by the Lyon Clerk Depute, whose time and labour have been freely expended, not in assisting me with the information which his post places within his reach, but in hunting for the blemishes incidental to such a work, and in making the most of them when discovered ; they have been corrected in this edition. It is inevitable that I should occasionally be led into error by following the recognised Scottish Authorities, as the verification of every extract would more than exhaust the energies of a lifetime. I have studiously

b

continued the exposure of the sham Scottish baronetcies, and this it would seem is a cause of offence, though it might have been removed long ago, had the details necessary to substantiate each discredited descent been publicly forthcoming. No one who knows anything of the nature of Scottish genealogical services, and the often consequent confirmation of arms or grant of supporters, will accept such quaint proceedings as even negative proof, unless the evidences on which these acts are founded can be and are supplied. I shall probably soon have occasion to return to this subject elsewhere.

I have been enabled in almost every instance to detect and correct the few important errors which exist in the parliamentary return on which this work is founded—at any rate those which occur since the Union—a list of them will be found at page xvii. For this singular advantage I am indebted to the Rev. A. B. Beaven, M.A., who, together with Thomas J. Hercy, esq., of Cruchfield, and Mr. W. D. Pink of Leigh, has also revised the whole of the proof-sheets. I am under the greatest obligation to these gentlemen for their valuable additions and important corrections, without which I should have lacked much of the confidence I now possess in this compilation.

It may cause surprise that this particular volume has been compiled by Englishmen, and not, as would seem more natural, by Scotchmen, who might be supposed to be more conversant with the history of their parliamentary representatives. Indeed, it has prac-tically been suggested that this section of the work should have been omitted sooner than that it should have been attempted by myself. If this principle were logically applied, no Peerage compiled by an Englishman would be allowed to contain the Scottish honours, even though as in the present case no Scotsman were found to record them! My object in this compilation has been also to render my Peerage more complete in this particular. I deem myself, however, most fortunate in securing the co-operation of the gentlemen I have named, and I much doubt, from the scarcity of such literature to which I have already alluded, whether an editorial quartett could be found on the other side of the Tweed, not only able, but also willing to assist *con amore* in the production of a work of so un-remunerative though valuable a character as this, which, even if it repay the cost of printing, can never in all probability repay the cost of labour, and may therefore claim, with justice, to be a present to the Scottish people.

"The compilation of an Index," it has been truly observed, "is one of those useful labours for which the public, commonly better pleased with entertainment than with real service, are rarely so forward to express their gratitude as we think they ought to be. It has been considered as a task fit only for the plodding and the dull; but with more truth it may be said that this is the judgment of the idle and the shallow." It is easy to sneer at a work compiled by "scissors and paste;" but it has avowedly from the first been my object in *Collectanea*—from which this work is reprinted, with additions and corrections—not to add to the mass of "unindexed raw material," but to render that which already exists available for my fellow genealogists. Nor is it the least object that will be gained by the publication of this annotated list, that any student interested in the subject will be henceforth spared the tedious drudgery of the necessary preliminary research, and can at his leisure, by reference to Wills and Charters, elucidate further still this branch of the history of his nation.

JOSEPH FOSTER.

21, *Boundary Road, London, N.W.,*
1 *June,* 1882.

PARLIAMENTS AND CONVENTIONS OF THE ESTATES OF SCOTLAND.

REPRINTED FROM THE PARLIAMENTARY RETURN.

IN the Parliament of Scotland the Estates sat and voted together as one Chamber. There was no division into an Upper and Lower House. The following Return, therefore, contains only the names and dates of election, so far as they can be ascertained, of the elected or representative Members of the Parliaments of Scotland, with the names of the shires or burghs for which they were respectively returned.

The beginnings of Parliamentary representation in Scotland are associated with the rise of the burgesses into political importance, as the Third Estate of the realm, in the early part of the fourteenth century. Their presence in the Great Council of the nation is first clearly ascertained on the occasion of the Parliament held at Cambuskenneth, 15th July 1326, when the earls, barons, burgesses, and freeholders, in full Parliament assembled, granted to King Robert Bruce, in consideration of his great services, and for the due support of the Royal dignity, the tenth penny of all rents and profits of lands, estimated according to the old extent or valuation of King Alexander III.; the King conceding in return the important constitutional limitation that no tax or impost should be levied by the Crown without the consent of the Parliament. It has generally been supposed that thenceforward the burgesses appeared by their Commissioners in every Parliament; but this does not admit of being satisfactorily determined, inasmuch as no sederunts or rolls of Members have been preserved of the many Parliaments which assembled between that date and the middle of the following century.

Only a very few lists of Commissioners for Burghs are extant of earlier date than the beginning of the sixteenth century. Before that time the records contain the names of those only who, at the beginning of each Session, were elected Members of the committees on which great part of the business of the Parliament was devolved—the Committee of Articles [*Domini ad articulos inquirendos*], by which all measures were discussed and prepared for receiving legislative sanction; and the Judicial Committee for hearing of causes and appeals *Domini auditores ad causas et querelas audiendas et ad judicia contradicta*], which,

[xiii]

co-ordinately with the Lords of Council, discharged the functions of a supreme civil tribunal till the institution, in 1532, of a permanent high court of judicature, under the name of the Court of Session.

By the small barons and freeholders, who were regarded as of the same estate with the greater barons, the feudal obligation to give suit and presence in the King's High Court of Parliament was always felt to be a burden; and as early as the time of James I., in 1427, an Act was passed for their relief, granting them authority to elect representatives. This statute, however, remained inoperative. In 1457 and 1503 Acts were passed for relief of the more inconsiderable of the freeholders, granting exemption, except when specially summoned, to those of them whose holdings were below a specified value. In 1567 there was renewed legislation on the subject of the election of Commissioners, but it was not till 1587 that the representation of the shires was actually established. It was then ordained "that the Commissioners of all the Sheriffdoms be elected at the first head court after Michaelmas yearly;" that they be "authorised with sufficient commissions, sealed and subscribed by six at least of the barons and freeholders" of the shire; and that "the compearance of the said Commissioners of the shires in Parliaments, or General Councils, shall relieve the whole remanent small barons and freeholders of the shires of the suit and presence due in the said Parliaments." From that time onwards the Commissioners for the shires are found in the roll of every Parliament.

Besides the Parliaments, Conventions of the Estates were frequently called together for the despatch of urgent business. At first they consisted of the Privy Council, with a few additional Members specially summoned, and their sittings rarely exceeded one or two days. In 1567 it was enacted that Provosts of Burghs, or Commissioners for Burghs, should be present in every Convention, and especially when taxation was to be imposed. This was, for a time, very imperfectly observed; but, gradually, the representation of the burghs became more regular, and the representation of the shires being established towards the close of the sixteenth century, the composition of the Convention of Estates became at length substantially identical with that of the Parliament. The Convention which met 14th March 1689 was turned into a Parliament, without re-election of Members. The Conventions have therefore been included in this Return.

PEDIGREES OF THE GOVERNING FAMILIES.

DISTRICTS OF BURGHS—SCOTLAND,

1707—1832.

ABERDEEN DISTRICT . . Aberdeen, Montrose, Brechin, Arbroath, Bervie.
ANSTRUTHER EASTER DISTRICT Anstruther Easter, Pittenweem, Craill, Anstruther Wester, Kilrenny.
AYR DISTRICT . . . . Ayr, Irvine, Rothesay, Inverary, Campbeltown.
DUMFRIES DISTRICT . . Dumfries, Kirkcudbright, Annan, Lochmaben, Sanquhar.
DYSART DISTRICT . . Dysart, Kirkcaldy, Burntisland, Kinghorn.
ELGIN DISTRICT . . . Elgin, Banff, Cullen, Kintore, Inverury.
GLASGOW DISTRICT . . . Glasgow, Dumbarton, Renfrew, Rutherglen.
HADDINGTON DISTRICT. . Haddington, Jedburgh, Dunbar, N. Berwick, Lauder.
INVERNESS DISTRICT . . Inverness, Nairn, Forres, Fortrose.
LINLITHGOW DISTRICT . . Linlithgow, Selkirk, Lanark, Peebles.
PERTH DISTRICT . . . Perth, Dundee, St. Andrews, Cupar, Forfar.
STIRLING DISTRICT . . Stirling, Inverkeithing, Dunfermline, Culross, Queensferry.
TAIN DISTRICT . . . Tain, Dingwall, Dornoch, Wick, Kirkwall.
WIGTOWN DISTRICT . . Wigtown, Whithorn, New Galloway, Stranraer.

Since 1832.

AYR DISTRICT . . . . Ayr, Irvine, Campbelltown, Inverary, Oban.
BORDER BURGHS . . . See Hawick.
DUMFRIES DISTRICT . . Dumfries, Sanquhar, Annan, Lochmaben, Kirkcudbright.
ELGIN DISTRICT . . . Elgin, Cullen, Banff, Inverury, Kintore, Peterhead.
FALKIRK DISTRICT . . . Linlithgow, Lanark, Falkirk, Airdrie, Hamilton.
HADDINGTON DISTRICT. . Haddington, Dunbar, North Berwick, Lauder, Jedburgh.
HAWICK OR BORDER BURGHS . Hawick, Galashiels, Selkirk.
INVERNESS DISTRICT . . Fortrose, Inverness, Nairn, Forres.
KILMARNOCK DISTRICT . . Renfrew, Rutherglen, Dumbarton, Kilmarnock, Port Glasgow.
KIRKCALDY DISTRICT . . Dysart, Kirkcaldy, Kinghorn, Burntisland.
LEITH DISTRICT . . . Leith, Portobello, Musselburgh.
MONTROSE DISTRICT . . Inverbervie, Montrose, Aberbrothock, Brechin, Forfar.
ST. ANDREWS DISTRICT . . Anstruther East, Anstruther West, Craill, Cupar, Kilrenny, Pittenweem, St. Andrews.
STIRLING DISTRICT . Inverkeithing, Dunfermline, Queensferry, Culross, Stirling.
WICK DISTRICT . . Kirkwall, Wick, Dornock, Dingwall, Tain, Cromarty.
WIGTOWN DISTRICT . Wigtown, New Galloway, Stranraer, Whithorn.

PRINCIPAL CORRECTIONS

OF THE

PARLIAMENTARY RETURN SINCE THE UNION.

By Rev. A. B. BEAVAN.

1707. Page 8. Ross of Kilravock, *read Rose* of Kilravock.

1708. ,, 17. PERTHSHIRE—*omitted*, Lord James Murray, of Dowallie, March 1708-9, *vice* Dugald [Stewart (appointed a lord of session).

Ross-shire—Lieut. Charles Ross, *read Lieut.-Genl.* Charles Ross.

Orkney and Shetland—Lord Alexander Douglas, *omit Lord.*

1713. ,, 35. Aberdeen—Sir Andrew Cumming, knt., *read Sir Alexander Cumming,* bart.

1714-15. ,, 49. Orkney and Shetland—Sir James Moodie, *omit sir.*

Wigtown—Sir Patrick Vanse, knt., *omit sir* and *knt.*

1722. ,, 60. Roxburgh—Sir Gilbert Elliot, bart., of Stobs, re-elected, etc., *read* Sir Gilbert [Eliott, bart., of Stobs, *vice* Sir Gilbert Elliot, of Minto, appointed a lord of session.

1727. ,, 70. Aberdeen—For 13 July 1731, *read* 3 July 1732.

Sir A. Grant was not expelled the house until 5 May 1732, and the new writ was issued [22nd same month.

1731. ,, 71. Orkney and Shetland—Sir Robert Douglas, of St. Olla, knt., *omit sir* and *knt.*

1747. ,, 107. Caithness-shire—*read* Dornoch, Tain, Dingwall, Wick, Kirkwall, district of [burghs—Sir H. Monro.

1754. ,, 122. Nairn, Fortrose, etc.—James Campbell, *read John.*

1768. ,, 148. Kinross-shire—Robert Adams, *read Adam.*

1780. ,, 174. Footnote—Robert Backie, *read Baikie.*

1784. ,, 185. Banffshire—Sir James Duff, bart., *omit bart.*

1790. ,, 190. Berwickshire—Patrick Thorne, *read Patrick Home.*

1796. ,, 211. Edinburghshire—Robert Dundas, esq., of Melville, re-elected after appointment as chief baron, etc., *read* Robert Dundas, esq., of Melville, *vice Robert Dundas,* [*of Arniston,* appointed chief baron, etc.

1796. ,, 212. Forfarshire—Sir James Carnegie, bart., *read Sir David Carnegie.*

1818. ,, 281. Linlithgowshire—Sir Alexander Hope, K.C.B., *read G.C.B.*

1833. ,, 349. Stirlingshire—Vice-Adl. Charles Fleming, *read Fleeming.*

1841. ,, 392. Forfarshire—John F. Gordon, etc., G.C.B., *read G.C.H.*

1857. ,, 441.⎫ Haddington—F. W. Charteris, esq., *add,* commonly called Lord Elcho.
1859. ,, 458.⎭

1592. page 540, 1596 conv., page 543, and 1597 conv., page 544. The laid of Pitarrow (Carnegie), *read* [the laird of Pitarrow, Wishart.

1643 conv., page 562. Anstruther Wester—Norman Farson (Sess I.), *read* Norman Fairfull—this [on the authority of the Lyon clerk depute.

ADDENDA.

The identification of the following names from WILLIS' NOTITIA PARLIAMENTARIA *were unfortunately omitted from the alphabetical list:—*

Argyll.

Archibald, Marquis of —— *co. Aberdeen,* 1658-9.

Archibald, 8th earl (on the death of his father, Archibald, 7th earl, 1638), created Marquis of Argyll by patent 15 Nov. 1641, was chiefly instrumental in bringing over Charles II. to Scotland in June 1650, and at the king's coronation at Scone, 1 Jan. 1650-1, placed the crown on his majesty's head. On 8 July 1660 he was committed to the Tower by the king's orders, where he remained until December, when he was sent to Edinburgh Castle by sea; was tried for "compliance with the usurpation," found guilty of high treason, and sentenced on the 25th May that he should be beheaded at the Cross of Edinburgh on Monday the 27th. After the sentence was pronounced he said, " I had the honour to set the crown upon the king's head, and now he hastens me to a better crown than his own." Buried at Kilmun. By his wife Margaret, dau. of William Douglas, 2nd Earl of Morton, he had 2 daus. and 3 sons, of whom [the eldest, Archibald, 9th earl, who also was executed 30 June 1685.

Barclay.

David (col.) —— *Forfar and Kincardine* 1654-5, 1656-8.

Of Urie by purchase 1647-8, major in the Swedish service, served with distinction under Gustavus Adolphus, col. in the civil war, governor of Strathbogie Castle, turned cavalier 1666, and suffered imprisonment (son of David Barclay, of Mathers, by Elizabeth, dau. of Sir John Livingstone, of Dunipare); buried at Urie 12 Oct. 1686, aged 76; he m. 26 Jan. 1648 (contract 24 Dec. 1647) Katherine, dau. of Sir Robert Gordon, of Gordonstoun; she d. Mar. [1663, having had with other issue Robert, the author of the " Apology."

Okey.

John (col.) —— *Linlithgow, Queensferry, &c.* 1654-5 (WILLIS). See also M.P. [England.

The well-known regicide; M.P. Bedford 1658-9; executed at Tyburn 19 April 1662.

Duff.

Robert William, of Fetteresso, etc. —— *Banffshire.* See page 107.

A junior lord of the treasury, June 1882.

[xviii]

MEMBERS OF PARLIAMENT—SCOTLAND.

Abercromby ——, see also Duff.

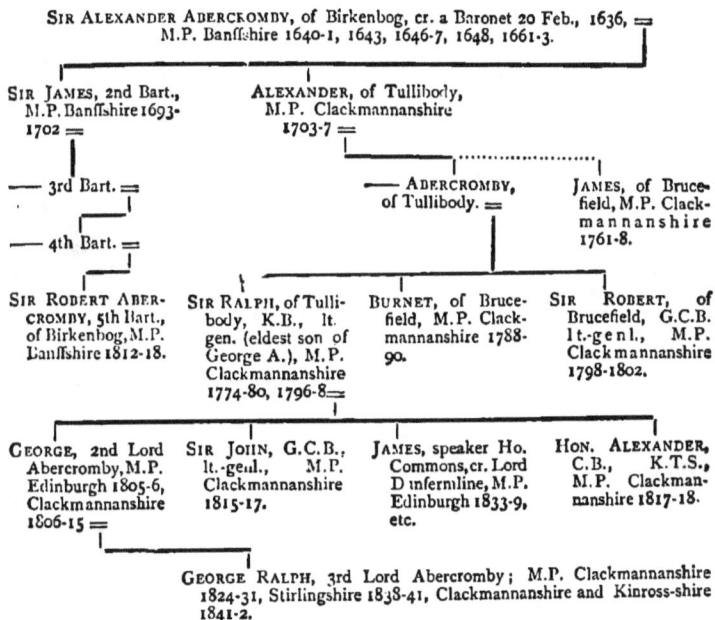

SIR ALEXANDER ABERCROMBY, of Birkenbog, cr. a Baronet 20 Feb., 1636, ⚌
M.P. Banffshire 1640-1, 1643, 1646-7, 1648, 1661-3.

SIR JAMES, 2nd Bart., M.P. Banffshire 1693-1702 ⚌	ALEXANDER, of Tullibody, M.P. Clackmannanshire 1703-7 ⚌

—— 3rd Bart. ⚌

—— 4th Bart. ⚌	—— ABERCROMBY, of Tullibody. ⚌	JAMES, of Bruce-field, M.P. Clackmannanshire 1761-8.

SIR ROBERT ABER-CROMBY, 5th Bart., of Birkenbog, M.P. Banffshire 1812-18.	SIR RALPH, of Tulli-body, K.B., lt.-gen. (eldest son of George A.), M.P. Clackmannanshire 1774-80, 1796-8⚌	BURNET, of Bruce-field, M.P. Clack-mannanshire 1788-90.	SIR ROBERT, of Brucefield, G.C.B. lt.-genl., M.P. Clackmannanshire 1798-1802.

GEORGE, 2nd Lord Abercromby, M.P. Edinburgh 1805-6, Clackmannanshire 1806-15 ⚌	SIR JOHN, G.C.B., lt.-genl., M.P. Clackmannanshire 1815-17.	JAMES, speaker Ho. Commons, cr. Lord Dunfermline, M.P. Edinburgh 1833-9, etc.	HON. ALEXANDER, C.B., K.T.S., M.P. Clackman-nanshire 1817-18.

GEORGE RALPH, 3rd Lord Abercromby; M.P. Clackmannanshire 1824-31, Stirlingshire 1838-41, Clackmannanshire and Kinross-shire 1841-2.

Alexander (sir), of Birkenbog —— *Banffshire* 1640-1 (then younger); 1643 [conv.; 1646-7 & 1648 (as the laird of Birkenbog), 1661-3.
Son of Alexander Abercromby, grand falconer in Scotland to Charles I., was created a Baronet of Nova Scotia 20 Feb. 1636, by his 3rd wife, Elizabeth, dau. of Sir James Baird, of Auchmedden, Knt. (see Foster's Baronetage); he was father of Sir James and Alexander,
[mentioned below.

Abercromby.

Alexander, of Glasshaugh —— *Banffshire* 1706-7 ; 1707-8 (first parlt. of Great [Britain) ; *Banffshire* 1708-10, 1710-13, 1713-15, 1715-22, 1722-7. Died 6 Jan. or 7 May 1729, see Historical Register 1729, pp. 6, 31.

Alexander (Mr.), of Tullibody, advocate —— *Clackmannanshire* 1703-7

>2nd son of Sir Alexander Abercomby, Bart., aforesaid. He succeeded to Tullibody, on the death of Mr. George Abercromby, of Skeith, who d. unm. 26 June 1699, aged 74. He died 1755, aged 84, having m. Mary, dau. of Alex Dufl of Braco (of Earl Fife's family), and [was grandfather of the illustrious Lt.-Genl. Sir Ralph Abercromby, K.B. See below.

Alexander (col.), 2nd Regt. Foot Guards —— *Clackmannanshire* 1817-18.

>Youngest son of Lt.-Genl. Sir Ralph Abercromby, and therefore brother of the 2nd Lord Abercromby, of General Sir John Abercromby, G.C.B., and of Lord Dunfermline. He served the campaign of 1799 in Holland as a volunteer with the 92nd ; with the 52nd in the Ferrol 1800 ; A.D.C. to Sir John Moore in Sicily 1806-7 ; proceeded to the Peninsula 1819 ; commanded 28th at the battle of Busaco, and before Lisbon ; commanded a brigade at the battle of Albuera, the 28th at Arroyo de Molino and Almarez ; A.Q.M.G. at the battles of Vittoria, the Pryenees and Orthes. Also A.Q.M.G. in the campaign of 1815 ; served at Quatre Bas and Waterloo, at the storming of Peronne and capture of Paris, C.B. Knight of Maria Theresa of Austria, of Tower and Sword of Portugal (7 Oct. 1814), and of St. George of Russia (4th class) ; b. 4 March 1784, and died 27 Aug 853. See [Foster's Peerage.

Burnet, of Brucefield —— *Clackmannanshire* 1788-90.

>Next brother to Lt.-General Sir Ralph Abercomby, K.B., and General Sir Robert Abercromby, G.C.B., etc. Was a captain East India Company Service, and d. s.p. in [London, 24 March 1792.

George, of Tullibody, advocate —— *Edinburgh* city 1805-6 ; *Clackmannanshire* [1806-7, 1812, until appointed Escheator of Munster, s.b. 7 Aug. 1815.

>Eldest son of Lt.-Genl. Sir Ralph Abercromby ; succ. as 2nd baron on the death of his mother, 11 Feb. 1821 ; his son, George Ralph, next mentioned, succ. as 3rd Lord Aber- [cromby, 14 Feb. 1843. See Foster's Peerage.

George Ralph (lt. col.) —— *Clackmannanshire* 1824-6 (then capt. 3rd Dragoon Guards), 1830-1 ; *Stirlingshire* 1838-41 ; *Clackmannanshire & Kinross-shire,* [1841, until he accepted *Chiltern hundreds* shortly before 18 Feb. 1842.

>Eldest son of the before-named, whom he succ. as 3rd Lord Abercromby, b. 30 May 1800, and d. 25 June 1852. His son George Ralph is (1881) 4th Lord Abercromby s.p. See [Foster's Peerage.

James (sir), of Birkenbog, Knt. —— *Banffshire,* 1693 to 1702.

>Succ. as 2nd Baronet, and d. 20 Sept. 1734, leaving issue by his wife, dau. of Arthur [Gordon, of Straloch. See Foster's Baronetage.

Abercromby.

James (col.) —— *Dysart* (now *Kirkcaldy*) *burghs*, 16 January to 21 Sept., 1710.

Probably identical with Sir James Abercromby, knt. (who died 14 Nov. 1724), natural son of the (then) late Duke of Hamilton, deputy-governor of Dunkirk under Major-General [Hill, *temp.* Q. Anne.

James (col.), of Glasshaugh —— *Banffshire*, 1734-41 ; 1741-7 (then capt.) ; [1747-54 (then col.).

Died at Glasshaugh, Banffshire, 23 April 1781, aged 75, a general of Foot, col. 44th Regiment, and deputy governor of Stirling Castle (Gent's Mag. 1781, p. 242). His mother was Helen, 2nd dau. and co-heir of George, son of John Meldrum, of Leathers, by John Duff, of Maldavit, Banffshire. He m. his third cousin, Mary, dau. of William Duff, esq., of Dipple and of Braco, and had issue. His great-grandson, Arthur Abercromby, succeeded to Glasshaugh, and assumed that surname in lieu of his patronymic Duff. See Foster's Peerage, [article "Earl Fife."

James, of Brucefield —— *Clackmannanshire* 1761-8.

Probably a brother of George Abercromby, of Tullybody, aforesaid.

James, a Privy Councillor —— *Edinburgh city*, 1833-4, (master of the Mint [1834); 1835-7 ; 1837 until created Baron Dunfermline 7 June 1839.

Third son of Lt.-Genl. Sir Ralph Abereromby, and brother of the 2nd lord. Called to the bar at Lincolns Inn 1801 (and a bencher), shortly after appointed a commissioner in bankruptcy. Hon. D.C.L. Oxon 1810 ; M.P. Midhurst 1807-12 ; Calne 1812-30 ; Judge Advocate General 1827-8 ; chief baron of the Exchequer Scotland 1830, the last who held that office ; Master of the Mint July to Dec. 1834 ; Speaker of the House of Commons 1835-9 ; Dean of Faculty Glasgow University 1841 ; created Lord Dunfermline 7 June 1839 ; b. 7 Nov. 1776 ; d. 7 April 1585, leaving an only son Ralph, at whose death 12 July 1868, the title [expired. See Foster's Peerage, article "Abercromby," and also M.P. England.

John (lieut.-genl. sir, G.C.B.) —— *Clackmannanshire* 1815 until his death shortly [before 11 April 1817.

Next baother of George, 2nd Lord Abercromby, and of James Lord Dunfermline, nomi-[nated G.C.B. 7 April 1815 ; died at Marseilles 14 Feb. 1817.

Ralph (sir), of Tullibody, K.B. —— *Clackmannanshire* 1774-80 (then younger of Tullibody, and Lt.-Col. 3rd Regt. of Horse) ; 1796 (then a knight) ; accepted [the *Chiltern hundreds* shortly before 26 Feb. 1798.

Eldest son of George Abercromby, of Tullibody (d. May 1800, aged 95), by Mary, dau. of Ralph Dundas, of Manour, co. Peebles. K.B. 22 July, 1795, P.C. Ireland, lt.-genl. in the army, commander-in-chief of troops serving in Mediterranean ; d. 28 March 1801, aged 66, on board H.M.S. *Foudroyant*, in Aboukir Bay, of wounds received at the battle of Aboukir in Egypt. In consideration of his services the House of Commons ordered a monu-ment to be erected to his memory in St. Paul's Cathedral ; his widow was created Baroness Abercromby 28 May 1801 ; his sons were George 2nd Lord Abercromby, Genl. Sir John Abercromby, G.C.B., James Lord Dunfermline, and lastly Col. the Hon. Alex. Abercromby, [C.B., all mentioned above.

Abercromby.

Robert (lt.-genl. sir), of Brucefield, K.B. —— *Clackmannanshire*, 1798 to 1802.

Youngest son of George Abercromby, of Tullibody, and youngest brother of Sir Ralph Abercromby ; entered the army as ensign 44th Foot in July 1758, and served with his regt. in N. America ; served as a volunteer at the battle of Ticonderoga 8 July 1785, at the siege of Niagara, &c., at Montreal, when the colony was surrendered by the French. Served in N. America 1776-83, and was present at the battles of Brooklyne, Brandywine, and German-town ; also at the siege of Charlestown, and at Yorktown, when it was attacked by the French and American armies, and surrendered to them. A.D.C. to the King 1781, col. 75th Foot 12 Oct. 1787, until his death. Governor and Com.-in-Chief Bombay 1790, major-general, present at the reduction of Tippoo's army, K.B. 1792, succ. Lord Cornwallis as commander-in-chief of the army in India 1793, present at the action at Batina, in Rohil-cund, lieut.-gen. 1797, on staff N. America, Governor of Edinburgh Castle 1801, general 1802; b. 21 Oct. 1740 ; d. unm. at Airthrey, nr. Stirling, 3 Nov. 1827 ; the senior if not the [oldest general in the British service ; Gent's Mag., vol. 97, pt. ii., p. 559.

Robert, of Birkenbog and Forglen —— *Banffshire* 1812-18.

Succ. as 5th Baronet on the death of his father Sir George 1831, and d. 6 July 1855, leaving issue ; his grandson is present Sir Robert John Abercromby, Bart. See Foster's [Baronetage.

Aberdeen.

The provost of —— *Aberdeen* 1540 *bis*, 1560.

Abernethy.

Lancelot, of —— *Edinburgh* 1440 ——, 1463, 1464.

Abirkerdo.

David——*Dundee* in 2 parliaments 1468, in the latter chosen an auditor of com-
[plaint.
George —— *Dundee* 1468.

Acheson.

—— (laird of Gosford), *Haddington Constabulary*, 1625 conv.

Probably identical with Sir Archibald Acheson of Gosford, Haddington. Created a Baronet of Nova Scotia 1 Jan. 1628, a Master in Chancery Ireland, Lord Glencairnie of session Scotland 1626-7, extraordinary lord 1628, Sec. of State for Scotland at his death, 9 Sept. 1634 (see Funeral Certificates Ireland, ed. Foster p. 1); ancestor of Earl Gosford. [See Foster's Peerage and M.P. Ireland, p. 2.

John —— *Dunbar* 1583.
John (Mr.) —— *Dunbar* 1612, 1617.

Adair.

Robert (sir), of Kinhilt——*Wigtownshire* 1639-41, 1649-50.

Son of William Adair of Kinhilt, co. Wigtown, who is said to have settled in co. Antrim, Ireland. Sir Robert was served heir to his father and grandfather, 19 Feb. 1629, and was also of Ballymena, co. Antrim. He d. 1 March 1665, w. d. 15 Feb. 1665, m. Jean, sister to Archibald Edmondstone, of Duntreath, and had 4 sons & 3 daus. ; his grandson Sir Robert was knighted at the battle of the Boyne by William III., see M.P. Ireland. His descendant, Sir Robert Shafto Adair, was cr. a baronet 2 Aug. 1838, and was father of Lord Waveney. [See Foster's Peerage and M.P. England.

Adam.

—— ADAM, of Maryburgh =   ROBERT ADAM, of London, M.P. Kinross-shire 1768-74.

WILLIAM ADAM, of Woodstone, co. Kincardine, and of Blair Adam, co. Kinross (eldest son of John Adam), M.P. 1780-1812 =

SIR CHARLES ADAM, K.C.B., Admiral R.N., M.P. Clackmannanshire & Kinross-shire 1831-41 =

WILLIAM PATRICK ADAM, of Blair Adam, P.C., Gov. of Madras 1880, until his death, 24 May, 1881, M.P. Clackmannanshire & Kinross-shire 1859-80.

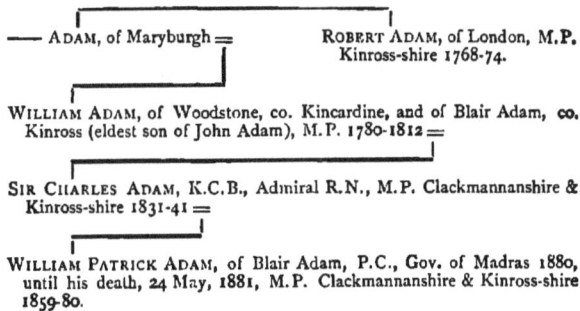

Charles (sir), of Barns, rear-admiral of the white —— *Kinross-shire* 1831-2, *Clackmannanshire* and *Kinross-shire* 1833-4, 1835-7 (a lord of the Admiralty [1835), 1837-41 (then a knight and a lord of the Admiralty).

Eldest son of Rt. Hon. William Adam mentioned below (and brother of Lieut.-General Sir Frederick Adam, G.C.B., G.C.M.G., Governor of Madras, who d. 17 Aug. 1853), b. 6 Oct. 1780, d. 16 Sept. 1853, at Greenwich Hospital. K.C.B. 1835, Admiral of the White 1848, Governor of Greenwich Hospital 1847, Lord-Lieut. Kinross-shire 1839, and one of the elder brethren of the Trinity House 1840, a lord of the Admiralty 1835-41, 1846-7 ; m. 4 Oct. 1822, Elizabeth, daughter of Patrick Brydone, Esq., of Lennell, and had with an only dau. an only son, Rt. Hon. Wm. Patrick Adam, Governor of Madras, 1880. See below.

Robert, of Dowhill, architect in London —— *Kinross-shire* 1768-74.

Eldest of three brothers, architects, was 2nd son of William Adam, of Maryburgh, co. Fife, architect (who died 24 June 1748), and his wife, Mary, dau. of Mr. Robertson, of Gladney, Fifeshire ; educated at Edinburgh University, F.R. and A.S. London and Edinburgh, architect to George III. 1762, until elected for Kinross-shire 1768 ; b. at Kirkcaldy, co. Fife, 3 July 1728, d. 3 March 1792, bur. in Westminster Abbey. The pall was supported by the Duke of Buccleuch, Earl of Coventry and Lauderdale, Viscount Stormont, Lord Frederick Campbell and Mr. Pulteney (Gent's Mag. 1792, p. 283). His senior brother John (father of William M.P., next mentioned), d. 25 June 1792, his younger brother James, also architect to George III., d. 20 Oct. 1794. See also Westminster Abbey registers, ed. Col. Chester, p 449.

Adam—*continued.*

William of Woodstone, co. Kincardine and of Blair Adam, co. Kinross ——
Wigtown-burghs 1780-4 (treasurer and paymaster of the Ordnance 1783);
Elgin-burghs 1784-90 ; *Ross-shire* 1790, (younger of Blair), until he accepted
the Chiltern hundreds, 1794 ; *Kincardineshire* 1806-7 ; (returned also for that
shire and for *Kinross-shire*) 1807, until he accepted the Chiltern hundreds
[shortly before 26 Feb. 1812.

> Son of John Adam, of Maryburgh, formerly an architect at Leith (who d. 25 June 1792),
> by his wife Jean (who d. 15 Dec. 1795), daughter of John Ramsay, esq. (eldest son of
> William Adam of Maryburgh, by Mary Robertson aforesaid), d. 17 Feb. 1839, Lord-Lieut.
> co Kinross, Lord Chief Commissioner of the Jury Court of Scotland 1815-39, a bencher of
> Lincoln's Inn, etc., called 1782, M.P. Gatton 1774-80. For particulars of his duel with Mr.
> Fox 29 Nov. 1778, see Gent's Mag. for that year, p. 610. Treasurer of the Ordnance 1780-2,
> 1783, auditor to the Duke of Bedford, in 1790 he was one of the managers appointed to
> draw up and conduct the articles of impeachment against Mr. Warren Hastings ; Solicitor-
> General to the Prince of Wales 1802, Attorney-General 1805, Chancellor and Keeper of
> Great Seal to Prince of Wales 1806, a councillor for the Duchy of Cornwall, and a state
> councillor for the Prince, appointed for his principality of Scotland 1806, counsel to East
> [India Company 1802, P.C. 1815, see below.

William Patrick, of Blair Adam —— *Clackmannanshire* and *Kinross-shire* 1859-
65 (a lord of the Treasury 20 April 1865), 1865-8, 1868-74 (a lord of the
[Treasury 1869), 1874-80 (a privy councillor) ; 1880.

> P.C. 1873, governor of Madras ; educ. at Rugby and Trin. Coll., Cambridge, B.A. 1846 ;
> barrister-at-law, Inner Temple, 1849 ; major Fife vols. ; private sec. to gov. of Bombay
> (Lord Elphinstone) 1853-8 ; a lord of the Treasury 1865-6, 1868-73 ; chief commissioner
> of works 1873-4, 1880, and paymaster-general 1873-4 ; J.P. and D.L. Kinross and Fife ;
> governor of Madras 1880, until his death at Ootacamund, 24 May, 1881 ; gazetted C.I.E. on
> the day of his death (son of Adm. Sir Charles Adam, K.C.B., M.P., governor of Green-
> wich Hospital, by Elizabeth, dau. of Patrick Brydone, esq.) ; b. 14 Sept. 1826 ; m. 23
> Feb. 1856, Emily (C.I.), dau. of Gen. Sir William Wyllie, G.C.B., and had with other
> [issue a son, Sir Charles Elphinstone Adam, cr. a baronet 20 May 1882.

Adamson.

Andrew —— *Lanark* 1357.

George —— *Dunbar* 1640-1 ; 1650 (or Thomas Purves).

Henry —— *Perth* 1581, 1596 conv.

James —— *Perth* 1594 conv. bis. ; 1597 conv. ; 1604, 1605, 1607, 1608.

James —— *Perth* 1617.

Adamson—*continued.*

John —— *Edinburgh* 1571 conv.

William, bailie of Edinburgh —— 1528.

William —— *Edinburgh* 1540, 1534.

Adie.

David (or Ædie) of Newark, —— *Aberdeen* 1678 conv. (then bailie), 1685-6 [late bailie, in absence (1685) of Sir George Skene of Fintry, provost.

James —— *Perth* 1597 conv., 1602 conv.

Affleck.   See also Auchinleck.

James —— *Dundee* 1596 conv.

William —— *Dundee* 1617 conv.

Agnew.   See also Vans-Agnew.

SIR PATRICK AGNEW, of Lochnaw, Knt. Bart., M.P. Wigtownshire 1628-33 =

SIR ANDREW, 2nd Bart., M.P. Wigtownshire 1643, 1644, 1645-7, 1648-9, 1665, 1667, 1669-72 =

SIR ANDREW, 3rd Bart., M.P. Wigtownshire 1685, 1689, 1702 =

—— 4th Baronet =

—— 5th Baronet =

—— 6th Baronet =

—— AGNEW =

SIR ANDREW, 7th Baronet, posthumous son of Andrew Agnew, M.P. Wigtownshire 1830-7 =

SIR ANDREW, 8th Bart., M.P. Wigtownshire 1856 to 1868.

Agnew.

Andrew (sir) —— *Wigtownshire* 1643 conv. (sheriff of Galloway); 1644 conv. (laird of Lochnaw); 1645-7 conv.; 1648-9 (then styled "appearand of Lochnaw," sheriff of Galloway), 1665 (then of Lochnaw, Knt. Bart.), 1667 [conv.; 1669 until his death shortly before 5 March 1672.

Succ. as 2nd Bart. on the death (1661) of his father Sir Patrick (see below), a member of the commission for governing the kingdom (Scotland) 1649, sheriff of Kirkcudbright as well as Wigtown, 'uring the commonwealth ; he m. (contract 22 March 1625) Anne, dau. of Alexander Stewart, 1st Earl of Galloway, and d. in 1671, having had 2 sons and 2 daus.

Andrew (sir), of Lochnaw, Knt. Bart. —— *Wigtownshire* 1685, 1689 conv.; 1689 [until his death shoitly before 4 June 1702.

Succ. as 3rd Bart. on the death (1671) of his father Andrew last mentioned ; refused the test 1682, and was deprived of the hereditary sheriffdom, but reinstated after the revolution 1689 ; m. 1656 Jane, dau. of Sir Thomas Hay, of Park, formerly of Lochloy, and d. 1701, [having had 3 sons and a dau.

Andrew (sir), of Lochnaw, Bart. —— *Wigtownshire* 1830-1, 1831-2, 1833-4, [1835-7.

Posthumous son of Andrew Agnew (who d. 11 Sept. 1792, having m. 21 May in that year Hon. Martha de' Courcy, eldest dau. of John 26th Lord Kingsale), succ. as 7th Bart. on the death (1809) of his grandfather Sir Stair, and d. 12 April 1849. See Foster's Baronetage.

Andrew (sir), of Lochnaw, Bart. —— *Wigtownshire* 1856-7, 1857-9, 1859 65, [1865-8 (see foot-note).

Patrick (sir), of Lochnaw, Knt. Bart. —— *Wigtownshire* 1628-33.

Knighted by James VI., and cr. a Bart. of Nova Scotia by Chas. I., 28 July 1629, with remainder to his heirs male, heritable sheriff of Galloway, as his ancestors had been for two centuries, and continued so until 1747, when heritable jurisdictions were finally abolished in Scotland. In the family history of "Agnew of Lochnaw," his wife is stated to have been [Margaret dau. of David Macgill, of Cranston Riddell. See Foster's Baronetage.

AGNEW, Sir ANDREW, of Lochnaw, co. Wigtown (1629, N.S.), vice-lieut. since 1852, M.P. 1856-68, capt. late 4th Light Dragoons ; succ. his father as 8th Baronet in 1849; b. 2 Jan., 1818; m. 20 Aug., 1846, Lady Louisa Noel, eldest dau. of Charles, 1st Earl of Gainsborough, and has 5 sons and 7 daus.

(1) Andrew Noel, J.P., and D.L., bar.-at-law I.T. 1874. b. 14 Aug., 1850.
(2) Henry de Courcy, J.P., b. 1 Nov., 1851.
(3) Charles Hamlyn, lieut. 21st R. Fusiliers ; b 21 June, 1859.
(4) Quentin Graham Kinnaird, 2nd lieut. R. Ayr and Wigtown mil., b. 8 Jan., 1861.
(5) Gerard Dalrymple, b. 24 April, 1862.
(6) Madeline Diana Elizabeth, m. 7 Feb., 1867, to Thomas Henry Clifton (B. Donnington), M.P. North Lanc. ; he d. 31 Mar., 1880.
(7) Arabella Frances Georgiana, ⎫ twins.
(8) Carolina Charlotte, ⎭
(9) Louisa Lucia, m. 10 July, 1877, to Duncan MacNeill, Esq.
(10) Mary Alma Victoria, m. 19 Aug., 1875, to Hon. Arthur Fitzgerald Kinnaird, Master of Kinnaird.
(11) Rosina Constance.
(12) Violet Margaret Maud.

Lochnaw Castle, Stranraer, Wigtownshire.

Aikenhead.

Patrick (sir), merchant burgess —— *Dunfermline* 1697 until his death shortly
[before 18 May 1699.

Aikman.

James —— *Edinburgh* 1473 —— 1504

Ainslie.

Adam, late bailie —— *Jedburgh* 1689 conv. ; 1689, until his death shortly before
[10 Aug. 1700.

Andro, provost —— *Jedburgh* 1681-2, 1685-6, then of Black Hill, trafficking merch.
[and late provost.

James (Heneslie) —— *Jedburgh* 1579.

John (Aynslie or Heneslie) —— *Jedburgh* 1579.

Airth.

George —— *Cupar* 1617.

James —— *Pittenweem* 1639-41.

Walter —— *Pittenweem* 1621, —— 1644, 1645-7.

Aitkin.

Edward (Mr.) —— *Dunbar* 1599 conv. ; 1603.

James —— *Culross* 1648-9.

Alexander.

Alexander, bailie —— *Aberdeen* 1667 conv.

Alexander Alexander, bailie in Aberdeen, admitted an honorary burgess of Stirling, 8
Aug. 1672, (burgh records). Alexander, son of A. A., was a regent in Marischal College,
Aberdeen ; admitted minister of Glass, Banffshire 1679, deprived 1690, resumed 1693, etc.
[See Rogers' "House of Alexander."

Archibald —— *Perth* 1605 conv.

Second son of William Alexander, of Menstry, Clackmannanshire, said to be the grandfather
of Wm. Earl of Stirling; a merchant in Stirling, a bailie of Dunfermline 1591, and of Stirling
1593, Dean of Guild of Stirling 1599, one of the burgh commissioners to parlt. 1600, apptd 26
June 1601, (a Commissioner to the Conventioune of Burrowis to be holden at Sanct Androis,)
appears on the roll of convention held at St. Andrews 30 June same year ; 31 Aug. he was
returned to the "Conventioune of the Nobilitie and Estaittis of this realme to be held at
Perth on 10 Septr.;" returned to the convention of estates May 1605, and in Aug. following, and again in 1606 was sent as commissioner to the convention of burghs ; d. 13 Sept.
1621; will dated 13 April 1621 ; m. (deed 7 June 1589 to marry Aug. following) Elizabeth,
dau. of Robert Alexander, burgess of Stirling, and had a son and dau. See below. See
[Rogers' "House of Alexander."

B*

Alexander.

Boyd, of Southbar —— *Renfrewshire* 1796 to 1802 ; *Glasgow burghs* 1803-6.

Fourth son of Claud Alexander of Newtown, co. Renfrew, and Joanna dau. of Alexander Cuninghame of Craigends ; entered the Hon. East India Company's service, purchased the estates of Southbar and Boghall, co. Renfrew ; b. Jan. 1758, and d. s.p. 1825, having m. his [cousin Camilla, dau. of Boyd Porterfield, of that ilk.

Claud (lieut.-col.), of Ballochmyle, Mauchline, Ayrshire —— *S. Ayrshire* 1874-80 [and since 1880.

Of Ballochmyle, Ayrshire (eldest son of late Boyd Alexander, of Ballochmyle and Southbar, by his wife, Sophia Elizabeth Hobhouse, sister of John, Lord Broughton, G.C.B.), educ. at Eton and Christ Church, Oxford ; J.P., D.L. cos. Ayr and Renfrew ; Colonel (h.p.) late Grenadier Guards, served in the Crimean War (medals), M.P. (conservative) co. Ayrshire since 1874 ; contested that division 1868 ; b. 15 Jan. 1831 ; m., 12 Feb. 1863, Eliza, dau. of late Alexander Speirs, esq., of Elderslie, M.P., L.L. Renfrewshire, and has an only [son and heir, Claud, b. 24 Feb. 1867.

David —— *Anstruther Easter* 1645-6? (also 1646-7).

Younger brother of John and Robert Alexander (see below) and 3rd son of William Alexander, a burgess of Anstruther, a fellow of the Fishery Society of Great Britain and Ireland, styled " Capt. David Alexander, master of a ship of Anstruther, called the James," in letters of reprisal granted by Charles I. under the Great Seal 20 April 1626, etc., etc. ; a deputy of the Vice-Adml. of Scotland (Alexander, Earl of Linlithgow), served heir to his brother James 4 March 1642 ; taken prisoner by Cromwell's soldiers when they despoiled Anstruther, [7 Aug. 1651. See Rogers' " House of Alexander."

John —— *Anstruther Easter* 1639-40 ; Andrew Martin was elected in his stead [23 July 1641 " quha hes keipit nane dyattis becaus so debilitat."

Probably brother of David above named and of Robert, who represented Anstruther Easter.

Robert —— *Stirling* 1579, 1584 conv., 1594 parlt. and conv.

A Robert Alexander was described as " dene of Gild " of Stirling, 25 July 1576. Robert Alexander, burgess of Stirling, and Katherine Mount his wife made a renunciation of the [lands of Levilandis, had issue. See Rogers' " House of Alexander."

Robert —— *Anstruther Easter* 1612, 1617, 1625 conv., 1628-33, —— 1645.

Brother of John and David Alexander aforesaid ; a merchant in Anstruther Easter, a Fellow of the Fishery Society ; m. Christian, yr. dau. of Sir John Anstruther of Anstruther. See [Rogers' " House of Alexander."

Robert, merchant, burgess —— *New Galloway* 1685-6.

William, lord provost of Edinburgh —— *Edinburgh city* 1754-61.

Of Edinburgh, banker (2nd son of John Alexander of Blackhouse and Boghall, Ayrshire), admitted a burgess and guild brother of Edinburgh 13 June 1733 ; elected lord provost 1752, and in 1753 ; he died 25 July, 1761, having married Marione Louisa de la Croix, of a Huguenot family ; she died 1 January 1773, having had with other issue a son, William, who by his 1st wife (Christian, only dau. of John Aitchison of Rocksolach and Airdrie, co. Lanark) had with 2 daus. 2 sons, of whom the elder, Sir William, b. 18 May, 1755 ; Q.C. 1800, master in chancery, 1809-24 ; was appointed lord chief baron of the Exchequer 19 Jan. 1824 (and then knighted P.C.), resigned Jan. 1831, and died unm. 29 June, 1842 [bd. in the chapel of Roslin Castle.

Alison.

Robert —— *Jedburgh* 1585.

William —— *Jedburgh* 1543 bis, then provost.

Allansone.

Andrew —— *Aberdeen* 1469, 1471.

Allardice. See also Barclay.

Alexander, of Dunnottar —— *Aberdeen* (now *Montrose*) *burghs* 1792-6, 1796 [until his death shortly before 5 Jan. 1802.

He d. 1 Nov. 1801, having m. 20 Oct. 1794 (G.M.) Hannah, 5th dau. of Alexander Innes, esq., of Cowie, co. Kincardine, and had an only child, Eleanor, mother of Archibald, 2nd [Marquis of Ailsa. See Foster's Peerage.

George, of that ilk, merchant —— *Kintore* 1702-7, sat in 1st parlt. of Great [Britain 1707-8.

Second son of Sir John Allardice of Allardice (by Mary, styled Lady Mary Graham, elder dau. and co-heir of Lord Kinpont, son and heir of William, Earl of Airth and Menteith), Master of the Mint; b. 17 Aug. 1672; d. 17 Oct. 1709, having m. Anne, eldest dau. of James Ogilvy, 4th Earl of Findlater and Seafield, Lord High Chancellor of Scotland ; she d. [27 Aug. 1735, having had issue, represented by Robert Barclay Allardice, esq.

John, fear of that ilk —— *Kincardineshire* 1607 (the laird of Allardice as a [minor baron); 1612.

John (Allerdes), provost —— *Aberdeen* 1702-7.

Alves.

William, commissar of Dumfries —— *Sanquhar* 1702, 1702-7.

Ancram.

Charles, Earl of—— See Kerr and England M.P.

Anderson.

Arthur, of Norwood, Surrey, and No. 51, St. Mary Axe, London —— *Orkney* and [*Shetlandshire* 1847-52.

Son of Robert Anderson, of Lerwick, Shetland ; entered the navy, but qu.tted the service in 1815 for a commercial life ; chairman and one of the founders of P. & O. Steam Navigation Co., &c. ; a director and chairman of Crystal Palace ; d. at Norwood 28 Feb. 1868, [aged 76 ; having m. 1822 Mary Ann, dau. of C. Hill, of Scarborough, she d. 1864.

David —— *Cupar* 1617 conv., 1625 conv., 1630 conv., 1639-41, then town clerk.

George, of St. Vincent Street, Glasgow —— *Glasgow* 1868-74, 1874-80 (then of [*London*), and since 1880 (see foot-note).

A NDERSON, GEORGE, of Glasgow (son of George Anderson, of Luscar, co. Fife), educated at Edinburgh High School and St. Andrews University, formerly a merchant in Glasgow, M.P. (liberal) for that city since 1868, and late Major 4th Lanark R.V. ; b. 19 Nov. 1819 ; m. 22 Aug. 1877, Mary Brown, eldest dau. of Thomas Clavering, esq., Glasgow, and has a dau.
Mary Clavering.
Clubs—Reform, Western, Glasgow.

Anderson.

Henry —— *Perth* 1596 conv.

James —— *Cupar* 1587, 1590 conv., 1593 conv., 1594.

James —— *Cupar* 1640.

James (sir), of Glasgow, knt. —— *Stirling burghs* 1852-7, 1857-9.
> Son of John Anderson, of Stirling, merchant; lord provost of Glasgow, Nov. 1848, knighted on the Queen's visit to that city Aug. 1849 ; d. at Blairvadick, Dumbartonshire, [8 May 1864. aged 63 ; he m. 1831, Janet, only dau. Robert Hood, esq., of Glasgow.

John, merchant, late bailie —— *Dunfermline* 1678 conv.

John —— *Cupar* 1585 conv.

John, bailie —— *Inverurie* 1681-2, 1685-6, 1689 conv. ; 1689 his seat was declared [vacant 28 April 1693, because he had not signed the assurance.
> Commissioner for Inverury to the convention of burghs 1671, then bailie ; bailie of [Inverury, 1677-8.

John, of Dowhill, merchant, burgess —— *Glasgow* 1689 conv., 1689 to 1702.
> Provost of Glasgow 1681.

John, younger, of Westerton —— *Dornoch* 1692 to 1702.

Mathew, provost —— *Kirkcaldy* 1678 conv., 1685-6 "elder of Ridburne, [provost."

Thomas —— *Cupar* 1456.

Thomas —— 1479.

Walter —— *Montrose* 1583.

William —— *Perth* 1593 conv.

William of Newtoune (provost) —— *Glasgow* 1655 conv. ; 1667 conv.; 1669-74, [then of Newtoune

Angus.
Andro, town clerk —— *Selkirk* 1681-2.

Annand.
Alexander —— *Elgin* 1594 conv.

John —— *Elgin* 1579, 1581, 1583.

Annand—*continued*.

William —— 1583.

Anstruther.

(JOHN ANSTRUTHER, M.P. Anstruther Easter 1597 conv., 1600) probably
identical with John A., whose great-grandson =

SIR PHILIP ANSTRUTHER, knighted 1650, sat in convention parlts. for
Fifeshire 1665, 1667, 1678, then styled knight baronet =

| SIR WILLIAM, M.P. Fifeshire 1681-2, 1689 conv., 1689 1702, 1702-7 =

SIR JOHN, M.P. Anstruther-Easter 1702-7, Anstruther-Easter burghs 1708-12, 1713-15, Fifeshire 1715 to 1741. = | ANSTRUTHER =

PHILIP, lt.-gen., governor of Minorca (son of Sir James A. of Airdrie) M.P. Anstruther-Easter burghs 1715-41, 1747-54. | SIR ROBERT, of = Balcaskie, cr. a Baronet 28 Nov., 1694, M.P. Anstruther-Easter 1681-2, Anstruther-Wester 1702-7, Fifeshire 1709-10. |

(SIR) JOHN, M.P. Anstruther-Easter
burghs 1766-74, 1780-3, 1790-3 =

| (SIR) PHILIP PATERSON, M.P. Anstruther-Easter burghs 1774-8. | SIR JOHN, cr. a Bart. 18 May, 1798, M.P. Anstruther-Easter burghs 1783-90, 1796-7, 1806-11 = | ROBERT, of Baltully, M.P. Anstruther-Easter burghs 1793-4 |

| SIR JOHN CARMICHAEL ANSTRUTHER, 2nd Bt., M.P. Anstruther-Easter burghs 1811-18. | —— CARMICHAEL ANSTRUTHER, 3rd Bart. = |

| SIR WYNDHAM CHARLES JAMES CARMICHAEL ANSTRUTHER, 4th Bart. (son of Sir Wyndham A.), M.P. S. Lanarkshire 1874-80. | SIR ROBERT ANSTRUTHER, of Balcaskie, 5th Bart., descended from the original patentee— M.P. Fifeshire 1864-80. |

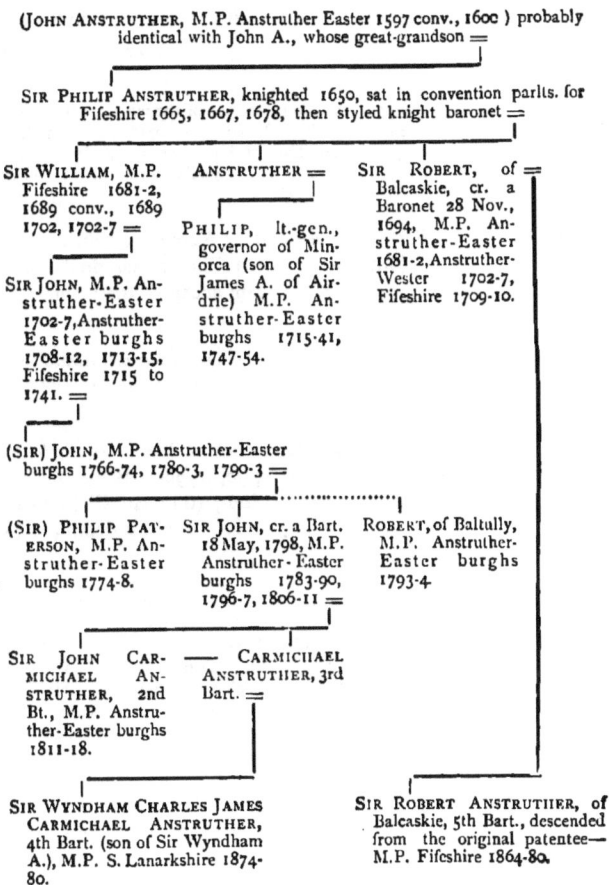

John —— *Anstruther Easter* 1597 conv. ; 1600.
    Probably the John Anstruther served heir of his father Andrew (who fell at the battle of
Pinkie 1547), and of his grandfather John Anstruther of that ilk, and is said to have died
[at a great age in 1610. Great-grandfather of Sir Philip, named below.

Anstruther—*continued.*

John (sir) of Anstruther —— *Anstruther Easter* 1702-7; *Anstruther Easter* (now St. Andrews) *burghs* 1708-10 (styled Sir John Anstruther, younger of that ilk); 1710 until unseated in 1711, 1713-15 (then styled a Baronet); *Fifeshire* 1715-22 (an officer of the Crown 1717, styled 'John Anstruther of Anstruther); 1227-7 (also styled Anstruther of Anstruther); 1727-34 (styled a Baronet); [1734-41 (styled a Knight).

> Son of Sir William Anstruther, see below; master of the works in Scotland 1717; died 6 Oct. 1753 (G.M.), or 30 Sept. 1753 (L.M.), having married, Jan. 1717, Lady Margaret Carmichael, eldest dau. of James, 2nd Earl of Hyndford, she d. 1721, leaving an only [surviving son Sir John, next mentioned.

John (Sir) of Anstruther, Bart. —— *Anstruther Easter* (now St. Andrews) *burghs* 1766-8, 1768-74, 1780 (until he accepted Chiltern hundreds shortly before 1 Jan. 1783), 1790 to 1793, when he again accepted the Chiltern hundreds.

> Son of the preceding Sir John Anstruther, and father of Sir John Anstruther, Bart., next [mentioned, he died 4 July 1799. See Foster's Baronetage.

John (sir) of Lincoln's Inn, London, counsellor at law —— *Anstruther Easter* (now St. Andrews) *burghs* 1783-4, 1784-90, 1796-7; (Chief Justice Supreme Court of Judicature, Calcutta, 1797); 1806-7 (then late C. J., Bengal); 1807 [until his death (26 Jan. 1811).

> Second son of the preceding Sir John Anstruther, by his wife Janet, dau. of James Fall of Dunbar, merchant, Barrister-at-Law, L.I., 1779, P.C. (19 Nov. 1806), took a leading part in the impeachment of Warren Hastings. M.P. Cockermouth, 1790-6 (see M.P. England), a Justice for co. Merioneth, etc., 1793-7, knighted 4 October 1797, cr. a Baronet of Great Britain 18 May 1798, general receiver of Bishop's rents, Scotland, Chief Justice Bengal 1797 to 1806, born at Elie House, Fifeshire, 27 March 1753, died in Albemarle St., [London, 26 June 1811.

John (sir) of Anstruther (2nd) Bart. —— *Anstruther Easter* (now St. Andrews) [*burghs* 1811, 1812, until his death (28 Jan. 1818.

> Elder son of the preceding Sir John Anstruther, Bart., assumed the additional surname and arms of Carmichael on succeeding as heir of entail to the last Earl of Hyndford, 1817; d. 2 Jan. 1818 and m. 11 Jan. 1817 Jessie, dau. Maj.-Genl. David Dewar of Gilston House, co. Fife. (she rem. 27 March 1828 to Robert Bullock Marsham, D.C.L., Warden Merton Coll. Ox., who died 27 Dec., 1880, aged 94,) and left a posthumous son Sir John, b. 6 Feb. 1818, [and d. Nov. 1831.

Anstruther—*continued*.

Philip (sir) of that ilk, Knt., Bart. —— *Fifeshire* 1665 conv.; 1667 conv.;
[1678 conv.; (then styled Baronet).

Younger son of Sir Robert Anstruther (gentleman of the bedchamber to James I., P.C.,
Charles I., Ambassador to Germany; buried in Westminster Abbey, 9 Feb. 1644-5; knighted
1650; like his father and uncle Sir William, he was a zealous royalist, he had a command in
the Royal army when invading England, and was taken prisoner at the battle of Worcester,
his estates were sequestered by Oliver Cromwell, and so continued untill the Restoration
(it may be that the representative in the convention of 1678 was Sir Philip his 4th son &
namesake); he d. 1702, having m. Christian, dau. of Gen. Sir James Lumsden, of Innergelly,
co. Fife. and had 5 sons, Sir William (see below), Sir James, of Airdrie, Sir Robert of Bal-
[caskie, Bart., Sir Philip of Anstrutherfield, and Sir Alexander, Bart.
    That Sir Philip Anstruther was a baronet is by no means certain; the baronetages
state that he was knighted in 1650, and that two of his sons, Sir William and Sir
Robert, were created Baronets of Nova Scotia in 1694. There is however no evidence
at present of a baronetcy having been conferred upon the eldest son; see Sir William
Anstruther below, and Sir John (eldest son of Sir William) Anstruther above (see also
"Foster's Baronetage").

Philip (lieut.-genl.) —— *Anstruther Easter* (now St. Andrews) *burghs* 1715-22,
(lieut.-col. of the foot guards 1715) 1722-7 (then of Airdrie), 1727-34, 1734-41
[(then col.), 1747-54 (then lieut.-genl.)

Col. 26th Foot, Governor of Minorca, only son of Sir James Anstruther of Airdrie
[aforesaid, died unm. 11 Nov. 1760. See Foster's Baronetage·

Philip, lieut. (1st King's) dragoon guards —— *Anstruther Easter* (now St.
Andrews) *burghs* 1774, until he accepted the Chiltern hundreds shortly before
[9 Jan. 1778.

Elder brother of Sir John Anstruther, (cr. a Baronet 18 May 1798, see above), assumed his
[wife's maiden name of Paterson, and died s.p. 5 Jan. 1808. See Foster's Baronetage.

Robert (sir) of Balcaskie, Knt. Bart. (1694) —— *Anstruther Easter* 1681-2
(then third lawful son of the laird of Anstruther, merchant burgess); *Anstruther*
[*Wester* 1702-7; *Fifeshire* 1710.

Third son of Sir Philip Anstruther aforesaid, cr. a baronet of Nova Scotia 28 Nov. 1694,
[died March 1737, ancestor of Sir Robert Anstruther of Balcaskie 1881. See below.

ANSTRUTHER, Sir Robert, of Balcaskie, co. Fife, Bart. (1654 N.S.), educ. at Harrow, Lt.-Col.
late Grenadier Guards, served 1853-62, Lord Lieutenant Fifeshire, D.L. Caithness, M.P. (liberal)
Fifeshire 1864-80; b. 28 Aug., 1834; m. 29 July, 1857, Louisa, eldest dau. of Rev. William Knox
Marshall, preby. of Hereford, etc., and has 4 sons and a dau.

(1) Ralph William, lieut. R.E.; b. 5 July, 1858.　(4) Arthur Wellesley, b. 5 March, 1864.
(2) Henry Torrens, b. 27 Nov., 1860.　(5) Mary Evelyn.
(3) Robert Hamilton, R.N.; b. 10 June, 1862.
Balcaskie, Pittenween, co. Fife.—1, *Eccleston Sq., S.W.*

Anstruther—*continued.*

Robert, of Baltully (esq.) —— *Anstruther-Easter* (now S. Andrews) *burghs*
[1793, until he accepted the Chiltern hundreds 1794.
Probably brother of Sir John Anstruther aforesaid (created a baronet 18 May 1798), lt.-col.
68th regt., col. of the Tay Fencibles.

Robert (sir), of Balcaskie, bart. —— *Fifeshire* 1864-5, 1865-8, 1868-74, 1874-80
[(see foot-note preceding page).

William (sir 1695-6), of that ilk, one of the Senators of the College of Justice
[(1702) —— *Fifeshire* 1681-2, 1689 conv. ; 1689 to 1702, 1702-7.
Brother of Sir Robert Anstruther of Balcaskie afsd. and eldest son of Sir Philip Anstruther
aforesaid. An ordinary lord of session at the revolution 1689, and P.C., Master of the
Household 1694, a lord of Justiciary 1704, d. 24 January 1711, said to have been created a
[Baronet ; ancestor of Sir Wyndham C. J. Carmichael Anstruther, Bart., next mentioned

Wyndham Charles James Carmichael (sir), of Cormiston Towers, Libberton
[by Biggar], Lanarkshire, bart. —— *S. Lanarkshire* 1874-80.
5th baronet (on the death of his father, Sir John, 15 Sept. 1869) heritable carver of the
Royal Household in Scotland ; b.   , 1824 ; m. 4 Sept. 1872, Janetta, only dau. of
Robert Barbour, esq., of Bolesworth Castle, Cheshire, and has a son, Wyndham Robert, b.
[26 March 1877. See Foster's Baronetage.

Arbuthnott.

Alexander of Knox —— *Kincardineshire,* 1689 conv. ; 1689 to 1702.
Only son of Si Robert 1st Viscount Arbuthnott (by his 2nd wife, Catherine, 3rd dau]
of Hugh, 8th Lord Lovat, widow of Sir Jno. Sinclair of Dunbeath), m. Jean dau. of Patrick
Scot of Rossie, and had with 3 daughters—a son Alexnnder, a commissioner of Customs 1742,
who d. in Edinburgh 7 Oct. 1764, aged 83, leaving issue by his wife Janet, dau. of John
Ronald of Larnie ; ancestor of late Adml. Sir Alex. Dundas Young Arbuthnott, K.B.,
[etc. See Foster's Peerage.

Alexander (Mr.) advocate provost —— *Bervie* 1702-4.
Hon. Alexander (Arbuthnott) Maitland of Pitrichie, advocate 18 Dec. 1697, a baron of the
Court of Exchequer, Scotland, 1707 (3rd son of Robert, 2nd Viscount Arbuthnott) ; m. Jean.
eldest dau. of Sir Charles Maitland, of Pitrichie, co. Aberdeen (and heir of her brother Sir
Charles Maitland, who died 1704) ; she d. 22 Oct. 1746, leaving a son, Charles Maitland,
[M.P. Aberdeen 1748.

Hugh (Genl. 1857), of Hatton —— *Kincardineshire,* 1826-30 (then col.),
1830-1 (then major-general), 1831-2, 1833-4, 1835-7, 1837-41, 1841-7, 1847-
[52, (then lieut-general), 1852-7, 1857-9 (then general), 1859-65.
Gen. the Hon. Sir Hugh Arbuthnott, K.C.B. 1862 (2nd son of John 7th Viscount
Arbuthnott), col. 79th regt. 1862, col. 38th regt. 1843 ; entered the service 1796, served¯
with the 49th regt. at the Helder 1799, in the Baltic and at battle of Copenhagen 1801, at
siege and capture of Copenhagen 1807, in Spain, at battle of Corunna, etc., served in the
peninsula under the Duke of Wellington, comd. 52nd regt. at battle of Busaco, died unm.
[11 July 1868, aged 88.

Arbuthnott.

—— laird of —— *Kincardineshire* 1621.

> Sir Robert Arbuthnott of Arbuthnott (son of Andrew), died s.p. Sept. 1631, having m.
> [Mary, eldest dau. of William, 3rd Lord Keith, son of William, 3rd Earl Marischal.

Argyll.

(Archibald) marquis of —— *Co. Aberdeen* 1658-9 (WILLIS). See addenda, page xviii.

Armitstead.

George —— *Dundee* 1868, until he accepted the Chiltern hundreds, shortly
[before 7 Aug. 1873, and since 1880 (see foot-note).

Arnot.

David —— *Kirkcudbright* 1621.

David (sir) of that ilk —— *Kinross-shire* 1689 conv. ; 1689 to 1702.

> Playfair states that Sir David Arnot, 2nd Baronet of that ilk, was a member of the Prince
> [of Orange's Convention Parliament in 1689, sitting for Kinross.

John —— *Edinburgh* 1586 conv. ; 1587, 1588 conv. ; 1590 conv.

John (sir) of Birswick, provost of Edinburgh —— *Edinburgh* 1608, 1609 conv.

John, commissary clerk —— *St. Andrews* 1612.

Robert, merchant, councillor —— *Perth* 1639-41 ; 1643 conv.; 1644-7 (then
[provost).

Arthur.

Henry —— *St. Andrews* 1621.

Asher.

Alexander, advocate —— *Elgin burghs* 1881 (see foot-note).

Asson.   See **Easson**.

A RMITSTEAD, GEORGE, of London and Dundee, merchant (2nd son of George Armitstead, Esq.,
of Easingwold, Yorks, and of Riga, merchant), J.P. Perthshire, J.P. D.L. Forfar, M.P. (liberal)
Dundee 1868-73, and since April 1880 ; b. February 1824 ; m. May 1848, Jane Elizabeth, eldest dau.
of Edward Baxter, Esq., of Kincaldrum, co. Forfar.
Kinloch Laggan, Kingussie, Scotland.
'Clubs—Reform ; New Liberal, Edinburgh ; Eastern, Dundee, etc.

A SHER, ALEXANDER, of Edinburgh, D.L., (2nd son of late Rev. William Asher, D.D.,
minister of Inveravon, Banffshire), educated at the Universities of Aberdeen and Edinburgh,
advocate 1861, advocate depute 1870-4, Solicitor-General Scotland 1881, contested Glasgow and
Aberdeen Universities 1880 ; b. 27 Jan. 1835 ; m. 31 March 1870, Caroline Julia, eldest dau. late Rev.
Charles Henry Crawfurd, rector of Old Swinford, co. Worc.   See Foster's Baronetage.
31, *Heriot Row, Edinburgh.   Clubs—Devonshire, University, Edinburgh.*

Atkinson.

John —— *Haddington* 1479.

Auchinleck.   See also Affleck.

William —— *Dundee* 1612, 1617.

George, of Balmanno —— *Perthshire* 1617 conv. (the laird), 1617 parlt.

Auchmutie.

John —— *Stirling* 1583, 1584 conv.

John Auchmoutie of Auchmoutie, m. Isabel, yst. dau. of Sir David Wemyss, of Wemyss.

Auld.

John —— *Irvine* 1543.

Auldliston.

—— the laird of —— *Linlithgowshire* 1621.

Austin (Oisteane).

Alexander —— *Edinburgh* 1587, 1588 conv.; 1590 conv.; 1596 conv.

Joseph (master), late magistrate of the burgh of Perth —— *Perth burghs* [1708-10.

Ayr.

The provost of —— *Ayr* 1567.

Ayton.

Ayton, laird of —— *Fifeshire* 1644.

Sir John Ayton, of Ayton, m. 1636 Elizabeth, 4th dau. of Sir John Wemyss, Bart., cr. Earl [of Wemyss 25 June, 1633.

John of —— 1483.

John —— *Haddington* 1645-7, 1650 (or John Sleigh).

John, bailie —— *Bervie* 1678 conv.

Aytoun.

Roger Sinclair, of Inchdairnie —— *Kirkcaldy burghs* 1862-6, 1865-8, 1868-74.

AYTOUN, ROGER SINCLAIR, of Inchdairnie, co. Fife, J.P., D.L. (son of John Aytoun, Esq., of Inchdairnie, by his wife, Margaret Anne, dau. of James Jeffray, Esq., M.D.), M.A. Trin. Coll. Cambridge, 1848 ; M.P. (liberal) Kirkcaldy 1862-74 ; b. 18 Feb. 1823.
Inchdairnie, Kirkcaldy, co. Fife.—33, *Upper Brook St., S.W.*
Club—Brooks'.

B.

Bagenoch.

John —— *Inverurie* 1621.

Baikie.

Robert (esq.), of Tankerness —— *Orkney and Shetland* 1780, until unseated, s.b. [23 Feb. 1781.

Of Hall of Tankerness, co. Orkney (son of James Baikie, provost of Dingwall during the rebellion of 1745, by his wife Janet Douglas, of Egilshay), d. 4 April 1817, having m. 1785 [Mary, dau. of Thomas Balfour, esq., of Huip, and had 4 sons and 3 daus.

Baillie.

Charles (H.M. advocate for Scotland) —— *Linlithgowshire* 5 Feb. to 23 Apl. [1859.

Brother of George 10th Earl of Haddington, became Hon. by patent of precedency 5 July 1859, Sol.-Genl. Scotland and Lord Advocate 1858. Lord Jerviswood of sess. 1859, lord of justiciary 1862-74, Sheriff Stirlingshire, d. 23 July 1879, see Foster's Peerage. Son [of George Baillie, esq. See below.

George —— *North Berwick* 1621.

George, of Jerviswood —— *Berwickshire* 1691 to 1702; *Lanarkshire* 1702-7; 1707-8 (1st parlt. Great Britain); *Berwickshire* 1708-10, 1710-13, 1713-15 [1715-22 (an officer of the crown 1717), 1722-7, 1727-34.

A lord of the admiralty 1714-17, of the treasury 1717-24, d. at Oxford 6 Aug. 1738, aged 75, having m. 17 Sept. 1692 Grizel, dau. of St. Patrick Hume or Home, Bart., created Earl of Marchmont, etc. (23 April 1697), she d. 6 Dec. 1746, aged 81, bd. at Mellerstain; he had a son Robert, who d. young, and 2 daughters, viz., Grisel, d. s. p. 6 June 1759, aged 67, having m. 26 Aug. 1710, to Sir Alexander Murray, of Stanhope, Bart., M.P., and Rachel (2nd dau.), b. 23 Feb. 1696, m. to Charles Lord Binning. See "Earl Haddington," Foster's [Peerage.

George, of Jerviswood, co. Berwick —— *Berwickshire* 1796 to 1802 (then [younger), 1802-6, 1806-7, 1807-12, 1812-18.

Elder son of Hon. George Baillie-Hamilton, of Mellerstain, at Jerviswood, and father of the 10th Earl of Haddington and the before-named Hon. Charles Baillie. Capt. Hopetoun [Fencible regt. 1793, d. 11 Dec. 1841. See "Haddington," Foster's Peerage.

Baillie—*continued.*

Henry James (younger), of Tarradale and Redcastle —— *Inverness-shire* 1840-1, [1841-7, 1847-52, 1852-7, 1857-9, 1859-65, 1865-8 (see foot-note).

Hugh —— *North Berwick* 1587.

Hugh ——*Fortrose* 1678 conv.

John (lieut. col.), of Leys —— *Inverness burghs* 1830-1, 1833 until his death s. b. [17 May in that year.

> Died 20 Apl. 1833, aged 60. Director East India Co. 1823. Lieut. Col. Bengal Establishment 1815, entered 1790, prof. of Arabic and Persian languages and of the Mahomedan law in the College of Fort William, political agent Bundlecund 1803-7, resident at Lucknow 1807-15, M.P. Hedon 1820-30; his dau. heir Annie m. to John Frederick Baillie, esq., of [Leys, son of Peter Baillie next mentiond.

Peter (younger), of Dochfour, banker and merchant in Bristol —— *Inverness* [1807 until his death shortly before 4 Nov. 1811.

> Eldest son of Evan Baillie of Dochfour, Inverness, he died 1 Sept. 1811, having m. 9 March 1797, Elizabeth, dau. of John Pinney, Esq., of Somerton Erleigh, Somerset, and had 2 sons [and 2 daus.

William —— *Inverness* 1581.

William (sir), of Lamington, knt. —— *Lanarkshire* 1612.

William (sir), of Lamington, knt. —— *Lanarkshire* 1639-41 (absent at New- [castle during 2nd sess. 1640-1) ; 1645-7 and 1648 as laird of Lamington.

> Son and heir of Sir William (Maxwell) Baillie, of Lamington, by his wife Elizabeth, dau. of Henry Stuart, of Craigie Hall, Linlithgowshire. He m. Grissel, dau. of Sir Claud Hamilton, [of Elieston, bro. of James 1st Earl of Abercorn, and had a son Samuel.

William, of Lamington —— *Lanarkshire* 1689 conv. ; 1689 to 1702, 1702-7.

> Son of Sir Samuel Baillie afsd. by Janet, dau. of John, Lord Belhaven : succ. his grandfather Sir William ; m., 1stly, Marjary, dau. of John, 1st Lord Bargany, and had a son William; he m., 2ndly, 16 Oct. 1691, Henriet, only dau. of Wm. Lindsay, 16th Earl of Crawford and 2nd Earl of Lindsay, by his 1st wife Mary, eldest dau. of James Johnstone, Earl of Annandale and Hartfell, and sister of Wm. 1st Marquis of Annandale, and had [daughters only.

BAILLIE, Right Hon. HENRY JAMES, of Redcastle, Inverness-shire (only son of Col. Hugh Duncan Baillie, of Redcastle and Tarradale, Ross-shire, M.P. Rye and Honiton ; by his wife Elizabeth, dau., heir of Rev. Henry Reynett, D.D.), M.P. (conservative) co. Inverness 1840-68; joint sec. to Board of Control 1852 ; Under Sec. of State India 1858-9 ; Lieut. Ross-shire; b. March 1804, m., 1st, 29 Dec., 1840, Hon. Philippa Eliza Sydney, dau. of Percy 6th Visct. Strangford, she d.   1854, leaving issue ; he m., 2ndly, 6 Aug., 1857, Clarissa, eldest dau. of late George Rush, Esq., of Elsenham Hall, Essex, and Farthinghoe Lodge, Northants.

Redcastle, Killearnan, Inverness-shire.—Elsenham Hall, Bishop Stortford.
Clubs—Carlton, Travellers.

Baillie—*continued.*

William (younger), of Polkemmet —— *Linlithgowshire* 1845-7 (see foot-note).

Baine.

Walter, merchant in Greenock —— *Greenock* 1845-7.

Baird.

Andrew —— *Banff* 1628-33; 1639-40, then bailie.

A red-hot Covenanter, member of the famous assembly of 1638. See Stevenson's History.
[His dau. Janet m. Jan., 1637, to Gilbert Mair, of Airds.

James (sir), of Auchmedden, knt., sheriff principal —— *Banffshire* 1665 conv.;
[1669-72.

Eldest son of George Baird, of Auchmedden (by Anne, dau. of Sir Alexander Fraser, of Saltoun), high sheriff Banff 1658, one of the two barons named by co. Aberdeen to meet the English Commissioners at Dalkeith after the battle of Worcester; d. 17 July 1691, aged 72; [having m. 1641, Christian, only dau. of Walter Ogilvie, of Boyne.

James, younger of Auchmedden —— *Banffshire* 1678 conv.

Predeceased his father, Sir James Baird, 20 July 1681, aged 33; he m. 16 Feb. 1669-70, Catherine, younger dau. of George Hay, 2nd Earl of Kinnoull; she d. at Auchmedden, 11 Jan. [1733, aged 92; he had 3 sons and 3 daus.

James, ironmaster of Gartsherrie, Lanarkshire —— *Falkirk burghs* 1851-2, [1852-7.

James Baird, of Auchmedden, co. Aberdeen, Kudydart, co. Inverness, and Cambusdoon, co. Ayr. J.P., D.L., (4th son of Alexander Baird, of Lochwood, co. Lanark,) d. 20 June 1876, m., 1st, 1852, Charlotte, dau. of Robert Lockhart, Esq., of Castle Hill, co. Lanark, (Sinclair, Bart.,) she d. 1857; he m., 2ndly, 8 Dec. 1859, Isabella Agnes, dau. of Admiral James Hay, of Belton, E. Lothian (M. Tweeddale).

John (sir), of Newbyth, knt., senator of the College of Justice —— *Aberdeenshire* [1665 conv.; 1667 conv.

Son of James Baird, of Byth, co. Aberdeen, and elder brother of Sir Robert Baird, of Saughton; cr. a Baronet 28 Feb. 1695-6. He sold the lands of Byth in Aberdeenshire, and purchased those of Foord and Whitekirk in Haddingtonshire, which were formed into a barony, and called Newbyth. Advocate 1647, a lord of Session and knighted 1664, a lord of Justiciary 1667-81, appointed a judge at the Revolution, died in Edinburgh 27 April 1698, aged 78. His son Sir William was created a Baronet 4 Feb. 1680. See Foster's Baronetage.

BAILLIE, Sir William, of Polkemmet, co. Linlithgow (1823, U.K.); M.P. co. Linlithgow, 1845-7; Lieut.-Col. Edinburgh city art. vols. since 1866; capt. late royal Midlothian yeo. cav. 1852-72; s. his father (Sir William) as 2nd Baronet in 1854; b. 2 Feb. 1816; m. 14 April 1846, Mary, eldest dau. of Stair Hathorn Stewart, Esq., of Physgill, co. Wigton, s.p.
Polkemmet, Linlithgow.

Baird—*continued.*

John —— *Cullen* 1669-72.

Son of James Baird, of Bankheid, a bailie of Cullen, left 3 sons.   "Baird History," p. 95.

John, younger of Newbyth —— *Edinburghshire* 1715-22.

Succeeded as 2nd Bart. on the death of his father, Sir William, 17 Feb. 1737, and died [s.p. 1745, when the title expired. See Foster's Baronetage.

Robert, of Newbyth —— *Haddington burghs* 1796, until he accepted the [Chiltern hundreds shortly before 10th March, 1802.

Father of Sir David, 2nd Bart. of Newbyth of the 2nd creation, and elder brother of Genl. Sir David Baird, G.C.B., cr. a bart. 13 April, 1809, etc. He d. 10 June 1828. See [Foster's Baronetage.

William, of Gartsherrie —— *Falkirk burghs* 1841 until he accepted the Chiltern [hundreds shortly before 2 May, 1846.

Of Elie, co. Fife (eldest son of Alexander Baird, of Lochwood, co. Lanark, by Jean Moffat his wife), d. 8 March, 1864, aged 68, having m. Janet Johnstone, and had 6 sons & 5 daus.

Balfour.

—— **laird of Burleigh** —— 1599 conv.

Sir Michael Balfour, of Burleigh, P.C. (son, heir of Sir James Balfour, of Pittendreich and Monquhany, co. Fife, who died 1583, by Margaret only dau. of Michael Balfour, of Burleigh, Ambassador to the Duke of Tuscany and Lorraine 1606, cr. Baron Balfour of Burleigh 16 July 1607, etc., d. 15 March 1619; he m. twice, and had an only dau. and heir. See [Foster's Peerage.

—— **laird of Burleigh** —— *Fifeshire* 1645.
Possibly John, afterwards 3rd Lord Balfour.

Bartholomew (sir), of Redheugh —— 1608.

David (sir), of Forret, senator of the College of Justice —— *Fifeshire* 1685-6.

Fourth son of Sir Michael Balfour, of Denmiln. Advocate 1650, Lord of Session 1674. [and knighted, a lord of Justiciary 1675, a commiss. for the plantation of Kirks 1685.

Duncan —— *St. Andrews* 1583 bis, 1588 conv.; 1594 conv. —— 1612, bailie.

George (sir), of 6, Cleveland Gardens, Hyde Park, London, Major-General royal artillery —— *Kincardineshire* 1872-4, 1874-80, since 1880 (see foot-note.)

BALFOUR, Genl. Sir George, K.C.B., 1870, (son of Capt. George Balfour, of Montrose, R.N.,) educated at Military Academy, Addiscombe, entered Madras Artillery 1825, Col. comdt. R.A. 1880 (retired list), Consul Shanghai, 1843-6, member Madras Military Board, 1849-57, Inspector-Genl. Ordnance Madras, 1857-9, member Military Finance Commission, India, 1859, 1860, president 1860-2, Ass. Compt.-Genl. War Office 1868-71, M.P. (liberal) Kincardineshire since 1872; b. 8 Dec., 1809; m. 28 June, 1848, Charlotte, 3rd dau. of late Joseph Hume, Esq., M.P.
6, *Cleveland Gardens, Hyde Park, W.*
Club—City Liberal.

Balfour—*continued.*

Henry (major), of Dunbog —— *Fifeshire* 1702-7.

3rd son of John, 3rd Lord Balfour of Burleigh, a major of dragoons, had a son Henry, of
[Dunbog. See note to Genl. Nesbitt Balfour, below.

James, of Whittinghame and Balgonie —— *Anstruther Easter* (now St. Andrews)
[*burghs* 1826-30, 1830-1. *Haddingtonshire* 1831-2, 1833-4.

Son of John Balfour, esq., of Balbirnie, co. Fife, died 19 April 1845, and m. (then of
Gorton, N.B.) 19 Jan. 1815, Lady Eleanor Maitland, dau. of James 8th Earl of Lauderdale;
[she d. 23 May 1869.

James Maitland, younger, of Whittinghame —— *Haddington burghs* 1841-7.

Of Whittinghame and Strathconan, N.B., eldest son of James Balfour, Esq., last named ;
b. 5 Jan. 1820, d. 23 Feb. 1856, having m. 15 Aug. 1843, Lady Blanche Gascoyne Cecil,
[2nd dau. of James 2nd Marquis of Salisbury ; she d. 16 May 1872, leaving issue.

John, of Trenaby —— *Orkney and Shetlandshire* 1790-6, 1820-6.

Eldest son of William Balfour, esq., of Trenabie, b. 6 Nov. 1750, d. s.p. 1842, having
m. 1783, Henrietta, sister of Sir Richard Joseph Sullivan, Bart., and widow of Col.
[Alexander McClellan.

John Blair, Solr.-Genl. Scotland, 1880 —— *Clackmannan* and *Kinross* since
.   [1880 (see foot-note).

Michael (sir), of Denmiln —— *Fifeshire* 1643-4 conv.

Married Jean Durham, of Pitkerro, and had with 2 daus., 5 sons, viz.—1. Sir James, Lord
Lyon, cr. a Bart. 22 Dec. 1633 ; 2. Sir Alexander, succ. as 3rd Bart. ; 3. Michael, ancestor
of Balfour of Randerston ; 4. Sir Andrew, an eminent physician ; 5. Sir David, mentioned
[above

Nesbitt (col.), A.D.C. to the King —— *Wigtown burghs* 1790-6.

A general 25 Sept. 1803, col. 39th foot, M.P. Arundel 1797-1802, died 10 Oct. 1823.
By his will directed that his nephew, William Stewart (3rd son of Robert Stewart of St.
Fort, co. Fife, by Ann Stewart, dau. of Henry Balfour of Dunbog) should assume the
[additional surname of Balfour. See also M.P. England.

Thomas (younger), of Elwick —— *Orkney and Shetlandshire* 1835-7.

Eldest son of William Balfour, of Trenabie, capt. R.N. and vice-lieut. of Orkney, b.
[2 April, 1810, died unm. 1838.

Balmanno.

. **Robert** —— 1473.

BALFOUR, RT. HON. JOHN BLAIR, Lord Advocate Scotland 1881, Solr.-Genl. for Scotland 1880-1
(son of Rev. Peter Balfour, minister of Clackmannan, by his wife, Jane Ramsay, dau. of John
Blair, esq., of Perth), educ. at Edinburgh University, advocate 1861, Q.C. 1880, D.L. Edinburgh,
M.P. (liberal) Clackmannan and Kinross since Nov., 1880 ; b. 11 July, 1837 ; m. 1st, 4 Aug., 1869,
Lilias Oswald, dau. of Lord Mackenzie, of Session, in Scotland ; she d. 19 June, 1872, leaving a son
Patrick, b. 23 April, 1870 ; he m. 2ndly, 6 April, 1877, Hon. Marianne Eliza, yr. dau. of James, Baron
Moncrieff, lord justice clerk, Scotland, since 1869, and has a son James Moncrieff, b. 6 July, 1878.

14, *Great Stuart Street, Edinburgh.*
Clubs—Devonshire, University and Liberal, Edinburgh.

Balnaves.

Henry —— *Perth* 1597 conv.

His namesake, Henry Balnaves, Lord Halhill of session 1538, Sec. of State 1543, in which year he was imprisoned in the Castle of Blackness. Accessory to the murder of Cardinal Beatoun, 29 May 1546, and in 1547 undertook with his associates to deliver Mary into the hands of the English, as also the Castle of St. Andrews; he was imprisoned at Rouen; his forfeiture was rescinded in 1556; re-appointed to a seat on the Bench 1563; the Regent
[Murray granted him the lands of Letham in Fife., etc. etc.

Bannatyne.

Hector, laird of Kaimes —— *Buteshire* 1617 (?), 1628-33, 1639-41 (then [younger), 1648.

Son of Ninian Bannatyne (and Mary, dau. of Duncan Campbell, of Auchinbreck), he m.
[Elizabeth, dau. of Patrick Stuart, of Rosslyn and Balshegray.

James —— *Ayr* 1569 conv.

"Burges of Air heritabill feur of the landis," in King's Kyle, 4 June 1576.

Ninian of Kames —— *Buteshire* 1667 conv.; 1669-74; 1678 conv.; 1681-2.

Son of Hector Bannatyne, aforesaid, He m. Elizabeth, eldest dau. of Sir James Stewart,
[Bart., of Bute, and had issue.

William —— *Lanark* 1545.

Bannerman.

Alexander —— *Aberdeen* 1833-4, 1835-7, 1837-41, 1841-7.

Eldest son of Thomas Bannerman, of Aberdeen, wine mercht., (brother of Sir Alexander Bannerman, 6th Bart.,) shipowner, banker, and merchant at Aberdeen, and provost, M.P. as above; lieut. governor Prince Edward Island 1851-4, knighted 3 Feb. 1851; governor of the Bahamas 1854-7, and of Newfoundland 1857-64; b. 8 Oct. 1788, d. s.p. 30 Dec. 1864, having m. 14 Jan., 1824, Margaret, 2nd dau. of Alexander Gordon, esq.; she d. 24 Dec. 1878. See
[Foster's Baronetage.

Barbour.

Robert, dean of Guild —— *Inverness* 1667 conv.

Barclay. See also addenda, page xviii.

James William, merchant, of 60, Dee St., Aberdeen —— *Forfarshire* 1872-4, [1874-80 and since 1880 (see foot-note).

John, dean of Guild —— *Cupar* 1669-72.

Robert (Mr.), provost —— *Irvine* 1639-41, 1643 conv., 1645-6, 1649, 1650, [1651.

In 1643 was of the Committee of Management for Ayrshire, and in 1646 for Committee of
[War. (Robertson's Ayr.)

BARCLAY, JAMES WILLIAM, of Aberdeen, merchant, shipowner, and farmer (son of late George Barclay, of Cults, Aberdeen, builder, by Margaret, dau. of James Massie), educated at University ·· of Aberdeen, Town Councillor Aberdeen, 1862-5, 1868-71, M.P. (Liberal) Forfarshire since 1872; b. 15 April 1832; m. 1st, 25 June 1863, Jane, dau. of John Smith, of Strathdon, she d. 3 Nov. 1865; he m. 2ndly, 12 April 1882, Lilian Alice, 2nd dau. of Augustus Henry Novelli, esq., of London; by his 1st wife he has an only surviving dau. Florence.
Aberdeen. Club—Reform.

Barclay—*continued.*

Robert, of Urie —— *Kincardineshire* 1788-90, 1790-6, 1796 until his death
[shortly before 8 June 1797.

Eldest son of Robert Barclay, of Urie, by his wife, Una, dau. of Sir Ewen Cameron, of
Lochiel ; d. at Urie, nr. Stonehaven 8, April 1797, aged 65 ; he m. 1st, Lucy, dau. of David
Barclay, of London, and 2ndly Sarah Anne, only dau. of James Allardice, of Allardice, and
[left issue extinct in the male line.

—— laird of Johnston-Barclay —— *Kincardineshire* 1650-1.

Barron.

James —— *Edinburgh* 1560, 1567, 1568, 1569 conv.

Patrick —— *Edinburgh* 1478, 1479 bis., 1482, 1483, —— 1526.

Barry.

Andrew —— 1526.

Baxter.

William Edward, merchant, of Dundee —— *Montrose burghs* 1855-7, 1857-9.
1859-65, 1865-8, 1868-74, 1874-80 (then of Kincaldrum, Forfarshire), and
[since 1880 (see foot-note).

Bayne.

Alexander, provost —— *Dingwall,* 1661-3, 1669-70.

Donald (sir) of Tulloch, Councillor —— *Dingwall* 1681-2 ; *Ross-shire* 1685-6.

John, younger, of Tulloch, Councillor —— *Dingwall* 1702-7.

Ranald —— *Dingwall* 1593.

Beattie.

Henrie, merchant trafficker, bailie —— *Dysart* 1669-74.

Robert —— *Montrose* 1644.

William, bailie —— *Bervie* 1685-6 ; 1689 conv. ; 1689 to 1702.

Bec. See also Bervic.

Andro —— *Edinburgh* 1367.

BAXTER, Rt. Hon. William Edward, of Kincaldrum, co. Forfar, and of Dundee, merchant,
P. C. 1873 (eldest son of Edward Baxter, of Kincaldrum, a merchant at Dundee, by Euphemia, dau.
of late Wm. Wilson, Esq., of Dundee), educated at University of Edinburgh, D.L. Forfar, M.P. (liberal)
Montrose since March 1855, Secretary to the Admiralty Dec. 1868 to 1871, joint Secretary to the
Treasury 1871 to Aug. 1873; b. June 1825; m. Nov. 1847, Janet, eldest dau. of late J. Home
Scott, Esq., of Dundee, and has 2 sons and 5 daus. (1) Edward Armitstead, b. Sept. 1848, (2) George
Washington, b. Nov. 1853, (3) Mary Euphemia, (4) Jessie Scott, (5) Alice Jane, m. 26 Jan. 1882, to
Major Alfred Gaselee, 4th Punjab Inf., (6) Edith Eleanor, (7) Rosa Elizabeth.
Kincaldrum, Forfar.
Clubs—Devonshire, Reform.

Scotch Members.   D *

Beniston.

Thomas —— *Pittenweem* 1579.

Belfrage.

Andrew, bailie —— *Dunfermline* 1681-2.

Bell

Andrew —— *Linlithgow* 1612 conv. and parlt. (then bailie), 1621, 1628-33;
[1630 conv.

George —— *Linlithgow* 1640, 1643-4 conv.; 1645, 1645-6 (then provost), 1648.

James —— *Glasgow* 1597 conv., 1612, —— 1643-4 conv. 1644 (then provost).

John, merchant, burgess, and late provost —— *Glasgow* 1661-3.

John, provost —— *Glasgow* 1681-2.

Lawrence —— *St. Andrews* 1357.

Patrick——*Glasgow* 1625 conv., 1639-41, then provost.

Robert —— *Linlithgow* 1646-7 (or James Gibbesone).

William —— *Stirling* 1545, 1546.

Belshes.

Alexander (sir), laird of Toftis —— *Berwickshire* 1644-7 (as laird of Toftis);
[1650-1, then senator of the College of Justice.

Served heir of his father, John Belches, of Tofts (now Purves Hall), Berwickshire.
[16 May 1632, knighted and apptd. Lord Tofts of Session, 2 July 1646, d. 1656.

John Wishart (sir), of Fettercairn (afterwards Stuart), Bart —— *Kincardineshire*
[1797 to 1802; 1802-6 as Sir John Stuart.

Only son of William Belches, esq., (by his wife and cousin Emilia, only surviving child
of John Belches, of Invermay, by his wife Mary Stuart, 2nd dau. of Sir George
Wishart, Bart., so created 17 June 1706, with remr. to the heirs of his body); became
3rd Baronet on the death of his great-uncle, Sir William Stuart, 1777; assumed that
surname in lieu of Wishart Belches (? Belches-Wishart), Oct. 1797, M.P. as above, a
baron of the Exchequer in Scotland 1807, d. 5 Dec. 1810, having m. 9 Nov. 1775, Lady
Jane Leslie, eldest dau. of David, Earl of Leven and Melville; she d. 28 Oct. 1829,
[leaving an only dau

Bennet.

James, captain, merchant trafficker —— *Inverkeithing* 1667 conv.; 1669-74,
[1678 conv.

William (Captain), of Grubbet —— *Roxburghshire* (or sheriffdom of Teviotdale),
1693 to 1702 (then younger); 1702-7, 1707-8, (first parliament of Great
[Britain.)

Sir William Bennet, cr. a Baronet of Nova Scotia 18 Nov. 1670, with remr. to the heirs
male of his body. Charles, eldest son of Hon. Alexander Stuart, of Dunearn (4th son of
[James, 3rd Earl of Moray), m. a dau. of Sir William Bennett, of Grubet, Bart.

Benson.
Patrick —— *Perth* 1560.

Cavendish-Bentinck.
William Henry, commonly called Lord William Bentinck —— *Glasgow* 1836-7; 1837 until he accepted the Chiltern hundreds shortly before
[24 June 1839.
A general in the army (second son of William Henry, 3rd Duke of Portland, K.G.), G.C.B. G.C.H. Gov.-Gen. of India 1827-35, Col. 11th Dragoons, Clerk of the Pipe in the Exchequer, M.P. Camelford 1796, Notts 1796-1803, 1812-14, 1816-26, Kings Lynn 1826-28; [m. and d. s.p. 17 June 1839. See Foster's Peerage, and M.P. England.

Bertrame.
George —— 1466, when elected an auditor of complaint.

Walter (Bartrahame) —— *Edinburgh* 1479, 1479 bis, 1482, 1483, 1485, [1492 bis.

William —— *Lanark* 1468.

Bervic. See also Bec.
Thomas —— *Edinburgh* 1445.

Bethune.
—— laird of Balfour —— *Fifeshire* 1621.
Probably David, 11th laird; b. 1574; m. Margaret Wardlaw, dau. of the laird of Torrie.

—— laird of Creiche —— *Fifeshire* 1644-5-6.
Possibly David Betoun, of Creich, who m. Margaret, dau. of Wm. Cunningham, 8th Earl [of Glencairn, she rem. to —— Chisholm, of Cromlix.

Alexander (Betoun) ——*Kilrenny* 1612.

Alexander (Beatoun), merchant, burgess —— *Kilrenny* 1641.
Alexander Bethoune, younger, appears in commission 23 Oct. 1641, James Beatone is found in the roll 15 July 1641. The 11th laird had a brother Alexander, who resided at Anstruther, and was father of Alexander, who m. —— dau. of William McDouall, of [Garthlands.

David, of Balfour —— *Fifeshire* 1702-7.
Son of Bethune, of Bandon; m. 1709 his cousin Anne, dau. cf David Bethune, 14th laird of Balfour. On the death of his brother-in-law, James Bethune, 15th laird, at Rheims 1719, [as stated below, he succ. to Balfour, and d. 1731.

George, brother german to the laird of Balfour, actual trader in the burgh ——
Kilrenny 1689 conv., 1689; his seat was declared vacant 25 April 1693, because
[he had not taken the oath of allegiance and signed the assurance.
Possibly the youngest son of John, 12th laird.

James (Mr.), younger, of Balfour, advocate —— *Kilrenny* 1702-7.
Succ. his father David, 14th laird, in 1709, joined the Stuarts in 1715, escaped to the Continent, and d. s. p. at Rheims 1719, having m. Anne, dau. of Major-Genl. Hamilton, of [Rood House, East Lothian.

Bissett.

Patrick, bailie —— *Lanark* 1661-3, 1665 conv., 1667 conv. (then provost), 1669-72 (then bailie).

Black.

Adam, bookseller and publisher in Edinburgh —— *Edinburgh* 1856-7, 1857-9, [1859-65.

Son of Charles Black of Edinburgh, builder; Lord Provost of Edinburgh for five consecutive years, 1843-8, J.P., D.L.; succeeded Thos. Babington Macaulay as M.P. Edinburgh in 1856; d. 24 Jan. 1874, aged 90, having m. 1817, Isabella, dau. of J. Tait,

Alexander, —— *Anstruther Easter* 1649, in absence of William Hamilton —— [*Anstruther Easter* 1661-3 (councillor).

John, bailie —— *Dysart* 1704-7.

Thomas —— *Montrose* 1367.

William —— *Anstruther Wester* 1648.

Blackburn.

Peter —— *Edinburgh* 1641.

Peter, of Killearn —— *Stirlingshire* 1855-7, 1857-9 (a lord of the treasury 1859), [1859-65.

Eldest son of John Blackburn, esq., of Killearn (by Rebecca Leslie, dau. Rev. Colin Gillies of Paisley), senior brother of Sir Colin Blackburn (cr. Lord Blackburn of Appeal 16 Oct. 1876); ed. at Eton, cornet 2nd Life Guards 1830, retd. as lieut. 1837, J.P., and D.L. co. Stirling; contested Edinburgh 1847, and Glasgow 1852; a Lord of the Treasury March to June 1859, died 20 May 1870, aged 59, having m. 1838, Jean, dau. [of Rt. Hon. James Wedderburn, Sol.-Gen. Scotland 1818, and had issue.

William —— *Inverkeithing* 1593 ——, 1617, 1621, 1628-33.

Blackwood.

John —— *Glasgow* 1727, unseated March 1728.

Blair. See also Hunter-Blair.

—— the laird of —— *Argyllshire* 1621, 1630 conv.

Bryce, laird of Blair, retoured heir to his father John 10 April 1610, and d. 4 Feb. 1639; [married Annabel Wallace.

—— laird of Ardblair —— *Perthshire* 1650-1.

James Blair, of Ardblair, etc., by charter from Charles I. 1626; m. —— dau. of Sir John [Blair, of Balgillo; d. before 1660.

—— laird of Balthyock —— *Perthshire* 1648.

Sir Thomas Blair, of Balthyock, retoured heir to his father Alexander 1621; knighted by Charles I.; had charters of lands 1637, 1642; d. about 1652, having m. 1st Margaret, dau. of Sir John Ayton, of that ilk, co. Fife, 2nd Margaret, dau. of Sir Alexander Gibson, of [Durie, relict of Thomas Fotheringham, of Pourie.

Blair—*continued.*

Alexander —— provost of —— *Perth* 1504.

Alexander Blair, of Balthyock, Perthshire, served heir to his father Thomas 1493 ; died 1509, having m. Jean, dau. of Andrew, 3rd Lord Gray, she rem. to Thomas, 3rd Lord Lovat.

Bryce, late provost —— *Annan* 1685-6, 1689 conv., 1689 until his death shortly [before 28 June 1698.

Edward (Mr.) —— *Culross* 1630 conv.

Gawin, of Braxfield —— *Lanark* 1617, 1621.

Writer to the signet ; 3 Aug. 1613 had a charter of the barony of Braxfield, which was purchased from Alexander Somerville ; he d. 1632—for his brother, Rev. James Blair, minister of Port Montgomerie, had a charter of the barony of Braxfield 16 June of that year.
[M'Kerlie's Galloway.

James —— *Ayr* 1617 conv. and parlt., 1628-33, 1630 conv.

Probably son of John, laird of Blair, and brother of Bryce, M.P. 1621.

James, of Penninghame —— *Wigtownshire* 1837-41.

M.P. Saltash 1818-20, Aldeburgh 1820-6, Minehead 1826-30. Died 9 Dec. 1841, having m. 27 Dec. 1815, Elizabeth Catherine, dau. of Lieut.-Genl. the Hon. Edward Stopford, son [of James, 1st Earl of Courtoun. See M.P. England.

Patrick —— *Perth* 1597 conv.

Patrick, 3rd son of Alexander Blair (1581), acquired the lands and barony of Pittendreich, [Perthshire ; m. —— Cargill, and had 6 sons and 3 daus.

Patrick, of Littleblair, sheriff —— *Orkney & Zetlandshire* 1663 (then sheriff [depute), 1669-72.

3rd son of Patrick Blair, of Pittendreich, Perthshire, lieut.-col. in the army, sheriff of [Orkney ; his only dau. Margaret m. to James Blair, of Ardblair.

William, of that ilk —— *Ayrshire* 1669-72, 1678 conv. (the laird), 1685-6 (the [laird), 1689 (the laird), conv., until his death shortly before 20 May 1690.

William, laird of Blair, retoured heir to his father John 5 Feb. 1664, commanded a troop of horse in Perthshire, which he raised at his own expense in the Revolution, was taken [prisoner by Lord Dundee.

William, of Blair —— *Ayrshire* 1829-30, 1830-1, 1831-2.

Only son of Major Hamilton Blair (son of William Scott, advocate, alias Blair) ; contested Ayrshire 1832 ; d. 21 Oct. 1841, having m. Madalene, dau. of John Fordyce, esq., of [Ayton, co. Berwick ; she d. 1817, leaving issue.

Blindsele.

Robert, alderman —— *Aberdeen* 1482, 1483.

Blyth.

Richard —— *Dundee* 1567 bis.

Bolton.

Joseph Cheney, of Carbrook, co. Stirling —— *Stirlingshire* since 1880.

Of Carbrook, co. Stirling, merchant, vice-chairman, Glasgow Chamber of Commerce, M.P. (liberal) Stirlingshire since 1880; his 3rd son Samuel m. 27 April 1881, Mary Susan, [dau. of John, son of late rear adml. Sir John Hindmarch, K.C.B.

Bonar.

[1471.

Wilyame —— *St. Andrews* 1456, 1468 (chosen an auditor of complaints),

Bonkill.

Alexander (Bonkle) —— *Edinburgh* 1472, 1479.

William —— *Dunbar* 1579.

Bontine.

William Cuningham, of Ardoch —— *Dumbartonshire* 1796, until he accepted [the Chiltern hundreds shortly before 15 May, 1797.

Elder son of Robert Cunninghame-Grahame, esq., of Gartmore, co. Perth, receiver-genl. for Jamaica. As the eldest son of his father, he became by an old entail the possessor of the estate of Ardoch, bearing the name and arms of Bontine during the lifetime of his father ; [he m. twice, and d. Nov. 1845.

Hugh (Buntine) (major), of Kilbryde —— *Ayrshire* 1690 to 1702.

Greatly distinguished at the battle of Philiphaugh, 13 Sept. 1645 ; Cromwell apptd. him muster master of horse in Scotland, acquired the lands of Kilbryde 1670. built his house in Kilwinning 1681, he disponed his barony of Kilbryde to his nephew William Baillie, of [Monckton 1714, —— *Robertson.*

Nicoll (Buntine), of Ardoch —— *Dumbartonshire* 1685-6.

Borthwick.

James —— *Edinburgh* 1649-50.

James, deacon of the Chirurgeons —— *Edinburgh* 1661, retired 19 Aug. 1662, [unable to attend on account of professional duties.

Boswell.

Hendrie (Boisivill) bailie —— *Kirkcaldy* 1667 conv.

James —— *Kinghorn* 1621.

John —— *Kinghorn* 1579, —— 1617.

[Robertstone).

John —— *Kinghorn* 1649 (or Mr. Robert Cunynghame), 1650-1 (or James

John, bailie and dean of Guild —— *Kirkcaldy* 1689 conv. ; 1689 to 1702.

John (Mr.) —— *Sanquhar* 1689 conv. ; 1689 until his death s.b. 24 Oct. 1692.

(Sir John) laird of Balmuto —— a minor baron 1599 conv.

See Douglas' Baronage, p. 310.

Bothwell.

Francis (Mr.) —— *Edinburgh* 1524, 1525, 1526, 1528, 1531, 1532, 1535.

Elder son of Richard Bothwell, provost of Edinburgh temp. James III., apptd. a lord of Session on its institution, 27 May. 1532, provost of Edinburgh 1535. He m. Janet, dau. and co-heir of Patrick Richardson of Meldrumsheugh, and got with her lands in the regality of Broughton ; his dau. Janet, by Sir Archibald Napier, of Merchistoun, was mother of John Napier, the inventor of logarithms ; his elder son Richard was provost of Edinburgh temp. Q. Mary, and his younger son Adam Bothwell, Bishop of Orkney 1562, a Lord of Session 1565 until his death 23 Aug. 1593, leaving with issue a son John, created Lord, Holyrood [House, 20 Dec. 1607, extinct on the death of his son John, 1635.

Bouverie.

Edward Pleydell —— *Kilmarnock burghs,* 1844-7, 1847-52, 1852-7 (V. P. board of trade April, and president poor law board Aug. 1855), 1857-9, 1859-[65, 1865-8, 1868-74. (See foot-note.)

Bower.

Alexander —— *Dundee* 1650, 1651.

Alexander Bower, of Kincaldrum, co. Forfar, was son of —— Bower of Methie and Kin-[caldrum, by the dau. of Thomas Sinclair, of Roslyn.

Bowmont & Cessford.   See **Innes-Ker**, page 193.

Bowring.

John, LL.D. London —— *Kilmarnock burghs* 1835-7.

Of Claremont, Devon, J.P. D.L. (eldest son of late Charles Bowring, esq., of Larkbeare, Devon, by Sarah, dau. of Rev. Thomas Lane, of St. Ives, Cornwall) ; contested Blackburn 1832 and 1834, and Kirkcaldy 1841 ; knighted at Buckingham Palace 16 Feb. 1854, H.M. plenipotentiary, commander-in-chief, governor and vice-admiral, Hong Kong, 1854-9, Grand Cross of the order of Leopold of Belgium, etc., envoy extraordinary to Siam, LL.D. Gröningen, F.R.S., M.P. as above and Bolton, co. Lancashire 1841-9 ; b. at Exeter 17 [Oct. 1792, d. 23 Nov. 1872, leaving issue. See " Annual Register Obituary," p. 169.

B OUVERIE, RT. HON. EDWARD PLEYDELL, of East Lavington, Wilts, J.P. (2nd son of William, 3rd Earl of Radnor, by his 2nd wife, Anne Judith, 3rd dau. late Sir Henry Paulet St. John Mildmay, Bart.), M.A., Trin. Coll. Camb., 1838, Bar.-at-Law, I.T. 1843, Under Sec. Home Department 1850-52, Chairman of Committees 1853-5, Vice-President Board of Trade 1855, President Poor-Law Board 1855-8, a Church. Estates Commissioner 1860-65 ; b. 26 April 1818 ; m. 1 Nov. 1842, Elizabeth Anne, youngest dau. of Gen. Robert Balfour, of Balbirnie, co. Fife, and has 2 sons and 3 daus.

(1) Walter, Capt. 2nd Wilts R.V. since 1876 ; b. 5 July 1848 ; m. 22 Feb. 1876, Mary, dau. of Rev. William Bridgeman-Simpson (E. BRADFORD), she d. 18 Jan. 1880, leaving 2 daus.

(2) Edward Oliver, b. 12 Dec. 1856.   (3) Anne.

(4) Eglantine ; m. 6 Dec. 1864, to Augustus Keppel Stephenson, H.M. Procurator-General and Solicitor-General to the Treasury s.p.   (5) Ruth.

Manor House, Market Lavington, Wilts.—44, *Wilton Crescent, S.W.*

Club—Brooks'.

Bowsie.

David (or William) —— *Crail* 1579.

Boyd.

Robert, lord provost of Glasgow —— 1575 conv., as a baron.

Robert, Lord Boyd, ancestor of Lord Kilmarnock, had charters of bailary and justiciary of the regality of Glasgow 2 Jan. 1573-4 ; a visitor of the university of Glasgow 1578, etc.
[See Douglas' Peerage.

Boyle.

```
JOHN BOYLE, of Kelburne, M.P.        JAMES BOYLE,  M.P.  Irvine
Buteshire 1678, conv. 1681-2,        1681-2, 1685-6.
1685 =
   |
DAVID BOYLE, of Kelburne, M.P. Buteshire 1689, conv. 1689, until cr.
Lord Boyle 31 Jan. 1699 ; cr. Earl of Glasgow 12 April, 1704 =
   |
—— 2nd Earl =
   |
—— 3rd Earl =            —— BOYLE =
   |                        |
= —— 4th Earl =          DAVID BOYLE, of Maress (son
   |                     of Hon. Patrick Boyle), Lord
   |                     Justice Clerk, M.P. Ayrshire
   |                     1807-11.
JAMES BOYLE-CARR (son of   GEORGE FREDERICK (son of
George, 4th Earl), M.P. Ayr-   George, 4th Earl), M.P. Bute-
shire 1839-41, 1841 until he   shire Feb. to July 1865 ; suc.
became 5th Earl of Glasgow   as 6th Earl of Glasgow 11 March
6 July 1843.                 1869.
```

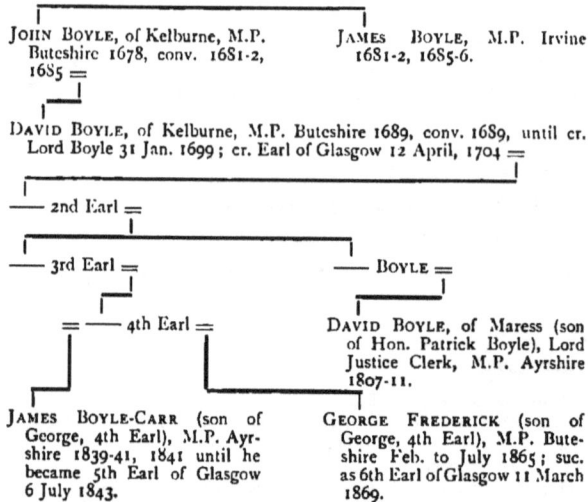

David, of Kelburne —— *Buteshire* 1689 conv. ; 1689 until created Lord Boyle
[31 Jan. 1699.

Elder son of John Boyle, of Kelburne, mentioned below, and whom he succeeded 7 Oct. 1685, P.C. 1695, treasurer depute 1703, cr. Earl of Glasgow, etc., 12 April, 1704, a commissioner for the treaty of the Union ; high commissioner to General Assembly of the Church of Scotland 1706-10, a representative peer 1707-8, 1708-10, lord register of Scotland 1708-14 ;
[d. 1 Nov. 1733. See Foster's Peerage.

David, of Maress, advocate, sol.-general for Scotland —— *Ayrshire* 1807
[until appointed a lord of session shortly before 22 March 1811,

Youngest son of Hon. Patrick Boyle, of Shewalton, advocate 1793, sol.-general 1807, a lord of session 28 Feb. 1811, and a lord of Justiciary, Lord Justice Clerk Nov. 1811, president of Court of Session, P.C.; b. 26 July 1772, d. 4 Feb. 1853, leaving issue. See E. Glasgow, Foster's Peerage. His grandson David, heir-presumptive to the earldom 1881.

Boyle—*continued.*

George Frederick —— *Buteshire* February to July 1865.

Sixth and present Earl of Glasgow, M.A., Oxon, D.L. Bute, and co. Ayr, contested Buteshire 1865, clerk of the registers and rolls in Scotland 1879, has two daughters. See
[Foster's Peerage.

James, merchant trafficker, provost —— *Irvine* 1681-2, 1685 6.

James Boyle (brother of John Boyle mentd. below), of Montgomeriestown. J.U.; m. Janet, dau. of Robert Barclay, provost of Irvine ; they had a son James, cashier of excise in Scotland [1707, a commissioner of excise 1709-14.

James (Boyle-Carr), commonly called Viscount Kelburne —— *Ayrshire* 1839-41, [1841 until he succeeded as 5th Earl of Glasgow (6 July 1843).

Elder son of George, 4th Earl of Glasgow, G.C.H., and half-brother of George Frederick, 6th Earl, sheriff principal Renfrewshire, assumed the additional surname of Carr by R.L., 2 Aug. 1823, contested Ayrshire 1837 ; d. s.p. 11 March 1869, having m. 4 Aug. 1821, Georgiana, dau. of Edward Hay-Mackenzie, esq., of Newhall and Cromarty. See Foster's
[Peerage.

John, of Kelburne —— *Buteshire* 1678 conv. ; 1681-2, 1685.

Eldest son of David Boyle of Halkshill, who m. Grizel, dau. and heir of John Boyle of Kelburn ; tacksman of excise 1684, d. 7 Oct. 1685 ; father of David Boyle mentd. above, cr.
[Earl of Glasgow. See Foster's Peerage.

Roger, Lord Broghill, president of his highness' council in Scotland —— *Edin*-
[*burgh* 1656 8. See also Ireland M.P.

1st Baron Broghill in Ireland, so cr. 28 Feb. 1628-9, M.P. co. Cork 1654-5, and was elected also 1656, but sat for Edinburgh as above, governor of Limerick in civil war, cr. Earl of Orrery at the Restoration 5 Sept. 1660 and made president of Munster, lord [justice 1660 and 1661 ; d. 6 Oct. 1679, aged 59. See Foster's Peerage, E. Cork.

Bredy.

Alexander —— 1653 (WILLIS).

One of the representatives for Scotland in the " barebones " or little parliament, July—
[Dec. 1653.

Brisbane.

John, of Bishoptoune —— *Renfrewshire* 1644-5 (then laird of Bishoptoune) 1650.

Son of John Brisbane of Bishoptoune, who died 1635 ; he married twice, and left daughters
[only.

John, younger, of Bishoptoune —— *Ayrshire* 1704-7.

Son of James Brisbane of that ilk, formerly Shaw ; his mother was Elizabeth, dau. of John Brisbane, and his wife was Elizabeth, grand-dau. of the same John ; he married (contracts 17 and 26 Oct. 1685) Margaret, dau. of Sir Archibald Stewart, of Blackhall, and had issue ; ancestor of Lieut.-Gen. Sir Thomas Makdougall-Brisbane, G.C.B., G.C.H., cr.
[a bart. 8 March 1836.

Brissie.

Benjamin, of Dolphinton —— *East Lothian* 1654-5 (WILLIS).

Brodie.

ALEXANDER BRODIE, of Lethen, M.P. Nairnshire 1646-7, 1649 =

SIR ALEXANDER BRODIE (son of David), M.P. Elgin and Forres-shire 1643-4, conv. 1645, 1646-7, 1649, 1650 =

(JAMES, of Kinlee, 3rd son) =

JAMES, M.P. Elgin and Forfarshire 1689 conv., 1689 to 1702, 1702-7.

GEORGE, of Aslisk (son of Joseph), M.P. Nairnshire 1693 to 1702, Forres 1703-7 =

(JAMES, of Whitehill) =

JAMES, of Brodie, M.P. Elginshire 1720.

ALEXANDER, of Brodie, Lord Lyon, King of Arms, M.P. Elginshire 1720-41, Caithness-shire 1741-7, Inverness burghs 1747-54.

ALEXANDER, younger, of Lethen (son of Alexander, of Duncarn), M.P. Nairnshire 1735-41.

JAMES, of Brodie (son of James of Spynic), M.P. Elginshire 1796-1802, 1802-6, 1806-7.

ALEXANDER, of Arnhall (3rd son of James of Spynie), M.P. Nairnshire 1785-90, Elgin burghs 1790-6, 1796-1802.

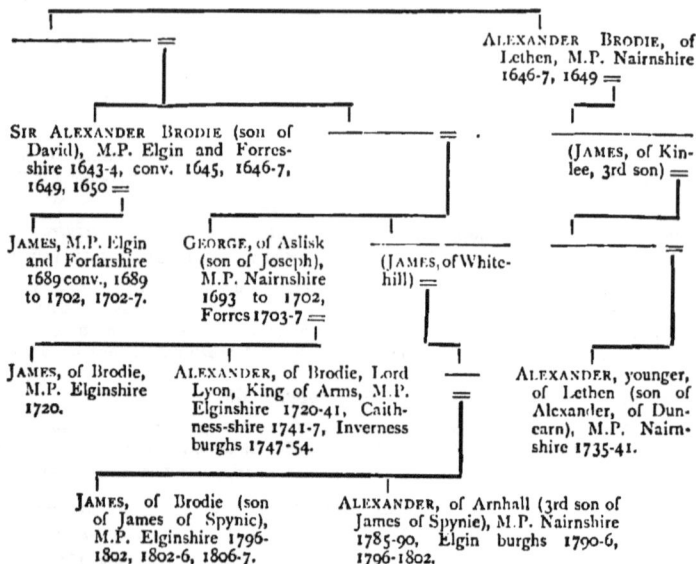

Alexander (sir), of that ilk —— *Elgin & Forresshire* 1643-4 conv.; 1645; [1646-7 (laird of Brodie); 1649 (then a knight), 1650.

Eldest son of David Brodie, of Brodie, by his wife Katherine, dau. of Mr. Thomas Dunbar, of Grange, dean of Moray; b. 25 July 1617; Lord Brodie of Session 22 June 1649; refused to act under Cromwell, and did not sit from Nov. 1649 to Dec. 1658; a commissioner to treat with Charles II. at Breda, as to his return to Scotland; commissary-general 1650; died 1679, having m. 28 October 1635, Elizabeth, dau. of Sir Robert Innes, widow of John [Urquhart, of Craigston, tutor of Cromarty, and had an only son James, mentioned below.

Alexander, of Lethen —— *Nairnshire*, 1646-7 (laird of Lethen), 1649.

2nd son of David Brodie, of Brodie, by his wife Janet, dau. of John Hay, of Lochloy and Park; purchased Lethen, etc., 1630-4; m. Margaret, dau. of James Clerk, of Balbirnie, co. [Fife, and d. 7 Nov. 1672, leaving issue.

Alexander, of Brodie, lord lyon king of arms, North Britain —— *Elginshire* 1720-2, 1722-7; (lord lyon, 1727); 1727-34; 1734-41; *Caithness-shire* 1741-7, [*Inverness burghs* 1747, until his death (9 March 1753-4).

2nd son of George Brodie, of Aslisk 1683, and of Brodie 1708 (see below); Lord Lyon, Scotland, 1727; b. 17 Aug. 1697, d. 9 March, 1753-4, having m. 3 Sept. 1724, Mary Sleigh, and left a son Alexander, died young, 1759; and a dau. Emilia, m. to Jno. Macleod, o [Macleod.

Brodie—*continued.*

Alexander, younger, of Lethen —— *Nairnshire* 1735-41.

Eldest son of Alex. Brodie, of Duncarn 1691, and of Lethen 1703 ; by his wife Sophia, dau. of Sir Hugh Campbell, of Calder (E. CAWDOR) ; died 28 April 1770 ; having m. 1754, [Henrietta, dau. of Col. Wm. Grant, of Ballindalloch, and had issue.

Alexander, late of Madras —— *Nairnshire* 1785-90. *Elgin burghs* 1790-6, 1796 [to 1802.

3rd son of James Brodie, of Spynie, who was grandson of Joseph of Aslisk ; 2nd son of David of Brodie ; acquired a considerable fortune at Madras, purchased Arnhall, Kincardine-shire ; b. 3 March 1748, d. 15 Jan. 1812, having m. 16 Aug. 1793, Elizabeth Margaret, dau. Hon. James Wemyss, of Wemyss Castle , she d. 19 July, 1800, leaving an only child, [Elizabeth, m. 11 Dec. 1813 to George 5th Duke of Gordon, G.C.B.

George, of Aslisk, " now heritor of Moynes " —— *Nairnshire* 1693 to 1702. [*Forres* 1703-7 then provost.

2nd son of Joseph Brodie, of Aslisk, by his 2nd wife ; succeeded to Aslisk 1683, and to Brodie 1708, mar. (contr. 10 Dec. 1692), Emilia, 5th dau. and co-heir of James Brodie, of Brodie (next mentioned), he died before 6 Jan. 1716, leaving with other issue, Alexander, [Lord Lyon, named above.

James, of that ilk —— *Elgin & Forfarshire* 1689 conv. ; 1689 to 1702, [1702-7.

Only son of Alexander Brodie, lord of session aforesaid, b. 15 Sept. 1637, m. (contract 16 July), 31 July 1659, Mary, dau. of Wm. Ker, 3rd Earl of Lothian, and died March [1708, leaving 9 daus.

James, of Brodie —— *Elginshire* 1720, until his death shortly before 29 Dec. [following.

Elder brother of Alexander Lord Lyon aforesaid, and eldest son of George Brodie, of [Aslisk and Brodie, also aforesaid ; died unm.

James, of Brodie —— *Elginshire* 1796-1802, 1802-6, 1806-7.

F.R.S. and L.S., Lord-Lieut. Nairnshire (eldest son of James Brodie, of Spynie, and grandson of James Brodie, of Whitehill, brother of George Brodie, of Brodie, who d. 1716) ; b. 31 Aug. 1744, d. 17 Jan. 1824, having m. 6 March 1768, Lady Margaret Duff, dau. of William 1st Earl of Fife, she was burnt to death at Brodie House, 24 April 1786, leaving [issue.

William, of Whitewreath —— *Forres* 1693 to 1702.

Broghill.   See Boyle.

Brolton.

Thomas —— *Lanark* 1540 bis.

Broun or Brown,

—— laird of Colstoun —— *Haddingtonshire* 1593 as a minor baron.

George Broun, 16th laird of Colstoun, m. Jean Hay, dau. of John 3rd Lord Yester, ancestor of the Marquis of Tweeddale, and d. 1603. His grandson St. Patrick was cr. a [Bart. of Nova Scotia 16 Feb. 1686. See Foster's Baronetage—CHAOS.

—— laird of Carlsluithe —— *Kirkcudbright* stewartcy, 1645-6.

John, son of John Broun (d. 1625), of Carsluith, who m. (contract) 26 March 1591, Janet, sister of Wm. Gordon, of Craichlaw, parish of Kirkcowan, " was alive in 1649, according to [the old valuation roll." Paterson's Ayr.

Adam —— *Jedburgh* 1641, 1644.

Merchant and dean of guild, Edinburgh 1647.

Andro —— *Perth* 1504.

George —— *Dundee* 1644 conv.

George —— *Haddington* 1649 in absence of John Sleigh.

Hugh —— *Edinburgh* 1596 conv.

Hugh —— *Inveraiy* 1689 conv., 1689 to 1702.

James —— *Kilrenny* 1651.

John (sir), of Fordell —— *Perthshire* 1649-50.

Sir John Broun of Fordel, eldest son of John of Fordel, and Catherine, widow of Sir John Lindsay of Balinscho and Woodhead, younger son of David, Earl of Crawford, dau. of John Lindsay of Balcarres and Menmuir, Lord Privy Seal, Secretary of State, Senator of the College of Justice, etc. He was knighted by Charles I. at Edinburgh, 6 Nov. 1641, was Major-General, Member of Committee of Estates, etc. Sir John was defeated, and taken prisoner by the English under General Lambert, on Sunday, 20 July 1651, near Inverkeithing, was sent to Leith, and died of fever 1 Sept. He m. (contract), 11 Feb. 1648, Mary, elder dau. and heir of Colonel Sir James Scott of Rossie, Fife, by Antonia, dau. of Sir Francis Willoughby, Governor of Dublin Castle, and had a posthumous son, John, who died in boy-hood, and a dau., Antonia, heiress of Rossie, her father's property being sequestrated and sold. She m., in June 1667, Alex. Dunlop of that ilk, co. Ayr, and had issue. Fordel was granted by charter, 19 July 1493, by George Brown, Bishop of Dunkeld, descended from the Browns of Midmar, co. Aberdeen, to his brother, Richard Brown, and Elizabeth Arnot [his wife and their heirs male, etc.

Broun or Brown—*continued.*

John (Mr.) —— *Jedburgh* 1645-6, 1649.

John —— *Burntisland* 1649, in absence of John Gardine.

Robert —— *Irvine* 1621, 1628-33, 1646-7, 1648.

Robert, bailie —— *Innerkeithing* 1650.

William —— *Haddington* 1581, 1586 conv.

William, provost —— *Inverary* 1678 conv., 1681-2.

Brownhill.

Adam, of —— *Edinburgh* 1367.

Bruce.   See also Cumming.

—— laird of Airth, minor baron in parlt. 1592, 1593 *bis.*

> Sir Alexander de Brus, of Airth, m. Janet, dau. of Alexander, 5th Lord Livingston, and was succ. by his grandson Sir John in 1603, ancestor of the Bruce baronetcies.   See Foster's
> [Baronetage.

Alexander (sir 1670-2), of Broomhall —— *Culross* 1661-3, 1669-74, 1678 conv., [1685-6 ; *Sanquhar* 1692 until expelled from parlt. 12 June 1702.

> Only son of Robert Bruce, of Broomhall, a lord of session 1649; served heir of his father 20 Feb. 1655, joint receiver-gen. of supply and excise 1693-5 ; expelled from parlt. "for a speech made against the presbytery ; " took his seat in parlt. as 4th Earl of Kincardine, 10 [Oct. 1706; ancestor of the Earl of Elgin and Kincardine. See Foster's Peerage.

Andrew, of Earlshall —— *Fifeshire* 1665 conv., 1667 conv.

> Andrew, son of Sir Andrew Bruce, of Earlshall, by Helen, dau. of Patrick 7th Lord Gray, m. 1st — dau. of Mr. James Reid of Pitlethie, relict of Sir Charles Arnot, of that ilk, and [2ndly his cousin, — Bruce, and had issue.

Anthony —— *Stirling* 1585, 1592, 1593, 1593 conv., *bis.*

Bruce—*continued.*

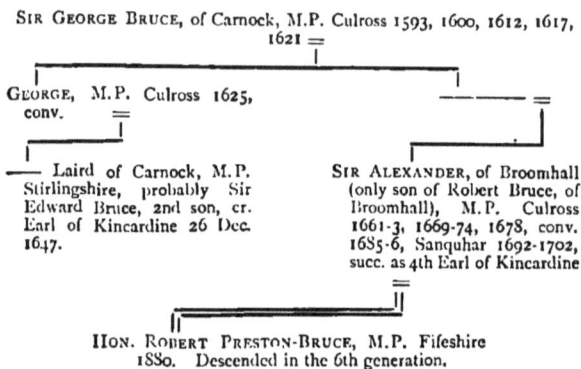

SIR GEORGE BRUCE, of Carnock, M.P. Culross 1593, 1600, 1612, 1617,
1621 =

GEORGE, M.P. Culross 1625,
conv. =

—— Laird of Carnock, M.P.
Stirlingshire, probably Sir
Edward Bruce, 2nd son, cr.
Earl of Kincardine 26 Dec.
1647.

SIR ALEXANDER, of Broomhall
(only son of Robert Bruce, of
Broomhall), M.P. Culross
1661-3, 1669-74, 1678, conv.
1685-6, Sanquhar 1692-1702,
succ. as 4th Earl of Kincardine

HON. ROBERT PRESTON-BRUCE, M.P. Fifeshire
1880. Descended in the 6th generation.

David, of Clackmannan —— *Clackmannanshire* 1678 conv., 1685-6, 1689 conv.,
1689 ; his seat was declared vacant 28 April 1693, because he had not signed
the assurance, and again 21 May 1700, because he had not signed the
[association.

Eldest son of Sir Henry Bruce, of Clackmannan (see below); he m. Margaret, dau. of
[George Mackenzie, 1st Earl of Cromarty, and d. s.p.

George (sir), of Carnock, knt. —— *Culross* 1593, 1600, 1612 (then a knt.), 1617,
[conv. and parlt., 1621.

2nd son of Sir Edward Bruce, of Blairhall ; knighted by James VI., a commissioner to treat
of union with England 1604, settled at Culross, where he established coal and salt works ; d. 6
May 1625, leaving issue, among others a 2nd son, Robert Bruce, of Broomhall, father of
Sir Alexander above named, ancestor of the Earl of Elgin and Kincardine.   See Foster's
[Peerage.

George —— *Culross* 1625 conv.

George Bruce, of Carnock, was served to his father 14 July 1625, member of Convention,
held at Edinburgh 27 Oct., 1 and 2 Nov. 1625 ; m. Mary, dau. of Sir John Preston, of Valleyfield, Bart., and had a son, Sir Edward (who probably represented co. Stirling in the convention 1644, see above), cr. Earl of Kincardine 26 Dec. 1647, and dying 1662, his brother
Alexander succ. as 2nd earl.   This line failed on the death of the 2nd earl's son Alexander,
3rd earl, Nov. 1705, and the title reverted to Sir Alexander Bruce, of Broomhall, above
[mentioned.

Bruce—*continued.*

SIR WILLIAM BRUCE, of Balcaskie, M.P. Fifeshire 1669-74, Kinross-shire 1681-2, 1685-6, cr. a Baronet 21 Oct. 1668 =

|
SIR JOHN, 2nd Bart., M.P.
Kinross-shire 1702-7, 1707-8.　　　　　Anne =

|
SIR JOHN (HOPE) BRUCE, 3rd Bart., M.P. Kinross-shire 1727-34, 1741-7.

Henrie (sir), of Clackmannan, knt., sheriff —— *Clackmannanshire* 1661-3, 1667 [conv., 1669-74, then sheriff.

Son of Robert Bruce, of Clackmannan ; knighted by Charles II.; m. Mary, dau. of Sir [Alexander Shaw, of Sauchie, and had with other issue, David mentioned above.

Henry Austin, of 1 Queen's Gate, London —— *Renfrewshire* 1869, until cr. Lord [Aberdare 23 Aug. 1873. (See foot-note.)

—— laird of Carnock —— *Stirlingshire* 1644 conv.

Probably Sir Edward Bruce (2nd son of George Bruce, who represented Culross in the Convention 1625), created Earl of Kincardine and Lord Bruce of Torry 26 Dec. 1647, with [remr, to his heirs male.

John, of Wester Abden, baillie —— *Kinghorn* 1678 conv.

John, of Kinross —— *Kinross-shire* 1702-7, (1st parlt. of Great Britain) 1707-8.

Only son of Sir William Bruce (2nd son of Robert Bruce of Blairhall), mentioned below. Succ. his father as 2nd Bart. 1710, m. May 1687, Christian, dau. of John Leslie, Duke of [Rothes, and dowager of James, 3rd Marquis of Montrose.

BRUCE, HENRY AUSTIN, Baron Aberdare, of Duffryn, co. Glamorgan (U.K.), so created 23 Aug. 1873, P.C., bar.-at-law, L.I. 1837, hon. D.C.L. Oxon. 1880, police magistrate Merthyr Tydvil, 1847-52, M.P. 1852-68, M.P. Renfrewshire 1869-73, under secretary of state (home department) 1862-4, secretary, 1869-73, lord president of the council 1873-4, second church estates commr. 1865-6, vice-president of the council 1866-7, president univ. coll. of Wales since 1875, president R. hist. soc. : (2nd son of John Bruce Bruce-Pryce, of Duffryn, co. Glamorgan, paternally KNIGHT); b. 16 April, 1815 ; m. 1st, 6 Jan. 1846, Annabella, only dau. of Richard Beadon, esq., of Clifton, Glouc. ; she died 28 July, 1852, having had a son and 3 daus. He m. 2ndly, 17 Aug. 1854, Nora Creina Blanche, youngest dau. of late Lieut.-Gen. Sir William Napier, K.C.B. (B. NAPIER), by whom he has 2 sons and 7 daus. See Foster's Peerage.

Duffryn, Aberdare, co. Glamorgan.—1, *Queen's Gate, Kensington, W.*
Club—Athenæum.

Bruce—*continued.*

John (sir), of Kinross, Bart. —— *Kinross-shire* 1727 34, 1741-7.

3rd and youngest son of Sir Thomas Hope, 4th Bart. of Craighall, by his wife Anne, only dau. of Sir Wm. Bruce, of Kinross, Bart , and eventually sole heir of her brother Sir John aforesaid. Sir William (see below) entailed his estate, failing issue of his son's body, to his dau. Anne and the heirs male of her body whomsoever succeeding to bear the name and arms of Bruce of Kinross. Sir John Hope succ. his brother Sir Thomas (Hope) Bruce of Kinross and Craighall, Bart., and became Sir John Bruce of Kinross (and Craighall), the 7th Bart. of his family, comd. a regt. of Foot, Governor of Bermuda 1721-7, d. 5 June 1766, one of the oldest lieut.-genls. in the British service; m. 1st Charlotte, dau. of Sir Charles Halkett, of Pitferran, Bart., he m. 2nd Marianne, daughter of Rev. William Denune of Pencaitland, East Lothian [(of the Catboll family). See " Hope Pedigree " in Foster's Baronetage.

Patrick, of Bunzoin —— *Cupar* 1702-7.

Robert (Brus.) —— *Stirling* 1504, 1526.

—— laird of Clackmannan —— *Clackmannanshire* 1617.

Probably Sir Robert Bruce, knighted by James VI., married twice and had issue—his [grandson Sir Henry, M.P.

Robert, merchant, bailie —— *Kinghorn* 1681-2, 1685-6.

Robert, of Kennet —— *Clackmannanshire* 1820, until he accepted the Chiltern [hundreds shortly before 13 July 1824.

Eldest son of Alexander Bruce, of Kennet, and grandson of Robert Bruce, Lord Kennet of session 1764, and a lord of justiciary 1767, served in the Peninsula and at Waterloo, claimed (through his gt. grandmother) the barony of Balfour, which was allowed (subject to the attainder of the 5th Lord), by the committee for privileges in the House of Lords 23 July 1868; he d. 13 Aug. 1864, aged 69, and the attainder of 1715 was reversed by act of parlt. 19 March 1869, in favour of his son Alexander Hugh Bruce, who became 6th Lord Balfour, of Burleigh. [See Foster's Peerage.

Robert Preston (commonly called Hon. Robert Preston), 2nd son of the Earl [of Elgin —— *Fifeshire* since 1880. (See foot-note.)

Thomas —— *Stirling* 1628-33, 1630 conv.

Thomas, of Weltown, provost —— *Stirling* 1639-41, 1643-4 conv., 1644-5, 1649 [(late provost), 1649 or John Shorte.

B RUCE, Hon. Robert Preston (2nd son of James, 8th Earl of Elgin, K.T., by his 2nd wife, Lady Mary Louisa Lambton, c.i., dau. of John George, 1st Earl of Durham), educated at Eton and at Balliol College, Oxford, Capt. Fife Arty. Mil. since 1877, M.P. Fifeshire since 1880, heir presumptive to the Earl of Elgin ; b. 4 Dec. 1851.
22, *Eaton Square, S.W.*

Bruce—*continued.*

William (sir), of Balcaskie —— *Fifeshire* 1669-74; *Kinross-shire* 1681-2, 1685-6.

2nd son of Robert Bruce, of Blairhall, by Jean Preston. He took a prominent part in the restoration of Charles II., and was appointed clerk to the bills 1660, acquired the lands of Balcaskie, co. Fife, and was cr. a Bart. of Nova Scotia, with that designation, 21 Oct. 1668; master of the king's works. Designed and completed the palace of Holyrood House. Purchased the lands and barony of Kinross from the Earl of Morton, and from which he took his designation. He m. 1st, Mary, dau. of Sir James Halkett, of Pitferrane, Bart., and 2ndly Magdalen Scot; by his 1st wife he had a son, Sir John Bruce, 2nd Bart. aforesaid, and a dau., Annie, m. 1st to Sir Thomas Hope, of Craig Hall, Bart., mother *inter alia* of Lieut.-Gen. of Sir John (Hope) Bruce, Bart. aforesaid. She re-m. to Sir John Carstairs, of Kilconquhar, [and had a son and 3 daus.

Brunton.

David —— *Lanark* 1585.

Bryce.

John —— *Dumfries* 1687.

Buchan.   See Hepburn.

Buchanan.

Arthur, of Sound —— *Orkney and Zetlandshire* 1667, conv.

George, of that ilk —— *Stirlingshire* 1643-4, conv. ; 1644-5, 1645-6, as laird of [Buchanan 1649-50, 1650.

Sir George, 21st laird of Buchanan (son of Sir George) Col. of Stirlingshire regt, died a prisoner 1651, having been taken at the battle of Innerkeithing ; he m. Elizabeth, dau. of [— Preston of Craigmiller, and had a son John, next mentd., and 3 daus.

John, of that ilk —— *Stirlingshire* 1661-3.

John, 22nd and last laird of Buchanan, m. 1st, Mary, dau. of Henry Erskine, Lord Cardross, and had a dau. ; he m. 2ndly, Jean, dau. of Mr. Andrew Pringle, a minister, and had [another dau. ; he d. Dec. 1682.

John, of Ardoch —— *Dumbartonshire* 1821-6.

Only son of Thomas Buchanan, esq., of Ardoch, co. Dumbarton, by his 1st wife Margaret Buchanan, vice.-lieut. Dumbartonshire ; b. 8 Jan. 1761, d.   having m. 1 Nov. 1785, Elizabeth, dau. of John Parkes, esq., of Netherton, co. Worc. ; she d. 4 Sept. 1807 ; grand- [father of Thomas John Buchanan, now of Ardoch.

Neil, merchant, late in Glasgow, now in London —— *Glasgow burghs* 1741, until [his death shortly before 26 March 1744.

Of Hillington, co. Renfrew, 4th and youngest son of George Buchanan, of Glasgow, merchant. (See Foster's Baronetage.) d. 13 Feb. 1743-4, having had a son and 3 daus., of the latter Anne (eldest) m. to John Oswald, Bishop of Raphoe 1763-80, and Maria (youngest) [m. to Robert Oliphant, of Rossie, postmaster-genrl. Scotland 1767.

Buchanan—*continued*.

Thomas Ryburn (esq.), of 10, Moray Place, Edinburgh —— *Edinburgh* [since 1881.

Of the Inner Temple, bar.-at-law 1873 (3rd son of late John Buchanan, formerly a Glasgow merchant), educated at High School of Glasgow, and Sherborne School, B.A. Balliol College, Oxford 1870, M.A. double first-class in moderations in 1867, a first-class in the final school of *Literæ Humaniores* in 1869, and gained Stanhope prize for an English historical essay in 1868, fellow of All Souls College since 1871, contested Haddingtonshire at the general [election 1880; b. 2 April 1846, unm.

Walter (younger), merchant in Glasgow —— *Glasgow* 1857, 1857-9, 1859-65.

Of Shandon, Hellensburgh, co. Dumbarton, eldest son of Andrew Buchanan, esq., of Glasgow, by Margaret, dau. of J. Cockburn, esq., of Edinburgh. A merchant in Glasgow J.P.D.L., co. Dumbarton, and a magistrate for Lanark; educated at Glasgow University; b. 1797; d. 1877, having m. 1st, 1824, Mary, dau. of John Hamilton, esq., of Middleton, and [2ndly, 1851, Christina Laura, dau. of James Smith, esq., of Jordan Hill; she d. 1853.

Bully.

Williame —— *Edinburgh* 1440.

Bunsch.

Alexander —— *Perth* 1468, 1478 bis., 1483.

Andrew —— *Perth* 1526.

Burgh.

Johnne de —— *Stirling* 1357.

Burnesyde.

John —— *Culross* 1650-1.

Burnett.

—— laird of Leys, 1605 conv., a minor baron —— *Kincardineshire* 1621, laird of [Leys Burnet.

Alexander Burnett, of Leys, m. Katharine, dau. of Alexander Gordon, of Lessmoir, co. Aberdeen, and d. 1619, having had with 8 daus. 5 sons, of whom the eldest, Sir Thomas, knighted circa 1625, was created a baronet of Nova Scotia 21 April 1626. See Foster's [Baronetage.

Thomas (sir), of Leys, knight baronet —— *Kincardineshire* 1689 conv., 1689 [to 1702, 1702-7, 1707-8 (1st parlt. of Great Britain).

3rd Baronet, and son of Sir Alexander, 2nd Bart., a strenuous opponent of the Union; m. Margaret, dau. of Robert, 2nd Viscount Arbuthnott; d. 1714, having had issue; ancestor [of Sir Robert Burnett. But see Foster's Baronetage.

Bury, Viscount. See Keppel.

C.

Cadyock.
Richard, of —— *Montrose* 1357.

Cadyow.
Johnne, of (master) —— *Aberdeen* 1440.

Caird.
James, of Baldoon —— *Stirling burghs* 1859-65. See foot-note.

Cairmunt.
Samuel, bailie —— *Kirkcudbright* 1681-2.

Cairns.
Bartholomew (Carnys) —— *Edinburgh* 1479.

Calder.
James, merchant burgess, councillor ——*Elgin* 1669-72 ; *Elgin* and *Forres-shire*
[1685-6, of Moortoune.

Sir James Calder, of Muirtown, Morayshire, Bart. of Nova Scotia, so cr. 5 Nov. 1686, with remainder to his heirs male (eldest son of Thomas Calder, provost of Elgin 1665, by his wife Margaret Sutherland); m. Grizel, dau. of Sir Robert Innes, of Innes, Bart., and d. [1711, leaving issue. See Foster's Baronetage.

Caldwell.
John, of that ilk —— *Renfrewshire* 1690, until his death s.b. 12 June 1700.

Callander.
Alexander, of Crichton —— *Aberdeen* (now Montrose) *burghs* 1790, until his
[death s.b. 18 May 1792.

4th son of Alexander Callander and his wife Margaret, youngest dau. of David Ramsay, of Lethendie, etc.; younger brother of Sir John Callander, bart ; born at Westertown, co. Stirling, 20 and bap. there 21 Aug. 1741; d. unm. 5 April 1792, bur. at W.

CAIRD, JAMES, of Cassencary, co. Kirkcudbright, C.B., F.R.S., 1875 (son of James Caird, of Stranraer N.B.), J.P. D.L., co. Wigton, M.P. Dartmouth 1857-9 (see England M.P.) and as above, *Times* agricultural commissioner 1850-1, chairman royal sea fishery commission 1864-5, a member of the fishery board 1861, senior commissioner for inclosures, etc., England and Wales 1865, Indian famine commissioner 1878, president of the statistical society 1880-2; b. 1816; m. 1st, 1843, Margaret, dau. of Capt. Henryson, R.E., she d. 1863, leaving 3 sons and 2 daus. ; he m. 2ndly, April 1865, Elizabeth Jane, dau. of late Robert Dudgeon, esq., of London.
Cassencary, Creetown, N.B.
Clubs—Reform, Athenæum, Political Economy.

Callander—*continued*.

James Henry, of Ardkinglass —— *Argyllshire* 1833-4.

Of Craigforth, co. Stirling, and Ardkinglass, co. Argyll (elder son of Lieut.-Col. George Callander, of Craigforth) ; b. 18 August 1803, d. at Newcastle-on-Tyne 31 Jan. 1851, having m. 1st, 29 August 1837, Hon. Jane Plumer Erskine, youngest dau. of David Montague, Lord Erskine ; she d. 30 March 1846, leaving 3 daus.; he m. 2ndly, 1 July 1847, Charlotte Edith Eleonora, only dau. of late John George Campbell, Esq., of the Islay family, and had [2 sons. See Chart Pedigree, page 49.

John, merchant burgess —— *Kirkcudbright* 1686.

Cameron.

Charles, LL.D., of Glasgow —— *Glasgow* 1874-80, and since 1880 (see foot-note).

Donald, of Lochiel, residing at Achnacarry House, near Fort William —— *Inverness-shire* 1868-74, 1874-80 (a groom in ordinary in waiting 1874), and [since 1880 (see foot-note).

James —— 1474.

Campbell.　See also Argyll.

Alexander (Mr.), of Glenstrae —— *Argyllshire* 1678, conv.

Alexander (younger), of Calder —— *Nairnshire* 1693 (vice his father, Sir Hugh [Campbell, of Calder, infirm), until his death s.b. 6 June 1700.

Sir Alexander Campbell died in Isla, 27 Aug. 1697, having m. 1689, Elizabeth, only dau. of Sir John Lort, Bart., and co-heir of her brother, Sir Gilbert Lort, of Stackpole Court, co. Pembroke, Bart. ; she d. 28 Sept. 1714, bd. in Westminster Abbey; father of John Campbell, named below, etc., etc. See Chart Pedigree, page 53, and Foster's Peerage, [E. CAWDOR.

CAMERON, CHARLES, of Glasgow (son of late John Cameron, of Glasgow and Dublin), educated at Madras College and at St. Andrews N.B., entered Trin. Coll. Dublin, 1858, first senior medical prizeman Dublin University School 1861, etc., prize essayist and gold medallist Dublin Pathological Society, 1862, B.A. same year, M.B. and Master in Surgery (took first places), M.D. M.A. 1865, LL.D. 1871, has never practised, M.P. (liberal) Glasgow since 1874 ; b.　　　　1841 ; m. 1869, Frances Caroline, youngest dau. of late J. W. Macauley, M.D.
　　261, West George Street, Glasgow.—80, St. George's Square, S.W.

CAMERON, DONALD, of Lochiel (eldest son of late Donald Cameron, of Lochiel, by Lady Vere Catherine Louisa Hobart (pp.), sister of the 5th and 6th Earls of Buckinghamshire), educated at Harrow, in diplomatic service 1852-9, Groom-in-Waiting to the Queen 1874-80, M.P. (conservative) Inverness-shire since Dec. 1868 ; b. 5 April, 1835 ; m. 9 Dec. 1875, Lady Margaret Elizabeth Montagu-Douglas Scott, 2nd dau. of Walter Francis, 5th Duke of Buccleuch, K.G., and has 3 sons.
　　(1) Donald Walter, b. 4 Nov. 1876.　　　(2) Ewen Charles, b. 18 Feb. 1878.
　　(3) Allan George, b. 27 July 1880.
　　Achnacarry, Fort William, N.B.　　　　　　*Clubs—White's and Carlton.*

Campbell—*continued.*

CAMPBELL OF CESSNOCK.

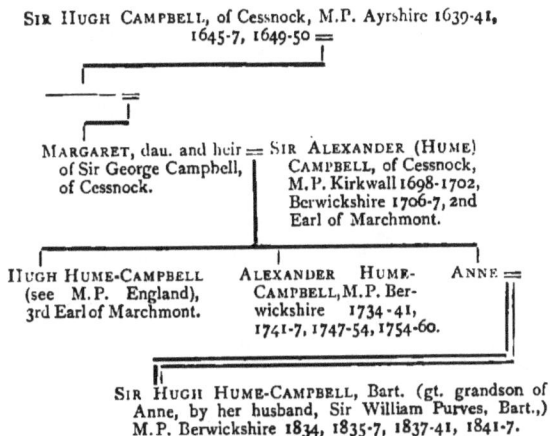

SIR HUGH CAMPBELL, of Cessnock, M.P. Ayrshire 1639-41,
1645-7, 1649-50 =

MARGARET, dau. and heir = SIR ALEXANDER (HUME)
of Sir George Campbell,   CAMPBELL, of Cessnock,
of Cessnock.   M.P. Kirkwall 1698-1702,
Berwickshire 1706-7, 2nd
Earl of Marchmont.

HUGH HUME-CAMPBELL   ALEXANDER HUME-   ANNE =
(see M.P. England),   CAMPBELL, M.P. Ber-
3rd Earl of Marchmont.   wickshire 1734-41,
1741-7, 1747-54, 1754-60.

SIR HUGH HUME-CAMPBELL, Bart. (gt. grandson of
Anne, by her husband, Sir William Purves, Bart.,)
M.P. Berwickshire 1834, 1835-7, 1837-41, 1841-7.

Alexander (sir), of Cessnock, senator of the College of Justice —— *Kirkwall* 1698-
[1702 (as Sir Alexander Home); *Berwickshire* 1706-7.

2nd Earl of Marchmont (on the death of his father, Patrick Hume, 1st Earl 1 Aug.
1724), K.T. 1725, advocate 1696, knighted by the style of Sir Alexander Campbell of
Cessnock, having assumed that surname by reason of his marriage. Ordinary lord of
session in place of Sir Colin Campbell of Aberuchill 1704, with title of Lord Cessnock
(which he resigned in favour of his brother Sir Andrew Hume in 1714), a commissioner of
the Exchequer, P.C. Raised 400 of the Berwickshire militia, and joined the Duke of
Argyll at Stirling, on the breaking out of the rebellion in 1715; envoy-extraordinary to
Denmark and Prussia 1715, lord clerk register 1716-33, first ambassador to the Congress
at Cambray 1721, P.C. England 1726, a representative peer 1727; d. in London 27
February 1740, aged 65, having m. 29 July 1697, Margaret, dau. and heir of Sir George
Campbell of Cessnock, co. Ayr, and had issue, Alexander, M.P. (see below), and Hugh,
[Lord Polwarth.

Alexander (capt.), late 75th foot —— *Nairnshire* 1784, until his death, s.b.
[22 Dec. 1785.

Grandson of (Sir) Alexander, M.P. Nairnshire, named above, and son of John Campbell,
M.P.; he died Nov. 1785, having m. Frances, only dau. of Philip Medows, esq., (E.
MANVERS); she d. July 1769, leaving a son who became Gen. Sir Henry Frederick
Campbell, K.C.B., G.C.H., M.P. See Foster's Peerage, E. CAWDOR, and Chart Pedigree,
[page 53.

Campbell—*continued*.

CAMPBELL OF MONZIE.

ROBERT CAMPBELL, of Finab, M.P. Argyllshire, 1766-8, 1768-72 =

ALEXANDER CAMPBELL, of Monzie, M.P. Anstruther Easter 1797 to 1802, 1802-6, Stirling burghs 1807-12, 1812-18 =

ALEXANDER CAMPBELL, of Monzie, M.P. Argyllshire 1841-3.

Alexander (genl.), of Monzie —— *Anstruther Easter* (now S. Andrew) *burghs* 1797-1802 (major-genl.), 1802-6 (lt.-genl.), *Stirling burghs* 1807-12, 1812-18, [then general.

Son of Robert Campbell of Finab, M.P., (derived from Archibald Campbell of Monzie, 4th son of Sir Duncan Campbell, 1st Baronet of Glenorchy, ancestor of the Earls of Breadalbane). He died at Leamington, 24 Feb., 1832. Col. 32nd foot 1813-32, 13th foot 1804-13, major-genl. 1794, lieut.-genl. 1801; served in Canada under Genl. Carleton 1776, and under Genl. Burgoyne 1777, in N. America until 1782; captain of light infantry in the campaigns of 1793 and 1794, the latter under the Duke of York, etc. etc.—served under Sir Ralph Abercromby in West Indies, 1796, etc. etc.; by his wife Christina Menzies [he left a son next named. See Chart Pedigree above.

Alexander of Monzie —— *Argyllshire* 1841, until he accepted the *Chiltern* [*hundreds;* s.b. 8 Sept. 1843.

Alexander Cameron-Campbell, esq., of Monzie Castle, co. Perth, and Inverawe, co. Argyll, (only son of Genl. Alex. Campbell M.P., aforesaid), 15th Hussars, assumed the additional surname of Cameron on his marriage; b. 30 Dec. 1812, d. 5 Jany. 1869, having m. 29 May 1844, Christina, only child of Sir Duncan Cameron, Bart., of Fassifern, and had [issue. See Chart Pedigree above.

Alexander Hume, —— *Berwickshire* 1734-41, 1741-7, 1747-54, 1754 (lord [clerk Register of Scotland 1756), until his death, s.b. 1 Jan. 1761.

4th son of Alexander, 2nd Earl of Marchmont, aforesaid, and younger brother of Hugh 3rd Earl (see POLWARTH, England M.P.) Solicitor to the Prince of Wales 1741, etc.; b. 15 Feb. 1708, d. s.p. 19 July 1760, aged 53, having m. 16 July 1737, Miss Elizabeth Pettis, [who d. 6 Sept. 1770. See Chart Pedigree, preceding page.

Archibald (Sir), K.B. (1788), of Inverneil, Inverness-shire, lt.-col. of forces in India, —— *Stirling burghs* 1774-80, 1789 90, 1790, until his death, s.b. 4 May [1791.

Of Inverneil (younger brother of Sir James Campbell, M.P. Stirling, see below, and 2nd son of James Campbell, commissary of the Western Isles of Scotland, and chamberlain of Argyll, by his wife Elizabeth, dau. of James Fisher, of Durren, provost of Inverary), col. 74th Highlanders, hereditary usher of the White Rod for Scotland, governor of Jamaica 1782, and of Fort St. George (Madras) 1785-9, K.B., invested 30 Sept. 1785, installed 1788, governor and commander-in-chief of the forces on the coast of Coromandel, in the East Indies. Maj-Genl. 1782; b. 21 August, 1739, d. s.p. in London 31 March 1791; buried in Westminster Abbey. He m. 1779 Amelia, dau. of Allan Ramsay, esq., of Kinkell, the portrait painter, (son of Allan Ramsay the poet), she d. 8 July 1813, [buried with her husband

Campbell—*continued.*

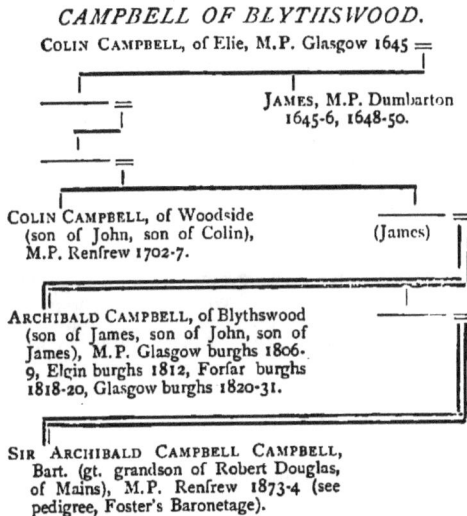

CAMPBELL OF BLYTHSWOOD.

COLIN CAMPBELL, of Elie, M.P. Glasgow 1645 =

JAMES, M.P. Dumbarton
1645-6, 1648-50.

COLIN CAMPBELL, of Woodside
(son of John, son of Colin),
M.P. Renfrew 1702-7.

(James)

ARCHIBALD CAMPBELL, of Blythswood
(son of James, son of John, son of
James), M.P. Glasgow burghs 1806-
9, Elgin burghs 1812, Forfar burghs
1818-20, Glasgow burghs 1820-31.

SIR ARCHIBALD CAMPBELL CAMPBELL,
Bart. (gt. grandson of Robert Douglas,
of Mains), M.P. Renfrew 1873-4 (see
pedigree, Foster's Baronetage).

Archibald, of Blythswood —— *Glasgow burghs* 1806-7, 1807, until he accepted the *Chiltern hundreds*, s.b. 30 June 1809; *Elgin burghs* 1812; *Perth burghs* [1818-20; *Glasgow burghs* 1820-6, 1826-30, 1830-1.

(Son of James Campbell, formerly James Douglas of Mains). Of Blythswood, co. Renfrew L.L., (to which he succeeded on the death of his elder brother Lt.-Col. John Campbell, who fell at Martinique Feb. 1794), major 1st Royals; d. unm. 13 June 1838, aged 75, when Blythswood passed to Archibald, father of Sir Archibald Campbell Campbell, Bart. [M.P., the present possessor. See Foster's Baronetage, and Chart Pedigree above.

Archibald Campbell, of Blythswood, Renfrewshire —— *Renfrewshire* 1873-4. [See foot-note, and Chart Pedigree above.

Archibald Islay (Sir), of Succoth, Bart. —— *Argyllshire* 1851-2, 1852-7.

3rd Bart. (eldest son of John Campbell, M.P. Dumbarton), on the death of his grandfather Sir Archibald, 2nd Bart., 23 July, 1846; b. 15 May, 1825, d. s.p. 11 Sept., 1866, having m. 1 July, 1858. Lady Agnes Grosvenor, 7th dau. of Richard, Marquis of Westminster; she re-m. 5 December, 1871, to Philip Frank, M.D. See Foster's Peerage and Baronetage, [and also Chart Pedigree, page 57, post.

CAMPBELL, SIR ARCHIBALD CAMPBELL, of Blythswood, co. Renfrew, J.P., D.L., vice-lieut., Baronet, so created 4 May, 1880, capt. and lieut.-col. late Scots Guards, col. commanding Renfrew militia since 1878; contested Renfrewshire 1874, and again in 1880; b. 22 Feb., 1837; m . 7 July, 1864, Hon. Augusta Clementina Carrington, dau. of Robert John, 2nd Lord Carrington. *Blythswood House, Renfrew, N.B. ; 2, Seamore Place, May Fair, W.*

Campbell—*continued.*

CAMPBELL, DUKE OF ARGYLL.

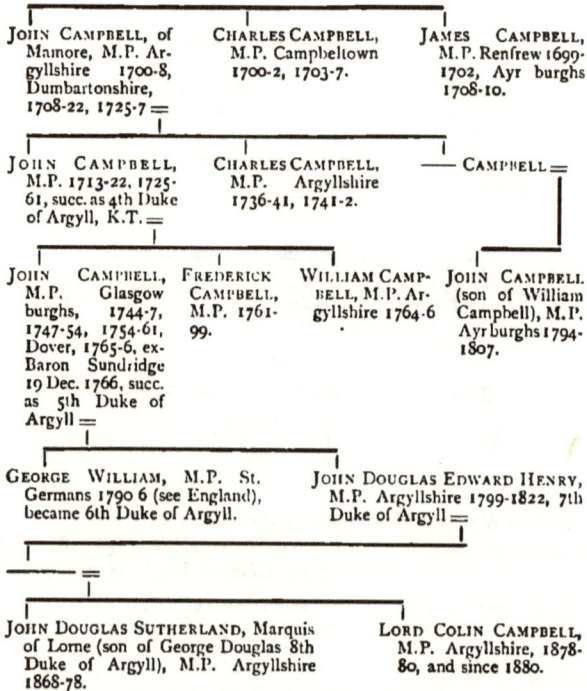

JOHN CAMPBELL, of Mamore, M.P. Argyllshire 1700-8, Dumbartonshire, 1708-22, 1725-7 =	CHARLES CAMPBELL, M.P. Campbeltown 1700-2, 1703-7.	JAMES CAMPBELL, M.P. Renfrew 1699-1702, Ayr burghs 1708-10.

JOHN CAMPBELL, M.P. 1713-22, 1725-61, succ. as 4th Duke of Argyll, K.T.=	CHARLES CAMPBELL, M.P. Argyllshire 1736-41, 1741-2.	—— CAMPBELL =

JOHN CAMPBELL, M.P. Glasgow burghs, 1744-7, 1747-54, 1754-61, Dover, 1765-6, ex-Baron Sundridge 19 Dec. 1766, succ. as 5th Duke of Argyll =	FREDERICK CAMPBELL, M.P. 1761-99.	WILLIAM CAMPBELL, M.P. Argyllshire 1764-6.	JOHN CAMPBELL (son of William Campbell), M.P. Ayr burghs 1794-1807.

GEORGE WILLIAM, M.P. St. Germans 1790 6 (see England), became 6th Duke of Argyll.	JOHN DOUGLAS EDWARD HENRY, M.P. Argyllshire 1799-1822, 7th Duke of Argyll =

——— ==

JOHN DOUGLAS SUTHERLAND, Marquis of Lorne (son of George Douglas 8th Duke of Argyll), M.P. Argyllshire 1868-78.	LORD COLIN CAMPBELL, M.P. Argyllshire, 1878-80, and since 1880.

Charles (Mr.), brother-german to the Earl of Argyll —— *Campbeltown* 1700-2,
[1703-7.

Col. in the Army. Second brother of Archibald 1st Duke of Argyll, whom he supported in the expedition against James VII. He was taken prisoner, and the Marquis of Atholl resolved to hang him, but he was eventually taken to Edinburgh ; forfeited on his own confession, 21 Aug. 1685, and banished. His forfeiture was rescinded in 1689; he m. Sophia, 2nd dau. of Alexander Lindsay, 1st Earl of Balcarres ; this lady was the means of accom-[plishing the Earl of Argyll's escape from Edinburgh Castle. See Chart Pedigree above.

Charles (capt.), of Auchnacreive —— *Argyllshire* 1736-41, 1741 until his death
[s.b. 5 Feb., 1741-2.

Second son of Hon. John Campbell, of Mamore, and next brother of John 4th Duke of_ [Argyll, he d. unm. Jan. 1742. See Chart Pedigree above.

Coline —— *Glasgow* 1645.

Probably identical with Colin Campbell, of Elie, provost of Glasgow 1636. See Campbell Blythswood, in Foster's Baronetage; see Chart Pedigree, preceding page.

Campbell—*continued.*

CAMPBELL OF ARDKINGLASS.

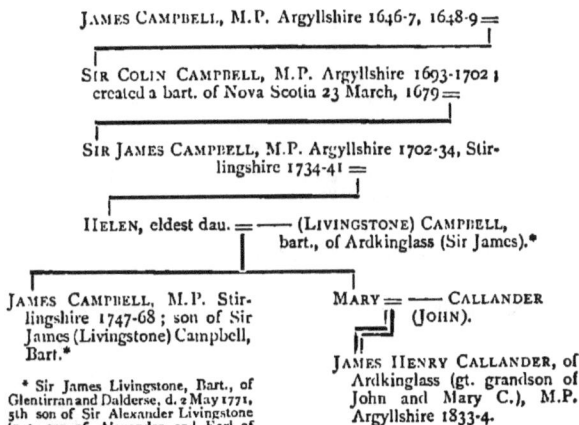

JAMES CAMPBELL, M.P. Argyllshire 1646-7, 1648-9 =

SIR COLIN CAMPBELL, M.P. Argyllshire 1693-1702 ; created a bart. of Nova Scotia 23 March, 1679 =

SIR JAMES CAMPBELL, M.P. Argyllshire 1702-34, Stirlingshire 1734-41 =

HELEN, eldest dau. = —— (LIVINGSTONE) CAMPBELL, bart., of Ardkinglass (Sir James).*

JAMES CAMPBELL, M.P. Stirlingshire 1747-68 ; son of Sir James (Livingstone) Campbell, Bart.*

* Sir James Livingstone, Bart., of Glentirran and Dalderse, d. 2 May 1771, 5th son of Sir Alexander Livingstone (nat. son of Alexander and Earl of Callendar) who was created a baronet of Nova Scotia 20 July 1685, and died July 1695.

MARY = —— CALLANDER (JOHN).

JAMES HENRY CALLANDER, of Ardkinglass (gt. grandson of John and Mary C.), M.P. Argyllshire 1833-4.

Colin (Sir), of Aberuchill —— *Inverary* 1669-74, (then provost) ; *Perthshire* 1690-1702, knight baronet, senator of the College of Justice and privy [councillor

Sheriff depute Argyllshire 1668, senator of the College of Justice as Lord Aberuchill 1689, lord of justiciary, P.C. 1690, acquired the barony and castle of Kilbryde 1669, estimated his losses inflicted by the Highland army under Lord Dundee at £17,201 Scots, compensation was granted him by Act of Parliament, but he never received it ; cr. Bart. of Nova Scotia between 23 Jan. 1667, and 16 May 1668, and between the years 1672 and 1703 he registered his arms in the Lyon office four times ; (son of James Campbell, of Aberuchill, who fell at the battle of Worcester, and his wife Ann, dau. of Patrick Hepburn, of Wooling ;) he d. at Edinburgh, 16 Feb. 1704, having m. 1st, Margaret, dau of Alexander Foulis, of Ratho, and 2ndly, Catherine, dau. of Sir John Mackenzie, of Tarbert, Bart., (E. CROMARTY,) and had [issue.

Colin (Sir), of Ardkinglass, knight baronet —— *Argyllshire* 1693-1702.

Created a Bart. of Nova Scotia 23 March 1679, with remainder to the heirs male of his body (s. of James Campbell, of Ardkinglass, M.P.) ; d April, 1709, having m. Helen, dau. of Sir Patrick Maxwell, of Newark, co. Renfrew, and had a son, Sir James, 2nd Bart., M.P. [See chart pedigree above.

Colin, of Woodside, provost —— *Renfrew* 1702-7.

Son of John Campbell, of Woodside, d. 1746 ; both his sons died s.p. See Campbell of [Blythswood, Foster's Baronetage, and chart pedigree, page 47 ante.

SCOTCH MEMBERS.   G

Campbell—*continued*.

CAMPBELL OF AUCHINBRECK.

SIR DUNCAN CAMPBELL, 2nd Bart., M.P. Argyllshire 1628-33,
1639-41, 1643 =

SIR DOUGALL CAMPBELL, 3rd
Bart., M.P. Argyllshire 1649.   =

SIR DUNCAN CAMPBELL, 4th Bart. (son of Archibald Campbell), M.P. Argyllshire 1689-1700 =

SIR JAMES CAMPBELL, 5th Bart., M.P. Argyllshire 1702-8.

Colin, commonly called Lord Colin, of Inverary Castle, Inverary, Argyllshire, [gentleman —— *Argyllshire* 1878-80 ; and since 1880.

> Fifth and youngest son of George Douglas, 8th Duke of Argyll, K.T.; b. 8 March, 1853 ; m. 21 July, 1881, Gertrude Elizabeth, youngest daughter of Edmund Maghlin Blood, esq., [of Brickhill, co. Clare. See chart pedigree, page 48.

Daniel (or Donald), of Ardintenie, councillor —— *Inverary* 1702-7, sat also in 1st parlt. of *Great Britain* 1707-8 ; *Glasgow burghs* 1716-22 (of Schawfield, [merchant), 1722-7, 1728-34.

> Daniel Campbell, 1st of Schawfield (2nd son of Walter Campbell, capt. of "Skipnish,") purchased Ardentenny, from his nephew (the son of his sister) ; one of the Scots Commissioners who signed the Treaty of Union ; m. twice, and d. 8 June, 1753, aged 82, leaving [issue. See chart pedigree, page 59.

Daniel, of Schawfield, (esq.) —— *Lanarkshire* 1760-1, 1761-8.

> Grandson of Daniel Campbell, M.P., last named (and eldest son of John Campbell, a commissioner of Inland Revenue, by his 2nd wife, Lady Harriet Cunyngham); d. unm. 13 May, 1777. See chart pedigree, page 59.

Dougall (Sir), of Auchinbreck —— *Argyllshire* 1649.

> Third Bart. on the death of his father Sir Duncan, M.P., in 1645 ; resigned the command of his regiment in Ireland, and declared for the king ; d. s.p. shortly after the Restoration. [See chart pedigree above.

Dugall (col.), of Ballimore —— *Argyllshire* 1754-61 (captain) 1761, until ap- [pointed master of the revels in Scotland, s.b. 17 Jan. 1764.

> 2nd son of Archibald Campbell, of Ballimore ; he m. Christian Drummond, and d. 30 Dec. [1764, having had a son Duncan, of Lochnell, M.P. See chart pedigree, next page.

Campbell—*continued.*

CAMPBELL OF LOCHNELL.

```
        |
SIR DUNCAN CAMPBELL, of Lochnell,            |    =
  knt., M.P. Argyllshire 1747-54.            |
                                             |
        |
     DUGALD CAMPBELL, of Ballimore,
       M.P. Argyllshire 1754-64 =
                   |
        |
     DUNCAN CAMPBELL, of Lochnell,
       M.P. Ayr burghs 1809, 1812-18.
```

——, laird of Glenorchy, a minor baron in parlt. 1592 ; (*Argyllshire*) 1593, 1599 [conv.

Sir Duncan Campbell, of Glenorchy (son of Sir Colin Campbell), knighted by James VII. at the coronation of Queen Anne, 18 May 1590, heritable keeper of the forest of Mamlorn 1617, sheriff of Perthshire, cr. a Baronet of Nova Scotia 30 May 1625, d. June 1631, ancestor of the Earls of Breadalbane. See Foster's Peerage, and also chart pedigree, page 58, post.

Duncan (sir), knight baronet —— *Argyllshire* 1628-33 (fear of Auchinbreck, but [not styled knight baronet) ; 1639-41 (then baronet), 1643 conv.

Son of Sir Dugald Campbell, of Auchinbreck, knight (1617) and baronet, so cr. 12-24 Jan. 1628 ; he espoused the parlt. cause in his father's lifetime, was a commissioner for the debts of the nation and for English supply 1641, a commissioner to Ireland, and commanded a regiment there in 1644, was recalled to oppose the Marquis of Montrose, and was killed in 1645 ; he m. twice ; his eldest son became Sir Dugald, 3rd baronet, M.P., his 2nd son Archibald was father of Sir Duncan, 4th baronet, M.P. See chart pedigree, preceding page.

Duncan, of Carrick —— *Dumbartonshire* 1639-41, 1648 " laird of Carrick."

Duncan (sir), of Auchinbreck —— *Argyllshire* 1689 conv. ; 1689 parlt. until [his death s.b. 28 Nov. 1700.

4th Baronet (son of Archibald Campbell of Knockemelie), m. Henrietta, dau. of Alexander Lindsay, 2nd Earl of Balcarres, and had a son, Sir James, M.P. See chart pedigree, pre- [ceding page.

Duncan (sir), of Lochnell, knt. —— *Argyllshire* 1747-54.

7th of Lochnell (son of Alexander Campbell by his wife Margaret Stewart), knighted by Q. Anne ; d. s.p. 10 March, 1765, having m., 1st, Isabella, widow of Roderick Macleod of Macleod, and dau. of Kenneth Mackenzie, 3rd Earl of Seaforth ; he m., 2ndly, Margaret, [dau. of Daniel Campbell, of Schawfield. See chart pedigree above.

Duncan (general), of Lochnell —— *Ayr burghs* 1809 (then lieut.-gen.), 1812-18.

8th of Lochnell, and also of Barbreck (son of Col. Dugald Campbell of Ballimore, M.P., master of the revels in Scotland), col. 91st Highlanders 1796, general in the army 1819 ; d. s.p. Apr. 1837, having m., 1st, 6 July 1792, Hon. Eleonora, widow of Sir George Ramsay, bart., of Barnff, and dau. of George (Fraser) Lord Saltoun ; she d. he m., 2ndly, 14 May 1808, Augusta, dau. of Sir William Murray, bart., of Ochtertyre ; [she d. 12 Mar. 1846. See chart pedigree above.

Campbell—*continued.*

Frederick, commonly called Lord Frederick; counsellor at law —— *Ayr burghs* and *Glasgow burghs* 1761-8, sat for the latter (keeper of the privy seal, Scotland, in 1765); *Glasgow burghs* 1768-74 (lord clerk register of Scotland 1768), 1774-80; *Argyllshire* 1780-84, 1784-90, 1790-96, 1796, until he acc.
[the *Chiltern hundreds*, s.b. 30 Oct. 1799.

F.S.A. 1792, F.R.S. 1793 (3rd son of John, 4th Duke of Argyll, K.T.), counsellor-at-law P.C. 1765, chief secretary to Viscount Townshend, lord-lieut. Ireland 1767, and was M.P. St. Canice 1767 (see Ireland M.P.), lord clerk register of Scotland, confirmed to him for life 1771, laid the foundation stone of the general register house 1774, col. Argyllshire Fencibles 1778, unduly elected for Dumbartonshire 1780; a vice-treasurer, Ireland, and a member of Board of Control 1786, treasurer of the Middle Temple 1803; d. 8 June 1816, aged 87, having m. 28 Mar. 1769, Mary, dau. of Amos, and sister of Sir William Meredith, of Henbury, Cheshire, bart., dowager of Lawrence, 4th Earl Ferrers; she was burnt to death [at Combe Bank, near Tunbridge, 25 July 1807. See chart pedigree, page 48.

George (sir), D.C.L., K.C.S.I., of Edenwood —— *Kirkcaldy burghs* 1875-80,
[and since 1880. See foot-note.

George Pryse, captain, R.N., 2nd son of John, Lord Cawdor —— *Nairnshire*
[1820-6, 1830-1, a groom of the bedchamber 1831.

Died a rear-admiral 12 Jan. 1858, s.p., having m. 13 Oct. 1821, Charlotte, 2nd dau. of [General Isaac Gascoyne. See chart pedigree, next page.

Henry Frederick, col. 1st regiment Foot Guards —— *Nairnshire* 1796-1802,
[1806-7.

General Sir Henry Frederick Campbell, K.C.B., G.C.H. (only son of Capt. Alexander Campbell, M.P.), col. 88th foot 1824. 25th foot 1831; b. 10 July 1769, d. 2 Sept. 1856, having m. 10 Apr. 1808, Emma, dau. of Thomas Williams, esq., of Temple House, Berks, and Craig-y-don, Anglesey, and widow of Lieut.-Col. Thomas Knox; she d. 20 Mar. 1847, leaving with 2 daus. an only son, Col. Campbell, of Evenley Hall, Northants. See chart [pedigree, next page.

Hugh of Loudoun —— *Irvine* 1579 (provost), 1587 (provost); sheriff of Ayr;
[sat as a minor baron in conv. 1597 and 1599.

Sir Hugh Campbell, Lord Campbell, of Loudoun, so cr. 30 June 1601, P.C. (elder son of Sir Matthew Campbell, of Loudoun); d. 15 Dec. 1622, leaving an only son by his first wife, [ancestor of the Earls of Loudoun. See chart pedigree, page 56.

CAMPBELL, Sir George, K.C.S.I. (eldest son of late Sir George Campbell, of Edenwood, co. Fife, only brother of John, Lord Campbell, M.P. (see post), Lord Chancellor of England, Bar.-at-Law, I.T. 1854, Bengal C.S. 1842-68, Lieut.-Governor Bengal 1869-74, Hon. D.C.L. Oxon 1870, member of Indian Council 1874-5, late Judge Supreme Court, Calcutta, M.P. (liberal) for Kirkcaldy burghs since 1875; b.   1824; m.   1854, Letitia, dau. of late Thomas Gowan Vibart, Esq., B.C.S., and has 2 sons and 2 daughters.

(1) George, b.   , 1861.   (3) Margaret Julia.
(2) Archibald Gowan, b.   , 1868   (4) Elizabeth Jane.
13, *Cornwall Gardens, S. W.*   *Clubs—Athenæum, Brooks', and Reform.*

Campbell—*continued.*

CAMPBELL OF CALDER.

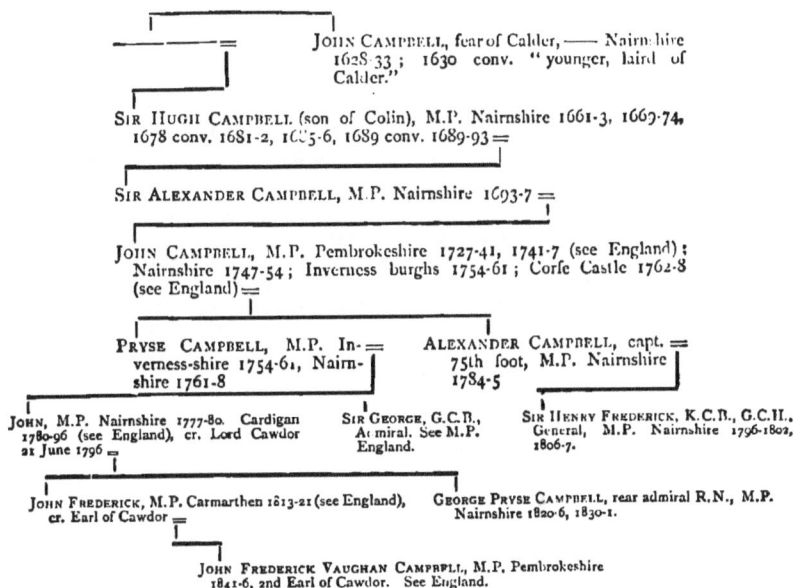

JOHN CAMPBELL, fear of Calder, —— Nairnshire 1628-33 ; 1630 conv. "younger, laird of Calder."

SIR HUGH CAMPBELL (son of Colin), M.P. Nairnshire 1661-3, 1669-74, 1678 conv. 1681-2, 1685-6, 1689 conv. 1689-93 =

SIR ALEXANDER CAMPBELL, M.P. Nairnshire 1693-7 =

JOHN CAMPBELL, M.P. Pembrokeshire 1727-41, 1741-7 (see England): Nairnshire 1747-54 ; Inverness burghs 1754-61 ; Corfe Castle 1762-8 (see England) =

PRYSE CAMPBELL, M.P. Inverness-shire 1754-61, Nairnshire 1761-8 = | ALEXANDER CAMPBELL, capt. = 75th foot, M.P. Nairnshire 1784-5

JOHN, M.P. Nairnshire 1777-80. Cardigan 1780-96 (see England), cr. Lord Cawdor 21 June 1796 = | SIR GEORGE, G.C.B., Admiral. See M.P. England. | SIR HENRY FREDERICK, K.C.B., G.C.H., General, M.P. Nairnshire 1796-1802, 1806-7.

JOHN FREDERICK, M.P. Carmarthen 1813-21 (see England), cr. Earl of Cawdor = | GEORGE PRYSE CAMPBELL, rear admiral R.N., M.P. Nairnshire 1820-6, 1830-1.

JOHN FREDERICK VAUGHAN CAMPBELL, M.P. Pembrokeshire 1841-6, 2nd Earl of Cawdor. See England.

Hugh (sir), of Cessnock —— *Ayrshire* 1639-41, 1645-7 (laird of Cessnock), [1649-50, then a knight.

Son of George Campbell, of Cessnock, he m. Elizabeth, younger dau. and co-h. of George Campbell, MASTER of Loudoun, and d. 20 Sept. 1686, aged 71, appointed Lord Justice Clerk and Lord of Session by parlt. in 1649, but declined those offices ; was heavily fined, and in 1665 was imprisoned in Edinburgh Castle. where he remained 2 years ; imprisoned again in 1683, with his eldest son Sir George ; tried for treason (the Bothwell rising) in the following year, and acquitted, and also in 1685 (the Rye House plot). and found guilty ; he was attainted, and his estates were forfeited ; they were, however, restored to his son, Sir George, [by act of parliament in 1690. See chart pedigree, page 45.

Hugh (sir), of Calder, knt. —— *Nairnshire* 1661-3 (then sheriff), 1669-74, 1678 conv., 1681-2, 1685-6, 1689 conv., 1689 until 28 Apr. 1693, when his seat [was delared vacant because he had not signed the assurance.

Nephew of Sir John Campbell, M.P. (son of Colin Campbell, by his wife Margaret Brodie); knighted 1660, d. 11 March 1716, having m. 1662, Harriet, dau. of James Stewart, 3rd Earl of Moray, father of Sir Alexander Campbell, M.P. before named. See chart [pedigree above.

Campbell—*continued*.

Hugh Purves-Hume (sir), of Marchmont and Purves, bart. —— *Berwickshire* [1834, 1835-7, 1837-41, 1841-7.

7th baronet on the death of his father, 9 Apr. 1833; b. 15 Dec. 1812 ; m. twice, and has an [only dau. See Foster's Baronetage, and chart pedigree, page 45, ante.

Ilay, lord advocate of Scotland —— *Glasgow burghs* 1784, until appointed lord [president of the Court of Session, s.b. 26 Feb. 1790.

Sir Ilay Campbell, solicitor-gen. 1783, lord advocate 1784, M.P. Glasgow burghs 1784-9, lord rector Glasgow University, D.C.L. 1784, lord President of the Court of Justice in Scotland by the title of Lord Succoth 1789-1808, was cr. a baronet on his retirement from office 17 Sept. 1808 (elder son of Archibald Campbell, of Succoth), b. 25 Aug. 1734, d. 28 Mar. 1823, having m. in 1766 Susan Mary, dau. of Archibald Murray, of Murrayfield (Lord Henderland of Session and Court of Justiciary, 1783-95, M.P. co. Peebles), and had issue. [See Foster's Baronetage, and also chart pedigree, page 57.

James (Mr.), provost —— *Dumbarton* 1645-6, 1648-50.

3rd son of Colin Campbell, of Elie, married, and died s.p. See Campbell of Blythswood, [Foster's Baronetage, and chart pedigree, page 47.

James —— *Linlithgow* 1649 (2nd session); or James Crawford, 1649 (3rd [session).

James, of Ardkinglass —— *Argyllshire* 1646-7 (laird of Ardkinglass), 1648-9.

Married Isabel, dau. of Sir Robert Campbell, of Glenorchy, and was father of Sir Colin [Campbell, of Ardkinglass, Bart., M.P. See chart pedigree, page 49.

James, provost —— *Glasgow* 1678 conv.

James (Mr.), brother to the Earl of Argyll —— *Renfrew* 1699-1702 —— *Ayr* [*burghs* 1708-10 (then burgess of Rothesay).

Of Burnbank and Boquhan (youngest brother of Archibald, 1st Duke of Argyll), captain of dragoons, attained the rank of colonel, eloped with Mary, dau. of Sir George Wharton (marriage annulled by act of parliament 20 Dec. 1690), m. Margaret, 3rd dau. of David Lesly, Lord Newark, the celebrated commander; she d. 19 Apr. 1755, having had issue. [See chart pedigree, page 48.

James (sir), of Auchinbreck, Bart. —— *Argyllshire* 1702-7, sat in 1st parlt. of [Great Britain 1707-8.

Fifth Bart. on the death of his father, Sir Duncan Campbell, M.P. 1700. He d. at Lochgair 14 Oct. 1756, æt. 78, having m. thrice, and had issue. See Foster's Baronetage, [and chart pedigree, page 50 ante.

Campbell—*continued.*

James (sir), of Ardkinglass, Bart. —— *Argyllshire* 1702-7 (fear of Ardkinglass), sat in 1st parlt. of Great Britain 1707-8 (then younger of Ardkinglass), and by the same designation for *Argyllshire* 1708-10, and as a Bart. 1710-18, 1713-15, 1715-[22, 1722-7, 1727-34; *Argyllshire* and *Stirlingshire* (sat for latter) 1734-41.

A commissioner equivalent, commissary of musters Scotland, governor of Stirling Castle, commissioner of customs England and Scotland. died 5 July 1752, aged 86, when the title became extinct (son of Sir Colin Campbell, of Ardkinglass, Bart., M.P.); he m. 1st Margaret, dau. and co-heir of Mr. Adam Campbell, heiress of Gargunnock, co. Stirling, and 2ndly Anne, dau. of John Callendar, of Craigforth, and widow of Col. Blackader, and had issue by his 1st wife, 3 daus., of whom the eldest, Helen, married, as shown in the chart pedigree, and was mother of Sir James Campbell, M.P., next named. See chart pedigree, page 49.

James, of Ardkinglass —— *Stirlingshire* 1747-54 (then capt. younger), 1754-61, [1761-8, governor of Stirling Castle, 1763.

3rd Bart. (on the death, 2 May, 1771, of his father, Sir James Campbell, alias Livingstone, of Ardkinglass); he died 21st Nov., 1788, having m., 1752, Katherine, dau. and coheir of Walter Campbell, receiver-gen. of customs, and had, with other issue, a son, Sir Alexander Campbell, who m. 1792, Marianne, only dau. of John Cheape, esq., of the Sauchie family. She d. 23 Oct. 1849, having re-m. 8 Dec. 1817, as 3rd wife to Thomas, 11th Earl of Strathmore, who died 22 Aug. 1846. On the death of Sir Alexander in 1810, the Livingstone [baronetcy became extinct. See chart pedigree, page 49.

James (col.), of Rowallan —— *Ayrshire* 1727-34, 1734-41 (of Shankstown).

Sir James Campbell, of Lawers (3rd and youngest son of James 2nd Earl of Loudoun), lieut.-col. Scots Greys, and served under Marlborough, at Malplaquet, 11 Sept. 1709, col. Scots Greys 1717, a groom of the bedchamber to George II., governor of Edinburgh Castle 1738, K.B. for services at the battle of Dettingen 16 June 1743, commanded the British horse at the battle of Fontenoy 30 Apl. 1745, and mortally wounded. He m. Jean, eldest dau. of David Boyle, 1st Earl of Glasgow (by his 2nd wife Jean, dau. and heir of William Mure of Rowallan), and had with a dau. a son, James Mure=Campbell, M.P., who succ. as [5th Earl of Loudoun. See chart pedigree, next page.

James of Calder —— *Inverness burghs* 1754-61.

Probably an error for John Campbell, of Lord Cawdor's family. See chart pedigree, [page 53.

James, major west fencible regt. —— *Stirling burghs* 1780-4, 1784, until he [accepted the *Chiltern hundreds*, s.b. 21 Aug. 1789, then a knight.

Sir James Campbell, of Inverniel, co. Argyll (elder brother and heir of Genl. Sir Archibald Campbell, K.B. M.P.), knighted 9 May 1788, hereditary usher of the White Rod for Scotland; born 16 Jany. 1737; d. Apl. 1805, having m. 16 July, 1761, Jane, dau. of John Campbell, esq., of Askom, co. Argyll; she d. Aug. 1805. Their eldest son, Lieut.-Genl. Sir James Campbell, G.C.H., was cr. a Bart. 3 Oct. 1818, and d. s.p. 5 June following, bd. in [Westminster Abbey.

Campbell—*continued.*

CAMPBELL, EARL OF LOUDOUN.

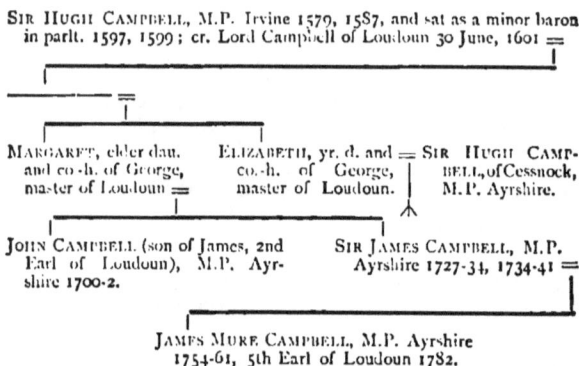

SIR HUGH CAMPBELL, M.P. Irvine 1579, 1587, and sat as a minor baron in parlt. 1597, 1599 ; cr. Lord Campbell of Loudoun 30 June, 1601 ═

```
┌─────────────────────────────────────────────────────────┐
│                          ═
        ┌────────────┴───────────────────┐
```

MARGARET, elder dau. and co.-h. of George, master of Loudoun ═	ELIZABETH, yr. d. and ═ SIR HUGH CAMP- co.-h. of George, | BELL, of Cessnock, master of Loudoun. | M.P. Ayrshire.

JOHN CAMPBELL (son of James, 2nd Earl of Loudoun), M.P. Ayr- shire 1700-2.

SIR JAMES CAMPBELL, M.P. Ayrshire 1727-34, 1734-41 ═

JAMES MURE CAMPBELL, M.P. Ayrshire 1754-61, 5th Earl of Loudoun 1782.

James Mure (capt.), of Rowallan —— *Ayrshire* 1754-61.

Fifth Earl of Loudoun (on the death of John, 4th Earl, 27 Apl. 1782), son of (Sir) James Campbell, M.P. He assumed the surname of Mure on succeeding to his grandmother's (the Countess of Glasgow's) estate, major-genl. 1781 ; born 11 Feb. 1726 ; d. 28 Apl. 1786, having m. 30 Apl. 1777, Flora, eldest dau. of John Macleod of Rasay, co. Inverness; she d. 2 Sept. 1780, leaving an only child Flora, Countess of Loudoun in her own right.   See chart
[pedigree above.

James Alexander, of Stracathro House, Brechin —— *Glasgow and Aberdeen* [*Universities* since 1881.   See foot-note.

Johne —— *Dundee* 1646.

John fear of Calder —— *Nairnshire* 1628-33, 1630 conv., younger, laird of [Caddell or Calder.

Sir John Campbell, 5th of Calder (son of Sir John Campbell) ; m. Elizabeth, eldest dau. of Thomas Urquhart, of Cromarty, and had 2 daus.; uncle of Sir Hugh, M.P. See chart
[pedigree, page 53.

John of Ardchattan —— *Argyllshire* 1644—1661-3.

CAMPBELL, JAMES ALEXANDER, of Stracathro House, co. Forfar (elder son of late Sir James Campbell, of Stracathro, Forfarshire, and of Glasgow, merchant, by his wife Janet, dau. of Henry Bannerman, of Manchester), educated at High School, Glasgow, and the University of Glasgow, Hon. LL.D., J.P. Forfar and Lanark, M.P. (conservative) Glasgow and Aberdeen Universities since 1880, brother of Henry Campbell-Bannerman, M.P. ; b. 20 Apl. 1825 ; m. 25 Apl. 1854, Ann, dau. of Sir Samuel Morton Peto, Bart., and has a son and 3 daus.

(1) James Morton Peto, b. 29 Jan. 1863.
(2) Nora Jane,
Stracathro House, Brechin, N.B.

(3) Hilda Sophia.
(4) Elsie Louisa.
Club—Carlton.

Campbell—*continued.*

CAMPBELL OF SUCCOTH.

JOHN CAMPBELL, of Succoth, M.P. Argyllshire 1681-2.

SIR ILAY CAMPBELL, M.P. Glasgow burghs 1784-9, cr. a baronet 17 Sept., 1808 =

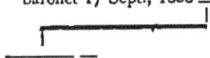

JOHN CAMPBELL, M.P. Dumbarton 1826-30 (son of Sir Archibald, 2nd Bart.) =

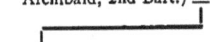

SIR ARCHIBALD ISLAY CAMPBELL, 3rd Bart., M.P. Argyll-shire 1851-7.

John (sir), fear of Glenorchy —— *Argyllshire* 1661-3.

> Fourth bart. (son of Sir Robert Campbell, 3rd bart. M.P.); d. June 1686; leaving a
> [son, John M.P., cr. Earl of Breadalbane next named. See chart pedigree, next page.

John (younger) of Glenorchy —— *Argyllshire* 1669-74.

> 1st Earl of Breadalbane, cr. 28 June, 1677 (son of Sir John Campbell, M.P., last-named),
> implicated in the massacre of Glencoe, and on that account imprisoned in Edinburgh Castle,
> a representative peer 1713, then aged 78 ; d. 1716, leaving issue. See Foster's Peerage, and
> [also chart pedigree, next page.

John (sir), of Carrick —— *Argyllshire* 1669-74, 1678 conv., 1681-2, 1689 conv.
[(then capt. of Carrick), 1689 to 1702, (a knt. 1695.)

John, of Succoth —— *Argyllshire* 1681-2.

Ancestor of Sir Ilay Campbell, bart., M.P.

John (Mr.) of Shankstown —— *Ayrshire* 1700-2.

Col. John C. of Shankstown, 2nd son of James 2nd Earl of Loudoun, d. s.p. See chart
[pedigree, preceding page.

John (Mr.), of Mamore, brother-german to the Earl of Argyll —— *Argyllshire*
1700-2, 1702-7; sat in 1st parlt. of Great Britain 1707-8; *Dumbartonshire*
[1708-10, (Master John) 1710-13, 1713-15, 1715-22, 1725-7 (on petition).
Brother of Archibald 1st Duke of Argyll; joined his father in his invasion of Scotland
1685 ; surrendered himself, and was capitally convicted (on his own confession), commuted
to banishment ; his forfeiture was rescinded in 1689. Surveyor of works, Scotland, groom
of the bedchamber, unduly elected 1722, seated on petition Jan. 1725; d. 7 April 1729,
leaving, with other issue, John, 4th Duke next named. Douglas' Peerage ; see chart
[pedigree, page 48 *ante.*

H

Campbell—*continued.*

CAMPBELL, EARL OF BREADALBANE.

SIR DUNCAN CAMPBELL, of Glenorchy, sat as a minor baron 1592, M.P.
Argyllshire 1593, 1599, cr. a Baronet 30 May, 1625 =

SIR ROBERT CAMPBELL, of Glenorchy, 3rd Bart., M.P.
Argyllshire 1639-41, 1643, 1644-7 =

SIR JOHN CAMPBELL, of
Glenorchy, 4th Bart., M.P.
Argyllshire 1661-3 =

SIR JOHN CAMPBELL, of   JOHN, Earl of Ormelie, M.P.
Glenorchy, 5th Bart., M.P.   Perthshire 1833-4, succ. as
Argyllshire 1669-74.   2nd Marquis of Breadalbane.

John (Lieut.-Gen.), of Mamore —— *Buteshire* 1713-15, (of South Garachtie, then
col.); *Elgin burghs* 1715-22, (of Mamore) 1725-7 (on petition); *Dumbartonshire* 1727-34, (of Alambeg) 1734-41, (of Mamore) 1741-7, 1747-54 (then
maj.-gen.) 1754-61, (then lieut.-gen.) 17 (*sic.*) April 1761, succ. as 4th Duke
[of Argyll, 15 April, 1761.

John, 4th Duke of Argyll, P.C., K.T. 1765 (eldest son of John Campbell, of Mamore, M.P.),
Lieut.-Col. 1712. at Dunkirk 1715, A.D.C. to John, Duke of Argyll and Greenwich, during
the rebellion 1715, had command of the 21st Scots Fusiliers, Brig.-Gen. at the battle of
Dettingen 1741, Maj.-Gen. 1744, and served a campaign in Germany. He commanded the
troops in the West of Scotland in 1745, Lieut.-Gen. 1747. commanded Scots Greys 1752-70,
Governor of Limerick 1761-70; groom of the bedchamber to George II. and George III.;
a representative peer 1761, Gen. 1765; d. 9 Nov. 1770, aged 77, having m. 1720, Hon. Mary
Bellenden (maid of honour to Caroline, Princess of Wales), 3rd dau. of John, 2nd Lord
Bellenden; she died housekeeper of Somerset House 18 Dec. 1736, leaving issue. See chart
[pedigree, page 48.

John, lord provost of Edinburgh (1722) —— *Edinburgh* 1721, 1722-7 (then
[late lord provost) 1727-34.

Master of the works, groom of the bedchamber, and commissioner of customs England
and Scotland, pension £100 per annum. Probably brother of Daniel of Shawfield, M.P.;
[he died 16 April (? 1 June) 1739. See chart pedigree, next page.

John, of Calder —— *Nairnshire* and *Pembrokeshire,* 1734-41 (sat for the latter
[in the English parlt.) ; *Nairnshire* 1747-54; *Inverness burghs* 1754-61.

Of Cawdor, Nairnshire, and Stackpole Court, co. Pembroke, M.P. 1727-47, Corfe Castle
1762-68 (see England), lord of the admiralty 1736, lord of the treasury 1746, lieut.-col.
horse guards, groom of the bedchamber 1727; the member for the Inverness burghs in
1754-61 is styled James in the parliamentary return, but this is an error; (son of Sir
Alexander Campbell, M.P.); d. at Bath 6 Sept. 1777, having m. 30 April 1726, Mary,
eldest dau. and co-heir of Lewis Pryse, esq., of Gogarthan, and had with other issue Pryse
[Campbell, M.P., and Capt. Alex. Campbell, M.P. See chart pedigree, page 53.

Campbell—*continued.*

CAMPBELL OF SCHAWFIELD.

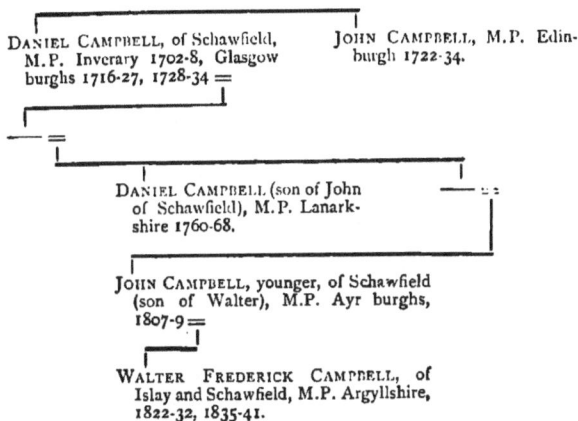

DANIEL CAMPBELL, of Schawfield,
M.P. Inverary 1702-8, Glasgow
burghs 1716-27, 1728-34 =

JOHN CAMPBELL, M.P. Edin-
burgh 1722-34.

=

DANIEL CAMPBELL (son of John
of Schawfield), M.P. Lanarkshire 1760-68.

JOHN CAMPBELL, younger, of Schawfield
(son of Walter), M.P. Ayr burghs,
1807-9 =

WALTER FREDERICK CAMPBELL, of
Islay and Schawfield, M.P. Argyllshire,
1822-32, 1835-41.

John, younger, of Calder —— *Nairnshire* 1777-80.

Lord Cawdor of Castlemartin, co. Pembroke, in the Peerage of Great Britain, so cr. 21 June 1796, (eldest son of Pryse Campbell, M.P.), M.P. Cardigan (see England), F.S.A. 1794, F.R.S. 1795; d. 1 June 1821, having m., 27 July 1789, Lady Isabella Caroline Howard, eldest dau. of Frederick, 5th Earl of Carlisle ; she d. 8 March 1848, leaving 2 sons, viz., John Frederick, 2nd Lord, and Admiral George Pryse Campbell, M.P., see chart
[pedigree, page 53.

John, lieut.-col., Lord Loudoun's regiment of foot (1747) —— *Glasgow burghs* 1744-7, (then major of brigade and capt. of a company in R.N. British Fusiliers), 1747-54, (then lieut.-col.) 1754-61, then lieut.-col. and provost [of Dumbarton.

F. M., John, 5th Duke of Argyll (9 Nov. 1770), lt.-col. 54th regt. 1745, lt.-col. 42nd Highlanders 1749, A.D.C. to the King 1755, col. 56th regt. Dec. 1755, of 14th dragoons 1757, of Argyllshire fencibles 1759 and major-gen., lieut.-gen. 1761, commander-in-chief of the forces in Scotland 1762, col. 1st regt. foot 1765, commander-in-chief Scotland 1767-78, gen. 1778, col. 3rd foot guards 1782, field-marshal 1796, M.P. Glasgow burghs as above, M.P. Dover 1765 (then Marquis of Lorne) until cr. Baron Sundridge in the English peerage 19 Dec. 1766; bapt. June 1723 ; d. 24 May 1806, æt. 83, having m., 3 March 1759, Elizabeth, 2nd dau. of John Gunning, of Castle Coote, co. Roscommon (dowager of James, 6th Duke of Hamilton and Brandon), she was cr. Baroness Hamilton of Hameldon, co. Leic., 4 May 1776 ; she [d. 20 Dec. 1793, leaving issue. See chart pedigree, page 48.

Campbell—*continued.*

John —— *Ayr burghs* 1794, 1796-1802 (then of Lincoln's Inn, London, Coun-
[sellor-at-Law), 1802-6 (then a master in Chancery) 1806-7.

Of Liston Hall, Essex, 1802, a master in Chancery, 2 June 1801, until accountant-genl.
29 Nov. 1819 (younger son of William Campbell, of Liston Hall, who was a younger
brother of John, 4th Duke of Argyll); he died in London, 31 Jan. 1826, having married
[twice, and had issue. See chart pedigree, page 48.

John (col.), younger, of Schawfield —— *Ayr burghs* 1807 until his death, s.b. 11
[May 1809.

Son of Walter Campbell, of Schawfield (who died 1816), by his 1st wife Eleonora Kerr
(gt. granddaughter of 1st Marquis of Lothian); d. 15 March 1809, having m. 14 June 1796,
Lady Charlotte Campbell, dau. of John 5th Duke of Argyll; she d. 1 Apl. 1861, having
[re-md. 17 March 1818 to Rev. Edward John Bury. See chart pedigree, page 59.

John, of Blairhall —— *Stirling burghs* 15 July 1818, until declared void, s.b.
[29 March 1819.

John, younger of Succoth —— *Dumbartonshire* 1826-30.

Eldest son of Sir Archibald Campbell, 2nd Bart. (son of Sir Ilay Campbell, M.P., Lord
Succoth); b. 28 May 1798, o.v.p. 3 July 1830, leaving a son, Sir Archibald Islay Campbell,
[3rd Baronet M.P. See Foster's Baronetage, and chart pedigree, ante.

John, commonly called Earl of Ormelie —— *Perthshire* 1833, until he succeeded
[as Marquis of Breadalbane, s.b. 5 May 1834.

John, 2nd Marquis and 5th Earl (29 March 1834), K.T., F.S.A., Scotland, F.R.S.,
M.P. Okehampton, June 1820-26 (then Lord Glenorchy), d. s.p. 8 Nov 1862, when the English
honours expired. He m. 23 Nov. 1821, Eliza, eldest dau. of George Baillie, Esq., of
[Jerviswood (E. HADDINGTON); she d. 28 Aug. 1861. See chart pedigree, page 58.

John sir), attorney-general for England, knt., —— *Edinburgh* 1834, 1835-7
[(then attorney-genl.), 1837-41.

Sir John Campbell, Baron Campbell, of St. Andrews, co. Fife, so created by patent 30
June 1841, P.C. England and Ireland, bencher L.I., K.C. 1807, M.P. Stafford 1830, Dudley
1832, see England, solicitor-gen., and knighted 1832, attorney-gen. 1834, 1835, and 1837,
M.P. Edinburgh 1834-41, lord chancellor of Ireland 1841, chancellor of the duchy of
Lancaster 1846, chief justice Queen's bench 1850, lord high chancellor of England 1859; b.
15 Sept. 1779; d. 23 June 1861, having m. 8 Sept. 1821, Hon. Mary Elizabeth Scarlett,
dau. of James, Baron Abinger, and created Baroness Stratheden, of Cupar, co. Fife, 22 Jan.
[1836; she d. 25 Mar. 1860, having had 3 sons and 4 daus.

John Douglas Edward Henry, commonly called Lord John Campbell, of
Ardencaple, 2nd lawful son of John, Duke of Argyll —— *Argyllshire* 1799-
1802, 1802-6, 1806-7, 1807-12, 1812-18, 1818-20, 1820 until he accepted the
[*Chiltern hundreds*, s.b. 14 March 1822.

7th Duke of Argyll (on the death of his brother 22 October 1839), F.R.S. 1819, b. 21
Dec. 1777, d. 26 April 1847, having m. thrice; father of George Douglas 8th Duke of Argyll,
[K.T., see chart pedigree, page 48.

Campbell—*continued*.

John Douglas Sutherland, commonly called Marquis of Lorne ; of Inverary Castle, Argyllshire —— *Argyllshire* 1868, 1868-74, until he accepted the [*Chiltern hundreds,* s.b. 31 Aug. 1878.

Marquis of Lorne K.T., G.C.M.G., P.C., Governor General of the dominion of Canada since 1878, (grandson of the 7th Duke of Argyll, M.P.), b. 6 Aug. 1845, m. 21 March 1871, H.R.H. Princess Louise Caroline Alberta, 4 dau. of Her Majesty Queen Victoria. See [chart pedigree, page 48.

Peter (col.), of South Garrachtie —— *Buteshire* 1722-7 ; *Elgin burghs* 1728-34 ; [*Buteshire* 1734-41.

Called Patrick in parliamentary returns 1722, 1728. Peter was of the Household and dep.-gov. of Portsmouth in 1733 ; died lieut.-gov. 18 Feb. 1750-51, also 1st gent. of the beer buttery, and lieut.-gen. 1743. Col. John Campbell (afterwards 4th Duke of Argyll), M.P. [Buteshire 1713-15 ; is also described as of South Garrachtie, see above.

Pryse, younger, of Calder —— *Inverness-shire* 1754-61, *Nairnshire* 1761-8, a lord [of the treasury 1766.

Of Cawdor Castle, co. Nairn, and of Stackpole Court, co. Pembroke, (son of John Campbell of Cawdor, M.P.); M.P. Cardigan 1768 (see England) ; d. in his father's lifetime 4 Dec. 1768 ; m. 20 Sept. 1752, Sarah, 3rd dau. and co-h. of Sir Edmund Bacon, 4th Bart.; she d. 20 May 1767, leaving with issue a son John, M.P., created Lord Cawdor, see chart [pedigree, page 53.

Richard Frederick Fotheringham, of Craigie Ho. co. Ayr —— *Ayr burghs* [since 1880. See foot-note.

Robert (sir), of Glenorchy, knight baronet —— *Argyllshire* 1639-41, 1643 conv. [1644-7 (the laird of Glenorchy).

Of Glenfalloch, 3rd Baronet on the death of his brother Sir Colin 2nd Bart. 6 Sept. 1640. He m. Isabel, dau. of Sir Lachlin Macintosh, of Torecastle, captain of the Clan Chattan ; [father of Sir John Campbell, Bart., M.P.

Robert (lt.-col.) of Finab —— *Argyllshire* 1766-8, 1768 until appointed receiver- [general and cashier of the customs s.b. 20 Feb. 1772.

Died rec.-gen. 7 April 1790, probably son of (? Patrick) Campbell, of Monzie, by Mary, sister of Wm., Viscount Strathallan ; he m. 26 Mar. 1749, Susanna, youngest dau. of Charles Erskine, Lord Tinwald of Session (by his 1st wife, Grizel Grierson, heiress of Barjarg), and had a son, [Alexander, M.P., see chart pedigree, page 46.

CAMPBELL, RICHARD FREDERICK FOTHERINGHAM, of Craigie House, Ayr (eldest surviving son of late James Campbell, Esq., of Craigie, advocate, by his 2nd wife, Grace Elizabeth, dau. of Genl. Hay, C.B.), educated at Rugby, capt late 8th Madras Cavalry, served on staff in Indian mutiny ; Major Ayrshire Yeomanry since 1873 ; Vice-Lieut. of Ayrshire, M.P. (liberal) Ayr burghs since 1880 ; b. 1831 ; m. 1869, Arabella Jane, dau. of late Archibald Argyll Hay, Esq., and widow of Charles Tennent, Esq.

Craigie House, Ayr, N.B.—3, *Hereford Gardens, W.*
Clubs—Devonshire, Brooks', and Junior United Service.

Campbell—*continued.*

Walter Frederick, of Islay and Schawfield —— *Argyllshire* 1822-6, 1826-30,
[1830-1, 1831-2, 1835-7, 1837-41.
J.P., D.L., co. Lanark (eldest son of Col. John Campbell, youngcr, M.P.), b. 10 Apr. 1798,
[d. 8 Feb. 1855, having m. twice, and left issue. See chart pedigree, page 59.

William —— *Inverness* 1612.

William —— *Dumbarton* 1650.

William, cornet of Duke of Argyll's regiment of Horse —— *Glasgow burghs*
[1734-41.

William (lord) —— *Argyllshire* 1764, until appointed governor of Nova Scotia,
[s.b. 12 Dec. 1766.
Post captain R.N. (youngest brother of John, 5th Duke of Argyll), governor of South
Carolina 1773 and at the breaking out of the American war, served as a volunteer at the
attack on Charlestown 28 June 1776, d. 5 Sept. 1778, having m. 7 Apr. 1763, Sarah, dau. of
Ralph Izard of Charlestown, So. Carolina ; she d. 4 Sept. 1784, leaving a son and 2 daus.
[See chart pedigree, page 48.

Campbell-Bannerman.

Henry, of London —— *Stirling burghs* 1868-74 (then Henry Campbell, merchant
[in Glasgow), 1874-80, and since 1881.   See foot-note.

Cant.

Henry —— *Edinburgh* 1473, 1476, 1478 bis, 1479, 1483, 1484, 1485, 1490,
[1492.

Carkettill.

John —— *Haddington* 1583 bis.

Carmichael.   See also Dundee.

Daniel (sir), of Hyndford —— *Lanarkshire* 1649-50, 1689 conv. (then of
[Mauldslie), 1689, died before 4 April 1693.
Of Hyndford and Mauldslie (2nd son of Sir James Carmichael, 1st Lord Carmichael,
treasurer depute to Charles II.); m., 11 July 1661, Anna Scott, 2nd dau. of the laird of
[Ardross, co. Fife, and died s.p.
James —— *Edinburgh* 1558.

James —— *Dundee* 1593.
(James Carmichael of Hyndford (2nd son of Gavin C.), m. Marion, dau. of Sir Hugh
Campbell, of Loudoun ; their eldest son, Walter, who died 1616, was father of Sir James,
[1st Lord Carmichael.)

CAMPBELL-BANNERMAN, HENRY, of Gennings Park, Kent, J.P., and J.P. for Lanarkshire,
secretary to the admiralty May 1882 (younger son of late Sir James Campbell, of Stracathro,
Forfarshire aforesaid), educated at Glasgow University, M.A. Trin. Coll. Camb. 1861, assumed the
additional surname of Bannerman 1872, M.P. (liberal) Stirling burghs since 1868 (brother of James
Alexander Campbell, M.P.), financial secretary War Office 1871-4, 1880-2 ; b. 7 Sept. 1836, m. 13 Sept.
1860, Sarah Charlotte, only dau. of late Major-General Sir Charles Bruce, K.C.B.
Gennings Park, Maidstone ; 6, *Grosvenor Place, S.W.*
Clubs—Brooks', Devonshire, Oxford & Cambridge, and Reform.

Carmichael—*continued.*

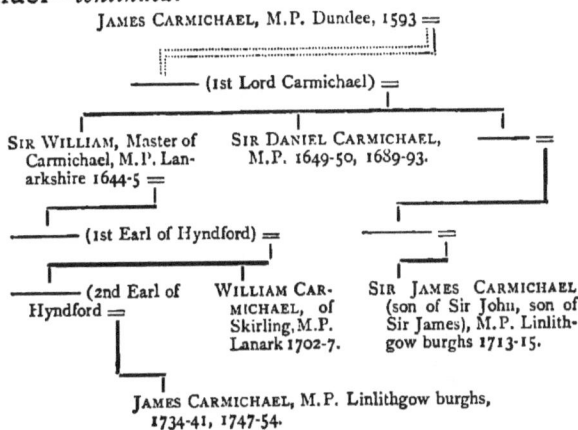

JAMES CARMICHAEL, M.P. Dundee, 1593 =

————— (1st Lord Carmichael) =

SIR WILLIAM, Master of	SIR DANIEL CARMICHAEL,	————— =
Carmichael, M.P. Lan-	M.P. 1649-50, 1689-93.	
arkshire 1644-5 =		

————— (1st Earl of Hyndford) =   ————— =

————— (2nd Earl of	WILLIAM CAR-	SIR JAMES CARMICHAEL
Hyndford =	MICHAEL, of	(son of Sir John, son of
	Skirling, M.P.	Sir James), M.P. Linlith-
	Lanark 1702-7.	gow burghs 1713-15.

JAMES CARMICHAEL, M.P. Linlithgow burghs,
1734-41, 1747-54.

James (sir), of Bonnytown, bart. ——— *Linlithgow burghs* 1713-15, *Linlithgow-* [*shire* 1713 (10 Sept.) until unseated 8 April 1714.
Son of Sir John Carmichael (son of Sir James, 3rd son of James, 1st Lord Carmichael), by his wife Henriet, 3rd dau. of James Johnstone, Earl of Annandale. He was served heir of his father, Sir John, and of his grandfather, Sir James, 12 April, 1692; d. 17 July 1727, having m. Margaret, elder dau. and heir of William Baillie, of Lamington; she d. in Edinburgh 14th Sept. 1759, æt. 63, having had a son, Sir William (Baillie), who d. s.p. 1738, and a daughter Henrietta, m., 17 Oct. 1741, to Robert Dundas, of Arniston, lord [president of court of session.

James, son of James, earl of Hyndford ——— *Linlithgow burghs* 1734-41, 1741 [(2 June) until unseated 25 Jan. following; 1748-54.
3rd son of James, 2nd Earl of Hyndford, d. unm. 1754.

(Sir John), laird of Carmichael, ——— a minor baron in convention 1593 bis; [1594 parlt. and conv., bis; 1596 conv., bis; 1597 conv. bis.
Elder son of John Carmichael of Carmichael, a knight in 1587, warden of the middle marches, ambassador to Denmark 1588, and capt. of the guard, ambassador to Q. Eliz. 1590, warden of the west marches 1598; murdered 16 June 1600; m. Margaret, dau. of Sir [George Douglas, of Pittendreich (E. ANGUS).

Robert, of Corp, provost ——— *Sanquhar* (co. Dumfries) 1665 conv. (then bailie), [1667 conv. (provost), 1669-72, 1678 conv.; 1681-2, 1685-6.

William ——— *Edinburgh* 1504.
"William Carmichael (ancestor of Sir John, M.P.) had a charter of the lands of Cruki-stane, 7 Dec. 1509, wherein he is designed burgess of Edinburgh, and died 1530." DOUGLAS.

William ——— *Dundee* 1526, 1535.
Probably son of the preceding William.

William (sir) ——— *Lanarkshire* 1644-5.
MASTER of Carmichael (father of John 1st Earl of Hyndford), one of the gens d'armes to Louis XIII., commanded the Clydesdale regt. against Montrose at the battle of Philiphaugh 1646; d. Aug. 1657, having m. Grizel, dau. of William Douglas, 1st Marquis of Douglas, [and had issue.

Carmichael—*continued.*

William (Mr.), advocate, —— *Lanark* 1702-7.

Of Skirling (2nd son of John 1st Earl of Hyndford), advocate 1694 ; d. at Edinburgh 29 Dec. 1759, æt. 88 ; he m. 1st 17th April 1709, Helen, only child of Thomas Craig of Riccarton, and had issue ; he m. 2ndly Margaret Menzies, who d. s.p. at Saltcoats. co. Had-
[dington, 17 June 1776.

Carnegie or Carnegy.

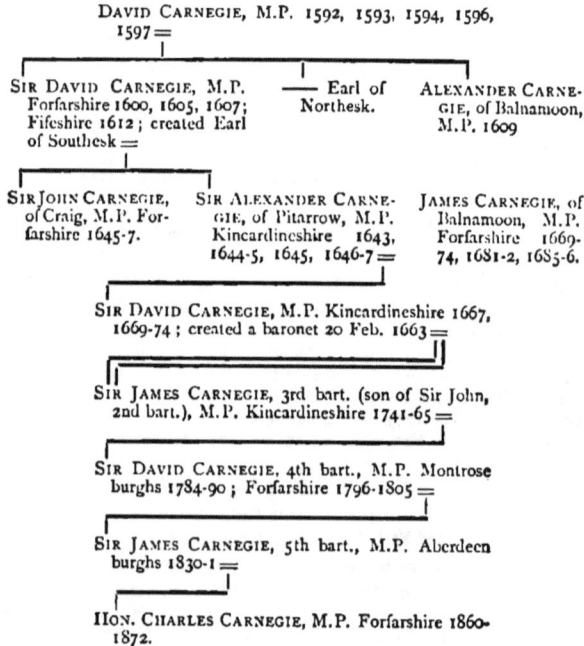

DAVID CARNEGIE, M.P. 1592, 1593, 1594, 1596, 1597 =

SIR DAVID CARNEGIE, M.P. Forfarshire 1600, 1605, 1607; Fifeshire 1612; created Earl of Southesk =

—— Earl of Northesk.

ALEXANDER CARNE-GIE, of Balnamoon, M.P. 1609

SIR JOHN CARNEGIE, of Craig, M.P. For-farshire 1645-7.

SIR ALEXANDER CARNE-GIE, of Pitarrow, M.P. Kincardineshire 1643, 1644-5, 1645, 1646-7 =

JAMES CARNEGIE, of Balnamoon, M.P. Forfarshire 1669-74, 1681-2, 1685-6.

SIR DAVID CARNEGIE, M.P. Kincardineshire 1667, 1669-74 ; created a baronet 20 Feb. 1663 =

SIR JAMES CARNEGIE, 3rd bart. (son of Sir John, 2nd bart.), M.P. Kincardineshire 1741-65 =

SIR DAVID CARNEGIE, 4th bart., M.P. Montrose burghs 1784-90 ; Forfarshire 1796-1805 =

SIR JAMES CARNEGIE, 5th bart., M.P. Aberdeen burghs 1830-1 =

HON. CHARLES CARNEGIE, M.P. Forfarshire 1860-1872.

Alexander (sir), of Pitarrow, —— *Kincardineshire* 1643 conv. ; 1644-5, 1645,
[1646-7.

4th son of Sir David Carnegy, M.P. (1st Earl of Southesk); d. March 1682, will proved 6 July 1683, having m. Margaret, sister of Sir Robert 1st Visct. Arbuthnott. See Foster's
[Peerage, E. SOUTHESK.

The parliamentary return states that Carnegie laird of Pitarrow sat in parlt. as a minor baron 1592, 1596 conv., and 1597 conv.; but as Lord Carnegie only purchased those lands about 1631, from Mr. James Wishart of Pitarrow and his brother Sir John Wishart, it is pro-
[bable that the laird of Pitarrow was a Wishart, not a Carnegie.

(Alexander) —— minor baron 1609 conv. ; laird of Balnamoon.

Youngest brother of David, Earl of Southesk and John, Earl of Northesk ; his will dated at Edinburgh 25 Aug. 1657 (d. Oct. follg.), proved 10 Dec. 1658 ; m. Giles Blair of Bla-
[thayock, and had 2 sons.

Carnegie or Carnegy—*continued.*

Charles —— *Forfarshire* 1860-5, 1865-8, 1868-72 ; inspector of constabulary
[Scotland 1872.

Son of Sir James Carnegie, 5th bart., M.P., and brother of James, 9th Earl of Southesk,
K.T. (restored 1855), had precedence as son of an earl granted him by patent 30 Aug. 1855,
[late 23rd and 73rd regts.; b. 14 May 1833.

(David) —— minor baron 1592, 1593 conv., 1594 bis, 1596 bis, 1597 conv.

Of Panbride and of Colluthie, &c., j.u. (2nd son of Sir Robert C., of Kinnaird, a senator
of the College of Justice), bred to the law P.C. Scotland 1592, an octavian (*i.e.*, one of the
eight commissioners of the treasury) 1595 ; d. 19 April 1598, leaving 2 daus. by his wife
[Elizabeth, dau. of William Ramsay, of Colluthie ; by his 2nd wife he left 4 sons and 3 daus.

David (sir), laird of Kinnaird, a lord of the articles —— *Forfarshire* 1600 (a
[minor baron), 1605 conv., 1609 conv., *Fifeshire* 1612.

Earl of Southesk (eldest son of David Carnegie of Colluthie, M.P.), knighted by James I.
1603, a commissioner for the projected Union of England and Scotland 1604, a visitor of
St. Andrew's University 1609 ; cr. Lord Carnegie of Kinnaird 14 April, 1616, lord of session
5 July following, an extraordinary lord 16 Feb. 1626—Nov. 1628 ; one of the royal commissioners to the General Assembly held at Perth 1617, etc. ; cr. Earl of Southesk, Lord Carnegie
of Kinnaird and Leuchars, on the coronation of Charles I. at Holyrood, 22 June, 1633, P.C.
1641 ; one of the Committee of Estates 1645, 1648, 1651 ; sheriff of Forfarshire—fined £3,000
sterling by Cromwell's Act of Grace and Pardon 1654—died at Kinnaird Feb. 1658, having
m. (contract dated 8 Oct. 1595) Margaret, dau. of Sir David Lindsay of Edzell, she d.
[9 July, 1614, having had with other issue Sir Alexander, M.P.

David (sir), of Pittaro, knight baronet —— *Kincardineshire* 1667 conv. (then
[younger), 1669-74.

Created a baronet of Nova Scotia 20 Feb. 1663, etc. (in the lifetime of his father, Sir
Alexander, M.P.), d. Nov. 1708, having married thrice and left issue, ancestor of the present
[Earl of Southesk. See Foster's Peerage.

David (sir), of Southesk, bart. —— *Montrose* (now Aberdeen) *burghs* 1784-90,
[*Forfarshire* 1796-1802, 1802 until his death s.b. 24 June, 1805.

4th baronet (eldest son of Sir James, M.P.), F.R.S. 1799, b. 22 Nov. 1753, d. 25 May,
[1805, leaving with other issue Sir James, M.P. See "Southesk," Foster's Peerage.

James of Balnamoon —— *Forfarshire* 1669-74, 1681-2, 1685-6.

Son of Sir John Carnegie of Balnamoon, served heir-male of David Carnegie fiar of
Balnamoon, his uncle, 4 Nov. 1662 ; d. 25 April, 1700, having m. 1st Margaret, dau. of Sir
Alexander Carnegie of Pitarrow, and 2ndly Jean, dau. of David Fotheringham of Powrie,
[relict of John Carnegie of Boysack, she d. Nov. 1705.

James (Mr.), of Findhaven (Phinheavin) —— *Forfar* 1669-74, *Forfarshire* 1686,
[1698-1702, 1702-7.

2nd son of David 2nd Earl of Northesk. He d. at Edinburgh 10 March, 1707, bd. in
the Abbey Church, m. (contract 10 Feb. and June, 1674) Anna, 2nd dau. of Margaret
Lundin, lady of that ilk, and Robert Maitland, brother of John, Duke of Lauderdale, she d.
[3 Sept. 1694, leaving issue,

Carnegie or Carnegy—*continued*.

James (sir), of Pitarrow, bart. —— *Kincardineshire* 1741-7, (a capt. of foot [1744); 1747-54, 1754-61, 1761 until his death s.b. 7 June, 1765.

3rd baronet (eldest son of Sir John Carnegie), heir-male of his family on the death of James 5th Earl of Southesk, 1729); served at Fontenoy 11 May, 1745. and at Culloden 16 April, 1746; d. 30 April and bd. 4 May 1765, leaving with other issue Sir David, M.P. See [Foster's Peerage.

James (sir), of Southesk, bart. —— *Aberdeen* (now Montrose) *burghs* 1830-1.

5th baronet (elder son of Sir David, M.P.), b. 28 Sept. 1799, d. 30 Jan. 1849, having m., 14 Nov. 1825, Charlotte, dau. of David Lysons, of Hempstead Court, co. Glouc., author of "Magna Britannia," etc. ; she d. 10 April, 1848, having had with other issue, James, [9th Earl of Southesk, and Charles, M.P.

John (sir), laird of Craig —— *Forfarshire* 1645-7.

3rd son of David 1st Earl of Southesk. David, son of Sir John C., was served heir-male of his father 22 May, 1656; d. 22 Nov. 1654 ; m. (contr. 27 Oct. 1632) Jane, dau. of [Sir John Scrymgeour of Dudhope, knt.

John (sir), of Boysack, knt. —— *Forfarshire* 1661-3.

(2nd son of John, 1st Earl of Northesk) ; m. Margaret, dau. of Sir Alex. Erskine of Dun, [and died circa 1677, leaving 2 sons and a dau.—his grandson John, M.P.

John, merchant trafficker, provost —— *Forfar* 1678 conv. (then bailie), 1681-2, 1685-6, 1689 conv., 1689 until his death, s. b. 7 March, 1698, then of [Ballindargs.

Of Ballindargs by purchase ; only son of Thomas Carnegy (by Margaret, eldest dau. of Alexander Carnegy of Bearhill, near to Brechin) ; he m. Elizabeth, dau. of John Dickson, [merchant in Forfar.—*Nisbet*, vol. ii., p. 242, facing 245.

John, of Boysack —— *Forfarshire* 1708-10, 1710-13, 1713-15 (an officer of the [crown, 1714) ; 1715 until expelled the house, s. b. 30 July, 1716.

Solicitor-general Scotland 1714-16 [son of John Carnegy (son of Sir John, M.P.), by his wife Jean, dau. of David Fotheringham of Powrie], advocate before 1708, expelled the house 22 June, 1715, "for being in open rebellion" ; m. Margaret, dau. of —— Skene of [Grange, co. Fife ; dead before 14 May, 1750, leaving issue.

Robert, merchant burgess —— *Bervie* 1670.

Probably a brother of Sir David Carnegie, bart., M.P. ; dead before 28 June, 1671.

Carre.　See Ker.

Carrick.

Alexander —— *North Berwick* 1585.

Carruthers.

James, provost —— *Annan* 1681-2.

John (Mr.) of Denbie —— *Lochmaben* 1702-7.

Carstairs.

Andrew —— *St. Andrews* 1650 (or James Sword): 1661-3, then dean of [guild.

Cathcart.

—— laird of Cairltoune —— *Ayrshire* 1625 conv.

Hew Cathcart (son of John of Carleton), m., 16 Sept. 1587, Janet Chalmers, lady Water-[head, and had a son John who succeeded him. See Foster's Baronetage.

Charles, lt.-col. and quartermaster-general of the forces in India —— *Clack-[mannanshire* 1784 until his death s.b. 29 Nov. 1788.

Charles Allan Cathcart, brother of William Schaw, 1st Earl Cathcart, K.T., b. 28 Dec. 1759, d. on his voyage to China, 10 June, 1788. For an account of his services see Douglas' [Peerage of Scotland, vol. i. p. 345.

Hugh, of Carleton —— *Ayrshire* 1702-7.

Sir Hew Cathcart, baronet of Nova Scotia, so cr. 20 June, 1703 (son of Hew Cathcart of Carleton, by his wife Grizel Agnew of Lochnaw); he m. 1695   dau. of Sir Patrick [Broun of Colstoun, bart., and had issue.

Cavelin.

Henry —— *Linlithgow* 1468.

Cavers.

—— the laird of —— *Roxburghshire* 1644, 1645-6.

It is uncertain whether the laird of Cavers here referred to was Sir Thomas Ker or Sir [William Douglas the sheriff of Teviotdale.

Chaipland.

Richard —— *Haddington* 1644, conv. and parlt. (? also 1646-7), 1648.

Chalmers.

Alexander (Chamer) —— *Aberdeen* 1467, 1468 (an auditor of complaint); [1469 (then alderman), 1479.

Of Murthill 1495, provost Aberdeen 1443, 1495, and during several intervening years.

Alexander —— *Perth* 1525, *Aberdeen* 1526.

Son of Thomas Chalmers of Balnacraig, co. Aberdeen, who was provost 1512.

James, of Gaitgirth —— *Ayrshire* 1628-33.

Of Gadgirth (son of James Chalmers by his wife Isobel, dau. of Sir Patrick Houston of that ilk), of age Oct. 1616, admitted a burgess of Ayr 1618, bailie of Kyle Stewart 1632, sheriff principal co. Ayr 1632, one of the Scots Commissioners in the Ripon treaty, etc. [1640; m. Isobel, dau. of John Blair of that ilk.

Johne —— *Perth* 1468, an auditor of complaint, etc.

Sir John Chalmer of Gadgirth, co. Ayr; sat in 1st parlt. James IV., 1484, as "dominus [Gaitgirth"; he m. Elizabeth, dau. of Sir James Hamilton of Cadzow, and had issue.

Chalmers—*continued*.

Patrick, of Auldbar —— *Montrose burghs* 1835-7, 1837-41, 1841 until accepted [Chiltern hundreds, s.b. 16 April, 1842.

J.P., D.L. co. Forfar, capt. 3rd dragoon guards, contested Montrose burghs, 1832, (elder son of Patrick Chalmers of Aldbar by his wife Frances Inglis) ; d. unm. 23 June, 1854, aged 52.

Thomas (de Camera) —— *Aberdeen* 1435.

Provost Aberdeen 1412, and many years subsequently.

Charteris.   See also Lord Elcho.

Andro —— *Perth* 1467 bis, 1468 (an auditor of complaint), 1469, 1471, 1473, [1479.

Of Kinfauns, provost of Perth 1465-71, 1473, 1475, 1484, etc., etc., until his death 1503.

Francis (younger), provost of Jedburgh —— *Haddington burghs* 1780, 1780-4. 1784 until 23 May, 1787, when he was declared ineligible to sit, being then the eldest son of a peer of Scotland, *i.e.*, by the death, 29 April, 1787, [of his uncle David, the attainted Lord Elcho.

Francis, Lord Elcho (only son of Francis 6th Earl of Wemyss), b. 31 Jan. 1749, d. v.p. 20 Jan. 1808, having m., 18 July 1771, Susan (a maid of honour to the Queen), 2nd dau. of Anthony Tracy-Keck, of Gt. Tew, Oxon ; she d. 25 Feb. 1835, aged 90, and had, with 4 [daus., an only son, Francis, who became 7th Earl of Wemyss.

John (sir) —— *Dumfries sheriffdom and stewartry of Annandale* 1621, 1625 conv. (laird of Hempisfield, *i.e.* Amisfield) ; 1628-33 (then styled Sir John).

Elder son of John Charteris of Amisfield (by his wife Janet, dau. of Sir James Douglas of Drumlanrig—M. QUEENSBERRY) ; a warden of the marches ; he m. Margaret, dau. of John [Fleming, Earl of Wigton, and had a son, Sir John, M.P.

John (sir), of Amisfield —— *Dumfries sheriffdom and stewartry of Annandale* [1639 (then fear of Amisfield), 1641 (then styled Sir John).

Sir John was strongly attached to the Stewarts, and suffered much ; a parliament commissioner to confirm Ripon treaty 1641, banished 1646, was engaged with Montrose, imprisoned in Edinburgh Castle ; he m. Catherine, dau. of William Crichton, Earl of Dumfries, and had [issue.

Patrick —— 1524.

Provost of Perth 1521-3, 1525 and 1527,—apparently son of John Charteris, provost of [Perth in 1507, and grandson of Andrew, M.P.

Cheislay.

John (sir), of Kerswall —— *Lanarkshire* 1649-50.
[Sir John Cheislay of Kerswall, m. Elspeth, sister of Sir James Carmichael, Lord Carmichael.]

Robert (sir), lord provost —— *Edinburgh* 1696-1702.

Provost Edinburgh 1694-6

Chernside.

Robert —— *Glasgow* 1593; parlt. and conv.

Cheyne.

John —— *Aberdeen* 1593, 1594 conv. and parlt.

John (Mr.), of Arnotischyre —— *Aberdeenshire* 1617.

Walter —— *Kintore* 1617.

Chisholm.

Alexander William, of Chisholm, commonly called "The Chisholm" ——
Inverness-shire 1835-7, 1837 until he accepted the Chiltern hundreds,
[s.b. 12 June, 1838.

Died unm. 8 Sept. 1838, aged 28 ; elder son of "The Chisholm" (William), by his wife
Eliza, dau. of Duncan Macdonell of Glengarry ; she rem.   1819 to Sir Thomas Ramsay
[of Balmain, bart., who d.   1830.

Michael (Mr.) —— *Edinburgh* 1571 conv.

Christie.

David, of Balsillie —— *Dysart* 1685, 1689 conv., 1689-90 (merchant trafficker),
[1702 (then of Balsillie) until his death, s.b. 23 Aug. 1703.

Clarges.

Thomas (Dr.) —— *Ross, Sutherland,* and *Cromarty* 1656-8, *Banff, Cullen,* and
[*Aberdeen,* and also *Peebles, Selkirk, Jedburgh* 1658-9 (WILLIS).

Sir Thomas Clarges, of city of Westminster (son of John de Glarges or Clarges), knighted
at Breda, May 1660, for his efforts to restore Charles II.   Unduly elected for Tregony 1660 ;
M.P. Oxford University 1689-90, 1690-5 (see ENGLAND) ; m. Mary, 3rd dau. of George, and
sister and co-h. of Edward Procter, esq., of Norwell Woodhouse, Notts. ; he died in
Piccadilly 4 Oct. 1695, leaving an only son, Sir Walter Clarges, bart., so created 30 Oct. 1674.

Cleghorne.

Edward, goldsmith ——*Edinburgh* 1681-2.

Clelland.

Robert (Mr.), burgess of Pittenweem and of this burgh —— *Anstruther*
[*Wester* 1689 conv., 1689-1702.

Clephane.

David, col. in the army, and lt.-col. 20th regt. of foot —— *Kinross-shire* 1803-6,
(then lt.-col.), 1807 until appointed a commissioner of excise in Scotland,
[s.b. 25 July 1811.

John —— *Burntisland* 1586, conv.

Probably John Clephane of Carslogie, lost the bulk of his estate.

Clephane—continued.

Nicol (Clapen) —— *Burntisland* 1599, conv.

Robert (Claipen) —— *Anstruther-Easter* 1593.

William Douglas McLean, of Kirkness —— *Kinross-shire* 1802 until [appointed lieut.-governor of Grenada, s.b. 23 Aug. 1803.
Assumed the additional surname of McLean by R. L. 6 Nov. 1790 (*London Gazette*, p. 659), maj.-gen. in the army, 1801, col. 3rd foot guards, died in Grenada 4 Nov. 1803, m.   dau. of   Maclean, of Torloisk of Mull, and left with other issue a dau. [Margaret, m. 24 July, 1815, to Spencer Joshua Alwyne, 2nd Marquis of Northampton.

Clerk.

Alexander —— *Edinburgh* 1567, 1569 conv., 1579 (then provost and of [Balbirnie), 1581 provost, 1583 provost.

Alexander, merchant burgess —— *Edinburgh* 1621, 1630 conv., then provost.

George (sir), of Pennicuik, bart. —— *Edinburghshire* 1811-12, 1812-18, 1818-20 (a lord of the admiralty 1819), 1820-6, 1826-30 (clerk of the ordnance 1827, of the council of the lord high admiral 1828, a lord of the admiralty [1829), 1830-1, 1831-2, 1835-7. See also England M.P.
Sir George Clerk, 6th baronet, P.C. 1845, F.R.S. 1819, advocate 1809, hon. D.C.L. Oxon. 1810, chairman of royal academy of music, M.P. Stamford 1838-47, and Dover 1847-52, contested Dover 1852, lord of the admiralty 1819-27, 1828-30, of the council to the lord high admiral 1827-8, under-sec. home dept. July-Nov. 1830-5, sec. treasury 1841, master of the mint and vice-president board of trade 1845-46; d. 23 Dec. 1867, aged 80, having m., 13 Aug. 1810, Maria, 2nd dau. of Ewan Law, esq., of Horsted Place, Sussex (B. ELLEN- [BOROUGH) ; she d. 7 Sept. 1866, having had issue. See Foster's Baronetage.

Johnne —— *Montrose* 1357.
Merchant burgess and chief magistrate of the royal borough of Montrose, one of the [hostages for David Bruce in 1357.—PLAYFAIR.

John (sir), of Pennycuik, knight bart. —— *Edinburghshire* 1690 to 1702.
Sir John Clerk of Pennycuik House, Edinburgh, knight baronet of Nova Scotia, so cr. 24 March, 1679 (eldest son of John Clerk of Pennycuik by his wife Mary, dau. of Sir William Gray of Pittendrum), d.   1722, having m. twice, and had with other issue a [son and successor Sir John, M.P. See Foster's Baronetage.

John (Mr.), younger of Pennycuik —— *Whithorn* 1702-7, sat also in 1st [parliament of Great Britain 1707-8.
Sir John Clerk, 2nd baronet (on the death of Sir John, M.P., 1722), F.S.A. 1725, F.R.S. 1728, a celebrated antiquary, a commissioner for the Union, a baron of the exchequer in Scotland 1707 until his death, 4 Oct. 1755; m. twice and had issue. See Foster's Baronetage.

Patrick —— *Rutherglen* 1357.

William —— *Haddington* 1468.

Cluiston.

William —— *Wigtown* 1673-4.

Clunes.

Alexander —— *Cromarty* 1661.

Cochrane.

—— of Barbachla —— *Linlithgowshire* 1643-4 conv.

Alexander Dundas Ross Wishart-Baillie of Lamington —— *Lanarkshire* [1857. See foot-note.

Alexander Forrester, capt. R.N. —— *Stirling burghs* 1800-2, 1802-6, seated [on petition 28 Feb. 1803.

Hon. Sir Alexander Forrester Inglis Cochrane, G.C.B., admiral 1819, com.-in-chief Plymouth 1821-4, lieut. R.N. 1778, wounded in the action between Sir George Rodney and M. de Guichen, 17 April 1780, etc., M.P. as above, rear-admiral 1804, defeated French fleet off St. Domingo, Feb. 1806, received thanks of both houses of parliament and corporation of London, together with the freedom of the city and a valuable sword, K.B. 29 Mar. 1806, together with Lt.-Gen. Beckwith reduced Martinique, took the islands of St. Thomas, Santa Cruz, Guadaloupe, gov. and commander 1810-13, etc. (son of Thomas, 8th Earl of Dundonald) ; b. 22-3 April, 1758 ; d. 26 Jan. 1832, having m. April, 1788, Maria, dau. of David Shaw, esq., widow of Capt. Sir Jacob Wheate, Bart. (ext.), R.N. ; she d. 18 Mar. 1856, having had with 2 daus. 2 sons, of whom the elder Admiral Sir Thomas John [Cochrane, G.C.B., father of Lord Lamington last-named.

Andrew, son late Thomas, Earl of Dundonald —— *Stirling burghs* 1791-6, 1796 [until appointed governor of Dominica, s.b. 3 May, 1797.

Hon. Andrew James Cochrane-Johnstone, col. in the army, capt.-gen. and governor of Dominica, etc., M.P. Grampound, 1807-8, 1812-14, until expelled the house (see England M.P.) ; b. 24 May, 1767 ; m. 1st, 20 Nov. 1793, Lady Georgiana Hope-Johnstone, dau. of James 3rd Earl of Hopetoun, when he assumed the additional surname of Johnstone ; she d. 17 Sept. 1797. He m. 2ndly, 21 Mar. 1803, Amelia Constance Gertrude Etienette, only dau. and heir of Baron de Clugny, governor of Guadaloupe, and widow of Raymond Godet, of Martinique. By his 1st wife he had with a son who d. young, a dau. Elizabeth, m. [28 Mar. 1816, to William John, 9th Baron Napier, who d. 11 Oct. 1834.

COCHRANE-WISHART-BAILLIE, ALEXANDER DUNDAS ROSS, BARON LAMINGTON, of Lamington, co. Lanark, so cr. 3 May, 1880, D.L. Haddington and Lanark, M.P. Isle of Wight 1870-80, Bridport 1841-6, 1847-52, Lanarkshire 1857, Honiton 1859-68 (see ENGLAND), co-heir (j.m.) of the barony of Wharton (1548) ; (elder son of Adml. Sir Thomas John Cochrane, G.C.B.), b. 24 Nov. 1816 ; m. 4 Dec. 1844. Annabella Mary Elizabeth, dau. of Andrew Robert Drummond, esq., of Cadland, Hants (V. STRATHALLAN), and has a son and 3 daus.

(1) Hon. Wallace Charles Alexander Napier, lieut. Leic. mil., b. 29 July, 1860.

(2) Constance Mary Elizabeth, m. 7 Feb. 1867, to Reginald Windsor, Earl Delawarr.

(3) Hon. Amy Augusta Frederica Annabella, m. 15 July, 1880, to the Marquis Francesco Nobile Vitelleschi, an Italian senator.

(4) Hon. Violet.

26, Wilton Crescent, S.W., and Lamington, Biggar, Lanarks.
Club—Carlton.

Cochrane—*continued.*

SIR WILLIAM COCHRANE, M.P. Ayrshire 1644 conv., 1644-7,
Ayrshire and Renfrewshire 1656-8, cr. Earl of Dundonald ═

═

SIR JOHN COCHRANE, M.P. Ayrshire 1667, 1669-74, 1681-2 ═

WILLIAM COCHRANE (son of William ═
Lord Cochrane). M.P. Renfrew 1689
conv., 1689-98, Dumbartonshire 1702-
7, Wigtown burghs 1708-10, 1710-13.

THOMAS COCHRANE (son of William Cochrane)
M.P. Renfrewshire 1722-7, succeeded as 8th
Earl of Dundonald ═

ADMIRAL SIR ALEXANDER FOR-   ANDREW COCHRANE-JOHNSTONE,
RESTER INGLIS COCHRANE,   M.P. Stirling burghs 1791-6,
G.C.B., M.P. Stirling burghs   1796-7 (see M.P. England).
1800-2, 1802-6 ═

ALEXANDER DUNDAS ROSS COCHRANE-WISHART BAILLIE
(son of Admiral Sir Thomas John Cochrane, G.C.B.),
M.P. Lanark 1857 (see also M.P. England), cr. Lord
Lamington 3 May, 1880.

George —— *Ayr* 1585 conv., 1593, 1597 conv,

James, merchant burgess —— *Edinburgh* 1641.

John (sir), of Ochiltree, knt. —— *Ayrshire* 1667 conv., 1669-74, 1681-2.

2nd son of William 1st Earl of Dundonald, an associate of Monmouth, escaped to Holland
upon the discovery of the Rye House plot. On the death of King Charles he accompanied
the Duke of Argyll to Scotland to take part in an intended invasion of that country, was forfeited 1685, and he and his son John were betrayed to the royalists. Sir John was ransomed
by his father, and his forfeiture was rescinded at the revolution 1689 ; a farmer of the poll
tax 1693 ; he m. Margaret, dau. of Sir William Strickland of Boynton, Yorks, bart., and
[had issue.

Michael —— *Wigtown* 1600.

Thomas (major), of Wester Stanely —— *Renfrewshire* 1722-7.

8th Earl of Dundonald 9 July 1758 (7th son of William Cochrane, elder son of Sir John,
M.P., of Ochiltree), commissioner of excise Scotland 1730-61 ; d. at La Mancha, Peebles,
[27 June, 1778, having m. twice and had issue. See Douglas' Peerage.

Walter (Mr.), of Dumbreck, merchant provost —— *Aberdeen* 15 April, 1693,
[until his death, s.b. 5 Dec. 1694.

Cochrane—*con'inued.*

—— laird of Cowdoun —— *Ayrshire* 1644 conv., 1644-7; *Ayrshire and Renfrew-*
[*shire* 1656-8, as Lord William (WILLIS).

Sir William Cochrane (2nd son of Alexander Blair, who took the name of Cochrane by reason of his marriage with Elizabeth, dau. and heir of William Cochrane of Cochrane); cr. Lord Cochrane of Dundonald 27 Dec. 1647; fined £5,000 under the Act of Grace and Pardon 1654; P.C. after the Restoration : commissioner of the treasury and exchequer ; cr. Earl of Dundonald, Lord Cochrane of Paisley and Ochiltree 12 May, 1669, with special remainder (see FOSTER'S Peerage) ; m. Euphcme, dau. of Sir William Scott of Ardoss, co.
[Fife, and she d. 1686, leaving issue.

William (Mr.), of Kilmarnock —— *Renfrew* 1689 conv., 1689-98, *Dumbarton-*
shire 1702-7, *Wigtown burghs* 1708-10, 1710-13, accepted a crown office of
[profit 1712.

Brother of John, 2nd Earl of Dundonald, joint keeper of the signet 1712 ; m. Grizel, dau. of James Graham, 2nd marquis of Montrose, and d. 1717, having had with 5 daus. a son
[Thomas, who succeeded as 6th Earl of Dundonald.

Cockburn.

—— laird of Clerkington —— *Haddington constabulary* 1644-7.

(Perhaps son of Sir Richard Cockburn of Clerkington, sec. of state 1591, lord of session
[same year, knighted 1594, lord privy seal, P.C. 1610, d. 1626.)

Adam, of Ormiston —— *Haddington constabulary* 1678 conv., 1681-2, 1689
[conv., 1689 until appointed lord justice clerk, 28 Nov. 1692.

Younger son of John Cockburn of Ormiston, M.P. (and heir of his brother John, who d. s.p. 26 Dec., 1671). P.C., treasurer depute (chancellor of the exchequer) 1699 until the accession of Queen Anne, lord justice clerk again 1705-10, and a lord of session 1705 until his death, 16 Apl. 1735, aged 79 ; he m. Susan, dau. of John Hamilton, 4th Earl of Haddington.

Archibald (sir), of Langton —— *Berwickshire* 1678 conv., 1685-6 (then elder),
[1689 conv., 1689-1702.

2nd Baronet d. 1705, retoured heir of his father (Sir William, M.P.) in the office of principal usher 10 Dec. 1657, heritable sheriff Berwickshire 1686, left issue. See Foster's
[Baronetage.

Archibald, of Borthwick —— *Berwickshire* 1685-6.

Probably son of the 2nd Baronet M.P. last named ; he m. 1684, Elizabeth, dau. of Sir
[George Mackenzie, and had with other issue a son Sir Archibald, 3rd baronet, who d. s.p.

Harry —— *Haddington* 1605 conv., 1612, 1617 conv.

Harie (Mr.), merchant provost —— *Haddington* 1681-2.

James —— *Haddington* 1572 conv. (then provost), 1579 (called also John),
1585 conv. and parlt., 1592, 1593, 1594 parlt. and conv. ; 1599 conv. bis,
[1600.

James (Mr.) —— *Haddington* 1617, 1621, 1625 conv. (then advocate), 1628-33,
[1630 conv.

SCOTCH MEMBERS. K

Cockburn—*continued.*

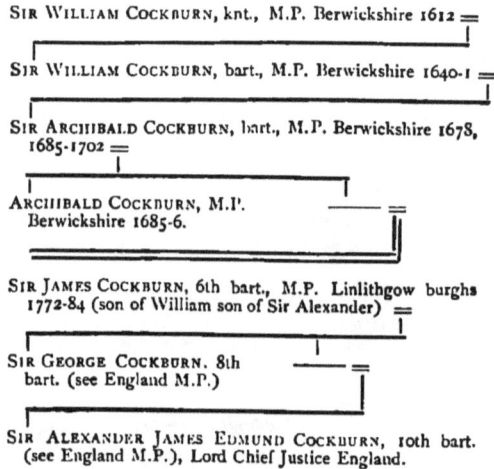

SIR WILLIAM COCKBURN, knt., M.P. Berwickshire 1612 =

SIR WILLIAM COCKBURN, bart., M.P. Berwickshire 1640-1 =

SIR ARCHIBALD COCKBURN, bart., M.P. Berwickshire 1678, 1685-1702 =

ARCHIBALD COCKBURN, M.P. Berwickshire 1685-6.　　　　=

SIR JAMES COCKBURN, 6th bart., M.P. Linlithgow burghs 1772-84 (son of William son of Sir Alexander) =

SIR GEORGE COCKBURN. 8th bart. (see England M.P.)　　　　=

SIR ALEXANDER JAMES EDMUND COCKBURN, 10th bart. (see England M.P.), Lord Chief Justice England.

James (sir), of Langton, bart. ——*Linlithgow burghs* 1772-4, 1774-80, 1780-4.

6th Baronet (son of William Cockburn of Ayton); sold Langton 1757; d. 26-7 July, 1804, aged 75, having m. twice and left issue, with a daughter, 5 sons, viz. :—(1) Major-Gen. Sir James Cockburn, 7th Bart., G.C.H. ; (2) Admiral Sir George Cockburn, 8th Bart., G.C.B., P.C. ; (3) Very Rev. Sir William Cockburn, 9th Bart., dean of York ; (4) Alexander, father of Sir Alexander James Edmund Cockburn, 10th Bart., lord chief [justice of England ; (5) General Sir Francis Cockburn, governor of Honduras.

John (sir), of Ormistoun —— 1608.

Son of John Cockburn of Ormistone, whom he succeeded in 1583 ; extraordinary lord of session 4 July, 1588 ; knighted and appointed justice clerk 1591, resigned 1623. On the death of his brother-in-law Sir Lewis Bellenden ordinary lord of session, 1593; d. June, 1623 ; m. Elizabeth, widow of James Lawson of Humbie, and dau. of Sir John Bellenden of [Auchinoule, lord justice clerk and a lord of session ; probably father of John M.P. 1648-9.

John, of Skraling —— 1608.

Probably related to Sir James Cockburn of Skirling, a commissioner for Mary, Queen of [Scots.

——, laird of Ryslaw —— *Berwickshire* 1625 conv.

John or James Cockburn of Ryslaw, is said to have been created a baronet of Nova Scotia in 1628, but no evidence of this creation has been discovered. See "CHAOS," [Foster's Baronetage.

John, provost *Haddington* 1643 conv.

John, of Ormistoun —— *Haddington constabulary* 1648-9.

Probably son of Sir John, lord justice clerk, etc., M.P. ; m. Margaret Hepburn, and had [a son Adam, M.P.

Cockburn—*continued.*

COCKBURN OF ORMISTON.

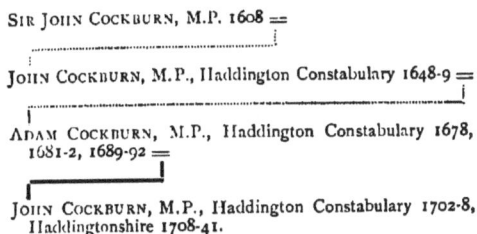

SIR JOHN COCKBURN, M.P. 1608 ==

JOHN COCKBURN, M.P., Haddington Constabulary 1648-9 ==

ADAM COCKBURN, M.P., Haddington Constabulary 1678, 1681-2, 1689-92 ==

JOHN COCKBURN, M.P., Haddington Constabulary 1702-8, Haddingtonshire 1708-41.

John, of Ormiston —— *Haddington constabulary* 1702-7 (then younger), 1st parlt. Great Britain, 1707-8, *Haddingtonshire* 1708-10, 1710-13, 1713-15, [1715-22 (an officer of the crown 1717), 1722-7, 1727-34, 1734-41.

Son of Adam Cockburn, M.P., lord justice clerk. Sold his estate 1748, a lord of the admiralty 1717-32, d. 11 Nov., 1758, having m. 1700, Beatrix, dau. of John Carmichael, 1st Earl of Hyndford. He had a son George, capt. R.N., comptroller of the navy 1756 until his death, 23 July, 1770, having m. Caroline, Baroness Forrester, who d. 25 Feb. 1784, [leaving 2 daus., who both married and died s.p.

Stephen —— *Haddington* 1492.

William (sir), of Langton, knt. —— *Berwickshire* 1612.

Knighted before 1609 ; had a grant of the office of principal usher, 1595 ; m. Helen, 5th dau. of Alexander, 4th Lord Elphinstone (she rem. to Henry Rolls of Woodneston), and [had a son, Sir William, M.P.

William (sir), of Langton, knight-baronet —— *Berwickshire* 1640-1.

Son of Sir William Cockburn, M.P. ; created a baronet of Nova Scotia 22 Nov. 1627 ; m. Margaret dau. of Sir Archibald Acheson, Bart., of Glencairny, co. Armagh (E. GOSFORD), father of Sir Archibald Cockburn, M P., and ancestor of Sir Alexander Cockburn, 10th baronet, and lord chief justice of England (see M.P, England), at whose death, 20 [Nov. 1880, the title expired.

Colebrooke.

Thomas Edward (sir), of Crawford, baronet —— *Lanarkshire* 1857-9, 1859-65, 1865-68, *N. Lanarkshire* 1868-74, 1874-80, and since 1880. [See foot-note.

COLEBROOKE, SIR THOMAS EDWARD, of Ottershawe Park, Surrey (1759 G.B.), LL.D., M.P. Taunton 1842-52 (see England M.P.), and as above ; contested Taunton 1852 ; lord-lieutenant Lanarkshire 1869, succ. his uncle as 4th baronet in 1838 ; (only son of Henry Thomas Colebrooke, F.R.S., Member of Council at Calcutta) ; b. 19 Aug. 1813 ; m. 15 Jan. 1857, Elizabeth Margaret, 2nd dau. of John Richardson, esq., of Kirklands, co. Roxburgh, and has had 2 sons and 3 daus.

(1) Edward Arthur, b. 12 October, 1861.
(2) Roland John, b. 22 July, 1864.
(3) Margaret Ginevra.   (4) Helen Emma.   (5) Mary Elizabeth.
Seats—Abington House, Lanark, N.B., and Ottershawe Park, Surrey.
Town House—14, South Street, Park Lane, W.

Collace.

—— of Balnamoon —— *Forfarshire* 1612.

Collinson.

* **John** (Collisone) —— *Aberdeen* 1531 —— 1596 c·qv.

Colquhoun.

Alexander, of Luss —— the laird of Luss sat as a minor baron in convention
[1605; *Dumbartonshire* 1612; certified unable to attend.

3rd son of Sir John Colquhoun of Luss, and heir of his elder brother. He m. (contract dated at Glasgow 18 Aug. 1595) Helen, dau. of Sir George Buchanan of that ilk, and had with other issue 2 sons, Sir John, M P., and Sir Humphrey, M.P. ; died 23 May, 1617, will [dated 16th and 17th same month.

Archibald, of Killermont, lord advocate of Scotland —— *Elgin burghs* 1807 until he accepted the Chiltern hundreds, s.b 13 July 1810; *Dumbartonshire* 1810-12, 1812-18 (clerk register of Scotland 1816), 1818-20, 1820 until his death, s.b. [19 Feb. 1821.

Of Killermont, co. Dumbarton [only son of John Campbell of Clathic, co. Perth, provost of Glasgow (and his wife Agnes Colquhoun, heiress of Killermont), son of Archibald Coates of Glasgow by Jean Campbell, heiress of Clathic]; sheriff of Perthshire, lord advocate 1807-16, lord clerk register 1816 ; d. 8 Dec. 1820, having m. Mary Anne, sister of William Erskine, [Lord Kinnedder of Session, and had with other issue a son John, M.P.

Humphrey (sir), of Balvie —— *Dumbartonshire* 1639-41, 1643-4 conv. (then a [knight), 1645-7 (as laird of Balvie).

2nd son of Alexander Colquhoun, M.P., m. Margaret, 2nd dau. and coheir of Gilbert, 8th [Lord Somerville, and d. s.p.

Humphrey (sir), of Luss —— *Dumbartonshire* 1702-7.

4th Baronet, lt.-col. militia Argyllshire, Dumbarton and Bute, a commissioner of supply, had a re-grant of the baronetcy 29 April, 1704. voted against the Union ; (son of Sir James, 3rd bart., who d. 1688) ; d. 1718, having m. (contr. 1 and 4 April, 1684) Margaret, eldest dau. of Sir Patrick Houston of that ilk, Bart., and had an only child, Anne, m. 29 Jan. 1702 to James Grant of Pluscardine, ancestor of the Earl of Seafield, and also father of Sir James [Colquhoun, cr. a baronet of Great Britain 27 June, 1786.

James (major), younger, of Luss —— *Dumbartonshire* 1799-1802, 1802 until [accepted the Chiltern hundreds, s.b. 22 Feb. 1806.

Sir James Colquhoun, 3rd Baronet (on the death of his father Sir James, 2nd Bart., 23 April, 1805), major Dumbartonshire vols. 1804; b. 28 Sept. 1774, d. 3 Feb. 1836, having m. (contract dated 11 June, 1799) Janet, dau. of Rt. Hon. Sir John Sinclair, Bart., she d. 21 [Oct. 1846, leaving with other issue a son, Sir James, M.P.

Colquhoun—*continued.*

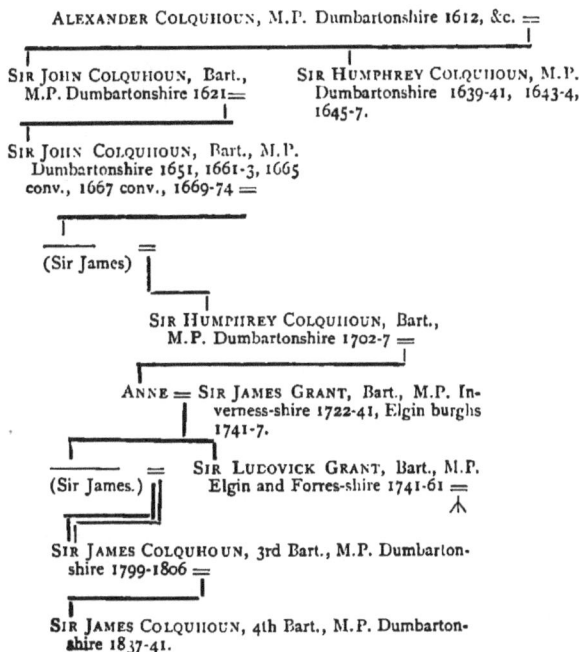

ALEXANDER COLQUHOUN, M.P. Dumbartonshire 1612, &c. =

SIR JOHN COLQUHOUN, Bart., M.P. Dumbartonshire 1621=

SIR HUMPHREY COLQUHOUN, M.P. Dumbartonshire 1639-41, 1643-4, 1645-7.

SIR JOHN COLQUHOUN, Bart., M.P. Dumbartonshire 1651, 1661-3, 1665 conv., 1667 conv., 1669-74 =

(Sir James) =

SIR HUMPHREY COLQUHOUN, Bart., M.P. Dumbartonshire 1702-7 =

ANNE = SIR JAMES GRANT, Bart., M.P. Inverness-shire 1722-41, Elgin burghs 1741-7.

(Sir James.) = SIR LUDOVICK GRANT, Bart., M.P. Elgin and Forres-shire 1741-61 =

SIR JAMES COLQUHOUN, 3rd Bart., M.P. Dumbartonshire 1799-1806 =

SIR JAMES COLQUHOUN, 4th Bart., M.P. Dumbartonshire 1837-41.

James (sir), of Luss, bart.—— *Dumbartonshire* 1837-41.

4th Baronet (on the death of his father Sir James, M.P.), contested Dumbartonshire 1832, lord lieut. co. Dumbarton 1837-73; b. 7 Feb. 1804, d. 18 Dec. 1873, having m. 14 June, 1843, Jane, 2nd dau. of Sir Robert Abercromby, Bart.; she d. 3 Aug. 1844, leaving an only [son Sir James, 5th Baronet.

John (sir), laird of Luss —— *Dumbartonshire* 1621.

Son of Alexander Colquhoun, M.P.; cr. a baronet of Nova Scotia 30 Aug. 1625, together with a grant of three miles square of land in Nova Scotia, and d. about 1649; he m. (contr. 30 June and 6 July, 1620), Lilias, dau. of John Graham, 4th Earl of Montrose; and had with [other issue John, M.P., next named.

John (sir), of Luss, knt. —— *Dumbartonshire* 1651 (laird of Luss), 1661-3, [1665 conv., 1667 conv., 1669-74.

Sir John, 2nd Bart., lt.-col. Argyllshire regt. of militia 1669, a commissioner of supply 1651; d. about 11 April, 1676, his will proved 27 Feb. 1677; he m. (contr. 17 Feb. 1636) Margaret, dau. of Sir Gideon Baillie of Lochend, co. Haddington; she re-m. 1 Apl. 1677 to [Archibald Stirling of Garden, and d. 20 July, 1679, leaving issue

Colquhoun—*continued.*

John Campbell, of Garscadden and Killermont —— *Dumbartonshire* 1833-4, [*Kilmarnock burghs* 1837-41.

Eldest son of Archibald Campbell Colquhoun, M.P. Newcastle-under-Lyne 1842 (see England M.P.), contested Kilmarnock burghs 1841 ; b. 23 Jan. 1803, d. 17 April, 1870, having m. 10 Sept. 1827, Hon. Henrietta Maria Powys, dau. of Thomas, 2nd Lord Lilford ; [she d. 21 Jan. 1870, leaving 2 sons.

William, of Craigtoun —— *Dumbartonshire* 1689 conv., 1689 ; his place was [declared vacant 21 May, 1700, because he had not signed the association.

Married Mary Stirling of Law ; his only dau. Margaret m. (contr. 11 July, 1732) to Alan [Colquhoun of Kenmure, and had issue.

Coltrane.

William, provost —— *Wigtown* 1681-2, 1685-6, 1689 conv., 1689-1702, 1702-7, [then of Drummorrell provost.

Of Drummorell, co. Wigtown (2nd son of Patrick Coltrane of Culmazie and Airless provost of Wigtown); he had with 3 daus. a son Patrick who had sasine of his father's lands [of Meikle Arrow, 16 Aug. 1710.

Colvile.

[James (sir) —— 1531, 1535, 1536; 1532 lord of articles and 1535.]

Eldest son of Sir Robert Colville of Ochiltree, who fell at Flodden ; a commissioner of parliament 24 April and 13 May, 1531, 15 Dec. 1535, 29 April, 1536 ; a lord of articles 13 July, 1532, and 7 June, 1535 ; one of the judges (Lord Easter Wemyss) appointed at institutions of college of justice 25 May, 1532 ; comptroller before 1527 till 1538 ; died [1541, and declared forfeited after death 15 May, 1541, rescinded 12 Dec. 1543.

—— laird of Easter Wemyss, sat as a minor baron in convention 1596.

Sir James Colvile of Easter Wemyss (son of Sir James Colville by his wife Janet Douglas), served in the wars in France under Henry, king of Navarre ; cr. Lord Colvile of Culross [about 5 May, 1606 ; d. 1620, leaving issue. See Foster's Peerage.

John —— *Stirling* 1590 conv.

Probably a younger son of Sir James Colville of Ochiltree, M.P., first named.

Robert, of Ochiltree —— *Kinross-shire* 1754-61.

Robert Colvile of Ochiltree m. Janet, 2nd dau. of Sir Peter Wedderburn of Gosford, Bart., and had a son Robert, b. 29 June, 1728.—? if identical with the above, or with Robert Colvill who assumed the title of Lord Ochiltree and voted at the general elections of 1784 and 1787, but his vote for the election of 1788 was rejected; stated that he was son of John [Colvill, wright at Ely, co. Fife.

Congalton.

Adam, of —— *Haddington* 1357.

Son of Sir John Congalton ; he was one of the barons who became surety for King David's [ransom 1357, had a son Henry.

Conqueror.

Dionys —— *Perth* 1579, 1583.

Cook.

James, baillie —— *Pittenweem* 1685-6.

Cor.

Clement —— *Edinburgh* 1593 conv. bis, 1594 parlt. and conv. bis, 1596
[conv., 1598 conv. bis, 1599.

Cornwall.

Nicol, of Bonhard —— *Linlithgow* 1593 parlt. and conv. bis, 1594 conv., 1596
[conv., 1597 (provost of Linlithgow), 1598 conv., 1599 conv., 1600.

Nicol Cornwall m. Mary, dau. of Sir Archibald Stewart, of Castlemilk, and had issue.

—— laird of Bonhard —— *Linlithgowshire* 1625 conv.

Corsan.

John —— *Dumfries* 1621.

Of Meikleknox, provost of Dumfries 45 years, d. 1629, aged 75; by his wife Janet
[Maxwell, of Lord Maxwell's family, he had a son John, M.P. (*Nisbet.*)

John (Mr.) —— *Dumfries* 1628-33, *Kirkcudbright* 1640-1, 1649 (Carsane).

Of Bardennoch and Meikleknox, advocate, (son of John Corsane, M.P.), provost of Dumfries ; m. Margaret, dau. and co-h. of Robert Maxwell of Dinwiddy, and d. 1671, leaving issue.
[(*Nisbet.*)

Corsell.

John —— *Dumfries* 1617.

Cossar.

Adam (Cosoure) —— *Stirling* 1449, —— 1467, 1469.

Couper.

John (sir), of Gogar —— *Edinburghshire* 1681-2.

John Couper of Nether Gogar, was served heir of his father (who styles himself in his will
"Ion Coupar of gogar") 27 Oct. 1640, knighted before 26 Aug. 1643, a commissioner of
supply and a member of committees of war ; by his wife Margaret Inglis of Otterston he had
[2 daus.

Coutts.

James —— *Edinburgh city* 1762-8.

3rd son of John Coutts, provost of Edinburgh and banker (who m., 10 Apl. 1730, Jean, 2nd
dau. of Sir John Stuart of Allanbank) ; b. 10 Mar. 1733, d. at Gibraltar 19 Feb. 1778, having
m. Polly Peagrim, niece of George Campbell, banker in the Strand (originally a goldsmith),
and became a banker as Campbell & Coutts ; she d. 28 Mar. 1760, leaving an only dau.,
[m. to her cousin Sir John Stuart of Allanbank, Bart.

Cowan.

Charles, of Valleyfield, co. Edinburgh —— *Edinburgh* 1847-52, 1852-7, 1857-9.
[See foot-note.

COWAN, CHARLES, of Edinburgh, paper maker (eldest son of Alexander Cowan of Edinburgh, by
Elizabeth, dau. of George Hall of Liverpool, merchant), J.P. Midlothian and Edinburgh ; b. 1801,
m. 1824, Catharine, dau. of late Rev. William Menzies, she d. 1872, leaving with other issue a son.
(1) Charles William, of Valleyfield, Midlothian, late capt. Queen's Edinburgh militia ; b. 1835, m.
1861, Margaret, dau. of Robert Craig, esq., and has with other issue a son Alexander, b. 1863.
Logan House, Midlothian, N.B. ; Wester Lea, Murrayfield, Edinburgh.

Cowan—*continued.*

James, of 35, Royal terrace, Edinburgh, paper maker —— *Edinburgh* 1874-80
                                            [and since 1880. See foot-note.
John —— *Stirling* 1625 —— 1651.
Walter —— *Stirling* 1588 conv., 1596 conv., 1597 conv. bis.

Cowper.

Patrick —— *Dunfermline* 1628-33, 1630 conv.
William —— *Cupar* 1488.

Crab.

Johnne —— *Aberdeen* 1357, 1367.

Craig.   See also Gibson-Craig.

Alexander (Mr.), —— *Banff* 1621.
Robert, of Riccarton —— *Edinburghshire* 1693-1702.
> Apparently grandson of Sir Lewis Craig, lord of session 1605, who died 6 June, 1622 ;
> he was probably father of James Craig, of Riccarton, who m. Christian, dau. of Robert
>   [Dundas, of Arniston, and had issue.
William, provost —— *Dumfries* 1678 conv., 1681-2.

Craigie.

David, of Over Sanday, merchant burgess, provost ——*Kirkwall* 1681-2, 1685-6.
Hugh, Gairsay —— *Orkney and Zetlandshire* 1661 until his death, s.b. 15
                                            [April, 1663.
James (Mr.), younger, of Dumbarnie —— *Perthshire* 1698-1702.
> [2nd son of John Craigie of Dumbarnie, by his wife, Susan, dau. of Sir John Inglis of
>   [Cramond, Bart.]
Robert, of Glendoig, lord advocate of Scotland —— *Wick burghs* 1742-7.
> Lord president court of session 1754 (son of Lawrence Craigie of Kilgraston, by his
> wife Margaret Scrimgeour) ; advocate 1710 ; lord advocate 1742 ; a commissioner of
>   [fisheries and manufactures, Scotland, 1755 ; d. 10 March, 1760.
William (sir), of Gairsay —— *Orkney and Zetland stewartry* 1681-2, 1689 conv.
                                            [1689-1702, a knight in 1690.
> Sir William Craigie of Gairnie, m. Anne, dau. of Sir Robert Hamilton of Silvertonhill,
>   [Bart., by his wife, Hon. Anne Hamilton (B. BELHAVEN).

Craigie-Hall.

—— the laird of —— sat as a minor baron in conv. 1597, See KYNYNMOUND.

Craigengelt.

—— the laird of —— *Stirling* 1567.

COWAN, JAMES, of Edinburgh, paper maker (brother of Charles Cowan, late M.P., sons of late
    Alexander Cowan, esq., of Pennicuik afsd.), educated at high school and university of Edin-
burgh, lord provost of Edinburgh 1872-4, b. 1816, m. 1841 Charlotte, dau. of Duncan Cowan, esq.
    110, *St. George's Square, S. W. ; 35, Royal Terrace, Edinburgh.*
    Clubs—Reform, Devonshire, —— University, Edin.

Cranstoun.

Thomas, of —— *Edinburgh* 1445.
Probably son of Thomas Cranston, who was ambassador to Eric, king of Denmark, 1426 ;
[warden of the marches 1459 ; d. about 1470.

Thomas —— *Lauder* 1646-7.
Possibly youngest son of William 1st Lord Cranstoun.

William —— *Edinburgh* 1439, 1449, 1456, 1458, 1462, 1463 (of Swynhop),
[1464,

William (sir) —— sat as a minor baron for Roxburghshire 1608 conv.
Lord Cranston, so cr. 17 Nov. 1609 (son of John Cranstoun of Moriestoun) ; capt. of the
guard to James VI., by whom he was knighted ; d. June, 1627 ; m. Sarah, eldest dau
[and co-h. of John Cranstoun of Cranstoun, and had issue

Craufurd and Crawford.

Andrea —— 1474.

David —— *Ayr* 1587, 1590 conv.
Son of David Crawford and grandson of Bartholomew Crawford of Kerse, he died 1600,
leaving issue only, having entailed his estate upon the heir male, Crawford of Balgregan.

Edward Henry John, younger, of Auchenames —— *Ayr burghs* 1852-7.
[1857-9, 1859-65, 1865-8, 1868-74. See foot-note.

James —— *Ayr* 1583.

James —— *Linlithgow* 1649, 1650, or James Campbell.

John (sir) —— of Kilbirny, knt. —— *Ayrshire* 1644 conv. and parlt. (laird of
[Kilbirny), 1661 (then a knight).
Sir John Crawfurd, said by Mr. Crawfurd in his "History of Renfrew" to have been made
a baronet of Nova Scotia 1642 (the patent is not recorded in the great seal register), and
he is so designated in the Lyon Office ; died M.P. Ayrshire 1661, but styled a knight,
having m. 1st, Margaret, dau. of Robert, Lord Burleigh, and 2ndly, Magdalene, dau. of
David, Lord Carnegie, by whom he had 2 daus., of whom the younger, Margaret, m. 27 Dec.
[1664 to Hon. Patrick Lindsay, and had a son John, M.P., next mentioned.

CRAUFURD, EDWARD HENRY JOHN, of Auchenames, Ayrshire, J.P., D.L. cos. Ayr and
Bute, M.P. as above ; B.A. Trin. Coll. Camb. 1841, M.A. 1844; bar.-at-law I. T. 1845,
(eldest son of John Craufurd, esq., of Auchenames, by Sophia Marianne, dau. of Maj.-Gen. Horace
Churchill) ; b. 9 Dec. 1816 ; m. 6 Oct. 1863, Frances, only sister of Sir Paul William Molesworth,
Bart., and has a son and 3 daus.
(1) Hugh Ronald George, b. 16 July, 1873.
(2) Mary Beatrice. (3) Katherine Yseult. (4) Frances Guenevere.
Crosbie Castle and *Auchenames House, West Kilbride, N.B.* 107, *St. George's Square, S.W. ;* 3, *Essex
Court, Temple, E.C.*
Clubs—Oxford & Cambridge, Brooks'.
SCOTCH MEMBERS.   1

Craufurd and Crawford—*continued*.

John, of Kilbirnie —— *Aryshire* 1693-1702, 1702 until cr. viscount of Garnock,
[10 April, 1703.

John, Viscount Garnock, P C. (eldest son of Hon. Patrick Lindsay afsd., 2nd son John 1st Earl of Lindsay), cr. viscount of Mount Crawford 10 April, 1703, changed to Garnock 26 Nov. same year; born 12 May, 1669, d. 24 Dec. 1708; bd. at Kilbirny 13 Jan. 1709; m. Margaret, only dau. of James Stewart, 1st Earl of Bute; she d. 27 April, [1738, having had issue.

John, of Auchenames —— *Renfrewshire* 1774-80, *Glasgow burghs* 1780-4, 1784-90.

John Craufurd of Drumsoy and Auchenames (elder son of Patrick Craufurd, M.P.), M.P. Old Sarum 1768 (see England M.P.), the friend of Charles James Fox; d. unm. in London [26 May, 1814.

Nicholas —— *Linlithgow* 1524 bis, 1525, 1526, elected a lord of the articles [in parliament 1528.

Nicholas Crawford of Oxengangs, justice clerk 20 Nov. 1524 until 1535; was appointed a [lord of session 27 May, 1532, at the institution of that court.

Patrick, of Auchenames —— *Ayrshire* 1741-7, 1747-54, *Renfrewshire* 1761-8.

Eldest son of Patrick Craufurd of Edinburgh (by his wife Jane, dau. of Archibald Crau-furd of Auchenames and Crosbie ; d. 10 Jan. 1778, having m. twice, and left with other [issue a son John, M.P.

Thomas —— *Glasgow* 1578 conv.

Probably of the family of the Crawfurd of Claslochie and Powmill, descended from [Thomas, 2nd son of Archibald Crawfurd of Crawfurdland, who died 1476.

Crichton.

—— laird of Ruthven —— *Forfarshire* 1644, conv. and parlt.

David (sir), of Lugtoun, knt. —— *Edinburghshire* 1621 (the laird), 1639-41 (Sir [David).

David Crichton of Lugtoun had a charter of the barony of Sanquhar and Langniddrie, etc., [2 Dec. 1602.

James (of Crechton), provost —— *Edinburgh* 1478 bis, (1479 the provost,) [1488 bis (then of Ruthven), 1489 (then of Ruthven-david).

James Crichton (brother of George, Earl of Caithness), had a charter of the lands of [Ruthven 29 April 1452.

James (Creichtoun), of Frendraught —— *Aberdeenshire* 1625 conv. (the laird), [*Banffshire* 1639-40, re-elected 1641.

Son of James Crichton of Frendraught; he m., 25 Feb. 1619, Elisabeth, eldest dau. of John Gordon, 12th Earl of Sutherland, and had a son James cr. viscount of Frendraught [and lord of Crichton (in his father's lifetime) 29 Aug. 1642.

James, of St. Leonards, sheriff at Dumfries —— *Dumfries sheriffdom and* [*stewartry of Annandale* 1661-3.

2nd son of William, 1st Earl of Dumfries, and 6th Lord Crichton of Sanquhar.

Crichton—*continued.*

John —— *Sanquhar* 1628-33.
Doubtless John Crichton of Rayhill, 3rd son of William 3rd Lord Crichton of Sanquhar, had a charter of confirmation of the lands of Rayhill, 16 May 1611 ; m. Mary, dau. of Sir John [Carmichael of Crawford, and was father of William, 1st Earl of Dumfries.

Robert, bailie —— *Whithorn* 1641
See note Douglas' Peerage, vol. i. 450.

William —— *Sanquhar* 1645-7.

William, of Craufurdtown —— *Dumfries* (or Nithsdale), *sheriffdom and stewartry* [*of Annandale* 1690 until his death, s.b. 13 May, 1702.

Crombie.

Thomas, of Kemnay —— *Aberdeenshire* 1628-33, 1630 conv., 1639-40, 1644 [conv. (the laird.)

Crosbie.

John (Corsbie) —— *Kirkcudbright* 1644.

Cruickshank.

Robert, of Banchory, merchant burgess, provost —— *Aberdeen* 1694-1702.

Crum.

Alexander, of Thornliebank, Glasgow —— *Renfrewshire* since 1880. See foot-[note.

Crum-Ewing.

Humphrey Ewing, of Strathleven, merchant in Glasgow —— *Paisley* 1857-9, [1859-65, 1865-8, 1868-74. See foot-note.

Cullane.

Alexander —— *Stirling* 1594 conv., 1597 conv.

Culrossie.

—— the laird of —— *Sutherlandshire* 1641.

CRUM, ALEXANDER, of Thornliebank, near Glasgow, J.P., D.L., cos. Lanark and Renfrew, hon. col. 3rd Renfrewshire rifle volunteers, contested Glasgow 1874, M.P. Renfrewshire as above, (eldest son of late Walter Crum, F.R.S., of Thornliebank, by Jessie. dau. of late William Graham of Burntshiel, co. Renfrew), b. 8 April 1828, m. 4 June 1863, Margaret Nina, eldest dau. of late Rt. Rev. Alexander Ewing, LL.D., D.C.L., bishop of Argyll, and has three sons, Walter Ewing, b. 22 July 1875, Alexander Stewart, b. 20 March 1867, John Ludovick, b. 21 May 1874.
Thornliebank, Glasgow. *Clubs—Windham* and *Devonshire.*

CRUM-EWING, HUMPHREY EWING, of Strathleven, co. Dumbarton, J.P., D.L., and lord-lieut., also J.P. cos. Lanark, Renfrew, and Argyll, assumed the additional surname of Ewing under the will of his uncle James Ewing of Strathleven in 1853 (son of Alexander Crum of Thornliebank), b. 16 July, 1802, m. 1825, Helen, dau. of Rev. John Dick, D.D., of Glasgow, and has had 3 sons and a dau.
  (1) Alexander, D.L. co. Dumbarton, col. Lanarkshire R.V., m. 1859 Jane, only dau. of Vice-Admiral O'Grady of Erinagh House, co. Clare, and has issue.
  (2) John Dick, D.L. co. Dumbarton.
  (3) Humphrey, d. 12 Mar. 1878, having m. Jessie, dau. of Neil Robson, esq.
  (4) Jane Coventry, m. 5 July, 1854, to Maj.-Gen. John Bayly, C.B. (M. ANGLESEY), and has issue.
Ardincaple, Helensburgh, N.B. ; 68, George Sq., Glasgow. Clubs—Reform, Union.

Cumming.

SIR ALEXANDER PENROSE CUMMING-GORDON, Bart., M.P. Inverness burghs 1802-3 =	GEORGE CUMMING, M.P Inverness burghs 1803-6, 1818-20, 1820-6.
SIR WILLIAM GORDON GORDON CUMMING, Bart, M.P. Elgin burghs 1831-2	CHARLES LENNOX CUMMING-BRUCE, M.P. Inverness 1831-7, Elgin and Nairnshire 1840-68.

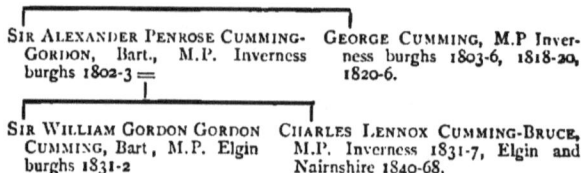

Alexander (sir), jun., of Culter —— *Aberdeenshire* 1709-10, 1710-13, 1713-15, [1715-22, then styled "younger of Culter knt."

Sir Alexander Cumming of Coulter, Aberdeenshire. baronet of Nova Scotia, so cr. 28 Feb. 1695, advocate 1691, ruined by the South Sea Bubble 1720, (son of Alexander Cumming of Coulter by Helen, dau. of James Allardice of that ilk). d. at Coulter 25 Feb. 1725, aged 55, bd. in the kirk there ; he m. 1st Elizabeth, 2nd dau. of Sir Alexander Swinton, lord Mersington of Session, she d. 1709, he m. 2ndly Elizabeth, dau. of Wm. Dennis of Pucklechurch, co. Glouc. Sir Alexander had issue by both marriages ; the baronetcy became extinct on the death of his grandson Sir Alexander, 3rd Bart., 1793. See Foster's Baronetage, "CHAOS."

Cumming-Gordon.

Alexander Penrose, of Altyre and Gordonstown —— *Inverness burghs* 1802 [until he accepted the Chiltern hundreds, s.b. 26 Dec. 1803.

Sir Alexander Penrose Cumming-Gordon (son and heir of Alexander Cumming of Altyre and Grace Pearce, niece and sole heir of John Penrose of Penrose, Cornwall), heir of entail of the last Sir William Gordon, Bart., of Gordonstoun, and in compliance with his testamentary injunction assumed the additional surname and arms of Gordon ; cr. a baronet 21 May 1804, d. 10 Feb. 1806, having m., 9 Sept. 1773, Helen, dau. of Sir Ludovic Grant, Bart., and aunt to Sir Lewis and Sir Francis, 5th and 6th Earls of Seafield ; she d.　Jan. 1830-2, having had with other issue 2 sons, Sir William, 2nd Bart., M.P., and Charles Lennox [Cumming-Bruce, M.P.

Andrew (Cuming) —— *Bervie* 1672-4.

Cumming-Bruce.

Charles Lennox, of Roseisle and Kinnaird ——— *Inverness* 1831-2, 1833-4, 1835-7 ; *Elgin and Nairnshire* 1840-1, 1841-7, 1847-52, 1852-7, 1857-9, [1859-65, 1865-8.

2nd son of Sir Alexander P. Cumming-Gordon, Bart., afsd., joint-sec. board of control 1852 and 1858-9 ; b. 20 Feb. 1790, d. 1 Jany. 1875. He assumed the additional surname and arms of Bruce on his marriage, 21 June, 1820, with Mary, only dau. of James Bruce of Kinnaird, co. Stirling, and granddau. of the famous Abyssinian traveller of that name, [and had a dau. Mary Elizabeth, died Countess of Elgin 7 July 1843.

Cumming.

David (Comyn) —— *Cupar* 1357.

George, of London —— *Inverness burghs* 1803-6, 1818-20, 1820-6.

Brother of Sir Alexander Penrose Cumming-Gordon, Bart., M.P., bred in the naval service of the East India Company, became a merchant in London, and d. 1 May 1834, [aged 81.

Cumming—*continued.*

Jasper —— *Inverness* 1587.

Clerk of the diocese of Morny, a notary public. .

William (or Robert) —— *Inverness* 1583.

A notary public 1574.

William, merchant burgess, late provost of Elgin —— *Banff* 1669-72.

William Gordon Gordon (sir), of Altyre and Gordonstown, bart. —— *Elgin* [*burghs* 1831-2.

2nd Baronet on the death of his father Sir Alexander, M.P., 10 Feb., 1806 ; b. 20 July, 1787 ; d. 23 Nov., 1854 : having married twice and left issue. See FOSTER's Baronetage.

Cunninghame or Cunynghame.

—— laird of Ballindalloch —— *Stirlingshire* 1645.

Alexander —— *Irvine* 1571 conv.

Probably father of the 3rd laird of Corsehill, was a great supporter of James VI.

(Alexander) laird of Corsehill —— *Ayrshire* 1630 conv.

Alexander Cunninghame of Corsehill m. Anne, dau. of John Craufurd of Kilbirnie, and [his son Alexander was served his heir in 1646, and created a baronet 1672.

Alexander, merchant trafficker —— *Crail* 1641, 1649, 1651.

Alexander (Mr.), of Chirrielands,·merchant burgess —— *Irvine* 1689 conv.

Alexander, of Collelane, late provost —— *Irvine* 1689 to 1702, 1702 until his [death, s.b. 14 July, 1705

Alexander Cunninghame, of Collelan, a commissioner of supply Ayrshire 1704 ; m. at Paisley, 17 Apl. 1686, Margaret Walkinshaw ; he died at Sheins, near Edinburgh, 13 July, [1705, having had issue.

Alexander, of Craigends —— *Renfrewshire* 1734-41, 1741 until his death, s.b. [23 Dec. 1742.

Son of William Cuningham of Craigends, M.P., died 1 Sept. 1742, having m. 1st Ann, dau. of Sir John Houstoun of that ilk, and 2ndly Katherine, dau. of Sir John Campbell of [Houston.

Allane —— *Crail* 1621.

Cuthbert (Mr.) —— *Dumfries* 1643 conv.

David (sir), of Milncraig, bart. —— *Lauder* 1702-7.

Sir David Cunyngham, of Milncraig, co. Ayr, and of Livingstone, co. Linlithgow, advocate (said to be descended from William, 2nd son of Alexander, 1st Earl of Glencairn), was created a baronet of Nova Scotia 3 Feb. 1702, with remainder "to his heires successive ;" m. 1st Hon. Isabella Dalyrmple, youngest dau. of James 1st Viscount Stair, and 2ndly Elizabeth, dau. of Sir Robert Baird, Bart., of Saughton Hall, and had issue, [father of Sir James, M.P.

Cunninghame or Cunynghame—*continued.*

Gabriel —— *Glasgow*, 1628-33 1630 conv., 1640.

Provost of Glasgow, 16*23*-39, younger son of John Cunyngham of Baidland, in Dalry.

Henry —— *Anstruther Wester* 1641, *Kilrenny* 1643 conv.

Henry, of Boquhan —— *Stirlingshire* 1708-10 ; *Stirling burghs* 1710-13, 1713-15, 1715-22 (then younger), 1722-7 (then provost of Inverkeithing), *Stirlingshire and Stirling burghs* 1727 (then provost) ; sat for the county until
[1734.

Commissary-general of musters, and a commissioner of forfeited estates, governor of Jamaica 1734 until his death 12 Feby., 1735-6, aged 59, M.I. (see Inscription by Archer, p. 42). Son of William Cunninghame of Boquhan, co. Stirling, by his wife Margaret, dau.
[of David 2nd Lord Cardross.

Herbert —— *Dumfries* 1600, 1612.

(James) laird of Glengarnock —— 1605 conv.

Sir James Cunninghame of Glengarnock, Ayrshire ;   m. Catherine, dau. of James
[Cuninghame, 7th Earl of Glencairne, and had issue.

James (sir), of Milncraig, bart. —— *Linlithgowshire* 1715-22.

2nd Baronet on the death of his father, Sir David, and died unmarried 1 Feb. 1747.

John (Mr.), of Brownhill, advocate —— *Ayrshire* 1665 conv.

Sir John Cuninghame of Lambrughton and Caprington (son of William C. of Brownhill), a celebrated lawyer ; cr. a baronet of Nova Scotia 19 Sept. 1669 ; died 1684, leaving issue.
[See FOSTER's Baronetage.

John (sir), of Lambrughton, knt. —— *Ayrshire* 1681-2.

Sir John Cunyngham of Lambrughton, and after of Caprington, by purchase from the Chancellor Glencairn, who had bought it from the creditors of Sir William Cunningham (descended from Thomas Cunninghame, of Baidland, in Dalry, whose son Adam m. the heiress of Caprington), was a lawyer of some distinction, created a baronet of Nova Scotia 21 Sept. 1669, with remainder to the heirs male of his body ; m. Margaret, dau. of William
[Murray of Polmaise and Touchadam, Stirlingshire, and d. 1684, leaving issue.

Nicoll —— *Sanquhar* 1621.

Robert —— *Dumfries* 1583.

Robert (Mr.) —— *Kinghorn* 1612, 1628-33, 1639-41 (then bailie), 1644 conv.,
[1644-7, 1648-9 (or John Boswall) —— 1661 (bailie).

Robert, late provost —— *Irvine* 1665 conv. (provost), 1667 conv. (then provost),
[1669 until his death, s.b. 24 Oct. 1673

Robert —— *Dumbarton* 1667 conv.

William —— *Ayr* 1571 conv.

William —— *Glasgow* 1592, *Dumbarton* 1593.

Cunninghame or Cunynghame—*continued.*

William —— *Kinghorn* 1593.

(William) laird of Caprington —— *Ayrshire* 1617 conv. and parlt.

William Cunninghame of Caprington had a charter of lands and barony of Cumnock 26 July, 1602, to him and his wife Agnes, dau. of Sir Hugh Campbell of Loudoun, sheriff of
[Ayr, and had a son Sir William.

William (sir), of Cunynghamehed, knt. —— *Ayrshire* 1628-33, 1639-40, unable
[to attend sessions 2 and 3 through sickness.

Created a baronet 1627 (son of John Cunninghame of Cuninghamehead by Mary Edmon-
[stone), married twice and died 1640, leaving issue.

William (sir), of Cunynghamehed, knt. —— *Ayrshire* 1648-9, 1650.

Died 1670 (son Sir William, M.P., last named) ; m. Aug. 1661 Ann, sister of David, Lord
[Ruthven, and had issue.

William, of Craigane —— *Renfrewshire* 1643 conv

Of Craigends, died July, 1647.

William, provost —— *Ayr* 1661-3, 1665 conv., 1667 conv., 1669-74 (then of
[Brownhill), 1681-2.

Probably a brother of John, M.P. 1665.

William, younger of Craigends —— *Renfrewshire* 1689 conv., 1689-1700, did not
[sign the association.

Son of Alexander C., of Craigends (by his wife Janet, dau. of William Cuninghame of Achinyards) ; m. Christian, dau. of Sir John Colquhoun, bart., of Luss, and had with other
[issue a son Alexander, M.P.

William Augustus (sir), of Livingstone, bart. —— *Linlithgowshire* 1774-80 (a
[clerk comptroller of the household 1779), 1780-4, 1784-90.

Of Livingston and Milncraig, 4th Baronet (on the death of his father Sir David, 10 Oct. 1767); capt. Duke of Buccleuch's southern regt. of fencibles, comptroller of the green cloth 1779, receiver-general land rents Scotland 1806 ; d. 17 Jan. 1828, having m. 1st, 21 Oct. 1768, Frances, dau. and heir of Sir Robert Myrton of Gogar, Bart., she d. 14 Nov. 1771, leaving issue ; m. 2ndly, 27 June, 1785, Mary, only dau. and sole heir of Robert Udny, of Udny,
[Aberdeen, and had further issue.

William James Montgomery (sir), of Corsehill and Kirktonholm, Ayrshire,
[bart. —— *Ayr burghs* 1874-80. See foot-note.

M ONTGOMERY-CUNINGHAME, SIR WILLIAM JAMES, "of Corsehill, Ayrs." (1672, N. S.), major late (h. p.) rifle brigade, served throughout Crimean war, V.C., K.M., major royal Ayrs. and Wigtown militia since 1873, M.P. Ayr burghs 1874-80 ; s. his father as 9th Baronet in 1870 ; b. 20 May, 1834 ; m. 22 April, 1869, Elizabeth, younger dau. of Edward Bourchier Hartopp, esq., of Dalby Hall, Melton Mowbray, and has had with other issue 2 sons and 4 daus.

(1) Thomas Andrew Alexander, b. 30 March, 1877.
(2) Edward, b. 30 May, 1878.
(3) Edith. (4) Marjory Eva Charlotte. (5) Violet Jessie. (6) A dau. b. 26 June, 1880.

Seat—Glenmoor, Ayr. Town House—68, Eccleston Square, S.W.
Club—Carlton.

Cupar.

Nicholas, rector of the schools —— 1357.

—— the provost of —— *Cupar* 1567.

Alexander, provost —— *Inverness* 1661-3, 1678 conv., then late provost.

James —— *Inverness* 1617.

John —— *Inverness* 1593.

John, merchant trader, provost —— *Inverness* 1685-6, 1689 conv., 1689-1702.

Currie.

Donald (sir), of Cluny, Aberfeldy, Perthshire, K.C.M.G. —— *Perthshire* since
              [1880. See foot-note.

CURRIE, SIR DONALD, K.C.M.G. (1881), of Cluny and Garth Castle, Perthshire, and of London, shipowner, one of H.M's. lieuts. for the city of London, C.M.G. 1877 for services in settlement of Diamond Fields dispute, etc., M.P. as above, (3rd son of James Currie of Belfast, by Elizabeth, dau. of Donald Martin), b.   1825, m.   1851, Margaret, dau. of Mr. John Miller of Ardencraig, Buteshire.

Cluny and *Garth Castle, Perthshire;* 13, *Hyde Park Place, London, W.*
Clubs—Reform, and *City Liberal.*

D.

Dairsie.

John (Mr.) —— *Anstruther Wester* 1640.

Dalkeith.

William Henry Walter Montagu-Douglas-Scott, commonly called Earl of
[Dalkeith —— *Edinburghshire* 1853-7, 1857-9, 1859-65, 1865-8, 1874-80.
K.T. (eldest son of William, 5th Duke of Buccleuch, K.G.); lord-lieut. co. Dumfries
since 1858, lt.-col. Midlothian yeomanry 1856-72, lieut.-genl. royal company of (the Queen's
body guard) archers in Scotland; contested Edinburghshire 1868 and 1880; b. 9 Sept. 1831;
[m. and has issue. See Foster's Peerage.

Dalglish.

Robert, merchant in Glasgow —— *Glasgow* 1857-9, 1859-65, 1865-8. 1868-74.
Of Kilmardinny, Dumbartonshire, J.P. D.L. co. Lanark, (son of Robert Dalglish,
provost of Glasgow,) died 20 June, 1880, aged 72, having m. 1843 —— Stephenson, and had
[issue.

Dallas.

George, of St. Martin's, writer to the signet —— *Cromarty-shire* 1665 conv.,
[1667 conv., 1669-74 (then W.S.), 1678 conv., 1681-2, 1685-6.

Hugh —— *Fortrose* 1665 conv.

Robert, of Lincoln's Inn, London, K.C. —— *Kirkcaldy burghs* 1805-6.
Rt. Hon. Sir Robert Dallas (elder brother of Sir George Dallas, Bart., M.P.), M.P. St.
Michael's, Cornwall, 1802 (see England); called to the bar of Lincoln's Inn, was counsel for
the defence of Lord George Gordon and of Warren Hastings), K.C. 1795, chief justice
Chester 1804-13, solr.-gen. 4, and knighted 19 May, 1813, a judge of common pleas 1813,
chief justice 1818 (eldest son of Robert Dallas of Kensington and his wife Elizabeth, dau.
of Rev. James Smith, minister of Kilbirny, Ayrshire), b. 16 Oct. 1756, d. 25 Dec. 1824,
having m. 1st Charlotte, dau. of Lt.-Col. Alexander Jardine, consul-gen. at Corunna, he m.
[2ndly Giustina, dau. of Henry Davidsor of Tulloch Castle, co. Ross, and had issue.

Dalmeny.

Archibald Primrose, commonly called Lord Dalmeny —— *Stirling burghs*
[1833-4, 1835-7 (a lord of the admiralty), 1837-41, 1841-7
Born 2 Oct. 1809; d. 23 Jan. 1851; leaving with other issue a son, Archibald, 5th Earl of
[Rosebery, under-secretary of State, home department. See Foster's Peerage.

Dalrymple.

Adolphus John (sir), of Highmark, co. Wigtown, bart. —— *Haddington burghs*
[1826-30 (then lt.-col.), 1830-1, 1831-2. See also M.P. England.
Genl. in the army 1860, A.D.C. to the king, 2nd Bart. on the death (9 Apl. 1830) of his
father, Gen. Sir Hew Whitefoord Dalrymple, Bart.; M.P. Weymouth 1817-18, Appleby
1819-26, Brighton 1837-41, contested Brighton 1832, 1835 and 1841 (see England); b.
3 Feb. 1784, d. s.p. 3 Mar. 1866, having m., 23 June, 1812, Anne, dau. of Sir James Graham
[of Kirkstall, Bart., she d. 10 May, 1858.

Dalrymple—*continued.*

Charles, of New Hailes —— *Buteshire* 1868-74, 1874-80 (then of Ardencraig, [bar.-at-law), and since 1880.   See foot-note.

David (sir), of Hailes, knight baronet —— *Culross* 1697-1702 (then Mr. and an advocate), 1702-7 (then a bart.); sat in 1st parlt. Great Britain 1707-8, *Haddington burghs* 1708-10 (Queen's advocate Scotland 1709), 1710-13, 1713-15, [1715 (crown office of profit 1720) until his death, s.b. 5 Jan. 1721-2.

> Hon. Sir David Dalrymple of Hailes, Haddington, advocate 1688. cr. a baronet of Nova Scotia 8 May 1700, with remainder to his heirs male successive for ever, solr-gen. to Q. Anne, Queen's advocate 1709, lord advocate 1720, (5th son of Sir James, M.P., 1st Visct. Stair—see Foster's Peerage) ; m. 4 April 1691, Janet, dau. of Sir James Rocheid, of Innerleith, relict of Alexander Murray, esq., of Melgund (by whom she had a posthumous son, Sir Alexander Murray, Bart., N.S., so cr. 29 Jan. 1704); he d. 3 Dec. 1721, having [had issue a son, Sir James, M.P., male line extinct 19 June 1808.

George (Mr.), son of John, Viscount Stair —— *Stranraer* 1703-7.

> Of Dalmahoy, co. Edinburgh (5th son of John, 2nd Viscount Stair) ; advocate 1704 ; a Baron of the Court of Exchequer, Scotland, 1708 ; d. 29 July. 1745 ; having m. 23 April 1720, Euphame, eldest dau. of Sir Andrew Myrton, of Gogar, co. Edinburgh, bart.; she d. 8 July, 1761, leaving with 4 daus. 2 sons, John, 5th Earl of Stair, and Major-Gen. [William, M.P.

Hugh (sir), of North Berwick, lord president of session —— *New Galloway* 1696-1702, (then advocate and one of the commissioners of Edinburgh) ; [*North Berwick* 1702-7.

> Hon. Sir Hew Dalrymple, of North Berwick (3rd son of Sir John, M.P., 1st Viscount Stair), dean of faculty of advocates 1695-8 ; lord president of the court of session 1698-1737; one of the commissioners to settle the Articles of Union ; created a baronet of Nova Scotia 29 April, 1698, with remainder to his heirs male ; he d. 1 Feb. 1737 ; having m. 1st, 12 March, 1682, Marion, d. of Sir Robert Hamilton, of Presmennan, one of the lords of session (B. BELHAVEN). He m. 2ndly, Elizabeth, dau. of John Hamilton, Esq., of Olivestob, and widow of John Hamilton, of Bangour; she d. 21 March, 1742.   By his first wife he had [with other issue 5 sons.

DALRYMPLE, CHARLES, of Newhailes, Midlothian, to which he succeeded in 1849, when he assumed the name of Dalrymple under the will of his great-grandfather Lord Hailes ; M.A. Trin Coll. Camb. 1865, bar.-at-law L.I. 1865, J.P. and D.L. co. Haddington, J.P. Midlothian and Ayrshire, capt. Ayr and Wigtown mil. since 1862 (2nd son of Sir Charles Dalrymple Fergusson, Bart.), b. Oct. 1839, m. 7 April, 1874, Alice Mary, 2nd dau. of Sir Edward Hunter-Blair, Bart., and has a son and dau.

(1) David Charles Herbert, b. 29 Mar. 1879.   (2) Christian Elizabeth Louisa.
Newhailes, Musselburgh, N.B.; Ardencraig, Isle of Bute, N.B.; 39°, Onslow Sq., S.W.
Club—Carlton, S.W.

Dalrymple—*continued.*

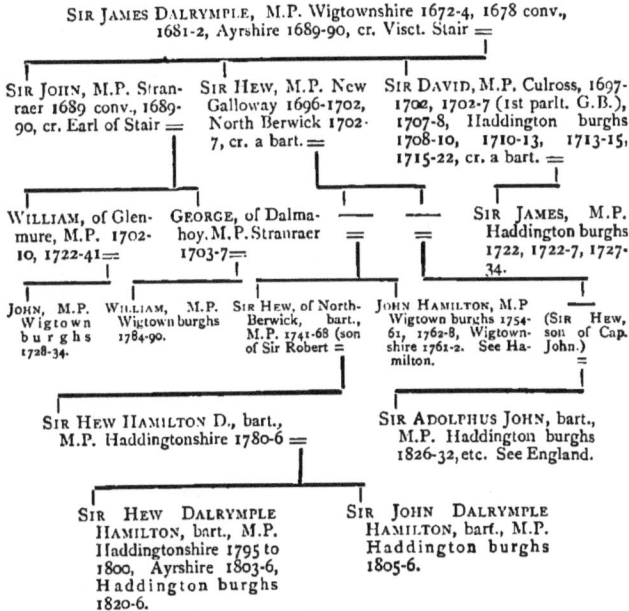

SIR JAMES DALRYMPLE, M.P. Wigtownshire 1672-4, 1678 conv.,
1681-2, Ayrshire 1689-90, cr. Visct. Stair =

SIR JOHN, M.P. Stranraer 1689 conv., 1689-90, cr. Earl of Stair =

SIR HEW, M.P. New Galloway 1696-1702, North Berwick 1702-7, cr. a bart. =

SIR DAVID, M.P. Culross, 1697-1702, 1702-7 (1st parlt. G.B.), 1707-8, Haddington burghs 1708-10, 1710-13, 1713-15, 1715-22, cr. a bart. =

WILLIAM, of Glenmure, M.P. 1702-10, 1722-41 =

GEORGE, of Dalmahoy. M.P. Stranraer 1703-7 =

SIR JAMES, M.P. Haddington burghs 1722, 1722-7, 1727-34.

JOHN, M.P. Wigtown burghs 1728-34.

WILLIAM, M.P. Wigtown burghs 1784-90.

SIR HEW, of North-Berwick, bart., M.P. 1741-68 (son of Sir Robert =

JOHN HAMILTON, M.P Wigtown burghs 1754-61, 1762-8, Wigtownshire 1761-2. See Hamilton.

(SIR HEW, son of Cap. John.) =

SIR HEW HAMILTON D., bart., M.P. Haddingtonshire 1780-6 =

SIR ADOLPHUS JOHN, bart., M.P. Haddington burghs 1826-32, etc. See England.

SIR HEW DALRYMPLE HAMILTON, bart., M.P. Haddingtonshire 1795 to 1800, Ayrshire 1803-6, Haddington burghs 1820-6.

SIR JOHN DALRYMPLE HAMILTON, bart., M.P. Haddington burghs 1805-6.

Hew (sir), of North Berwick, bart. —— *Haddington burghs* 1741-7 (seated on petition 27 Jan. 1742); *Haddingtonshire,* 1747-54, 1754-61; *Haddington* [*burghs,* 1761-8.

2nd Baronet (on the death of his grandfather Sir Hew Dalrymple, M.P. in 1737); an advocate, 1730; king's remembrancer in the exchequer for Scotland 1768; d. 23 Nov., 1790. He married 12 July, 1743, Miss Sainthill; she d. 31 Dec., 1747, leaving 2 sons, of whom [the younger, Sir Hew, became 3rd Bart., M.P.

Hew Hamilton (sir), of North Berwick, bart. —— *Haddingtonshire* 1780-4; (then junior) 1784, until appointed auditor of the Excise in Scotland, 1786.

3rd Baronet (on the death of his father, Sir Hew, M.P., 23 Nov., 1790); assumed the additional surname of Hamilton in 1796, on inheriting the Bargeny estates from his uncle John (Dalrymple) Hamilton, M.P.; d. 13 Feb. 1800, having m. his cousin Janet, dau. of William Duff, esq., of Crombie, and had with other issue a son, Sir Hew Dalrymple-
[Hamilton, M.P. See page 93.

Dalrymple—*continued.*

James (sir), of Stair, lord president of the session —— *Wigtownshire* 1672-4, 1678, conv. 1681-2; *Ayrshire*, 1689, until he took the oath as Viscount [Stair, etc., 1 May, 1690.

Sir James Dalrymple, of Stair (descended from William de Dalrymple, 1450) ; advocate 1648 ; knighted by Charles II. at the Restoration ; lord of session as Lord Stair 1657-71; created a Baronet of Nova Scotia 2 June, 1664, with remainder to the heir male of his body ; president of the court of session 1671-81 ; M.P. co. Wigtown, 1681 ; he attended the Prince of Orange into England 1688 ; re-appointed president of the council 1689; created Viscount of Stair, Lord Glenluce and Stranraer, 21 April, 1690 ; b. at Drummurchie, in Carrick, May, 1619 ; d. 25 Nov., 1697 ; having m. 21 Sept., 1643, Margaret, eldest dau. of James Ross, of Balniel, co. Wigtown ; she d. 1692, having had 5 sons (see Foster's Peerage), [of whom Sir John M.P. (Earl of Stair), Sir Hew, M.P., and Sir David, M.P.

James (sir), of Hailes, bart. —— *Haddington burghs* 1722, 1722-7, 1727-34.

2nd Baronet (on the death of his father, Sir David, M.P., 1721); auditor-general Scotland ; b. 24 July, 1692, d. 24 Feb. 1751, having m. Lady Christian Hamilton, youngest [dau. of Thomas, 6th Earl of Haddington ; she d. 30 June 1770, leaving issue.

Johnne, of —— *Edinburgh* 1445, 1458.

John de Dalrumpill, bailie of the burgh of Edinburgh, had a safe conduct to pass through England with Crichton the chancellor, on his embassy to France and Burgundy, 23 April, 1448 ; had a charter to him and his heirs of a third of the barony of Bolton, in the con- [stabulary of Haddington, 12 Aug., 1459. DOUGLAS.

John (sir), younger, of Stair —— *Stranraer* 1689 conv., 1689-90, advocate.

John, 2nd Viscount ; advocate 1672 ; king's advocate 1686-90; a lord of session and lord justice clerk 1688 ; was one of the three commissioners sent by the convention parliament (of which he was a member) with the offer of the crown to the Prince and Princess of Orange 1689 ; and was one of the six persons excepted by James VII. out of his intended act of indemnity ; a principal sec. of state 1691-5, when he resigned on account of the massacre of Glencoe, P.C. Queen Anne ; created Earl of Stair, Viscount Dalrymple, Lord Newliston, Glenluce, and Stranraer, 8 April, 1703, with remainder to the issue male of his father (Sir James Dalrymple. M.P., Viscount Stair) ; d. 8 Jan. 1707 ; having m. Elizabeth, dau. and heir of Sir John Dundas, knt., of Newliston, co. Linlithgow ; she d. 25 May,1731, leaving with other issue a son William, M.P. His male line failed on the death of his great- [grandson, John William Henry, 7th Earl, 22 Mar. 1840.

John, capt.-lieut. of the Earl of Stair's regiment of dragoons —— *Wigtown burghs* [1728-34.

2nd son of William Dalrymple, of Glenmure, M.P. (and brother of William, Earl of Dumfries and Stair, and of James, 3rd Earl of Stair) ; capt. Inniskillin regiment of [dragoons ; died unm. at Newliston 23 Feb. 1742.

John, younger, of Fordel and Cleland, commonly called Viscount D.—— *Wigtown-shire* 1841-7 ; (capt. Scots fusilier guards) 1847-52, (then younger of Fordel and Cleland) ; 1852, (Viscount Dalrymple) until accepted the stewardship of [Manor of Northstead, Yorks, s.b. 9 Feb. 1856.

10th Earl Stair, K.T. (on the death of his father, North Hamilton, 9th Earl, 9 Nov., 1864), late 1st life guards ; lord high commissioner to the Church of Scotland 1869-71. etc.; became Viscount Dalrymple by courtesy 10 Jan. 1853; lord-lieut. Wigtownshire 1857, Ayrshire [1870 ; major-general royal archers, Scotland. See Foster's Peerage.

Dalrymple—*continued.*

John —— *Haddington burghs* 1805, until he accepted the *Chiltern hundreds*
[s.b. 17 April, 1806.

> Major-gen. Sir John Hamilton-Dalrymple, of Bargeny and North Berwick, 5th baronet
> (bro. of Sir Hew, 4th baronet, M.P. see below); d. 26 May, 1835 ; he m. 30 July, 1806,
> Charlotte, only dau. of Sir Patrick Warrender, bart., M.P. ; she d. 14 April, 1871, leaving
> [issue. See Foster's Baronetage.

John Hamilton (lieut-gen. sir), of Cousland, bart. —— *Edinburghshire*
[1833-4.

> Sir John Hamilton Dalrymple, K.T. 5th bart. (on the death, 26 Feb. 1810, of his father
> Sir John, a baron of the Court of Exchequer, Scotland), and succeeded his kinsman, John
> William Henry, as 8th Earl of Stair 22 Mar. 1840, keeper of the great seal of Scotland
> 1840-1, gen. in the army, col. 46th regt., was created Baron Oxenfoord, of Cousland, co.
> Edinburgh, in the peerage of the U.K. 16th Aug. 1841, with remainder to his brother North ;
> b. 14 June, 1771 ; d. s. p. 10 Jan. 1853, having m. 1st, 23 July, 1795, Harriet, eldest dau.
> of Rev. Robert Augustus Johnson, of Kenilworth, co. Warwick ; she d. 16 Oct. 1823. He
> m. 2ndly, 8 June, 1825, Hon. Adamina Duncan, 3rd dau. of Adam, 1st Viscount Duncan
> [(E. CAMPERDOWN) ; she d. 1 Aug. 1857.

William (Mr.), of Glenmure —— *Ayrshire* 1702-7 (of Drongan), 1st parlt. of
Great Britain 1707-8 ; *Clackmannanshire* 1708-10 (then styled Master
William) ; *Wigtown burghs* 1722-7 (then styled Col.) ; *Wigtownshire and
Wigtown burghs* 1727 ; sat for the county until 1734 ; *Wigtownshire* 1734-
[41, then Col. William of Sleudonall.

> Col. in the army, 2nd surviving son of John (M.P.) 1st Earl of Stair ; d. 3 Dec. 1744,
> having m. 26 Feb. 1698, his cousin Penelope, Countess of Dumfries ; she d. 1 March, 1742,
> [leaving with other issue a son John, M.P.

William (major genl.), brother-german to John (5th) Earl of Stair —— *Wigtown*
[*burghs* 1784-90.

> Gen. Dalrymple, col. 47th regt. 1794 ; lt.-gov. Chelsea hospital 1798 (son of hon. George
> Dalrymple, of Dalmahoy) ; d. 23 Feb. 1807, aged 72, having m. 13 Sept. 1783, Marianne
> Dorothy, 2nd dau. of Sir Robert Harland of Sproughton Hall, Suffolk, Bart.; she d. 28 Oct.
> [1785, leaving issue.

Dalrymple-Hamilton.

Hew Hamilton (sir), of Bargeny and North Berwick, bart. —— *Haddingtonshire* 1795-6 (then younger) ; 1796, until he accepted the *Chiltern hundreds*,
s.b. 12 May, 1800 ; *Ayrshire* 1803-6, 1806-7, 1811-12, 1812-18 ; *Haddington*
[*burghs* 1820-6.

> 4th baronet (on the death of his father Sir Hew, M.P., see page 90), lieut.-col. Ayrshire
> [militia; b. 3 Jan. 1774, d. 23 Feb. 1834, leaving an only dau. See Foster's Baronetage.

Dalyell.

Thomas (genl.), of Binns —— *Linlithgowshire* 1678 conv., 1681-2 (genl.), 1685, [and d. s.b. 1 Oct. same year.

Gen. Dalyell (only son of Thomas Dalyell of Binns, by Janet, eldest dau. of Edward Bruce, Lord Kinloss) ; a commander in the Royalist army, taken prisoner at the battle of Worcester, served the Czar of Muscovy during the Commonwealth, and after the restoration became com.-in-chief of the forces in Scotland, P.C. 1666 ; he m. Agnes Ker of Cavers, and [had a son Thomas, cr. a baronet. See "Chaos," Foster's Baronetage.

Dalzell.

Gawen —— *Perth* 1605 conv.

Probably a brother of the 1st Earl of Carnwath.

John (sir), of Glenae, Bart. —— *Dumfries* (or Nithsdale) *sheriffdom and* [*stewartry of Annandale* 1686, 1689, until his death s.b. 24 Feb. 1690.

2nd son of Sir Robert Dalzell, Earl of Carnwath, so created 1639. See that title in Foster's Peerage. The title of baronet is in all probability wrongly applied, for the printed lists state the original patentee to have been his son Robert. See below and lists of Nova Scotia [baronets in Foster's Baronetage.

Robert -—— *Wigtown* 1587.

Probably father of the 1st Earl of Carnwath.

Robert (sir), of Glenae, knt. bart. —— *Dumfries* (or Nithsdale) *sheriffdom and stewartry of Annandale* 1665 conv. (then younger knt.), 1667 conv., 1669-74, [1681-2, 1685 until his death s.b. 8 April, 1686.

Created a baronet of Nova Scotia 11 April, 1666 (only son of Sir John aforesaid), his grandson Robert succ. as 6th Earl of Carnwath ; joined the rebellion of 1715 ; taken prisoner at Preston 14 Nov. of that year ; his estate forfeited and sentenced to death, which latter was respited ; the grandson of the attainted Earl, Lt.-Genl. Robert Alexander Dalzell, [was restored by Act of Parliament 26 May 1826, and became 7th Earl.

Damer.

George, son to Lord Milton —— *Anstruther Easter burghs* 1778-80. See also [M.P. England.

2nd and last Earl of Dorchester (of that creation), Viscount Milton, Baron Milton of Milton Abbey, Dorset, and Baron Milton of Shrone hill, Ireland (succeeded 12 Feb. 1798) ; lord lieut. and custos rot. Dorset and a P.C. Ireland ; sec. to Earl Fitzwilliam, Ireland ; M.P. Cricklade 1768-74, Dorchester 1780-91, Malton 1792-8 (see England) ; B. 28 March [1746, d. unm. 6 March 1808.

Darroch.

William —— *Stirling* 1567, 1568, then provost.

Dashwood.

Henry Watkin —— *Wigtown burghs* 1775-80.   See also England M.P.

Sir Henry Watkin Dashwood, 3rd Bart. (10 Nov. 1779), of Kirtlington Park, Oxon, D.C.L.; gent. of the Privy Chamber to Geo. III.; M.P. Woodstock 1784-1820 (see England); of Brazenose College, Oxford, cr. M.A. 29 April 1766; and D.C.L. 8 July 1773 (eldest surviving son of Sir James Dashwood, Bart., M.P., D.C.L.); b. 30 Aug. 1745; d. 10 June 1828, having m. 17 July 1780, Mary Helen, dau. of John Graham, of the Supreme Court, [Calcutta; she d. 1796, leaving issue.

Davidson.

Duncan, of Tulloch —— *Cromartyshire* 1790-6.

Died s.p. 15 Aug. 1799, aged 66 (younger son of Alexander Davidson, of Davidston, co. [Cromarty); m. Sarah, dau. of Dr. Chandler.

Duncan, of Tulloch —— *Cromartyshire* 1826-30 (then younger), 1831-2.

Of Tulloch Castle, Ross-shire J.P. and D.L., served as lieut. in grenadier guards, a dean of faculty of Marischal College, Aberdeen, lord lieut. co. Ross (eldest son of Henry Davidson, of Tulloch, J.P. D.L.), d. 18 Sept. 1881, aged 81, having m. 1st, 20 June 1825, Hon. Elizabeth Diana Macdonald, eldest dau. of Godfrey, 3rd Lord Macdonald, she d. 9 June 1839, leaving issue; he m. 2ndly,   1841, Eleonora Dalrymple, 3rd dau. of Sir James Fergusson, Bart., she d. 26 Dec. 1845; he m. 3rdly,   1846, Arabella, dau. of Hugh Rose-Ross, Esq., of Cromarty, she d. 1847; he m. 4thly,   1849, Mary, eldest dau. of John Mackenzie, Esq., (of Gairloch,) she d.   he m. 5thly, 14 Apl. 1877, Sarah Justina, eldest dau. of late Lt.-Col. Jasper Taylor Hall, formerly of the Coldstream [Guards, and had issue. See Landed Gentry.

Lawrence —— *Sanquhar* 1643 conv., 1649.

Patrick —— *Linlithgow* 1488.

Robert —— *Dundee* 1644, 1649 (Mr. George Haliburton in his absence), 1651.

Dawe.

Andrew —— *Crail* 1640, 1643 conv., 1645, (? also 1646-7), 1648.

John (Daw), bailie —— *Crail* 1665 conv. (late bailie), 1667 conv. (bailie).

Dawling.

James (elder), councillor —— *Queensferry South*, 1639-41, 1644 conv.

Dempster.

George, of Dunnichen, advocate, provost of St. Andrews —— *Perth burghs* 1761-8, (sec. to the Order of the Thistle 1766), 1769-74, 1774-80 (then [provost of St. Andrews) 1780-4, 1784-90.

Advocate 1 March 1755, a director East India Company, purchased the estate of Skibo, co. Sutherland 1786; b. Dundee Feb. 1732, d. unm. 13 Feb. 1818.   See Gent's Mag v. [88, p. 566.

John (sir), of Pitliver, trafficking merchant, provost —— *Inverkeithing* 1681-2, [1685-6; *Fifeshire* 1689 conv. (then Mr.), 1687 to 1702 (knighted 1690-3).

Eldest son of John Dempster, advocate, by his wife Janet Kirkcaldy of Grange. Sir John left an only child, Jean, m. as 1st wife to Sir James Campbell, of Aberuchill, 2nd Bart.

Dempster—*continued.*

Robert, bailie —— *Brechin* 1639-41.

Denham.   *See* Steuart-Denham.

Denholme.

William (sir), of Westheills —— *Lanarkshire* 1690-1702.

Dennistoun.

Alexander, younger, of Golfhill —— *Dumbartonshire* 1835-7.
> J.P. cos. Dumbarton and Lanark, (eldest son of James Dennistoun, of Golfhill, by Mary Finlay); d. 15 July, 1874, aged 84, having m. 1822, Eleanor, dau. of John Thomson, esq., of [Liverpool, and had issue.

John, a merchant in Glasgow —— *Glasgow* 1837, 1837-41, 1841-7.
> Brother of the last-named, contested Glasgow 1847, died 9 Sept. 1870, aged 66.

James —— *Edinburgh* 1643 conv.

Desborrow.

Samuel (esq.) —— *Edinburgh* 1654-6 (a commissioner of revenue); *Mid-Lothian* 1656-8 (one of his Highness's council in Scotland); 1658-9, chancellor and [keeper of the great seal of Scotland (WILLIS).
> Related to Maj.-Genl. "Lord" Desborough, one of the councillors for the kingdom of Scotland 4 May 1655 ; keeper of great seal, etc., same year (see Noble's Cromwell, ii. 254).

Dewar.

James, merchant trafficker, bailie, —— *Burntisland* 1675-4, 1678 conv., 1681-2.

Dick.

Andrew (capt.), steward —— *Orkney and Zetland stewartry* 1678 conv.
> 3rd son of Mr. John Dick of Braid (by his wife Nichola, dau. of Sir George Bruce, of Carnock), steward-principal and chamberlain of Orkney and Zetland 30 July, 1669 ; [m. Francisca Nairne.

James (sir), of Priestfield, provost —— *Edinburgh* 1681-2.
> Sir James Dick, of Priestfield, bart. [younger son of Alexander Dick, of Heugh (who was 4th son of Sir William Dick, of Braid), by Helen, dau. of Sir James Rochead, of Innerleath, bart.], and of Edinburgh, merchant, created a bart. of Nova Scotia by Charles II. 2 Mar. 1677, lord provost of Edinburgh 1682-3 ; he entailed the estates of Prestonfield and Corstorphine in 1699 on the 2nd and younger son successively of his dau. Janet by the said Sir William Cunningham and their issue male, and Queen Anne granted him a baronet's patent, 22 Mar. 1707, the dignity to go with the entail of the estates, and the possessor to bear the name and arms of Dick only ; he made a similar entail 1710, and d. 1728, aged 85, having m. Anne, dau. of Andrew Paterson, of Dunmore, co. Fife, and had with other issue a dau., [Janet, m. to Sir William Cunningham, of Lambrughton. See Foster's Baronetage.

John —— *Queensferry* 1646-7, 1649.
> Possibly son of Sir William Dick, and father of John and Andrew, M.P.

John, actual trafficker; provost —— *Stirling* 1693, until expelled from parliament [15 July 1695, for menacing another member.
> Probably brother of Andrew, M.P.

Dickinson.

David, bailie —— *Forfar* 1661.

Dickson.

Andrew —— *Inverkeithing* 1649, 1651.

James, of Broughton —— *Linlithgow burghs* 1768, until his death s. b. 9 Jan. [1772.

A merchant in London ; died 1771.

John, of Wingiston —— *Peebles* 1568.

John —— *Peebles* 1612, 1617.

John —— *Sanquhar* 1645.

John (Mr.), of Busbie —— *Lanarkshire* 1649.

John, of Hartrie, senator of the College of Justice (1 Nov. 1649) —— *Peebles-shire* [1649-50.

Of Kilbucho 1630, and of Hartrie 1633 ; advocate 1649, deputy clerk register to Sir Alexander Gibson of Durie, "one of the commissioners for the shire of Peebles from 1644 to the cessation of Scottish parliaments in 1651, and a member of the various committees of estates to whom the parliament intrusted the government of the country during its intervals. ["BRUNTON and HAIG," m. and had issue.

John, of Kilbucho, the younger —— *Peebles-shire* 1747-54, 1754-61, 1761 until [his death s. b. 31 Dec. 1767.

Died 2 Dec. 1767.

Patrick —— (*Peebles?*) 1583.

Robert (Mr.), eldest son of Mr. John Dicksone, minister of Kells —— *New* [*Galloway* 1661-3 (John or Robert), 1667 conv. (of Bughtrig), 1669-74.

Robert (sir), of Inveresk —— *Edinburghshire* 1702-7.

Sir Robert Dickson of Sornbegg, cr. a baronet of Nova Scotia 28 Feb. 1695, after of [Inveresk.

William, of Kilbucho, lieut.-col. 42nd regt. of royal highlanders, —— *Linlith-* [*gow burghs* 1802-6.

Lieut.-governor of Cork 1808, lieut.-col. 42nd highlanders 1795, col. in the army 1803, [and brigadier-general ; died in Edinburgh 18 May, 1815.

Dingwall.

Donald, merchant burgess, late dean of Guild —— *Dingwall* 1685-6.

Dingwall-Fordyce.

Alexander, of Culsh and Brucklay, commander R.N. —— *Aberdeen City* 1847-52.

3rd son of William Dingwall-Fordyce, younger, of Culsh ; b. 4 March 1800 ; d. 1864, having m. 14 July 1835, Barbara, 5th dau. of James Thorn, esq., of Halifax, N.S., and had with other issue a son William, next named.

Dingwall-Fordyce—*continued.*

William, of Brucklay Castle, New Dee, Aberdeenshire —— *Aberdeenshire* 1866-8, *East Aberdeenshire* 1868-74, 1874 until his death s.b. 24 Dec, 1875.

J.P., D.L., cos. Aberdeen and Kincardine ; b. 31 March 1836 ; d. 26 Nov. 1875, having m. April 1870, Christine, eldest dau. of Robert Horn, esq., dean of the faculty of advocates, [and had issue.

Dixon.

Joseph (esq.), advocate —— *Glasgow burghs* 1831-2.

Advocate 11 March 1827, contested Glasgow 1832 (son of Jacob Dixon, esq., of [Dumbarton], died   1844.

Dobie.

Richard —— *Edinburgh* 1608.

Don.

Alexander (sir), of Newton bart. —— *Roxburghshire* 1814-18 (then younger [1818-20, 1820 until his death s.b. 8 May 1826.

6th baronet (on the death of his father, Sir Alexander, 5 June 1815); married twice, and [died 11 April 1826, leaving issue. See DON-WAUCHOPE in Foster's Baronetage.

Donaldson.

Alexander, provost —— *Whithorn* 1661-3, 1665 conv.

David —— *Brechin* 1664.

David, elder, late bailie —— *Brechin* 1665 conv.

David, younger, dean of Guild —— *Brechin* 1678 conv., 1681-2, bailie.

Doock.

Robert, provost —— *Ayr* 1678 conv.

Douglas.

Alexander (Mr.), provost —— *Banff* 1641, 1643 conv., 1644-5, 1649-50, 1651, [1656-8 (WILLIS).

Alexander of Spynie —— *Elgin* and *Forreshire* 1669-74.

Alexander (sir), of Eagleshay —— *Orkney and Zetland stewartry* 1702-7 ; 1st parlt. Great Britain 1707-8 (then a knight), *Orkney* and *Shetlandshire* 1708-10 [(lord of Egilshay), 1710-13.

Archibald, provost —— *Edinburgh* 1526 —— 1560.

Douglas—*continued.*

DOUGLAS OF CAVERS.

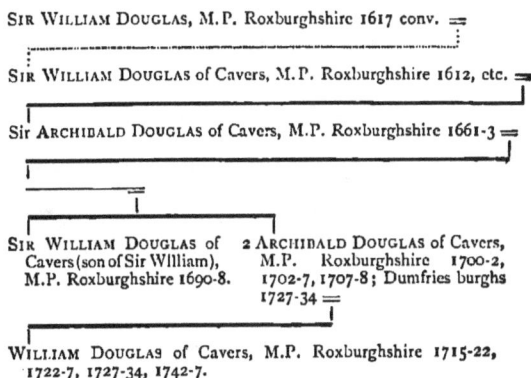

SIR WILLIAM DOUGLAS, M.P. Roxburghshire 1617 conv. ⚌

SIR WILLIAM DOUGLAS of Cavers, M.P. Roxburghshire 1612, etc. ⚌

Sir ARCHIBALD DOUGLAS of Cavers, M.P. Roxburghshire 1661-3 ⚌

SIR WILLIAM DOUGLAS of Cavers (son of Sir William), M.P. Roxburghshire 1690-8.

2 ARCHIBALD DOUGLAS of Cavers, M.P. Roxburghshire 1700-2, 1702-7, 1707-8; Dumfries burghs 1727-34 ⚌

WILLIAM DOUGLAS of Cavers, M.P. Roxburghshire 1715-22, 1722-7, 1727-34, 1742-7.

Archibald (sir), of Whittinghame —— the laird of Whittinghame sat as a minor [baron 1604, 1604, conv.; *Haddington constabulary* 1605, 1607, 1608.
Sir Archibald Douglas, of Whittinghame, a lord of session 8 Aug. 1590, upon the resignation of his father, William Douglas, of Whittinghame, a lord of session and probably M.P.; accompanied James to Norway on his marriage in 1589; knighted and admitted a privy councillor 29 May 1603 ; resigned his seat on the bench May 1618 ; m. and left issue, a son Archibald, who d. 28 Nov. 1660, leaving his sister Elizabeth, Viscountess Kingston, his [heir.

Archibald, of Tofts —— *Berwickshire* 1617.

Archibald —— *Roxburghshire* 1644 conv.
? Brother of Sir William Douglas, of Cavers, who died 1676.

Archibald (sir), of Cavers, knt. —— *Roxburghshire* 1661-3,
Also of Denholm and Spittal (son of Sir William Douglas, knt., M.P., named below) ; had a command in the parliament army ; m. Fachel, dau. of Sir James Skene, of Hallyards, [president of the court of session, and had a son, Sir William.

Archibald, of Cavers, heritable sheriff of Teviotdale —— *Roxburghshire* (or sheriffdom of Teviotdale) 1700-2, 1702-7, sat in 1st parlt. of Great Britain [1707-8 ; *Dumfries burghs* 1727-34, then styled " elder of Cavers."
Brother of Sir William Douglas, of Cavers, and 2nd son of Sir William Douglas, also of Cavers ; receiver-genl. Scotland 1705-18 ; postmaster-genl. 1725 ; d. 1741, having m. Anna, [dau. of Francis Scott, of Gorrenbery, and had with other issue William, M.P.

Archibald (major-genl.), of Kirktown —— *Dumfries burghs* 1754-61 (then lt.-col. of the regiment of dragoons commanded by Sir Robert Rich) ; *Dumfries-* [*shire* 1761-8, 1768-74 (then major-genl.
General in the army 19 March 1778, col. 13th dragoons 1758 until his death at Dublin [about Oct. 1778, leaving a son

Douglas—*continued.*

DOUGLAS—MARQUIS OF QUEENSBERRY.

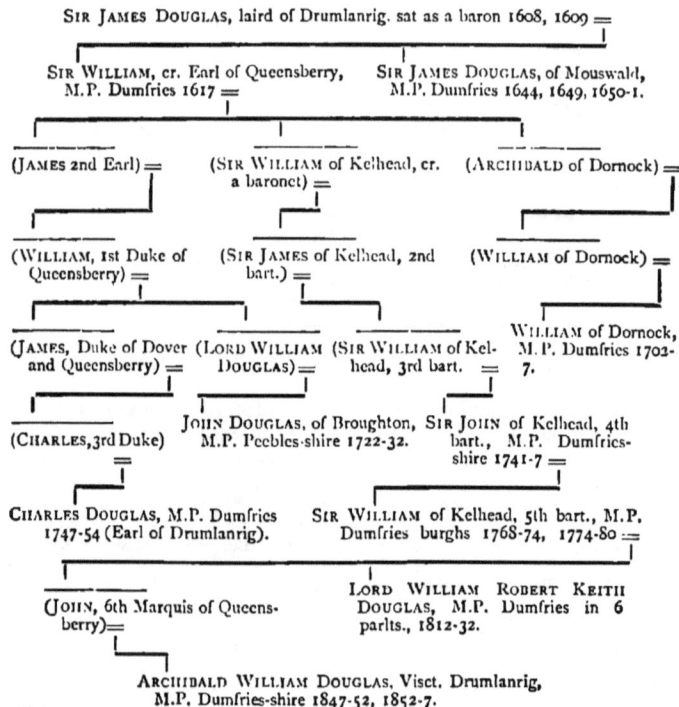

SIR JAMES DOUGLAS, laird of Drumlanrig. sat as a baron 1608, 1609 =

SIR WILLIAM, cr. Earl of Queensberry,   SIR JAMES DOUGLAS, of Mouswald,
M.P. Dumfries 1617 =   M.P. Dumfries 1644, 1649, 1650-1.

(JAMES 2nd Earl) =   (SIR WILLIAM of Kelhead, cr.   (ARCHIBALD of Dornock) =
                a baronet) =

(WILLIAM, 1st Duke of   (SIR JAMES of Kelhead, 2nd   (WILLIAM of Dornock) =
Queensberry) =   bart.) =

                                      WILLIAM of Dornock,
(JAMES, Duke of Dover (LORD WILLIAM (SIR WILLIAM of Kel- M.P. Dumfries 1702-
and Queensberry) =   DOUGLAS) =   head, 3rd bart. =   7.

               JOHN DOUGLAS, of Broughton, SIR JOHN of Kelhead, 4th
(CHARLES,3rd Duke)   M.P. Peebles-shire 1722-32.   bart., M.P. Dumfries-
=   shire 1741-7 =

CHARLES DOUGLAS, M.P. Dumfries   SIR WILLIAM of Kelhead, 5th bart., M.P.
1747-54 (Earl of Drumlanrig).   Dumfries burghs 1768-74, 1774-80 =

                          LORD WILLIAM ROBERT KEITH
(JOHN, 6th Marquis of Queens-   DOUGLAS, M.P. Dumfries in 6
berry)=   parlts., 1812-32.

ARCHIBALD WILLIAM DOUGLAS, Visct. Drumlanrig,
M.P. Dumfries-shire 1847-52, 1852-7.

Archibald, of Douglas —— *Forfarshire* 1782-4, 1784-90.

Baron Douglas, of Douglas, co. Lanark, so cr. 8 July 1790 (eldest son of Sir John Stewart, of Grandtully, Bart.—see Foster's Baronetage—by his wife, Jane Douglas, only sister and heir of Archibald, Duke of Douglas); col. Forfar mil. ; lord lieut. Forfarshire ; b. 10 July 1748; d. 26 Dec. 1827, leaving with other issue Charles, M.P., succ. as 3rd lord.

Charles, of Kellwood, commonly called Lord Charles D., 2nd son to Charles, Duke of Queensberry and Dover —— *Dumfries-shire* 1747-54, 1754, until he became (by the death of his brother) the eldest son of a peer of Scotland 19 [Oct. same year.

Earl of Drumlanrig (on the death of his brother Henry, 19 Oct. 1754); b. 17 July 1726 ; [d. unm. 24 Oct. 1756.

Douglas—*continued*

Charles, second son of the deceased Archibald, Lord Douglas, of Douglas —— [*Lanarkshire* 1830-1, 1831-2 (then of Douglas Castle).

3rd Lord Douglas (on the death of his brother Archibald 27 Jan. 1844), son of Archibald, [M.P., afsd. ; major Forfarshire militia ; b. 26 Oct. 1775 ; d. unm. 10 Sept. 1848.

David —— *Edinburgh* 1646-7, 1648.

George (col.), brother to (Robert) Earl of Morton —— *Linlithgow burghs* 1708-10, 1710-13, 1715-22 ; *Orkney and Shetlandshire* 1713-15, 1722-7, 1727 [(then of St. Olla) until he succ. as Earl of Morton s.b. 7 May 1730.

13th Earl of Morton (son of James, 10th Earl) ; a col. in the army ; vice-admiral of [Scotland 1733 ; d. 4 Jan. 1738, aged 77, leaving with other issue a son Robert, M.P.

George (sir), of Springwood Park, bart. —— *Roxburghshire* 1784-90 (then captain 1st foot guards), 1790-6 (then a baronet), 1796-1802, 1802-6.

2nd Baronet (on the death of his father, Admiral Sir James Douglas, M.P.; served in 21st regt. and 1st foot guards 1771-89 ; b. 1 March 1754 ; d. 4 June 1821, having m. 16 Oct. 1786, Lady Elizabeth Boyle, dau. of John, 3rd Earl of Glasgow ; she d. 15 Feb. 1801, leaving [issue.

George Henry Scott (sir), of Springwood Park, Roxburghshire —— *Roxburgh-* [*shire* 1874-80.

Grandson of Sir George Douglas, bart., M.P., last named, capt. late 34th regt., lt.-col. Border rifle volunteers ; a brigadier general (Queen's body guard) royal company of archers ; contested Roxburghshire 1880 ; b. 19 June 1825 ; m. and has issue. See Foster's Baronetage [His eldest son, James Henry, lieut. 2nd R. Scots fusiliers, fell in Zulu war 23 July 1879.

Hector —— *Tain* 1621.

James, of —— *Haddington* 1479.

James (sir), laird of Drumlanrig, sat as a minor baron 1608, 1609 conv.

Only son of Sir William Douglas, of Hawick, and grandson of Sir James Douglas of Drumlanrig ; he d. 16 Oct. 1615, having m. Mary, eldest dau. of John, 5th Lord Fleming, and had with other issue Sir William, cr. Earl of Queensberry, and Sir James, M.P., of [Mouswald.

James (sir), of Spott, knt. —— *Haddington constabulary* 1612.

James Douglas, commendator of Pluscardine, natl. son of James, Earl of Morton, had a charter, 31 Jan. 1577-8, of the lands of Easter Spott, co. Edinburgh, etc., from George [Home, fiar of Spott. Douglas, vol. ii., 271, note.

James, of Mouswall —— *Dumfries sheriffdom and stewartry of Annandale* 1644, (laird of Mouswall,—see William, M.P.) 1649, 1650-51.

Probably identical with Sir James Douglas of Mouswald, 2nd son of Sir James, M.P.

James (lt.-genl.), of Skirling —— *Peebles-shire* 1685-6

A col. 1685, lt.-gen. 1686, ? killed at Steinkirk 1692.

Douglas – *continued.*

James (sir), of St. Olla —— *Orkney and Shetlandshire* 1754-61, 1761-8, then
[a knt.

Sir James Douglas, adm. of the white, knighted as messenger who brought the announcement of the surrender of Quebec 16 Oct. 1757, commanded a fleet at the Leeward Islands 1761, took Dominica, and the same year had a broad pendant at the siege of Martinique, and was created a baronet 27 June 1786 (son of George Douglas of Frearshaw, co. Roxburgh); d. 2 Nov. 1787, having m. 1st, 1753, Helen. dau. of Thomas Brisbane, of Brisbane, co. Renfrew; she d. 20 Mar. 1766. He m. 2ndly, Lady Helen Boyle, dau. of John, 2nd Earl
[of Glasgow; she d. s.p. 17 Oct. 1794.

John —— *Crail* 1585.

John (Mr.), councillor —— *Elgin* 1639-40, 1643 conv., 1645 (then provost), 1650
[(or Mr. John Hay).

John, of Broughton, brother-german of William, Earl of March —— *Peebles-shire*
[1722-7 (styled "master"), 1727 until his death s. b. 28 April 1732.
Grandson of William, 1st Duke of Queensberry; d. unm. 21 March 1732.

John (sir), of Kelhead —— *Dumfries burghs* 1735, unseated on petition,
[*Dumfries-shire* 1741-7.
Sir John Douglas, 3rd Bart. (son of Sir William Douglas, Bart.); committed to the Tower on suspicion of favouring the Stuarts 14 Aug. 1746, liberated March 1748; d. at Drumlanrig 13 Nov. 1778; m. Christian, 6th dau. of Sir William Cunningham, of Caprington, co. Ayr, Bart.; she d. Nov. 1741, leaving with other issue a son, Sir William, M.P., father of Sir
[Charles, who succ. as 5th Marquis of Queensberry. See that title, Foster's Peerage.

Robert (sir), of Blackerstoun —— *Berwickshire* 1661-3.

[Elizabeth, dau. and heir of —— Douglas, of Blackerston, m. as 1st wife to Sir Robert
[Sinclair, of Longformacus, cr. a baronet of Nova Scotia 10 Dec. 1664.]

Robert (Mr.), brother-german to James, Earl of Morton —— *Kirkwall* 1702-7,
[*Wick burghs* 1708-10.
12th Earl of Morton on the death of his brother James, Dec. 1715. He d. unm. 17 March
[1730.

Robert, of Strathendrie —— *Fifeshire* 1703 until his death s. b. 25 April 1706.
Married Susan, dau. of John, 3rd Lord Balfour of Burleigh, and had issue.

Robert (col.), of St. Olla, younger son of George, Earl of Morton ——
Orkney and *Shetlandshire* 1730-4, 1734-41; (brother-german to James, Earl
[of Morton), 1741 (then colonel) until his death s.b. 19 Feb., 1746-7.
3rd son of George Douglas, M.P. (afterwards 13th Earl of Morton); A.D.C. to the king, with rank of colonel, July, 1743; had a company in 3rd regt. foot guards; fell at Fontenoy
[30 April 1745.

William, of Whittingham —— *Haddington constabulary* 1605.
Possibly father of Sir Archibald, M.P., who succeeded him as a lord of session 8 Aug.
[1590, or more probably a brother of Sir Archibald.

William (sir), sheriff —— *Roxburghshire* 1617 conv.
Probably father of the next named Sir William, M.P.

Douglas—*continued.*

William (sir), of Cavers, knt. —— *Roxburghshire* 1612 (then younger), 1617 parlt., (Mr. William); 1621, (Mr. William); 1628-33, (Sir William of Cavers, sheriff), 1639-40 (then sheriff-principal, he was absent in England on state business in 1640-1, during sessions 2 and 3), 1644, 1645-6 (see Cavers), 1650 1 [(laird of Cavers).

Said to have died 1658 ; probably son of Sir William Douglas, sheriff of Roxburghshire, M.P. aforesaid; father of Sir Archibald Douglas, M.P., by his wife Anne Douglas, of [Whittingham.

William (sir) —— *Dumfries sheriffdom* and *stewartry of Annandale* 1617, [("the laird of Drumlanrig ").

Earl of Queensberry, etc. ; so created 13 June 1663 (see Foster's Peerage) ; served heir of his father, Sir James Douglas, of Drumlanrig, 17 Oct. 1615 ; entertained King James VI. [in his house at Drumlanrig 1617 ; d. 8 March 1640, leaving issue.

William, of Mouswall —— *Dumfries sheriffdom* and *stewartry of Annandale* [1644 (laird of Mouswall), 1648-9.

William (Mr.), of Egilshaw, —— *Orkney* and *Zetland* 1667 conv.

William (sir), of Cavers, heritable sheriff of Teviotdale, —— *Roxburghshire* (or *[sheriffdom of Teviotdale)* 1690, until his death s.b. 2 Aug. 1698.

Eldest son of Sir William Douglas, knt., of Cavers ; he m. Elizabeth, dau. of John [Douglas of Newcastle, and d. s.p.

William, of Dornock —— *Dumfries* (or *Nithsdale) sheriffdom* and *stewartry of [Annandale,* 1702-7.

Probably son of William Douglas of Dornock, who was son of Archibald, brother of [James, 2nd Earl of Queensberry.

William (younger), of Kirkness —— *Kinross-shire* 1715-22.

Probably elder son of Sir Robert Douglas of Kirkness ; died s. p. m.

William, of Cavers —— *Roxburghshire* 1715-22, *Dumfries burghs* 1722-7. (younger), *Roxburghshire* 1727-34, (an officer of the crown 1728), 1742-7.

Eldest son of Archibald Douglas, M.P.; keeper of the general register of Hornings 1728, [storekeeper Custom House Ireland; died unm. Jan. 1748.

William (younger), of Kelhead —— *Dumfries burghs* 1768-74, 1774-80.

Sir William Douglas, of Kelhead, 4th baronet (on the death of his father, Sir John, M.P.); d. 16 May, 1783, leaving with other issue a son, Sir Charles, who succeeded as 5th Marquis of Queensberry. See that title Foster's Peerage and Lord William Douglas, M.P., next [named.

William Robert Keith, youngest brother of Charles, Marquis of Queensberry —— *Dumfries,* 1812-18, (" youngest son of late Sir William Douglas, of Kelhead, bart.") 1818-20 (then of London, merchant) 1820-6 (a lord of the [admiralty 1822, 1824), 1826-30, 1830-1, 1831-2.

Lord William Robert Keith Douglas, precedence of the son of a marquis granted him by patent 4 May 1837 ; a lord of the admiralty Feb.-March 1822, 1824-7 ; died 5 Dec. 1859, having m. 24 Nov. 1821, Elizabeth, eldest dau. of Walter Irvine, esq.; she d. 25 April 1846.

Dow.

—— !aird of Bandeth —— *Stirlingshire* 1646-7.

Downie.

Robert, of Appin —— *Stirling burghs* 1820-6, 1826-30.
Died 10 Sept. 1841, aged 70.

Downing.

George (esq.) —— *Edinburgh* 1654-5 (scout master general), *Peebles, Selkirk, Jedburgh*, etc., and also for *Carlisle* 1656 ; elected to sit for the latter (WILLIS).

Sir George Downing, of East Hatley, co. Cambridge, created a baronet 1 July 1663 (son of Rev. Calybut Downing), secretary of the treasury, teller of the exchequer, a commissioner of customs, ambassador to Holland during the Protectorate, and again 1670-2 ; M.P. Morpeth 1660-81 (see England M.P.); d. 1684, having m. Frances Howard, sister of Charles, 1st Earl of Carlisle ; she d. 10 July 1683 ; buried at Chetoden ; their grandson,
[Sir George, 3rd bart., was the founder of Downing College, Cambridge.

Drumlanrig.

Archibald William Douglas, commonly called Viscount ; —— *Dumfries-shire* 1847-52, 1852, (comptroller of the household 1853), until he succeeded as
[Marquis of Queensberry, s. b. 12 Feb. 1857.

7th Marquis of Queensberry, P.C., (on the death of his father John, 6th Marquis, 19 Dec. [1856), 2nd life guards ; b. 18 April 1818, d. 6 Aug. 1858, leaving with other issue, John [Sholto, 8th and present Marquis of Queensberry. See Foster's Peerage.

Drummond.   See also Home.

Adam, of Megginch —— *Perthshire* 1690-1702.

Adam Drummond, 9th baron of Lennoch, and 2nd of Megginch, (son of John Drummond, of Lennoch and Megginch, by his wife Jean, dau. of Colin Campbell, of Aberuchill, uncle of John, Earl of Loudoun), P.C. Scotland, a commissioner to enquire into the massacre of Glencoe ; m. Alison, eldest dau. of John Hay of Haystoun, and had with other issue a son
[John, M.P.

Adam, of Megginch —— *Aberdeen* (now *Montrose*) *burghs* 1779-80, 1780-4.

11th of Lennoch, and 4th of Megginch, resided at Drummond Castle, capt. in the army, served in first American war, M.P. Lymington, St. Ives, and Shaftesbury (see England M.P.); d. s.p. 17 June 1786, having m.   Feb. 1755, Lady Catherine Ashe, widow of Wm. Ashe, esq., M.P., Heytesbury, and younger dau. of Henry (Powlett), 4th Duke of Bolton, she d.
[8 Oct. 1774.

Charles —— *Linlithgow* 1567, 1568, 1572 conv.

George (sir), of Milnab, provost —— *Edinburgh* 1685-6.

3rd son of James Drummond, 5th laird of Mylnab, by his wife Marion, dau. of Anthony Murray, of Dollerie, provost of Edinburgh in 1684 ; m. 1st Elizabeth Hay of Monckton, near [Edinburgh, and 2ndly Helen, dau. of Sir William Gray, of Pittendrum, and had issue.

George Harley, of Drumtochty —— *Kincardineshire* 1812, 1812-18, 1818-20.

Elder son of George Drummond of Stanmore, Middx. (by his wife Martha, 5th dau. of Rt. Hon. Thomas Harley, M.P., P.C.); b. 23 Nov. 1783, d. 23 July 1853, leaving issue.
[See VISCOUNT STRATHALLAN, Foster's Peerage.

James —— *Perth* 1585, 1592, 1593, 1597 conv., 1600.

[Lord Maderty, so cr. 31 Jan. 1609, (2nd son of David, 2nd Lord Drummond), gent. of [the bedchamber 1585, ancestor of Viscount Strathallan. See Foster's Peerage.

Drummond—*continued.*

James, of Strathallan —— *Perthshire* 1812 (of Drumness), 1312-18, 1818-20 (then of Strathallan), 1820, until accepted stewardship of manor of East [Hendred, Berks, s. b. 6 April 1824.

James Andrew John Lawrence Charles, 6th Viscount Strathallan, on the reversal of the attainder by Act of Parliament, 17 June 1824, many years chief of the British settlement at Canton, a representative peer; (son of Hon. William Drummond, son of William 4th [Viscount, attainted 4 June 1746); b. 24 March 1767, d. 14 May 1851, leaving issue.

John (sir), of Burnebank, knt. —— *Perthshire* 1665 conv., 1667 conv.

Probably elder brother of Sir Wm. Drummond, M.P., cr. Viscount Strathallan.

John (Mr.), of Lundy —— *Fifeshire* 1678 conv.

John, of Megginch —— *Perthshire* 1727-34.

Son of Adam Drummond M.P.; m. 1712, Bethia, dau. of James Murray, esq., of Denchar, [and was father of Adam, M.P.

John, of Quarrill —— *Perth burghs* 1727-34, 1734-41, 1741 until his death [s. b. 20 Jan. 1742-3.

A commissioner of treaties with the Emperor of Germany; died 20 Dec. 1742.

Samuel, of Carlowrie —— *Linlithgowshire* 1644 conv. (laird of Carlowrie), 1644-5.

Thomas, of Riccartoune —— *Linlithgowshire* 1661, 1665 conv.

Son of William Drummond, of Riccarton, M.P. He m. Elizabeth, dau. of Sir Thomas [Nicholson, of Carnock; and had with other issue Thomas, M.P.

Thomas, of Riccarton —— *Linlithgowshire* 1685-6, 1689 conv., 1689 until his [death s. b. 5 Oct. 1699.

Son of Thomas, M.P., last named.

William, of Riccartoun —— *Linlithgowshire* 1628-33, 1630 conv. (then laird of [Riccartoun), 1639-40.

Fourth son of Sir William Drummond, by his wife Jean, dau. of Sir Archibald Stirling, of [Keir, and had a son Thomas, M.P., 1661.

William (lieut.-genl. sir), of Cromlix —— *Perthshire* 1669-74, 1678 conv., [1681-2 (then a knight), 1685-6.

Viscount of Strathallan and Lord Drummond of Cromlix, so cr. 6 Sept. 1684 (youngest son of John, 2nd Lord Maderty); a celebrated Royalist general, had a command "in the engagement" 1648; served in Ireland under the Marquis of Ormond, taken prisoner at the battle of Worcester, but escaped; lieut.-genl. in the Muscovite army. After the Restoration he was appointed major-genl. of the forces in Scotland 1666, imprisoned for twelve months in Dunbarton Castle; general of the Ordnance 1684, general of the forces in Scotland, and a lord of the treasury on the accession of James VII.; d. Jan. 1688, leaving [issue.

Duff.   See also Fife, Macduff, and Grant-Duff.

DUFF, EARL OF FIFE.

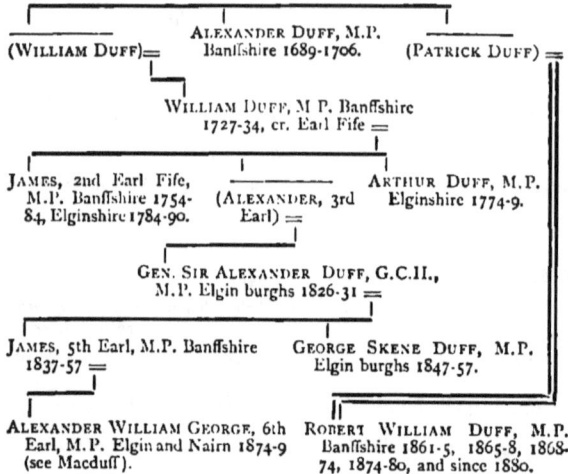

```
                        ALEXANDER DUFF, M.P.
(WILLIAM DUFF)=         Banffshire 1689-1706.        (PATRICK DUFF) =

                        WILLIAM DUFF, M P. Banffshire
                        1727-34, cr. Earl Fife =

JAMES, 2nd Earl Fife,                         ARTHUR DUFF, M.P.
M.P. Banffshire 1754-    (ALEXANDER, 3rd      Elginshire 1774-9.
84, Elginshire 1784-90.   Earl) =

                    GEN. SIR ALEXANDER DUFF, G.C.H.,
                    M.P. Elgin burghs 1826-31 =

JAMES, 5th Earl, M.P. Banffshire      GEORGE SKENE DUFF, M.P.
1837-57 =                             Elgin burghs 1847-57.

ALEXANDER WILLIAM GEORGE, 6th     ROBERT WILLIAM DUFF, M.P.
Earl, M.P. Elgin and Nairn 1874-9  Banffshire 1861-5, 1865-8, 1868-
(see Macduff).                     74, 1874-80, and since 1880.
```

Alexander, of Braco —— *Banffshire* 1689 conv. ; 1689-1702, 1702 until his [death s.b. 25 June, 1706.

Uncle of William 1st Earl Fife, and eldest son of Alexander Duff, of Keithmore. He [m. Margaret, dau. of Sir Wm. Gordon, Bart., of Lesmore, and had issue.

Alexander, of Drummuir —— *Inverness* 1702-7, *Inverness burghs* 1708-10, then [provost of Inverness.

Descended from William, 3rd son of Adam Duff, of Clunybeg, ancestor of Lachlan Duff- [Gordon-Duff, M.P.

Alexander (lieut.-genl.), of Delgaty Castle, col. 92nd regt. foot —— *Elgin* [*burghs* 1826-30, 1830-1.

General Sir Alexander Duff, G.C.H. (2nd son of Alexander, 3rd Earl Fife), entered the army as ensign 66th foot, May 1793, capt. 88th regt. 1794, served in Flanders 1794-5, East Indies 1798 and in Egypt, in South America 1806, and commanded the centre column in the attack on Buenos Ayres. Col. 25 May, 1808 ; major-genl. 1811, lieut.-genl. 1821, general 1838, col. 37th foot 1831, G.C.H. 1834, lord lieut. Elginshire ; d. 21 March 1851, aged 77 ; m. 16 March, 1812, Anne, younger dau. of James Stein, esq., of Kilbagie ; she d. 13-14 Feb. 1859, leaving with other issue 2 sons, James (M.P.) succ. as 5th Earl of [Fife, and George Skene Duff, M.P.

Arthur, of Ortown, brother-german to James, Earl of Fife —— *Elginshire* 1774, antil he accepted the stewardship of the Manor of East Hendred, Berks, [s. b. 29 April 1779.

An advocate, 7th and youngest son of William, 1st Earl Fife ; d. unm. 20 April 1805.

Duff—*continued.*

George —— *Cullen* 1593.

George Skene —— *Elgin burghs* 1847-52, 1852-7, 1857, until he accepted the [*Chiltern hundreds* s. b. 19 Dec. in same year.

Brother of James, 5th Earl Fife, and son of Genl. Sir Alex. Duff, G.C.H., M.P., lord lieut. Elgin 1856, formerly R.H. guards, HEIR PRESUMPTIVE TO THE EARLDOM, had the [precedence of the son of an earl granted him by patent 2 June 1857 ; unm.

James, son to the Lord Braco —— *Banffshire* 1754-61, 1761-8 (Viscount Macduff) [1768-74 (Earl Fife), 1774-80, 1780-4, *Elginshire* 1784-90.

2nd Earl Fife (on the death of his father 30 Sept. 1763), cr. Baron Fife in the peerage of Great Britain 19 Feb. 1790, lord lieut. Banffshire ; d. s.p.m. 24 Jan. 1809, having m. 5 June 1759, Lady Dorothea Sinclair, only child of Alexander, 9th Earl of Caithness.

James (sir), of Kinstair, lieut.-col. 1st foot guards —— *Banffshire* 1784, until he [accepted the Chiltern hundreds s.b. 22 Jan. 1789.

General in the army, col. 50th foot, knighted 30 April, 1779, as proxy for Sir James [Harris, K.B. (afterwards Earl of Malmesbury, and died 5 Dec. 1839, aged 87.

Lachlan, Duff-Gordon-Duff, of Drummuir and Park —— *Banffshire* 1857-9, 1859, until accepted Chiltern hundreds s.b. 1 May 1861. See foot-note.

James, residing at Delgaty Castle —— *Banffshire* 1837-41, 1841-7, 1847-52 (then of Skene House), 1852-7, 1857 (then Earl Fife) until he accepted the [stewardship of the manor of Hempholme s.b. 30 June same year.

5th Earl Fife, K.T. (son of Genl. Sir Alexander Duff, G.C.H., M.P.) ; lord-lieut. co. Fife 1856-7 ; created Baron Skene, of Skene, co. Aberdeen, in the peerage of the United Kingdom, 1 Oct. 1857; b. 6 July 1814; d. 7 Aug. 1879, leaving issue. See Foster's Peerage.

Robert William, of Fetteresso, Culter, Glasshaugh, and Auchinderan —— *Banffshire* 1861-5 (then lieut. R.N., etc.), 1865-8, 1868-74, 1874-80, and [since 1880. See foot-note.

DUFF-GORDON-DUFF, LACHLAN, of Drummuir and Park, co. Banff, J.P., vice-lieut. and convener, co. Banff, M.P. as above, late major 20th regt., assumed additional name of Duff March 1858 (eldest son of Lt.-Col. Thomas Gordon, formerly Duff) ; b. 1 June 1817 ; m. 6 March 1847, Jane Ellen, dau. of Thomas Butterfield, Esq., of Bermuda, and has had 2 sons and 2 daus.

(1) Thomas Duff ; b. 11 Aug. 1848 ; m. 2 Feb. 1875, Pauline Emma, dau. of Charles Tennant, Esq., of Glen, co. Peebles.
(2) Archibald Hay, b. 6 April 1863.
(3) Mary Louisa, d. 1868.   (4) Helen Elizabeth.
Drummuir Castle, Keith, and *Park House, Banff, N.B.*
Club—United Service.

DUFF, ROBERT WILLIAM, of Fetteresso Castle, co. Kincardine, J.P., D.L., of Culter House, co. Aberdeen, and Glasshaugh, co. Banff, J.P., D.L., comr. R.N. 1870, resumed his patronymic in 1861, M.P. as above (son of Arthur Abercromby, who assumed that surname in lieu of Duff—see "Earl of Fife," Foster's Peerage) ; b. 8 March 1835 ; m. 21 Feb. 1871, Louisa, youngest dau. of Sir William Scott, Bart., of Ancrum, co. Roxburgh, and has issue.

Fetteresso Castle, co. Kincardine ; Culter House, co. Aberdeen ; Glasshaugh, co. Banff ; 16, *Lowndes Square, S. W.*
Club—Brooks'.

Duff—*continued.*

William, bailie —— *Inverness* 1681-2.

William, of Braco —— *Banffshire* 1727-34.

Earl Fife and Visct. Macduff, so cr. 26 April 1759, having been cr. Lord Braco 28 July 1735, all in the peerage of Ireland (son of William Duff, of Dipple, co. Banff); d. 30 Sept. [1763, leaving with other issue James, M.P., 2nd Earl, and Arthur, M.P.

Dumfries.

Johnne —— 1440.

Dunb.

Robert of —— 1475.

Dunbar. See also Enterkine.

Alexander —— *Nairn,* 1617.

Alexander, of Boath —— *Nairnshire* 1643 conv.

Alexander, of Westfield, sheriff-principal of Moray —— *Elgin and Forres-shire* [1696-1702, 1702 until his death s. b. 16 Feb. 1703.

Son of Robert Dunbar of Westfield; he m. Margaret, dau. of Sir James Calder of Muirtown, and had two sons, who both d. unm., and a dau. Elizabeth, m. to Sir Wm. Dunbar of [Hempriggs.

David (sir), of Baldoon, knt. and bart. —— *Wigtownshire* 1650-1 (laird of [Baldoon), 1665 conv. (then knt. bart.), 1681-2.

Cr. a baronet 13 Oct. 1664; m. Mary Montgomerie, dau. of Hugh, 7th Earl of Eglinton; [she d. Sept. 1687, leaving issue.

George (Mr.) —— *Cullen* 1661.

James —— *Forres* 1587 —— 1628-33.

James (Mr.), of Hempriggs, formerly Sutherland, brother-german to the Lord Duffus —— *Caithness-shire* 1706-7, 1710-13 (laird of Hempriggs).

Hon. Sir James Dunbar, Bart. (2nd son of James Sutherland, 2nd Lord Duffus); m. Elizabeth, only surviving child and heiress of Sir William Dunbar of Hempriggs, co. Caithness, relict of Sir Robert Gordon of Gordonstown; he assumed the name of Dunbar in lieu of his patronymic; was cr. a baronet 10 Dec. 1706; and had issue. See Douglas' [Peerage, vol. i., 447.

John, of Moynes —— *Nairnshire* 1617, 1628-33.

[Sir Alexander Dunbar of Cumnock and Westfield had by his 2nd wife Janet Leslie a son [John of Moynes.]

John (Mr.), bailie —— *Forres* 1639-41.

Dunbar—*continued.*

[Ninian], laird of Grangehill —— *Elgin and Forres-shire* 1646-7.

Son of Mark Dunbar of Durris; m. twice, and had with other issue a son Sir Robert, M.P.

Patrick, of Ballnaferrie —— *Elgin and Forres-shire* 1665 conv., 1667 conv.

Patrick, of Machrimore —— *Kirkcudbright stewartry* 1693-1702.

Married dau. of   Macdowall, of Freugh; served heir 1663 of his father, John
[Dunbar of Machrimore, who m. a dau. of John Madowall of Logan.

Patrick, of Bowermadden —— *Caithness shire* 1727-34.

Robert (sir), of Grangehill —— *Elgin and Forres shire* 1669-70.

Son of Ninian Dunbar, M.P., knighted by Charles II., 1660: m. Grisel Brodie of that
[ilk, and had a son Robert.

Robert, of Grangehill —— *Elgin and Forres-shire* 1703, until his death, s. b.
[16 June, 1704.

Son of Sir Robert Dunbar, M.P., last named ; he m. Catherine, dau. of James Brodie of
[that ilk, and had issue

Thomas, of Grange —— *Elgin and Forres-shire* 1681-2, 1689 conv. 1689, until
[his death, s. b. 1 Dec. 1696.

William (Mr.) —— *Forres* 1646-7, 1648.

William, of Hempriggs —— *Caithness-shire* 1678 conv.

Sir William Dunbar, of Hempriggs (son of John Dunbar), cr. a raronet of Nova Scotia
10 April, 1700; m. Margaret, dau. of Alexander Sinclair, of Lathron, and d. 1711, leaving
[issue. See "Chaos." Foster's Baronetage.

William (sir), of Mochrum, Bart. —— *Wigtown burghs* 1857-9, 1859-65, a lord of
[the treasury 1859, and commissioner for auditing public accounts 1865.

Seventh baronet (son of James Dunbar, 21st light dragoons), keeper of the great seal of
H.R.H. the Prince of Wales in Scotland, 1862-5, and of his privy seal 1859-65 ; a member
of the duchy of Cornwall, etc., member of the Scottish bar; b. 2 March 1812; m.
7 Jan. 1852, Catherine Hay, eldest dau. of James Paterson, esq., of Carpow, co. Perth,
[and has 2 sons. See Foster's Baronetage.

Duncan.

Adam Duncan-Haldane, commonly called Visct. Duncan —— *Forfarshire*
1854-7 ; (a lord of the Treasury 1855), 1857-9, 1859 until he succeeded as Earl
[of Camperdown 22 Dec. same year. See also M.P. England.

2nd Earl of Camperdown, M.P. Southampton 1837-41, Bath 1841-2, etc. ; a lord of the
Treasury 1855-8 ; b. 25 March 1812 ; d. 30 Jan. 1867, leaving issue. See Foster's Peerage.

George, of Dundee, mercht. —— *Dundee* 1841-7, 1847-52, 1852-7, then of the
[Vine.

A linen draper, died 6 Jan. 1878, aged 86.

Walter —— *Kinghorn* 1617.

William—— *Dundee* 1583, 1585 conv.

Duncoll.

William of —— *Dumfries* 1357.

Dundas.

Charles —— *Orkney and Shetlandshire* 1781-4 (on petition).

> Baron Amesbury, of Kintbury Amesbury, and Barton Court, Berks ; so cr. 16 May 1832, M.P. Richmond, Yorkshire 1775-80, 1784-6, Berkshire 1794. and for ten successive parlts., until raised to the peerage (see England M.P.) ; nominated speaker of the House of Commons in 1802. One of the six counsellors of state to the Prince of Wales, as great steward of Scotland, col. of the white horse volunteer cavalry, counsellor-at-law (son of Thomas Dundas, M.P., and brother of General Thos. Dundas, M.P.) ; b. 5 Aug. 1751, d. 30 June 1832, having m, 1st, Anne, dau. and sole heir of Ralph Whitley of Aston Hall, Flints. He m. 2ndly, 25 Jan. 1822, his cousin Margaret, dau. of Charles Barclay, esq. (E. LAUDERDALE), widow 1st. of Charles Ogilvy, and 2ndly, of Major Archibald Erskine (E. [BUCHAN] ; she d. 14 April, 1841. By his 1st wife he had an only daughter.

David (sir), of Ochtertyre, co. Perth, knt. Q.C. —— *Sutherlandshire* 1840-1, (Q.C. of the Inner Temple), 1841-7 (solr.-genl. 1846), 1847-52 (judge-advocate genl. 1849, described as Sir David Dundas, knt. of Ochtertyre, co. Perth), 1861-5, 1865, until he accepted the Chiltern hundreds s. b. 27 May, [1867.

> Eldest surviving son of James Dundas, Ochtortyre, co. Perth, by Elizabeth, dau. of William Graham, esq., of Airth, co. Stirling. B.A. Christ Church, Oxford 1820, M.A. 1822, bar.-at-law, I.T. 1823, Q.C. 1840, sol.-genl., and knighted 1846, P.C. 1849, judge advo.-genl. [1849-52 ; d. unm. 30 March 1877, aged 78.

Frederick, of 24, Hanover sq., London, —— *Orkney* and *Shetlandshire* 1837-41, 1841-7, 1852-7, 1857-9, 1859-65, 1868, until his death s. b. 11 Jan. 1873.

> Of Papdale, Orkney (only son of Hon. Charles Lawrence Dundas (see M.P. England), brother of Lawrence 1st Earl of Zetland), lord-lieut. of Orkney, contested Orkney and Shetlandshire 1847 ; b. 14 June 1802, d. s.p. 26 Oct. 1872, having m. 2 June 1847, Grace, eldest dau. of Sir Ralph St. George Gore, bart., she d. 15 Jan. 1858. See ZETLAND, Foster's [Peerage.

George of that ilk —— *Linlithgowshire* 1639-41, 1643-4 conv., 1650.

> Eldest son of Sir Walter Dundas, M.P. " He appears to have been deeply engaged on the parliament's side in the troublesome reign of King Charles I , and was by them made a privy councillor for life 13 Nov. 1641, also one of the committee of parliament for stating the public debts, one of the planters of kirks, one of the commissioners for concerting the Ripon treaty, one of the committee for trying Montrose and other loyalists, all in the said year 1641, one of the committee for settling the sale of coals in 1644, one of the commissioners for visiting the Universities in 1649, and one of the colonels in Linlithgowshire for putting the kingdom in a posture of defence, etc., etc. He m. Elizabeth, dau. of Sir Alex-[ander Hamilton, of Innerwick, and had issue." See Douglas' Baronage.

George (Mr.), of Manour —— *Linlithgowshire* 1644 conv. (laird of Manour), [1644-7, 1648 (laird of Manour).

> Second son of David Dundas, of Dudingston, bred a lawyer, acquired the estate of Manour in Perthshire 1628, high sheriff co. Linlithgow 1637, one of the parliament committee 1640, one of the commissioners for the Uxbridge treaty 1644, one of the new commissioners for planting of kirks, same year, etc., etc., a commissioner of excise 1649 ; he subsequently adhered to the royal cause, and his estate was sequestrated ; he m. Margaret, [dau. of William Livingstone of West Quarter, and had isssue. See Douglas' Baronage.

Dundas—*continued.*

DUNDAS OF THAT ILK.

SIR WALTER DUNDAS of that ilk, sat as a minor baron 1609—Linlithgowshire 1612, 1617, 1621, 1628-33 ═

GFORGE DUNDAS, M.P. Linlithgowshire 1639-41, 1643-4, 1650 ═

GEORGE DUNDAS ═

GEORGE DUNDAS, M.P. Linlithgowshire 1722-7, 1741-3 ═

COL. JAMFS DUNDAS, M.P. Linlithgowshire 1768-74 ═

GEORGE DUNDAS, C.M.G. (son of Thomas son of George), M.P. Linlithgowshire 1847-52, 1852-7, 1857-9.

George, of Duddington —— *Linlithgowshire* 1649-50

Nephew of the last named George and elder son of James Dundas, of Dudingstone, by his
wife Isabel, dau. of Thomas Maule, Lord Panmure, a commissioner for visiting universities
[1649, etc., etc. ; m. Catherine Monypenny, of Pitmillie, and had a son John.

George, of Dundas —— *Linlithgowshire* 1722-7, 1741 until appointed master of
[the king's works in Scotland s.b. 13 May 1743.

Eldest son of George Dundas, by his wife Margaret Hay ; m. Alison, dau. of Gen. James
[Bruce, of Kennet, and had with other issue a son James, M.P.

George (younger), of Dundas —— *Linlithgowshire* 1847-52, 1852-7, 1857 until
[appointed lieut.-gov. of Prince Edward Island s.b. 5 Feb. 1859.

George Dundas, C.M.G. (1877), served with rifle brigade in Bermuda, Nova Scotia, and
the Mediterranean ; retired 1844 ; lieut.-gov. Prince Edward Island Jan. 1859 to 1870,
lieut.-gov. St. Vincent 1874-8, Windward Islands 1876, 1878-9 (eldest son of James Dundas,
of Dundas, who d. 9 March 1881) ; b. 12 Nov. 1819, d. s p. 18 March, 1880, having m. Mary
[only dau. Rev. W. Atkinson, incumbent of Gateshead Fell, co. Durham.

George Heneage Lawrence, capt. R.N. —— *Orkney* and *Shetlandshire*
[1818-20, 1826-30.

Rear-adml. Dundas, C.B. (1815), lieut. on board H.M.S. the ill-fated Queen Charlotte,
and for his intrepidity was appointed to the Calpe 14 ; took part with the combined squadrons
in the actions on 6th and 13th July 1801, and received the thanks of the com.-in-chief, etc.
etc. ; received post rank 3 Aug. same year, etc., etc. ; rear-adml. of the blue on the
accession of William IV., a lord of the admiralty 1821, M.P. Richmond 1802 (see England),
[(4th son of Thomas, 1st lord of Dundas) ; b. 8 Sept. 1778, d. unm. 6 Oct. 1834.

Dundas—*continued.*

DUNDAS, VISCOUNT MELVILLE, etc., etc.

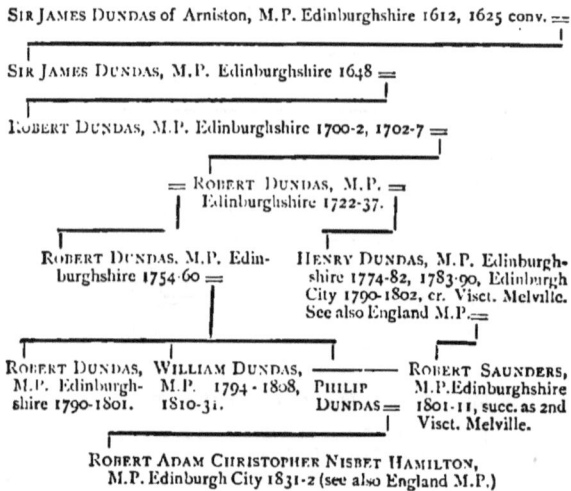

SIR JAMES DUNDAS of Arniston, M.P. Edinburghshire 1612, 1625 conv. ==

SIR JAMES DUNDAS, M.P. Edinburghshire 1648 =

ROBERT DUNDAS, M.P. Edinburghshire 1700-2, 1702-7 =

= ROBERT DUNDAS, M.P. = Edinburghshire 1722-37.

ROBERT DUNDAS, M.P. Edinburghshire 1754-60 =

HENRY DUNDAS, M.P. Edinburghshire 1774-82, 1783-90, Edinburgh City 1790-1802, cr. Visct. Melville. See also England M.P.==

ROBERT DUNDAS, M.P. Edinburghshire 1790-1801.

WILLIAM DUNDAS, M.P. 1794-1808, 1810-31.

—— PHILIP DUNDAS=

ROBERT SAUNDERS, M.P.Edinburghshire 1801-11, succ. as 2nd Visct. Melville.

ROBERT ADAM CHRISTOPHER NISBET HAMILTON, M.P. Edinburgh City 1831-2 (see also England M.P.)

Henry, of Melville, advocate —— *Edinburghshire* 1774-80 (advocate for Scotland 1775, a keeper of the signet for Scotland 1777 and also 1779), 1780-2, 1783-4 (treasurer of the navy 1783 and 1784), 1784-90 (then treasurer of the navy), *Edinburgh city* 1790-6 (P.C., a principal secretary of state 1791, a commissioner for India 1793), 1796-1802 (keeper of the privy seal of Scotland 1800), [1802 (12 July), until created Viscount Melville, etc., 24 Dec. same year.

Henry, Viscount Melville, of Melville, co. Edinburgh, and Baron Dunira, co. Perth, so cr. 24 Dec. 1802, advocate 1763, sol. gen. Scotland 1773, lord advocate 1775-83, P.C. 1782, M.P. Newton I.W. 1782 (see England), treasurer of the navy 1782-3 and 1783-1801, president of the board of control East India Company 1793-1801, secretary of State Home Department 1791-4, secretary for war 1794 to 1801, first lord of the Admiralty 1804-5, impeached of malversation whilst treasurer of the navy by the House of Commons in 1805, was tried by his peers in Westminster Hall, and acquitted, struck off P.C. 6 May 1805, restored 1806 (son of Robert, Lord Arniston, of session, M.P.); b. 28 April 1739, d. 28 May 1811, leaving an only son, who succeeded as 2nd Viscount. See MELVILLE, [Foster's Peerage.

James (sir), of Arniston —— *Edinburghshire* 1612, 1625 conv.

Son of George Dundas, of that ilk, by his 2nd wife, Catherine, dau. of Lawrence, 3rd Lord Oliphant ; knighted by James VI., governor of Berwick ; by his 2nd wife, Mary, dau. of [George Home of Wedderburn, had with other issue a son, Sir James, M.P., next named

Dundas—*continued.*

James (sir), laird of Arniston —— *Edinburghshire* 1648.

Lord Arniston, of session, ordinary lord 4 June 1662, resigned 18 Nov. 1663, "declining to subscribe a declaration that it should be unlawful to take up arms against the king, and abjuring the national and solemn league and covenant;" knighted by Charles I. 16 Nov. 1641 (elder son of Sir James Dundas, M.P., last named) ; d. 1679, leaving with other issue,
[Robert, lord of session, M.P. See MELVILLE, Foster's Peerage.

James, of Mortoune —— *Linlithgowshire* 1669-74.

Probably eldest son of James Dundas, of Morton, by his wife Elizabeth, dau. of James
[Hamilton, of Westport.

James —— *Linlithgowhires* 1770-74 (on petition).

Colonel James Dundas, of Dundas (eldest son of George Dundas, M.P.) ; m. 22 April 1748, Jean Maria, eldest dau. of William, Lord Forbes ; she d. 28 July, 1774, leaving issue.
[Great-grandfather of George Dundas, C.M.G., M.P.

John, of Newliston —— *Linlithgowshire* 1617.

Sir John Dundas, of Newliston (son of Sir James Dundas, of Newliston), living 1599-1633; m. Agnes, dau. of William, Lord Gray (she re-m. as 2nd wife to Sir Archibald Primrose,
[lord register), and had an only daughter.

Lawrence (sir), of Kerse, bart. —— *Linlithgow burghs* 1747 (22 July) until unseated 16 March following ; *Edinburgh city* 1768-74, 1774-80, and March
[1781 until his death, s. b. 29 Oct. same year.   See also England M.P.

Of Upleatham, Yorks (younger brother of Thomas Dundas, M.P.), M.P. Newcastle-under-Lyne, 1762-8 (see England), commissary-general 1748-59, cr. a baronet 23 Nov. 1762 (with remainder to the issue male of his brother Thomas, M.P.) ; d. 21 Sept. 1781, having m. 9 April 1738, Margaret, only dau. of Brig.-Gen. Alex. Bruce, of Kennet (B. BALFOUR);
[she d. 11 Oct. 1802, aged 87, leaving an only son Thomas, M.P., cr. Lord Dundas.

Robert (sir), of Arniston, knt., senator of the college of justice —— *Edinburgh-*
[*shire* 1700-2, 1702-7.

Eldest son of Sir James Dundas, M.P. ; ordinary lord of session 1 Nov. 1689 until his death, 25 Nov. 1726 ; he m. Margaret, dau of Sir Robert Sinclair, of Stevenson, bart., and
[had with other issue, Robert, M.P., next named.

Robert, of Arniston, king's advocate in Scotland —— *Edinburghshire* 1722-7,
[1727-34, 1734 until appointed a lord of session 10 June 1737.

Eldest son of Robert Dundas, M.P., last named ; advocate 26 July, 1709, solicitor-gen. 1717, lord advocate 1720-5, dean of the faculty of advocates 9 Dec. 1721, until lord of session 10 June 1737, lord president 10 Sept. 1748; b. 9 Dec. 1685; d. 26 Aug. 1753, leaving by his 1st wife a son, Robert, M.P., and by his second wife a son, Henry, M.P., cr. Viscount
[Melville, aforesaid.

Robert, of Arniston —— *Edinburghshire* 1754 (lord advocate 1754), until [appointed lord president of the court of session (14 June 1760).

Eldest son of Robert Dundas, M.P., last named ; advocate 18 Feb. 1737, solicitor-general 1742-6, dean of the faculty of advocates, 25 Nov. 1746 until elevated to the bench, lord advocate 1754, a commissioner for fisheries and manufactures Scotland 1755, lord president of the court of session 14 June 1760 until his death, 13 Dec. 1787; b. 18 July 1713 ; m. twice,
[and he left with other issue a son, Robert M.P., next named, and William, M.P.

SCOTCH MEMBERS. P

Dundas—*continued.*

DUNDAS, EARL OF ZETLAND.

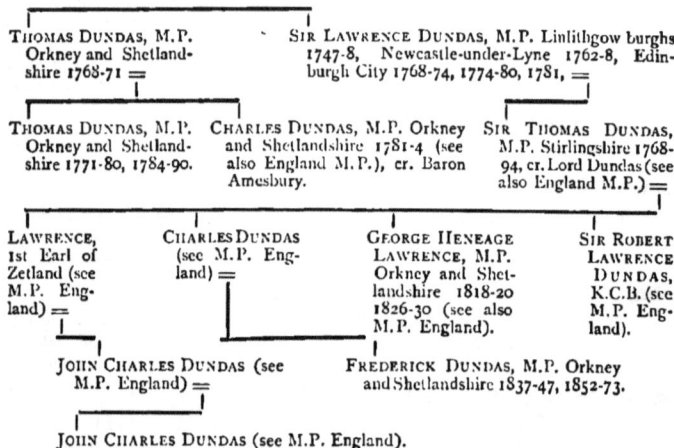

THOMAS DUNDAS, M.P. Orkney and Shetland-shire 1768-71 ═══   ` SIR LAWRENCE DUNDAS, M.P. Linlithgow burghs 1747-8, Newcastle-under-Lyne 1762-8, Edin-burgh City 1768-74, 1774-80, 1781, ═══

THOMAS DUNDAS, M.P. Orkney and Shetland-shire 1771-80, 1784-90.   CHARLES DUNDAS, M.P. Orkney and Shetlandshire 1781-4 (see also England M.P.), cr. Baron Amesbury.   SIR THOMAS DUNDAS, M.P. Stirlingshire 1768-94, cr. Lord Dundas (see also England M.P.) ═══

LAWRENCE, 1st Earl of Zetland (see M.P. England) ═══   CHARLES DUNDAS (see M.P. England) ═══   GEORGE HENEAGE LAWRENCE, M.P. Orkney and Shetlandshire 1818-20 1826-30 (see also M.P. England).   SIR ROBERT LAWRENCE DUNDAS, K.C.B. (see M.P. England).

JOHN CHARLES DUNDAS (see M.P. England) ═══   FREDERICK DUNDAS, M.P. Orkney and Shetlandshire 1837-47, 1852-73.

JOHN CHARLES DUNDAS (see M.P. England).

Robert, of Arniston, king's advocate for Scotland —— *Edinburghshire* 1790-6, 1796 (joint clerk and keeper of the general registers for seisins and other writs in Scotland 1799), until appointed chief baron of the exchequer in Scotland [s.b. 1 June 1801

Eldest son of Robert Dundas, M.P., last named, advocate 1779. sol.-genl. 1784, lord advocate 1789; b. 6 June 1753, d. 17 June 1819, having m. May 1787, Hon. Elizabeth Dundas, dau. [of Robert, 1st Viscount Melville ; she d. 18 March 1852, leaving issue.

Robert, of Melville —— *Edinburghshire* 1801-2, 1802-6, 1806-7 (a commissioner for Indian affairs 1807), 1807 (chief secretary to L.L. Ireland 1809, president of the commissioners for the affairs of India 1810) until he succeeded as 2nd [Viscount Melville, 28 May, 1811.

Robert, 2nd Viscount Melville, K.T., 1821, P.C., deputy privy seal, deputy keeper of the register of seisins, M.P. Hastings and Rye (see England), keeper of the (signet) privy seal of Scotland 1811-21, lieut.-genl. of the royal archers (the Queen's body guard) of Scotland, D.L. cos. Edinburgh and Linlithgow, chancellor of the university of St. Andrew 1814-21, governor of the bank of Scotland 1811-21, a commissioner for manufactures in Scotland, a commis-sioner for the custody of the regalia of Scotland, an elder brother of the Trinity-house of London, a vice-president of the marine society, F.R.S. 1817, F.R.A.S., president of the board of control 1807, chief secretary Ireland 1809-10, first lord of the admiralty 1812-27, 1828-30 (only son of Henry Dundas, M.P., created Viscount Melville); b. 14 March 1771, d. 10 June 1851 ; assumed the additional name of Saunders on his marriage (29 Aug. 1796) with Anne, dau. of Richard Huck Saunders, M.D., (niece and co-heir of Admiral Sir Charles [Saunders, K.H. ;) she d. 10 Sept. 1841, leaving issue.

Dundas—*continued.*

Robert Adam, of Whiterigg —— *Edinburgh city* 1831-2.

Robert Adam Christopher-Nisbet-Hamilton, of Bloxholme Hall, and Well Vale, co. Linc., and of Archerfield and Biel, N.B. ; exchanged his name of Dundas for that of Christopher by R.L., 20 Jan. 1836, and took the additional surnames of Nisbet-Hamilton in 1854, on the accession of his wife to the Belhaven and Dirleton estates ; J.P., D.L., cos. Linc. and Haddington, M.P. Ipswich 1826-30, 1835-7, Edinburgh 1831-2, North Linc. 1837-57 (see England M.P.), chancellor duchy of Lancaster 1852, F.R.S. 1833 (elder son of Philip Dundas, govr. and treasr. Prince of Wales Island) ; b. 9 Feb. 1804, d. 9 June 1877, having m. 28 Jan. 1828, Lady Mary Bruce, eldest dau. of Thomas, 7th Earl of Elgin, and had an only dau. [Constance.

Thomas, of Fingask —— *Orkney and Shetlandshire* 1768, until appointed a [commissioner of police in Scotland, s.b. 31 Jan. 1771.

Of Fingask, and of Carron Hall, co. Stirling, the latter by purchase (elder brother of Sir Lawrence Dundas, bart., M.P.) ; d. 16 April 1786, leaving with other issue (see Foster's [Peerage, E. ZETLAND), a son, Thomas, M.P.

Thomas (capt.), eldest son of Thomas Dundas, of Fingask (the former M.P. Orkney) —— *Orkney and Shetlandshire* 1771-4, 1774-80 (then styled [younger), 1784-90 (then styled colonel).

Of Fingask and Carron Hall, maj.-genl. in the army, rendered distinguished service in the reduction of the French West India Islands, col. 68th regt., at the capture of Martinique, St. Lucia, and Guadaloupe (elder brother of Charles, Lord Amesbury aforesaid, son of Thomas Dundas, M.P., before named) ; b. 30 June 1750, d. (at Guadaloupe) 3 June 1794, aged 44 ; monument in St. Paul's cath. ; m. and had issue (see E. ZETLAND, Foster's Peerage).

Thomas (sir), of Kerse, bart. —— *Stirlingshire* 1768-74 (then of Castle Cary, esq.) 1774-80, 1780-4, 1784-90 (then of Kerse, baronet), 1790 until created ·Baron Dundas, 13 Aug. 1794.

Thomas, Lord Dundas, so created 13 Aug. 1794 (only son of Sir. Lawrence Dundas, Bart. M.P.), lord lieut. and vice-admiral of Orkney and Shetland, president of the society of antiquaries Scotland, councillor of state to Prince of Wales, M.P. Richmond (see England); [b. 16 Feb. 1741, d. 14 June 1820, leaving issue, (see E. ZETLAND in Foster's Peerage).

Walter (sir), of that ilk, knight —— sat as a minor baron in convention 1609 (the laird of Dundas). *Linlithgowshire* 1612 (the laird), 1617, 1621 (the [laird), 1628-33.

Sir Walter Dundas, of Dundas (son of George Dundas of that ilk), knighted by James VI. at the baptism of Prince Henry (b. at Stirling 19 Feb. 1593-4) ; m. 1st Janet, dau. of Sir Alexander Oliphant, of Kelly, and 2ndly Anne Monteith, of Carse, and had with other issue [George, M.P.

Dundas—*continued.*

William —— *Anstruther Easter* (now *St. Andrews*) *burghs* 1794-6 (counsellor-at-law in London) ; *Wick burghs* 1796-1802 (a commissioner for the affairs of India 1797) ; *Sutherlandshire* 1802-6 (P.C. secretary-at-war 1804), 1806-7, 1807 until acc. Chiltern hundreds s.b. 2 May 1808 ; *Elgin burghs* 1810 until acc. Chiltern hundreds s.b. 13 April 1812 ; *Edinburgh* 1812, 1812-18 (keeper of the signet Scotland 1814), 1818-20 (keeper of the general register of sasines [in Scotland 1819), 1820-6, 1826-30, 1830-1.

Third son of Right Hon. Robert Dundas, M.P., bar.-at-law, L.I. 1788 ; a commissioner for India 1797-1803, P.C. 25 June 1800, sec.-at-war 1804-6, lord clerk register 1821-45, etc., as above ; d. s.p. 14 Nov. 1845, having m. 1 June 1813, Mary, dau. of Col. James Archibald Stuart-Mackenzie (E. WHARNCLIFFE); she d. 9 March 1855.   (See E. MELVILLE, [Foster's Peerage.)

Dundee.

—— the provost of —— *Dundee* 1526 (William Carmichael) —— 1568.

Dunlop.

Alexander Murray, of Corsock, advocate —— *Greenock* 1852-7, 1857-9, 1859- [65, 1865-8.

Alexander Colquhoun-Stirling-Murray-Dunlop, of Corsock, co. Kirkcudbright (eldest son of Alexander Dunlop, esq., of Kepoch, by Margaret Colquhoun, of Kenmure, co. Lanark); advocate 1820, assessor to Greenock, author of "Treatises on Scottish Poor Law," and framer of "The Claim of Rights" for Scottish Church, and of "The Protest," made on the occasion of disruption, afterwards legal adviser to Free Church of Scotland ; assumed the additional name of Murray in 1849, assumed also the surnames of Colquhoun-Stirling in 1867 ; b. 27 Dec. 1798 ; d. 1 Sept. 1870, having m. 18 July 1844, Eliza Esther, only child [of John Murray, esq., of Edinburgh, and had issue.

Allan —— *Irvine* 1644-5.

Allan, younger of Craig (provost) —— *Irvine* 1661.

Colin, of Tollcross —— *Glasgow* 1835, until he accepted the Chiltern hundreds [s.b. 17 Feb. 1836.

Died unm. 27 July 1837, at the Clyde iron works, and was succeeded by his nephew, James [Dunlop, of Tollcross.

James (lieut.-genl.), of Dunlop —— *Kirkcudbright stewartry* 1812-18 (then major- [general) 1818-20, 1820-6.

Son of John Dunlop, of Dunlop (by his wife Frances Anne, dau. of Sir Thomas Wallace, of Craigie, bart.), at siege of Cannanmore, East Indies, Nov. 1789, at first siege of Seringa-patam 1790, severely wounded, military secretary to governor of Bombay 1794, etc., etc., served in Mysore war 1798, brigadier-general western district 1804, major-genl. 1810, and was placed on the staff of the army in the Peninsula, commanded a brigade, lt.-genl. 1814, col. 75th foot 1827 ; d. March 1832, having m. 1802, Julia, dau. of Hugh Baillie, esq., and [had a son, Sir John, M.P.

Dunlop—*continued*.

John (sir), of Dunlop, bart. —— *Kilmarnock burghs* 1833-4 (capt.); *Ayrshire* [1835-7, 1837 until his death, s.b. 1 May 1839, then a baronet.

Sir John Dunlop, bart., so cr. 28 April 1838 (son of General James Dunlop, M.P.); d. 3 April 1839; he m. 1st, 17 Nov. 1829, Charlotte Constance, dau. of Major-Genl. Sir Richard Downes Jackson, K.C.H., and 2ndly, 29 Dec. 1835, Lady Harriet Primrose, dau. of Archibald John, Earl of Rosebery; she d. s.p. 8 March 1876. By his 1st wife he had an only son, [Sir James Dunlop, 2nd baronet, who died s.p. 10 Feb. 1858.

Dunning.

Robert (Dunnyn) —— 1472, 1475, 1482 bis.

Dykes.

James, bailie —— *Perth* 1661-3, in absence of Mr. John Patersone, of Benchills, [provost.

E.

Eassone or Asson.

George, merchant, bailie —— *Dysart* 1703 until his death s.b. 4 Nov. 1704.

John, merchant, provost —— *St. Andrew* 1681-2, 1685-6, late provost.

Edgar.

Alexander, provost —— *Haddington* 1696-1702, 1703-7, late provost.

Edward, merchant —— *Edinburgh* 1640-1, 1646-7.

John, of Wedderlie —— *Berwickshire* 1681-2.

> Son of John Edgar, of Wedderlie, j.u. Elizabeth, dau. of John Edgar, of Wedderlie ; he
> m. Jean or Joanna, dau. of Thomas Robertson, merchant, of Edinburgh and of Lochbank,
> [and d. 1683, leaving issue.

Edinburgh.

The Provost of —— *Edinburgh* 1479 (see Bertram and Crichton), 1491, 1528,
[1532, 1535, 1543, 1544, 1546, 1560, 1568, 1593 conv.

Edmonstone.

(Andrew) laird of Edmonstone, sat as a minor baron in the conventions of 1597
[and 1599.

> Son of Sir John Edmonstone of that ilk, who d. 1592 ; he m. Mary Gordon, and was
> [succeeded by his son John, who was a knight, in 1619.

Archibald, of Duntreath —— *Stirlingshire* 1628-33.

> Son of William Edmonstone, of Duntreath, etc.; he m. Jean, dau. of Archibald Hamilton,
> [of Halcraig, co. Lanark, and had issue.

Edmonstone —*continued.*

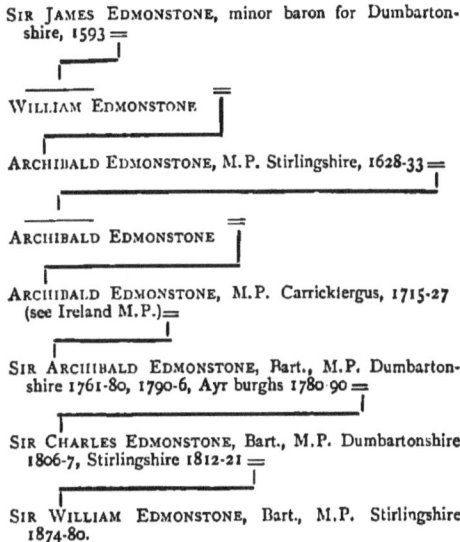

SIR JAMES EDMONSTONE, minor baron for Dumbartonshire, 1593 =

WILLIAM EDMONSTONE =

ARCHIBALD EDMONSTONE, M.P. Stirlingshire, 1628-33 =

ARCHIBALD EDMONSTONE =

ARCHIBALD EDMONSTONE, M.P. Carrickfergus, 1715-27
(see Ireland M.P.)=

SIR ARCHIBALD EDMONSTONE, Bart., M.P. Dumbartonshire 1761-80, 1790-6, Ayr burghs 1780 90 =

SIR CHARLES EDMONSTONE, Bart., M.P. Dumbartonshire
1806-7, Stirlingshire 1812-21 =

SIR WILLIAM EDMONSTONE, Bart., M.P. Stirlingshire
1874-80.

Archibald (sir), of Duntreath, bart. —— *Dumbartonshire* 1761-8 (then younger),
1768-74, 1774-80 (then a baronet) ; *Ayr burghs* 1780-4, 1784-90 ; *Dumbarton-*
[shire 1790-6.

     Sir Archibald Edmonstone, Bart. (son of Archibald Edmonstone, of Duntreath), so cr.
20 May 1774 ; b. 10 Oct. 1717 ; d. 20 July 1807 ; having m. 1st, Oct. 1753, Susannah, dau. of
Roger Harenc, esq., of Foots Cray, Kent ; she d.   ; he m. 2ndly, Hester,
dau. of Sir John Heathcote, Bart., of Normanton Park, Rutland ; she d. s.p.
     [1796 ; by his 1st wife he had with other issue Sir Charles, M.P., next named.

Charles (sir), of Duntreath, bart. —— *Dumbartonshire* 1806-7 (younger) ; *Stirling-*
[shire 1812-18, 1818-20, 1820 until his death s. b. 24 May 1821.

     2nd baronet (eldest surviving son of Sir Archibald, M.P., last named), one of the six clerks
in Chancery 1797-1807 ; b. 9 Oct. 1764 ; d. 1 April 1821 ; having m. 1st, June 1794, Emma,
5th dau. of Richard Wilbraham-Bootle, esq. (E. LATHOM) ; she d. 30 Nov. 1797, leaving
him a son and successor ; he m. 2ndly, 4 Dec. 1804, Hon. Louisa Hotham, youngest dau. of
Beaumont, 2nd Lord Hotham ; she d. 20 Aug. 1840, having (re-married Feb. 1832 to
     [Charles Woodcock, esq.), had with other issue Sir William, M.P.

(James), laird of Duntreath —— sat as a minor baron for Dumbartonshire 1593.

     Sir James Edmonstone (only surviving son of Sir William Edmondstone, of Duntreath,
whose will bears date 1 March 1580) ; justice deputy under the Earl of Argyll 1578 ; tried
for high treason, but pardoned ; m. 1st Helen, dau. of Sir James Stirling, of Keir, and 2nd
in 1585, Margaret, dau. of Sir John Colquhoun, of Luss, and d. about 1618, having had issue

Edmonstone—*continued*.

William (sir), of Colzium House, Kilsyth, co. Stirling —— *Stirlingshire* 1874-80.
[See foot-note.

Eizat.

Alexander —— *Culross* 1643 conv.

Elcho. See also **Wemyss.**

Francis Wemyss Charteris, commonly called Lord —— *Haddingtonshire* 1847-52, 1852-7 (a lord of the treasury 1853), 1857-9, 1859-65, 1865-8, [1868-74, 1874-80, and since 1880 (see also England M.P.)

> Lord Elcho, eldest son of Francis, 8th Earl of Wemyss (see Foster's Peerage), B.A. Oxon., LL.D. Edinburgh, a lord of the treasury 1852-5, M.P. East Gloucestershire 1841-6, lieut.-col. commanding London Scottish Volunteers 1859-79, A.D.C. to the Queen, an ensign-general (Queen's body guard) royal company of archers ; b. 4 Aug. 1818, m. and has [issue.

Eliott-Lockhart.

Allan, of Borthwickbrae —— *Selkirkshire* 1846-7, 1847-52, 1852-7, 1857-9, 1859 [until he accepted the Chiltern hundreds, s.b. 1 Aug. 1861.

> Eldest son of William Eliott-Lockhart, M.P., next named ; advocate 1824, J.P., D.L. cos. Lanark and Roxburgh, lord lieut. of Selkirk ; d. 15 March 1878, aged 75, having m. 12 April 1830, Charlotte, 5th dau. of Sir Robert Dundas, bart., of Beechwood, and had 5 sons [and 6 daus.

William, of Borthwickbrae —— *Selkirkshire* 1806-7, 1807-12, 1812-18, 1818-20, [1820-6, 1826-30.

> Eldest, son of John Eliott of Borthwickbrae ; he m. 1792, Marianne, only child of Allan [Lockhart of Cleghorn, co. Lanark, and d. 1832, leaving with other issue Allan, M.P.

EDMONSTONE, Sir William, of Duntreath, co. Stirling, D.L. (1774 G.B.), C.B., M.P. as above, admiral R.N. (retired list 1880), wounded in the Archipelago 1826, superintendent of Woolwich Dockyard 1866-71 ; succeeded his half-brother, Sir Archibald, as 4th baronet, in 1871 ; b. 29 Jan. 1810; m. 13 July 1841, Mary Elizabeth, dau. of late Lt.-Col. John Whittle Parsons, C.M.G , and has with 8 daus. an only son.
(1) Archibald, b. 30 May 1867.
Seats—Duntreath and Colzium, Stirling.
Club—Carlton.

Eliott.

WILLIAM ELIOTT, of Stobs, M.P.
Roxburghshire 1640-51 =

GAVIN ELLIOT =

SIR GILBERT ELIOTT, Bart., M.P.
Roxburghshire 1661-74 =

SIR GILBERT ELLIOT, of Minto,
Bart., M.P. Roxburghshire, 1702-1707 =

SIR WILLIAM ELIOTT, Bart.. M.P. Roxburghshire 1689-93=

SIR GILBERT ELLIOT, Bart., M.P. Roxburghshire 1722-6 =

JOHN, M.P. Cockermouth 1766-8 (see England).

SIR GILBERT ELIOTT, Bart., M.P.
Roxburghshire, 1708-15, 1726-7.

SIR GILBERT ELLIOT, Bart., M.P.
Selkirkshire 1753-65, Roxburghshire 1765-77 =

SIR GILBERT ELLIOT, Bart., M.P. co. Roxburgh 1777-84 (see also England); cr. Earl of Minto =

GILBERT, 2nd Earl, M.P. Roxburghshire 1812-14, as Viscount Melgund =

ADMIRAL SIR GEORGE ELLIOT, K.C.B..M.P. Roxburghshire,1833-1834 =

JOHN EDMOND ELLIOT M.P. Roxburghshire 1837-41, 1847-59.

WILLIAM HUGH, 3rd Earl, M.P. Hythe 1837-41 (see England), Greenock 1847-52, Clackmannan and Kinross-shire 1857-9, as Viscount Melgund =

ADMIRAL SIR GEORGE AUGUSTUS ELLIOT, K.C.B., M.P. Chatham (see England).

ARTHUR RALPH DOUGLAS ELLIOT, M.P. Roxburghshire since 1880.

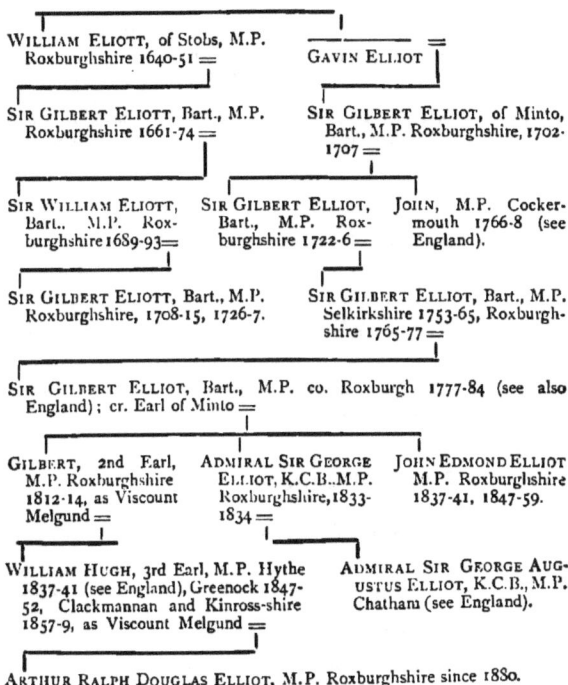

Gilbert (sir), of Stobs, knight and bart. —— *Roxburghshire* 1661-3 (knight), [1667 conv., 1669-74 (bart.)

Sir Gilbert Eliott, of Stobs, bart., so created 3 Dec. 1666, (son of William Eliott, of Stobs, M.P.), knighted at Largo 14 Feb. 1651; m. twice, and had (with other issue, see [Foster's Baronetage), a son, Sir William, M.P.

Gilbert (sir), of Stobs, bart. —— *Roxburghshire,* 1708-10, 1710-13, 1713-15, [1726-7.

3rd baronet on the death of his father, Sir William, M.P.; d. 27 May 1764, having m. Eleanor, dau. of William Eliot, of Wells, Roxburghshire; she d. 1728, leaving with other issue a son, Sir John, 4th bart., and a son, Genl. Sir George Augustus Eliott, K.B , the celebrated governor [and defender of Gibraltar, created Lord Heathfield.

William, of Stobs —— *Roxburghshire* 1640-1, 1643 conv., 1645-7 (the laird), 1650-1 (the laird).

Eldest son of Gilbert Eliott, of Stobs, whose 2nd son, Gavin, was ancestor of the Earl of Minto, etc.; he m. Elizabeth, dau. of Sir James Douglas, of Cavers, and had with other issue [a son, Sir Gilbert, M.P., cr. a baronet.

SCOTCH MEMBERS. Q

Eliott—*continued.*

William (sir), of Stobs, bart. —— *Roxburghshire* 1689 conv., 1689 until 25 April 1693, when his seat was declared vacant because he had not taken the [oath of allegiance and signed the assurance.

2nd baronet (eldest son of Sir Gilbert Eliott, of Stobs), baronet, M.P.; m. Margaret, dau. of Charles Murray, of Haldon, esq., and d. 1694, leaving with other issue, Sir Gilbert, M.P. [1708-15.

Ellice.

Edward, of Invergarry —— *S. Andrews burghs* 1837-41, 1841-7, 1847-52, 1852-7, [1857-9, 1859-65, 1865-8, 1868-74, 1874-80.

Of Invergarry, co. Inverness, J.P. D.L., J.P. cos. Banff and Fife, M.A. Trin. Coll. Camb. 1831; contested Inverness 1835, M.P. Huddersfield May to Aug. 1837 (see England); (eldest son of late right hon. Edward Ellice, M.P. Coventry 1832-63); d. 2 Aug. 1880, aged 70, having m. 1st,   1834, Catherine Jane, dau. of Lieut.-Genl. Robert Balfour, of Balbirnie, she d.   1864; he m. 2ndly,   1867, Eliza Stewart, dau. of late Thomas Campbell Hagart, esq., of Bantaskine, co. Fife, and widow of Alexander [Spiers, esq., of Elderslie, co. Renfrew.

Elliot.   See also Visct. Melgund.

Arthur Ralph Douglas (hon.) —— *Roxburghshire* since 1880.

2nd son of William, 3rd Earl of Minto, B.A. Trin. Coll. Cambr. 1868, M.A., in due course; [bar.-at-law, I.T. 1870; b. 17 Dec. 1846. See Foster's Peerage.

George, capt. R.N. —— *Roxburghshire* 1833-4.

Adm. the Hon. Sir George Elliot, K.C.B. (2nd son of Gilbert, 1st Earl of Minto, see below); genl. of the mint in Scotland, and a lord of the Admiralty; contested Roxburghshire 1835; b. 1 Aug. 1784; d. 24 June 1863; having m. Dec. 1810, Eliza Cecilia, dau. of James Ness, esq., of Osgodby, co. York; she d. 23 May 1848, having had with other issue a son, [Adml. Sir George Augustus Elliot, K.C.B., M.P. See England.

Gilbert (sir), of Minto and Headshaw, knt., bart. —— *Roxburghshire* 1702-7.

Son of Gavin Elliot, of Grange; declared guilty of treason, and forfeited, 16 July 1685, for being accessory to the rebellion of 1679, rescinded by act of parlt. 22 July 1690, and knighted, clerk P.C.; created a baronet of Nova Scotia 19 April 1700, lord of session with the title of Lord Minto, 28 June 1705, and a lord of justiciary; d. 1 May 1718, having m. twice, and left with other issue Sir Gilbert, M.P., next named, and John, M.P. Cockermouth. [See England.

Gilbert (sir), of Minto, bart. —— *Roxburghshire* 1722, until appointed to [Crown office of profit s.b. 6 July 1726.

2nd baronet, advocate 26 July 1715, a lord of session 4 June 1726, a lord of justiciary 13 Sept. 1733, justice clerk 3 May 1763 until his death 16 April 1766, aged 73, leaving with [other issue Sir Gilbert, M.P., next named.

Elliot—*continued.*

Gilbert (sir), of Minto, bart. —— *Selkirkshire* 1753-4, 1754-61, styled "the younger" (a lord of the Admiralty 1756), 1761 (treasurer of the chamber 1762) until accepted Chiltern hundreds s.b. 13 June 1765; *Roxburghshire* 1765-8 (keeper of the signet for Scotland 1767), 1768-74 (treasurer of the [navy 1770), 1774 until his death 11 Feb. 1777.

3rd baronet ; d. 11 Feb. 1777 ; having m. 14 Dec. 1746, Agnes, dau. of Hugh Dalrymple-Murray-Kynynmound, esq., heiress of Melgund, co. Forfar, and of Lochgelly and Kynyn-[mound in Fife ; she d. 1778, leaving with other issue Sir Gilbert, M.P., cr. Earl of Minto.

Gilbert (sir), of Minto, bart. —— *Roxburghshire* 1777-80, 1780-4.

Sir Gilbert, 4th bart., M.P. Morpeth, Helston, and Berwick-on-Tweed (see England) P.C. 1793 ; viceroy of kingdom of Corsica 1795-7 ; cr. Baron Minto, of Minto, co. Roxburgh, in the Peerage of G. B., 20 Oct. 1797, and by roy. lic. was authorised to bear an aug-mentation to his coat armour, viz., on a chief, the arms of the island of Corsica ; envoy-extraordinary to Vienna 1799 ; president board of control India, 1806 ; gov.-genrl. Bengal 1807-13 ; cr. Earl of Minto and Viscount Melgund, in the Peerage of the U. K., 24 Feb. 1813 ; b. 23 April 1751 ; d. 21 June 1814 (bur. in Westminster Abbey) ; having m. 3 Jan. 1777, Anna Maria, dau. of Sir George Amyand, bart. ; she d. 8 March 1829. having had with 3 daus. 3 sons, viz., Gilbert, 2nd earl (see Visct. Melgund, M.P.), Adml. Sir [George, K.C.B., M.P. (see England), and Hon. John Edmund, M.P.

John Edmund, of Belses, Roxburghshire —— *Roxburghshire* 1837-41, 1847-52, [1852-7, 1857-9.

3rd son of Gilbert, 1st Earl of Minto ; contested Roxburghshire 1841 ; sometime E.I.C.S., secretary of board of control 1847-52 ; b. 30 March 1788 ; d. 4 April 1862 ; having m. 3 Oct. 1809, Amelia, dau. of James Henry Casamajor, esq., of Madras ; she d. 23 July 1872, [leaving issue.

Robert, late bailie —— *Selkirk* 1661-3.

William —— *Selkirk* 1621, 1628-33. —— 1644, 1644-5, 1648.

Elphinstone-Fleeming.

Charles, of Biggar and Cumbernauld, (vice-adml.) —— *Stirlingshire* 1802, [(capt. R.N.) 1802-6, 1806-7, 1807-12, 1832-5.

2nd son of John, 11th Lord Elphinstone ; admiral of the blue 1837; served in the Mediterranean 1794, West Indies 1796, and in East Indies, on French coast 1803, etc.; contested Stirlingshire 1835 ; gov. of Greenwich Hospital 1839 ; assumed the name of Fleeming 1799 ; d. 30 Oct. 1840, having m. June 1816, Catalina Paulina Alesandro (she re-m. 1849, to Capt. James Edward Katon, R.N.), and had with 3 daus., a son John, 14th [Lord Elphinstone, who d. unm. 13 Jan. 1861.

Elphinstone.

George —— *Glasgow* 1583.

George Keith (sir), K.B. —— *Dumbartonshire* 1781-4 (chamberlain and sec. of the principality of Scotland 1783), 1784-90; *Stirlingshire* 1796, until created [an English peer 15 Dec. 1801.

> Baron Keith, of Stonehaven Marischal, co. Kincardine, in the Peerage of Ireland 16 March 1797, so cr. with remainder to the male issue of his daughter ; cr. a peer of the United Kingdom, as Baron Keith, 15 Dec. 1801, also Baron Keith of Banheath, co. Dumbarton, with remainder to his daughter ; further advanced 1 June, 1814, to the dignity of Viscount Keith (4th son of Charles, 10th Baron Elphinstone), G.C.B.; invested 1794, installed 1803, F.R.S. 1790, admiral of the blue 1801, commanded the naval forces at the capture of the Cape of Good Hope, admiral of the white 1805, keeper of signet and councillor of state for Scotland, treasurer and comptroller of the household to Duke of Clarence ; d. 10 March. 1823, aged 76, having m. 1st, 9 April, 1787, Jane, dau. and sole h. of William Mercer, of Aldie, co. Perth ; she d. 12 Dec. 1782, leaving a dau. Margaret, who succeeded as Baroness Keith (see Foster's Peerage). He m. 2ndly, 10 Jan. 1808, Hester Maria, eldest dau. and co-h. of Henry Thrale, of Streatham, co. Surrey, she [d. 31 March, 1757, leaving an only dau.

James —— *Inverurie* 1669-74.

> Of Glack (eldest son of James Elphinstone, also of Glack); admitted a burgess of [Inverurie 1671, dead before 1676 ; uncle of Sir James, next named.

James (sir), of Logie —— *Aberdeenshire* 1693-1702.

> Sir James [eldest son of William Elphinstone, of Milntown of Durno (2nd son of James, of Glack, aforesaid), by his wife, Margaret Forbes], acquired Logie Durno about 1670 ; writer to the Signet 1671, a judge of the commissary court of Edinburgh 1696, with remainder to his son ; cr. a baronet 2 Dec. 1701, "for his pure zeall to King William's government," a commissioner of the Signet 1720 ; d. March 1722, having m. Cecilia, dau. of John [Denholm, of Muirhouse (son of West Shield), and had a son and dau.

Richard, of Airth —— *Stirlingshire* 1681-2.

> Eldest son of Sir Thomas Elphinstone of Calder hall, muster master general of Scotland ; in November 1672 deputy keeper of privy seal, major Earl of Mar's regt. of Militia 1678, in which year he succeeded his father as muster master general ; sold Calder hall in 1677 ; b. 3 Oct. 1652; m. 14 Dec. 1674, Jean Bruce, heiress of Airth; she d. 20 March, 1683, having [had issue.

Enterkine.

(David Dunbar), laird of —— *Ayrshire* 1625 conv.

Erskine. See also Loughborough.

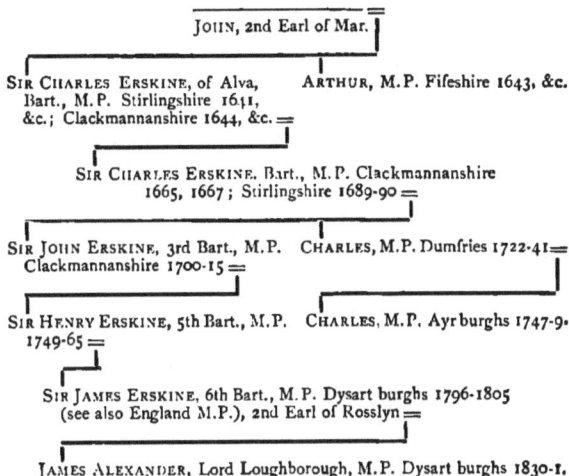

JOHN, 2nd Earl of Mar.

SIR CHARLES ERSKINE, of Alva,   ARTHUR, M.P. Fifeshire 1643, &c.
Bart., M.P. Stirlingshire 1651,
&c.; Clackmannanshire 1644, &c. =

SIR CHARLES ERSKINE. Bart., M.P. Clackmannanshire
1665, 1667; Stirlingshire 1689-90 =

SIR JOHN ERSKINE, 3rd Bart., M.P.   CHARLES, M.P. Dumfries 1722-41=
Clackmannanshire 1700-15 =

SIR HENRY ERSKINE, 5th Bart., M.P.   CHARLES, M.P. Ayr burghs 1747-9.
1749-65 =

SIR JAMES ERSKINE, 6th Bart., M.P. Dysart burghs 1796-1805
(see also England M.P.), 2nd Earl of Rosslyn =

JAMES ALEXANDER, Lord Loughborough, M.P. Dysart burghs 1830-1.

Alexander (sir), of Dune —— *Forfarshire* 1630 conv. (the laird), 1639-41, 1645 [(the laird).

Alexander (sir), of Cambo, knight and baronet, lyon king-of-arms —— *Fifeshire* [1710-13, 1713-15.

2nd baronet on the death of his father, Sir Charles Erskine, who was also lord lyon king-of-arms; served heir of his father 12 Oct. 1686, lord lyon 27 July 1681 (the day of his coronation), had a grant of the office of lord lyon to himself and his son 29 Jan. 1702, a joint keeper of the signet 1711, joined the Earl of Mar in the rebellion of 1715, surrendered himself and was imprisoned in Edinburgh Castle; d. 1735, aged 70, having m. 1680, his cousin, Lady Mary Erskine, eldest dau. of Alexander, 6th Earl of Kellie, and had issue; his great-grandson, Sir Charles, became 8th Earl of Kellie 1797, on whose death, 1799, his uncle Thomas succeeded as 9th Earl, and on his death s.p. 7 Feb. 1828, his brother Methven [became 10th Earl, and also d. s.p. the year following, when this line terminated.

Arthur, of Scotscraig —— *Fifeshire* 1643-4 conv., 1645 (the laird), 1648-9.
Sir Arthur Erskine, of Scotscraig, 6th son of John, 2nd Earl of Mar, K.G.

Charles (sir), of Cambuskenneth —— *Stirlingshire* 1641; (of Bandeath) *Clack-* [*mannanshire* 1644, 1649-50; *Stirlingshire* 1650.

4th son of John, 2nd Earl of Mar, K.G. (by his 2nd wife, Mary Stewart, 2nd dau. of Esmé, Duke of Lennox); d. in Edinburgh 8 July 1663, bur. at Alva, having m. 1639, Mary, eldest dau. of Sir Thomas Hope, of Craighall, bart., and had with other issue a son, Sir [Charles, M.P.

Erskine—*continued.*

Charles (sir), of Alva and Cambuskenneth —— *Clackmannanshire* 1665 conv., 1667 conv. ; *Stirlingshire* 1689 conv., 1689 until his death s.b. 4 June 1690.

Sir Charles Erskine, of Alva (son of Sir Charles, M.P., aforesaid) ; b. 4 July 1643 ; cr. a baronet 30 April 1666 ; he m. Christian, dau. of Sir James Dundas, of Arniston, knt., and [had with other issue 2 sons, Sir John, M.P., and Charles, M.P., next named.

Charles, of Barjarg —— *Dumfries-shire* 1722-7 (an officer of the crown 1725), 1727-34 (styled " master "), 1734-41 (lord advocate 1737) ; as burgess and provost of Lochmaben he was also returned for the *Dumfries burghs*, but elected to sit for the shire ; returned 1741 for the *Wick burghs* (then of Tinwald [and lord advocate for Scotland) ; this election was however declared void.

Charles Erskine, of Tinwald, Dumfries, and of Alva ; advocate 1711 ; M.P. Dumfries 1722, 1727, 1734 ; solicitor-gen. Scotland 1725, lord advocate 1737, a lord of session, with title of Lord Tinwald, 29 Nov. 1742, lord justice clerk for life 1748 (son of Sir Charles, last named) ; d. 5 April 1763, aged 83 ; having m. 1st, 21 Dec. 1712, Grizel Grierson, heiress of Barjarg, co. Dumfries ; he m. 2ndly, 26 Aug. 1753, Elizabeth, dau. of William Harestanes, esq., of Craigs, Kirkcudbright, relict of Dr. William Maxwell, of Preston ; she d. 24 Oct. 1806, aged 90. By his first wife he had with other issue a son, Charles, M.P., [next named.

Charles, counsellor-at-law —— *Ayr burghs* 1747 until his death s.b. 29 Dec. 1749.

Admitted to the Middle Temple 24 Aug. 1733, and to Lincoln's Inn 22 June, 1743 (eldest [son of the preceding Charles, Lord Tinwald) ; b. 23 Oct. 1716 ; d. unm. 25 June 1749.

David, of Dun —— *Forfarshire* 1689 conv., 1689 until his death s.b. 26 May, [1698.

Father of David Erskine, of Dun, ordinary lord of session 1710, and of justiciary 1714, who d. 26 May 1725, aged 85.

Henry (major-gen. sir), of Alva, bart. —— *Ayr burghs* 1749-54 ; *Anstruther Easter burghs* 1754-61 (keeper of the king's private roads, gates, and bridges, and conductor or guide of his royal person in all the royal progresses 1757), 1761, then a maj.-gen. (secretary of the Order of the Thistle 1765) until his [death s.b. 17 Jan. 1766.

Sir Henry Erskine, 5th bart., lieut.-gen. in the army, D.Q.M.G. with rank of lieut.-col. of forces commanded by his uncle, Gen. the Hon. James St. Clair, on the expedition to Port l'Orient, where he was wounded, 21 Sept. 1746, etc. ; commanded royal Scots 1762 (son of Sir John Erskine, bart., M.P.) ; d. 9 Aug. 1765 ; having m. 1761, Janet, dau. of Peter Wedderburn, of Chesterhall, above-named, and sister of Alexander, Earl of Rosslyn, high chancellor of Great Britain ; she d. June 1767, having had with other issue a son, Sir James, [6th bart., G.C.B., M.P. ; succeeded as 2nd Earl Rosslyn 3 Jan. 1805

Erskine—*continued.*

Henry, lord advocate of Scotland —— *Haddington burghs* 1806; *Dumfries* [*burghs* 1806-7.

Hon. Henry Erskine, of Amondell, co. Linlithgow (brother of David, 11th Earl of Buchan, and of Thomas, lord chancellor of England, cr. Lord Erskine; sons of Henry David, 10th Earl of Buchan), advocate 1768, king's advocate 1783, dean of the faculty of advocates 1786, etc., etc., lord advocate of Scotland 1783-4, 1806-7, and state counsellor of the Prince of Wales for Scotland; b. 1 Nov. 1746; d. 8 Oct. 1817; having m. twice, and had with other [issue a son, Henry David, 12th Earl of Buchan.

James (advocate), of Grange —— *Aberdeen burghs* 1715, unseated 22 July same [year, *Clackmannanshire* 1734-41; *Stirling burghs* 1741-7, then advocate.

Hon. James Erskine, 2nd son of Charles, 5th Earl of Mar; advocate 1705, lord Grange of session 1707-34, lord justice clerk 1710-14, sec. to the Prince of Wales; d. in London 24 Jan. 1754; having m. Rachel, sister of Major Chiesly, of Dalry; their grandson, John Francis, [succeeded as 7th Earl of Mar.

James St. Clair (sir), of Sinclair, bart. —— *Dysart burghs* 1796-1802, 1802 [until he succeeded as 2nd Earl Rosslyn 2 Jan. 1805.

Lt.-Gen. Sir James St. Clair-Erskine, 6th bart., G.C.B., P.C., D.C.L. (son of Lt.-Gen. Sir Henry Erskine, 5th bart., M.P.), succeeded as 2nd Earl Rosslyn on the death of his uncle, Alexander (Wedderburn), 1st earl, 3 Jan. 1805; assumed by R.L. 9 June 1789 the additional name of St. Clair on succeeding to his cousin Col. Paterson St. Clair, and the arms by R.L. 14 Feb. 1805; M.P. Castle Rising 1782-4, Morpeth 1784-90, 1790-6 (see England); director of chancery in Scotland 1785 for life, lord president of the council 1834-5, counsellor of state to the king in Scotland, lord-lieut. Fifeshire, lieut.-gen. 1814, col. 9th regt., served at Minorca, at the siege of Copenhagen, and in the Zealand expedition, etc.; d. 18 Jan., 1837, aged 75; having m. 1790, Henrietta Elizabeth, eldest dau. of Hon. Edward Bouverie, M.P. (E. RADNOR); she d. Aug. 1810, leaving with other issue James Alexander, Lord Lough- [borough, M.P. 1830-1. See Foster's Peerage.

John, of Dun—— *Montrose* 1563 (provost), 1567, 1568, 1569 conv., then provost.

Probably son of John Erskine, of Dun, superintendent of Angus and Mearns, (the celebrated reformer,) by his wife Elizabeth, youngest dau. of David, 7th Earl of Crawford; query if he [m. Margaret, dau. of James, 5th Lord Ogilvy, of Airly.

John, of Balgony —— *Stirlingshire* 1630 conv.

Query father of Sir John Erskine, of Balgonie, who m. Margaret, dau. of Sir Charles [Halket, bart., of Pitferran.

John (sir), of Alva, knt. baronet —— *Clackmannanshire* 1700-2; *Burntisland* 1702-7, sat in the 1st parlt. of Great Britain 1707-8, *Clackmannanshire* [1713-15.

Sir John Erskine, 2nd bart (son of Sir Charles, M.P.), advocate 1700; d. 12 March, 1739, aged 67, having m. Hon. Catherine St. Clair, 2nd dau. of Henry, Lord Sinclair, and had with [other issue, Sir Henry, bart,.M.P.

Erskine—*continued.*

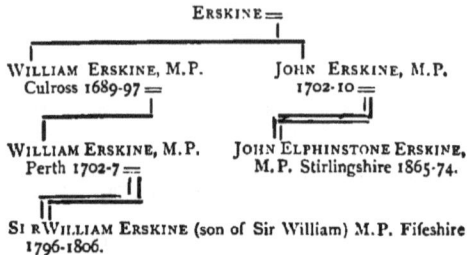

ERSKINE =

```
                    |
    ┌───────────────┴───────────────┐
WILLIAM ERSKINE, M.P.          JOHN ERSKINE, M.P.
Culross 1689-97 =                  1702-10 =
    ┌───────┘                         ║
WILLIAM ERSKINE, M.P.          JOHN ELPHINSTONE ERSKINE,
Perth 1702-7 =                 M.P. Stirlingshire 1865-74.
    ║
SIR WILLIAM ERSKINE (son of Sir William) M.P. Fifeshire
1796-1806.
```

John (col.), deputy governor of Stirling Castle, merchant burgess —— *Stirling* 1702-7 (lieut.-col.), sat in 1st parlt. of Great Britain 1707-8; *Stirling burghs* [1708-10 (col.).

John Erskine, of Carnock, co. Fife, commander of a company of foot under the Prince of Orange, whom he accompanied to England at the Revolution of 1688, and by whom he was appointed lieut.-gov. of Stirling Castle; a lieut.-col. of foot, and gov. of Dumbarton Castle (son of David, 2nd Lord Cardross, by his 2nd wife, Mary Bruce, of Carnock); b. at Cardross 30 March 1662; d. at Edinburgh 13 Jan. 1743, having m. 1st, 14 March 1690, Jane, dau. and heir of William Mure, of Caldwell, co. Renfrew; she d. s.p. in May 1689. He m. 2ndly, 5 Jan. 1691, Anna, elder dau. and co-h. (with her sister the Countess of Bute) of William Dundas, of Kincavel, co. Linlithgow; she d. 29 June 1723. He m. 3rdly, 28 April, 1725, Lillias, eldest dau. of Sir John Stirling, of Keir, and widow of John Murray, of Touchadam and Polmaise; she d. s.p. 27 March, 1729. He m. 4thly, 25 Nov. following, Mary, dau. of Charles Stuart, of Dunearn; she d. 12 Sept. 1772, having had an only son [Charles, who predeceased her. By his 2nd wife, Anna Dundas, he had 6 sons and a dau.

John Elphinstone (vice admiral), of London —— *Stirlingshire* 1865-8, 1868-74.

Admiral R.N. 1869, commanded the channel squadron 1859-64, A.D.C. to the Queen 1856-7 (son of David Erskine, of Cardross, who was great-grandson of John Erskine, M.P., [last named); b. 13 July 1806.

Thomas (sir) —— sat as a minor baron in convention 1602.

Sir Thomas Erskine, K.G. (son of Sir Alexander, of Gogar, governor of Edinburgh Castle, P.C. vice-chamberlain of Scotland 1580), killed Alexander Ruthven, brother of the Earl of Gowrie, on the treasonable attempt on the person of James VI. at Perth, 1600; cr. Baron of Dirleton 1603, and Viscount of Fentoun by patent 18 May 1606, being the first raised to that degree of nobility in Scotland, with remainder in default of issue male to his heirs male whatsoever, and was cr. Earl of Kellie 12 March 1619, with remainder to his heirs male [whatsoever, bearing the name of Erskine; he d. 12 June 1639, having had an only son.

Thomas —— *Stirling burghs* 1728-34 (appointed to a crown office of profit [1729); *Stirlingshire* 1747; *Clackmannanshire* 1747-54:

Elder son of John, attainted Earl of Mar; capt. in the army 1729, commissary of stores at Gibraltar; d. s.p. at Gayfield, 16 March 1766, having m. 1 Oct. 1741, Lady Charlotte Hope, [8th dau. of Charles, 1st Earl of Hopetoun, she d. 24 Nov. 1788.

Erskine—*continued.*

(Thomas), laird of Pittodrie —— *Aberdeenshire* 1630 conv

Succeeded 1625 ; m. Isabel, dau. of Alexander Seton, of Meldrum, and had issue (? the
[next named M.P.)

—— laird of Ballhaggardie —— *Aberdeenshire* 1644.

Query if identical with Thomas Erskine, of Pittodrie, who m. 1643, Helen, dau. of Sir
[William Auchinleck, of Balmanno, and had issue.

William (Mr.), son of the deceased David, Lord Cardross —— *Culross* 1689
nv., 1689 until his death, s.b. 15 May 1697.

William Erskine, of Torry, co. Aberdeen, col. in the army, deputy-gov. of Blackness
Castle (brother of John Erskine, M.P., gov. of Stirling Castle) ; m. Magdalen, dau. of Sir
[James Lumsden, of Innergelly, Fife, and had with other issue a son William, M.P.

William, capt. royal regt. North British dragoons —— *Perth burghs* 1722-7,
[seated on petition.

Col. William Erskine, of Torry, lieut.-col. commanding 7th regt. dragoons at Fontenoy
1745, where he was wounded (son of William, M.P., last named) ; b. 19 May 1691 ;
m. Henrietta, relict of Robert Watson, of Muirhouse, co. Edinburgh, 2nd and youngest
dau. of William Baillie, esq., of Lamington, and had with 2 daus. an only son, Sir William
[father of Sir William, M.P.

William (sir), of Torry, baronet —— *Fifeshire* 1796-1802, 1802-6.

Major-Gen. Sir W. Erskine, 2nd baronet (son and heir of Lieut.-Gen. Sir Wm. Erskine,
who was knighted 27 July, 1763, and cr. a baronet 28 July 1791), served in Flanders 1793
and 1794 as major 15th regt. of dragoons, and A.D.C. to his father ; b. 30 March 1770 ;
[d. unm. at Brozas, 13 Feb. 1813.

Evelyn.

Lyndon, of London —— *Wigtown burghs* 1809-12.   See also England and
[Ireland M.P.

Of Keynsham Court, Hereford ; M.P. Dundalk 1813-18, St. Ives 1820-6 ; admitted to
Lincoln's Inn 11 Nov. 1778, bar.-at-law King's Inns, Hilary 1781 (eldest son of Francis
Evelyn, esq., of Dublin) ; m. Elizabeth, dau. of John Pimlot, esq., of Marple and Brad-
[shawe, co. Lanc., and died s.p. 30 April 1839.

Ewart.

John, provost —— *Kirkcudbright* 1661.

Possibly father of the next named.

John, late provost —— *Kirkcudbright* 1689 conv., 1689 until his death, s. b. 28
[Feb. 1700.

Son of John Ewart of Mullock, co. Kirkcudbright, and grandson of John Ewart (who died
[1630) ; he died 1697, leaving issue.

Ewart—*continued*.

William (Mr.), provost —— *Kirkcudbright* 1678 conv.

William, of London —— *Dumfries burghs* 1841-7, 1847-52, 1852-7, 1857-9, [1859-65, 1865-8. See also England M.P.

William Ewart, of Broadleas, Wilts, J.P., D.L. (2nd son of William Ewart, of Liverpool, mercht., by Margaret, dau. of Christopher Jacques, esq., of Bedale, Yorks); educated at Eton; B.A., Ch. Ch. Oxford, 1821; took the university prize for English verse 1819; bar.-at-law M.T. 1827; M.P. Blechingley 1828-30, Liverpool 1830, 1831-7, Wigan 1839-41; d. 23 Jan. 1869, aged 71, having m. 15 Dec. 1829, his cousin Mary Anne, eldest dau. of [George Augustus Lee, esq., of Sing'eton, near Manchester.

Ewing.

Archibald Orr —— *Dumbartonshire* 1868-74, 1874-80, and since 1880. See [foot-note.

James, of Dunoon Castle, lord provost of Glasgow —— *Glasgow* 1833-4. See [also England M.P.

M.P. Wareham 1830-1; contested Glasgow 1835; died 6 Dec. 1853, aged 78; left issue.

ORR-EWING, ARCHIBALD, of Ballinkinrain, co. Stirling, J.P., D.L., and of Lennoxbank, co. Dumbarton, J.P., M.P., as above, J.P. co. Lanark (7th son of William Ewing, of Ardvullan and Dunoon, co. Argyll, and of Glasgow, mercht.); b. 4 Jan. 1819; m. 27 April 1847, Elizabeth Lindsay, only dau. of James Reid, esq., of Berridale, co. Dumbarton, and of Caldercruix, co. Lanark, and has had 5 sons and 2 daus.

(1) William, b. 14 Feb. 1848; m. 18 Nov. 1873, Maud, dau. of Wm. Williams, esq., of Aberpergwm, and widow of Wyndham Lewis, esq., of the Heath and Newhouse, co. Glam.
(2) Archibald Ewart, b. 22 Feb. 1853; m. 30 Oct. 1879, Hon. Mabel Addington, youngest dau. of William Wells, Viscount Sidmouth.
(3) James Alexander, b. 22 March 1857.
(4) John, b. 29 March 1859.
(5) Charles Lindsay, b. 8 Sept. 1860.
(6) Janet Edith, m. 9 Jan. 1878, to Arthur Gray Hazelrigg (eldest son of Sir A. G. Hazelrigg, bart.), major and lieut.-col. R. Scots fusiliers; served in Crimea 1854-5, and in Zulu war 1879, and d. 16 July 1880, leaving a son.
(7) Elizabeth Constance Lindsay, d. 6 Feb. 1878.
*Seats—Ballinkinrain Castle, Killearn, N.B., and Lennoxbank, Jamestown, co. Dumbarton.
Club—Carlton.*

F.

Fairfull or Fairfool.

Norman —— *Anstruther Wester* 1641, 1643 conv. (Farson), 1644 conv., 1644,
[1645-6.

Fairlie.

Alexander, of Braid —— 1597.

Robert, son and heir, m. Margaret, dau. of Alex. Dalmahoy.

Falconer.

Sir Alexander Falconer, M.P. Kincardineshire, 1643-7, cr. Lord Halkertoun	Sir David Falconer, M.P. Kincardineshire, 1667 =	Sir John Falconer, M.P. Kincardineshire 1678-86

Sir Alexander Falconer, M.P. Kincardineshire, 1678.	Sir David Falconer, M.P. Forfarshire, 1685-6.

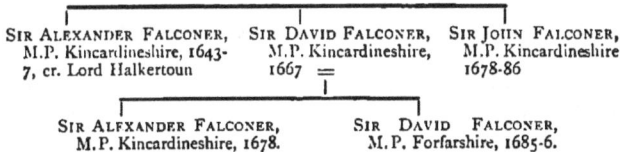

Alexander (sir), of Halkertoun, senator of the college of justice —— *Kincar-*
[*dineshire* 1643-4 conv. ; 1644-5, 1645-7.

Lord Falconer, of Halkertoun, so cr. 20 Dec. 1647 (eldest son of Sir Alexander Falconer, of Halkertoun, by Agnes, eldest dau. of Sir David Carnegie, of Colluthie) ; ordinary lord of session 1639, chosen a judge by the king and parliament Nov. 1641, a commissioner for the plantation of kirks 1644, and a commissioner of exchequer 1645, deprived of his seat in the college of justice 1649, but re-appointed at the Restoration 1660, and continued until his death, 1 Oct. 1671 ; he m. Anne, only child of John, 9th Lord Lindsay, of the Byres, and had [a son and dau.; his line failed on the death of his grandson David, 3rd Lord, Feb. 1724.

Alexander (sir), of Glenfarquhar, knt. and bart. —— *Kincardineshire* 1678 conv.

Created a baronet 20 March, 1670-1 (son of Sir David Falconer. M.P.), the baronetcy ex-
[pired on the death of his son Alexander, 4th Lord Halkertoun 17 March, 1727.

Alexander, merchant trafficker, son of Colin, lord bishop of Moray —— *Nairn*
[1685-6.

[Colin Falconer, bishop of Argyll and Moray, was son of William Falconer, of Dinduff,
[4th son of Sir Alexander Falconer, of Halkertoun 1544.]

David (Mr.) elder, of Glenfarquhar —— *Kincardineshire* 1667 conv.

Sir David Falconer, of Glenfarquhar (brother of Sir Alexander, Lord Halkertoun) ; m. Margaret, dau of —— Hepburn, of Bearford, and had 2 sons, Sir Alexander, M.P., cr. a [baronet, and Sir David, M.P., next named.

Falconer—*continued.*

David (sir), of Newtown, knt., lord president of the session —— *Forfarshire* 1685 [until his death s.b. 12 Jan. 1686.

Sir David Falconer, of Newton, a commissary of Edinburgh, and knighted, lord of session 1676, with title of Lord Newton, a lord of justiciary 1678, president 1682, lord of articles and commiss. of trade ; d. 15 Dec. 1685, aged 46, having m. 1st, Elizabeth, dau. of Robert Nairn, of Muckersy, sister of Robert, 1st Lord Nairn ; he m. 2ndly, 16 Feb. 1678, Mary, dau. of George Norvell, of Boghall, Linlithgow, by whom he had, with 4 daus., 3 sons, [of whom the eldest, David, succeeded as 5th Lord Falconer.

Eliseus —— *Montrose* 1367.

James (sir), of Phesdoe, senator of the college of justice —— *Kincardineshire* [1702 until his death s.b. 19 June 1705.

Said to be son of Sir John Falconer, one of the wardens of the mint, who d. Nov. 1682, but see next entry. Advocate 1674, re-admitted 1676, an ordinary lord at the revolution 1689, [a lord of judiciary 1690 ; d. in Edinburgh 9 June 1705.

John (sir), of Ballnakellie, knt. —— *Kincardineshire* 1678 conv., 1681-2, 1685 [until his death s.b. 18 May 1686.

Master of the mint *temp.* Charles II. (brother of Sir Alexander, M.P., 1st Lord Halkertoun, and also of Sir David, M.P., of Glenfarquhar) ; m. 1st, Esther Briot, and 2nd, Barbara Jaffray, [and had issue.

John, of Phesdoe —— *Kincardineshire* 1734-41.

John Falconer, of Phesdoe, advocate (the last of his line), d. at Leith 21 Nov. 1764, [aged 91, leaving his estate to Capt. the Hon. George Falconer.

Samuel (Mr.) —— *Forres* 1617.

Fall.

James (capt.), merchant, of Dunbar —— *Haddington burghs* 1734-41. Elected [1741 (double return).

Died 25 Dec. 1743; his dau. Janet, d. 17 Feb. 1802, aged 75, having m. 4 Oct. 1750, [to Sir John Anstruther, of Anstruther, bart., who d. 4 July 1799, aged 81

Robert (Faa), merchant burgess, bailie —— *Dunbar* 1693-1702.

Falla.

George, of (Fawla) —— *Edinburgh* 1458.

Fallisdaill.

Thomas —— *Dumbarton* 1600, 1612, 1621.

Falside.

Johne of (Fauside) —— *Edinburgh* 1468.

Farquhar.

James, of Johnstone and Inverbervie —— *Aberdeen* (now *Montrose*) *burghs* 1802, [1802-6, 1807-12, 1812-18. See also Ireland M.P.
Of Johnstone Lodge, co. Kincardine, J.P., D.L., M.P. Portarlington 1824-30, a proctor in Doctors Commons, dep. registrar of the diocese of Rochester, and of Admiralty Court 1810 (2nd son of John Farquhar, of Aberdeen, merchant, by his wife, Rachel Young); b. at Aberdeen, 1 Aug. 1764; d. s.p. in London, 4 Sept. 1833, having m. 19 May 1795, Helen, dau. of Alex. Innes, of Breda and Cowie, commissary of Aberdeen; she d. 19 Feb. 1851, aged 80.

Robert —— *Forres* 1612.

Robert (Mr.), late provost —— *Aberdeen* 1645-7.
Sir Robert Farquhar, of Mounie, a zealous Covenanter, knighted by Charles II.; commissary-general for the northern shires; disponed Mounie in 1633 to Patrick, eldest son of [Alexander Farquhar, of Tonley.

Farquharson.

Archibald, of Finzean —— *Elgin burghs* 1820-6.
Died s.p. 1841, said to be chief of the clan.

Robert, of Finzean, Aboyne —— *Aberdeenshire West* since 1880.
M.D. Edin. 1858, M.R.C.P. London 1872, fellow 1877; assistant physician to St. Mary's Hospital, London, and lecturer; formerly assistant surgeon Coldstream guards, and medical officer to Rugby school (son of Francis Farquharson, of Finzean, Aberdeenshire, and his wife, [Alison Mary Ainslie); b. 1837.

Fergus.

John, of Strathore —— *Kirkcaldy burghs* 1835-7; *Fifeshire* 1847-52, 1852-7, [1857-9.
Of Kirkcaldy, co. Fife, J.P., D.L., merchant and manufacturer (son of Walter Fergus, [provost of Kirkcaldy); d. 23 Jan. 1865.

Ferguson.

George (capt. R.N.), of Pitfour —— *Banffshire* 1833-4, 1835-7.
Rear-Adml. Ferguson (natural son of George Ferguson of Pitfour), J.P., D.L. cos. Banff and Aberdeen, etc.; d. 15 March 1867, aged 81; having m. 1st, 26 May 1812, Elizabeth Holcombe, only dau. and heir of John Woodhouse, esq., of Yatton Court, co. Hereford; he m. 2ndly, 5 April 1825, Hon. Elizabeth Jane Rowley, eldest dau. of Clot-[worthy, 1st Lord Langford; she d. 12 Aug. 1864, leaving issue.

James, of Pitfour —— *Banffshire* 1789-90; *Aberdeenshire* 1790-6, 1796-1802, 1802-6, 1806-7, 1807-12, 1812-18, 1818-20, 1820 until his death s.b. 17 Oct. [same year.
Descended from William Ferguson, M.P. Inverurie 1661-3; d. 6 Sept. 1820, aged 85; son of James Ferguson, of Pitfour, a lord of session, who m. 28 Jan. 1733, Hon. Anne [Murray, dau. of Alexander, 5th Lord Elibank.

Robert —— *Inverkeithing* 1579, 1587.

Ferguson—*continued.*

Robert, of Raith —— *Fifeshire* 1806-7 (younger); *Kirkcaldy burghs* 1831-2, 1833-4; *Haddingtonshire* 1835-7; *Kirkcaldy burghs* 1837 until his death s.b. [27 Jan. 1841

> Lord-lieut. co. Fife (son of William Ferguson, of Raith, by his wife Jane, dau. of Ronald Crawford, esq., of Restalrig); he m. Mary, only child and heir of William Hamilton-Nisbet esq., of Dirleton, co. Haddington (divorced wife of Thomas, 7th Earl of Elgin); he d. s.p.] [3 Dec. 1840, uncle of the next named

Robert (lt.-col.), of Raith —— *Kirkcaldy burghs* 1841, 1841-7 (then younger), 1847-52, 1852-7, 1857-9, 1859 until he accepted the stewardship of the manor [of Hempholme s.b. 25 July 1862.

> Son of Genl. Sir Ronald C. Ferguson, G.C.B., next named ; lt.-col. commanding 79th Highlanders ; succeeded to the estates of Novar, Ross-shire, and Muirtown, Morayshire 1864, when he assumed the additional surname of Munro, J.P., D.L. Ross-shire; b. 20 Aug. 1802; d. 28 Nov. 1868; having m. 7 May 1859, Emma, dau. of late James Henry Mande- [ville, esq., of Merton, Surrey, and had issue.

Ronald Crawford (lt.-gen. sir), of Muirtown, K.C.B. —— *Kirkcaldy burghs,* 1806-7, 1807-12 (brigr-genl.), 1812-18 (major-genl.), 1818-20 (lt.-genl. and [K.C.B.), 1820-6, 1826-30. See also England M.P.

> Genl. Sir Ronald C. Ferguson, G.C.B., col. 79th regt. 1828; M.P. Nottingham 1830-2, 1832-7, 1837 until his death (see England) ; entered the army as ensign 53rd regt. of foot 1790, capt. 1793 ; served in Flanders, at Valenciennes, Dunkirk, etc., wounded ; lt.-col. 2nd batt. 84th regt. at the reduction of the Cape of Good Hope 1794, etc. ; brig.-genl. and commanding York district 1804-5 ; commanded Highland brigade at the recapture of the Cape of Good Hope 1806 ; major-genl. commanding a brigade under Sir Arthur Wellesley ; served at the battles of Roleia and Vimiera ; col. of the Sicilian regt. 1809 ; lt.-genl. 1813, and the following year was appointed 2nd in command of the troops in Holland ; K.C.B. 1815, G.C.B. 183—, genl. 1830 (son of William Ferguson, of Raith, aforesaid); b. in Edinburgh 8 Feb. 1773, and d. 10 April 1841 ; having m. Jean, natural daughter of Genl. Sir Hector Munro, [K.C.B., of Novar, co. Ross, and had a son, Col. Robert, M.P.

William, younger, of Badifurrow —— *Inverurie* 1661-3.

> 2nd son of William Ferguson, in Crichie, bailie in Inverurie, laird of Badifurrow 1655-86; infeft his son William in Badifurrow in 1655 ; he m. 1st, Jean, sister to Sir James Elphin- stone, of Logie (and had a son, James, of Pitfour, great-grandfather of James, M.P.); he m. [2nd, Lucretia Burnett.

Ferguson-Davie.

Henry Robert (genl. sir), of Creedy, bart. —— *Haddington burghs* 1847-52, 1852-7, 1857-9, 1859-65, 1865-8, 1868-74, 1874 (then a genl. in the army) until he accepted the stewardship of the manor of Northstead, co. York, s.b [3 Aug. 1878.

> J.P., D.L. Devon, J.P. Somerset ; col. 73rd regt. since 1865 (retired list 1877); cr. a baronet 9 Jan. 1847 ; assumed the additional surname and arms of Davie by R.L. 9 Feb- [1846; m. and has issue. See Foster's Baronetage.

Fergusson,

Adam (sir), of Kilkerran, bart. —— *Ayrshire* 1774-80, 1781-4 (a commissioner [for trade and plantations 1781); *Edinburgh city* 1784-90 ; *Ayrshire* 1790-6.

3rd bart., LL.D. (son of Sir James, M.P., 2nd bart., a lord of session) ; claimed the Earldom [of Glencairn, etc., 1796 ; d. s.p. 23 Sept. 1813. aged 81. See Foster's Baronetage.

Alexander (Mr.), of Isle, advocate —— *Dumfries* (or *Nithsdale*), *sheriffdom and [stewartry of Annandale* 1702-7.

Admitted advocate 20 Dec. 1685 ; married a dau. of Sir Robert Dalzell, of Glenae, bart.

Alexander, of Craigdarroch —— *Dumfries burghs* 1715-22.

Married Anne, dau. of Sir Robert Laurie, of Maxweltoun, and was ancestor of Rt. Hon. [Robert Cutlar Fergusson, M.P.

James (sir), of Kilkerran, bart. —— *Sutherlandshire* 1734, 1734 until appointed [a lord of session 1736.

2nd bart., advocate 1711, lord of session 7 Nov. 1735, and of justiciary 3 April 1749 as Lord Kilkerran ; d. 20 Jan. 1759, aged 71 ; having m. (contracts dated 3 and 8 Sept. 1726) Jean Maitland, only child of James. Lord Maitland (son of John, 5th Earl of Lauderdale) ; she d. 4 March 1766, leaving with other issue Sir Adam, M.P., 3rd bart., and George, Lord [Hermand of session.

James (sir), of Kilkerran, bart. —— *Ayrshire* 1854-7, 1859-65, 1865-8.

Rt. Hon. Sir James Fergusson, Bart., K.C.M.G., C.I.E. ; governor of Bombay since 1880 ; hon. col. 1873; lt.-col. commandant 1st adm. batt. Ayrshire volunteers 1854-73; late lieut. and capt. grenadier guards ; wounded at Inkerman ; under-secretary for India 1866, home department 1867; governor South Australia 1868-73, and New Zealand 1873-4 ; b. 18 March [1832 ; m. twice, and has issue. See Foster's Baronetage.

John, of Craigdarroch —— *Dumfries sheriffdom and stewartry of Annandale* 1649.

Robert, of Craigdarroch —— *Dumfries sheriffdom and stewartry of Annandale* [1649, 1650, 1651, 1661-3, 1665 conv., 1667 conv., 1669-72, 1678 conv.

Robert Cutlar, of Orroland and Craigdarroch —— *Kirkcudbright stewartry* 1826-30, 1830-1, 1831-2, 1833-4 (advocate-genl. or judge martial of the forces [1834), 1835-7, 1837 until his death s.b. 31 Dec. 1838.

Rt. Hon. Robert C. Fergusson, P.C. 1834 ; barrister-at-law Lincoln's Inn 1797 ; practised at Calcutta, and for a short while acting attorney-genl. there ; judge advocate genl. 1834, 1835-8 ; underwent 12 months' imprisonment in the king's bench prison for attempting to assist O'Connor in his escape during his trial for high treason at Maidstone 1798-9 (son of Alexander Fergusson, of Craigdarroch, advocate) ; d. in Paris 16 Nov. 1838, aged 69; [having m. 17 May 1832, Marie Josephine Auger ; she d. 1 Sept. 1858, leaving issue.

William, of Craigdarroch —— *Dumfries sheriffdom and stewartry of Annandale* [1640-1.

Fife.   See also **Duff** and **Macduff.**

Johnne of —— *Aberdeen* 1456, 1458.

Fife—continued.

James (earl) —— *Banffshire* 1768-74, 1774-80, 1780-4; *Elginshire* 1784-90.

2nd Earl Fife, lord-lieut. co. Banff; cr. Baron Fife in the peerage of Great Britain 19 Feb. 1790; d. s.p. 24 Jan. 1809; having m. 5 June 1759, Lady Dorothea Sinclair, sole [heir of Alexander, 9th Earl of Caithness; she d.   See chart pedigree, p. 106.

James (earl), of the kingdom of Ireland —— *Banffshire* 1818-20 (a lord of the [bedchamber 1819), 1820, 1826 until unseated 2 April 1827.

4th Earl Fife, K.T., G.C.H., K.S.F. of Spain; major-genl. in the Spanish army, wounded at Talavera and Fort Matagorda; lord-lieut. co. Banff; cr. Baron Fife of the United Kingdom 28 April 1827; d. s.p. 9 March 1857; having m. 9 Sept. 1799, Mary Caroline, 2nd dau. of [John Manners; she d. 20 Dec. 1805. See chart pedigree, p. 106.

James (earl), residing at Duff House, co. Banff —— *Banffshire* 1837-57 (see James Duff), 30 March 1857, until he accepted the stewardship of the manor [of Hempholme s.b. 30 June same year.

5th Earl Fife, K.T., lord-lieut. co. Banff 1856-7; cr. Baron Skene, of Skene, co. Aberdeen, in the peerage of the United Kingdom, 1 Oct. 1857; b. 6 July 1814; d. 7 Aug. 1879; having m. 16 March 1846, Lady Agnes Georgiana Elizabeth Hay, dau. of William George, [17 Earl of Erroll; she d. 18 Dec. 1869, leaving issue. See chart pedigree, p. 106.

Fingask or Fingass.

William —— *Dumfries* 1685 until his death s.b. 31 May 1686.

Finlay.

Alexander Struthers, of Castle Toward —— *Argyllshire* 1857-9, 1859-65, 1865 [until he accepted the Chiltern hundreds s.b. 3 March 1868. See foot-note.

Kirkman, lord provost of Glasgow —— *Glasgow burghs* 1812-18. See also [England M.P.

M.P. Malmesbury 1818-20; rector of Glasgow University 1819; m. Janet, dau. of Robert Struthers, and d. at Castle Toward 4 March 1842, aged 74, leaving with other issue a son, [Alexander, M.P.

Finlayson.

John —— *Dundee* 1590 conv., 1594 conv., 1597 conv., bis.

FINLAY, ALEXANDER STRUTHERS, of Castle Toward, co. Argyll, J.P., D.L., and a commissioner of supply, J.P., D.L. Buteshire (5th son of late Kirkman Finlay, M.P.); b. 21 July 1806; m. 3 Jan. 1840, Maria, dau. of Colin Campbell, esq., of Colgrain, Dumbartonshire, and has 2 sons.
 (1) Colin Campbell, b. 12 July 1843.
 (2) Alexander Kirkman, b. 24 Sept. 1844.
Seat—*Castle Toward, Innellan, Greenock, N.B.*
Club—*Union.*

Finnie.

William, of Newfield —— *North Ayrshire* 1868-74. See foot-note.

Fisher.

Thomas —— *Edinburgh* 1599 conv., 1600, 1608.

Fitch.

Thomas (col.) —— co. *Inverness* 1658 (WILLIS). See also England M.P.

Fleming. See also Elphinstone.

James —— *Glasgow* 1569 conv., 1571 conv.

Patrick, of Barochane —— *Renfrewshire* 1628-33.

Robert —— *Edinburgh* 1644 conv.

William —— *Perth* 1567, 1568, 1579 (then bailie), 1587.

Fletcher.

Andrew (sir), Lord Innerpeffer, senator of the college of justice —— *Forfarshire* [1646-7, 1648 (laird of Innerpeffer).

> Ordinary lord of session 18 Dec. 1623; a lord of session 1641; a commissioner of exchequer 1645; one of the committee of estates and of the committee of war for co. Haddington, 1647, and also in 1648 (son of Robert Fletcher, burgess of Dundee); he m. —— dau. of Peter Hay, of Kirkland of Megginch, brother of George, 1st Earl of Kinnoul, [and d. March 1650, leaving issue Sir Robert, father of Andrew, M.P., next named.

Andrew, of Saltoun —— *Haddingtonshire* 1681-2; *Haddington constabulary* [1702-7.

> Son of Sir Robert Fletcher, of Salton, and grandson of Sir Andrew, M.P., lord of session; educated under Bishop Burnet, then parish minister of his native place; when in parliament, he so strongly opposed the measures of the court, that he fled to Holland, whereupon he was outlawed and his estates confiscated; in 1685 he landed in the west of England with Monmouth; afterwards went to Spain, and subsequently fought against the Turks in the Hungarian army; the revolution restored him to his country, etc.; he d. unm. in London 16 Sept. 1716. ROSE's [Biog. Dic.

Andrew, younger, of Salton —— *Haddington burghs* 1747-54 (auditor of the [exchequer in Scotland 1751), 1754-61; *Haddingtonshire* 1761-8.

Nephew of the last named, son of Henry Fletcher, brother and heir of Andrew, M.P.

FINNIE, WILLIAM, of Newfield, Aryshire, J.P., D.L., M.P. as above, LL.B. Trin. Coll., Camb., 1852, barrister-at-law, Inner Temple 1852 (only surviving son of James Finnie, of Newfield, by his wife Marianne, dau. of William Brown, provost of Kilmarnock; b. 6 Nov. 1827; m. 17 March 1853, Antoinette, youngest dau. of George Burnand, esq., of Tewin Water, Herts.
Seats—Newfield, Kilmarnock, N.B.
Clubs—Reform; Western, Glasgow; University, Edinburgh.

Fletcher—*continued.*

George, dean of guild —— *Dundee* 1665 conv.

James, provost —— *Dundee* 1639-41.

James, of Salton —— *Haddington constabulary* 1678 conv.
Possibly a son of Sir Robert Fletcher.

James, merchant bailie —— *Dundee* 1685-6, 1689 conv., 1689 until his death
[s.b. 19 May 1702.

Robert (Flesheour) —— *Dundee* 1596 conv., 1597 conv., 1599 conv.

Focart.

Thomas (Fokert) —— *Edinburgh* 1467 bis.

Forbes.

—— laird of Brux —— *Aberdeenshire* 1621.
Probably descended from a brother of the 1st Lord Forbes.

—— laird of Reresse (Rires) —— *Fifeshire* 1630 conv.
(Elizabeth, dau. of Robert Forbes, of Rires, co. Fife ; m. as 2nd wife to Alexander, 10th
[Lord Forbes.

Alexander, merchant burgess —— *Inverurie* 1678 conv.

Arthur, of Echt —— *Aberdeenshire* 1645-6 (laird), 1649-50.

Arthur (sir), of Craigievar, bart. —— *Aberdeenshire* 1732-4, 1734-41, 1741-7.
4th bart. on the death of his father, Sir William ; d. 1 Jan. 1773, aged 64 ; having m.
1st, 1721, Christina, eldest dau. of —— Ross, of Arnage, provost of Aberdeen, and had
2 daus. ; he m. 2ndly, Margaret, dau of —— Strachan, of Balgall, and widow of John
[Burnett, of Elrich, co. Aberdeen, and had issue.

Duncan, of Culloden —— *Inverness* 1625, 1628-33, 1639-40, 1649.
Purchased the barony of Culloden from the laird of Mackintosh in 1626 ; d. 14 Oct. 1654
aged 82 ; having m. Janet, eldest dau. of James Forbes, of Corsinday, and had with
[issue a son, John, M.P.

Duncan, of Culloden —— *Nairnshire* 1678 conv. (younger), 1681-2 ; *Inverness-
shire* 1689 conv., 1689-1702 ; *Nairnshire* 1702 until his death s.b. 20 June
[1704.

Son of John Forbes, of Culloden, M.P. ; he m. (contract dated 1668) Mary, dau. of Sir
Robert Innes of that ilk, and had with other issue 2 sons, John, M.P., and Duncan, M.P.

Forbes—*continued*.

FORBES OF CULLODEN.

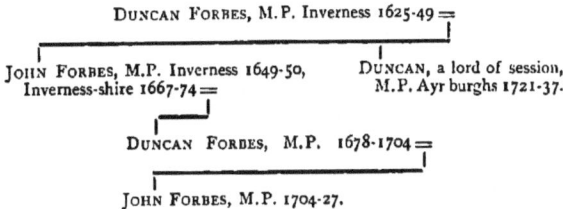

DUNCAN FORBES, M.P. Inverness 1625-49 =

JOHN FORBES, M.P. Inverness 1649-50,
Inverness-shire 1667-74 =

DUNCAN, a lord of session,
M.P. Ayr burghs 1721-37.

DUNCAN FORBES, M.P. 1678-1704 =

JOHN FORBES, M.P. 1704-27.

Duncan, a lord of session —— *Ayr burghs* 1721-7; *Inverness burghs* 1722-7 (then styled "master," king's advocate 1725), 1727-34, 1734 until appointed [president of court of session 1737.

Lord president of the court of session 1737, advocate 1709, sheriff Midlothian, deputy lord advocate 1716, lord advocate 1725, succeeded to the estate of Culloden on the death of his brother John, M.P., in 1735; distinguished for his services in aiding the suppression of the rising of '45; b. at Bunchrew, near Inverness, 10 Nov. 1685; d. in Edinburgh 10 Dec. 1747; [having m. Mary, dau. of Hugh Rose, of Kilravock, and had issue.

Francis, of Thornhill, provost —— *Forres* 1665 conv.

John, of Pitsligo —— *Aberdeenshire* 1612.

Sir John Forbes, of Pitsligo (only son of Alexander Forbes, of Pitsligo); m. Christian, eldest dau. of Walter, 1st Lord Ogilvy, of Deskford, and d. Sept. 1625, leaving a son, Alexander, [cr. Lord Pitsligo.

John, of Leslie —— *Aberdeenshire* 1639-41.

An active Covenanter (2nd son of William Forbes, of Monymusk, and Lady Margaret Douglas); obtained the lands of Leslie about 1620, from George Leslie of that ilk; he m. Jean [Leslie, sister of Patrick, 2nd Lord Lindores, and was succeeded by his son William.

John, of Culloden —— *Inverness* 1649, 1650; *Inverness-shire* 1669-74.

Provost of Inverness (son of Duncan, M.P., 1625, etc.); d. about 1688; having m. (contract dated 1643) Anna, eldest dau. of Alexander Dunbar, of Grange, and had a son, Duncan, M.P.

John, of Culloden —— *Nairnshire* 1704-7 (vice his father, Duncan), 1713-15; [*Inverness-shire* 1715-22; *Nairnshire* 1722-7.

"A commissioner equivalent" (elder brother of Duncan Forbes, M.P., lord president of the court of session); m. (contract dated 1699) Jean, dau. of Sir Robert Gordon, of [Gordonstown, and d. s.p. 1734.

John (sir), of Craigievar —— *Aberdeenshire* 1689 conv., 1689-1702.

2nd baronet (on the death of his father, Sir William, M.P.); m. Margaret, youngest dau. [of the laird of Auldbar, and had with other issue Sir Robert, M.P.

Robert (sir 1703-4), of Learnie, advocate merchant —— *Inverurie* 1700-7.

3rd son of Sir John, M.P., last named; he m. Margaret, dau. of Sir James Elphinstone, [bart., M.P., of Logie Durno.

Forbes—*continued.*

FORBES OF CRAIGIEVAR.

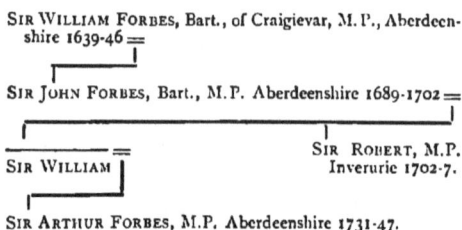

SIR WILLIAM FORBES, Bart., of Craigievar, M.P., Aberdeenshire 1639-46 =

SIR JOHN FORBES, Bart., M.P. Aberdeenshire 1689-1702 =

SIR WILLIAM ==

SIR ROBERT, M.P.
Inverurie 1702-7.

SIR ARTHUR FORBES, M.P. Aberdeenshire 1731-47.

Samuel (sir), of Foveran —— *Aberdeenshire* 1693-1702.

Cr. a baronet 10 Aug. 1700 ; one of his daus. m. —— Chalmers, of Auldbar, and had
issue ; Jean, dau. of Sir Alexander Forbes, of Foveran, m. to Capt. James Macfarlane, and
had issue ; Samuel Forbes, of Knapperny, cousin-german of Sir Alexander Forbes, of Foveran,
bart. ; m. Margaret, dau. of Hew Crawford, of Jordan Hill, and had a son, Sir John Forbes,
[bart.

William (sir), of Craigievar, knt. and bart. —— *Aberdeenshire* 1639-41, 1644
[(the laird), 1645-6.

Cr. a baronet 20 April 1630 ; sheriff of Aberdeen 1647 ; commanded a troop of horse in the
parliamentary service (son of William Forbes, of Edinburgh, merchant, who completed the
building of Craigievar Castle) ; d. 1648 ; having m. Bethia, dau. of Sir Archibald Murray,
of Blackbarony, bart. (she re-m. to Sir Alexander Forbes, knt., of Tolquhoune), and had
[with other issue a son, Sir John, M.P.

William, younger, of Leslie —— *Aberdeenshire* 1649.

Son of John Forbes, M.P., of Leslie ; d. 12 Nov. 1670, aged 55 ; bur. in Leslie kirkyard ;
[having had sons, John and David.

William, of Callendar —— *Stirlingshire* 1835-7, 1837 until unseated, 30 April
1838, 1841-7, 1847-52, 1852 until his death s.b. 5 March 1855.

Vice-lieut. co. Stirling; eldest son of William Forbes, of London, merchant, and of
Callendar and Almond, co. Stirling, by purchase ; d. 10 Feb. 1855, aged 49 ; having m.
14 Aug. 1832, Lady Louisa Antoinette Wemyss, dau. of Francis, Earl of Wemyss.

Forrest.

Henry —— *Linlithgow* 1540 bis, 1544, 1545.

James —— *Jedburgh* 1645.

John —— *Linlithgow* 1583 bis, 1585.

(——) —— *Linlithgow* 1472.

Forrester or Forster.

Alexander (Forster) —— *Stirling* 1524, 1525, 1526 (provost), 1535 (provost).

Forrester or Forster—*continued.*

Alexander, of Garden —— *Stirling* 1569 conv. (then provost).

[Probably a son of Sir Duncan Forrester, of Garden, king's comptroller.]

Alexander —— *Tain* 1643 conv.

Alexander —— *Fortrose* 1672, took the oath of allegiance, and signed the
[declaration 25 June of that year.

Possibly identical with Alexander next named.

Alexander, of Edertaine, late provost —— *Tain* 1672.

David, merchant burgess —— *Whithorn* 1681-2, 1685-6.

Duncan —— *Stirling* 1482, 1488 bis, 1489, 1490, 1491 bis, 1492 bis.

George (sir), of Corstorphine, sheriff —— *Edinburghshire* 1625 conv. (laird)
[1628-33.

Lord Forrester, of Corstorphine, so cr. 22 July 1633, having been cr. a baronet 17 March
1625 (son of Henry Forrester, of Corstorphine, M.P.); he m. Christian, dau. of Sir Wm.
[Livingstone, of Kilsyth, and d. 1654, leaving 5 daus.

George, merchant burgess, councillor —— *Dundee* 1669-74.

Henry, of Corstorphine —— 1597.

Son of James Forrester, of Corstorphine; m. Helen Preston, of the Craigmiller family, and
[had a son, George, Lord Forrester, M.P.

John —— *Tain* 1665 conv. (dean of guild), 1678 conv., 1681-2 (merchant and
[heritor, late bailie), 1685-6.

Matthew (Forster) —— *Stirling* 1468, 1471, 1474, 1476, 1478 bis, 1479.

Robert (Forster) —— *Stirling* 1543.

Robert, of Boquhane —— *Stirling* 1569 conv. (Forster younger), 1578 conv.,
[1585 conv., then provost, 1587 provost.

Forus or Forhous.

John —— *Haddington* 1567, 1568.

Forret.

David —— *St. Andrews* 1599 conv.

James —— *Glasgow* 1600, 1604, 1605 parliament and conv. 1607.

Forsyth.

William —— *Forres* 1621.

Fortrose. See also Mackenzie.

Kenneth Mackenzie, of Seaforth, commonly called lord ——— *Inverness burghs* [1741-7; *Ross-shire* 1747-54, 1754-61.

Eldest son of William, 5th and attainted Earl of Seafield; d. in London 18 Oct. 1761, aged 43; bur. in Westminster Abbey; he m. 11 Sept. 1741, Lady Mary Stewart, eldest dau. of Alexander, 6th Earl of Galloway; she d. 18 April 1751, leaving with 6 daus. an only son, [Kenneth, M.P., next named.

Kenneth Mackenzie, lord visct. of the kingdom of Ireland ——— *Caithness-shire* [1768-1774.

Grandson of William, 5th and attainted Earl of Seafield, and son of Kenneth last named; cr. Baron of Adelve, co. Wicklow, and Visct. of Fortrose, 18 Nov. 1766, and Earl of Seafield 3 Dec. 1771, both in the peerage of Ireland; col. 78th regt. of Highlanders, which he raised; d. on his passage to the East Indies with his regt. Aug. 1781; he m. 7th Oct. 1765, Lady Caroline Stanhope, eldest dau. of William, 2nd Earl of Harrington; she d. 9 Feb. 1767, [aged 20, leaving a dau.

Fothringham.

——— laird of Powrie-Fothringham ——— *Forfarshire* 1621.

David, of Powrie ——— *Forfarshire* 1665 conv.

John ——— *Dundee* 1569 conv.

Thomas ——— 1482 (of Powrie), 1483 (? Dundee), 1484, 1485 (? Dundee).
? if married Elizabeth, eldest dau. of Sir Robert Arbuthnott, of Arbuthnott.

Foulis.

Alexander ——— *Linlithgow* 1469, 1471, 1472, 1474, 1476 bis, 1478 bis, 1479 [bis, 1483, 1484, 1488, 1489.

George ——— *Edinburgh* 1604, 1605, 1607, 1608, 1612, 1617, 1621.

Probably of Ravelstone, 2nd son of James Foulis (M.P. 1594), of Colinton, by his wife, Agnes Heriot, and grandfather of Sir John, of Ravelstone, cr. a baronet 15 Oct. 1661. See [Foster's Baronetage.

James ——— *Edinburgh* 1526.

Sir James Foulis chosen a lord of session 12 Nov. 1526, admitted 27 May 1532; acquired the lands of Colinton from William, Master of Glencairn, in 1519; conjunct advocate with Sir Adam Otterburn 1527, clerk register 1531-48, knighted 1539, one of the commissioners to negotiate a marriage between Mary and Prince Edward 1543, and d. before 4 Feb. 1549; son and heir of James de Foulis, who is said to have been a skinner in Edinburgh, by his wife Margaret, dau. of Sir James (or Thomas) Henderson, of Fordel, co. Fife; grandfather [of James, M.P.

Foulis—*continued.*

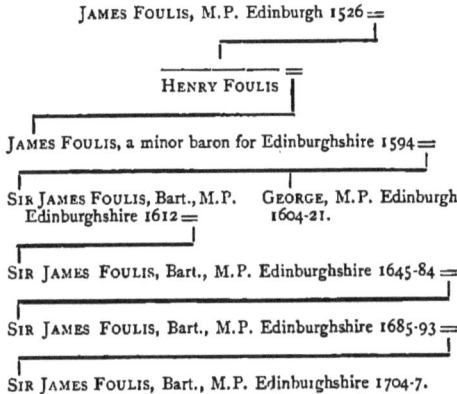

JAMES FOULIS, M.P. Edinburgh 1526 ==

HENRY FOULIS =

JAMES FOULIS, a minor baron for Edinburghshire 1594 ==

SIR JAMES FOULIS, Bart., M.P.   GEORGE, M.P. Edinburgh
Edinburghshire 1612 ==   1604-21.

SIR JAMES FOULIS, Bart., M.P. Edinburghshire 1645-84 ==

SIR JAMES FOULIS, Bart., M.P. Edinburghshire 1685-93 ==

SIR JAMES FOULIS, Bart., M.P. Edinburghshire 1704-7.

(James) laird of Colinton —— a minor baron—*Edinburghshire* 1594.

Son of Henry Foulis, of Colinton; he m. Agnes Heriot, of Lumphoy, and had with other issue Sir James, M.P., George, of Ravelstone, M.P., and Sir David, cr. a baronet 6 Feb.
[1619-20.

James (sir), of Colinton, knt. —— *Edinburghshire* 1612.

Eldest son of James, M.P., last named; m. Mary, dau. of Sir John Lauder, of Hatton, and relict of the laird of Cunninghamehead, and had a son, Sir Alexander, cr. a baronet
[7 June 1634, father of Sir James, M.P., next named.

James (sir), of Colinton —— *Edinburghshire* 1645-7, 1648, 1651 (laird), 1661-3, (then a senator of college of justice), 1665 conv., 1667 conv., 1672-4 (a [baronet), 1678 conv., 1681-2 and until his appointment as clerk register.

Sir James Foulis, 2nd bart. (son of Sir James Foulis, 1st bart.); knighted by Charles I. 14 Nov. 1641; a member of the committee of estates in 1646, etc.; was taken prisoner at Alyth 28 Sept. 1651, by a detachment of Monk's forces; a senator of the college of justice 14 Feb. 1661, a lord of the articles, a lord of justiciary with title of Lord Colville 1671, privy councillor 1674, lord justice clerk 22 Feb. 1684; d. in Edinburgh 19 Jan. 1688; having m.
[twice, and left issue, Sir James, M.P., next named.

James (sir), of Colinton, senator of the college of justice —— *Edinburghshire* 1685-6 (then of Redfoord), 1689 conv. (then of Colinton), 1689 until his seat was declared vacant 25 April 1693, because he had not taken the oath [of allegiance and signed the assurance.

Sir James, 3rd bart. (son of Sir James, 2nd bart., M.P., last named); col. of Midlothian militia, P.C. 1703; ordinary lord of session 10 Nov. 1674, and took his seat as Lord Reidfurd 27th; a commissioner for plantation of kirks 1685; opposed the union; d. 1711; having m. Margaret, dau. of John Boyd, dean of guild of Edinburgh, and had with other issue, a
[son, Sir James, M.P.

Foulis—*continued.*

James (sir), of Colinton, knt. —— *Edinburghshire* 1704-7.

4th bart. (son of Sir James, M.P., last named); d. July 1742.

Fox.

Charles James —— *Wick burghs* and *Westminster* 1784, elected to sit for the
[latter.   See M.P. England.

Fraser.   See also Mackenzie and Mackintosh.

Alexander (sir), of Philorth —— *Aberdeenshire* 1643 conv., 1648 (laird), 1661-3.

Lord Saltoun; Charles II. confirmed this dignity to him by patent dated at Whitehall 11 July 1670 (son of Sir Alexander Fraser, of Philorth); commanded a regt. in the
expedition into England to attempt the rescue of Charles I. 1648 ; wounded at the battle of
Worcester 1651 ; b. March 1604; d. 11 August 1693, aged 90; having m. twice, and left
[issue. See Foster's Peerage.

Alexander (sir), of Duris —— *Kincardineshire* 1669-70.

His dau. Carey m. as 1st wife to Charles Mordaunt, 1st Earl of Monmouth and 3rd Earl
[of Peterborough.

Archibald, of Lovat, vice Simon Fraser deceased —— *Inverness-shire* 1782-4.

Son of the attainted and executed Lord Lovat (by his 2nd wife, Primrose, sister of John,
4th Duke of Argyll) ; consul-general Algiers 1766 ; d. s.p.s. 8 Dec. 1815; father of Simon,
[M.P. 1796. See Foster's Peerage.

Finlay, bailie —— *Inverness* 1669-74.

Hew, of Belladrum —— *Inverness-shire* 1678 conv.

Hugh, younger, of Belladrum —— *Inverness-shire* 1685-6.

James (sir), of Brae —— *Inverness* 1646-7 (the laird), 1649.

4th son of Simon, 7th Lord Lovat.

Robert (Mr.), advocate —— *Wick* 1702-7.

Admitted advocate 6 Feb. 1686.

Simon, lt.-genl. of his most faithful majesty's armies in Portugal —— *Inverness-
shire* 1761-8 (then lt.-col. 78th regt.), 1768-74, 1774-80 (then major-genl.
[and of Lovat), 1780 until his death s.b. 28 March 1782.

Eldest son of the attainted and executed Lord Lovat (by his 1st wife, Margaret, 4th dau.
of Ludovic Grant, of Grant) ; restored in his estates subject to a money payment ; col. of a
regt. which he raised 1757, with which he served in America; brig.-genl. in Portugal ; col.
[71st regt.; died a lt.-genl. 8 Feb. 1782.

Simon, younger, of Lovat —— *Inverness-shire* 1796-1802.

Eldest son of Archibald Fraser, M.P.; d. unm. at Lisbon 6 April 1803, aged 38.

Fraser—*continued.*

Thomas, of Strichen —— *Inverness-shire*, including *Ross* 1639-40.

William, of Culbokie —— *Inverness-shire* 1649, 1650, 1651.

William (hon.) —— *Elgin burghs* **1722** until unseated 23 Jan. 1725.

Advocate 1713, brother of 12th Saltoun, d. 23 March 1727, leaving issue. See Foster's
[Peerage.

Fremantle.

William Henry, of London —— *Wick burghs* 1808-12.   See also England
[and Ireland M.P.

Rt. Hon. Sir William H. Fremantle, G.C.H. 31 Oct. 1827 (uncle of Sir Thomas F. Fremantle, bart., cr. Lord Cottesloe), P.C. 1822, treasurer of the household 1826, deputy keeper of Windsor Great Park 1831-50, A.D.C. to the Marquis of Buckingham when lord-lieut. of Ireland 1782, and subsequently his private secretary, Irish secretary in London 1789-1800, deputy teller of the exchequer, joint secretary to the treasury 1806, a commissioner of board of control India 1822-6, M.P. Enniskillen 1806, Harwich 1806-7, Saltash 1807, Buckingham 1812-27; d. s.p. 19 Oct. 1850, aged 84; having m. 21 Sept. 1797, Selina Mary, only dau. of Sir John Elwill, bart., and widow of Felton Lionel Hervey, esq. (E. BATHURST, etc.);
[she d. 22 Nov. 1841.

Fullarton.

—— of Corsbie —— *Ayrshire* 1643-4 conv., 1648.

James Fullarton of that ilk (son of James Fullarton and his wife Agnes, dau. of John Fullarton, of Dreghorn); head sheriff of Ayr 1645; disclaimed "the remonstrance" June 1651; m. Babare, eldest surviving dau. of John Cuninghame, of Cuninghamehead, and d. 1667,
[leaving issue.

Adam —— *Edinburgh* 1572 conv.

John, of Kinnaber —— *Forfarshire* 1693-1702.

Married Mary, 2nd dau. of Sir Charles Ramsay, 3rd bart., of Balmain.

William (col.), of Fullarton —— *Haddington burghs* 1787-90; *Ayrshire* Nov. 1796-1802, 1802 until appointed a commissioner for the government of the [island of Trinidad s.b. 5 April 1803.   See also England M.P.

Col. 23rd regt. F.R.S., M.P. Plympton 1779-80, Horsham 1793-6, commissioner of Trinidad Jan. to July 1803, " the prosecutor of Genl. Picton " (son of William Fullarton, esq.);
[d. 13 Feb. 1808, aged 54.

Futhie, or Fithie.

Alexander —— *Arbroath* 1651.

Henry, merchant burgess, provost —— *Arbroath* 1667 conv., 1669-74.

Fyfe.   See also Fife.

John, merchant burgess, councillor —— *Elgin* 1681-2.

William (Fyift), bailie —— *Banff* 1681-2.

SCOTCH MEMBERS.   T

G.

Galbraith.

David, of —— 1440.

Edward —— *Edinburgh* 1593 parliament and conv., 1594 conv. bis., 1596 conv.,
[1597.

Garden.

Alexander, of Troup —— *Aberdeenshire* 1768-74, 1774-80, 1780-4, 1784 until his
[death s.b. 28 Feb. 1786.

Eldest son of Alexander Garden, of Troup, by his wife Jean, dau. of Sir Francis Grant, of
[Cullen, bart. ; he d. unm. 1785.

Gardyne.

George, merchant burgess —— *Burntisland* 1639-41, 1644 conv., 1644-7, 1648-9,
[1650-1, 1661 until his death s.b. 21 June 1663.

John (Gardin) —— *Elgin* 1579.

John, of Lautoune —— *Forfarshire* 1667 conv.

Garlies.

Alan Plantagenet Stewart, commonly called lord —— *Wigtownshire* 1868
[until he succeeded as Earl of Galloway 2 Jan. 1873.

10th Earl of Galloway, lord high commissioner to Kirk of Scotland 1876, high commissioner
to general assembly 1857, lt.-col. commandant Ayr and Wigtown militia since 1873, capt.
late royal horse guards ; b. 21 Oct. 1835 ; m. 25 Jan. 1872, Lady Mary Arabella Arthur
[Cecil, 4th dau. of James, 2nd Marquis of Salisbury, K.G. See Foster's Peerage.

Garne.

James —— *Elgin* 1579.

Garoch.

Thomas, merchant burgess —— *Whithorn* 1678 conv.

Gartshore.

Alexander of that ilk —— *Dumbartonshire* 1685-6.

Of Glasgow, merchant, younger brother of Patrick and James Gartshore of that ilk.

Garoch.
Lawrence of —— *Aberdeen* 1357.

Gatmilke.
Robert of —— *Perth* 1357.

Ged or Gedd.
Alexander, bailie —— *Burntisland* 1689 conv. 1689-1702.

William —— *Burntisland* 1670 until his death s.b. 27 Oct. 1673.

Geddie.
James —— *Crail* 1587.

John, of St. Nicholas, bailie, provost —— *St. Andrews (city)* 1667 conv. 1669-74,
[1678 conv. (then provost).

Martin (Mr.) —— *St. Andrews* 1569 conv.

Gellie.
John —— *Fortrose* 1667 conv.

Gibson.
Alexander (sir), of Durie —— *Fifeshire* (1658-9, WILLIS) 1661 until his death
[s.b. 1 Oct. same year.

Died at Durie 6 Aug. 1661, aged 32; having m. 10 June 1651, Hon. Margery Murray, dau.
of Andrew, 1st Lord Balvaird (see Douglas' Peerage, vol. ii., p. 542); she d. 6 Aug. 1667,
having had 2 daus.; son of Sir Alexander Gibson, a senator of the college of justice, who
[d. June 1656.

Alexander —— *Cromarty* 1665 conv.; *Anstruther Easter* 1674.

Probably identical with Sir Alexander Gibson, of Pentland and Adiston (2nd son of Sir
John Gibson, of Pentland); a principal clerk of session and clerk to the privy council of
Scotland; he m. Helen, dau. of Sir James Fleming, of Rathobyres, Midlothian, and had
[issue.

James —— *Linlithgow* 1646-7 (or Robert Bell).

Gibson-Craig.
William, of Riccarton —— *Edinburghshire* 1837-41; *Edinburgh city* 1841-7 (a
[lord of the treasury 1846), 1847-52.

Rt. Hon. Sir William, P.C., 2nd bart. (on the death of his father, Sir James, 6 March
1850), a lord of the treasury 1846-52, lord clerk register 1862-78, and keeper of the signet for
Scotland; b. 2 Aug. 1797; d. 12 March 1878; having m. 29 Aug. 1840, Betsy Sarah, dau.
[of John Henry Vivian, esq., of Singleton, co. Glamorgan (B. VIVIAN), and had issue.

Gilbert.
Michael —— *Edinburgh* 1585.

Gilchrist.

Donald —— *Rothesay* 1649.

John —— *Renfrew* 1587.

Gill.

Johnne —— *Perth* 1357, 1367.

Gilliott.

Alexander (Gylyot) —— *Edinburgh* 1357.

Gillon.

William Downe, of Wallhouse —— *Linlithgow burghs* 1831-2 ; *Falkirk burghs* [1833-4, 1835-7, 1837-41.

Of Wallhouse, co. Linlithgow, and Hurtsmonceux, co. Sussex, J.P., D.L. (only son of Andrew Gillon, of Wallhouse, lt.-col. Scots greys, by his wife Mary Anne, dau. of William Downe, esq., of Downe Hall, Dorset) ; b. 31 Aug. 1801 ; d. 7 Oct. 1846 ; having m. 24 Oct. 1820, Helen Eliza, dau. of John Corse Scott, esq., of Synton, co. Roxburgh, and had issue.

Gilmour.

Alexander (sir), of Craigmiller, knt. and bart. —— *Edinburghshire* 1690-1702.

Cr. a baronet 1 Feb. 1678 ; b. 6 Dec. 1657 ; d. Oct. 1731, aged 74 ; he m. Grizel, dau. of George, 11th Lord Ross ; she d. at Inch 10 June 1732 ; having had with other issue a [son, Sir Charles, M.P.

Alexander (sir), of Craigmiller, bart. —— *Edinburghshire* 1761, 1761-8 (a clerk [comptroller of the household 1766), 1768-74.

3rd and last bart. (son of Sir Charles, M.P., next named) ; served in the foot guards ; d. [unm. in France 27 Dec. 1792.

Charles (sir), of Craigmiller, bart. —— *Edinburghshire* 1737-41, 1741-7 (paymaster of the board of works 1742, a commissioner for trade and plantations [1744), 1747 until his death s.b. 14 Feb. 1750-1.

2nd baronet (son of Sir Alexander, M.P. 1690) ; d. at Montpellier 9 Aug. 1750 ; having m. March 1733, Jean, dau. of Sir Robert Sinclair, bart., of Longformacus ; she d. 1 Feb. [1782, leaving a son, Sir Alexander, M.P.

John (sir), of Craigmiller, knt., president of the session —— *Edinburghshire* [1661-3, 1665 conv., 1667 conv., 1669 until his death s.b. 16 Jan. 1672.

Advocate 1628, nominated lord president of the court of session on the restoration 13 Feb. 1661, and took his seat 1 June in that year, P.C. and a lord of the exchequer, a member of the court of high commission 1664, resigned the presidential chair 22 Dec. 1670 (son of John [Gilmour, W.S.) ; m. four or five times, and d. 1671.

Gladstanes.

Herbert (Glaidstanis) —— *Kirkcudbright* 1579.

Gladstone.

William Ewart, of Hawarden Castle, Flintshire——*Edinburghshire* since 1880.
[See also England M.P.

Rt. Hon. William Ewart Gladstone, P.C. Sept. 1841, B.A. Oxon 1832, M.A. 1834, D.C.L. 1848, prime minister and chancellor of the exchequer since April 1880, of the council of education Scotland 1881, prime minister 1868-74, M.P. Newark 1832-45. Oxford university 1847-65, South Lancashire 1865-68, Greenwich 1868-80 (see England M.P.), D.L. co. Flint, junior lord of the treasury 1834-5, under-secretary for colonies 1835, secretary 1845-6, vice-president board of trade 1841-3, president 1843-5, chancellor of the exchequer 1852-5, 1859-66, 1873-4, lord high commissioner to the Ionian Islands 1858-9, lord rector of Edinburgh university 1859-65, Glasgow university 1877-9, governor of the Charterhouse, a life governor of King's college, London, a student of Lincoln's Inn 1833-9, late a trustee of British Museum (youngest son of Sir John Gladstone, bart.) ; b. 29 Dec. 1809; m. 25 July 1839, Catherine, eldest dau. of Sir Stephen Richard Glynn, bart. (ext.), of Hawarden Castle, [co. Flint, and has 4 sons and 3 daus. See Foster's Baronetage.

Glas.

John —— merchant burgess, provost —— *Perth* 1681-2, 1685-6.

Glasfurd.

Andrew, bailie —— *Cupar* 1685-6.

John —— *Cupar* 1649-50 (or John Jamieson).

Glasgow.

—— the provost of —— *Glasgow* 1560.

Glassford.

Henry, of Dougalston —— *Dumbartonshire* Feb. to Oct. 1806, 1807 until he acc. the stewardship of the manor of East Hendred, Berks, s.b. 13 July 1810.
Died 14 May 1819 ; son of John Glassford, of Dougalstoun, co. Dumbarton, merchant, [by his 2nd wife Anne, dau. of Sir John Nisbet, of Dean, bart.

Glen.

Andrew, merchant, provost (1661) —— *Linlithgow* 1651, 1661-3.

George —— *Linlithgow*, 1641.

James, merchant, provost (1639) —— *Linlithgow* 1625 conv., 1639-41.

Glendoning.

John, bailie —— *Kirkcudbright* 1667 conv., 1669-72 (provost).

Robert, bailie —— *Kirkcudbright* 1665 conv.

William, provost —— *Kirkcudbright* 1628-33, 1639-41 (provost), 1643 conv.,
1645-7, 1648.

Goldsmyth.

Johnne —— *Edinburgh* 1357

Good.

George (Gude) —— *Ayr* 1535, 1545.

Gordon. See also Haddo and Strathnaver.

—— laird of Badenscoth, sat as a minor baron in convention 1605.

Adam (sir), of Dalfolly —— *Sutherlandshire* 1689 conv., 1689 until his death [s.b. 25 Oct. 1700.

> Knighted 1695-6 (son of William Gordon, of Dalpholly, by a dau. of John Cor, of Michael Elphinstone); he m.   dau. of   Urquhart, of New Hall, and d. 21 Sept. 1700, leaving with other issue a son, Sir Wm. Gordon, of Dalpholly, afterwards of Invergordon, [M.P., cr. a baronet 8 Feb. 1704.

Adam (lt.-genl. lord), of Cuttieshillock and Woodtoun —— *Aberdeenshire* 1754-61, 1761-8, Kincardineshire 1774-80 (then major-genl.), 1780-4 (lt.-genl.) [1784, until he acc. the Chiltern hundreds s.b. 19 June 1788.

> 4th son of Alexander, 2nd Duke of Gordon, genl. in the army, col. 1st regt. of foot 1782, gov. of Edinburgh Castle 1796, of Tynemouth Castle 1778, col. 66th regt. 1763, 26th regt. of Cameronians 1775, served in Gen. Bligh's expedition to the court of France 1758, held a command in America 1765, commander-in-chief of the forces in Scotland 1789-98; d. s.p. 13 Aug. 1801, having m. 2 Sept. 1767, Jane, dau. of John Drummond, of Megginch, co. [Perth, dowager of James, Duke of Athole; she d. 22 Feb. 1795.

Alexander, of Erlestoane —— *Kirkcudbright stewartry* 1641.

> Son of John Gordon, of Earlston, by his 2nd wife, served heir to his father 23 Oct. 1628; a staunch royalist, said to have declined a baronetcy in 4 Jan. 1612; m. Elizabeth, dau. of John Gordon, of Pennynghame (grandfather of Alexander, 5th Vict. Kenmure), and d. Nov. 1653; his grandson, Sir William, was cr. a baronet 9 July 1706. See Foster's [Baronetage.

Alexander, of Cluny —— *Aberdeenshire* 1612.

> Sir Alexander Gordon, of Cluny, cr. a bart. 31 Aug. 1625, ? m. 1st Elizabeth, dau. of Sir William Douglas, 9th Earl of Angus; he m. also Violet, dau. of John Urquhart, of Cromarty; and lastly, 22 June 1641, Elizabeth, widow of Sir John Leslie, of Wardes, and [dau. of John Gordon, of Newton; she d. at Durham 2 Dec. 1642.

Alexander —— *Dornock* 1661.

? of the Embo family.

Alexander, provost —— *Aberdeen* 1689 conv., 1689 until his death s.b. 15 April [1693.

Alexander, of Gairthrie —— *Sutherlandshire* 1700-2, 1702-5.

Alexander, of Pitlurg —— *Aberdeenshire* 1702-7.

> Son of Robert Gordon, of Pitlurg, by his wife Jean, dau. of Sir Richard Maitland, Lord [Pitrichie. He m. Jean, dau. of James Gordon, of Ellon, and had a son and dau.

Gordon—*continued.*

Alexander (esq.), of Ardoch —— *Inverness burghs* 1722, 13 April until un-
[sealed 19 Oct. following.

Alexander Hamilton (lt.-genl. sir), of London, K.C.B. —— *East Aberdeenshire*
[1875-80, and since 1880.

General in the army K.L.H. & M. (2nd son of George, 4th Earl of Aberdeen), hon.
equerry to the Queen since 1862, D.Q.M.G. Crimea and 1855-60, comd. a division in
India 1867-70, also the Eastern district England 1871-2, col. 100th regt.; b. 11 Dec. 1817,
[m. and had issue. See Foster's Peerage.

Cosmo, advocate of Cluny —— *Nairnshire* 1774, until appointed a baron of the
[exchequer in Scotland 1777.

Admitted advocate 29 July 1758, Baron of the exchequer 1777, until he died 19 Nov. 1800
[(his younger brother, Alexander of Belmont, Tobago. died at Bath 11 Jan. 1801).

Douglas Gordon-Hallyburton, Lord. See **Halyburton.**

Douglas William Cope (lord), of London, lieut. Coldstream Guards —— *West*
[*Aberdeenshire* 1876-80, Huntingdonshire since 1880. See England M.P.

3rd son of Charles, 10th Marquis of Huntly, and heir presumptive to the titles, lieut. and
[capt. Coldstream Guards 1874-80; contested Hunts 1874; b. 11 Oct. 1851.

Edward Strathearn, Q.C., LL.D. of the University of Glasgow and Dean of
the Faculty of Advocates —— *Glasgow and Aberdeen Universities* 1869-74,
1874 (Queen's advocate for Scotland, March 1874), until appointed a lord
[of appeal in ordinary 17 Oct. 1876. See also England M.P.

Advocate 1835, sheriff of Perthshire 1858-66, solict.-genl. Scotland 1866-7, lord advocate
Scotland 1867-8, 1874-6, M.P. Thetford 1867-8 (see England), lord of appeal 17 Oct.
1876, P.C. (eldest son of John Gordon, major 2nd regt., by his wife Catherine, dau. of
Alexander Smith); d. 21 Aug. 1879, aged 65, having m. 1845, Agnes, only dau. of John
[McInnes, esq., of Auchenrcoch, co. Stirling, and had issue.

George —— *Aberdeen* 1588 conv.

George (sir), of Haddo, knt. and bart. —— *Aberdeenshire* 1669-74, 1678 conv.,
[1681-2, then a senator of the college of justice.

Sir George Gordon, 3rd baronet (on the death 1665 of his brother, Sir John, to whom his
father's estates had been restored in 1661), advocate 1668, P.C. 1678, a lord of session 8 Iune
1680, and raised to the president's chair 14 Oct. 1681, lord high chancellor of Scotland 1682-4.
and on 30 Nov. 1682 was elevated to the peerage, etc., as Earl of Aberdeen, Viscount of
Formartine, Lord Haddo, Methlic, Tarves, and Kellie, by letters patent dated at Whitehall,
setting forth the services of his ancestors, the suffering and death of his father in the royal
cause, and his own splendid abilities and faithful discharge of his official duties (son of Sir
John Gordon of Haddo, 1st bart.); b. 3 Oct. 1637; d. at Kelly 20 April 1720; having m.
Anne, eldest dau. of George Lockhart, of Torbrecks, heiress of her brother William. His
[son and heir, William, 2nd Earl, M.P.

George, son of Sir Robert G., of Embo (1689) —— *Dornock* 1685-6, 1689 conv.,
1689 parlt. ("George brother of John Gordon, of Embo"), until his death
s.b. 21 Dec. 1692; when he is styled "Capt. George Gordon, son of the
[deceased Sir Robert Gordon, of Embo."

Brother of John Gordon, M.P., sons of Robert Gordon, M.P.

Gordon—*continued.*

George (sir), of Edinglassie —— *Banffshire* 1681-2, 1685-6.

James, laird of Lesmoir, younger —— *Aberdeenshire* 1625 conv.

Son of Sir James Gordon, of Lesmoir, cr. a baronet 1 Sept. 1625. He m. —— dau. of [Sir Thomas Urquhart, of Cromarty, and d. in his father's lifetime, leaving 2 daus.

James, younger, of Creachlee —— *New Galloway* 1689 conv., 1689 until his [death s.b. 27 Aug. 1690.

(Sir John), laird of Lochinvar —— sat as a minor baron in the conventions [1594, 1597.

Son of Sir James Gordon, of Lochinvar; justiciary of the lordship of Galloway 1555, 1587; d. 23 Aug. 1604; m. 1st Juliana Home. of Wedderburn, and 2nd, in 1563, Elisabeth, dau. of [John, Lord Herries, father of Sir Robert, M.P., and had issue.

John, the goodman of Bucklee —— *Inverness-shire* 1617 conv., 1617 parlt., [including Caithness and Ross,

John, of Innermarkie —— *Banffshire* 1628-33.

John, of Cardines —— *Kirkcudbright stewartry* 1643 conv., 1645, the laird.

John (sir) —— *Sutherlandshire* 1681-2 (then John, eldest son, heir apparent of Sir Robert Gordon, of Embo, knt. and bart.), 1689 conv. (younger), 1689 parlt. (his name is included in the act of 25 April 1693 "concerning members who have not signed the assurance") until his death as Sir John Gordon, of [Embo, s. b. 10 May 1700.

3rd baronet of Embo, married and had issue.

John (sir), of Doall —— *Sutherlandshire* 1685-6.

John (Mr.), younger, of Carrell —— *Sutherlandshire* 1700-2.

John, provost of Aberdeen —— *Aberdeen* (now Montrose) *burghs* 1708-10

Probably 3rd and youngest son of Charles 1st Earl of Aboyne; died 22 July 1762.

John (sir), of Invergordon, bart. —— *Cromartyshire* 1742-7, 1754-61.

2nd bart. (son of Sir William Gordon, M.P.) ; registered arms in the Lyon office 1756; d. s.p. 25 May 1783. See Milne's list of Nova Scotia baronets, Foster's Baronetage, p. xiv.

John, of Kenmure —— *Kirkcudbright stewartry* 1781, until declared unduly [elected, 6 Feb. 1782.

Vice-lieut. Kirkcudbright stewartry, capt. 17th regt. of foot (2nd son of John, eldest surviving son of William, 6th and attainted Viscount Kenmure), restored by act of parlt. [17 June 1824 ; d. s.p. 21 Sept. 1840, aged 90, having m. Miss Morgan.

John Frederick, G.C.H., commonly called lord —— *Forfarshire* 1841-7, [1847-52.

Admiral R.N. (3rd son of George, 9th Marquis of Huntly), assumed the additl. surname of Hallyburton 1843; b. 15 Aug. 1799 ; d. s.p. 29 Sept. 1878, having m. 24 Aug. 1836, Lady Augusta Fitzclarence (precedency patent 24 May 1831), sister of George 1st Earl of Munster [and widow of Hon. John Kennedy-Erskine (M. AILSA) ; she d. 8 Dec. 1865.

Gordon—*continued.*

Ludovick (sir), of Gordonstown —— *Elgin and Forres-shire* 1649

2nd baronet (on the death of his father, Sir Robert Gordon, 1656) ; b. 15 Oct. 1624 ; d. 1686, having m. 1st, 1 Jan. 1644, Elizabeth, dau. and heir of Sir Robert Farquhar, of Menie, and had with other issue a son, Sir Robert, M.P. ; he m. 2ndly (contract 6 March [1669) Jean, dau. of John Stewart, of Ladywell, widow.

Robert —— *Inverness* 1586 conv.

Robert (sir), of Lochinvar, knt. —— *Kirkcudbright stewartry* 1612.

Entered as a baronet, 1 May 1626, in Milne's list, see Foster's Baronetage, which states that " he was made Governour of Nova Scotia, bot his patent does not invest him tytle baronet, bot he has power to create Judges, Generalls, Archbishops, Bishops, &c.," (son of Sir John, M.P.) ; m. Isobel, dau. of William Ruthven, 1st Earl of Gowrie ; d. Nov. 1628, [having had with other issue a son Robert, probably M.P

Robert —— *New Galloway* 1628-33, 1639-41 (of Knockbrax), 1643-4 conv.

Possibly son of Sir Robert, M.P., last named.

Robert (sir), knt. and bart. —— *Inverness-shire* 1630 conv.

Hon. Sir Robert Gordon, of Gordonstoun, the historian of his family (2nd son of Alexander, 11th Earl of Sutherland), gentleman of the bedchamber to King James 1606, knighted 1609, gentleman of the bedchamber to Charles I., who created him a baronet of Nova Scotia, with remainder to his heir male whatsoever, 28 May 1625, being the first of that order, sheriff principal of Inverness-shire 1629, vice-chamberlain 1630, P.C. Scotland 1634 ; b. 14 May, 1580 ; d. 1656, having m. 16 Feb. 1613 Louisa, only child and sole heir of John Gordon, Lord of Glenluce, dean of Salisbury, brother of George, 4th Earl of Huntly, and [had issue.

Robert (sir), of Embo —— *Sutherlandshire* 1649-50, 1661.

2nd bart. (on the death of his father, Sir John) ; d. 16 Oct. 1697 ; father of Sir John, M.P., [1681.

Robert (sir), of Langdale —— *Sutherlandshire* 1663 (? identical with Sir Robert [of Embo).

Robert, of Lumsdeall (Rumsdeall) —— *Sutherlandshire* 1661-2, 1678 (then [described as of Rogart).

Robert (sir 1673), of Gordonstoun, younger (1672) —— *Sutherlandshire* 1672-4, [1678 conv. (younger), 1681-2 (younger), 1685-6 (a knight, younger).

3rd bart. (son of Sir Ludovick, M.P.) ; b. 7 March 1647; d. 1701, having m. 1st Margaret, eldest dau. of William, 11th Lord Forbes, and relict of Alexander, 1st Lord Duffus ; he m. 2ndly, Elisabeth, only dau. of Sir Wm. Dunbar, of Hempriggs, bart., and [had with other issue a son, Sir Robert, M.P.

Robert (sir), of Gordonstown, knt. and bart. —— *Caithness-shire* 1715-22.

4th baronet (son of Sir Robert, M.P.), claimed the earldom of Sutherland ; d. 8 Jan. 1772, aged nearly 80, having m. 26 May 1734, Anne, only dau. of Sir William Maxwell, of Calder- [wood, bart. ; she d. 11 March 1808, aged 89.

William (lt.-col.), of Craig —— *Kirkcudbright stewartry* 1690 until his death [s.b. 12 April 1693.

Gordon—*continued.*

William (sir), of Dalfolly, knt. and bart. —— *Sutherlandshire* 1708-10, 1710-13, 1714-15, 1715-22, 1722-7 (then of Invergordon) ; *Cromartyshire* 1741 until [his death s.b. 30 Dec. 1742.

Of London, banker, created a baronet 8 Feb. 1704, purchased Inverbreakie, and called it Invergordon ; a commissioner for stating debts due to army (son of Sir Adam, M.P. 1689) ; m. Isabel, dau. and heir of Sir John Hamilton, of Halcraig, Lanark, and d. at Chelsea [9 June 1742, having had with 2 daus. a son, Sir John, who succeeded as M.P.

William, commonly called Lord William, brother-german to Alexander, Duke of Gordon —— *Elginshire* 1779-80, 1780-4 (vice-admiral of Scotland 1782), [*Inverness-shire* 1784-90. See also England M.P.

Son of Cosmo George, 3rd Duke of Gordon, K.T., served in 89th foot and 37th foot, depy. ranger St. James's Park and Hyde Park, 1778, and lt.-col. north fencible regt. same year, vice-admiral of Scotland 1782-95, recr.-genrl. duchy of Cornwall, M.P. Horsham 1792-6 ; b. 15 Aug. 1744, d. 1 May 1823, having m. 1 March 1781, Hon. Frances Ingram-Shepherd, 2nd dau. and co-heir of Charles, 9th Viscount Irvine ; she d. 29th Sept. 1841, [aged 80.

William, rear-admiral R.N. —— *Aberdeenshire* 1820-6 (of Minories), 1826-30, 1830-1, 1831-2, 1833-4, (capt. R.N.) 1835-7, 1837-41, 1841-7, (a lord of the Admiralty) 1847-52, (then rear-admiral) 1852 until he accepted the Chiltern [hundreds s.b. 22 Aug. 1854.

Brother of George, 4th Earl of Aberdeen, entered the navy 1794, com.-in-chief at the [Nore ; d. unm. 3 Feb. 1858, aged 73.

Goslintoun.

—— the laird of —— *Lanarkshire* 1625 conv.

Gourlay.

Robert (Mr.) —— *Culross* 1641, 1644, conv. 1645.

Govan.

John, bailie —— *Peebles* 1685-6.

Gower.   See also Stafford.

Francis Leveson, commonly called Lord —— *Sutherlandshire* 1826-30, (a lord of the treasury 1827, and chief secretary to the lord lieutenant of Ireland 1828), 1830-1, M.P. *S. Lancashire* 1835-44, as Lord Francis Egerton. [See also England M.P.

Francis Egerton, K.G. 7 Feb. 1855, D.C.L. (2nd surviving son of George Granville Leveson-Gower, 1st Duke of Sutherland) ; on the death of his grandmother, Lady Louisa Egerton, dau. and co-heir of Scroope, 1st Duke of Bridgewater, inherited the Bridgewater property, and assumed by R.L. 24 Aug. 1833, the surname and arms of Egerton only, was created Earl of Ellesmere, of Ellesmere, Salop, and Viscount Brackley, of Brackley, Northants, 1 July 1846, lord-lieut. Lancashire, lieut.-col. Duke of Lancaster's own regt. yeo. cav., M.P. Bletchingley 1822-6, South Lancashire 1835-7, 1837-41, 1841-4, carried the sceptre (as deputy for his mother) before George IV. on his visit to Scotland 1822 ; b. 1 Jan. 1800; d. 18 Feb. 1857, having m. 18 June 1822, Harriet Catherine, eldest dau. [of Charles Greville, esq. (E. WARWICK) ; she d. 17 April 1866.

Gower—*continued*.

Ronald Sutherland Leveson, commonly called Lord —— *Sutherlandshire* [1867-8, 1868-74.

> 4th son of George, 2nd Duke of Sutherland, K.G., a trustee of National Portrait Gallery; [b. 2 Aug. 1845; unm. See Foster's Peerage.

Graeme.

George (Mr.), of Inchbrackie —— *Perthshire* 1643-4 conv.

> Son of Patrick, M.P., fined and imprisoned during the Civil Wars 1641; m. Margaret, [dau. of Sir Alexander Keith, of Ludquhairn, and d. 1654, leaving issue.

David, of Orchill —— *Perthshire* 1724 until his death s.b. 28 April 1726.

> Died 14 March 1726, son of — Graeme, of Pitcairn, and Beatrix, heiress of Orchill.

David, of Gorthie (major-general) —— *Perthshire* 1764-8, (then col.), 1768 [until he accepted the Chiltern hundreds s.b. 11 June 1773.

> Col. 19th regt. of foot, m.-genl. 1763, lt.-genl. 1772, general 1783; died Jan. 1797, then [of Braco.

Mungo, of Gorthie —— *Perthshire* 1702-7, sat in first parlt. of Great Britain, [1707-8 —— *Kinross-shire* 16 Oct. 1710, until unseated 10 Feb. following.

Patrick, of Inchbrackie —— *Perthshire* 1612.

> Son of George Graeme, of Inchbrackie; he m. 1st Nichola Browne, of Fordell, and 2ndly [Margaret Scott, heiress of Monzie, Perths, and d. 1635, leaving issue.

Graham.

· —— laird of Monorgund —— *Forfarshire* 1646-7.

Alexander, of Drynie, late provost —— *Rosemarkie and Channurie of Ross or* [*Fortrose burgh* 1661-3.

David (sir), of Fintrie —— *Forfarshire* 1641.

> Son of David Graham and Barbara Scott; he m. Mary, dau. of Sir James Halliburton, of [Pitcur, and had a son John, M.P. 1678.

David (younger), of Fintrie —— *Forfarshire* 1702-7.

> Son of lt.-col James Graham; he m. Anna, eldest dau. of Robert Moray, of Abercairnie, [and had a son and 10 daus.

Graham—*continued.*

George, Lord of Dundaft —— *Stirlingshire* 1741 until his death s.b. 6 Feb.
[1746-7.

4th son of James, 1st Duke of Montrose; capt. R.N. and gov. of Newfoundland 1740;
[d. unm. at Bath 2 Jan. 1747.

George, of Kinross —— *Kinross-shire* 1780-4, 1790-6.

George Edward, of London —— *Kinross-shire* 1819-20, 1826-30.

Of Abington Pigotts, co. Cambridge; assumed the names of Foster-Pigott 12 March
1827, lt.-col. comm. Central Sussex Militia (son of John Graham, of Kernock, member
Supreme Council, Bengal, by Helen, dau. of William Mayne, of Powis, and sister of Sir
Wm. Mayne, created Lord Newhaven, 1776, extinct 1794); b. 3 Nov. 1771; d. 5 Nov.
1831; m. 1794, Mary, only dau. and heir of Rev. John Foster, D.D., provost of Eton; she
[d. 25 Nov. 1858, leaving issue.

Harie, of Breckness —— *Orkney and Zetland stewartry* 1685-6.

James, of Bucklyvie —— *Stirlingshire* 1702-7.

James, of Kirkstall, co. York —— *Wigtown burgh* 1805-6.   See also England M.P.

Sir James Graham, bart., so created 3 Oct. 1808, bar.-at-law Lincoln's Inn, recorder of
Appleby, M.P. Cockermouth 1802-5, 1807-12, Carlisle 1812-25 (see England M.P.), (son of
Thomas Graham of Edmund Castle, Cumberland); b. 18 Nov. 1753, d. 21 March 1825,
having m. 17 June 1781, Anne, only dau. of Rev. Thomas Moore, of Kirkstall; she d. 28
[Aug. 1821, leaving issue.   See Foster's Baronetage.

John, younger —— *Glasgow* 1583.

John, of Callendar —— 1583.

John —— *Glasgow* 1649-50, or George Porterfield.

John, of Fintry —— *Perthshire* 1678 conv.

(Son of David Graham, M.P. 1641); also a commissioner of supply for Forfarshire.

John, of Killearn —— *Stirlingshire* 1702-7.

John, younger, of Killearn —— *Stirlingshire* 1722-7.

Montagu William, commonly called lord; youngest son of the Duke of
[Montrose —— *Dumbartonshire* 1830-1, 1831-2.   See also England M.P.

J.P., D.L., captain Coldstream Guards, M.P. Grantham 1852-7, Herefordshire 1858-65
(see England); b. 2 Feb. 1807, d. s.p. 21 June 1878, having m. 14 Feb. 1867, Hon. Harriet
Anne Bateman-Hanbury, eldest dau. of William, 1st Lord Bateman, and widow of George
[Astley Charles Dashwood, esq.

Robert (sir), of Morphie, knt. —— *Kincardineshire* 1617, 1625 conv. (the laird)
[1628-33, 1639-41.

He m. Margaret, sister of John, 1st Viscount of Dundee.

Graham—*continued.*

Robert, of Gartmore —— *Stirlingshire* 1794-6.

Robert Cunninghame-Graham (son of Nicol Graham ot Gartmore, and his wife Lady Margaret Cunninghame, dau. of William, 12th Earl of Glencairn), receiver-genrl. for Jamaica, assumed the additl. surname of Cunninghame in 1796 ; m. 1st, Anne, dau. of Patrick Taylor, of Jamaica, and sister ot Sir John Taylor, bart. ; he m. 2ndly, Elizabeth, dau. of [Thomas Buchanan, esq., of Spital and Leny, and had issue.

Thomas (col.), of Balgowan —— *Perthshire* 1794-6 (lt.-col.), 1796-1802, [1802-6, 1806-7.

Baron Lynedoch of Balgowan, co. Perth, so created 3 May 1814, G.C.B. 1812, G.C.M.G., K.T.S. of Portugal, K.S.F. of Spain, a general in the army 1821, col. 1st foot 1834, governor of Dumbarton Castle 1829, extra A.D.C. to Lord Mulgrave 1793, (then 40 years of age,) col. comdt. 90th regt. (1794), which he raised, col. 1795 ; the French surrendered Malta to him after 2 years' blockade in Sept. 1800 ; served with Sir John Moore in Spain, during the campaign of 1808, and was in the retreat to Corunna. Lt.-genl. 1810, gained the memorable battle of Barossa 5 March 1811, commanded the left wing of the British army at the battle of Vittoria, commanded at the siege of St. Sebastian, etc., etc., had a command in Holland 1814, cr. Baron Lynedoch 17 May 1814, col. 14th foot 1826-34. Contested Perthshire 1811 and 1812, (only surviving issue of Thomas Graham, esq., of Balgowan, by Lady Christian Hope, 6th dau. of Charles, 1st Earl of Hopetown) ; d. s.p. 18 Dec. 1843, aged 94, having m. 26 Dec. 1774, Hon. Mary Cathcart, 2nd dau. of Charles, 9th Lord [Cathcart, she d. 26 June, 1792.

Thomas, of Kinross and Burleigh —— *Kinross-shire* 1811-12, 1818 until his [death s.b. 16 Sept. 1819.
Died 28 July 1819 "an East Indian," leaving two daughters.

William (sir), of Claverhouse —— *Forfarshire* 1628-33.

Son of John Graham, of Claverhouse, d. Oct. 1642, having m. Maria, dau. of Thomas Fotheringham, of Powrie, and was ancestor of John Graham, "bonnie Dundee," 1st [Viscount Dundee, so created 12 Nov. 1688, who fell at Killiecrankie 26 May 1689.

William, of Blaatwood, provost —— *Annan* 1669-72.

William, merchant in Glasgow —— *Glasgow* 1865-8, 1868-74. See foot-note.

GRAHAM, WILLIAM, J.P., D.L., co. Lanark, and of Glasgow, merchant, M.P. as above (eldest son of late William Graham, of Burnshiels, co. Renfrew, by Catherine, dau. of John Swanston, Esq.) ; b. 25 August 1817 ; m. Jan. 1846, Jane Catherine, dau. of late John Lowndes, Esq., of Arthurlie, co. Renfrew, and has with 5 daus. 2 sons.

(1) James Rutherford, b. 1849 ; (2) William, b. 1858.

44, Grosvenor Place, S.W.
Clubs—Windham, Travellers', Reform.

Granard.

George Forbes, commonly called Earl of Granard in the kingdom of Ireland [—— *Ayr burghs* 1741-7. See also M.P. England.

3rd Earl P.C. (3rd son of Sir Arthur, 2nd Earl), M.P. Queensborough (see England), had summons to Irish House of Lords 27 Feb. 1725, capt.-genl. and com.-in-chief Leeward Islands, etc., 1729, plenipotentiary to the court of Muscovy 1733, rear-adml. of the white 1734, and of the red the same year, vice-adml. of the blue 1736, com.-in-chief of squadron in West Indies 1738, governor counties Westmeath and Longford ; d. 29 Oct. 1765, aged 80, having m. Mary, elder dau. of William 1st Lord Mountjoy, and relict of Phineas Preston, [of Ardsallagh, co. Meath ; she d. 4 Oct. 1755, leaving issue.

Grant. See also **Macdowall-Grant** and **Macpherson-Grant**.

Alexander, of Grant —— *Inverness-shire* 1702-7, sat in 1st parlt. Great Britain 1707-8 ; *Inverness-shire* 1708-10 ; *Elgin* and *Forres-shire* 1710-13, 1713-15, [**1715** until his death s.b. 5 Jan. 1719-20.

Son of Ludovick Grant, M.P., and governor of Sheerness, a brig.-genl., high shf. Inverness, lord lieut. co. Inverness and Moray ; m. 1st Elizabeth Stuart, eldest dau. of James, Lord Downe, eldest son of Alexander, 4th Earl of Moray ; she d. s.p. and he m. 2ndly Anne (maid of honour to Queen Anne), dau. of John Smith, speaker of the House of Commons ; he [d. s.p. in Aug. 1719, bd. in the Abbey Church, Edinburgh.

Alexander (sir), of Dalvey, bart. —— *Inverness burghs* 1761-8.

Married and died s.p. (son of Patrick Grant, of Inverladinem). This baronetcy (created 10 Aug. 1688) is discredited, and it is believed that this Patrick was the first to receive it (service 22 Aug. 1752) since the death of the grantee, Sir James Grant of Dalvey, 1695. Sir Alexander had a grant of supporters from the Lyon office 8 July 1761, and it is seriously argued that this was the most direct recognition the crown could afford ; this is news indeed ! the crown and Lyon king of arms were evidently synonymous when George the [third was king ! ! !

Andrew —— *Perth* 1612.

Andrew, provost —— *Perth* 1650, 1650-1, or Patrick Ros.

Andrew, of Edinburgh —— *Leith burghs* 1878-80, and since 1880. See foot-note.

Archibald (sir), of Monymusk, bart. —— *Aberdeenshire* 1722-7 (then master), [1727 until expelled the house 22 May 1732.

2nd bart. (2nd son of Sir Francis Grant, Lord Cullen), advocate 1711, principal clerk and keeper of the Hornings 1749 ; d. at Monymusk 17 Sept. 1788, having had 4 wives. See [Foster's Baronetage.

G RANT, ANDREW, of Invermay House, Perthshire, educated at the High School and at the University of Edinburgh, a fellow of the University of Bombay, F.R.G.S., formerly an East India merchant in Bombay and Liverpool (son of Rev. James Grant, D.D., D.C.L., Oxon) ; b. June 1830 ; m. April 1872,   eldest dau. of Joseph Townsend, of Glasgow.

Invermay House, Bridge of Earn, N.B.
Clubs—Reform ; Oriental.

Grant—*continued.*

Charles (sen.) esq., of Waternish —— *Inverness-shire* 1802-6 (then of London), [1806-7 (of Waternish), 1807-12, 1812-18.

A distinguished East India director, a director South Sea Company, vice-president British and Foreign Bible Society 1804, etc., etc., (son of Alexander Grant, who fell at Culloden); d. 31 Oct. 1823, aged 77. For an extended account of his career see the "Gentleman's Magazine," vol 93, p. ii. p. 561 *et seq.* He m. 1770, Jane, dau. of Thomas Fraser, esq., of the Balnain family, and was father of Charles, M.P., Lord Glenelg, next [named, and of Sir Robert Grant, gov. of Bombay, G.C.II., P.C., M.P.

Charles, of Glenelg —— *Inverness burghs* 1811-12 (of Waternish), 1812-18 (a lord of the treasury 1814); *Inverness-shire* 1818-20 (chief sec. to lord-lieut. Ireland 1819), 1820-6 (vice-president board of trade 1823), 1826-30 (of Glenelg, treasurer of the navy and president of the board of trade 1828), 1830-1 (president board of control 1830), 1831-2, 1833-4, 1835, until a principal sec. [of state s.b. 15 May same year.

Baron Glenelg, of Glenelg, co. Inverness, so cr. 8 May 1835 (brother of Sir Robert Grant P.C., G.C.H., M.P., gov. of Bombay, sons of Charles Grant, M.P.), sec. of state, colonial dept. 1835-9, a commissioner of land tax, etc., see above ; b. 26 Oct. 1778 ; d. unm. 23 [April 1866.

Francis (col.), of Dunphaile —— *Elgin* and *Forres-shire* 1768-74.

Lt.-gen. Grant 1777 (son of Sir James Grant, M.P., of Pluscardine, afterwards Colquhoun) ; m.-gen. 1770, col. 63rd. regt. ; b. 10 Aug. 1717 ; m. Miss Cox, and d. 30 Dec. 1781, having [had issue.

Francis William, of Grant, col. of the Inverness-shire or 10th North British militia —— *Elgin burghs* 1802-6 (lt.-col.) ; *Inverness burghs* 1806-7 (col.) ; *Elginshire* 1807-12, 1812-18, 1818-20, 1820-6, 1826-30, 1830-1, 1831-2 ; *Elgin* and *Nairnshire* 1833-4, 1835-7, 1837 until he acc. the *Chiltern hundreds* [s.b. 25 April 1840.

6th Earl of Seafield (on the death of his brother Lewis 26 Oct. 1840), a representative peer 1841-53 (2nd son of Sir James Grant, 7th baronet, M.P.) ; b. 6 March 1778, and d. 30 July 1853, having married twice, and had with other issue a son, Francis William, M.P. [See Foster's Peerage.

Francis William, younger, of Grant —— *Inverness-shire* 1838 until his death [s.b. 30 March 1840.

Eldest son of the 6th Earl of Seafield last named ; b. 5 Oct. 1814 ; d. unm. 11 March [1840.

[James, of Grant —— 1681.]

Created Earl of Strathspey and Lord Grant, but died before the patent passed the seal, 1663 ; a member of the Scots' estates 1661, but not named in Parliamentary return ; father [of Ludovick, M.P. 1681-1707.

James, of Moynes —— *Nairnshire* 1667 conv.

Grant—*continued.*

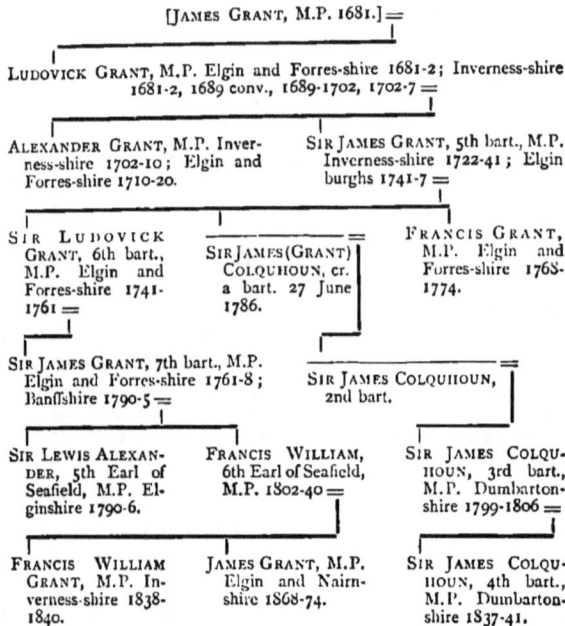

[JAMES GRANT, M.P. 1681.] =

LUDOVICK GRANT, M.P. Elgin and Forres-shire 1681-2; Inverness-shire
1681-2, 1689 conv., 1689-1702, 1702-7 =

ALEXANDER GRANT, M.P. Inverness-shire 1702-10; Elgin and
Forres-shire 1710-20.

SIR JAMES GRANT, 5th bart., M.P.
Inverness-shire 1722-41; Elgin
burghs 1741-7 =

SIR LUDOVICK
GRANT, 6th bart.,
M.P. Elgin and
Forres-shire 1741-
1761 =

SIR JAMES (GRANT)
COLQUHOUN, cr.
a bart. 27 June
1786.

FRANCIS GRANT,
M.P. Elgin and
Forres-shire 1768-
1774.

SIR JAMES GRANT, 7th bart., M.P.
Elgin and Forres-shire 1761-8;
Banffshire 1790-5 =

SIR JAMES COLQUHOUN,
2nd bart.

SIR LEWIS ALEXAN-
DER, 5th Earl of
Seafield, M.P. El-
ginshire 1790-6.

FRANCIS WILLIAM,
6th Earl of Seafield,
M.P. 1802-40 =

SIR JAMES COLQU-
HOUN, 3rd bart.,
M.P. Dumbarton-
shire 1799-1806 =

FRANCIS WILLIAM
GRANT, M.P. In-
verness-shire 1838-
1840.

JAMES GRANT, M.P.
Elgin and Nairn-
shire 1868-74.

SIR JAMES COLQU-
HOUN, 4th bart.,
M.P. Dumbarton-
shire 1837-41.

James (sir), of Grant, bart. —— *Inverness-shire* 1722-7, 1727-34, 1734-41 (then
[a baronet) ; *Elgin burghs* 1741 until his death s.b. 18 Feb. 1746-7.

Sir James Grant, of Pluscardine, assumed the designation of Sir James Colquhoun, of
Luss, co. Dumbarton, when he succeeded as 5th baronet, on the death (1718) of his father-
in-law, Sir Humphrey Colquhoun, bart. (so cr. 30 Aug. 1625). In 1704 Sir Humphrey
resigned his title of baronet into the sovereign's hands, in favour of himself and the heirs
male of his body ; whom failing, to James Grant, his son-in-law, and the heirs male of his
body (as therein named in fee); whom failing, to the other heirs of entail of the said Sir
Humphrey whomsoever, but with this express limitation, that he or his heirs so succeeding
to that estate and title shall be obliged to bear the name and arms of Colquhoun, of Luss.
It was also specially provided that the estates of Grant and Luss should not be conjoined ; a
new patent with the precedency of the former patent of 1625 was then conferred upon Sir
Humphrey. On the death of Sir James's elder brother, Brigadier-gen. Alexander Grant, in
1719 aforesaid, he resumed his paternal surname, and became Sir James Grant, of Grant,
retaining the baronetcy of Colquhoun, of Luss, but the estate of Luss went to his 2nd
surviving son (Sir James), according to the settlement in the entail of that estate. Sir James
(Colquhoun) Grant, of Grant (son of Ludovick Grant, M.P. 1681-1707) ; b. 28 July 1679 ;
d. 16 Jan. 1747, having m. 29 Jan. 1702, Anne, only dau. and sole heir of Sir Humphrey
Colquhoun, of Luss, aforesaid ; she d. 25 June 1724, having had with other issue 3 sons, of
[whom Sir Ludovick, M.P.

Grant—*continued.*

James (general), of Ballindalloch —— *Wick burghs* 1773-4 (late governor of [Florida), 1774-80 ; *Sutherlandshire* 1787-90, 1790-6 (lt.-genl.), 1796-1802.

General in the army 1796, col. 55th regt. ; d. at Ballindalloch, near Elgin, 13 April 1806, and was succeeded by his great-nephew, George Macpherson, afterwards Sir George [Macpherson-Grant, bart., so cr. 25 July 1838.

James (sir), of Grant, bart. —— *Elgin* and *Forres-shire* 1761-8 ; *Banffshire* 1790, until appointed receiver and cashier of the excise in Scotland s.b. 24 July [1795.

Sir James Grant, 7th baronet (on the death of his father, Sir Ludovick, M.P.), levied the first regt. of fencible infantry in 1793, and the 97th regt. in 1794, general cashier of excise, Scotland, L.L. Inverness 1794-1809 ; b. 19 May 1738 ; d. 18 Feb. 1811, having m. 4 Jan. 1763, Jean, only child of Alexander Duff, of Hatton, co. Aberdeen ; she d. 15 Feb. 1805, [having had with other issue Francis William, M.P.

James (lt.-col.), of Grant —— *Elgin* and *Nairnshire* 1868-74.

3rd son of Francis William, 6th Earl of Seafield, capt. late 42nd regt., vice-lieut. Elgin [since 1868 ; b. 27 Dec. 1817 ; m. thrice, and has issue. See Foster's Peerage.

John, of Moynes —— *Nairnshire* 1639-41.

Descended from James, 4th son of Duncan Grant, of Grant.

John, of Moynes —— *Nairnshire* 1661-3.

Lewis Alexander, younger, of Grant —— *Elginshire* 1790-6.

5th Earl of Seafield, on the death, 5 Oct. 1811, of James 7th Earl of Findlater and 4th Earl of Seafield ; succeeded as 8th baronet on the death of his father, Sir James, M.P., [18 Feb. same year ; b. 22 March 1767, d. unm. 26 Oct. 1840.

Ludovick, of that ilk —— *Elgin* and *Forres-shire* 1681-2 (of Freuchie) *Inverness-* [*shire* 1681-2 (laird), 1689 conv., 1689-1702, 1702-7.

Col. of a regt. of foot 1689, sheriff principal of Inverness (son of James Grant of that ilk, M.P.) ; m. 1st Janet, only dau. of Alexander Brodie, of Lethen, and 2ndly Jean, dau. of Sir John Houston of that ilk, and d. 1717, aged 66, and bd. in the Abbey Church, [Edinburgh ; father of Alexander, M.P., and of Sir James, M.P.

Ludovick (sir), of Grant, bart. —— *Elgin* and *Forres-shire* 1741-7, 1747·54, [1754-61.

6th baronet (on the death of his father, Sir James, M.P.), an advocate ; b. 13 Jan. 1707, d. 18 March, 1773, having m. 1st Marian, dau. of Sir Hugh Dalrymple of North Berwick, he m. 2ndly Lady Margaret Ogilvie, dau. of James, 5th Earl of Findlater and 2nd Earl of [Seafield ; she d. 20 Feb. 1757, having had with 7 daus. an only son, Sir James, M.P.

Grant—*continued.*

Robert, bar.-at-law of Lincoln's Inn, London —— *Elgin burghs* 1818-20, [*Inverness burghs* 1826-30. See also England M.P.

Sir Robert Grant, P.C., 1831 (brother of Charles, Lord Glenelg, aforesaid, and son of Charles Grant, M.P.), G.C.II., gov. of Bombay 1834-8; B.A. Magdalen Coll. Camb. 1801 (4th wrangler), M.A. 1806, bar.-at-law L.I. 1807, king's serjeant in duchy court of Lancaster a commissioner of bankrupts, M.P. Norwich 1830-2, Finsbury 1832—June 1834, a commissioner board of control 1831, judge advocate-gen. 1832; died gov. of Bombay, 9 July 1838, aged 57; m. Margaret, dau. of Sir David Davidson, of Cantray, co. Nairn (she re-m. 8 Aug. [1848 to Lord Joceline W. Percy, brother of the Duke of Northumberland), and had issue.

William, of Preston Grange, a lord of session —— *Elgin burghs* 1747, 1747-54, 1754 (then advocate for Scotland), until appointed a lord of session 14 Nov. [same year.

2nd son of Sir Francis Grant, of Cullen, M.P., advocate 1722, procurator for the Church of Scotland, and principal clerk to the general assembly 1731, solicitor-genrl. 1737, elected advocate 1746, but declared to have vacated by absence, lord of session 1754; d. at Bath [23 May 1764, bd. at Preston Pans, leaving 3 daus.

William (sir), of Beldorny —— *Banffshire* 1796-1802 (chief justice of Chester 1798, and master of the rolls 1801), 1802-6, 1806-7, 1807-12. See also [England M.P.

Son of James Grant, of Beldornie, a small farmer, afterwards collector of the customs in the Isle of Man, educated at the College of Aberdeen, and studied civil law at Leyden, a student of Lincoln's Inn 30 Jan. 1769. called to the bar 3 Feb. 1774, atty.-genrl. Canada, M.P. Shaftesbury 1790-6 (see M.P. England), a judge of the Carmarthen circuit 1793, solr.-general to the Queen 1795, chief justice Chester 1698, solr.-genrl. and knighted July 1799, master of the rolls 1801-17, commanded the Lincoln's Inn volunteer corps, lord rector of [University of Aberdeen 1809; d. unm. at Dawlish, Devon, 25 May 1832, aged 83.

Grant-Duff.

Mountstuart Elphinstone, of Eden —— *Elgin burghs* 1857-9, 1859-65, 1865-8, 1868-74, 1874-80, 1880 until appointed governor of the presidency of [Fort St. George, at Madras, s.b. 15 July 1881. See foot-note.

G RANT-DUFF, MOUNTSTUART-ELPHINSTONE, governor of Madras since 1881, M.A. Balliol Coll. Oxon 1853, LL.B. London, 1854, bar.-at-law I.T. 1854, lord rector of Aberdeen 1866-72, under-secretary of state India 1868-74, under-sec. of State for the Colonies 1880-1, a member of committee of council on education, Scotland, J.P. D.L. Moray, J.P. cos. Banff and Aberdeen, (elder son of James Cuninghame Grant-Duff, of Eden, N.B., by Jane Catherine, only child of Sir Whitelaw Ainslie); b. 21 Feb. 1829, m. 13 April 1859, Anne Julia, only dau. of E. Webster, esq., of Ealing, and has 4 sons and 2 daus.

(1) Arthur Cuninghame, b. 23 May 1861.
(2) Evelyn Mountstuart, b. 9 Oct. 1863.
(3) Adrian, b. 29 Sept. 1869.
Clubs—Athenæum, Brooks'.

(4) Hampden, b. 27 July 1874.
(5) Clara Annabel Catherine.
(6) Victoria Adelaide Alexandrine.

Gray.

Andrew —— *Perth* 1617 conv., 1617 parlt., 1621 (provost), 1625 conv., [1628-33, 1630 conv.

Andrew —— *Montrose* 1643-4 conv., 1649.

George (Mr.), town clerk —— *Haddington* 1639-41.

Gilbert, of Saphok, late provost —— *Aberdeen* 1663.

James —— *Lanark* 1617.

John —— *Dysart* 1650 (or David Symson).

Robert, of Skibo —— *Sutherlandshire* 1643-4.

Robert, of Ballone —— *Sutherlandshire* 1645, 1648 (the laird).

Robert —— *Dornoch* 1648.

William, bailie, late provost —— *Aberdeen* 1661, until his death s.b. 12 May [1663.

Greenlaw.

George (Girnelaw) —— 1464, 1467 ; (? *Haddington*) 1468, when elected an [auditor of complaint 1472 (—— Girnelaw) 1473 (no burgh named).

John (Girnelaw) —— 1466, when elected an auditor of complaint, 1467 (no [burgh named).

Greig.

David, present lord provost of the city of Perth —— *Perth* 1839-41.
A watchmaker and jellewer of Perth.

Symon (Greg) —— *Cupar* 1478.

Grierson.

Robert (sir), of Lag, knt. —— *Dumfries sheriffdom and stewartry of Annandale* [1628-33, 1639-41, 1643 conv., 1644-7, 1648.
Knighted in the lifetime of his father, Sir William, M.P. ; m. 1622, Margaret, eldest dau. [of Sir James Murray, of Cockpool ; d. about 1654, having had issue.

Robert (sir), of Lag, bart. —— *Dumfries* (or *Nithsdale*) *sheriffdom and stewartry* [*of Annandale* 1678 conv., 1681-2, 1685-6 (baronet).
Sir Robert Grierson, cr. a baronet 25 March 1685 (said to be son of James 2nd son of Sir Robert, M.P.), served heir to Sir John Grierson of Lag, knt., 9 April 1669 ; he m. Henri-etta, sister of William, 1st Duke of Queensberry, and d. 15 April 1736, having had [issue.

Grierson—*continued.*

(Sir William), laird of Lag —— *Dumfries sheriffdom and stewartry of Annan-*
[*dale* 1617 conv. and parlt., 1621, 1625 conv.

Knighted by James VI. about 1608 (son of Roger Grierson, of Lag) ; he m. 1593, Nicola Maxwell, sister of William, Lord Herries, and d. 1629, having had with other issue a son,
[Sir Robert, M.P.

William, of Bargattoune —— *Kirkcudbright stewartry* 1644, 1645, 1646-7,
[1648-9.

(? Married Elizabeth, widow of John Grierson, of Capenoch, and dau. of Sir James Murray,
[of Cockpool).

William (Grier) —— *Dumfries-shire* 1709-10, 1710 until unseated, Feb. 1711.

Sir Wm. Grierson, of Lag, 2nd baronet, disinherited by his father, died about 1740 ; he
[m. Ann, dau. of Sir Richard Mu-grave, bart., of Hayton ; she d. 16 Dec. 1749.

Grieve.

James Johnstone, merchant in Greenock —— *Greenock* 1868-74, 1874 (then of Levan, near Gouroch, Renfrewshire), until he accepted the Chiltern hun-
[dreds s.b. 25 Jan. 1878. See foot-note.

Patrick —— *Burntisland* 1607, 1608, 1612, 1617 conv. and parlt.

William, of London —— *Linlithgow burghs* 1790-6.

Grundiston.

David —— *Cupar* 1524.

Guthrie.

Alexander —— *Edinburgh* 1569 conv. bis.

Son of Andrew Guthrie, of Guthrie. He was one of the barons who subscribed to the articles agreed to by the general assembly of the kirk 1567, was assassinated in his house at
[Inverpeffer ; he m. Isabel, dau. of Wm. Wood, of Bonnytoun, and had issue.

James —— *Montrose* 1587.

James —— *Edinburgh* 1630 conv.

Malcolm —— *Dundee* 1472, 1479.

G RIEVE, JAMES JOHNSTONE, of Levan, Renfrewshire, J.P., provost of Greenock 18   , M.P. as above (2nd son of Robert Grieve, esq., of Kielator, Killin, co. Perth, by his wife Margaret, dau. of late James Johnstone, esq., of Alton, co. Dumfries) ; b.   1810 ; m. 1st   1833, Mary Jane, dau. of Andrew Richardson esq., of Halifax, N.S. ; he m. 2ndly,   1846, Anne, dau. of Col. Charles John Hill, and has issue,

Levan by Gouroch, N.B., 74, *Queen's Gate, S.W.*
Club—Reform.

H.

Haddo.   See also Gordon.

George John James Gordon, commonly called Lord —— *Aberdeenshire* 1854-7, 1857-9, 1859, until he succeeded as 5th Earl of Aberdeen 14 Dec.
[1860.

b. 28 Sept. 1816 ; d. 22 March 1864, leaving issue. See Foster's Peerage.

William, lord —— *Aberdeenshire* 1 June 1708 until s.b. 18 Jan. following, he being incapable of taking his seat, being the eldest son of a peer of Scotland.
[See also England M.P.

2nd Earl, K.T., a representative peer 1721-46 ; d. 30 March 1746, aged 70, leaving issue. [See Foster's Peerage.   Son of Sir George Gordon, bart., M.P. (see) cr. Earl of Aberdeen.

Haddington.

—— the bailie of —— *Haddington* 1543.

Adam, of —— *Haddington* 1357.

John —— *Perth* 1479, 1485.   See also Perth.

Hair.

James —— *Lanark* 1686.

Haldane.   See also Duncan.

George, younger, of Berecrofts, col. 3rd regt. of foot guards —— *Stirling burghs* 1747-54 (then capt.) 1754 until appointed governor of Jamaica, s.b. 3 March
[1758.

Brigadier-genl. Haldane died s.p. governor of Jamaica 26 July 1759, son of Patrick
[Haldane, M.P.

(James), of Gleneagles —— 1608.

James son of John Haldane (by his wife Isabel Hume) ; m. Margaret Murray, dau. of John,
[Earl of Tullibardine, father of Sir John, M.P., 1630.

(Sir John), laird of Gleneagles —— *Perthshire* 1630 conv., 1644-5.

Sir John (son of James, M.P.) ; m. Catherine, dau. of Sir John Wemyss, of Wemyss, and
[sister of the 1st Earl.

Haldane—*continued.*

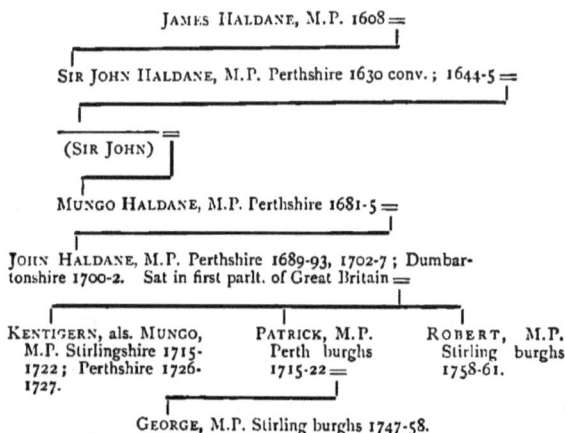

JAMES HALDANE, M.P. 1608 =

┌─────────────────────────────────┘
SIR JOHN HALDANE, M.P. Perthshire 1630 conv.; 1644-5 =

┌─────────────────────────────┘
(SIR JOHN) =

┌─────────────────────────────┘
MUNGO HALDANE, M.P. Perthshire 1681-5 =

┌─────────────────────────────┘
JOHN HALDANE, M.P. Perthshire 1689-93, 1702-7; Dumbartonshire 1700-2.   Sat in first parlt. of Great Britain =

┌──────────────────────┬──────────────────┬──────────────────┐
KENTIGERN, als. MUNGO,   PATRICK, M.P.   ROBERT,   M.P.
M.P. Stirlingshire 1715-   Perth burghs   Stirling   burghs
1722; Perthshire 1726-   1715-22 =   1758-61.
1727.

                    ┌─────────┘
            GEORGE, M.P. Stirling burghs 1747-58.

John, of Gleneagles —— *Perthshire* 1689 conv., 1689 bis., his seat was declared
vacant 28 April 1693 because he had not signed the assurance; *Dumbartonshire* 1700-2, *Perthshire* 1702-7, sat in first parliament of Great Britain
[1707-8.

Son of Mungo Haldane, M.P.; he m. 1st Mary Drummond, dau. of David, Lord
Maderty, and 2ndly Helen, dau. of Sir John Erskine of Alva, and was father of Kentigern
[M.P., Patrick M.P., and Robert M.P.

Kentigern (or Mungo), younger, of Gleneagles —— *Stirlingshire* 1715-22;
Dumbartonshire 1722, until unseated 3 Jan. 1724-5; *Perthshire* 1726-7.
Eldest son of John Haldane, last named; d. unm. 1 June 1759, aged 73.

Mungo (Haddin), of Gleneggies —— *Perthshire* 1681-2, 1685 until his death
[s.b. 19 May same year.

Son of Sir John Haldane, by his wife Margaret Fraser, dau. of Simon, Lord Lovat; he m.
[Anne Grant, and had with other issue John, M.P., who was father of John, M.P.

Patrick (master) —— *Perth burghs* 1715-22.

2nd son of John Haldane, M.P., 1689, advocate 1715, king's solicitor, one of the commissioners for forfeited estates, appointed lord of session 1721, but vacated before comple-
tion; d. at Duddingstone 10 Jan. 1769, aged 86, having m. Hon. Margaret Forrester, 3rd
[dau. of William, 4th Lord Forrester, and had a son George, M.P.

Robert, of Plean —— *Stirling burghs* 1758-61.

3rd son of John Haldane, M.P., 1689; d. s.p. 1 Jan. 1768, having m. at Gray's Inn
chapel, 29 Sept. 1742, Elizabeth, widow of Capt. Robert Holmes, and eldest dau. of Sir
[William Oglander, of Nunwell, I.W., and of Parnham, Dorset, bart.

Halgreen.

—— laird of —— *Kincardineshire* 1686.

Halkett.   See also Wedderburn.

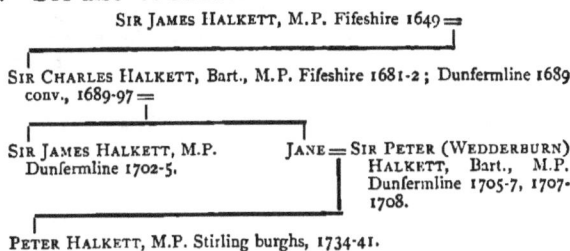

SIR JAMES HALKETT, M.P. Fifeshire 1649 ══

SIR CHARLES HALKETT, Bart., M.P. Fifeshire 1681-2 ; Dunfermline 1689
conv., 1689-97 ══

SIR JAMES HALKETT, M.P.   JANE ══ SIR PETER (WEDDERBURN)
Dunfermline 1702-5.   HALKETT, Bart., M.P.
                                             Dunfermline 1705-7, 1707-
                                             1708.

PETER HALKETT, M.P. Stirling burghs, 1734-41.

Charles *(sir)*, of Pitfirrane —— *Fifeshire* 1681-2 ; *Dunfermline* 1689 conv.,
[1689 until his death s.b. 12 Nov. 1697.

Cr. a baronet 25 Jan. 1662 (son of Sir James Halkett, M.P., 1649) ; m. Janet, dau. of
[Sir Patrick Murray, of Pitdennis, knt., and had a son, Sir James, M.P., 1702.

James *(sir)*, of Pitfirrane —— *Fifeshire* 1649.

Col. of horse,engaged with the Covenanters temp. Charles I. (son of Sir Robert Halkett) ;
he m. 1st   dau. of Sir Robert Montgomerie, of Skelmorley ; he m. 2ndly Anne,
dau. of Thomas Murray, provost of Eton, tutor to Charles I. ; by his 1st wife he had a son,
[Sir Charles, M.P.

James *(sir)*, of Pitfirrane, provost —— *Dunfermline* 1702 until his death s.b. 19
[May 1705.

2nd baronet, d. unm. March 1705, when the baronetcy expired ; son of Sir Charles, M.P.

John —— *Kirkcaldy* 1593.

Probably identical with Sir John Halkett (son of George Halkett, of Pitfirrane), knighted
by James VI., col. in the army of the states of Holland, and commanded a Scots regt. in
that service, president of the grand court-martial in Holland, fell at the siege of Bois-le-duc
[1628 ; m. Mary Van Loon, and had issue.

Peter *(sir)*, of Pitfirrane, bart. (alias Wedderburn), of Gosford —— *Dunfermline*
[1705-7 ; sat in 1st parlt. of Great Britain 1707-8.

Sir Peter Halkett, of Gosford, capt. of grenadiers (2nd son of Sir Peter Wedderburn, lord
of session), cr. a baronet 30 Dec. 1697, assumed the name of Halkett in lieu of his patronymic Wedderburn, by virtue of his marriage with Dame Jane Halkett, heiress of Pitfirrane,
eldest dau. of Sir Charles Halkett, Bart., M.P., afsd., and d. 20 March 1746, aged 86, having
[had with other issue a son, Peter, M.P.

Peter *(capt.)*, junior, of Pitfirrane —— *Stirling burghs* 1734-41.

2nd baronet (on the death of Sir Peter, M.P., last named), col. in the army, killed near
the river Monougahela, by the Indians, 9 July 1755 ; left a son Peter, 3rd bart., who died in
[1792. See Foster's Baronetage

Hall.

John (sir), of Dunglass, provost —— *Edinburgh* 1689 conv., 1690 until his
[death s.b. 5 Aug. 1696.
Of Dunglass, co. Haddington, by purchase 1687, a merchant burgess of Edinburgh (son
of Robert Hall), cr. a baronet 8 Oct. 1687, praeses of the Edinburgh committee to take the
oaths of the member of the university, to the confession of faith ; m. and had issue. See
[Foster's Baronetage.

Robert —— *Renfrew* 1628-33.

Robert (elder) —— Queensferry 1650, or Samuel Wilson.

Robert, of Fulbar, provost —— *Renfrew* 1667 conv., 1681-2, 1685-6.

Halliday

James (Mr.) —— *Dumfries* 1617.

John —— *Dumfries* 1593.

Halliwell.

George (Halywall) —— *Selkirk* 1585.

Halyburton or Haliburton.

—— laird of Pitcur —— *Forfarshire* 1617 conv. and parlt

Alexander —— 1475, 1476.

Douglas Gordon,(lord)of Pitcur —— *Forfarshire* 1832 (on petition), 1832-5,
[1835-7 (esq.), 1837-41 (lord).
Son of Charles, 4th Earl of Aboyne, and half-brother of George, 9th Marquis of Huntly;
[m. and d. s.p. 25 Dec. 1841. See Foster's Peerage.

George (Mr.) —— *Dundee* 1649, in absence of Robert Davidson.

Gilbert —— *Burntisland* 1663.

James —— *Dundee* 1563 (provost), 1567 (tutor of Pitcur and provost), 1569
conv. bis., 1572 conv. (provost), 1575 conv. (provost), 1578 conv., 1579
[(provost), 1581 (provost).
Died 1588 ; said to be descended from Walter, 2nd son of 1st Lord Halyburton.

James, of Pitcur —— *Forfarshire* 1702-7, sat in 1st parlt. of Great Britain, 1707-8.

James, of Firth —— *Orkney & Shetlandshire* 1746-7, 1747-54.

William —— *Haddington* 1468.

Thomas —— *Dundee* 1625 conv., 1630 conv. —— 1644.

Hamilton.

—— laird of Binning —— *Linlithgowshire* 1646-7, 1648.

—— laird of Boighall —— *Linlithgowshire* 1645-6.

Alexander (sir), of Innerwick —— a lord of the articles for *Haddingtonshire* 1600 (the laird), a minor baron 1608 conv., 1609 conv., *Haddington con-*
[*stabulary* 1612.

Son of Sir Alexander Hamilton (descended from Sir John, 2nd son of Sir Walter, 1st Baron Cadyow) ; he m. 1st Margaret, dau. and heir of Patrick Whitelaw of that ilk, he m. [2ndly Christian Hamilton, and d. about 1616, leaving issue.

Alexander, of Innerwick —— *Linlithgowshire* 1727-34, 1734-41.

Postmaster-general for Scotland (son of Alexander Hamilton, of Ballincrieff) ; m. Mary [Ker, dau. of William, 2nd Marquis of Lothian ; and d. 17 Nov. 1768, leaving issue.

Andrew —— *Glasgow* 1546.

Possibly of Silvertonhill, and son of Andrew, who died v.p.

Archibald (lord), of Motherwell, —— *Lanarkshire* 1708-10, 1718-22, 1722-7, [1727-34, an officer of the crown 1729. See also England.

Lord Archibald, of Riccartoun, and Pardovan, co. Linlithgow, and of Court Nichola, co. Longford, and Castle Confey, co. Kildare, youngest brother of James, 4th Duke of Hamilton (see E. SELKIRK, in Foster's Peerage), capt. R.N. 1693, distinguished himself at the battle of Malplaquet 1709, capt.-gen. governor, and vice-adm. of the Island of Jamaica 1710, 1715, a lord of the Admiralty 1729-38, 1742, etc., M.P. as above, and Queensborough 1735, Dartmouth 1742, gov. of Greenwich Hospital ; bap. 17 Feb. 1672-3, died senior capt. R.N. 5 April, 1754, having m. 1st, Anne, eldest dau. and co-heir of Charles, 2nd Lord Lucas, of Shenfield, Essex, and widow of Edward Cary, esq. ; she bd. at Taplow, Bucks ; he m. 2ndly, 17 Dec. 1718, widow of Sir Francis Hamilton, of Ireland, who d. 29 Mar. following (bd. in Westminster Abbey, 4 April) ; he m. 3rdly, 29 Sept. 1719, Lady Jane Hamilton, 5th dau. of James, 6th Earl of Abercorn, that d. 6 Dec. 1753, having had with 4 daus. 4 sons, who all died without male issue, of whom the youngest, Right Hon. Sir William, K.B., equerry to George III., M.P. Midhurst 1761, ambassador Naples 1764- [1800 ; m. and d. s.p. 8 April 1803.

Archibald, commonly called lord —— *Lanarkshire* 1802-6, 1806-7, 1807-12, [1812-18, 1818-20, 1820-6, 1826, until his death s.b. 16 Oct. 1827.

2nd son of Archibald, 9th Duke of Hamilton, and 6th Duke of Brandon ; b. 16 March [1769, d. unm. 4 Sept. 1827, *Gent's. Mag.*

Arthur, town clerk —— *Irvine* 1673.

Basil, of Baldoon —— *Kirkcudbright stewartry* 1741 until his death s.b. 31 Dec. [1742.

Basil Hamilton, of Baldoon, com. the first troop of horse under Viscount Kenmure, and behaved with great gallantry at Preston, where he surrendered, tried 31 May 1716, found guilty, and sentenced to be executed 13 July, reprieved, pardoned, and restored by Act of Parliament 1732 (son of Lord Basil Hamilton) ; d. 17 Nov. 1742, having m. Isabella, dau. of Col. the Hon. Alexander Mackenzie, M.P. (ancestor of extinct Baron Seaforth), 2nd son of Kenneth, 4th Earl of Seaforth (att.), and had with other issue an only surviving son, [Dunbar, s. as 4th Earl of Selkirk.

Hamilton—*continued.*

Claude, of Barnes —— *Dumbartonshire* 1689 conv., 1689-1702.

Gavin, of Raplock —— *Lanarkshire* 1628-33, 1630 conv.

Gavin, of Raplock —— *Lanarkshire* 1665 conv., 1667 conv.

George (sir), of Blackeburne —— *Caithness-shire* 1644.

George —— *Anstruther Easter burghs* 1712-13.

James (sir), of Lettrik —— *Lanarkshire* 1593 as a minor baron, 1600, as a lord
[of the articles (of Lettrik).
James —— *Linlithgow* 1597 conv.

Sheriff Linlithgow 1600, ? afterwards 1st Earl of Abercorn.

James, provost —— *Glasgow* 1617.

James, of Dalserfe —— *Lanarkshire* 1643-4 conv. (laird), 1644.

James (sir), of Orbiston —— *Dumbarton, Argyll,* and *Bute* 1654-5 (WILLIS).

Son of Sir John Hamilton, of Orbiston, M.P. 1645 ; he m. Jean Houston, and had issue.

James, merchant bailie —— *Dunbar* 1681-2.

James, of Aikenhead —— *Lanarkshire* 1690-1702, 1702-7.

Probably descended from Thomas, 3rd son of Sir John Hamilton, of Cadyow, aforesaid.

James (sir), of Rosehall, bart. —— *Lanarkshire* 1710-13, 1713-15, 1735·41,
[1741-7, 1747 until his death s.b. 18 May 1750.

Elder son of Sir Archibald Hamilton, bart., of Rosehall, so cr. 10 April 1703, and to
whom Sir James was served heir 17 March 1710 ; he.d. s.p. 15 March 1750, having m. 2
March 1707, Hon. Frances Stuart, 2nd dau. of Alexander, 5th Lord Blantyre. See Foster's
[Peerage. B. BELHAVEN.

John (sir), of Lettrik, knt. —— *Lanarkshire* 1605 (as a minor baron), 1612, 1617
[conv. and parlt., 1621, 1625 conv. (laird).

Natural son of John, 1st marquis of Hamilton, had a charter of the lands of Bargeny 23
May 1631, etc., etc. ; m. Jean, dau. of Alexander Campbell, bishop of Brechin, of the Ard-
[kinglass family, and had a son John, cr. Lord Bargeny 1639. See below.

John (sir), of Grange —— *Linlithgowshire* 1617 conv.

John (sir), of Preston, knt. —— *Haddington constabulary* 1621 (laird), 1628-33,
[1639-41 (knight).

Hamilton—*continued.*

John (sir), of Biel —— *Haddington constabulary* 1645-7.

Sir John Hamilton, of Broomhill, afterwards of Biel, cr. a baronet of Nova Scotia 6 Jan. 1635, cr. Lord of Belhaven and Stenton by patent 15 Dec. 1647, with remainder to his heirs male. Charles II. by patent 10 Feb. 1675 re-conferred the peerage on him for life, with remainder to Sir John Hamilton, who married his granddaughter (see Foster's Peerage), and the heirs male of his body, which failing, to his nearest heirs male whatsoever; he d. 1679, leaving by his wife Margaret, natural dau. of James, 2nd Marquis of Hamilton, 3 daus.
[and co-h.

John (sir), of Orbiston, knt., justice clerk —— *Renfrewshire* 1645.

Son of Sir John Hamilton, of Orbiston, by Christian, dau. of Sir Robert Dalzell of that ilk, knighted 1636 and appointed justice clerk, took his seat 11 Jan. 1637, a commiss. of exchequer 1 Feb. 1645, "joined Montrose after the victory of Kilsyth, for which act of malignancy it is said Mr. Mackail made him sit on the stool of repentance," joined the engagement and was deprived of his offices 1649; d. 1664; he m. 1st Rachel, dau. of James Bonar, of Rossie, co. Fife, and had 2 daus; he m. 2ndly Margaret, dau. of Sir John Hender-
[son, of Fordel, bart., and had a son, Sir James, M.P. 1654.

John, of Udston —— *Lanarkshire* 1649.

Son of John, who was son of John Hamilton, of Coltness(see BELHAVEN, Foster's Peerage);
· [m.——dau. of Sir Archibald Stewart, of Castlemilk, and had 2 sons and 6 daus.

John (sir), of Hallcraig —— *Cullen* 1696-1702.

Lord of session 1 Nov. 1689, knighted by King William (son of John Hamilton of Hall-craig, and Jean, 2nd dau. of William Mure, of Glanderston), imprisoned 1684; d. at Clys-
[dale 16 March 1706.

John, of Bargeny —— *Wigtown burghs* 1754-61 ; *Wigtownshire* 1761 until he accepted the stewardship of the manor of Old Shoreham s.b. 18 March 1762 ; [*Wigtown burghs* 1762-8.

Son of Sir Robert Dalrymple, of Castleton, knt. (o.v.p.), by his wife, Johanna Hamilton, only child of John, master of Bargeny, advocate 1735, assumed the name and arms of Hamilton of Bargeny on succeeding to that estate ; b. 4 Feb. 1715 ; d. s.p. 12 Feb. 1796, having m. 1st Lady Anne Wemyss, 3rd dau. of James, 4th Earl of Wemyss ; he m. 2ndly,
[1772, Margaret, youngest sister of Hugh, 12th Earl of Eglintoun.

John, of Pencaitland —— *Haddingtonshire* 1786-90, 1790 until appointed [receiver-general of the land tax in Scotland s.b. 26 Nov. 1795.

Of Pencaitland, Saltcoats and Dechmont, younger brother of William Hamilton-Nisbet, M.P. (sons of William Nisbet, of Dirleton, by his wife Mary, only child of Alexander Hamilton, of Dechmont) ; b. 22 Dec. 1751 ; d. s.p. 25 Dec. 1804, having m. 8 Oct. 1782, Janet, youngest dau. of Robert Dundas, of Arniston, lord president of the court of ses-
[sion, M.P.

Hamilton—*continued.*

John Glencairn Carter, of Dalzell —— *Falkirk burghs* 1857-9 ; *So. Lanarkshire* [1868-74 and since 1880. See foot-note.

Matthew —— *Glasgow* 1546.

Ninian —— *Crail* 1639-41 (bailie), 1644 conv. and parlt.

Paul —— *Buteshire* 1617.

Patrick (Mr.), of Little Preston —— *Edinburghshire* 1628-33, 1644 conv. (of [Preston), 1644.

4th son of Sir Thomas Hamilton, of Prestfield, and brother of Sir Thomas, 1st Earl of [Haddington.

Robert, of Bathgate —— *Linlithgowshire* 1612.

Robert (sir), of Silvertonhill, knt. —— *Lanarkshire* 1661-3 —— 1678 conv.

Sir Robert Hamilton, of Silvertonhill (son of Edward Hamilton, of Balgray, after of Silvertonhill, descended from Alexander, 2nd son of Sir James Hamilton, of Cadyow, ancestor of the Duke of Abercorn), cr. a baronet of Nova Scotia in or shortly before 1655, "the patent is not recorded in the general register, owing to the confusion and distraction of those times ; " m. Hon. Anne Hamilton, 2nd dau. of John, 1st Lord Belhaven, and had with other issue a son, Lt.-genl. Sir Robert Hamilton, 2nd baronet, col. 108th and 40th regt., and was in the service of the states of Holland, where he m. 1st, Aurelia Catherine van Hettingen, of Friesland ; he m. 2ndly, Isabel, dau. of John Hamilton, of Boggs, in Scotland ; [he d. in 1708, having had issue by his 1st wife.

Robert, bailie —— *Banff* 1665 conv.

Robert Baillie (major), of Langton Dunse —— *Berwickshire* 1874-80.

2nd son of George, 10th Earl of Haddington (see Foster's Peerage), bt.-major late 44th regt., major Berwickshire R.V. 1877, major E. Lothian yeomanry cavalry 1878-81 ; b. 8 [Oct. 1828 ; m. 18 July 1861, Mary Gavin, dau. of late Sir John Pringle, bart.

HAMILTON, JOHN GLENCAIRN CARTER, of Dalzell, co. Lanark, J.P., D.L., vice-lieut. Lanarkshire 1865, capt. 2nd life guards, retired 1860, major Queen's own Glasgow Yeomanry since 1856, M.P. as above, contested So. Lanarkshire 1874 (only surviving son of late Archibald James Hamilton, who served in the Peninsula and at Waterloo) ; b. 16 Nov. 1829; m. 29 March 1864, Lady Emily Eleanor Leslie-Melville, youngest dau. of David, Earl of Leven and Melville, and has had 4 sons and 4 daus.

(1) Archibald John, b. 24 May 1868, d. 20 May 1870.　　(5) Eleanor.
(2) Gavin George, b. 29 June 1872.　　(6) Alice Susan.
(3) Leslie. b. 19 Dec. 1873.　　(7) Helena Mabel.
(4) John David, b. 23 Dec. 1878.　　(8) Adele Emily Anna.

Dalzell, Motherwell, Scotland, 54, Eaton Place, S.W.
Clubs—Devonshire, Brooks', Arthur.

Hamilton—*continued.*

(Thomas, sir), laird of Drumcairn —— sat as a minor baron in convention 1594.

Sir Thomas Hamilton, of Drumcairn and Orchartfield (brother of Sir Andrew Hamilton, Lord Redhouse of session, who d. 1637, and of Sir John Hamilton, Lord Magdalen of session, who'd. 28 Nov. 1632, and eldest son of Sir Thomas Hamilton, lord of session 1607-8, and grandson of Thomas Hamilton, of Orchartfield and Ballincrief, Linlithgow, fell at the battle of Pinkie 10 Sept. 1547, said to descend from Hamilton, of Innerwick, a branch of the ducal house of Hamilton), studied law in France ; Lord Drumcairn of session 2 Nov. 1592, one of the octavians or eight commissioners of the treasury and exchequer 1595, king's advocate, lord clerk register of Scotland 16 May 1612, and secretary of state Oct. following, till 15 Feb. 1626, created Lord Binning and Byres 30 Nov. 1613, lord president of the court of session 1616, created Earl of Melrose 20 Mar. 1619, to him and his heirs male bearing the name of Hamilton, obtained a patent 27 Aug. 1627, suppressing the title of Melrose and creating him Earl of Haddington, to him and his heirs male with the former precedency, keeper of the privy seal 1626 ; d. 29 May 1637, aged 74; m. 1st, Margaret, dau. of James Borthwick, of New Byres, and had a dau.; and 2ndly, Margaret, dau. of James Foulis, of Colinton (bart.), and had issue. See Foster's Peerage.

Thomas (sir), of Preston, knt. —— *Haddington constabulary* 1661-3, 1665 conv., [1667 conv.

Died 1672, father of Sir William Hamilton, who was cr. a baronet of Nova Scotia 5 Nov. [1673, title extinct. See "CHAOS," Foster's Baronetage.

Thomas, merchant, bailie —— *Lanark* 1689 conv., 1689-1702.

Walter Ferrier, the younger, of Westport, major —— *Linlithgowshire* 1859-65.

Eldest son of Col. John Hamilton, of Westport, co. Linlithgow, etc., A.D.C. to lord lieut. Ireland ; b. 31 May 1818 ; d. 8 April 1872, having m. Barbara Agnes, dau. of James [Marshall, esq., and had 2 sons.

William —— *Ayr* 1540 bis., 1543 bis. (then provost), 1546 bis.

William —— *Anstruther Easter* 1643 conv., 1644, 1649.

William, of Orbiston —— *Dumbartonshire* 1678 conv. ; *Renfrewshire* 1681-2, [1685-6.

Son of Sir James Hamilton, of Orbiston ; he m. Elizabeth Cunninghame, dau. of William, [9th Earl of Glencairn, and d. s.p.s.

William —— *Edinburgh* 1670-4.

Wiliam (sir), of Whitelaw, senator of the college of justice —— *Queensferry* 1689 conv. (Mr.), 1689-1702 (advocate) ; *Queensferry* 1702 until his death s.b. [5 May 1705.

Advocate 1664, ordinary lord 19 Dec. 1693, and knighted shortly after by King William, justice clerk 31 Oct. 1704, until his death 14 Dec. following, 5th son of John Hamilton, of [Bangour, by his wife Margaret, dau. of James Hamilton, of West Park.

William, commonly called Lord; of Coats —— *Lanarkshire* 1734 until his death [s.b. 7 March 1735.

2nd son of the notorious Duke of Hamilton ; he d. s.p. 11 July 1734, having m. 30 April 1733, Frances, only dau. and heir of Francis Hawes, of Purley Hall, Berks ; she d. s.p. [31 March 1788, having re-m. May 1735 to William, 2nd Visct. Vane.

Hampseid.

George, bailie —— *Cullen* 1639-41.

Hannay.

John —— *Wigtown* 1581.

Patrick —— *Wigtown* 1639-41 (bailie), 1643 conv., 1644-5.

Harden.

William of —— *Dundee* 1367.

Hardy.

Robert, merchant bailie —— *Elgin* 1641.

Harper.

John (sir), of Cambusnethane, advocate —— *Lanarkshire* 1669-74.
    Admitted advocate 16 June 1649, re-admitted 8 January 1676 ; he m. —— dau. of Sir
        [John Hope, of Craighall, 2nd bart., senator of the college of justice.

Harrison.

James Fortescue, of Crawley Down Park, Sussex —— *Kilmarnock burghs*
        [1874-80. See foot-note.

Hart.

Edward —— *Edinburgh* 1586 conv.

Hartfell.

James, 2nd Earl of —— *co. Dumfries* 1654-5 (WILLIS).
    P.C., cr. Earl of Annandale and Hartfell 13 Feb. 1661, with precedency of 18 March 1643;
        [d. 17 July 1672, leaving a son William, cr. Marquis of Annandale 24 June 1701.

Hartrig.

John —— *Dumbarton* 1579.

Harvey.

Alexander —— *Inverurie* 1617.
    Married —— widow of Norman Leslie, of Inverurie, brewer

William (Hervie) —— *Edinburgh* 1583 bis.

H ARRISON, JAMES FORTESCUE, of Crawley Down, Sussex, J.P., D.L., bar.-at-law Lincoln's
    Inn 1864, M.P. as above (eldest son of late Henry Fortescue Harrison, esq., J.P.) ; b.
1819 ; m.   1837, Anne, dau. of William Humphries, esq., of Oxford, and had issue.
    (1) Henry William Fortescue, bar.-at-law, M.T., lieut. 17th Lancers ; d. unm.   1879, aged 41.

Crawley Down Park, Worth. 88, *Cornwall Gardens, S.W.*
Club—Reform,

Hastie.

Alexander, merchant —— *Glasgow* 1847-52 (lord provost of Glasgow), 1852-7.

Of Mains House, Milngavie, Dumbartonshire (son of Robert Hastie, of Glasgow, merchant), lord provost of Glasgow 1846-8 ; d. 13 Aug. 1864, aged 59, having m. Anne, eldest [dau. of Robert Napier, of West Shandon, co. Dumbarton, and had 2 daus.

Archibald, merchant in London —— *Paisley* 1836-7, 1837-41, 1841-7, 1847-52, [1852-7, 1857 until his death s.b. 11 Dec. same year.

An East India agent in London (son of W. Hastie); d. 10 Nov. 1857, aged 66.

Hay. See also Leith-Hay and Tweeddale.

Adam, of Soonhope, capt. 6th regt. of foot —— *Peebles-shire* 1767-8, 1775 until [his death s.b. 14 Dec. same year.

3rd son of John Hay, of Haystoun (by his wife Grizel Thomson) ; he m. 1st, Miss Britland, of Nottingham, and 2ndly, Caroline, sister of Sir Henry Harpur, 6th bart., of Caulke, [Derbyshire; he d. s.p. 15 Nov. 1775.

Adam, banker in Edinburgh —— *Linlithgow burghs* 1826-30.

Son of Sir John Hay, of Smithfield and Haystoun, bart. (see 'CHAOS,' Foster's Baronetage), banker in Edinburgh, and assumed the baronetcy on the death of his brother John, M.P. in 1838 (who had been admitted an advocate 29 June 1811, as son of John Hay, [banker, in Edinburgh] ; b. 14 Dec. 1795, d. 18 Jan. 1867, leaving issue.

Charles, of Blance, commonly called Lord Charles —— *Haddingtonshire* 1741-7.

Of Linplum 1751 (3rd son of Charles, 3rd Marquis of Tweeddale), served at the siege of Gibraltar, and afterwards in Germany as a volunteer, wounded at Fontenoy 30 April 1745, A.D.C. to George II., col. 33rd foot 1752, m.-genl. 1757, 2nd in command under General [Hopson in expedition to America 1757; d. unm. 1 May 1760.

George (or ? Francis), laird of Balhousie —— *Perthshire* 1644-5.

Francis Hay, of Balhousie 1643, (son of Peter Hay, of Kirkland of Megginch, brother of George, 1st Earl of Kinnoul), a writer to the signet, fined £2,000 sterling by Cromwell's Act of grace and pardon 1654 ; m. Margaret, dau. of James Oliphant of Bachilton, and had issue ; [his grandson, Thomas, M.P., cr. Visct. Dupplin.

George, of Nauchtane —— *Fifeshire* 1650, 1651.

James —— 1593 conv.

James (sir), of Smithfield —— *Peebles-shire* 1628-33 (esquire of the body of the [king], erroneously called John in parly. return; 1643 conv. (then a knight).

Sir James Hay, of Smithfield, cr. a baronet of Nova Scotia 20 July 1635 (only surviving [son of John Hay, of Smithfield), esquire of the body to James VI. 1624; d. 1654.

James (Mr.) —— *Banffshire* 1643 conv.

James (sir), of Linplum —— *Haddington constabulary* 1669-74.

Eldest son of Sir William Hay, of Linplum, brother of John, 1st Marquis of Tweeddale, he m. (contr. dated 4 Feb. 1661) Jean, eldest dau. of Sir Patrick Scott, of Thirlestane, bart., [and d. 1704, leaving 2 sons.

Hay—*continued.*

James (col.) —— *cos. Fife & Kinross* 1654-5 (WILLIS).

John (Mr.) —— *Elgin* 1617, 1621, 1628-33 (town clerk) —— 1646-7, 1648-50.

John, sheriff-depute, East Lothian —— *Haddingtonshire* 1669-74.

John, of Lochloy —— *Nairnshire* 1689 conv., 1689 until his death s.b. 10 April
[1693.

John, commonly called lord —— *Haddingtonshire* 1826-30, 1830-1. See also
[England M.P.

> Rear-admiral R.N., C.B., K.C.H., grand cross of the order of Charles III. of Spain, M.P.
> Windsor 1847-50 (see England), a lord of the Admiralty and Naval A.D.C. to the Queen
> (3rd son of George, 7th Marquis of Tweeddale); b. 1 April 1783, d. s.p. 26 Aug. 1851,
> having m. 2 Sept. 1846, Mary Anne, eldest dau. of Donald Cameron, of Lochiel, she d.
> [30 Nov. 1850.

John (sir), of Smithfield and Haystoun, bart. —— *Peebles-shire* 1831-2, 1833-4,
1835-7.

> 6th baronet by assumption (see 'CHAOS,' Foster's Baronetage), b. 3 Aug. 1788, d. s.p.
> [1 Nov. 1838, having m. Anne Preston, she d. 2 Sept. 1862.

John, post.-capt. R.N., commonly called Lord John —— *Wick burghs* 1857-9.
[See also England M.P.

> Vice-adm. R.N., K.C.B. 1881, K.L.H., M.P. Ripon 1866-71, a lord of the Admiralty
> 1866, 1868-71, and since 1880, commanding channel squadron 1877-9, 2nd in command
> 1875-7, served in China war 1842 and 1859-60, and Crimean war 1854-5, heir presumptive
> to the 10th Marquis of Tweeddale; b. 23 Aug. 1827 (4th son of George, 8th Marquis of
> Tweeddale, K.T., G.C.B.); m. 8 June 1876, Annie Christina, youngest dau. of Nathaniel
> [Grace Lambert, M.P. of Wenham Court, Bucks, and has a son and dau.

John Charles Dalrymple (admiral the Rt. Hon. Sir), of Craigenveoch,
[Scotland, bart. —— *Wigtown burghs* since July 1880. See also England.

> 3rd baronet, (son of Sir James Dalrymple Hay, see Foster's Baronetage), hon. D.C.L.
> Oxon 1870, entered the navy 1834, capt. 1850, rear-adml. 1866, adml. (retd. list) 1878, a
> lord of the Admiralty 1866-8, M.P. Wakefield 1862-5, contested 1865, M.P. Stamford
> [1866-80, contested 1880 (see England M.P.); m. and has issue. See Foster's Baronetage.

Patrick, merchant, provost —— *Perth* 1678 conv.

> 2nd son of Patrick Hay, of Pitfour, by his wife Elizabeth, dau. of Andrew Gray, of
> [Ballegarno.

Robert —— *Kirkcaldy* 1585 conv.

Robert, of Strowie —— *Perthshire* 1695-1702.

> J.P. and collector of Customs at Kirkcaldy (son of Francis Hay, of Strowie, by his wife
> Margaret, dau. of Patrick Seton, of Lathrisk, co. Fife); he m. twice, and left with a son
> [Andrew, who d. unm., 3 daus.

Thomas —— *Elgin* 1587.

Hay—*continued.*

Thomas, of Balhousie —— *Perthshire* 1693 until created Viscount Dupplin, [31 Dec. 1697.

> Viscount Dupplin, 2nd son of George Hay, of Balhousie, a commissioner for the Union, succeeded as Earl of Kinnoul 10 May 1709, a representative peer 1710, 1713, committed to Edinburgh Castle 1715, d. Jan. 1719; he m. Elizabeth Drummond, only dau. of William 1st Viscount Strathallan, and had a son George Henry, M.P. (see England), succeeded as 7th [Earl Kinnoul.

Walter —— *Dundee* 1593 conv.

William —— *Kirkcaldy* 1594 conv.

William, of Drummelzier, one of his majesty's privy council —— *Selkirkshire* [1685-6.

> Only son of John, 1st Earl of Tweeddale (by his 2nd wife); he m. Elizabeth, dau. of Alexander Seton, 1st Visct. Kingston, and had issue. See Foster's Peerage, M. TWEEDDALE.

William Montague, commonly called Lord William Hay —— *Haddington burghs* 1878 until he succeeded as Marquis of Tweeddale 29 Dec. same [year.

> 10th Marquis of Tweeddale, cr. Baron Tweeddale in the peerage of the United Kingdom 6 Oct. 1881, M.P. Taunton 1865-8 (see M.P. England), hereditary chamberlain Dunfermline, dep. commiss. Simla 18 , B.C.S. 1845-62; married and has issue. See Foster's [Peerage.

Heiton.

Johnne, of —— *Haddington* 1367 —— 1456.

Hendchyld.

Richard —— *Crail* 1357.

Henderson.

Frank, of Dundee —— *Dundee* since 1880. See foot-note.

George —— *Edinburgh* 1543.

> Possibly identical with George Henderson, of Fordell (son of George and grandson of James, who both fell at Flodden, next named), fell at the battle of Pinkie 10 Sept. 1547; he [m. Marian Scott, a maid of honour to Queen Mary.

HENDERSON, FRANK, town councillor, Dundee, since 1868, &c., M.P. as above (son of late Henry Henderson, leather merchant, Dundee); b. 1836; m. 1863 Ellen Isabella, dau. of David Scroggie, of Lawrancekirk, co. Kincardine.
Dundee.

SCOTCH MEMBERS.   Z

Henderson—*continued.*

James (Mr.) —— (? *Edinburgh*) 1504.

Probably first of Fordel (son of Robert Henderson), king's advocate 1494, was lord [justice clerk in 1508, fell at Flodden 9 Sept. 1513, leaving issue.

John (of Henrysone) —— *Lochmaben* 1645-7, 1648, 1661-3 late bailie.

Sir John Henderson, of Fordel, cr. a baronet 15 July 1664 ; m. Margaret, dau. of Sir [John Hamilton, of Orbiston, lord justice clerk, and died 1683, having had issue.

John (sir), of Fordel, bart. —— *Fifeshire* (on petition) Feb. 1780 to 1 Sept. following ; *Dysart and Kirkcaldy burghs* 1780-4 (younger of Fordel) ; *Stirling burghs* 1802 (double return) until unseated Feb. 1803, 1806-7. See also [England M.P.

5th baronet of Fordel (on the death of his father, Sir Robert, 19 Oct. 1781), M.P. Seaford 29 March 1785, unseated, and re-elected 21 March 1786, again unseated April 1786, advocate 1774, a director of the chamber of commerce 1789, provost of Inverkeithing 1802 (son of Sir Robert Henderson, bart.) ; d. 12 Dec. 1817, having m. May 1781,   dau. [of Genl. Robertson, of Newbigging, and governor of New York.

Robert (Mr.), of Holland —— *Orkney and Zetlandshire* 1617.

Possibly identical with Col. Sir Robert Henderson, brother of Sir John. Sir James, and [Sir Francis, sons of James Henderson, of Fordel.

Thomas ——*Jedburgh* 1587, 1593, 1594 conv.

Possibly identical with Sir Thomas Henderson, of Chesters, a lord of session 6 June 1622, and knighted, advocate depute 1606 (son of Dr. Edward Henryson, also a senator) ; d. 3 Feb. [1638.

Hepburn.

—— the laird of Wauchton (sat as a minor baron), —— *Haddingtonshire* 1593, 1593 conv., 1594 conv. ; *Haddington constabulary* 1594, 1598 conv., 1599 [conv., 1605 parlt. and conv., 1609 conv.

Adam (sir), of Humbie, senator of the college of justice —— *Haddington con-* [*stabulary* 1643-4 conv., 1648, 1650-1.

Clerk to the committee of estates June 1640, to oppose Charles I., a lord of session 13 Nov. 1641, knighted 15th, collector-genl. and treasurer to the army 1643, taken prisoner at Alyth [in Aug. 1651 ; d. s.p. 1656-8.

Archibald —— *Haddington* 1471, 1476.

James —— *Perth* 1583.

John —— *Haddington* 1483, 1484, 1485, 1488 bis.

John, of Wauchton —— *Haddington constabulary* 1650.

Married Mary Ross, elder dau. and co-h. of Sir Robert Innes of that ilk, bart., by his" [wife Jean, dau. of James, 6th Lord Ross, and had an only dau. Margaret.

Patrick (sir), of Wauchton, knt. —— *Haddington constabulary* 1639-41, 1643-4 [conv.

Robert (sir) —— *Haddington constabulary* 1621.

Hepburn—*continued*.

Robert, of Keith —— *Haddington constabulary* 1649-51.

Robert Rickart —— *Kincardineshire* 1768-74.

Of Hillhouse, nr. Edinburgh, lt.-col. of dragoons ; died 24 May 1804, aged 84.

Thomas Buchan (sir), of Smeaton Hepburn, bart. —— *Haddingtonshire* 1838-
[41, 1841-7.

3rd baronet, b. 30 Sept. 1804 ; married and has issue. See Foster's Baronetage.

William, of Beinstoun —— *Haddington constabulary* 1693-1702.

Heriot.

George —— *Edinburgh* 1585 conv., 1592, 1594 parlt. and conv. bis, 1596 conv.,
1597 conv. bis, 1598 conv. (the elder) bis, 1599 conv., 1600, 1602 conv.,
[1604, 1605 parlt. and conv., 1607.

George Heriot, jeweller to James VI., one of the wealthiest subjects in the kingdom, and
founder of the hospital in Edinburgh which bears his name ; m. 24 Aug. 1609, Alison, sister
[of Sir Archibald Primrose, bart., of Carrington, ancestor of Lord Roseberry.

Heron.

Patrick, of Heron —— *Kirkcudbright stewartry* 1727-34, 1734-41.

Died Oct. 1761.

Patrick, of Heron —— *Kirkcudbright stewartry* 1795-6, 1796-1802, 1802 until
[10 May 1803, when his name was erased by order of the house.

Grandson of Patrick, M.P.; he m. at La Mancha 18 Dec. 1775, Lady Elizabeth Cochrane,
dau. of Thomas, 8th Earl of Dundonald, and died at Grantham 9 June 1803, having had
[2 daus.

Herries.

Robert (sir), knt. —— *Dumfries burghs* 1780-4.

Of London, banker, col. city light horse volunteers, knighted 25 Feb. 1774, died at
[Cheltenham 25 Feb. 1815, aged 85.

Herring.

—— laird of Lethendie —— *Perthshire*, 1607, as a minor baron; 1608 conv.

Higgins.

William, merchant burgess —— *Linlithgow* 1689 conv., 1689 "he demitted his
[place 1700, having entered the ministry of the gospel."

Highgate.

Archibald (Hiegat) —— *Glasgow* 1586.

Hill.

James, merchant bailie —— *Queensferry* 1681-2.

Robert —— *Queensferry* 1643 conv., 1644-5.

Hog.

Roger (sir), of Harcarss, senator of the college of justice —— *Berwickshire* [1678 conv.

Son of William Hog of Bogend, advocate 1661, Lord Harcarse of session 1677, a lord of [justiciary 1678, he was succeeded by Alexander Gordon 19 June 1688, d. 1700, aged 65.

Holburne.

Francis, vice-admiral of the Red —— *Stirling burghs* 1761-8. See also England [M.P.

3rd son of Sir James Holburne, of Menstrie, bart. of Nova Scotia (so cr. 21 June 1706), admiral of the white, rear-admiral of Great Britain Oct. 1770, M.P. Plymouth 1768-71, and governor of Greenwich Hospital 1771, a lord of the Admiralty 1770; d. 15 July 1771, aged 67; he m. Frances, dau. of Guy Ball, esq., of Barbadoes, and widow of Edward Lascelles, esq., collector of the Island of Barbadoes (E. HAREWOOD); she d. 17 May 1761 (aged 42 ?), [leaving a son and 2 daus. by her 2nd marriage.

Holms.

William, of Glasgow and Sands, Perthshire, manufacturer, —— *Paisley* 1874-80, [and since 1880. See foot-note.

Home or Hume.

—— laird of Spott —— sat as a minor baron 1593 conv. (bis), 1594, conv. (bis), [1596 conv. (bis.), 1597 conv. (3), 1598 conv. (3), 1599.

—— laird of Blackadder —— *Berwickshire* 1617.

Alexander, of North Berwick —— sat as a minor baron 1590 conv., *Edinburgh* [1593 (bis), then provost, 1594 parlt., then provost, 1594 conv.

Sir Alexander Home, of North Berwick (2nd son of Patrick Home, of Polwarth), provost of Edinburgh 2 Oct. 1593, ambassador to England temp. James VI.; d. s.p. before 23 June [1608.

Alexander (Mr.) of St. Leonards, bailie —— *Lauder* 1639-40.

See pedigree, Drummond's Noble Families, vol. ii., p. 36.

HOLMS, WILLIAM, of Edinburgh, of Glasgow and London, spinner and manufacturer, M.P. as above, J.P. co. Lanark, and lt.-col. Lanarkshire arty. vols., (brother of John Holms, M P. Hackney, see England, sons of late James Holms of Saucel Bank, Paisley); b. 1827, m. 1857, Mary Lindsay McArthur, dau. of late John Buchanan, LL.D. Glasgow.

Club—Reform.

Home or Hume—*continued.*

HUME, EARL OF MARCHMONT.

SIR PATRICK HUME, laird of Polwarth,
Berwickshire, 1630, conv. ═

SIR PATRICK HUME, 1st Earl of Marchmont, M.P. Berwickshire, 1669-74, 1689-90, 1665 conv., 1667, and 1689 conv. ═

SIR ALEXANDER, 2nd Earl of Marchmont, M.P. Kirkwall, 1698-1702,
Berwickshire, 1706-7 ═

SIR ANDREW HUME, M.P. Kirkcudbright 1700-2, 1702-7, 1707-8.

ALEXANDER HUME-CAMPBELL, M.P. Berwickshire, 1734-41,
1741-7, 1747-54, 1754-61. See page 46.

Alexander, laird of Plandergaist —— *Berwickshire* 1648.

Alexander —— *Lauder* 1678 conv., 1685-6 (bailie).

Alexander (sir), advocate, —— *Kirkwall* 1698 to 1702, *Berwickshire* 1706-7,
[as Sir Alexander Campbell, of Cessnock. See that name.

2nd Earl of Marchmont (see Sir Alexander Campbell, of Cessnock, p. 45), brother of Sir
[Andrew, M.P., next named, and father of Alexander, M.P., 1734, &c., see p. 46.

Andrew (sir), advocate, son of the Earl of Marchmont, lord high chancellor of
Scotland —— *Kirkcudbright* 1700-2, 1702-7, sat in 1st parlt. of Great
[Britain 1707-8.

Of Kimmerghame, co. Berwick, a lord of session 1714, advocate 1696, sheriff-depute co.
Berwick, general collector of tonnage, etc. 1695 (4th son of Patrick 1st Earl of Marchmont);
[d. 16 March 1730, m. Elizabeth, dau. of John Douglas, esq., and had a son and 2 daus.

David (sir), laird of Wedderburne, knt. —— *Berwickshire* 1621 (the laird)
[1639-41, 1645-6 (the laird), 1649-50.

Only son of Sir George Home, M.P., next named, to whom he was retoured heir in
special 10 April 1617, fell with his only son George, M.P., at the battle of Dunbar, fighting
[against Cromwell, 3 Sept. 1650.

George (sir), laird of Wedderburne —— sat as a minor baron 1590 conv., 1592,
[*Berwickshire,* 1593 conv. (bis), 1594 conv. (3), 1604, 1605 conv.

Son of David Home, of Wedderburne, to whom he was retoured heir 6 Oct. 1574, warden
of the east marches 1578, comptroller 1597 ; he m. Jean, dau. of John Haldane, of Gleneagles,
[and d. 24 Nov. 1616, leaving with other issue a son, Sir David, M.P.

George —— *North Berwick* 1639-41, 1643-4 conv., 1644-5.

Probably son of Sir David Home, M.P., of Wedderburne, m. (contr. dated 14 Aug. 1635)
Katherine, dau. of Alexander Morison, of Preston Grange, a lord of session 1626-32, fell
[with his father at the battle of Dunbar, 3 Sept. 1650, had 2 daus.

George, of Whitfield —— *New Galloway* 1703-7.

Home or Hume—*continued.*

Harie (sir), laird of Hardrig —— *Berwickshire* 1648.

John (sir), of North Berwick —— sat as a minor baron 1608, 1609 conv. (the [laird); *Haddington constabulary* 1617, conv. and parlt.

4th son of Patrick Home, of Polwarth, his elder son, Sir George, was cr. a baronet of Nova Scotia, had a grant of the manor of Tully, co. Fermanagh 1641, and was served heir of his [father, Sir John, 10 Feb. 1642. See Lodge's Irish Peerage, vol. ii., p. 112.

John, of Renton —— *Berwick* 1628-33.

Sir John Home, of Renton (son of Alexander, to whom he was served heir 18 Jan. 1621), adhering to Charles I., his lands and property were pillaged and destroyed, knighted on the Restoration, P.C., nominated an ordinary lord of session 1663, and also lord justice clerk for life; he d. 1671, having m. Margaret, eldest dau. of John Stewart, commendator of Coldinghame (2nd son of Francis, 1st Earl of Bothwell), and had 3 sons, of whom the 2nd, Sir Patrick, was M.P., and the youngest, Henry, was ancestor of Mr. Home Drummond-
[Moray, M.P.

John (sir), of Blackadder, knt. —— *Berwickshire* 1639-40 (unable to attend sess. [2 and 3), 1643-4 conv. (as John Home), 1646-7 (the laird).

Sir John Home (son of Sir John Home and Mary Dundas), cr. a bart. of Nova Scotia 25 Jan. 1671, with remainder to the heirs male of his body; d. in France 23 Jan. 1675, having m. 1660, his cousin Mary, dau. of Sir James Dundas, of Arniston (V. MELVILLE); she d.
[1672, and had a son, Sir John, M.P., 1690.

John (col.), of Plandergaist —— *Berwickshire* 1661-3.

John (sir), of Blackadder —— *Berwickshire* 1690-1702, 1702 until his death s.b.
[4 April 1706.

2nd bart., ? married Catherine, dau. of Sir John Pringle, of Stichill; she died his widow
[6 June 1755.

Patrick (sir), laird of Polwarth —— *Berwickshire* 1630 conv.

Cr. a bart. of Nova Scotia 28 Dec. 1625, retoured heir in special of his father (Sir Patrick) 1 Feb. 1611; d. April 1648, having m. Christian, dau. of Sir Alexander Hamilton, of Innerwick (she re-m. to Robert, 3rd Lord Jedburgh), and had a son Patrick, Earl of
[Marchmont, next named.

Patrick (sir), of Polwarth, knt. and bart. —— *Berwickshire* 1665 conv., 1667 [conv., 1669-74, 1689 conv., 1689 until cr. Lord Polwarth 26 Dec. 1690.

Earl of Marchmont (eldest son of Sir Patrick Home, of Polwarth, M.P.), accompanied the Duke of Argyll in his unfortunate expedition to Scotland 1685, his estate confiscated, he himself attainted, and a high reward offered for his apprehension; he settled at Utrecht, and came over with the Prince of Orange 1688, and took his seat as member for Berwick; his forfeiture was rescinded by Parliament; P.C., cr. a peer of Scotland, by the title of Lord Polwarth, 26 Dec. 1690, "et hæredes masculos de corpore suo et hæredes dictorum suorum hæredum," when the king assigned to him an Orange ppr. ensigned with an imperial crown, to be placed in a surtout in his coat of arms; sheriff of Berwickshire 1692, an extraordinary lord of session 1693, high chancellor of Scotland 1696; cr. Earl of Marchmont, etc., 23 April 1697, to him and his heirs male whomsoever; b. 13 Jan. 1641; d. 1 Aug. 1724, [having m. Grizel, dau. of Sir Thomas Ker, of Cavers; she d. 11 Oct. 1703.

Home or Hume—*continued.*

Patrick (sir), of Renton, advocate —— *Berwickshire* 1702-7.

2nd son of Sir John Home, of Renton, M.P., 1628-33. See Foster's Baronetage, etc.

Patrick, of Wedderburn —— *Berwickshire* 1784-90, 1790-6.

He died 19 Dec. 1808, son of Ninian Home, of Billie, by his wife Margaret, eldest dau. of George Home, of Wedderburn 1695, who engaged in the rebellion 1715, taken at [Preston, tried and condemned, but pardoned.

Robert —— *Lauder* 1579.

William (sir), of Aytoun —— *Berwickshire* 1643-4 conv.

Home-Drummond.

Henry, of Blair Drummond —— *Stirlingshire* 1821-6, 1826-30, 1830-1 ; *Perth-* [*shire* 1840-1, 1841-7, 1847-52.

Henry Home-Drummond, of Blair Drummond, co. Stirling (son of George Home-Drummond, by his wife Janet, dau. of Rev. John Jardine, D.D.), vice-lieut. Perthshire ; b. 28 July 1783; d. 12 Sept. 1867, having m. 14 April 1812, Christian, eldest dau. of Charles Moray, esq., of Abercairny, co. Perth, and sister and heir of William Moray Stirling, esq., of Abercairny [and Ardoch ; she d. 29 Nov. 1864, having had 2 sons and a dau.

Home-Drummond-Moray.

Henry Edward, of Blair Drummond, Perthshire, capt. and lieut.-col. in her [majesty's regt. of Scots guards —— *Perthshire* 1878-80.

Eldest son of Charles Stirling Home-Drummond-Moray, esq., of Abercairny, Blair Drummond, and Ardoch ; b. 15 Sept. 1846 ; m. 23 Jan. 1877, Lady Georgina Emily Lucy [Seymour, dau. of Francis, 5th Marquis of Hertford, G.C.B.

Honyman.

Richard Bempde Johnstone (younger), of Armadale and Gromsey —— [*Orkney and Shetlandshire* 1812-18.

2nd baronet (on the death of his father, Sir William, 5 Jan. 1825) ; b. 4 May 1787 ; d. 23 Feb. 1842, having m. Elizabeth Campbell, who d. 31 Dec. 1874, having had an only dau.

Robert (capt. R.N.) —— *Orkney and Shetlandshire* 1796-1802 (lieut. R.N.) [1802-6.

Admiral Honyman (son of Patrick Honyman and half-uncle of the 2nd bart. M.P.), served under Sir Home Popham at the Rio de la Plata, and under Lord Gambier in the expedition to Copenhagen in 180 7, admiral 1825 ; d. 31 July 1848 ; he m. Margaret Henrietta, granddau. of Adml. Sir John Knight, K.C.B. ; she d. 30 Sept. 1880, aged 90, having [had issue.

Honyman—*continued*.

Robert, lt.-col. 39th regt. —— *Orkney and Shetlandshire* 1806-7.

Elder brother of Sir Richard, M.P., above named ; lt.-col. 18th foot, served as a volunteer in Egypt, major 93rd regt., which he led on the attack on the Dutch lines at the capture of the Cape of Good Hope, and was severely wounded, as lt.-col. 18th regt. he received the thanks of the commander-in-chief of the island of Jamaica for his services in suppressing a [mutiny of the black troops ; he died v.p. at Jamaica 26 Nov. 1808, aged 27.

Hope.

A. (sir) —— *Haddington constabulary* 1650.

Probably Sir Alexander Hope, of Grantoun, cupbearer to Charles I. (5th son of Sir Thomas Hope); b. 12 March 1611 ; m. Anna Bill, an English lady, and died s.p. 13 Feb. 1680,
[aged 69.

Alexander (genl., sir), of Waughton, G.C.B. —— *Dumfries burghs* 1796 (then lt.-col. 14th regt. of foot) until he accepted the stewardship of the manor of East Hendred s.b. 22 May 1800 ; *Linlithgowshire* 1800-2, 1802-6 (colonel), 1806-7, 1807-12, 1812-18, 1818-20 (G.C.B.), 1820-6 (lt.-genl.), 1826-30, [1830-1 (genl.), 1831-2 (of Craighall), 1833-4.

2nd son of John, 2nd Earl of Hopetoun (by his 3rd wife) ; b. 9 Dec. 1769 ; d. 19 May 1837 ; general in the army (1830), col. 14th foot (1835), lieut.-gov. of Chelsea hospital (1826), a commissioner R.M. College, &c., entered the army as ensign 63rd foot, dangerously wounded at action of Buren in Holland 8 June 1795, lost an arm, gov. of Tynemouth and Clifford Forts 1797, lieut.-gov. Edinburgh Castle 1798, D.A.G. to forces under Duke of York 1799, col. 1800, col. 5th West India regt. 1806, major-gen. 1808, col. 74th foot 18—, col. 47th foot 1813, of 14th foot 1835, and lt.-gen., D.Q.M.G. and inspector of army clothing, the 2nd gov. of R.M. College 1812-19, again lt.-gov. Edinburgh Castle 1819-26, invested G.C.B. 29 June 1813, hon. D.C.L. 1824 ; he m. 23 Oct. 1805, Georgiana Alicia, dau. of George Brown, esq., of Ellistoun, near Edinburgh, a commiss. of excise, and had with other issue a son George
[William, M.P. See England.

Archibald (sir), of Rankeillour, senator of the college of justice —— *Fifeshire* [25 April 1706 until his death s.b. 29 Oct. same year.

Younger son of Sir John Hope, of Craighall, 2nd bart., a lord of session 1689 and a lord of justiciary at the revolution 1690 (as Lord Rankeillour), knighted by William III.; b. 9 Sept. 1639 ; d. 10 Oct. 1706, having m. Margaret, dau. of Sir John Ayton, and had a son, Sir
[Thomas, M.P., who became 8th baronet in 1766.

Charles, of Hopetoun —— *Linlithgowshire* 1702, until cr. Earl of Hopetoun [15 April 1703.

Charles Hope K.T., cr. Earl of Hopetoun, Viscount Aithrie, and Baron Hope, in the peerage of Scotland, with remainder to the heirs male and female of his body, 15 April 1703, P.C. 1703, lord high commissioner 1723, a representative peer 1722 ; d. 26 Feb. 1742, aged 61, having m. Aug. 31 1699, Lady Henrietta Johnstone, only dau. of William, 1st Marquis of Annandale (ext.); she d. 25 Nov. 1750, having had with other issue a son
[Charles, M.P., next named.

Hope—*continued.*

Charles (Hope-Weir or Vere) of Craigiehall —— *Linlithgowshire* 1743-7, [(commissary of the musters of Scotland 1744), 1747-54, 1754-61, 1761-8.

Hon. Charles Hope-Vere, of Craigie Hall, governor of Blackness Castle (son of Charles, 1st Earl of Hopetoun, last named, see Foster's Peerage); b. 8 May 1710, d. 30 Dec. 1791, he does not appear by his franks to have used the additional surname of Vere until 1764, although it is stated that he assumed the name and arms of Vere on his 1st marriage, 26 July 1733, with Catherine, sole dau. and heir of Sir William Vere, of Blackwood, co. [Lanark, bart. (ext.); she d. 5 Dec. 1743, having had with other issue John, M.P. 1768.

Charles (maj.-genl.), of Waughton —— *Kirkcaldy burghs* 1790-6, *Haddington-shire* 1800-2 (col.), 1802-6, 1806-7, 1807-12, (maj.-genl.) 1812 until he [accepted the Chiltern hundreds s.b. 21 March 1816, then of Luffness.

Hon. Charles Hope, of Waughton, Haddington (brother of Genl. Sir Alexander Hope, G.C.B., M.P., and eldest son of John, 2nd Earl of Hopetoun by his 3rd wife), gen. in the army; b. 16 Oct. 1768, d. 1 July, 1828, having m. 30 April, 1807, Louisa Anne, dau. of George Finch-Hatton, esq. of Eastwell Park, Kent (E. WINCHILSEA); she d. 1 Mar. [1875, having had a dau. Elizabeth, m. to Louis Billard, esq., and d. 30 May, 1868.

Charles, king's advocate for Scotland, —— *Dumfries burghs* 1802 until he accepted the Chiltern hundreds s.b. 24 Jan. 1803, *Edinburgh city* 1803 until [appointed lord justice clerk s.b. 28 Jan. 1805.

Rt. Hon. Charles Hope, of Grantoun (eldest son of John Hope, of London, M.P. Linlithgow 1768), lord justice clerk 1804, and president of the court of session in Scotland 1811, deputy judge advocate 1786, sheriff of Orkney 1792, lord advocate 1801, P. C. 1822, lord justice clerk 1805, lord justice genl. 1836 (by act of parlt.), resigned 1841, lieut.-col. Edinburgh volunteers; b. 29 June 1763; d. 31 Oct. 1851, having m. 8 Aug. 1793, Lady Charlotte Hope, dau. of John, 2nd Earl of Hopetoun; she d. 22 Jan. 1834, having had [4 sons and 8 daus. See Foster's Peerage (E. HOPETOUN).

Charles —— *Linlithgowshire* 1838-41, 1841(a commiss. of Greenwich Hospital 1845), until appointed lieut.-governor of the Isle of Man s.b. 22 Aug. 1845.

Hon. Charles Hope, of Bridge Castle, Linlithgow, J.P. D.L. (3rd son of Gen. John, 4th Earl of Hopetoun, G.C.B.), lieut.-gov. Isle of Man 1845-60, m. and has issue. See [Foster's Peerage.

James (sir), of Kerse —— *Stirlingshire* 1649.
Probably identical with the next named.

James (sir), of Hopetoun, senator of the college of justice —— *Stirlingshire* [1649-50, *Lanarkshire* 1650.

Sir James Hope, of Hopetoun, governor of the mint 1641, lord of session 1 June 1649, commissioner for sale of forfeited estates 1654 (6th son of Sir Thomas Hope); b. 12 July 1614; died of the Flanders sickness 23 Nov. 1661; m. 1st, 14 Jan. 1638, Ann, only dau. and heir of Robert Foulis, of Leadhills, co. Lanark; she d. 1656, having had with other [issue a son John, M.P.

Hope—*continued.*

James (esq.) —— *Linlithgowshire* 1835-7, 1837 (then captain), until he accepted
[the Chiltern hundreds s.b. 14 June 1838.

Hon. James Hope-Wallace, of Featherstone Castle, Northumb., lieut.-col. Coldstream
guards, D.L. Linlithgow, assumed the additional final surname and arms of Wallace in
compliance with the will of Thomas Lord Wallace, 3 April 1844 ; (2nd son of Genl. John,
4th Earl of Hopetoun, G.C.B.); b. 7 June, 1807 ; d. 7 Jan. 1854, having m. 4 Mar. 1837,
Lady Mary Frances Nugent, dau. of George Frederick, 7th Earl of Westmeath, sister of the
Marquis of Westmeath ; she has resumed the surname of Hope only, and had 3 sons and
[4 daus.

John (sir) —— 1653 (Barebones parlt.).

2nd bart. of Craighall (on the death of his father, Sir John, 1646), called Sir James by
Willis—lord of session as Lord Craighall, 27 July 1623, P.C. 1645. commissioner for
administration of justice 1651 ; d. 28 April 1654, leaving issue. See Foster's Baronetage.

John, of Hopetoun —— *Linlithgowshire* 1681-2.

John Hope, of Hopetoun (son of Sir James Hope, M.P.), purchased in 1678 the barony
of Abercorn, with the office of heritable sheriff of co. Linlithgow, etc., resided at Niddry
Castle, lost in the "Gloucester" frigate, 5 May 1682, having m. Margaret Hamilton, eldest
dau. of John, 4th Earl of Haddington ; she d. 31 Dec. 1711, leaving with an only dau. an
[only son Charles, M.P., cr. Earl of Hopetoun. See Foster's Peerage.

John, of Culdraines (col.) —— *Kinross-shire* 1727-34, 1741-7 (then Sir John
[Bruce, bart., of Kinross).

3rd and youngest son of Sir Thomas Hope, 4th bart., of Craighall, by his wife Anne, only dau.
of Sir Wm. Bruce, of Kinross, bart., and eventually sole heir of her brother, Sir John Bruce, M.P.
aforesaid. Sir William Bruce (see page 40) entailed his estate, failing issue of his son's body,
to his dau. Anne and the heirs male of her body whomsoever succeeding to bear the name
and arms of Bruce of Kinross. Sir John Hope succ. his brother, Sir Thomas (Hope) Bruce
of Kinross and Craighall, bart., and became Sir John Bruce of Kinross (and Craighall),
the 7th bart. of his family, comd. a regt. of foot, governor of Bermuda 1721-7; d. 5 June 1766,
one of the oldest lieut.-genls. in the British service, succeeded by Sir Thomas Hope, M.P.,
1706. He m. 1st Charlotte, dau. of Sir Charles Halkett, of Pitfirran, bart., he m. 2nd
Marianne, dau. of Rev. Wm. Denune, of Pencaitland, East Lothian (of the Catboll familly).
[See "Hope Pedigree" in Foster's Baronetage.

John (esq.) —— *Linlithgowshire,* 1768 until unseated 27 March 1770.

Of London, merchant, 2nd son of Hon. Charles Hope-Vere, M.P. ; b. 7 April 1739 ; d.
21 May 1785, leaving with other issue Charles, M.P. 1802, and Sir William, M.P. 1800
[See "HOPETOUN" in Foster's Peerage.

John (esq.), of Craighall —— *Linlithgowshire* 1790-6, 1796 until he acc. the
[Chiltern hundreds s.b. 12 May 1800.

Ger. John, 4th Earl of Hopetoun (on the death of his half-brother, James, 3rd Earl, 29 May
1816), G.C.B., invested 26 April 1809, installed 1812, col. 42nd regt., succeeded to the chief
command at the battle of Corunna on the death of Sir John Moore ; commander-in-chief Ireland 1812, and for his numerous services in the Peninsula war was created Baron Niddry, of
Niddry Castle, co. Linlithgow, 17 May 1814.; b. 17 Aug. 1765 ; d. 27 Aug. 1823, leaving·
[issue. See Foster s Peerage.

Hope—*continued.*

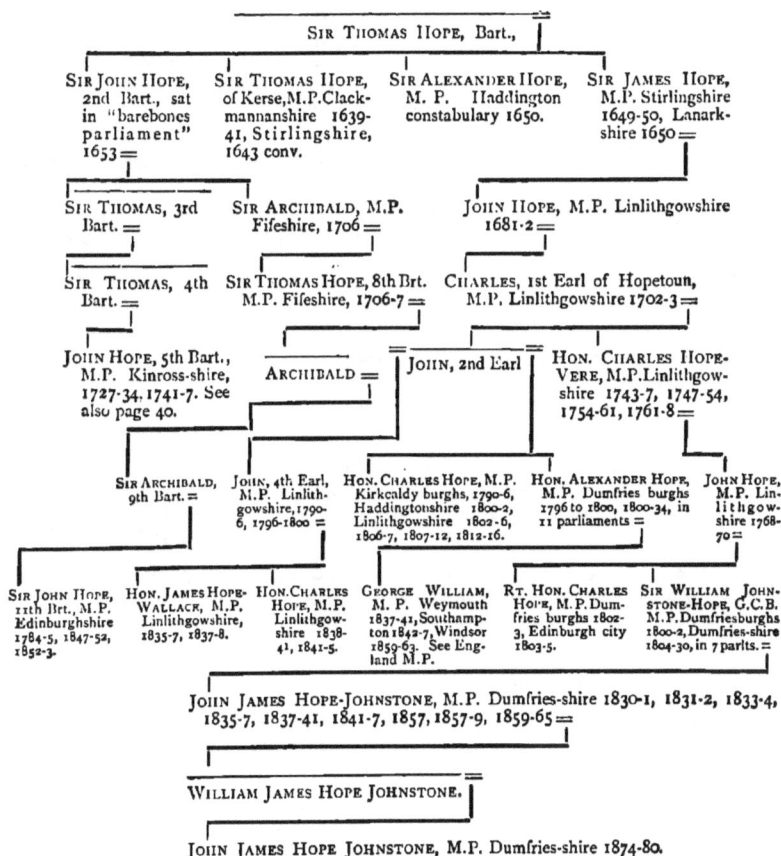

SIR THOMAS HOPE, Bart.,

SIR JOHN HOPE, 2nd Bart., sat in "barebones parliament" 1653 =	SIR THOMAS HOPE, of Kerse,M.P.Clackmannanshire 1639-41, Stirlingshire 1643 conv.	SIR ALEXANDER HOPE, M. P. Haddington constabulary 1650.	SIR JAMES HOPE, M.P. Stirlingshire 1649-50, Lanarkshire 1650 =

SIR THOMAS, 3rd Bart. =	SIR ARCHIBALD, M.P. Fifeshire, 1706 =	JOHN HOPE, M.P. Linlithgowshire 1681-2 =

SIR THOMAS, 4th Bart. =	SIR THOMAS HOPE, 8th Brt. M.P. Fifeshire, 1706-7 =	CHARLES, 1st Earl of Hopetoun, M.P. Linlithgowshire 1702-3 =

JOHN HOPE, 5th Bart., M.P. Kinross-shire, 1727-34, 1741-7. See also page 40.	ARCHIBALD =	JOHN, 2nd Earl	HON. CHARLES HOPE-VERE,M.P.Linlithgowshire 1743-7, 1747-54, 1754-61, 1761-8 =

SIR ARCHIBALD, 9th Bart. =	JOHN, 4th Earl, M.P. Linlithgowshire,1790-6, 1796-1800 =	HON. CHARLES HOPE, M.P. Kirkcaldy burghs, 1790-6, Haddingtonshire 1800-2, Linlithgowshire 1802-6, 1806-7, 1807-12, 1812-16.	HON. ALEXANDER HOPE, M.P. Dumfries burghs 1796 to 1800, 1800-34, in 11 parliaments =	JOHN HOPE, M.P. Linlithgowshire 1768-70 =

SIR JOHN HOPE, 11th Brt., M.P. Edinburghshire 1784-5, 1847-52, 1852-3.	HON. JAMES HOPE-WALLACE, M.P. Linlithgowshire, 1835-7, 1837-8.	HON.CHARLES HOPE, M.P. Linlithgowshire 1838-41, 1841-5.	GEORGE WILLIAM, M. P. Weymouth 1837-41,Southampton 1842-7,Windsor 1859-63. See England M.P.	RT. HON. CHARLES HOPE, M.P.Dumfries burghs 1802-3, Edinburgh city 1803-5.	SIR WILLIAM JOHNSTONE-HOPE, G.C.B. M.P.Dumfriesburghs 1800-2,Dumfries-shire 1804-30, in 7 parlts. =

JOHN JAMES HOPE-JOHNSTONE, M.P. Dumfries-shire 1830-1, 1831-2, 1833-4, 1835-7, 1837-41, 1841-7, 1857, 1857-9, 1859-65 =

WILLIAM JAMES HOPE JOHNSTONE.

JOHN JAMES HOPE JOHNSTONE, M.P. Dumfries-shire 1874-80.

John (sir), of Craighall, bart. —— *Edinburghshire* 1845-7, 1847-52, 1852 until [his death s.b. 25 June 1853.

11th baronet, of Craighall, co. Fife, and of Pinkie Ho., co. Edinburgh, vice-lieut. of that county, lt.-col. comdt. R. Midlothian yeomanry cavalry, depy.-gov. Royal Bank of Scotland, etc. ; b. 13 April, 1781, d. 5 June 1853, having m. 17 June 1805, Anne, dau. of Sir John Wedderburn, 6th baronet ; she d. 17 March 1867, leaving issue. See Foster's Baronetage.

Hope—*continued.*

John James (Hope-Johnstone), of Annandale —— *Dumfries-shire* 1830-1,
[1831-2, 1833-4, 1835-7, 1837-41, 1841-7, 1857, 1857-9, 1859-65.
John James Hope-Johnstone, of Annandale and Raehills, Dumfries, keeper of Loch-
maben, claimed the Annandale peerage, (eldest son of Vice-adml. Sir William Johnstone
Hope, G.C.B., M.P.) ; b. 29 Nov. 1796; d. 11 July, 1876, having m. 8 July 1816, Alicia
Anne, dau. of George Gordon, of Halhead, esq., and had issue ; grandfather of next named
                                                                                    [M.P.

John James (Hope-Johnstone), of Rae Hills, Dumfries-shire, younger of Annan-
[dale —— *Dumfries-shire* 1874-80.
Keeper of Lochmaben palace, capt. late grenadier guards (son of late Wm. James Hope-
[Johnstone, esq., eldest son of late John James Hope-Johnstone, M.P.), b. 5 Oct. 1842.

Thomas (sir), of Kerse, knt., sheriff principal —— *Clackmannanshire* 1639-41.
(Sir Alexander Shaw, of Sauchie, elected to serve in his absence if necessary) ;
[*Stirlingshire* 1643 conv., then senator of the college of justice.
2nd son of Sir Thomas Hope, of Craighall, bart., advocate 1631, knighted by
Charles I. 16 July 1633, col. of a troop of horse raised by the College of Justice, to attend
General Leslie, etc., a lord of session and lord justice general 13 Nov. 1641, etc., as above ;
[b. 6 Aug. 1606, d. 23 Aug. 1643, leaving issue.

Thomas (sir), of Rankeillour —— *Fifeshire* 1706-7.
8th baronet on the death of Sir John Bruce (Hope), M.P. in 1766, advocate 1701, (son of
Sir Archibald Hope, M.P.) ; m. Margaret, eldest dau. of James or Ninian Lowis, of Mer-
[chiston, and d. 17 April 1771, having had issue.

William Johnstone (vice-adml., sir), G.C.B. —— *Dumfries burghs* 1800-2 (capt.
R.N.), *Dumfries-shire* 1804-6, 1806-7 (a lord of the Admiralty 1807), 1807-12,
1812-18 (then rear-adml.), 1818-20 (K.C.B.), 1820-6 (vice-adml.), 1826-30
[G.C.B. and treasurer of Greenwich hospital.
Sir William Johnstone Hope, Vice-adml. of the red, G.C.B., P.C. 1830, K.T.S., knight
of Malta and of the Crescent, F.R.S., post-capt. Bellcrophon 74, in the defeat of the French
fleet off Ushant, at capture of the Helder 1798, sent home with despatches, com.-in-chief at
Leith 1813, 1816-18, K.C.B. 2 Jan. 1815, G.C.B. 4 Oct. 1825, lord of the Admiralty 1807-9,
1820-8, governor of Greenwich hospital 1828-31 (son of John Hope, M.P. 1768, and
brother of Rt. Hon. Charles Hope, of Grantoun, M.P.) ; b. 16 Aug. 1766 ; d. 2 May 1831,
having m. 1st, 8 July 1792, Lady Anne Hope-Johnstone, eldest dau. of James, 3rd Earl
Hopetoun ; she d. 28 Aug. 1818 ; he m. 2ndly, 30 Oct. 1821, Maria, Dowager-Countess
of Athlone, 2nd dau. of Sir John Eden, bart. ; she d. 4 Mar. 1851. By his first wife he
[had with other issue a son, John James Hope-Johnstone, M.P.

Horseburgh.

Alexander, of that ilk, —— *Peebles-shire* 1700-2, 1702-7.

Houstoun.

—— laird of —— *Renfrewshire* 1593 (as a minor baron), 1594 conv., 1609 conv.

Houstoun—*continued.*

SIR LUDOVICK HOUSTOUN, M.P. Dumbartonshire 1628-33, 1645, 1649, 1651, Renfrewshire 1639-41, 1645-7 =

SIR PATRICK, M.P. Renfrewshire 1661, Dumbartonshire 1678, 1681-2 =

SIR JOHN, 2nd Bart., M.P. Renfrewshire 1685-6,   PATRICK, M.P. Renfrew 1702-7, Stirlingshire 1689, 1689-1702 =   1698-9.

SIR JOHN, 3rd Bart., M.P. Linlithgowshire 1708-10, 1710-13, 1714-15.

Anthony —— Whithorn, 1643 conv.

Alexander, of Clerkington —— *Glasgow burghs* 1802 until unseated March [1803, 1809-12, 1818-20.

Probably brother of Gen. Sir Robert Houston, K.C.B., son of Col. Andrew Houston [Jordan Hill, co. Renfrew.

George, younger, of Johnstone —— *Renfrewshire* 1837, 1837-41.

D.L. co. Renfrew (only son of Ludovic Houstoun) ; b. 31 July, 1810 d. unm. 14 Sept. 1843.

John (sir), of that ilk, —— *Renfrewshire* 1685-6, *Stirlingshire* 1689 conv., (then [younger) 1689-1702, *Renfrewshire* 1702-7.

2nd baronet (on the death of his father, Sir Patrick, 1696), is said to have m. Anne, dau. of [John Drummond, Earl of Melfort, and had a son John, M.P.

John, of Houstoun —— *Linlithgowshire* 1708-10, 1710-13 (junior), 1714-15.

3rd baronet, died in London 27 July 1751, having m. 15 Feb. 1744, Hon. Eleanor Cathcart, eldest dau. of Charles, 8th Lord Cathcart ; she d. 3 Nov. 1769, aged 50, leaving a dau.

Ludovic (sir), of that ilk, knt. —— *Dumbartonshire* 1628-33, *Renfrewshire* 1639-41, *Dumbartonshire* 1645 (the laird), *Renfrewshire* 1645-7 (the laird), [1648 (the laird), *Dumbartonshire* 1649, 1651.

Died 1662, father of Sir Patrick Houstoun of that ilk, M.P., and cr. a baronet.

Patrick (sir), of that ilk, knight baronet —— *Renfrewshire* 1661 (fiar of that ilk) ; [*Dumbartonshire* 1678 conv., 1681-2 (knight and baronet).

Created a baronet of Nova Scotia 29 Feb. 1668 ; d. 1696, having m. Anne, 2nd dau. of Sir John Hamilton, Lord Bargeny ; she d. 1678, having had with other issue Sir John, M.P.

Patrick, provost —— *Renfrew* 1698 until his death, s.b. 18 Sept. 1699.

Probably 2nd son of Sir Patrick last named.

William (Mr.) —— *Dumbarton* 1587.

William —— *Whithorn* 1648.

Howard.

William, of London —— *Sutherlandshire* 1837, until he accepted the Chiltern
[hundreds s.b. 8 April 1840.   See also England M.P.

2nd son of Frederick, 5th Earl of Carlisle, K.G., M.P. Morpeth, 1806-7, 1807-12, 1812-18,
[1818-20, 1820-6, 1830-1, 1831-2 ; b. 25 Dec. 1781, d. unm. 25 Jan. 1843.

Howieson.

·—— (Houesoun) —— *Dundee* 1588.

Andrew —— *Kilrenny* 1645-6, 1650.

Alexander (Howiston) —— *Kilrenny* 1645.

Hume.   See also Home.

Joseph, of London —— *Aberdeen* (now Montrose) *burghs* 1818-20 ; (burgess of
Aberbrothock) 1820-6, 1826-30 ; *Montrose burghs* 1842-7 1847-52, 1852 until
[his death, s.b. 9 March 1855.   See also M.P. England and M.P. Ireland.

Of Burnley Hall, Norfolk, J.P., D.L. Middlesex, J.P. Westminster, vice-president
Society of Arts, F.R.S. and F.R.A.S., member College of Surgeons, Edinburgh 1796,
assist.-surgeon E.I.C.S. 1797, Persian interpreter to the army during the Mahratta war,
1802-7, etc., etc. ; M.P. Weymouth, Jan.—Sept. 1812, Middlesex 1830-7, contested the
county 1837, Kilkenny 1837-41, contested Leeds 1841 ; b. at Montrose Jan. 1777, d. 20 Feb.
[1855, having m. — Burnley, and had issue.

Hunter.

David —— *Forfar* 1643 conv.

Robert, provost —— *Ayr* 1685-6.

Of Dogland (son of James Hunter, of Abbotshill) ; m. 1657, Agnes, dau. of John Paterson,
[and had 6 sons and 5 daus.

William, bailie —— *Forfar* 1640-1.

Hunter-Blair.

James, of Dunskey, banker, citizen, burgess, and guild brother —— *Edinburgh
City* 1781-4, 1784 until he accepted the stewardship of the manor of East
[Hendred, Berks, s.b. 31 Aug. 1784.

Sir James Hunter-Blair, lord provost of Edinburgh 1784-6, banker, king's printer and
stationer for Scotland ; assumed the additional surname of Blair on his marriage ; created a
baronet of Great Britain 27 June 1786 (son of John Hunter, of Brownhill, Ayrshire, etc.) ;
b.   Feb. 1741 ; d. 1 July 1787, having m.   1770, Jane, dau. and heir of John
Blair, esq. of Dunskey, co. Wigtown, by Anne, sister and co-heir of David, 10th Earl of
[Cassilis (M. AILSA) ; she d. 2 Feb. 1817, having had with other issue a son James, M.P.

Hunter-Blair—*continued.*

James, esq., of Dunskey —— *Wigtownshire* 1816-18, 1818-20, 1820 until his [death, s.b. 30 July 1822.

Lt.-col. Ayrshire militia (3rd son of Sir James Hunter-Blair, Bart., M.P.); d. 24 June 1822.

James (lieut.-col. younger) of Blairquhan —— *Ayrshire* 1852 until his death, s.b. [30 Dec. 1854.

Lieut.-col. Scots fusilier guards (eldest son of Sir David Hunter-Blair, 3rd Bart.); b. 22 [March 1817; fell at the head of his battalion at the battle of Inkerman, 5 Nov. 1854.

Hutchinson.

John, provost —— *Arbroath* 1702-7.

Hutton.

John (Dr.), formerly physician-in-ordinary to his late majesty, King William III. [—— *Dumfries burghs* 1710, until his death, s.b. 9 May 1713.

"M.D. of Padua, F.R.C.P. 1690, M.D. Oxon, 9 Nov. 1695, accompanied William III. to Ireland, and was with him at the siege of Limerick and at the battle of the Boyne;" [d. Dec. 1712.

I.

Inglis.

Alexander —— *Perth* 1644 conv.

James —— *Glasgow* 1608, 1612, 1617 conv., 1621.

> Grandfather of Sir James Inglis, 1st bart., so created 22 March 1687, purchased lands of
> [Nether Cramond 1624.

Robert —— 1482.

Robert, goldsmith and deacon, convener of the incorporation —— *Edinburgh* 1702-7.

Innes.

Alexander, of Cockstoune —— *Elgin and Forres-shire* 1685-6.

> Created a baronet 20 March 1686; descended from Peter Innes of Keam; 3rd son of
> [Walter, 2nd son of Sir Robert Innes of that ilk. See CHAOS, in Foster's Baronetage.

Harie (sir), younger of that ilk —— *Elgin and Forres-shire* 1704-7.

> 4th baronet (son of Sir James, 3rd Bart., by his wife Margaret, dau. of Henry, Lord Ker);
> m. Jean, dau. of Duncan Forbes of Culloden, and d. 12 Nov. 1721, having had issue. See
> [DUKE OF ROXBURGHE, Foster's Peerage.

Hugh (sir), of Lochalsh and Cortoun, bart. —— *Ross-shire* 1809-12 ; *Wick burghs* 1812-18, 1820-6 (then a baronet), 1826-30; *Sutherlandshire* 1831 until his [death s.b. 14 Sept. same year.

> Created a baronet 20 Oct. 1818; only surviving son of Rev. Hugh Innes, by his wife
> [Jean, dau. of Thomas Graham; d. unm. 16 Aug. 1831, aged 67.

James, of Sandsyde —— *Caithness-shire* 1648 (the laird) —— 1665 conv.

Robert of that ilk —— *Elgin and Forres-shire* 1612.

> Son of Alexander Innes, of Cromy ; he m. Elizabeth, dau. of Robert, 3rd Lord Elphin-
> [stone, and had with other issue a son, Sir Robert, M.P. 1639, etc.

Robert (sir), of that ilk, knight baronet —— *Elgin and Forres-shire* 1639-41, [1648, the laird.

> Created a baronet of Nova Scotia 29 May 1625 ; a privy councillor for life (son of Robert
> Innes, M.P., 1612) ; m. Grizel, dau. of James Stewart, Earl of Moray; he died before the
> [Restoration, having had with other issue a son, Sir Robert, M.P.

Innes—*continued*.

Robert (sir), of that ilk —— *Elgin and Forres-shire* 1661-3, 1678, elder of that [ilk.

2nd baronet (son of Sir Robert, M.P. 1639, etc.) ; m. Mary, dau. of James, 5th Lord [Ross, of Halkhead, and had issue, ancestor of Duke of Roxburghe 1882.

Robert (sir), of Muiretoune —— *Elgin and Forres-shire* 1665 conv.

Son of Sir John Innes, of Cromy ; he m.   , dau. of his uncle, Sir Robert Innes, 1st [bart., M.P.

Robert (Mr.), of Blairtoun, councillor —— *Anstruther Easter* 1685-6.

Robert, bailie —— *Fortrose* 1681-2, 1685-6, 1689 conv., 1689 parlt.

Innes-Ker. See also Ker.

James Henry Robert, commonly called the Marquis of Bowmont and Cessford, [residing at Floors Castle, Roxburghshire —— *Roxburghshire* 1870-4.

Succeeded as 7th Duke of Roxburghe (K.T.) 23 April 1879; m. and had issue. See [Foster's peerage.

Inverpeffer.

William of —— *Dundee* 1367.

Irvine. See also Ramsay.

(Alexander) laird of Drum, a lord of the articles —— *Kincardineshire* 1600, [1604 (as a minor baron).

Founded several bursaries of philosophy and divinity at the Marischal College of Aberdeen, etc. (son of Alexander Irvine, of Drum, by his wife Elizabeth, 2nd dau. of William Keith, Earl Marischal) ; m. Marion, dau. of Robert Douglas, Earl of Buchan ; she endowed a [hospital in Aberdeen ; had a son, Sir Alexander, M.P.

Alexander (sir), of Drum —— *Aberdeenshire* 1628-33, 1643 conv.

Sheriff-principal of Aberdeen, lost severely by espousing the royal cause in the civil wars, had a patent from Charles I., creating him Earl of Aberdeen, but the rebellion broke out before it passed the great seal ; m. 1617, Magdalen, eldest dau. of Sir John Scrimgeour, of [Dudhope, knt., and had issue.

Irving.

Francis —— *Dumfries* 1617 conv., 1625 conv.

John —— *Dumfries* 1630 conv., 1639-41, late provost.

John, provost —— *Dumfries* 1661, 1665 conv., 1667 conv. (late provost), 1669- [74, provost.

J.

Jack.

Gideon, merchant burgess —— *Lanark* 1621, 1628-33, 1630 conv., 1639-41 (bailie), 1643-4 conv., 1644-5. 1646-7, 1648-9 (or Alexander Tennent [1649).

Jackson.

John —— *Renfrew* 1593.

Robert —— *Dunbar* 1644, 1645 (? also 1646-7).

Jaffray.

Alexander (Mr.), merchant trafficker, provost —— *Aberdeen* 1639-40.
An early benefactor of Marischal College ; d. Jan. 1644, father of Alexander next named.

Alexander —— 1649, 1649-50 (Alexander or John).
Alexander Jaffray, of Kingswells, laird of Ardtannies, director of the chancery of Scotland 1652, apptd. by Cromwell ; served heir of his father, Alexander, 1645, M.P. bailie and provost of Aberdeen ; one of the five Scottish members of the "Barebones" parliament ; declined a judgeship from the protector ; imprisoned after the restoration 1660 ; a commissioner for suppressing the rebellion which was put down by Argyll 1644 ; of the committee of war for co. Aberdeen 1644, 1646, and 1648, etc., etc. ; rather celebrated for his several religious conversions, being in turn a Presbyterian, an Independent, a Millenarian (fifth monarchy), and lastly, a member of the Society of Friends, and for his labours in this society he was imprisoned in Banff gaol for 10 months ; d. 1673, having m. 1st in 1632 (then aged 14) Jean, dau. of principal Dun ; she d. 1644, and he m. 2ndly 1647, Sarah, dau. of [Andrew Cant, minister of Aberdeen, and she d. 1673.

John —— *Aberdeen* 1649-50 (or Alexander) 1650.

Jameson.

Alexander —— *Cupar* 1612.

George, provost —— *Cupar* 1643-4 conv., 1644-7, 1648-50, 1651.

John —— *Rothesay* 1644 conv.

Robert —— *Ayr* 1581, 1602 conv.

Thomas —— *Perth* 1543 bis.

Jardine.

(Alexander), laird of Applegirth —— *Dumfries* (or *Nithsdale*) *sheriffdom and* [*stewartry of Annandale* 1645-6.

Alexander Jardine retoured heir to his father John 9 May 1643, see pedigree, Foster's [Baronetage.

Robert, of Castlemilk, Dumfries-shire —— *Dumfries burghs* 1868-74, and *Dum-* [*fries-shire* since 1880, see also England M.P. See foot-note.

Jeffrey.

Francis, lord advocate for Scotland —— *Forfar burghs* Jan. 1831, until unseated on petition 28 March following, and 1831-2 ; *Edinburgh city* 1833, and until appointed a lord of session and commissioner of the High Court of [Justiciary of Scotland s.b. 2 June 1834.

Lord Jeffrey was educated in the High School, Edinburgh, entered University of Glasgow 1787, and removed to Queen's Coll., Oxon 1791, advocate 1794, one of the original founders of the *Edinburgh Review*, editor 1802-29 ; it was during this period (in 1806) that occurred his memorable duel at Chalk Farm, with Mr. Moore ; lord rector of the University of Glasgow 1821 ; dean of the faculty of advocates 1829 ; returned for Malton April 1831, shortly before the general election of 1831, and again at the general election of 1831, but elected to sit for the Forfar burghs, lord advocate 1833, lord of session 1834, (eldest son of George Jeffrey, under-clerk in the court of session, by Henrietta, dau. of Mr. Loudoun of Lanarkshire); b. at the Lawn Market in Edinburgh 23 Oct. 1773, d. at Craigerook, near Edinburgh 26 Jan. 1850; he m. 1st, 1802, Catherine, dau. of Rev. Dr. Wilson, of St. Andrews, and 2nd, 1813, Charlotte, dau. of Charles Wilkes of New York, and great-niece [of Ald. John Wilkes of London.

Jedburgh.

The provost of —— *Jedburgh* 1506.

Jenkins.

John Edward, barrister-at-law —— *Dundee* 1874-80. See foot-note.

JARDINE, ROBERT, of Castlemilk, co. Dumfries, D.L., formerly a merchant in London and China, partner in Matheson and Co., M.P. Ashburton 1865-8, and as above (youngest son of David Jardine, esq., of Muirhousehead, co. Dumfries, and nephew of William Jardine, M.P., Ashburton 1841-3) ; b. 1826; m. 4 April 1867 Margaret Seton, eldest dau. of John Buchanan Hamilton, esq., of Leny, Perthshire ; she d. 7 March 1868, aged 21, leaving a son.
Robert William Buchanan, b. 21 Jan. 1868.
Castlemilk, Lockerbie, N.B., 24, *St. James' Place, S.W.*
Clubs—Brooks and Reform.

JENKINS, JOHN EDWARD, bar.-at-law, L.I. 17 Nov. 1864 ; agent-general in London for dominion of Canada 1874-5, M.P. as above, author of "Ginx's Baby," etc. (son of Rev. John Jenkins, D.D., presbyterian minister St. Paul's, Montreal, by Harriette, dau. of James Shepstone, of Clifton, esq.) ; b. 1838, m. 1867, Hannah Matilda, dau. of Philip Johnstone, esq., of Dalriada, Belfast.
20, *Southwell Gardens, S.W.*
Clubs—Reform and City Liberal.

Johnson.

John —— *Linlithgow* 1357.

Nicholas —— *Peebles* 1357.

Thomas —— *Inverkeithing* 1357.

Johnston or Johnstone. See also Cochrane, Hartfell, and Pulteney.

Alexander, of Elchieshields —— *Dumfries* (or *Nithsdale*) *sheriffdom and* [*stewartry of Annandale* 1693-1702.

Alexander, of Shield Hall —— *Kilmarnock burghs* 1841, until his death s.b. [29 May 1844.

A merchant and manufacturer of Glasgow, president of the Anti-Corn Law Association of Glasgow and the West of Scotland ; d. 9 May 1844, aged 54 ; m. 1816, Agnes Ronald, and [left issue.

Andrew, younger, of Renny Hill —— *Anstruther Easter burghs* (now *St.* [*Andrews*) 1831-2 ; *St. Andrews burghs* 1833-4, 1835-7.

Of Holton Halesworth, Sussex ; sold Renny Hill 1853 (son of Andrew Johnston), d. 24 Aug. 1862, aged 64, having m. 1st,   1827, Barbara, dau. of C. Pearson, esq., of Edinburgh; he m. 2ndly, 1 Aug. 1834, Priscilla, dau. of Sir Thomas Fowell Buxton, Bart., M.P.; she d. 18 June 1852, leaving with other issue a son Andrew, M.P. Essex 1868-74. See [England M.P.

Archibald (sir), of Warristown, senator of the college of justice —— *Edinburgh-shire*, 1643-4 conv., 1644-7, *Argyllshire*, 1648 (the laird), *Edinburghshire*, 1649.

Advocate 6 Nov. 1633, clerk and advocate or procurator to the General Assembly 1638 ; one of the commissioners who concluded the treaty of Ripon 1640, appointed an ordinary lord of session 14 June 1641, and knighted by Charles I. 15 Nov. 1641, king's advocate 1646, clerk register 1649, re-appointed 1657, sat as a peer in Cromwell's House of Lords, attempted to open a negotiation with Genl. Monk, on the restoration he escaped to Hamburgh, outlawed, forfeited and condemned to death 15 May 1661, taken at Rouen 1662, executed at the cross of Edinburgh 22 July 1663 (son of James Johnston, [merchant in Edinburgh, by Elizabeth, dau. of Sir Thomas Craig).

David, bailie —— *Annan* 1678, conv.

Edward —— *Annan* 1628-33.

George —— *Dumfries* 1644 conv. ; *Annan* 1645-7.

James (sir), of Westerhall —— *Dumfries* (or *Nithsdale*) *sheriffdom and stewartry* [*of Annandale* 1689 conv.; 1689 until his death s.b. 2 May 1700.

Knighted 10 Charles II. (son of James Johnstone, by Janet, dau. of Walter Scott, of Harden, who was 6th in descent from Matthew Johnstone, who had a grant of lands of Westeraw, co. Lanark, May 1455, and d. 1491, and who is stated to be a younger son of Sir Adam Johnstone, of Johnstone, ancestor of the Marquis of Annandale, ext.); m. Margaret, dau. of John Bannatyne, of Corhouse, and d. 1699, having had 2 sons, Sir John, M.P. cr. a [baronet 24 April 1700, and Sir William, 2nd bart., M.P.

Johnston or Johnstone—*continued.*

James, of Corhead —— *Dumfries* (or *Nithsdale*) *sheriffdom and stewartry of* [*Annandale* 1690, until his death s.b. 12 April 1693.

James, lord —— *Dumfries-shire* 1708, also for *Linlithgowshire* 1708, then described as of Over Carlowry, esq., commonly called "laird Johnston," but was rendered incapable of taking his seat for either, being the eldest son of a [peer of Scotland.

2nd Marquis of Annandale (on the death of his father William, 14 Jan. 1721); d. unm. [at Naples 10 Feb. 1730, bd. in Westminster Abbey 25 Sept. following.

James (sir), of Westerhall, bart. —— *Dumfries burghs* 1743-7, 1747-54.

3rd baronet, provost of Lochmaben, steward depute of Annandale 1743 (son of Sir William, M.P., 2nd bart.); d. 10 Dec. 1772, having m. 1719, Hon. Barbara Murray, dau. of Alexander, 4th Baron Elibank; she d. 15 March 1773, leaving issue, see Foster's [Baronetage.

James (sir), of Westerhall, bart. —— *Dumfries burghs* 1784-90. See also [England M.P.

4th baronet, lieut.-col. in the army, M.P. Weymouth 1791-4, claimed the marquisate of Annandale as heir male 12 June 1792, b. 23 Jan. 1726, d. s.p. 4 Sept. 1794, bd. in Westminster Abbey; he m. before 3 July 1759, Louisa Maria Elizabeth, dau. of —— Colclough, [and widow of Rev. — Merrick; she d. 9 April 1797, bd. with her husband.

James, of Straiton —— *Stirling burghs* 1830 1, 1831-2.

Born 15 Sept. 1802, d. 4 Sept. 1841.

James, of Alva —— *Clackmannanshire & Kinross-shire* 1851-2, 1852-7.

Of Alva, co. Clackmannan, D.L. and convener, and of Hangingshaw, co. Selkirk, D.L. and D.L. co. Stirling (son of James Raymond Johnstone, of Alva, and gt.-grandson of Sir James Johnstone, 3rd bart., M.P.); b. 4 July 1801, married twice, and has issue, see [Foster's Baronetage.

John —— *Edinburgh* 1581.

Possibly identical with John (son of John) Johnstone, warden of the west marches; justice general 1579; m. Margaret, dau. of Sir William Scott, of Buccleuch, and had a son, [Sir James, of Dunskelly.

(John) laird of Caskieben —— sat as a minor baron 1608.

Son of George Johnston of that ilk and Caskieben (who died 1593), by his wife Christian, dau. of William, 7th Lord Forbes; he m. 1st, Janet, dau. of — Turing, of Foveran, and 2nd, Katherine, dau. of William Lundy of that ilk, and d. 4 Feb. 1613, will dated 23 Jan. same year; father of Sir George Johnston, cr. a baronet 31 March 1626. [See Foster's Baronetage.

John —— *Dumfries* 1640, 1644 conv., 1644-7

John, of Elchieshields, bailie —— *Lochmaben* 1665 conv., 1667 conv., 1669-74, [1678 conv., 1681-2, provost.

Johnston or Johnstone—*continued.*

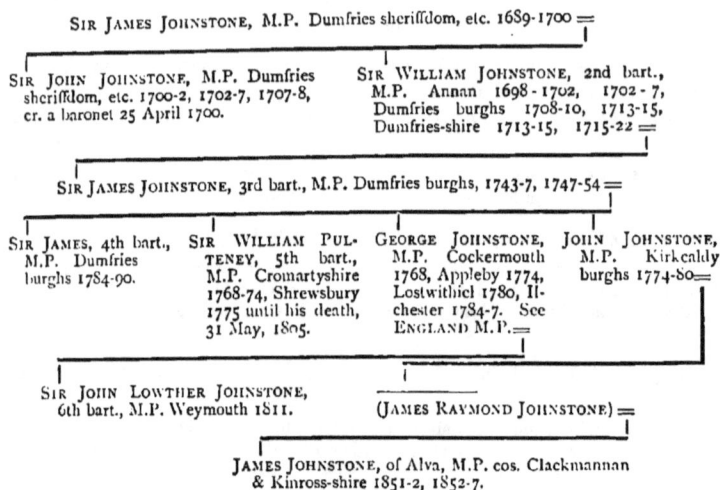

SIR JAMES JOHNSTONE, M.P. Dumfries sheriffdom, etc. 1689-1700 =

SIR JOHN JOHNSTONE, M.P. Dumfries sheriffdom, etc. 1700-2, 1702-7, 1707-8, cr. a baronet 25 April 1700.

SIR WILLIAM JOHNSTONE, 2nd bart., M.P. Annan 1698 - 1702, 1702 - 7, Dumfries burghs 1708-10, 1713-15, Dumfries-shire 1713-15, 1715-22 =

SIR JAMES JOHNSTONE, 3rd bart., M.P. Dumfries burghs, 1743-7, 1747-54 =

SIR JAMES, 4th bart., M.P. Dumfries burghs 1784-90.

SIR WILLIAM PULTENEY, 5th bart., M.P. Cromartyshire 1768-74, Shrewsbury 1775 until his death, 31 May, 1805.

GEORGE JOHNSTONE, M.P. Cockermouth 1768, Appleby 1774, Lostwithiel 1780, Ilchester 1784-7. See ENGLAND M.P.=

JOHN JOHNSTONE, M.P. Kirkcaldy burghs 1774-80=

SIR JOHN LOWTHER JOHNSTONE, 6th bart., M.P. Weymouth 1811.

(JAMES RAYMOND JOHNSTONE) =

JAMES JOHNSTONE, of Alva, M.P. cos. Clackmannan & Kinross-shire 1851-2, 1852-7.

John, of Clanchrie, provost —— *Glasgow* 1685-6.

John (sir), of Westerhall —— *Dumfries* (or *Nithsdale*) *sheriffdom and stewartry* [*of Annandale* 1700-2, 1702-7, 1707-8 (1st parlt. G.B.).

    Sir John Johnstone, of Westerhall (son of Sir James, M.P.), created a baronet of Nova Scotia 25 April 1700, with remainder to his heirs male for ever ; voted for the Union ; m. Rachel, eldest dau. and co-heir of James Johnstone, of Sheens, and d. at Tourney, 30 Sept. 1711, leaving a dau. Philadelphia, m. to James Douglas, of Dornock, and had issue; he was [succ. by his only brother Sir William, M.P. See Foster's Baronetage.

John, commonly called lord ; brother-german to George, Marquis of Annandale [—— *Dumfries burghs* 1741, until his death s.b. 20 Jan. 1742-3.
Younger son of William, 1st marquis by his 2nd wife, elected when under age ; b. 8 June [1721, d. unm. at Montpelier, 13 Nov. 1742.

John, of Donovan —— *Kirkcaldy burghs* 1774-80.

    John Johnstone, of Alva, co. Stirling, (by purchase,) n.c.s. commanded the artillery at Plassy, 23 June 1757 (son of Sir James, 3rd bart., M.P.); b. 28 April 1734, d. 10 Dec. 1795, having m. Elizabeth Caroline, dau. of Col. Keene, niece of Sir Benjamin Keene, minister at court of Madrid, and of Dr. Keene, bishop of Ely, and had with a dau. an only son, James . [Raymond Johnstone, of Alva, father of James, M.P. 1851-7.

Patrick (sir), lord provost —— *Edinburgh* 1702-7, 1707-8, (1st parlt. G.B.) [1709-10, 1710-13, then late lord provost.
Died 7 Sept. 1736, when he is styled a baronet, but this is probably an error.

Johnston or Johnstone—*continued.*

Peter, of Carnsalloch —— *Kirkcudbright stewartry* 1782-4, 1784, until he accepted the stewardship of the manor of East Hendred, Berks, s.b. 16
[Aug. 1786.

Bar.-at-law Lincoln's Inn 24 Nov. 1775, a commissioner of bankrupts, unduly elected for Kirkcudbright 1781 (son of Alexander Johnston); d. unm. 3 Oct. 1837, aged 38.

Robert, merchant, late provost —— *Dumfries* 1695-1702, 1702-7, provost.

William (sir), of Westerhall, bart. —— *Annan* 1698-1702 (2nd son of Sir James, of Westerhall, councillor), 1702-7 (of Sheenes, councillor), *Dumfries burghs* 1708-10, 1713 (then a baronet), 1713-15, *Dumfries-shire* 1713-15,
[1715-22.

2nd baronet (on the death of his brother, Sir John, M.P., 30 Sept 1711), he sat for the county and burghs of Dumfries throughout the parliament of 1713-15, owing to the petition against his return for the former being left undecided; d. 14 Oct. 1727, having m. Henrietta, dau. and co-heir of James Johnstone, of Sheens, and had issue, Sir James, [M.P. (see Foster's Baronetage), ancestor of Lord Derwent. See Foster's Peerage.

K.

Keith.

George (col.), of Aden —— *Aberdeenshire* 1661-3.

James (Mr.), son of the late John Keith "sometime in Auquhorsk" bailie
[—— *Kintore* 1661-3.

Robert —— *Montrose* 1625 conv.; 1628-33, 1639-40 provost.

Robert Murray (sir), of Murray Hall, knight of the bath —— *Peebles-shire*
[1775-80.

Lieut.-gen. in the army, col. 10th regt. of foot, nominated a knight of the bath 29 Feb.
1772, instituted by proxy 1772, being the first nomination to this order of a supernumerary
knight, ambassador-extraordinary to the courts of Dresden, Copenhagen, and Vienna, P.C.
29 April 1789, brother of Capt. Sir Basil Keith, R.N., governor of Jamaica 1773-7 (son of
"Ambassador Keith," of Craig, by Margaret Cunninghame, his wife); d. at Hammersmith
[22 June 1795, aged 63.

Kellie.

James, bailie, merchant —— *Dunbar* 1678 conv.

Robert, bailie —— *Dunbar* 1703-7.

Kennan.

James, bailie —— *Dumfries* 1689 conv., 1689 until his death s.b. 18 Feb.
[1695.

Kennedy.

—— laird of Kermuckis —— *Aberdeenshire* 1646-7.

—— laird of Bargany, sat as a minor baron 1597 conv.

Possibly Alexander Kennedy, of Bargany, who m. Mary, dau. of Sir John Gordon, of
Lochinvar, and descended from Sir Hugh Kennedy, of Ardstinchar, 4th son of Sir Gilbert
[Kennedy, of Dunure.

David, of Newark —— *Ayrshire* 1768-74.

10th Earl of Cassilis (on the death of his brother Thomas, 9th Earl, 30 Nov. 1775),
advocate 1752, a representative peer 1776-80, 1780-4, and 1784-90 (son of Sir John
[Kennedy, of Cullean or Colzean); d. unm. 18 Dec. 1792.

Hew —— *Ayr* 1621.

Kennedy—*continued.*

Hew —— *Ayr* 1643 conv., 1649-1650 (John Osburne in his absence), 1650-1.

Hugh, of Schelloch, provost —— *Stirling* 1689 conv., 1689 until his death s.b.
[3 April 1693.

John —— *Lochmaben* 1643 conv., *Ayr* 1644 conv. 1645-7, 1648, 1649 (John
[Osburne in his absence).

(Sir Thomas), laird of Culleane, a minor baron 1599, convention.

Hon. Sir Thomas Kennedy (2nd son of Gilbert, 3rd Earl of Cassilis), knighted at the
coronation of James VI. 29 July 1567, styled Master of Cassilis when he was taken prisoner
at the battle of Langside, May 1568; infeft in the lands of Cullean 1569, had charters to
himself and Elisabeth Macgill his spouse 1592 and 1597; murdered by John Moore, of
Auchindrain, Ayrshire, and others; he m. Elisabeth, eldest dau. of David Macgill, of
Cranston Riddell, king's advocate, widow of — Logan, of Restalrig, and had 3 sons, of
whom the eldest, Thomas, younger, of Cullean, to whom his brother James was served
[heir 18 May 1602, see DOUGLAS.

Thomas, of Halleaths —— *Lochmaben* 1685-6, 1689 conv., 1689 until his
[death s.b. 6. May 1695.

Thomas —— *Ayr burghs* 1720, until appointed to an office of profit by the
[crown s.b. Sep. 1721.
Of Dunure, Lord advocate of Scotland, temp. Q. Anne, a baron of the Exchequer, 1721, a
[great-uncle of the next named,

Thomas Francis, of Dunure —— *Ayr burghs* 1818-20 (then younger), 1820-6,
1826-30, 1830-1, 1831-32 (clerk of the ordnance 1831), 1833, until he accepted
[the stewardship of the manor of East Hendred s.b. 3 March 1834.

Of Dalquaharran Castle and Dunure, co. Ayr, J.P., D.L., P.C., advocate 1811, educated
at Harrow and Edinburgh, clerk of the ordnance 1832-3, a lord of the treasury 1833-4,
paymaster of the civil service Ireland 1837-50, a commissioner of woods and forests 1850-4
(son of Thomas Kennedy, by his wife Jane, dau. of John Adam, esq., of Blair Adam, co.
Kinross) b. 11 Nov. 1788, d. 1 April 1879, aged 90, having m. July 1820, Sophie, only sister
[of John, 1st Lord Romilly; she d. 9 Oct. 1879, leaving issue.

Keppel.

William Coutts, commonly called Viscount Bury, a privy councillor, treasurer
[of the household —— *Wick burghs* 1860-5. See also England M.P.

William Coutts, Viscount Bury, K.C.M.G., P.C., A.D.C. to the Queen, summoned to
parliament 6 Sept. 1876, in his father's barony, as Baron Ashford, of Ashford, under-sec.
war 1878-80, treasurer of the household 1859-66, late 43rd foot, lieut. Scots guards 1848-53,
supt.-genl. for Indian affairs in Canada 1854-6, M.P. Norwich 1857-60, Berwick 1868-74,
and as above, lieut.-col. civil service R.V. since 1860, pres. royal horticultural soc. 1865-75
(son and heir of George Thomas, 6th Earl of Albemarle); b. 15 April 1832, m. 15 Nov. 1855,
Sophia Mary, younger dau. of late Hon. Sir Allan Napier McNab, bart. (ext.), prime minister
of Canada, A.D.C. to the Queen (by his wife Mary, niece of Sir James Stewart, bart., chief
[justice Lower Canada 1838), and has issue.

Ker or Kerr.   See also Innes.

Andro—— *Linlithgow* 1579—1594 conv.—1605 conv.

(Sir Andrew), of Fernihurst —— minor baron 1597 conv., bis.

Sir Andrew Ker, created Baron Jedburgh, with remainder to his heirs male, etc., etc. etc., 2 Feb. 1622 ; heritable bailie of Jedburgh, confirmed by charter 15 March 1587, gent. of the bedchamber to James VI. 1591 (son of Sir Thomas Ker, of Fernihurst, by his 1st wife, Janet Kirkaldy), m. (contract 20 Oct. 1584) Anne, eldest dau. of Andrew Stuart, master of Ochiltree, niece of James, Earl of Arran, chancellor of Scotland, and d. 1631, without [surviving male issue.

Andrew (sir), of Greenhead, knt. —— *Roxburghshire* 1645 (the laird) 1648-9.

Created a baronet 31 July 1637, a commissioner for preserving peace on the borders 1641, a member of the committee of war, co. Roxburgh 1643-9, of the commission for the plantation of kirks 1649, a colonel in 1650, supported the covenant, and was imprisoned in Edinburgh castle at the Restoration, and fined £6,000 (served heir special of his father, Sir Andrew Kerr, of Greenhead 1617) ; d. about May 1665, having m. 1st, 1634, Elizabeth, dau. of Sir William Scott, of Harden (B. Polwarth), he m. 2ndly, 16 Aug. 1664, Katherine, widow of David Carnegie, of Craig, dau. of John, 1st Earl of Wemyss ; she d. at Dysart 24 Feb. 1668 ; by his 1st wife he had with other issue 2 sons, Sir Andrew, M.P., and Sir [William, M.P.

Andrew (sir), of Greenhead, knt., bart. —— *Roxburghshire* 1658-9 (Willis) [1669-74.

2nd bart., d. s.p. before June 1676, m. Jean, dau. of Sir Alexander Don, 1st bart. of [Newton,

Edward—— *Edinburgh* 1617 conv.

James (sir), of Hundelie —— *Roxburghshire* 1630 conv.

Sir James Kerr, of Crailing, half-brother of Sir Andrew Kerr, M.P., Lord Jedburgh, to whom he was served heir special 29 Oct. 1603; m. Mary. dau. and heir of James Rutherford, of Hundolie, ph. of Jedburgh, and d. 1645, leaving a son Robert, 3rd Lord Jedburgh, m. Christian, relict of Sir Patrick Hume, of Polwarth, dau. of Sir Alexander Hamilton, of [Innerwick, but d. s.p. 4 Aug. 1692.

James, of Bughtridge, convener of the trades of Edinburgh —— *Edinburgh city* [1747-54.

Of Bughtrig, ph. of Hownam, co. Roxburgh, and of Edinburgh, jeweller and goldsmith, deacon of the incorporation of goldsmiths 1734, convener of trades 1746, engraver to the mint and assay master 1745 ; commanded a company of gentlemen volunteers (son of Thomas Kerr, of Edinburgh, grandson of Sir Thomas Kerr, of Redden, co. Roxburgh"; brother of Robert, 1st Earl of Ancrum) ; d. at Drumsheugh, near Edinburgh, 24 Jan. 1768 ; m. 1st, 8 July 1725, Jean, dau. of Gavin Thomson, of Lowget, writer in Edinburgh ; she d. 10 Oct. 1746 ; he m. 2ndly, 6 Aug. 1750, Elizabeth, dau. of Lord Charles Kerr, of Cramon, director of chancery in Scotland, 2nd son of 1st Marquis of Lothian ; she d. 21 Feb. 1799, [aged 85, leaving issue. See Foster's Peerage.

Ker or Kerr—*continued.*

John —— *Linlithgow* 1467 bis.

John (sir), of Hirzell —— *Roxburghshire* 1605, 1607 ; sat as a minor baron.

Sir John led a foray into England Aug. 1657, exchanged his lands of Hirzell for those of Jedburgh Abbey 1611 (son of Walter Kerr, of Hirzell and Littledean, by his wife Eupheme Edmonstone) ; m. 1st (contract, 12 Jan. 1576) Julian, 3rd dau. of David Home, of Wedderburne, she divorced him 21 Feb. 1589, and re-m. to James Hop-Pringle, of Whitelaw ; he m. 2ndly, 5 March 1589-90, Margaret, dau. of Patrick Whitelaw of that ilk (the divorced wife, 2 Dec. 1589, of Sir Alexander Hamilton, of Innerwick); Sir John was dead in Aug. [1631, and had with other issue a son, Sir Mark, of Dolphingston.

John (Mr.) —— *Selkirk* 1617—1630 conv.

Possibly a younger brother of Sir Andrew Kerr, of Greenhead, 1st bart., who had a crown charter of Howdon 1614, and was a member of the committee of war for co. Roxburgh [1649.

(Sir John), laird of Lochtour —— *Roxburghshire* 1644 conv. and parlt.

Sir John Kerr, of Lochtour, knighted by Charles II. at Scone 2 Jan. 1651 (son of John Kerr, of Lochtour, and grandson of Gilbert Kerr, brother of Sir Andrew, M.P. 1648), m. 18 April 1640, Jean, dau. of John Kerr, of Littledean, co. Roxburgh ; she re-m. (contract 16 June 1652) to Sir John Wanchope, of Niddrie. See Herald and Genealogist, vol. vii.. 221

Ralph —— *Lauder* 1617.

Thomas —— *Aberdeen* 1583.

Called also James.

Thomas (sir), of Cavers —— *Roxburghshire* 1643-4 conv., 1648-9.

Sir Thomas Carre, of Cavers, knighted at Hollyrood House 2 June 1662, a member of the committee of estates and of war; fined £6,000 on the Restoration (son of George Carre, of Cavers); d. 1681, aged 88, having m. 1st, 1630 Agnes, dau. of Sir John Riddell of that ilk, but she d. 1635; he m. 2ndly, 1638, Grizel, dau. of Sir Robert Halkett, of Pitfirrane, co. [Fife ; she d. 1682, having had 4 daughters.

(William), laird of Cessford —— 1597 conv., 1599 conv., as a minor baron.

Warden of the middle march (2nd son of Sir Walter, M.P., though not named in parliamentary return) ; m. 1st, 1562, Janet, widow of James Tweedie, of Drummelzier, dau. of Sir James Douglas, of Drumlanrig; he m. 2ndly, Jean Johnston, relict of Alexander, Lord [Abernethy, of session, and d. Feb. 1600.

(William), laird of Newton —— *Roxburghshire* 1646-7, 1656-8 (Willis).

Served heir special of his father Robert (uncle of Robert, Earl of Ancrum), 22 May 1639; a member of the committee for war 1643 and 1649 ; lieut.-col. of the regt. of horse raised in the counties of Roxburgh and Selkirk ; m. Agnes, dau. and co-heir of John Abernethy, [Bishop of Caithness 1616-35, and had 3 daus.

Ker or Kerr—*continued.*

William (sir), of Greenhead —— *Roxburghshire* 1685-6, 1702-7, 1707-8 (1st
[parlt. Great Britain).

3rd bart. (on the death of his brother, Sir Andrew, M.P. 1669, to whom he was served heir special 15 June 1676); a commissioner of supply 1685—1704 ; col. of militia 1689 ;
[dead in 1721, leaving issue.

William (master), —— *Dysart burghs* 1715-22.   See also England M.P.

Lieut.-genl. Kerr (1739), col. 7th regt. of dragoons 1709-41, served under the Duke of Marlborough ; was wounded at Sheriffmuir 13 Nov. 1715, when his horse was shot under him ; groom of the bedchamber to George, Prince of Wales ; a commissioner equivalent 1715 ; M.P. Berwick 1710-13, 1723-7, unduly elected Montrose burghs 1722 (3rd son of Robert, 3rd Earl of Roxburgh); d. unm. 7 Jan. 1741.

Kidd.

John, merchant trafficker, bailie —— *Arbroath* 1678 conv., 1681-2, 1685-6.

Robert (Kyd) —— *Dundee* 1357.

Kinglassie.

Harrie —— *Inverkeithing* 1612 —— 1630.

Mark —— *Inverkeithing* 1639-41 (bailie), 1643-4 conv., 1644-7, 1618.

Kingorne.

David (Mr.) —— *Dysart* 1630 conv.

George —— *Pitenweem* 1630 conv.

Kinloch.

Francis, lord provost —— *Edinburghshire* 1678 conv.

Sir Francis Kinloch, of Gilmerton, Haddington (said to be son of Andrew Kinloch), merchant at Rochelle, purchased Gilmerton, Athelstaneford, and Markle, in Haddington-shire, and had a charter of the barony of Markle 24 July 1664, a commissioner of supply, lord provost of Edinburgh, created a baronet of Nova Scotia 16 Sept. 1686, with remainder to his heirs male ; d. Sept. 1691, having m. Magdalen McMath ; she d. 16 Nov. 1674,
[having had a son and 2 daus.   See Foster's Baronetage.

George, of Kinloch —— *Dundee* 1833, until his death, 28 March, same year.

Younger son of Capt. George Oliphant Kinloch, of Rosemount, and father of Sir George
[Kinloch, cr. a baronet 16 April 1873. See Foster's Baronetage.

John, merchant, bailie —— *Dundee* 1667 conv.

Kinnaird.

Arthur Fitzgerald, 3rd son of late (Charles) Lord Kinnaird —— *Perth* 1837, until he accepted the Chiltern hundreds, s.b. 19 Aug. 1839; 1852, 1852-7, 1857-9, 1859-65, 1865-8, 1868-74, 1874 until he succ. as Baron Kinnaird, s.b. [29 Jan. 1878.

10th Lord Kinnaird 7 Jan. 1878, descended from Sir George, M.P., next named. See [Foster's Peerage.

George (sir), of Rossie, knt. —— *Perthshire* 1661-3.

Knighted by Chas. II. 1661, P.C., cr. Lord Kinnaird, of Inchture 28 Dec. 1682, with remainder to the heirs male of his body (son of Patrick, M.P., next named); d. 29 Dec. 1689; he m. Margaret, dau. of James Crichton, of Ruthven, and had issue, ancestor of Arthur [Fitzgerald, 10th lord, last named.

Patrick, of Inchture —— *Perthshire* 1625 conv. (laird), 1643 conv.

Served heir of Patrick, his father, 10 Oct. 1604, and was father of Sir George, last [named

Kinross.

James —— *Inverness* 1579.

Kintore.

Richard —— *Aberdeen* 1467, 1471.

Kirkcaldy.

John —— *Kinghorn* 1585 conv., 1600.
(? of the Grange family.)

Kirkpatrick.

(Sir Thomas), laird of Closeburn —— *Dumfries-shire,* 1593, as a minor baron.

Sir Thomas Kirkpatrick, gent. of the Privy Chamber, knighted by James VI., joined the Lord Maxwell who fell at the battle of Dryffe Sands, had a patent of free denizen within the kingdom of England; he m. twice, 2ndly (contract 17 Dec. 1614), Dame Barbara Stewart, dau. of Sir Alexander Stewart, of Garlies, ancestor of the Earls of Galloway; by his 1st wife [(name unknown), he had a son, Thomas, M.P., next named.

Thomas, of Closeburne —— *Dumfries* (or *Nithsdale*) *sheriffdom and stewartry of Annandale* 1639-41, "in case of abscence, Sir John Charteris, of Amisfield."

Son of Sir Thomas, M.P.; m. Agnes, dau. of Sir John Charteris, of Amisfield, and had [with other issue, Robert, father of Sir Thomas, M.P., next named.

Kirkpatrick—*continued*

Thomas (sir), of Closeburn, knt., bart. —— *Dumfries* (or *Nithsdale*) *sheriffdom* [*and stewartry of Annandale* 1690-1702.

> Sir Thomas Kirkpatrick, of Closeburne, lt.-col. Dumfries-shire militia 1691 (son of Robert Kirkpatrick, by Grizel, dau. of Sir William Baillie, of Lamington) ; created a baronet of Nova Scotia, 26 Mar. 1685, with remainder to his heirs male ; m. 1st (contract dated 25 April, 1666), Isabel Sandiland, dau. of John, Lord Torpichen ; and 2ndly (contract dated 7 Dec. 1672), Sarah, dau. of Robert Fergusson, esq., of Craigdarroch ; and 3rdly, 1686, Grizel, dau. of Gavin Hamilton, esq., of Raploch, widow of   Inglis of Murdiestown, [and had issue. See Foster's Baronetage.

William, of Lochmaben —— *Dumfries burghs* 1736 until appointed a principal [clerk of the court of session, s.b. 19 June 1738.

> Of Alisland (3rd son of Sir Thomas Kirkpatrick, 2nd bart.) ; m. 21 Dec. 1746, Jean, dau. of Charles Erskine, of Alva, lord justice clerk (son of Sir Charles Erskine, of Alva, [bart.) ; he d. 22 May 1778 ; and had issue.

Kirktown.

Alexander —— *Jedburgh* 1617, 1628-33, 1630 conv.

Kirkwood.

Gilbert, goldsmith —— *Edinburgh* 1633.

James —— *Haddington* 1597 conv.

Kirkyntolach.

Adam of —— *St. Andrews* 1357.

Knollis, or Knowis.

Johne, of —— *Aberdeen* 1469, 1472, 1478 bis, 1488, 1490.

Kynneries.

—— the laird of —— *Inverness-shire* 1646-7.

Kynynmound.

—— laird of Craigie Hall —— 1597 conv. (a minor baron) ; *Fifeshire* 1600, a [lord of the articles.

L.

Laing.

Malcolm, advocate of Strenzie —— *Orkney* and *Shetlandshire* 1807-12.

Admitted advocate 9 July 1785 (eldest son of Robert Laing, of Kirkwall, in Orkney) ; [d. 6 Nov. 1818, aged 56.

John (Layng or Layne) bailie —— *Forres* 1661.

Thomas (Lang) —— *Dumfries* 1357,

Samuel, of Brighton —— *Wick burghs* 1852-7, 1859, until appointed an ordinary member of council of governor-general of India s.b. 1 Dec. 1860 ; 1865-8 ; *Orkney* and *Shetlandshire* 1873-4, 1874-80, and since 1880. See foot-note.

Lamb.

Thomas —— *Kirkcaldy* 1612, 1617, 1621.

William, bailie, merchant —— *Haddington* 1678 conv.

William —— *Haddington burghs* 1806-7. See also England M.P.

2nd Viscount Melbourne, the celebrated premier, P.C., a commissioner of exchequer loans, an elder brother of the Trinity House, and a governor of the Charter House, A.M. Trin. Coll. Camb. 1799, studied jurisprudence and politics under Prof. Millar, at Glasgow, admitted to Lincoln's Inn 21 July 1797, called to the bar 23 Nov. 1804, entered the House of Commons as member for Leominster, M.P. 31 Jan. until 24 Oct. 1806, Haddington burghs as above, and moved the address on the king's speech ; Portarlington 1807-12, Peterboro' 1816-18, 1818-19, Herts 1819-20, 1820-6, chief sec. to the lord-lieutenant of Ireland 1827, home secretary 1830-4, M.P. Bletchingley 1827, until he succeeded to the peerage on the death of his father, Sir Peniston Lamb, 1st viscount, 22 July 1828, prime minister July to Nov. 1834, and April 1835 till Sept. 1841 ; b. 15 March 1779, d. s.p.s. 24 Nov. 1848, having m. 3 June 1805, Lady Caroline Ponsonby, only dau. of Frederick, 3rd Earl of Bessborough ; [she d. 25 Jan. 1828, she was known as a novelist.

L AING, SAMUEL, of Hordle House, Hants, and of Crook, Isle of Orkney, J.P., D.L., B.A., St. John's College, Cambridge (2nd wrangler), 1832 formerly fellow, bar.-at-law L.I. 1840, a railway commissioner, chairman of the Brighton railway 1867, and of Sydenham palace compy. 1848-54 ; M.P. as above, contested Wick burghs 1868, financial sec. to the treasury 1859-60, finance minister of India 1860-2 (son of Samuel Laing, of Papdale, Orkney, by Agnes, dau. of Francis Kelly, of Kelly, Devon) ; b. 1812, m. 1841, Mary, dau. of Capt. Cowan, R.N., and had with other issue,

(1) Samuel, bar.-at-law, b. 1842, d. 1870, having m. 1869, Mary, 2nd dau. of T. W. Riddell Webster, esq., of Invereighty, co. Forfar, and had a son.

Crook, Kirkwall, N.B. ; Eastern Terrace, Brighton ; 36, *Wilton Crescent, S.W.*
Club—Reform.

Lamont.

—— laird of —— *Argyllshire* 1630 conv.

Archibald, of Inneryne —— *Argyllshire* 1685-6.

James, of Inneryne —— *Argyllshire* 1639-40.

James, of Knockdow —— *Buteshire* 1865-8. Sec foot-note.

Lanark.

—— the bailie of —— *Lanark* 1543.

Lauder.

—— laird of Bas —— a minor baron in parlt. 1592, 1593 conv. bis; 1594 conv.
[(4) 1597 conv., 1598 conv., 1599 conv., and 1605 conv.

(Probably Sir Robert Lauder, of Bas, father of Sir Robert Lauder, of Popil, knt.)

—— laird of Haltoun —— *Edinburghshire* 1621.

Alexander (provost) —— *Edinburgh* 1504 bis.

Andrew —— *Lauder* 1583 bis.

Charles, of Park, merchant —— *Lauder* 1681-2.

George (or John Levington) —— *North Berwick* 1649.

Hugh —— *Dunbar* 1587.

James —— *Dunbar* 1645, *Renfrew* 1645, scs. 2, *Dunbar* 1646-7 (or William
[Purves), 1648.

James —— *Dunbar* 1661-3 (and Thomas Purves, two of the bailies "conjunctly
and severally"); 1665 conv., 1667 conv. (merchant burgess, bailie) 1669-72;
Haddington 1690 (Mr., bailie, late provost), until his death s.b. 13 Aug.
[1696.

John (sir), of Fountainhall, senator of the college of justice —— *Haddington
constabulary* 1685-6, 1690-1702, 1702-7.

Sir John Lauder, of Fountain Hall, co. Haddington (grandson of Andrew Lauder and
Janet, dau. of Andrew Ramsay, of Polton), advocate 1668, counsel to the Duke of Monmouth at his trial 1686, appointed an ordinary lord of session as Lord Fountainhall at the
revolution 1689, and a lord of justiciary 1690, declined the appointment of lord advocate
1692 ; created a baronet of Nova Scotia 25 Jan. 1690, with remainder to his issue male; d.
20 Sept. 1722, having m. Margaret, 2nd dau. of Sir Alexander Seton, Lord Pitmedden of session, and had issue, ancestor of Sir Thomas North Dick-Lauder, see Foster's Baronetage.

LAMONT, JAMES, of Knockdow, co. Argyll, J.P., D.L., M.P. as above ; D.L. Bute, F.R.S. ~
F.R.G.S. (only son of late Alexander Lamont, esq., D.L. of Knockdow), b. 1828, m. 10 March,
1868, Adelaide Eliza, dau. of Sir George William Denys, 2nd bart., and had 2 sons and a dau.
(1) Norman, b. 7 Dec. 1869.   (2) Alexander, b. 24 Aug. 1872.   (3) Augusta.
Knockdow, Inellan, N.B. ; 4, *Queen St., May Fair, W.*
Clubs—Arthur and Union.

Lauder—*continued.*

John (sir), of Haltoun —— *Edinburghshire* 1685-6, 1689 conv., 1689-93 (as Sir John Maitland of Ravelrig), 1693, until he succeeded as Earl of Lauderdale [s.b. 28 Aug. 1696.

Sir John Maitland, of Ravelrig, 5th Earl of Lauderdale (on the death of his brother Richard, 1695), created a baronet of Nova Scotia 18 Nov. 1680, advocate 30 July 1680, lord of session 28 Oct. 1689, as Lord Ravelrig, P.C. at the Revolution, col. Edinburghshire militia, 1689, took his seat in parliament 8 Sept. 1696, supported the Union, general of the mint 1699 (2nd son of Charles, 3rd Earl of Lauderdale, by his wife Elizabeth, only dau. and heir of Richard Lauder, of Hatton), assumed the designation of " Lauder of Haltoun " 1693, in lieu of " Maitland of Ravelrig "; d. 30 Aug. 1710, having m. Margaret, only child of Alexander Cunningham, 10th Earl of Glencairn, she died 12 May 1742, leaving with other [issue a son Charles, 6th Earl. See Foster's Peerage.

Maurice —— *Dunbar* 1585.

Robert —— *North Berwick* 1600.

Thomas —— *North Berwick* 1579, 1583 —— 1612, 1617.

William, bailie of Edinburgh —— 1528.

William ——*Lauder* 1649.

Laurie.

John, of Maxwelltoun —— *Dumfries* (or *Nithsdale*) *sheriffdom and stewartry of* [*Annandale* 1643 conv.

Son of Stephen Laurie, of Maxwelltoun, which he purchased from the Earl of Glencairn, and father of Sir Robert Laurie ; cr. a bart. 27 March, 1685, who was grandfather of Sir [Robert, next named.

Robert (sir), of Maxwelltoun, bart. —— *Dumfries burghs* 1738-41.

4th baronet (on the death of his father, Sir Walter, at Carse, 5 May 1764) ; d. 28 Apl. 1779, having m. 4 Feb. 1733, Christian, dau. of Charles Erskine, lord alva of session and lord justice clerk of session (E. MAR) ; she d. 21 Aug. 1755. aged 40, leaving with 2 daus. a [son, Sir Robert, M.P., next named.

Robert (sir), of Maxwelltoun, bart. —— *Dumfries-shire* 1774-80 (then younger), 1780-4, 1784-90 (knight marshal of Scotland 1785), 1790-6, 1796-1802, 1802 [until his death s.b. 8 Nov. 1804.

General Sir Robert Laurie (5th bart. on the death of his father, Sir Robert, M.P., 28 Apl. 1779), col. 8th regt. dragoons, lieut.-col. 16th light dragoons; d. 10 Sept. 1804, having m. 1st, 18 July 1763, Hon. Mary Elizabeth Ruthven, dau of 6th Lord Ruthven, and had a son, vice-admiral Sir Robert, 6th bart., K.C.B., who d. unm. 7 Jan. 1848, and a dau. ; he m. [2ndly, 25 Apl. 1778, Judith, relict of Robert Wollaston, esq., dau of — Hatley, esq.

Law.

James —— *Kirkcaldy* 1644-5, 1649 in absence of John Williamson.

Lawson.

James —— *Edinburgh* 1526, 1531, 1532.

Senator of the college of justice 27 May 1532 (2nd son of Richard Lawson, of Hariggs, [lord justice clerk, M.P.), provost of Edinburgh 1534.

James, bailie —— *Anstruther Easter* 1678 conv.

Possibly of Cairnmuir, and son of James Lawson, of that place; m. Isabel, dau. of John [Muirhead, of Linhouse, and had a son John.

Richard (Mr.) —— *Edinburgh* 1479 bis, 1482, 1483 bis, 1484 bis, 1485, 1488, [1491, 1492, 1493.

Richard Lawson, of Hariggs (Highriggs), justice clerk about 1488 ; a counsellor appointed for managing the affairs of James IV., one of the commissioners to negotiate a treaty with the English commissioners 1490 and 1497 ; m. Janet Elphinston, and had with other issue a son, [James, M.P.

(Sir William), laird of Boghall —— *Linlithgowshire* 1625 conv.

Sir William Lawson, of Lochtulloch and Boghall (son of John Lawson and Christian Livingstone, of Kilsyth). "This Sir William dilapidate and put away most of his fortune before his death, and went to Holland to the wars."—*Scotstarbets Staggering State; d. May [1628.

Lawtie.

George —— *Cullen* 1646-7, 1648

James —— *Cullen* 1628-33.

Learmonth.

David (Leirmonth) —— *St. Andrews* 1524.

James —— *St. Andrews* 1524, 1535, 1540, 1543 (then provost), 1544.

James, of Dersie —— *St. Andrews* 1587, 1593 (the laird), 1600.

James (sir), of Balcomie, knt. —— *Fifeshire* 1625, conv.

Lord of session 8 Nov. 1627, a member of various parliamentary commissions 1633, re-appointed a judge by the king in 1641, elected president of court of session in 1643 and 1647, joined in the " Engagement," and was deprived of his offices ; a commissioner for the administration of justice 1655 (son of Sir John Learmonth, M.P., next named) ; died while [sitting on the bench 26 June 1657.

(Sir John), laird of Balcomie —— *Fifeshire* 1593 (as a minor baron), 1596, conv., [1604 and 1609, conv. (as a minor baron) ; *Fifeshire* 1612, then a knt.

Probably John Learmonth, of Balcomie, who m. Elizabeth Myrtone, dau. of the laird [of Randerston, and had a son, Sir James, M.P., last named.

Patrick (sir), of Dersie, knt. —— *St. Andrews* 1567, 1568 (then provost), 1569 [conv.

Patrick, of Dersie —— *St. Andrews* 1581 (the laird), 1585 conv.

Leighton

(————) —— *Montrose* 1578, conv.

Patrick —— *Montrose* 1612, 1630, conv.

Robert —— *Montrose* 1581, 1587.

Leith-Hay.

Andrew (sir) —— *Elgin burghs* 1833-4 (clerk of the ordnance 1834, then lieut-col.); 1835-7 (clerk of the ordnance 1835); 1837 (then a knt., younger, of Rannes), until appointed governor of Bermuda, s.b. 13 Feb. 1838; 1841-7.

Sir Andrew Leith-Hay, of Rannes and Leith Hall, co. Aberdeen, J.P., D.L., lieut.-col. in the army, K.H. 1834, a knight commander of the order of Charles III. of Spain, K.L.H., clerk of the ordnance 1834-8, governor of Bermuda 1838-41, served throughout the Peninsular war, of which he wrote a history ; (son of Gen. Alexander Leith-Hay, by his wife Mary Forbes ;) b. 17 Feb. 1785, d. 13 Oct. 1862, having m. 1816, Mary Margaret, dau. of William Clark, esq., of Buckland House, Devon ; she d. 28 May 1859, [leaving with other issue Col. Leith-Hay, C.B.

Leith.

John Farley, Q.C., of London —— *Aberdeen* 1872-4, 1874-80. See foot-note.

Thomas —— *Linlithgow* 1367.

William —— *Aberdeen* 1357, 1367.

Of Ruthrieston, provost of Aberdeen 1352 and 1355.

Lentron.

James —— *St. Andrews* 1646-7, or James Robertson.

Robert, merchant burgess, provost —— *St. Andrews City* 1665 conv.

LEITH, JOHN FARLEY, of Prittlewell Priory, Essex, M.A. Aberdeen 1825; bar.-at-law Middle Temple 1830; Q.C. 1872, and a bencher 1874, practises before the Privy Council, formerly an advocate Supreme Court, Calcutta ; M.P. as above (son of late James Urquhart Leith, capt. 68th regt., who fell in action near Orthes, by Mary Ann, dau. of Andrew Henderson, M.D., of Aberdeen) ; b. 5 May 1808 ; m. 1 June 1832, Alicia Amé, dau. of late Samuel Tompkins, of London, banker ; she d. 25 Sept. 1876, having had with other issue 3 sons and 4 daus.

(1) James Percy, late of Bombay, b. 7 March 1838.
(2) William Ernest Gordon, B.A. Trin. Hall, Camb., b. 19 Apl. 1855.
(3) Edward Tyrrell, of Bombay, L.L.M., bar.-at-law M.T., govt. prof. of law at Bombay University; b. 12 March 1842, m. 25 May 1875, Evelyn Mary, dau. of John Dawson, of London, and has a dau., Essyllt Amy.
(4) Mary Ann, m. 11 Nov. 1858 to Sir William Miller, of Manderston, bart., M.P.
(5) Helen.   (6) Emily.   (7) Alicia Amy.
Prittlewell Priory, Southend; 8, Dorset Sq., N.W.
Club—Brooks'.

Lepar.

John, provost —— *St. Andrews City* 1639-40, 1644-6.

Leslie.

Andrew, bailie —— *Elgin* 1661-3.

Son of William Leslie, merchant, of Elgin, of the Bucharn family; m. Margaret Hay, and [had a son James.

Charles (Mr.) —— *Perth burghs* 28 April 1722 (double return), until unseated [27 Oct. following.

Col. Earl Drumlanrig's regt., raised for service in States of Holland (brother of John, [8th Earl of Rothes); d. 16 Aug. 1769.

George, eldest son of William Leslie, of Burdsbank —— *Cullen* 1663, 1678 [(bailie), 1685-6 (late bailie).

Son of William Leslie, second goodman of Burdsbank, by his wife, Helen Munro, of [Milltoun; he m. Christian, dau. of Sir James Baird, of Auchmeddan, and had issue.

(John), laird of Balquhain —— *Aberdeenshire* 1593 (a minor baron) —— 1608 [of that ilk.

10th laird, sheriff-principal Aberdeen 1580-97, constable of the bishop's palace, Aberdeen (eldest son of William Leslie, 9th laird, by his wife Janet, widow of John, Earl of Atholl, dau. of John, 6th Lord Forbes); m. 1st (contract 15 Feb. 1564) Elizabeth, dau. of —— Grant, of Grant, whom it is said he divorced; he m. 2ndly (before 1595), Elizabeth, dau. of George Hay, 6th Earl of Errol, she divorced him 9 March 1597; he m. 3rdly, at Lethnal, 6 July 1598, Jean, dau. of Sir Alex. Erskine, of Gogar, sister of Thomas, 1st Earl of Kellie; it is said that all his 3 wives were alive at the same time, and were on one occasion all in the same [chapel of Garioch; he d. in 1622, leaving issue, father of John, M.P., next named.

John, of Bochane —— *Aberdeenshire* 1617; *Kintore* 1621.

11th laird, John Leslie, fiar of Balquhain, elected 1 Oct. 1616 (son of John, 10th laird, M.P.); he m. 1st, Marjory Gordon, widow of Robert Duguid, 5th baron of Auchinhove; he [m. 2ndly, Janet Innes, dau. of the laird of Auchintoul, and d. 1638, leaving issue.

John (sir), of Newton —— *Fifeshire* 1621 (the laird), 1633, then described as a [knight.

Of Newton, served heir of his brother George 5 July 1620, lord of session 13 Nov. 1641, knighted 2 days after by Chas. I. at Holyrood House, a commissioner of exchequer 1645, lt.-col. king's horse guards, concerned in the "engagement," and deprived of his offices 1649, killed with his son David at the storming of Dundee (by Genl. Monk) 1 Dec. 1651 (5th son of Andrew, 4th Earl of Rothes); m. Elizabeth, dau. of Patrick, 7th Lord Gray, and had [issue.

Norman —— *Kilrenny* 1621.

Patrick, bailie —— *Aberdeen* 1633, 1640-1 (provost), 1643 conv., 1644-5 (pro-[vost), 1648 (provost).

Sir Patrick Leslie, of Whitehall, in 1652.

Leslie—*continued.*

Thomas, of Stenton (captain), brother-german of John, Earl of Rothes —— *Kirkcaldy burghs* 28 April 1722 (double return) until unseated 27 Oct. following, and 1734-41 ; *Perth burghs* 1743-7 (then captain), 1747-54 (of Stenton), [1754-61, then barrack-master-general of Scotland.

Equerry to Prince of Wales 1742, capt. 46th regt. of foot, wounded and taken prisoner by the rebels at the battle of Preston 1745, barrack master Scotland 1748-69, died unm. [17 March 1772.

William, of Warthill —— *Aberdeenshire* 1861-5, 1865 until he accepted the [Chiltern hundreds s.b. 15 May 1866.

Of Warthill, co. Aberdeen, J.P., D.L., M.A. Aberdeen, a partner in Dent and Company, China (son of Wm. Leslie, of Warthill) ; b. 16 Mar. 1814, d. 4 Mar. 1880, having m. 16 Nov. 1848, Matilda Rose, 2nd dau. of late Wm. Rose Robinson. esq., of Clermiston, Midlothian, [and had, with 7 sons who died young, 5 daus.

Liberton.

William, of —— *Edinburgh* 1450.

Lincoln.

Henry Pelham Pelham-Clinton, commonly called Earl of —— *Falkirk burghs* 1846-7, 1847 until he succeeded as Duke of Newcastle 12 Jan. 1851. [See also England M.P.

5th Duke of Newcastle, K.G., 17 Dec. 1860, secretary of state for the Colonies 1852-4, 1859 64, commissioner of woods and forests, lord warden of the Stannaries 1862-4, chief secretary for Ireland 1846, secretary of state for war 1854, M.P. South Notts 1832-5, 1835-7, 1837-41, 1841-6 (son of Henry Pelham, 4th Duke, K.G.); b. 22 May, 1811; d. 18 Oct. [1864, leaving issue. See Foster's Peerage.

Lind.

George, lord provost of Edinburgh —— *Edinburgh* 1761 until appointed conservator of the privileges of the Scots nation in the Netherlands, and resident [there for the affairs of Scotland s.b. 27 Feb. 1762.

2nd son of George Lind, of Gorgie, by his 2nd wife, Joan, dau. of Hugh Montgomery, of [Smithton ; d. at Edinburgh 4 June 1763.

Lindsay.

Alexander —— *Perth* 1545.

David —— *Cupar* 1540, 1543 bis, 1544, 1545, 1548 (then provost). See Lord Crawford's "Lives of the Lindsays," vol. i. 209.

David (sir) —— *Cupar* 1571 conv., 1572 conv. (then provost), 1585 (then a [knight).

Probably identical with Sir David Lindsay, of Ratherlet, lyon king of arms 1568, half-brother of Sir David of the Mount. See Lord Crawford's "Lives of the Lindsays," vol. i. 467.

Lindsay—*continued.*

David (sir), of Edzell —— as a minor baron 1597 conv., 1598 conv. bis, 1599 [conv., 1605 conv. (laird of Edzell), 1608, then a knight.

> A lord of session, 2 Mar. 1598, P.C. 1603 (eldest son of Sir David Lindsay, of Edzell and Glenesk, 8th Earl of Crawford); m. 1st, Helen Lindsay, dau. of David, 9th Earl of Crawford, [m. 2ndly, Isobel Forbes, and d. before 16 Jan. 1610-11, leaving issue.

David —— *Brechin* 1621.

> Served heir of his father (Robert) as citizen and hereditary smith in Brechin 1605.

David, of Edzell —— *Forfarshire* 1678 conv.

> De jure 14th Lord Lindsay (son of John Lindsay, of Edzell); m. Agnes, dau. of James [Graham, brother, of Fintry, and d. 1698, having had issue.

Hugh (esq.), deputy chairman of the East India Company, residing in London [—— *Forfar burghs* 1820-6, 1826-30.

> Marshal of the Court of Admiralty, director East India Co. 1814-44, a commissioner for lieutenancy of London, served in the Navy under Lord Rodney and Lord St. Vincent, commander H.E.I.C.S. (son of James, 5th Earl of Balcarres); b. 30 Oct. 1765, d. 23 April 1844, m. 14 Jan. 1799, Jane, 2nd dau. of Hon. Alexander Gordon, Lord Rockville, of Session [(E. ABERDEEN), she d. 26 May, 1862, leaving issue

(James), of Belstanes —— *Lanarkshire* 1643-4 conv.

> Col. James Lindsay, of Belstain, co. Lanark, gov. of Edinburgh Castle 1641, of Berwick [Castle 1644-58.

James (lt.-col.), younger, of Balcarres —— *Fifeshire* 1831-2.

> Lt.-Gen. Lindsay served with grenadier guards at Walcheren 1809, at defence of Cadiz 1811, in Peninsula campaigns 1812-3, and under Lord Lynedoch in Holland, severely wounded at the assault upon Bergen-op-Zoom, contested Fifeshire 1835 (grandson of James, 5th Earl of Balcarres); b. 17 April, 1793, d. 5 Dec. 1855, leaving with other issue (see Foster's Peerage and Baronetage) 2 sons, viz., Sir Coutts Lindsay, 2nd bart., and Sir Robert James [Loyd-Lindsay, K.C.B., M.P. Berks. See England.

(Sir John), laird of Dunrod —— *Lanarkshire* 1593 (as a minor baron), 1596 [conv. (as a minor baron).

> 2nd son of Robert Lindsay, of Dunrod, served heir of his brother 1591, knighted at the [baptism of Henry, Prince of Scotland, 1594, and had a son Alexander, of Dunrod.

John —— *Anstruther Easter* 1641, 1650-1.

John, of Edzell —— *Forfarshire* 1649.

> Son of Alexander Lindsay, who was 2nd son of Sir David, M.P. 1597, etc.; m. Magdalen, [relict of Alexander, master of Spynie, 2nd dau. of John Carnegie, 1st Earl of Northesk.

Lindsay—*continued*

John (sir), of the royal navy, knt. —— *Aberdeen burghs* 1767-8.

> Rear-Adml. Sir John Lindsay, K.B., capt· R.N. 1757, knighted 10 Feb. 1764, princi-
> pally for his services at the attack on the Havannahs, invested with the Order of the Bath
> 11 March 1771, by the Nabob of Arcot (installed 1772) while serving in the East Indics,
> a lord of the admiralty 1783, rear-adml. 14 Sept. 1787 (son of Sir Alexander, and brother
> of Sir David Alexander, of Evelick, Perthshire, barts.) ; d. s.p.l. 7 June 1788, aged 51,
> bd. in Westminster Abbey, 16th ; he m. 19 Sept. 1768, Mary, only dau. of Sir William
> Milner, of Nunappleton, Yorkshire, bart. ; she d. 24 Oct. 1799, bd. with her husband, 30th.

Patrick, Lord Lindsay, of the Byres, provost of Edinburgh —— as a baron 1575
[conv.

> 6th Lord Lindsay, of the Byres, a lord of the congregation and a zealous reformer, one
> of the peers concerned in seizing the king's person at the raid of Ruthven 1582, and in the
> death of Rizzio, and also in the deposition of Q. Mary, sheriff of Fife by charter 1574, of
> the bailiary of St. Andrews 1580, which continued to his descendants till the abolition of
> heritable jurisdictions 1748 ; m. Euphemc, eldest dau. of Sir Robert Douglas, of Lochleven
> [(half-sister of the Regent Moray), and d. 11 Dec. 1589, leaving issue.

Patrick, lord provost of Edinburgh —— *Edinburgh City* 1734-41·

> . Governor of the Isle of Man, an officer in Sir Robert Rich's regt. of foot in Spain until
> the peace of Utrecht, when he settled in business in Edinburgh (only surviving son of
> Patrick Lindsay, rector of the Grammar School) ; d. 17 Feb. 1753, having m. 1st,
> Margaret, dau. of David Montier, merchant in Edinburgh, and had issue ; he m. 2ndly,
> Janet, dau of James Murray, of Polton ; she d. s.p. ; he m. 3rdly, 7 May 1741, Lady Mary
> [Lindsay, youngest dau. of William, 14th Earl of Crawford : she d. 20 April 1769.

Robert, of Dunrod —— *Rutherglen* 1579 (then provost).

> Probably elder brother of Sir John, M.P., 1593, and d. s.p.

Robert —— *Rutherglen* 1617·

Linlithgow.

(——) the provost of —— *Linlithgow* 1560.

George, Earl of —— *Perth sheriffdom* 1654-5 (English parlt.).

> 3rd Earl of Linlithgow, constable and keeper of the palace of Linlithgow and castle of
> Blackness 1642, and also as Earl of Linlithgow 1669, espoused the royal cause, and
> accordingly suffered with its reverses, col. royal regt. of horse guards, P.C. at the Restoration,
> justice-general of Scotland 1681, deprived at the revolution (son of Alexander, 2nd Earl of
> Linlithgow) ; d. 1 Feb. 1690, having m. 30 July 1650, Elizabeth, dowager of John, 2nd Earl
> [of Kinghorn, dau. of Patrick Maule, 1st Earl of Panmure ; she d. Oct. 1659, leaving issue.

Little.

Edward —— *Edinburgh* 1526.

William —— *Edinburgh* 1592 (then provost).

Livingstone.

Adam, lt.-col., late North British fusiliers —— *Argyleshire* 1772-4, 1774-80.

Henry —— 1469, 1479.

James (sir), of Kilsyth, knt., cr. viscount of Kilsyth 17 Aug. 1661 —— *Stirling-*
[*shire* 1661.

Viscount of Kilsyth and Lord Campsie, cr. as above, a zealous royalist, fined £1,500 by
Cromwell's act of grace and pardon (son of Sir Wm. Livingstone, of Kilsyth, M.P. 1599,
etc.) ; b. 25 June 1616, d. 7 Sept. 1661, having m. Eupheme, dau. of Sir David Cuninghame,
[of Robertland, and had issue, Sir William, M.P., afterwards 3rd visct.

John (sir), of Dunipace, knt. —— 1605 conv. (the laird, as a minor baron);
Stirlingshire 1607, 1609 conv. (the laird), 1612 (Sir John), 1617 conv. (the
[laird], 1617 parlt., 1621 (the laird), 1630 conv. (the laird).

John (Levington) —— *North Berwick* 1649 (or George Lauder) 1649.

Robert —— (*Lanark*) 1587.

William (sir) —— 1599 conv. (laird of Kilsyth) 1602 conv. ; *Linlithgowshire*
1605 (as a minor baron), and as a minor baron 1605 conv., 1608 (Sir William),
[and 1609 conv.

A lord of session 6 June 1609, accompanied the Duke of Lennox on an embassy to
France 1601, P.C. and vice-chamberlain of Scotland 1613, a commissioner for the plantation of Kirks 1621 (only son of Sir William Livingston, of Kilsyth, by Christina, dau. of
John Graham, 4th Earl of Monteith); d. 1627, m. twice, and had issue, Sir James, M.P.,
[cr. Visct. of Kilsyth.

William (Mr.), of Kilsyth —— *Stirlingshire* 1685-6, 1702.

3rd Visct. (on the death of his brother James 1706), a representative peer 1710 and 1713,
engaged in the rebellion 1715, was attainted of high treason, his estate and honours forfeited,
[and d. at Rome 12 Jan. 1733, s.p.s., having m. twice.

William —— *Aberdeen* (now *Montrose*) *burghs* 1711-13.

Married —— dau. of John Skene of that ilk.

Loch.

George, Q.C., of London —— *Wick burghs* 1868, until he accepted the steward-
[ship of the manor of Northsted, co. York, s.b. 28 Feb. 1872.

Of Drylaw, co. Edinburgh, F.G.S., J.P., D.L., co. Sutherland, J.P. co. Lanc., admitted
to the Middle Temple 25 April 1844, called to the bar Easter term 1847, Q.C. and a bencher
1863, treasurer 1875, attorney-genrl. to the Prince of Wales ; contested Falkirk burghs 1851,
Manchester 1852 (son of James Loch, M.P.) ; b. 6 July 1811, d. 18 Aug. 1877, aged 66 ;
having m.   1836, Catherine, eldest dau of Joseph Pilkington Brandreth, esq., M.D.,
[of Liverpool, and had 4 daus.

Loch—*continued*

James, of London, bar.-at-law —— *Wick burghs* 1830-1, 1831-2, 1833-4, 1835-7, [1837-41, 1841-7, 1847-52. See also England M.P.

Of Drylaw afsd., a fellow of the Geological, Statistical, and Zoological Societies of London, admitted to the faculty of advocates 1801, called to the bar of Lincoln's Inn 15 Nov. 1806, auditor to the Duke of Sutherland, Earl of Carnarvon. and Earl of Ellesmere (when Lord Francis Egerton), and to the trust estates of the Earl of Dudley and of Viscount Keith, M.P. St. Germains 1827-30, contested the Wick burghs 1852 (son of George Loch, of Drylaw, by his wife Mary, dau. of John Adam, esq , of Blair, co. Kinross, sister of Rt. Hon. Wm. Adam, M.P., whom see); b. 7 May 1780, d. 5 July 1855, having m. 1st, 10 Aug. 1810, Ann, youngest dau. of Patrick Orr, esq., and had issue, he m. 2ndly, 2 Dec. 1847, Elizabeth Mary, widow of George Macartney Greville, major 38th foot (E. WARWICK), eldest dau. of John Pearson, esq., of Tettenhall Wood, co. Staff., judge-advocate-general) ;
[she d. 29 Dec. 1848.

Lockhart.

Alexander Macdonald, of Carnwath —— *Lanarkshire* 1837-41.

3rd son of Sir Alexander Macdonald Lockhart, bart., D.L. ; b. July 1806, d. unm. 27 Oct.
[1861. See Foster's Baronetage.

Cromwell, of Lee —— *Lanarkshire* 1678 conv., 1681-2, 1685-6.

Eldest son of Sir William Lockhart, of Lee ; m. 1st,   dau. of Sir Daniel Harvey, ambassador-extraordinary at Constantinople, he m. 2ndly his cousin Martha, dau. and eventual sole heir of Sir John Lockhart, of Castlehill (she re-m. to Sir John Sinclair, of [Stevenson, bart.); d. s.p., and was succeeded by his brother Richard, M.P.

George —— *Ayr* 1605 conv.

Of Bar, Ayrshire.

George (sir), of Braidwood —— *Lanarkshire* 1658-9 (English parliament see WILLIS), 1681-2, 1685-6 (then of Carnwath), lord president of the session [1 Jan. 1686.

Sir George Lockhart, of Carnwath (son of Sir James Lockhart, M.P.), advocate to Oliver Cromwell 1658-60, sheriff of Lanark 1658-9, knighted 1663, advocate 8 Jan. 1656, dean of faculty 1672, lord president of the court of session 1686, P.C., and commissioner of the Exchequer ; assassinated in Edinburgh on his return from church Easter day 31 Mar. 1689, having m. 2 Sept. 1679, Philadelphia, youngest dau. of Philip, 4th Lord Wharton, and sister of Philip, Duke of Wharton ; she d. 3 July 1722 (having re-m. to Capt. John Ramsay, son [of the bishop of Ross), and had with other issue a son George, M.P., next named.

George, of Carnwath —— *Edinburghshire* 1702-7, 1708-10 (returned also for the [*Wigton burghs*) 1710-13, 1713-15.

A commissioner for settling the articles of Union, author of the " Memoirs of Scotland " (son of Sir George, M.P., last named) ; d. 17 Dec. 1731, having m. Euphemia Montgomerie, dau. of Alexander, 8th Earl of Eglintoun ; she d. at Tarnaway 1 Dec. 1738, having had issue.
[See Foster's Baronetage.

James (sir), laird of Lee —— *Lanarkshire* 1607.

Knighted by James VI. (son of James Lockhart, of Lee, by his 1st wife, Janet, dau. of Robert Hamilton, of Dalserfe), m. thrice, and had issue, ancestor of the baronets Lockhart [and Ross (see Foster's Baronetage), father of Sir James, M.P., next named.

Lockhart—*continued.*

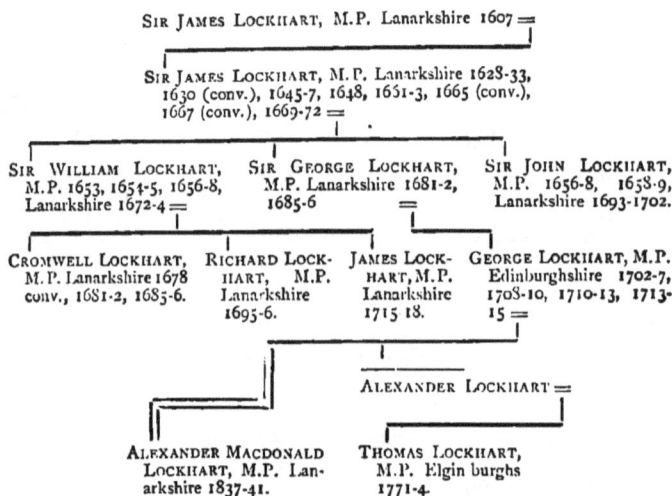

SIR JAMES LOCKHART, M.P. Lanarkshire 1607 =

SIR JAMES LOCKHART, M.P. Lanarkshire 1628-33,
1630 (conv.), 1645-7, 1648, 1651-3, 1665 (conv.),
1667 (conv.), 1669-72 =

| SIR WILLIAM LOCKHART, M.P. 1653, 1654-5, 1656-8, Lanarkshire 1672-4 = | SIR GEORGE LOCKHART, M.P. Lanarkshire 1681-2, 1685-6 = | SIR JOHN LOCKHART, M.P. 1656-8, 1658-9, Lanarkshire 1693-1702. |

| CROMWELL LOCKHART, M.P. Lanarkshire 1678 conv., 1681-2, 1685-6. | RICHARD LOCKHART, M.P. Lanarkshire 1695-6. | JAMES LOCKHART, M.P. Lanarkshire 1715-18. | GEORGE LOCKHART, M.P. Edinburghshire 1702-7, 1708-10, 1710-13, 1713-15 = |

ALEXANDER LOCKHART =

| ALEXANDER MACDONALD LOCKHART, M.P. Lanarkshire 1837-41. | THOMAS LOCKHART, M.P. Elgin burghs 1771-4. |

James (sir), laird of Lee, senator of the college of justice —— *Lanarkshire* 1628-33, 1630 conv. (the laird, younger), 1645-7 (the laird), 1648 (then senator of the college of justice), 1661-3, 1665 conv., 1667 conv., 1669 until [appointed lord justice clerk s.b. 20 March, 1672.

> Sir James Lockhart, knt. of Lee (eldest son of Sir James Lockhart, of Lee), gent. of the privy chamber to Charles I. and knighted, lord of the articles 1633, a commissioner of the exchequer 1645, a senator of the college of justice in 1646 as Lord Lee, commanded a regt. *ex parte regis* at the battle of Preston 1648, deprived of all his offices for his attachment to the royal family 1649, and was sent a prisoner to the tower of London 1651, on the Restoration he was reinstated as a lord of session, privy councillor 1661, lord justice clerk 1671; d. May 1674, aged 78, having m. 1st, Helen, dau. of Alexander Fairlie, of Braid, and 2ndly, Martha (maid of honour to Queen Mary, consort of Charles I.), dau. of Sir George Douglas, [of Mordington, brother of James, Lord Torthorwald, by whom he had issue.

James, of Lee —— *Lanarkshire* 1715 until his death s.b. 23 Dec. 1718.

> A commissioner equivalent (5th and youngest son of Col. Sir William Lockhart, M.P.); m. Dorothy, dau. and co-heir of Sir William Luckyn, of Waltham Abbey, Essex, and d. [19 Oct. 1718, having had issue. See Douglas' Baronage.

John —— *Ayr* 1567, 1575 conv., 1578 conv., 1579.

> Of Bar, Ayrshire; m. —— dau. of —— Mure, of Rowallan.

John —— *Ayr* 1604, 1605, 1607, 1609 conv., 1612.

> Of Bar, Ayrshire; m. Marion Cunningham (who d. Jan. 1623), he d. April 1614, will [dated at Ayr 16 April 1614, had a son John, who d. April 1624.

Lockhart—*continued*

John (sir), of Castlehill —— *Sheriffdom of Dumbarton, Argyle & Bute* 1656-8, *boroughs of Lannerick, Glasgow, etc.*, 1658-9 (Eng. parlt., see WILLIS), *Lanark* [*shire* 1693-1702.

3rd son of Sir James Lockhart, of Lee, M.P. 1628, etc.; advocate 4 Jan. 1656, re-admitted (after the restoration) 7 June 1662, a lord of session, as Lord Castlehill, 1665, and a lord of [justiciary 1671-8, restored 1683, had at least a son and dau. See Foster's Baronetage.

Richard, of Lee —— *Lanarkshire* 1695 until his death s.b. 26 Aug. 1696.

Of Lee, on the death of his brother Cromwell, M.P., he m. Jean, dau. of Sir Patrick Houstoun [of that ilk, bart., and d. s.p.

Robert —— *Lanark* 1612.

Stephen —— *Lanark* 1485, 1491, 1492 bis, 1493.

Thomas, counsellor-at-law, Lincoln's Inn —— *Elgin burghs* 1771-4.

Of Craighouse (eldest son of Alexander Lockhart, Lord Covington, of Session 1775); d. s.p. at Weymouth 22 July 1775, having m. Mary, dau. of Rev. Wm. Danby, D.D., of Swinton, Yorks, she re-m. 21 Sept. 1778 to F. M. William, 3rd Earl of Harcourt, G.C.B., [who d. s.p. 18 June 1830.

William (sir) —— (1653, 1654-5, 1656-8, Eng. parlt.—WILLIS) *Lanarkshire* [1672-74.

Sir William Lockhart, capt. of horse in the French service, returned to England and was appointed lieut.-col. in Earl Lanark's regt., said to have been cr. a baronet of Nova Scotia (see list, Foster's Baronetage), espoused the royal cause, and was taken prisoner by Gen. Lambert, comr. for administration of justice 1652, and one of the council of Oliver Cromwell, knighted by Cromwell, 10 Dec. 1654, ambassador to France 1655. and Brandenburg 1670, keeper of the signet of Scotland, com.-in-chief of the forces against Spain, was the principal personage in inducing the French to give up Dunkirk to the English army, and was constituted its governor (son of Sir James Lockhart, M.P. 1628, etc.); d. 20 Mar. 1675-6, having m. April 1654, Robina, dau. of John Sewster, of Wiston, Hunts, niece by her mother of Oliver Cromwell, and had with 2 daus. 5 sons, of whom the youngest, James M.P. [1715.

William, of Milltown Lockhart —— *Lanarkshire* 1841-7, 1847-52, 1852 until [his death s.b. 5 Jan. 1857.

Of Milton Lockhart, co. Lanark, D.L., dean of faculty of the university of Glasgow, lt.-col. comdt. Lanarkshire regt. yeo. cavalry (son of Rev. John Lockhart, D.D., by his 1st wife, Elizabeth Dinwiddie); d. s.p. 25 Nov. 1856, aged 69, having m. 16 April 1822, [Mary Jane, dau. of Sir Hugh Palliser, bart.

Logie.

George —— *Queensferry* 1648.

Loughborough. See also Erskine.

James Alexander St. Clair Erskine, commonly called Lord —— *Dysart* [*burghs* 1830-1. See also England M.P.

3rd Earl of Rosslyn (on the death of his father, James, 18 Jan. 1837, see Sir James Erskine, M.P. 1796-1805), P.C. gen. in the army, col. 7th hussars, master H.M. Buck-hounds, M.P. Grimsby Aug. 1831-1832, contested it 1832, under-secretary for war 1859; b. 15 Feb. 1802, d. 16 June 1866, having m. 10 Oct. 1826, Frances, dau. of Lt.-Gen. William [Wemyss (E. WEMYSS), she d. 30 Sept. 1858, leaving issue.

Lovell.

James —— *Dundee* 1568 (in the absence of the provost), 1569 conv., 1572
[conv.

Lowis.

William —— *Peebles* 1645   1646-7, 1649 (or James Williamson).

Ninian —— *Peebles* 1603.

Lowther.

John Henry, of Swillington, Yorks. —— *Wigton burghs* 1826-30, 1830-1.   See
[also England M.P.

2nd baronet (on the death of his father, Sir John, 11 May 1844), high shf. Yorks 1852,
D.L., N. and W. Ridings, M.P. Cockermouth 1816-1818, 1818-20, 1820-6, 1831-2, York
City 1835-7, 1837-41, 1841-7, and as above, contested York 1832 and 1833; b. 23 March
[1793, d. unm. 23 June 1868.

Luck.

William (Luik) —— *Forfar* 1650 (or Alexander Scot).

Lumsden.

Robert (Mr.) —— *Aberdeen* 1569 conv.

Lundie.

George —— *Dysart* 1644 conv.; *Forfarshire* 1650-1 (the laird).

(William) the laird —— 1590 conv., as a minor baron.

Represented King James VI. at the meetings of the general assembly of Church of
Scotland 1580 (son of Walter Lundy, M.P.. 1560, of that ilk, and of Elizabeth Lindsay);
m. 1st Christian, dau. of William, 2nd Lord Ruthven, and 2ndly Elizabeth, dau. of Robert
[Lundy, of Balgonie, co. Fife; he d. 13 April 1600, aged 78, leaving issue.

Lyell.

Walter —— *Montrose* 1651.

Lyon.

(——) laird of Troupe —— *Banffshire* 1648.

(Frederick) laird of Brigton —— *Forfarshire* 1644 conv., 1644-7

Possibly 3rd son of Patrick, 1st Earl of Kinghorn, who had a charter of those lands from
[his father, 31 July 1662.

James —— *Dundee* 1596 conv.

Lyon—*continued.*

James, of Auldbarr —— *Forfarshire* 1630 conv. (the laird), 1639 until his death
[s.b. 13 Aug. 1641.
Possibly 2nd son of Patrick, 1st Earl of Kinghorn.

John (Mr.), sheriff clerk of Forfar, merchant trafficker —— *Forfar* 1698-1702,
[1702-7.

Patrick —— *Dundee* 1587, 1592, 1593, 1598 conv. (3), 1602 conv.

Patrick (Mr.), of Auchterhouse —— *Forfarshire* 1702-7.
2nd son of Patrick, 3rd Earl of Kinghorn, fell at the battle of Sheriffmuir 13 Nov.
[1715 s.p.s.

Thomas (Master), of Deanside —— *Forfarshire* 1734 until he succ. as 8th of
[Earl of Strathmore and Kinghorn 14 Jan. 1735.
8th Earl of Strathmore and Kinghorn (6th son of John, 4th Earl); d. at Glamis Castle
18 Jan. 1753, having m. at Houghton-le-Spring 28 July 1736, Jean, dau. and heir of James
Nicolson, of West Rainton, co. Durham; she d. at Hetton 13 May 1778, having had with
[other issue a son Thomas, next named.

Thomas, of Hall Green, brother-german to the present Earl of Strathmore ——
Aberdeen (now *Montrose*) *burghs* 1768-74, 1774 until he accepted the
[stewardship of the manor of East Hendred, s.b. 11 Jan. 1779.
Hon. Thomas Lyon, of Hetton, co. Durham (3rd son of Thomas, 8th Lord Strathmore,
last named); d. 13 Sept. 1796, aged 55, having m. 13 Jan. 1774, Mary Elizabeth, dau. of
Farrer Wren, of Binchester, co. Durham; she d. 31 May 1811, having had 2 sons and
[6 daus.

William —— *Brechin* 1645-6.

M.

McAlexander.

Andrew —— *Tain* 1640-1.

Macalzean.

Thomas (Mr.) —— *Edinburgh* 1563.

Lord (Cliftonhall) of session 20 Oct. 1570, assessor for City of Edinburgh, deprived 1556, but restored the following year, provost of Edinburgh 1561 ; d. 5 June 1581, his only dau. and heiress Euphame, "Notorious in the annals of sorcery, was burned at Edinburgh [25 June 1591, being convicted of treasonably conspiring against the king's life," etc., etc.

Macartney.

George (sir), knight of the bath —— *Ayr burghs* 1774, until appointed governor of Grenada, s.b. 17 Jan. 1776.   See also England M.P. and Ireland M.P.

Earl Macartney, K.B., the friend of Lord Holland, M.A. Trin, Coll., Dublin, 1759, envoy-extraordinary to Russia 1764, knighted 19 Oct. of that year on taking leave ; the king of Poland conferred on him the most ancient and royal order of the White Eagle June 1766 ; envoy-extra. and min. plen. at St. Petersburg 20 Nov. 1767, M.P. Cockermouth 1768-9, Armagh 1769-76, constable of Toome and custos rot. Antrim, 1774, chief sec. of Ireland under Lord Townshend, LL., 1 Jan. 1769, P.C. Ireland 30 March following, nominated a knight of the bath 1772, installed by proxy 17 June same year, governor of Grenada, etc., 1775, until its capture 1779, when he was sent prisoner to France ; created Lord Macartney, baron of Lissanoure, co. Antrim, 19 July 1776, M.P. Beeralston, Devon, 1780, until governor of Fort St. George (Madras) at the end of that year ; appointed gov.-genl. of Bengal 1785, but declined to accept ; ambassador-extraordinary and min. plen. to Emperor of China 1792-4, P.C. 3 May 1792, created Viscount Macartney of Dervocks, co. Antrim, 19 July following, and Earl of Macartney March 1794, all in the peerage of Ireland ; he was raised to the English peerage as Baron Macartney, of Parkhurst, Surrey, and of Auchinleck in the stewartry of Kirkcudbright 8 June 1796, lord lieutenant co. Antrim, a trustee of the linen manufacture for Ulster, col. of a regt. of militia dragoons (only son of George Macartney, of Lissanoure, co. Antrim) ; d. s.p. 31 March 1806, M.I. Lissanoure ; he m. 1 Feb. 1768, Lady Jane Stuart, 2nd dau. of John, 3rd Earl of Bute, she [d. 28 Feb. 1828, aged 86.

Macaulay.

(——) laird of Ardincaple —— *Dumbartonshire* 1608 conv. (as a minor baron).

Sir Aulay McAulay, laird of Ardincaple (son and heir of Walter), died s.p. 1617.

Macaulay—*continued.*

Thomas Babington, of London —— *Edinburgh City* 1839-40 (secretary at war 1840); 1841-7 (paymaster-general of the forces 1846) 1852 until he accepted the stewardship of the manor of Hempholme, s.b. 9 Feb. 1856.
[See also England M.P.

Lord Macaulay, historian and critic, B.A. Trin. Coll., Cambridge 1822, M.A. 1825, fellow 1822, bar.-at-law Lincoln's Inn 1826, M.P. Calne 1830-2, a commissioner of bankruptcy, secretary to the Board of Control, M.P. Leeds 1832, member and legal adviser of the Supreme Council in India during the codification of Indian law, secretary at war and M.P. 1840 as above, published the "Lays of Ancient Rome" 1842, paymaster-general with a seat in the Cabinet 1846 etc.; created Lord Macaulay of Rothley Temple, co. Leicester, 10 Sept. 1857 (eldest son of Zachary Macaulay, the philanthropist, who married at Bristol 26 Aug. 1799, Selina, dau. of Thomas Mills, of Bristol, bookseller); b. at Rothley Temple, [co. Leicester, 25 Oct. 1800; died unm. 28 Dec. 1859, bd. in Westminster Abbey 9 Jan.

McBaith.

William, merchant burgess —— *Wick* 1661.

McBirny.

Thomas —— *Dumfries* (1648, 1649, 1650).

McBrair.

(——) laird of Almagill —— *Dumfries sheriffdom and stewartry of Annandale* [1646-7, 1648, 1651.

Archibald —— *Dumfries* 1581.

David, of Newarke and Almagill —— *Kirkcudbright stewartry* 1661-3.

Nicholas, alderman —— *Dumfries* 1504.

Patrick —— *Dumfries* 1579 (then provost).

Robert (alderman) —— *Dumfries* 1469.

Robert —— *Dumfries sheriffdom and stewartry of Annandale* 1630 conv.

MacClellan.

(Sir Robert) laird of Bombie —— *Wigtownshire* 1621.

Lord Kirkcudbright, so created 25 May 1633, to him and his heirs male, gent. of the bedchamber to James VI. and Charles I. (son of Sir Thomas MacClellan, of Bombie); died 1641, [married twice and left an only dau.

Samuel (sir), lord provost of Edinburgh —— *Edinburgh city* 1708 until his [death s.b. 25 Nov. 1709.

Died 22 Sept. 1709, father of James MacClellan, who voted as Lord Kirkcudbright at the general election 1741; it was subsequently declared that he had not established his claim.

William —— *Kirkcudbright* 1617.

Probably of Glenshannock; and if so, then brother of Sir Robert, 1st Lord Kirkcudbright, [and father of Thomas, 2nd Lord.

M'Combie.

William, farmer, of Tillyfour —— *West Aberdeenshire* 1868-74, 1874 until he
[accepted the Chiltern hundreds, s.b. 12 May 1876.
President of the Scottish Chamber of Agriculture, son of Charles M'Combie, of Tillyfour,
[by his wife Anne Black ; d. unm. 1 Feb. 1880, aged 75.

McCubie.

James, provost —— *Jedburgh* 1678 conv.

McCulloch.

Alexander, of Drumorell —— *Whithorn* 1669-74.
Son of Robert McCulloch, of Drummorall.

Andrew —— *Tain* 1649.

Godfrey (sir), of Mertoun, knight baronet —— *Wigtownshire* 1678 conv.
Of Myrton and Cardiness, son of John McCulloch; of Myrton [who was probably a son of
Sir Alexander, created a baronet of Nova Scotia 10 Aug. 1664 (patent not recorded),]
executed at the Cross of Edinburgh 26 March 1697, for having killed Wm. Gordon, of
[Cardiness; he is said to have left illegitimate issue.

James —— *Tain* 1648 ; *Findhorn* 1649 ; *Whithorn* 1649 and 1650.

John, of Myrtoune —— *Wigtownshire* 1641.
Possibly son of Alexander McCulloch, of Myrtoune ; he m. before 1638, Margaret Couper,
[and had issue.

John, merchant trafficker, provost —— *Stirling* 1685-6.

Thomas, bailie —— *Tain* 1639-41.

William, of Mertoune —— *Kirkcudbright stewartry* 1612 (the laird), 1617.
Probably son of Simon M'Culloch and Marion Gordon, whom he succeeded in 1581 ; he
m. 1st (contract 29 March 1574) Elizabeth Dunbar, and 2ndly (before 1584) Marie McCulloch,
[of Cardiness.

Macdonald.

James, of Langdale, co. Sutherland —— *Tain* (now *Wick*) *burghs* 1805-6, *Sutherlandshire* 1812, until he accepted the Chiltern hundreds, s.b. 6 March 1816.
[See also England M.P.
2nd baronet (on the death of his father, Sir Archibald Macdonald, 18 May 1826), M.P.
Newcastle-under-Lyne 1806-7, 1807-12, Calne 1816-1818, 1818-20, 1820-6, 1826-30, 1830-1,
Hants 1831-2, clerk of the privy seal, until appointed a commissioner of the India board
1831, lord high commissioner of the Ionian islands a few weeks before his death ; b. 14 Feb.
[1784, d. 29 June 1832, having married thrice, and left issue, see Foster's Baronetage.

McDouall.

Andrew (col.), of Logan and Culgroat —— *Wigtownshire* 1784-90, 1790-6,
1802 (then col.) until he accepted the Chiltern hundreds, s.b. 15 April, 1805.
Col. in the army (son of John McDouall, of Logan, by his wife Helen, dau. of George
Buchan, of Kello) ; m. Mary, dau. of James Russell, of Dumfries, and d. 3 May 1834, aged
[75, leaving issue,

McDouall—*continued.*

Uchtred, of Freugh —— *Wigtownshire* 1661-3.

Served heir of his father (John) 1669, "had several commands in the king's service both in Scotland and in Ireland ;" m. Agnes, dau. of Sir Patrick Agnew, of Lochnaw, and had
[issue.

MacDougall.

—— laird of McCairston —— 1597 conv., as a minor baron —— *Roxburghshire*
[1625 conv.

Henrie, of McCairston —— *Roxburghshire* 1665 conv., 1667 conv., 1678 conv.,
[1681-2.

McDowall.

James, of Garthland —— *Wigtownshire* 1643 conv., 1644-7, 1648 laird ——
[(1654-5, 1656-8, 1658-9 English parlt.—WILLIS).

Sir James McDowall. of Garthland, served heir of his father (Sir John) 1637 ; he m. Jane,
[dau. of Sir John Hamilton, of Grange, and had a son William, M.P.

William, of Garthland —— *Wigtownshire* 1689 conv., 1689 until his death s.b.
[31 Dec. 1700.

Son of Sir James, M.P., last named ; m. Grizel, dau. of A. Beatoun, and had at least 4
[sons.

William, of Castle Semple —— *Renfrewshire* 1768-74.

William MacDowall, of Castle Semple (son of Col. Wm. MacDowall, who purchased Castle Semple 1727), purchased Garthland in 1752, from his cousin, Wm. MacDowall ; m.
[Elizabeth, dau. of James Graham, of Airth, and had a son William, M.P., next named.

William, of Garthland —— *Renfrewshire* 1783-4, 1784 until he accepted the Chiltern hundreds s.b. 19 Oct. 1786 ; *Ayrshire* 1789-90 ; *Glasgow burghs* 1790-6, 1796-1802 ; *Renfrewshire* 1802-6, 1806-7, 1807 until his death s.b.
[2 May 1810.

Lord Lieut. Renfrewshire (eldest son of William Macdowall, of Castle Semple, M.P.,
[last named) ; d. unm. April 1810.

MacDowall-Grant.

David, of Arndilly —— *Banffshire* 1795-6.

Capt. R.N. (5th son of William MacDowall, of Castle Semple of Renfrew), m. Mary Eleanor, dau. of Alexander Grant, esq., of Arndilly, and d. 1840, having had 2 sons and 4
[daus.

Macduff. See also Fife, Duff, and Grant-Duff.

Alexander William George, commonly called Viscount, of Innes Ho. Elginshire —— *Elgin and Nairnshire* 1874 until he succ. as 6th Earl Fife s.b.
[18 Sept. 1879.

6th Earl Fife (7 Aug. 1879), P.C. 1880, capt. of corps of gentlemen-at-arms 1880-1,
[lord lieut. co. Elgin 1879 ; b. 10 Nov. 1849. See Foster's Peerage.

SCOTCH MEMBERS.   F F

Macduff—*continued.*

(James) Lord Viscount —— *Banffshire* 1761-8.

 2nd Earl Fife (on the death of his father, 30 Sept. 1763), M.P. Banffshire 1754-61, 1768-74, 1774-80, Elginshire 1784-90, cr. a peer of Great Britain 19 Feb. 1790, lord lieut. [Banffshire. See also DUFF, p. 107, and Foster's Peerage.

McFarlane.

William, provost —— *Dumbarton* 1681-2.

Macfie.

Robert Andrew —— *Leith burghs* 1868-74.   See foot-note.

Macgill.

(Sir James) laird of Cranston-Riddell —— *Edinburghshire* 1630 conv.

 Viscount of Oxfurd and Lord Macgill, of Cousland, so cr. 19 April 1661, but never took his seat, owing to the troubles of the times, cr. a baronet 19 July 1627, and a lord of session 3 Nov. 1629; his father, grandfather, and gt.-grandfather were also senators; a commissioner of Exchequer 1645 (son of David Macgill, Lord Cranston-Riddell, of Session); m. 1st, Catherine, dau. of Sir John Cockburn, of Ormiston, and 2nd, Christian, dau. of Sir William [Livingston, of Kilsyth; he d. 5 May 1663, leaving issue by both wives

M'Gillichoane.

John —— *Dingwall,* 1587.

McGillichrist.

John —— *Rothesay,* 1646-7.

MacGregor.

Donald Robert, of Woodburn, Edinburgh —— *Leith burghs* 1874 until he accepted the stewardship of the manor of Northstead, Yorkshire, s.b. 29 Jan. [1878.   See foot-note.

M ACFIE, ROBERT ANDREW, of Dreghorn Castle, Edinburgh, J.P., M.P. as above, and contested the Leith burghs 1859 and 1874 (eldest son of John Macfie, D.L., of Edinburgh, by Alison, dau. of Wm. Thorburn, of Leith, and grandson of Robert Macfie, of Langhouse, co. Renfrew); b. 4 Oct. 1811, m. 2 Jan. 1840, Caroline Eliza, dau. of 15th hussars, M.D., of 15th hussars, and of Courance Hill, co. Dumfries, surgeon 15th hussars, and has 2 sons and 3 daus.

 (1) John William, b. 1 Dec. 1844, m. 7 June 1867, Helen, dau. of late Major-General Charles Wahab.

Dreghorn Castle, Colinton, Edinburgh.

Clubs—Reform, University, Edinburgh.

M ACGREGOR, DONALD ROBERT, of Woodburn, Midlothian, and of Leith, merchant and ship-owner, moderator of the Leith High Constables, lt.-col. 1st Midlothian Rifle Volunteers, since M.P. as above (eldest son of late Lieut. Evan Macgregor, of Perth); b. 1824, m. 1851, Mary, only dau. of William Anderson, esq., of South Shields.

Woodburn, Edinburgh; 21, Gt. George St., W.

Mac Gregor—*continued*.

John, of London —— *Glasgow* 1847-52, 1852 until he accepted the stewardship [of the manor of Northstead, Yorkshire, s.b. 6 March 1857.

Of Carrick, Glasgow, high sheriff Prince Edward Island, member of Legislative Council, joint sec. to Board of Trade 1839-47, employed on several commercial missions to continental nations, *e.g.* to Germany, Austria, Paris, and Naples, author of several statistical works relating to commerce, original governor of the Royal British Bank and chairman of the Eastern Archipelago Company (eldest son of David MacGregor, of Drynie, Ross-shire); b. 1797, d. 23 April 1857, having m. 1833, Anne, dau. of Wm. Peard Jillard, esq., [of Oakhill, Somerset, she d. Oct. 1853.

McGuffock.

Hugh, of Rosco. —— *Kirkcudbright stewartry* 1689 conv., 1689-1702.

(Sir?) Hugh McGuffock, of Rusco (3rd and ygst. son of James Blair, of Dunskey), assumed the surname of McGuffock on his marriage (then of Kildonan) with Elizabeth, only dau. and sole heir of William McGuffock, of Rusco ; he m. 2ndly Margaret, 2nd dau. of Sir David Dunbar, of Baldoon, and had issue by both marriages ; gt.-grandfather of William, [who died M.P. Weymouth (see England) 5 April 1806.

McIntosh.

Lauchlan, of Torcastle —— *Inverness-shire* 1669-74, 1681-2, 1685-6.

? 19th chief of the clan (on the death of his father, William of that ilk, 22 Nov. 1660); [died 9 Dec. 1704, leaving an only son Lauchlan, who died s.p. 1731.

Mackay.

Alexander (hon.), of Strathlongue, col. 65th regt. —— *Sutherlandshire* 1761-8 ; *Wick burghs* 1768 until he accepted the Chiltern hundreds, s.b. 26 April [1773.

Lieut-genl. in the army 1777, commander-in-chief of the forces in Scotland 1780-92, col. 21st foot (R. Scots Fusiliers) 1770-92, governor of Stirling Castle 1788 92, taken prisoner by the rebels at the battle of Preston, col. 122nd foot 1762, of 65th foot 1764, maj.-genl. in America 1768, and in Great Britain 1770, governor of Tynemouth Castle and Clifford's Fort 1772, governor of Landguard Fort 1778 (2nd son of George, 3rd Lord Reay, by his 3rd marriage) ; he d. s.p. 31 May 1789, having m. at Ford 24 Dec. 1770, Margaret, dau. of Sir William Carr, of Etal, Northumberland, bart., she re-m. at Holyrood House 4 Oct. 1792 to [James Farquharson, of Invercauld.

George, of Skibo —— *Sutherlandshire,* 1747-54 (Captn. George, of Strathmore), [1754-61 ; master of the mint in Scotland 1756.

Brother of Genl. Mackay, M.P., last named, advocate 1737, d. at Tongue 25 June 1782, having m. at Embo 13 Dec. 1766, Anne, 3rd dau. of Eric Sutherland, only son of the attainted [Lord Duffus, and had with other issue a son Eric, who succ. as 7th Lord Reay.

Robert (Makke) —— *Kirkcaldy* 1600.

MacKeane.

Robert —— *Edinburgh* 1645-6.

McKenzie.   See also Macleod and Stuart.

(——) laird of —— 1598 conv. (as a minor baron), 1608.

Alexander (sir), of Coull —— *Ross-shire* 1693-1702.
2nd baronet (on the death of his father, Sir Kenneth) ; m. 1st Jean, dau. of Sir Robert Gordon, of Gordonstown ; he m. 2ndly Janet Johnson ; and d. 1702, leaving issue by both [wives. See Foster's Baronetage.

Alexander (master), of Fraserdale —— *Inverness-shire* 1710-13, 1713-15.
Alexander Mackenzie changed his name to Fraser, and was designed of Fraserdale (son of Roderick Mackenzie, M.P., 1700, Lord Prestonhall) ; attainted for engaging in the rebellion 1715 ; d. 3 June 1755, aged 72, having m. 1702, Amelia, eldest dau. and heir of Hugh. 10th Lord Lovat ; she unsuccessfully claimed that title, and had a son Hugh, who assumed the title of Lord Lovat on his mother's death, and d. at Edinburgh 9 Nov. 1770,
[aged 67.

MacKenzie-Fraser.

Alexander, maj.-genl. of Inverallochy —— *Cromartyshire* 1802-6 (then Alex. MacKenzie, 78th foot, etc.) ; *Ross shire* 1806-7, 1807 until his death s.b.
[28 Nov. 1809.
Alexander MacKenzie-Fraser, lieut.-genl. in the army, col. 78th highlanders, had from his aunts the estates of Inverallochy and Castle Fraser, and assumed the surname of **Fraser** by r.l.. 22 July 1803 (youngest son of Colin MacKenzie of Kilcoy, see Foster's Baronetage); d. at Walcheren 13 Sept. 1809, having m. Helen MacKenzie, sister of Francis, 1st Baron Seaforth; she d. 15 Jan. 1802, having had with other issue a son Charles, M.P., next named.

Charles, of Inverallochy and Castle Fraser —— *Ross-shire* 1814-18.
Charles Mackenzie-Fraser, of Castle Fraser, J.P., D.L., capt. coldstream guards, col. Ross-shire mil., served in Peninsula with 52nd regt. 1808-9 (son of Lieut.-Genl. Mackenzie-Fraser, M.P., last named) ; b. 9 June 1792 ; d. 7 March 1871, having m. 25 April 1817, Jane, dau. of Sir John Hay, bart., of Smithfield and Haystoune ; she d. 12 Jan. 1851, having [had issue. See Foster's Baronetage.

McKenzie.

Colin, of Kintail —— 1608.
Probably younger brother of Kenneth, 1st Lord Kintail.

Colin, of Redcastle —— *Inverness-shire* 1661-8.
Son of Roderick McKenzie, of Redcastle, m. twice, killed at Killearnan 1704. See [Douglas' Baronage, p. 399.

Francis Humberston, of Seaforth —— *Ross-shire* 1784-90, 1794-6.
Lord Seaforth, Baron McKenzie of Kintail, so cr. 26 Oct. 1797, col. 78th regt. of foot, which he raised 1793, lord lieut. Ross-shire, col. Ross-shire mil. 1798, governor of Barbadoes 1800-6, lieut.-genl. in the army 1808, F.R.S., F.L.S. ; b. 9 June 1754 ; d. s.p. m. 11 Jan. 1815, having m. 22 April 1782, Mary, dau. of Baptist Proby, D.D., Dean of Lichfield (brother of John, 1st Lord Carysfort) ; she d. 27 Feb. 1829, having had with other issue a son, William [Frederick, M.P.

McKenzie—*continued.*

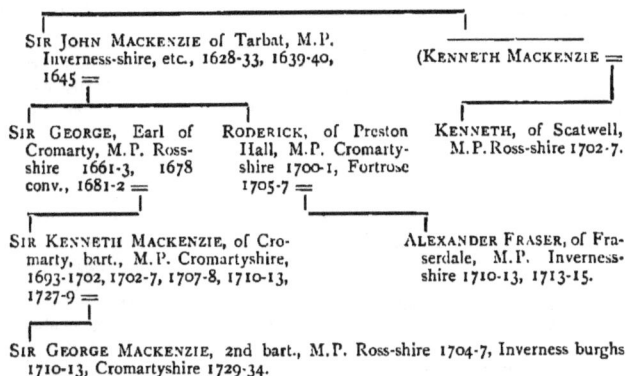

```
┌─────────────────────────────────────┬──────────────────────────┐
SIR JOHN MACKENZIE of Tarbat, M.P.
Inverness-shire, etc., 1628-33, 1639-40,          (KENNETH MACKENZIE =
1645 =                                                 │
```

| SIR GEORGE, Earl of Cromarty, M.P. Ross-shire 1661-3, 1678 conv., 1681-2 = | RODERICK, of Preston Hall, M.P. Cromarty-shire 1700-1, Fortrose 1705-7 = | KENNETH, of Scatwell, M.P. Ross-shire 1702-7. |

| SIR KENNETH MACKENZIE, of Cromarty, bart., M.P. Cromartyshire, 1693-1702, 1702-7, 1707-8, 1710-13, 1727-9 = | ALEXANDER FRASER, of Fraserdale, M.P. Inverness-shire 1710-13, 1713-15. |

SIR GEORGE MACKENZIE, 2nd bart., M.P. Ross-shire 1704-7, Inverness burghs 1710-13, Cromartyshire 1729-34.

George (sir), of Tarbat, senator of the college of justice —— *Ross-shire* 1661-3, [1678 conv., 1681-2.

Earl of Cromarty, so cr. 1 Jan. 1703; apptd. a lord of session 1 June 1661; deprived 16 Feb. 1664; justice-general 1678; P.C.; re-apptd. ordinary lord 1681 until 1689, having been appointed clerk register in the same year; cr. Viscount of Tarbat, Macleod, and Castlehaven 15 Feb. 1685; clerk register 1692-5; sec. of state upon the accession of Queen Mary 1703-5, and cr. Earl of Cromarty as above; justice-general 1705-10 (son of Sir John Mackenzie, of Tarbat, bart., M.P.; d. at New Tarbat 17 Aug. 1714, aged 84, having m. twice, and had with other issue Sir Kenneth, M.P. 1693. See also John, Lord Macleod.

George (sir), of Rosehaugh, advocate —— *Ross-shire* 1669-74; *Forfarshire* 1689 conv. (then of Rosehaugh and Newtyle), 1689 until his death 8 May 1691.

Eldest son of Hon. Simon Mackenzie, of Lochslyne, M.P.; admitted to the faculty of advocates 18 Jan. 1659; king's advocate 1666-86; restored 1688, and dismissed at the revolution; d. in London 8 May 1691; he m. 1st Elizabeth, dau. of John Dickson, of Hartree, a lord of session; he m. 2ndly 14 Jan. 1670, Margaret, dau. of   Halyburton of Pitcur (she re-m. to Roderick Mackenzie, of Prestonhall, a lord of session, brother of the 1st [Earl of Cromarty, last named), and had issue.

George (sir), of Grandvale —— *Ross-shire* 1704-7; *Inverness burghs* 1710-13, provost of Fortrose, (master George, of Inchculter); *Cromartyshire* 1729-34.

2nd baronet (on the death of his father, Sir Kenneth Mackenzie, of Cromarty, bart., M.P.); sold his estate of Cromarty to William Urquhart of Meldrum 1741; m. Elizabeth Reid, and [d. s.p. 1748. See Foster's Baronetage.

Hugh, merchant burgess —— *Dingwall* 1678 conv.

McKenzie—*continued.*

James Wemyss (sir), of Scatwell, bart. —— *Ross-shire* 1822-6, 1826-30, 1830-1.

Sir James Wemyss Mackenzie, 5th baronet, recorded his arms as a baronet in the Lyon office, lord lieut. co. Ross (son of Sir Roderick Mackenzie, 4th bart., descended from Sir Kenneth, M.P., 1702-7) b. 10 Aug. 1770; d. 5-8 March 1843, having m. 26 March 1810, Henrietta Wharton, only surviving dau. of William, and sister and sole heir of Major-Genl. John Randoll Mackenzie, M.P., of Suddie (who fell at Talavera), relict of Capt. Robert Pott. of Galallan; she d. 14 Nov. 1840, having had a son, Sir James John Randoll, [6th and present baronet.

John (sir), of Tarbett, knt. baronet —— *Inverness-shire including Caithness and Ross* 1628-33 (a knight); *Inverness-shire and Ross* 1639-40 (knight baronet); [*Inverness-shire* 1645 (laird).

Sir John Mackenzie, of Tarbat, cr. a baronet of Nova Scotia 21 May 1628 (son of Sir Roderick McKenzie, of Tarbat and Coigiach); d. 10 Sept. 1654, having m. Margaret, dau. and co-heir of Sir George Erskine, of Innerteil (a lord of session 1617-46). brother of 1st Earl of Kellie (she re-m. to Sir James Foulis, of Colinton, a lord of session and lord justice clerk); his son, Sir George, 2nd baronet, M.P., cr. Earl of Cromarty and Roderick, M.P.

John (Mr.), of Inverlawell —— *Ross-shire* 1665 conv.

Probably son of Rev. Thomas Mackenzie, of Inverlael, 9th son of John, archdeacon of [Ross.

John (Mr.), of Assint, provost —— *Fortrose* 1702 until his death s.b. 26 June [1705.

2nd son of Kenneth, 3rd Earl of Seaforth; m. Sibella, eldest dau. of Alexander McKenzie, [of Applecross, and left an only son Kenneth, who died s.p. 1723.

John Randoll (brig.-genl.) of Suddie —— *Tain* (now *Wick*) *burghs* 1806-7, 1807 until he accepted the Chiltern hundreds, s.b. 7 May 1808; *Sutherland-*[*shire* 1808 until his death s.b. 29 Sept. 1809.

Major-General Mackenzie (younger son of William Mackenzie of Suddley, by his wife Margaret, dau. of Sir Alexander Mackenzie of Coul, bart.), entered the marines; major 2nd batt. 78th regt. 1794; served with his regt. in India; col. 1803; brigadier-general on the northern staff; governor and commandant of Alderney; commanded a brigade in Portugal [1808; fell at the bat.le of Talavera 27-28 July 1809.

Kenneth, of Kintail —— 1607.

Lord Mackenzie, of Kintail, so cr. 19 Nov. 1609 (son of Colin McKenzie, 11th baron of Kintail); d. March 1611, having m. 1st Anne, dau. of George Ross, of Balnagowan; he m. 2ndly Isabel, dau. of Sir Gilbert Ogilvy of Powrie; she re-m. to Hon. John Seton of Barns, and d. Sept. 1618; his eldest son Colin was cr. Earl of Seaforth 3 Dec. 1623, with [remainder to his heirs male.

Kenneth, merchant burgess, bailie —— *Dingwall* 1689 conv., 1689 until 1698, [" not having qualified himself according to law.'

Possibly 2nd son of John Mackenzie, 1st of Gruinard; he m. the widow of Kenneth, 4th Earl of Seaforth, and died. s.p.

McKenzie—*continued.*

Kenneth (sir), of Cromarty —— *Cromartyshire* 1693-1702 (Mr.), 1702-7, 1707-8 (1st parlt. of Great Britain, then of Pharnez), 1710-13 (the laird), 1727 [until his death s.b. 25 March 1729.

> Sir Kenneth McKenzie, of Grandvale, and of Cromarty in 1665, cr. a baronet 8 Feb. 1704 (with the same precedence as his grandfather 21 May 1628); supported the Union (2nd son of Sir George, M.P., 1st Earl of Cromarty); d 13 Sept. 1728, leaving with other [issue 2 sons, Sir George, M.P. 1729, and Sir Kenneth, 3rd bart.

Kenneth, of Gairloch —— *Ross-shire* 1702 until his death s.b. 3 Oct. 1704.

> 8th baron of Gairloch, said to have been cr. a baronet of Nova Scotia by Douglas in 1703, by Playfair in 1723, by Burke's Peerage (1834) in 1629, and by the present (Sir) Kenneth 22 Feb. 1702-3. In Douglas' Peerage (E. CROMARTY) Alexander Mackenzie of Gairloch is said to have m. Barbara Mackenzie, sister of 1st Earl of Cromarty, and to have been father of Sir Kenneth Mackenzie (the supposed 1st) bart., of Gairloch. Kenneth Mackenzie m. Margaret, dau. of Sir Roderick Mackenzie of Findon, and d. Dec. 1703, aged 32, and his son Alexander was served heir, neither being styled "Sir." In 1723 this Alexander registered arms in the Lyon office without style or badge of a baronet, but in 1770 (his grandson) "Sir Hector" was served heir of his father, "Sir Alexander," who [had died in April of that year. See "CHAOS," Foster's Baronetage.

Kenneth, of Scatwell —— *Ross-shire* 1702-7.

> Built Findon House, said to have been created a baronet of Nova Scotia 22 Feb. 1702-3 (patent not recorded, and nothing seems to be known of the creation) (son of Kenneth M'Kenzie, of Scatwell, by his 2nd wife, Janet Ross); d. 1730, having m. 1st, Lilias, eldest dau. and heir of Sir Roderick Mackenzie, of Findon, she d. 21 Oct. 1703, having had issue; he m. 2ndly, Christian, eldest dau. of Roderick Mackenzie, minister and laird of Avoch, she d. s.p.; he m. 3rdly (contract 1707), Abigail, dau. of John Urquhart, of New- [hall, by whom he had a son and 2 daus. See Foster's Baronetage.

Roderick (sir), of Findon —— *Dingwall* 1672-4 (then Mr., advocate at Edin- [burgh), *Ross-shire* 1678 conv (Mr.), 1681-2 (then a knight).

> 4th son of Alexander Mackenzie, of Kilcoy, sheriff substitute, admitted advocate 7 Dec. 1672; m. Margaret Cathcart, widow, dau. of Alexander Mackenzie, of Bellaloan, and d. [1692, leaving a son and 4 daus.

Roderick (Mr.), of Preston Hall, senator of the college of justice —— *Cromar-* [*tyshire* 1700-1, *Fortrose* 1705-7.

> Lord Prestonhall of session 12 Jan. 1703; admitted advocate 6 Feb. 1666, a clerk of session 13 Nov. 1678, unduly elected for Cromartyshire 1698, justice clerk 1703-4, resigned his seat as ordinary lord June 1710, sheriff of Ross-shire 1710 (2nd son of Sir John Mackenzie, of Tarbert, bart., M.P.); d. 4 Feb. 1712, having m. 1st, Margaret, dau. of Alexander Burnet, archbishop of St. Andrews, he m. 2ndly, Margaret Haliburton, relict of Sir George [Mackenzie, of Rosehaugh, M.P., by this wife he had a son, Alexander, M.P. 1710, etc.

Symon, of Lochslyne —— *Inverness-shire* including *Ross* 1640-1.

> 4th son of Kenneth, 1st Lord Mackenzie, of Kintail; m. Elizabeth, dau. of Peter Bruce, D.D., principal of St. Leonard's College, St. Andrews, and had with other issue a son, Sir [George, of Rosehaugh, M.P. 1669, etc.

McKenzie—*continued.*

Thomas, of Pluscardine —— *Elgin and Forres-shire* 1645 (laird), 1661-3.

Elder brother of Symon, M.P., last named, had a charter to himself and Jean Grant, his wife, of the barony of Pluscardine 25 July 1636, his son Colin was served heir and heir male
[of his father May 1687.

Thomas, of Applecross, Ross-shire —— *Ross-shire* 1818-20, 1820 until his death
[s.b. 20 Dec. 1822.

Only son of John McKenzie, of Applecross and Loch Carron, esq., by Elizabeth, dau. of
[Alexander Elphinston, of Glack; he died unm. in Leicester Square 19 Oct. 1822.

Thomas, of Applecross, Ross-shire —— *Ross and Cromartyshire* 1837, 1837-41,
[1841-7.

A writer to the signet, sold the Applecross estate (son of Kenneth Mackenzie, esq., of Inverinate, by Anne, eventual heir (in her issue) of last-named Thomas, M.P.); b.   1793, m. 12 April 1817, Margaret, dau. of G. MacKenzie, esq., of Avoch, and d. 9 June 1856,
[leaving issue.

William Forbes, of Portmore —— *Peebles-shire* 1837-41, 1841-7 (a lord of the
[treasury 1845), 1847-52.

A lord of the treasury 1845-6, M.P. Liverpool. 1852, but unseated on petition (eldest son of Colin Mackenzie, of Portmore); b. 18 April 1807, d. 24 Sept. 1862, having m. 16 March 1830, Helen Anne. eldest dau. of Sir James Montgomery, of Stanhope, bart., and had an
[only son.

William Frederick, eldest son of Francis, Lord Seaforth —— *Ross-shire* 1812
[until his death s.b. 25 Oct. 1814.
Died 25 Aug. 1814.

Mackeson.

John —— *Crail* 1600, 1612, 1617, 1625 conv. (Mackieson), 1628-33, 1630
[conv.

McKie.

Adam —— *Wigtown* 1645-7, 1649, 1665 conv. (provost).

Alexander, of Palgowan —— *Kirkcudbright stewartry* 1704-7.

Son of John McKie, of Palgowan (by his wife, Elizabeth Dunbar); he is said to have m. Christian, widow of Major Thomas Young, of Leny, dau. of Sir James Dunbar. of Mochrum, although in sasine dated 9 Nov. 1731 his spouse is styled Mrs. Christian Douglas; he d.
[22 Feb. 1735, aged 85, leaving with other issue, John, M.P. 1741, etc.

James, town clerk —— *Whithorn* 1667 conv.

James (Mackie), of Ernespie —— *Kirkcudbright stewartry* 1857-9, 1859-65, 1865
[until his death s.b. 30 Jan. 1868.

Of Bargaly and Ernespie, co. Kirkcudbright, J.P., D.L., educated at Rugby, B.A. Oriel College, Oxford 1844, M.A. 1847, advocate 1847, capt. 1st Kirkcudbright Rifle Volunteers (son of John Mackie, M.P. 1850-7); b. 18 May 1821, d. 28 Dec. 1867, having m. 1853. Jane Wilson. only dau. of Archibald Horne, esq., of Edinburgh, and had
[issue.

McKie—*continued.*

John Ross, of Palgowan —— *Linlithgow burghs* 1741-7 (seated on petition); *Kirkcudbright stewartry* 1747-54, 1754-61 (styled John McKie), 1761-8, [treasurer and paymaster of the ordnance 1763 (then John Ross McKie).

Advocate 1730, served heir of his father (Alexander, M.P.) 9 May 1753, he assumed the additional surname of Ross; d. in London   Oct. 1797, aged 91, having m. 28 July 1755, [Hon. Jane Ross, eldest dau. of George, 13th Lord Ross, she d. s.p. 19 Aug. 1777.

John (Mackie), of Bargaly —— *Kirkcudbright stewartry* 1851-2, 1852-7.

Son of James Mackie, of Bargaly, J.P., D.L., m.   1817, Anne, eldest dau. of Peter Laurie, esq., of Ernespie, and d. 3 July 1858, having had with other issue a son, James, [M.P. 1857-68.

Patrick (sir), of Larg, knt. —— *Kirkcudbright stewartry* 1628-33, 1639-40, [absent in England during 2nd and 3rd sessions.

Youngest son of Patrick M'Kie, of Larg, by Margaret, eldest dau. of Sir Alexander Stewart, of Garlies, served under Gustavus, king of Sweden, and also under Leslie 1639; he m. 1st —— dau. of Sir Thomas Kennedy, of Culzean, and 2ndly —— dau. of Uchtred [McDowall, of Garthland, and had issue.

Thomas, town clerk —— *Wigtown* 1628-33.

William (McChie) —— *Kirkcudbright* 1612.

William (provost) —— *Wigtown* 1667 conv. (bailie), 1669-72 (provost).

Fraser-Mackintosh.

Charles, of Inverness —— *Inverness burghs* 1874-80, and since 1880. See foot-[note.

FRASER-MACKINTOSH, CHARLES, of Drummond, co. Inverness, J.P., assumed the additional surname of Mackintosh in compliance with the testamentary injunction of his maternal uncle, Eneas Mackintosh, R.N., practised as a solicitor 1853-67, M.P. as above (son of Alexander Fraser, esq., of Dochnalrug, co. Inverness, by Marjory, dau. of Capt. Alexander Mackintosh); b. 5 June 1828, m. 12 July 1876, Eveline May, only dau. of Richard D. Holland, esq., of Brooklands, Streatham, Surrey, and of Kilvean, co. Inverness.

Lockhardhill, co. Inverness ; 5, *Clarges Street, W.*   *Club—Devonshire.*

Mackintosh.

Æneas William, of Raigmore, Inverness-shire —— *Inverness burghs* 1868-74. [See foot-note.

James (sir), knt., some time recorder at Bombay in the East Indies —— *Nairn-* [*shire*, 1813-18. See also England M.P.

Rt. Hon. Sir James Mackintosh, P.C., D.C.L., profr. of general polity and the laws in the East India College at Haileybury 1818-27, knighted 21 Dec. 1803, on his appointment as recorder of Bombay, a member of the Royal Medical Society Edinburgh, M.D. 1787, entered at Lincoln's Inn 1792, barrister 1795, author of "Vindiciæ Gallicæ, or a Defence of the French Revolution," M.P. Knaresborough 1818-20, 1820-6, 1826-30, 1830-1, 1831-2, a commissioner for the affairs of India 1 Dec. 1830, lord rector of University of Glasgow 1822 and 1823 (son of Capt. John Mackintosh, of Kellachie); b. at Alldowrie, co. Inverness, 24 Oct. 1765, d. in London 30 May 1832, aged 69, having m. 1st,   1789, —— sister of Mr. Charles Stuart, dramatic author, she d. in Serle Street 8 April 1797, aged 33, leaving 3 daus.; he m. 2ndly, 10 April 1798, Catherine, 3rd dau. of John Bartlett Allen, of Cresselly, [co. Pembroke, she d. 1 May 1830, having had with 2 daus. a son Robert James.

M'Lagan.

Peter, of Pumpherston —— *Linlithgowshire* 1865-8, 1868-74, 1874-80, and since [1881. See foot-note.

McLaren.

Duncan, of Edinburgh, mercht. —— *Edinburgh city*, 1865-8, 1868-74, 1874-80, [1880 until he accepted the Chiltern hundreds, Jan. 1881. See foot-note.

M ACKINTOSH, ÆNEAS WILLIAM, of Raigmore, Inverness-shire, J.P., D.L., hon. col. Inverness Arty. Vols. since 1880, formerly lieut.-col. comdt., M.P. as above (son of late Lauchlan Mackintosh, esq., of Raigmore, by Margaret, dau. of late Sir Archibald Dunbar, bart.); b.   1819, m. 12 March 1856, Grace Ellen Augusta, dau. of late Sir Neil Menzies, bart., and had with other issue a son.
(1) Lauchlan (eldest son), d. at Eton 21 June 1880, aged 17.
Raigmore, Inverness, N.B.; 42, Brook St., W.

M 'LAGAN, PETER, of Pumpherston, Midlothian, J.P., and J.P., D.L., Linlithgowshire, F.R.S. Scotland, a member of the Council of the University of Edinburgh, educated there, M.P. as above (son of Peter M'Lagan, of Pumpherston); b.   1823, m.   1876, Elizabeth Ann, widow of John Henry Taylor, esq., of Ravensdeane, co. York, dau. of George Taylor, esq., of Headingley, Leeds.
Pumpherston, Midcalder, N.B.; Clifton Hall, Ratho, N.B.
Clubs—Windham, Junior Athenæum; and University, Edinburgh.

M cLAREN, DUNCAN, of Newington House, Edinburgh, lord provost 1851-4, J.P. and D.L. since 1836, President of the Edinburgh Chamber of Commerce since 1862, M.P. as above, contested Edinburgh 1852 (son of late John M'Laren; b.   1800, m. 1st,   1829, Grant, dau. of William Aitken, esq., of Haddington, she d.   1833; he m. 2ndly,   1836, Chistina, dau. of William Renton, esq., merchant, of Edinburgh, she d.   1841; by his 1st wife he had with other issue a son.
(1) John, lord of session, next named.
MR. McLAREN m. 3rdly, Priscilla, 2nd dau. of late Jacob Bright, of Rochdale, and sister of the Rt. Hon. John Bright, M.P., and had with other issue—
(2) Priscilla (ygst. dau.), m. 25 May 1877 to Andrea Honyman Rabagliatti, M.A., M.D., of Bradford.
Newington House, Edinburgh.
Clubs—Reform, Liberal, Edinburgh.

McLaren—*continued.*

John, of **Edinburgh**, sheriff of chancery in Scotland —— *Wigton burghs* 1880, *Edinburgh City* 1881 until appointed a lord of session 15 Aug. 1881. See
[foot-note.

McLean.

Lauchlan (sir), of Morvern —— *Tarbert sheriffdom* 1628-33.

Sir Lauchlan MacLean, of Morvaren, was cr. a baronet of Nova Scotia 13 Feb. 1632, with remainder to his heirs male whatsoever (for other dates of creation see list of Nova Scotia Baronets in Foster's Baronetage); served at the battle of Inverlochy, when Montrose defeated the rebels under Argyll, and also at the battle of Kilsyth; d. 18 April 1649. His male line failed on the death of his great-grandson, Sir Hector, 5th bart., unm. 1750. See
[Foster's Baronetage.

Lauchlan, of Brollace —— *Argyllshire* 1685-6.

Son of Donald McLean, of Brolas, in Mull, and nephew of the half-blood of Sir Lauchlan, M.P., last named; m. Isabella, dau. of Hector McLean, of Torloisk, and d. 1687, leaving
[issue. See Foster's Baronetage.

McLeod.

Daniel (capt.) —— *Tain* 1703-7.

See Alexander, son of Neil McLeod, 8th baron of Assynt. Douglas Baronage, p. 387.

Eneas (Mr.), of Cadboll —— *Cromartyshire* 1703-7.

Of Cadboll and Cambuscurry, signed the Articles of Union 1707 (younger son of Hugh McLeod); m. Margaret, eldest dau. of Sir Kenneth Mackenzie, of Scatwell, and had issue;
[grandson of Robert, M.P.

John, of Dunvegan —— *Inverness-shire*, including *Ross* 1640-1.

Eldest son of Sir Roderick McLeod of that ilk : commonly called John More, on account of his great size and strength; m. Sybilla, dau. of Kenneth, Lord Mackenzie, of Kintail, and
[d. 1649, leaving with other issue a son John, M.P.

John, of Dunvegan —— *Inverness-shire* 1678 conv., 1680, but unable to serve
[through indisposition.

2nd son of John McLeod, of Dunvegan, M.P., served heir special of his brother Roderick 11 Aug. 1664; m. Florence, 2nd dau. of Sir James Macdonald, 2nd bart. of Slate, and d.
[1693, leaving issue.

Norman of that ilk —— *Inverness-shire* 1741-7, 1747-54.

Son of Norman of that ilk, who m. Sept. 1703, Anne Fraser, dau. of Hugh, Lord Lovat; he m. 1st. Janet, dau. of Sir Donald Macdonald, 4th bart. of Slate, and had a son and a dau.; he m. 2ndly Anne, dau. of William Martin, of Inchture, and d. 1772, having had
[further issue.

M c LAREN, JOHN, Q.C., a lord of session Scotland since 1881, lord advocate 1880-1, advocate 1856, sheriff of chancery Scotland 1869-80, M.P. as above (son of Duncan McLaren, M.P., last named, by his 1st wife); b. 17 April 1831, m. 14 Dec. 1868, Ottilie Augusta, eldest dau. of late H. L. Schwabe, esq.

McLeod—*continued.*

Norman (col.), of Macleod —— *Inverness-shire* 1790-6.

20th laird of Macleod, lt.-col. 42nd regt., served with considerable distinction in India, commanded the forces on the Malabar coast, contested Milbourne Port, Dorset, 1796, (son of John and grandson of Norman MacLeod, M.P., last named); b. 4 March 1754, d. Aug. 1801, having m. 1st Mary Mackenzie, of Suddie, she d. 1782; he m. 2ndly Sarah, dau. of [N. Stackhouse, 2nd member of council Bombay, and had further issue.

John Mackenzie, commonly called lord (Macleod) —— *Ross-shire,* 1780-4.

Eldest son of George, 3rd and attainted Earl of Cromarty, major-genl. in the British army 1782, col. 71st regt. 1777, Count Cromarty and a commandant of the Order of the Tower and Sword (Sweden), engaged with his father in the '45, taken to London, pleaded guilty, pardoned 1748, entered the service of the king of Sweden, who cr. him Count Cromarty, etc., raised two battalions of Highlanders 1777, his estates were restored in 1784 on payment of £19,000; he d. s.p. 2 April 1789, aged 62, having m. 4 June 1786, Margery, eldest dau. of James, 16th Lord Forbes, she d. 4 Oct. 1842, aged 81, having re-m. 11 March 1794 as 2nd [wife to John, 5th Duke of Atholl, who d. 26 June 1778.

Robert Bruce Æneas, of Cadboll —— *Cromartyshire* 1807-12.

1st lord lieut. Cromartyshire 1794-1833, contested Sutherlandshire 1790 (son of Roderick McLeod, of Cadboll, and Lilias Mackenzie), b. 23 Jan. 1764, m. 27 July 1784, Elizabeth, dau. of Alexander Macleod, esq., of Harris; he d.   leaving a son Roderick, M.P.

Roderick, younger, of Cadboll —— *Cromartyshire* 1818-20; *Sutherlandshire* 1831-2, 1833-4, 1835-7, *Inverness burghs* 1837 until he accepted the Chiltern [hundreds, s.b. 4 March 1840.

Of Invergordon Castle, Ross-shire, D.L., Lord Lieutenant Cromartyshire 1833-53 (son of Robert B. Macleod, M.P., last named); d. 13 March, 1853, aged 67, having m. 1813, Isabella, dau. of William Cunninghame, esq., of Lainshaw, Ayrshire, she d. 15 Dec. 1878, [leaving issue.

McNaught.

John —— *Edinburgh* 1625 conv.

Probably son of Roger, next named.

Roger, —— *Edinburgh* 1594 conv., 1597 conv., 1605 conv.

Probably father of John aforesaid.

McNaughton.

John, councillor —— *Inverary* 1685-6.

Forfeited for joining Dundee (son of Sir Alexander McNaughton of that ilk).

M'Neill.

Duncan, lord advocate for Scotland —— *Argyllshire* 1843-7, 1847 until appointed [a judge of Supreme Court of Scotland, s.b. 6 June 1851.

Lord Colonsay, of Colonsay and Oronsay, co. Argyll, so created 26 Feb. 1867, P.C., sheriff of Perthshire 1824-34, solicitor-general for Scotland 1834-5, 1841-2, lord advocate 1842-6, dean of the faculty of advocates 1843-51, then lord of session as Lord Colonsay, lord justice-general and president of court of session 1852-67, J.P., D.L. co. Midlethian and Argyllshire (2nd son of John M'Neill, and brother of Sir John M'Neill, G.C.B., P.C.); d. unm. at Pau [31 Jan. 1874, aged 80.

Maconochie.

Alexander, lord advocate of Scotland —— *Anstruther Easter* (now *St. Andrews*) *burghs* 1818, 1818 until appointed lord of session and justiciary in Scotland, [s.b. 26 July, 1819. See also England M.P.

Alexander Maconochie-Welwood, of Meadowbank Ho., Midlothian and Garvock, co. Fife, D.L., advocate 2 March 1799, sheriff depute co. Haddington 1810, solicitor-general 1813, lord advocate 1816, lord of session 1 July 1819, M.P. Yarmouth, I.W., Feb. 1817 to March 1818 (son of Allan Maconochie, Lord Meadowbank of session); b. March 1777, d. 30 Nov. 1861, having m. 29 April 1805, Anne, eldest dau. of Rt. Hon. Robert Blair, lord [president of court of session, and had issue.

Macpherson-Grant.

George, of Ballindalloch and Invereshie —— *Sutherlandshire* 1809-12, 1816-18, [1818-20, 1820-6.

Sir George Macpherson-Grant (son of Capt. John Macpherson), inherited, 13 April 1806, as heir of his father's maternal uncle, Sir James Grant, the estate of Ballindalloch, co. Elgin, and assumed the surname of Grant; cr. a baronet 25 July 1838; b. 25 Feb. 1781, d. 24 Nov. 1846, having m. 26 Aug. 1803, Mary, eldest dau. of Thomas Carnegy, esq., of Craigo, co. Forfar; and had 3 sons and 2 daus (see Foster's Baronetage); grandfather of Sir George, [next named.

George (sir) of Ballindalloch Castle, bart. —— *Elgin* and *Nairnshire* 1879-80, [and since 1880. See foot-note.

MACPHERSON-GRANT, Sir George, of Ballindalloch, co. Elgin, and of Invereshie, co. Inverness (1838, U.K.), J.P. and D.L. cos. Banff, Elgin, and Inverness, convener of co. Banff since 1872, M.P. as above; s. his father (Sir John) as 3rd baronet in 1850; b. 12 Aug. 1839, m. 3 July 1861, Frances Elizabeth, younger dau. of Rev. Roger Pocklington, vicar of Walesby, Notts, and has had with other issue 3 sons and 2 daus.

(1) John, b. 22 Mar. 1863.
(2) George Bertram, b. 26 Jan. 1868.
(3) Alastair, b. 29 Sept. 1875.
(4) Eva.   (5) Mabel Lucy.
Ballindalloch Castle, co. Elgin, and Invereshie House, Inverness.

McTaggart.

John (sir), of Ardwell, bart. —— *Wigtown burghs* 1835-7, 1837-41, 1841-7, [1847-52 (then a baronet), 1852-7.

Created a baronet 21 Sept. 1841, contested Wigtown burghs 1832 (son of John M'Taggart, of Ardwell) ; b. 15 March, 1789; d. 13 Aug. 1867, having m. 6 April 1811, Susannah, 3rd dau. of late John Kymer, esq., of Streatham, Surrey; she d. 2 December 1864, leaving 2 daus.

Maitland.

Alexander (Mr.) —— *Bervie* 1705-7, 1707-8 (1st parlt. Gt. Britain).

Possibly 3rd son of Charles, 3rd Earl of Lauderdale or 2nd son of Robert, 2nd Visct. of [Arbuthnott.

Alexander Charles (sir) Ramsay-Gibson (-Maitland), of Clifton Hall —— [*Edinburghshire* 1868-74.

3rd bart., col. Stirlingshire militia, assumed in 1865 the surname of Ramsay before that of Gibson on inheriting the estates of Mr. Ramsay, of Barnton, co. Edinburgh, and Sauchie, co. Stirling ; b. 7 Jan. 1820 ; d. 16 May, 1876, having m. 3 Feb. 1841, Thomasina Agnes, eldest dau. of James Hunt, esq., of Pittencrief, co. Fife, and had 2 sons and 3 daus. See [Foster's Baronetage.

Anthony (Capt. R.N.) —— *Haddington burghs* 1813-18, *Berwickshire* 1826-30, [1830-1, 1831-2.

10th Earl of Lauderdale, G.C.B., K.C.M.G., admiral of the red, knight commander of the Ionian order, now K.C.M.G., contested Berwickshire 1832 (son of James, 8th earl) ; [b. 10 June 1785, d. unm. 22 March 1863. See Foster's Peerage.

Charles, fiar of Haltoun —— *Edinburghshire* 1669 until appointed lord treasurer [depute, s.b. 16 Jan. 1672.

3rd Earl of Lauderdale (on the death of his brother, John, Duke of Lauderdale, 24 Aug. 1682), lord (Haltoun) of session 8 June, 1670, treasurer depute 1672, master and general of the mint 1661-82, and P.C. 1661-82, readmitted 1686 (son of John, Earl of Lauderdale) ; d. 9 June 1691, having m. 18 Nov. 1652, Elizabeth, only dau. and heir of Richard Lauder, of Halton, co. Edinburgh, and had with other issue Richard, M.P., 4th Earl, and Sir John, [M.P., 5th Earl. See Foster's Peerage.

Charles, merchant burgess —— *North Berwick* 1678 conv., 1681-2, 1685-6 (then bailie).

Charles (sir) of Pittrichie —— *Aberdeenshire* 1685-6.

Probably son of Sir Richard Maitland elder, of Pitrichie, cr. a baronet 12 March 1672, with remainder to his heirs male. A Sir Charles, son of Sir Chas. Maitland, bart., d. 1704.

Charles, advocate of Pittrichie —— *Aberdeen* (now *Montrose*) *burghs* 1748, until ‾ [his death s.b. 27 March, 1751.

Advocate 1727, commissary of Glasgow, sheriff co. Edinburgh 1747-8 (only son of Hon. Alexander (Arbuthnott) Maitland, by his wife, Jean, eldest dau. of Sir Charles Maitland, of [Pitrichie, co. Aberdeen) ; d. s.p. at Edinburgh, 10 Feb. 1751.

Maitland—*continued.*

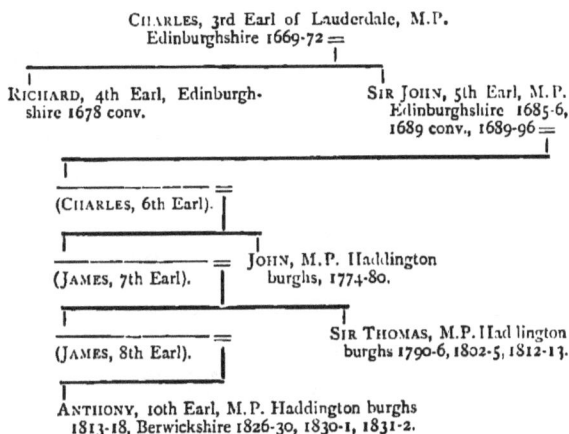

CHARLES, 3rd Earl of Lauderdale, M.P.
Edinburghshire 1669-72 =

RICHARD, 4th Earl, Edinburghshire 1678 conv.

SIR JOHN, 5th Earl, M.P.
Edinburghshire 1685-6,
1689 conv., 1689-96 =

(CHARLES, 6th Earl). =

(JAMES, 7th Earl). = JOHN, M.P. Haddington
burghs, 1774-80.

(JAMES, 8th Earl). = SIR THOMAS, M.P. Haddington
burghs 1790-6, 1802-5, 1812-13.

ANTHONY, 10th Earl, M.P. Haddington burghs
1813-18, Berwickshire 1826-30, 1830-1, 1831-2.

David, of Soutra, bailie —— *Lauder* 1689 conv., 1689-1702.

John, bailie —— *Lauder* 1667 conv., 1669.

John (sir), of Ravelrig —— *Edinburghshire* 1685-6, 1689 conv., 1689 until he succeeded (then Sir John Lauder) as Earl of Lauderdale, s.b. 28 Aug. 1696.

5th Earl of Lauderdale (on the death of his brother Richard 1695), advocate 30 July 1680, knighted and cr. a baronet of Nova Scotia 18 Nov. 1680, lord (Ravelrig) of session 28 Nov. 1689, P.C. at the revolution, col. Edinburghshire militia 1689, took his seat in parliament 8 Sept. 1696, supported the Union, assumed the designation of "Lauder of Haltoun" 1693, in lieu of "Maitland of Ravelrig;" d. 30 Aug. 1710, having m. Margaret, only child of Alexander Cunningham, 10th Earl of Glencairn, she d. 12 May 1742, leaving [with other issue a son Charles, 6th earl. See Foster's Peerage.

John (captain), brother of the Earl of Lauderdale —— *Haddington burghs* 1774 [until his death s.b. 23 Feb. 1780.

Lt.-col. 71st regt. 1779, major of marines 1775, lost a hand in Adml. Boscawen's engage-ment with De la Clue 1759, clerk of the pipe in the exchequer, Scotland, 1769, served with great distinction in the American war (8th son of Charles, 6th Earl of Lauderdale); d. at [Savannah, 12 Oct. 1779.

John, advocate, of Argrennan, in the stewartry of Kirkcudbright —— *Kirkcud-* [*bright stewartry* 1874-80. See foot-note.

M AITLAND, JOHN, of Argrennan, co. Kirkcudbright, B.A. University Coll., Oxon, 1864, educated also at Universities of St. Andrews and Edinburgh, admitted advocate 1685, M.P. as above, son of Edward Francis Maitland, Lord Barcaple, of session, and nephew of Thomas Maitland, M.P., (Lord Dundrennan, of session); b. 4 May 1841.

Barcaple, Argrennan, Ringford, N.B.; Ainslie Place, Edinburgh.

Clubs—Savile, Reform.

Maitland—*continued.*

Richard, of Gogar —— *Edinburghshire* 1678 conv.

4th Earl of Lauderdale (on the death of his father, Charles, 9 June 1691) styled of Over Gogar, and knighted, P.C. 1678, general of the mint jointly with his father, lord justice general 1681-4, retired to St. Germains at the revolution, was outlawed by the court of justiciary 23 July 1694; d. s.p. 1695, having m. Anne, 2nd dau. of Archibald Campbell, 9th Earl of Argyll; she re-m. to Charles, 7th Earl of Moray, and d. s.p. 18 Sept. 1734,
[aged 70.

Thomas (lt.-genl.) —— *Haddington burghs* 1790-6, 1802, 1802 (a commissioner for the affairs of India 1803), until appointed governor of Ceylon s.b. 14 Feb. 1805; 1812 (then lt.-genl.), until appointed governor of Malta s.b. 16 July
[1813.

Rt. Hon. Sir Thomas Maitland, G.C.B., 1815, installed 1821, G.C.M.G., P.C., lt.-genl. in the army 1811, col. 10th regt. 1811, governor of Ceylon 1805-13, of Malta, commander of the forces in the Mediterranean, and lord high commissioner of Ionian Islands 1813, knight grand cross of the Ionian order, now G.C.M.G., grand master 1818, brigadier-general St. Domingo 1797, West Indies 1798, major-general in the army 1805 (son of James, 7th Earl [of Lauderdale); d. unm. at Malta 17 Jan. 1824.

Thomas, of Dundrennan —— *Kirkcudbright stewartry* 1845-7 (solicitor-general Scotland 1846), 1847, until appointed a judge of court of session s.b. 20 Feb.
[1850.

Lord Dundrennan, of session 1850-1, advocate Dec. 1813, solicitor-genl. Scotland 18.0-1, 1846-50 (eldest son of Adam Maitland, of Dundrennan Abbey); b. 9 Oct. 1792, d. 10 June 1851, having m. 3 July 1815, Isabella Graham, dau. of James McDowall, of Garthland, M.P.;
[she d. 27 Aug. 1864, leaving issue.

Malcolm.

John (sir), bart. —— *Kinross-shire* 1711-13.
Probably the 2nd baronet (son of Sir John of Balberdie, so cr. 25 July 1665, and d. 8 Feb. 1692); m. Emilia, dau. of John Balfour, 3rd Lord Balfour, of Burleigh, and d. March 1729,
[leaving issue; see CHAOS, Foster's Baronetage.

Maleson.

Thomas (Malyssoun) —— *Kintore* 1579.

Man.

Alexander —— *Bervie* 1681-2.

Manderston.

Archibald —— *Berwick* 1479.

Manson.

Alexander, bailie —— *Wick* 1678 conv., 1681-2, 1685-6.

Alexander, of Bridgend —— *Caithness-shire* 1693-1702.

George, bailie —— *Cupar* 1678 conv.

Thomas —— *Dornoch* 1646-7.

Mar.

Johnne, of —— *Aberdeen* 1456.

David —— *Aberdeen* 1567, 1568.

Marjoribanks. See also Robertson.

Charles, of Lees —— *Berwickshire* 1833 until his death s.b. 13 Jan. 1834.

> 2nd son of Sir John Marjoribanks, bart., M.P., and brother of David, Lord Marjoribanks. E.I.C.C.S. president of committee on trade with China; b. 15 July 1794, d. unm. 3 Dec. [1833.

Edward (hon.) —— *Berwickshire* since 1880.

> Eldest son of Lord Tweedmouth, bar.-at-law I. T. 1874, contested West Kent 1874; b. 8 July 1849, m. 9 June 1873, Lady Fanny Octavia Louisa Spencer-Churchill, 3rd dau. of [John Winston, 7th Duke of Marlborough, K.G., and has issue. See Foster's Peerage.

John (sir), of Lees, bart. —— *Buteshire* 1812-18 (then younger); *Berwickshire* [1818-20, 1820-6.

> Served in grenadier guards, lord provost of Edinburgh 1814 and 1825, cr. a baronet 6 May 1815 (son of Edward Marjoribanks, of Hallyards); b. 13 Jan. 1763, d. 5 Feb. 1833, having m. 15 April 1791, Alison, eldest dau. of William Ramsay, esq., of Barnton, Midlothian, and [had with other issue, Charles, M.P., and David Robertson, M.P.

Thomas —— *Edinburgh* 1540, 1546 bis.

> Lord Ratho of session, and clerk register 8 Feb. 1549, advocate 1524, acquired the lands of Ratho, co. Renfrew, charter 27 Sept. 1540, lord provost of Edinburgh 1540; m. Janet Purves, and d. about 1567, having had at least 4 sons and 3 daus.; viz., John, Robert, [Thomas, James, Margaret, Jennet, and Bessie.

Markham.

Henry (col.) —— *Linlithgow, etc.* 1656-8 (WILLIS).

> Col. in the parliamentary army, governor of Belvoir castle for 3 years, wounded at the battle of Naseby, commissioner for letting lands in Ireland ; son of Sir Anthony Markham, [of Sedgbrook, and younger brother of Sir Robert, cr. a baronet 15 Aug. 1642.

Martin.

Andrew —— *Anstruther Easter* 1641, 1645, 1646-7 (or David Alexander) 1665 [conv., bailie.

Henry (master) ——1469.

Robert (Mr.) —— *Elgin* 1667 conv.

Thomas —— *Anstruther Easter* 1630 conv.

SCOTCH MEMBERS.   H H

Mason.

James —— *Montrose* 1568 (in the absence of the provost), 1583.

Masterton.

James —— *Stirling burghs* 1768-74, barrack-master-general for Scotland 1769.

Of Newston (son of John Masterton, of Edinburgh, merchant), a col. in the army, said [to have been A.D.C. to the Duke of Cumberland, at Culloden, died 7 Feb. 1778.

Matheson.

Alexander (sir), of Ardross, Ross-shire, bart. —— *Inverness burghs* 1847-52, 1852-7, 1857-9, 1859-65, 1865-8. *Ross-shire and Cromartyshire* 1868-74, [1874-80, and since 1880 (esq.), see foot-note.

James (sir) of Achany and the Lews —— *Ross* and *Cromartyshire* 1847-52, 1852-7 (then a baronet), 1857-9 (F.R.S.), 1859-65, 1865-8. See also England M.P.

Sir James Matheson, of the Lews, co. Ross, baronet, so cr. 15 Jan. 1851, L.L. Ross 1866-78, J.P., D.L., co. Sutherland, M.P. Ashburton 1843-7, and as above, vice-president Caledonian asylum, London. F.R.S. (2nd son of Donald Matheson); b. 17 Nov. 1796, d. s.p. at Mentone 31 Dec. 1878, having m. 9 Nov. 1843, Mary Jane, 4th dau. of (Hon.) Michael Henry Perceval, esq., of Spencer Wood, Canada; she d. 23 Nov. 1876. See [Foster's Baronetage, 1880.

John —— *Crail* 1593.

Mauchane.

John, bailie of Edinburgh —— 1528.

Maule.

—— laird of Melgum —— *Forfarshire* 1650-1.

Henry Maule of Melgund (son of Henry Maule, of Balgreggy and Easter Innerpeffer), [m. Margaret Durham, of Petkenon, and had a son, James, M.P.

MATHESON, ALEXANDER (SIR), of Ardross and Attadale, Ross-shire, cr. a baronet 15 May 1882, M.P. Inverness 1847-68, and co. Ross and Cromarty since 1868 as above, director bank of England, and a commissioner of the lieutenancy for London. J.P., D.L., co. Ross, Cromarty, and Inverness, (son of John Matheson, of Attadale, and Fernaig, J.P., D.L.); b. 26 Jan. 1805; m. 1st, 2 Feb. 1841, Mary, only dau. of James Craufurd Macleod, esq., of Geanis, Ross-shire. she d. s.p. 28 April 1841; he m. 2ndly, 19 July 1853, Lavinia Mary Stapleton, sister of Miles, 8th Lord Beaumont, she d. 30 Sep. 1855, having had a son and dau.

(1) Kenneth James, D.L., Ross, b. 12 May 1854.

(2) Mary Isabella, m. 20 Apl. 1881, to Wallace Charles, yst. son of Col. Alexander Houstoun, of Clerkington, co. Haddington.

SIR ALEXANDER m. 3rdly, 17 April 1860, Eleanor Irving, 5th dau. of late Spencer Perceval, esq (E. EGMONT), of Ealing, Middx., and has 3 sons and 4 daus.

(3) Alexander Perceval, b. 6 Feb. 1861.

(4) Roderick Mackenzie Chisholm, b. 26 Dec. 1861.   (5) Torquhill George, b. 4 Feb. 1871.

(6) Eleanor Margaret.   (7) Anna Elizabeth.   (8) Flora.   (9) Hylda Nora Grace.

Ardross Castle, Alness, N.B., Doucraig, Strome Ferry, N.B.; 16 South St., W. *Club—Reform.*

Maule—*continued.*

Fox, eldest son of William, Baron Panmure —— *Perthshire* 1835-7, *Elgin burghs* 1838-41, *Perth* 1841-7, (vice president board of trade 1841, sec.-at-war 1846-7), 1847 (sec.-at-war 1847-52, president of India board 1852) until [he s. as 2nd Lord Panmure, 13 April 1852.

> 11th Earl of Dalhousie, K.T., G.C.B., P.C. (on the death of his cousin, James Andrew, 10th Earl, 19 Dec. 1860), having succeeded as 2nd Lord Panmure as afsd., keeper of the privy seal Scotland, lord-lieut. co. Forfar, com. royal military asylum, capt. 79th Highlanders, under-sec. of state home dept. 1835-41, contested Perthshire 1837, vice-president board of trade 1841, sec.-at-war 1846-52 and 1855-8, assumed the surname of Ramsay after that of Maule 1861 (son of William Maule, M.P., cr. Baron Panmure) ; b. 22 Apl. 1801, d. s.p. 6 July 1874, having m. 4 April 1831, Hon Montagu, eldest dau. of George, 2nd Lord [Abercromby, she d. s.p. 11 Nov. 1853.

Henry (Mr.), of Kellie —— *Brechin* 1689 conv., 1689 to 1702.

> Youngest son of George, 2nd Earl of Panmure (and next brother of James, 4th and attained earl, who d. s.p. 11 Apl. 1723), he engaged in the rebellion of 1715, and d. at Edinburgh, June 1734 ; he m. 1st, 30 March 1695, Mary, only dau. of William Fleming, 5th Earl of Wigton, and had with other issue a son, William, M.P. 1735 ; he m. 2ndly (cont. 27 Jan. 1704) Anne Lindsay, sister of John, Viscount of Garnock, and had with other issue a son John, [M.P. 1739, etc.

James, fiar of Melgum —— *Forfarshire* 1667 conv.

> Probably son of Henry Maule, of Melgund ; he m. Marion, dau. of Sir John Ogilvy, of [Inverquharitie.

John, of Inverkellor —— *Aberdeen* (now *Montrose*) *burghs* 1739-41, 1741-7, 1747 until appointed a baron of the exchequer Scotland, s.b. 20 June, 1748.

> Of Inverkeilor; advocate 1725, keeper of the register of sasines 1737, a baron of the [exchequer Scotland 1748 (son of Henry Maule, M.P. 1689) ; d. unm. 2 July 1781.

Lauderdale, lt.-col. 79th regt. —— *Forfarshire* 1852 (surveyor-general of the [ordnance 1853) until his death s. b. 11 Oct. 1854.

> Next brother to Fox Maule, M.P., Earl of Dalhousie ; b. 27 March 1807, d. at Varna, [in Turkey, 1 Aug. 1854, unm.

William —— *Edinburgh* 1596 conv.

> Probably 2nd son of Thomas Maule, of Panmure, by his wife, Margaret, dau. of Sir [George Halyburton, of Pitcur.

William, of Panmure —— *Forfarshire* 1735-41, 1741-7, 1747-54 (then earl), 1754-61, 1761-8, 1768-74, 1774-80, 1780 until his death s. b. 11 Feb. 1782.

> Earl of Panmure of Forth and Viscount Maule of Whitechurch, in the peerage of Ireland, so cr. 6 April 1743, with remainder to his brother John ; served at the battles of Dettingen and Fontenoy, comd. 25th regt. 1747, 21st R. Scots fusiliers 1752, 2nd in comd. at Gibraltar 1756, col. 2nd regt. of dragoons or Royal Scots greys 1770, major-general 1755, lt.-genl. 1758, general 1770 (son of Hon. Harry Maule, M.P.) ; d. unm. 4 Jan. 1782, aged 82, when [the titles expired.

Maule—*continued.*

William, of Panmure —— *Forfarshire* 1796, 1805-6, 1806-7, 1807-12, 1812-18, 1818-20, 1820-6, 1826-30, 1830-1, 1831 until cr. Baron Panmure, 10 Sept. [same year.

> Baron Panmure, of Brechin and Navar, co. Forfar, so cr. 10 Sept. 1831, assumed the surname and arms of Maule in lieu of Ramsay, on succeeding to the estates of the Earl of Panmure (2nd son of George, 8th Earl of Dalhousie); b. 27 Oct. 1771, d. 13 Apl. 1852, having m. twice, and had with other issue (see Foster's Peerage—DALHOUSIE) 2 sons, Fox [and Lauderdale Maule, M.P., afsd.

Mawar.

Mark —— *Elgin* 1593.

Maxwell.   See also **Stirling**.

Adam, merchant burgess —— *North Berwick* 1661-3.

Alexander (sir), of Monreith, knt. and bart. —— *Wigtown burghs* 1713-15.

> 2nd baronet (on the death of his father, Sir William, M.P. 1667); m. 29 Dec. 1711, Lady Jean Montgomerie (d. 20 Feb. 1745), dau. of Alexander, 9th Earl of Eglintoun, and d. [23 May 1730, leaving issue.

George (sir), of Nether Pollok —— *Renfrewshire* 1649-50.

> Of Auldhouse, and afterwards of Pollok, by devise of his cousin, Sir John Maxwell, bart., of Nether Pollok (who was created a baronet of Nova Scotia 25 Nov. 1630, and d. s.p.s. 1 Nov. 1647), a zealous covenanter, knighted by Charles II., rector of Glasgow university 1654-8, fined £4,000 on the Restoration, imprisoned in Stirling Castle 1665-70 (son of John Maxwell, of Auldhouse); d. April 1677, having m. (contract 24 Dec. 1646), Annabella, dau. of Sir Archibald Stewart, of Blackhall, bart., she d. 1692, having had with other issue a son, Sir John, M.P. See STIRLING-MAXWELL and HERON-MAXWELL, Foster's [Baronetage.

George, of Munches —— *Kirkcudbright stewartry* 1665 conv., 1667 conv.

> 6th son of Alexander Maxwell, of Logan; m. 1st Margaret Macqueen, and had a son John, he m. 2ndly (contract 9 June 1655), Barbara, dau. of James Maxwell, of Tinwald, and [had a son George, of Munches, ancestor of that family.

Herbert Eustace (sir), of Monreith, co. Wigtown —— *Wigtownshire* since [1880. See foot-note.

MAXWELL, SIR HERBERT EUSTACE, of Monreith, co. Wigtown, D.L. (1681 N.S.), capt. royal Ayrs. militia, M.P. as above, succ. his father as 7th baronet in 1877; b. 8 Jan. 1845, m. 20 Jan. 1869, Mary, eldest dau. of late Henry Fletcher-Campbell, esq., of Boquhan, co. Stirling, and has 2 sons and 3 daus.
(1) William, b. 23 Sept. 1869.
(2) Aymer Edward, b. 26 Oct. 1877.
(3) Ann Christian.   (4) Winifred Edith.   (5) Beatrice Mary.
Monreith, Whauphill, Scotland; 71, *Prince's Gate, S.W.*
Clubs—St. Stephen's, Carlton.

Maxwell—*continued.*

(Sir James), laird of Calderwood —— *Lanarkshire* 1593, 1594 and 1596 conv.
[(as a minor baron), 1617 conv. and parlt., 1621.

Sir James Maxwell, 9th of Calderwood, co. Lanark (son of John Maxwell, of Calderwood, who it is said sat in Scots parlt. 1560,) sheriff depute Lanarkshire 1607, d. Sept. 1622, having m. 1st, Helena, dau. of John Porterfield, esq., of Porterfield, co. Renfrew, she d. Aug. 1573, having had 2 daus.; he m. 2ndly (contract 12 Feb. 1579) Isabel, dau. of Sir Alexander Hamilton, of Innerwick, and had with 6 daus. 3 sons, of whom the second, Sir James, cr. a baronet of Nova Scotia 18 Mar. 1627, with remainder to his heirs male whatsoever; he m. 3rdly, 8 Sept. 1610, Margaret, dau. of James Cuninghame, 7th Earl of Glencairn (ext.), relict of Sir James Hamilton, of Evandale (her will dated 2nd Oct. 1622),
[and had issue.

John —— *Dumfries* 1585.

(Sir John), laird of Pollok Maxwell —— *Renfrewshire* 1593 as a minor baron.

Son and heir of Sir John Maxwell, who d. 20 Feb. 1577; he m. 1st (contract 6 July 1569), Margaret, dau. of Wm. Cuninghame, of Caprington, he m. 2ndly (contract at Stirling 17 Sept. 1592), Marjory, dau. of Sir Wm. Edmonstone, of Duntreath; he fell at an encounter
[at Lockerbie 1 Nov. 1595, leaving issue.

(Sir John), laird of Pollok Maxwell —— *Renfrewshire* 1617.

Sir John Maxwell, knight baronet, so cr. 25 Nov. 1630; governor of Dumbarton Castle, 1634; d. s.p.s. 1 Nov. 1647; having m. 1st Isobel Campbell, dau. of Hew, Lord Loudoun, she d. Jan. 1612; he m. 2ndly Grizel, dau. of John Blair, of Blair, she d. s.p.s. April 1642.

John (sir), of Pollok —— *Renfrewshire* 1689 conv., 1689-93, 1695-6, 1698 until
[appointed lord justice clerk 6 Feb. 1699.

Sir John Maxwell, Lord Pollok of session, cr. a baronet of Nova Scotia 12 April 1682, as the person succeeding to the late baronet in his lands and heritage (terris suis hereditate), and as nearest agnate, and to the heirs male of his body, and by further patent dated 27 March 1707 (Reg. Mag. Sig. lib. 82, No. 148), the said title was new granted and extended to him and the heirs male of his body, whom failing, to his other heirs of entail whatsoever contained in his infeftment of his lands and estate; fined £93,600 Scots, for refusing to take "the test," and imprisoned July 1683, the fine was remitted on the accession of William and Mary, made P.C., a lord of the treasury and exchequer Scotland 1696, ordinary lord of session, and took his seat as Lord Pollok 17 Feb. 1699, lord justice clerk 1699-1703, lord rector of Glasgow 1691-1717, D.D. 1710 (son of Sir George Maxwell, M.P.); b. Jan. 1648, d. s.p. 4 July 1732, having m. (contract dated 23 Feb. 1671), Marion, dau. of Sir James Stewart, of Kirkfield, knt., and sister of Sir James Stewart, of Goodtrees, lord advocate of
[Scotland, she d. 1706.

John, younger, of Cardoness —— *Kirkcudbright stewartry* 1742-7.

Major John Maxwell, of Cardoness (son of Col. William Maxwell, of Newlands, M.P.); m. Miss Irving, of Bonshaw, and d. Feb. 1754, having had a son, Sir David, cr. a baronet
[9th June 1804. See Foster's Baronetage.

John, younger, of Pollok —— *Renfrewshire* 1818-20, 1820-6, 1826-30; *Lanark-*
[*shire* 1833-4, 1835-7.

8th baronet (on the death of his father, Sir John, M.P., 30 July 1844); lt.-col. Renfrewshire mil., contested Lanarkshire 1831; b. 12 May 1791, and d. s.p. 6 June 1865, having m. 14 Oct. 1839, Lady Matilda Harriet Bruce, dau. of Thomas, Earl of Elgin and Kincardine, she d. 31 Aug. 1857. See STIRLING-MAXWELL, Foster's Baronetage.

Maxwell—*continued.*

John (sir), of Pollok, bart. —— *Paisley* 1833 until he accepted the Chiltern hundreds s.b. 24 March 1834.

> 7th baronet (on the death of his father, Sir James, 1785), master of the Renfrewshire and Lanarkshire foxhounds, contested the latter county 1830 and Renfrewshire Jan. 1837; b. 31 Oct. 1768, d. 30 July 1844, having m.   1788, Hannah Anne, dau. of Richard Gardiner, [esq., of Aldborough, Suffolk, she d. 21 July 1841, leaving issue, John M.P. 1818, etc.

John Maxwell Heron-, of Kirouchtree, Newton Stewart —— *Kirkcudbright-*
[*shire* since 1880. See foot-note.

John Shaw Heron (sir), of Heron and Springkell —— *Dumfries burghs*
[1807-12.

> 4th baronet (on the death of his father, Sir William, 4 March 1804), lieut.-gen. in the army, lieut.-col. 23rd light dragoons, assumed on the death of his father-in-law the additional surname and arms of Heron; b. 29 June 1772, d. 29 Jan. 1830, having m. 4 Jan. 1802, Mary, only surviving child and heir of Patrick Heron, esq., of Heron, in the stewartry of Galloway. M.P. Kirkcudbright, she d. 18 June 1856. having had issue. See Foster's
> [Baronetage.

Patrick, of Newark —— *Renfrewshire* 1639-41, 1645-6 (laird).

> "Cousin" of John, 8th Lord Maxwell.

Richard, deacon of the hammermen —— *Edinburgh* 1639-41.

(Robert 4th) lord —— *Edinburgh* 1524 (provost).

> 4th lord (on the death of his father, who fell at Flodden 9 Sept. 1513), knighted and appointed steward of Annandale 10 June 1513, warden of the west marches 1517, provost of Edinburgh 1524, and chosen one of the lords of articles, as above—"a solitary instance, it is believed, of a peer being so elected;" P.C. 21 June 1526, an extraordinary lord of session 17 Nov. 1533, one of the lords of the regency 1536; he proposed in parliament that permission should be granted to all to read the Bible in the vulgar tongue, and that was granted; [he d. 9 July 1546, having m twice, and left issue.

Robert (sir), of Orchardtown, knt. bart. —— *Kirkcudbright stewartry* 1669-74
[(then younger), 1681-2 (then a baronet).

> The baronetcy was created 30 June 1663 (son of Sir Robert Maxwell, of Spottis, 2nd son of John, 4th Lord Herries); d. before 26 Oct. 1681, the title became dormant on the death [s.p. of Sir Robert Maxwell, 7th bart., 21 Sept. 1786.

HERON (MAXWELL), JOHN MAXWELL, of Kirouchtree, co. Kirkcudbright, J.P., D.L., and for co. Wigtown, capt. 1st (royal) regt., retd. 1868 (h.p.), has abandoned the final surname of Maxwell, M.P. as above (son of Rev. Michael Maxwell-Heron, of Heron and Kirouchtree, see Foster's Baronetage); b. 6 Sept. 1836, m. 12 Nov. 1868, Margaret, 2nd dau. of William Stancombe, esq., of Blount's Court, Wilts, and has issue.

Kirouchtree, Newton Stewart, Scotland.
Club—Junior United Service.

Maxwell—*continued.*

Wellwood Herries, of Munches —— *Kirkcudbright stewartry* 1868, 1868-74.
[See foot-note.

William —— *Glasgow* 1568.

William —— *Lochmaben* 1612.

William, of Monreith —— *Wigtownshire* 1667 conv. 1669-72.

    d. unm. 1679, succeeded by his uncle William, who was retoured heir male of entail and
                       [provision 2 June 1681, cr. a baronet 8 Jan. 1681.

William, of Cardoness —— *Kirkcudbright stewartry* 1702-7.

    Col. William Maxwell, of Newlands (son of William Maxwell, minister of Minnigaff); m.
    1696, Nicholas, only dau. of William Stuart, of Castle Stuart (son of John, Earl of Gallo-
    [way), he d. 1752, aged 89, leaving with other issue a son John, M.P. 1742.

William (sir), of Monreith, bart. —— *Wigtownshire* 1805-6, 1806-7, 1807-12
(then of Camphart, younger of Monreith, lt.-col. 26th regt.), 1822-6 (then a
[bart.), 1826-30.

    5th baronet (on the death of his father, Sir William. Feb. 1812), lieut.-col. 26th Camero-
    nians, of which he raised a battalion and commanded the regiment at the battle of Corunna,
    where he lost his left arm, wounded in the knee at the siege of Walcheren ; b. 5 Mar. 1779,
    d. 22 Aug. 1838, having m. 23 April 1803, Catherine, youngest dau. of John Fordyce, esq.,
    [of Ayton, co. Berwick, she d. 19 July 1857, having had issue. See Foster's Baronetage.

William, of Carriden —— *Linlithgow burghs* 1807-12.

Meiklejohn.

Robert —— *Edinburgh* 1643 conv., 1644.

William —— *Burntisland* 1621, 1625 conv., 1630 conv

Meldrum.

Robert (Mr.), of Tillibody —— *Clackmannanshire* 1648.

MAXWELL, WELLWOOD HERRIES, of Munches, co. Kirkcudbright, J.P. and D.L., and convener
of the stewartry since 1880; advocate 1839, M.P. as above (elder son of late John Herries
Maxwell); b. 15 Oct. 1817, m. March 1844, Jane Home, eldest dau. of Sir William Jardine, bart., of
Applegirth, co. Dumfries, and has had, with other issue, 4 sons and 5 daus.
    (1) William Jardine Maxwell, b. 4 March 1852, m. 29 March 1877, Dorothea FitzGerald Maitland,
        dau. of late Charles Lionel Maitland-Kirwan, of Gelston Castle, N.B., and has issue.
    (2) Wellwood, of Kirkennan, b. 28 Dec. 1857.
    (3) Alexander, b. 26 June 1860. (4) Hugh, b. 12 May 1862.
    (5) Jessie Jane, m. 20 Aug. 1868, to Charles George Hood-Kinnear, esq., and has issue.
    (6) Clementina.
    (7) Agnes, m. 29 Aug. 1878, to Lionel Maitland-Kirwan, esq., and has issue.
    (8) Margaret. (9) Catherine Helen.
Munches, Dalbcattie, and Terraughtie, Dumfries, N.B.

Melgund.   See also Elliot.

William Hugh Elliot, commonly called Viscount —— *Greenock* 1847-52, [*Clackmannanshire* and *Kinross-shire* 1857-9.   See also England M.P.

3rd Earl of Minto (on the death of his father, Gilbert, 2nd Earl, 31 July 1859), M.P. Hythe 1837-41, contested Rochester 1841, Glasgow, 1852 ; b. 19 March 1814, m. 20 May 1844, his cousin, Emma Elinor Elizabeth, only dau. of Gen. Sir Thomas Hislop, bart. (ext.), G.C.B., she d. 21 April 1882, having had with other issue (see Foster's Peerage) a son [Arthur, M.P. (see p. 122).

Gilbert, of Minto, lord viscount —— *Roxburghshire* 1812 until he succ. as 2nd [Earl of Minto 21 June 1814.   See also England M.P.

2nd Earl of Minto (on the death of his father, Gilbert, 1st Earl, 21 June 1814), P.C., G.C.B., lord privy seal 1846-52 gov. of Naval College Portsmouth, an official trustee British Museum, envoy-extraordinary and minister-plenipotentiary to Berlin 1832-4. 1st lord of admiralty in Lord Melbourne's 2nd administration 1835-41, assumed the additional surname and arms of Murray-Kynynmound, M.P. Ashburton, 1806-7 ; b. 16 May 1782, d. 31 July 1859, having m. 28 Aug. 1806, Mary, dau. of Patrick Brydone, esq., of Lennuel House, Berwick, afore- [said, she d. 21 July 1853, having had issue.   (See Foster's Peerage.)

Melville.

(Sir James), of Halhill —— 1594 (the laird) conv. bis. (as a minor baron), 1599 [conv.

A statesman and historian, served under the Duke of Montmorenci. great constable and chief minister of France, served 3 years at the court of the Elector Palatine, P.C. to Q. Mary until imprisoned in Lochleven Castle, P.C. to James VI., gentleman of the chamber to Anne his queen, author of " The Memoirs " (younger brother of Robert, 1st Lord Melville); d. 13 Nov. [1617, leaving issue.

James (Mr.), of Halhill —— *Fifeshire* 1690-1702, *Kinghorn* 1702 until his death [s.b. 18 June 1706.

Robert (sir) —— 1602 conv. (as a minor baron), 1605 conv. (the elder).

Lord Melville. of Monymaill, so cr. 30 April 1616 (2nd son of Sir John Melville, of Raith), served at the court of France temp. Henry II., P.C. 1562, ambassador to England 1566, etc., hereditary keeper of the palace of Linlithgow 1567, espoused the cause of Mary, Queen of Scots, and was taken prisoner on the surrender of Edinburgh Castle April 1573, treasurer depute 1582-96, knighted Oct. 1582. ambassador to England with the master of Gray, Jan. 1587, to endeavour to prevent the execution of Q. Mary, vice-chancellor Scotland 1589, an extraordinary lord of session 11 June 1594 until 26 Feb. 1601 (as Lord Murdocairnie) when he resigned in favour of his son next named, a commissioner for the projected union 1604 ; [d. 1621, aged 94, having m. twice, and left a son, Sir Robert, M.P.

Robert (sir), the younger —— 1605 conv. (as a minor baron).

2nd Lord Melville, P.C. (on the death of his father, Robert, last named 1621), admitted an extraordinary lord of session on the resignation of his father 26 Feb. 1601, as Lord Burntis- land, removed Feb. 1626, a royal commissioner to open parliament 1633 ; m. twice, and d. [s.p. 9 March 1635.

Robert, of Carskeirdoe —— *Cupar* 1689 conv., 1689 until his death s.b. 13 July [1693.

Menteth.

James, provost of Stirling —— 1504.

Of Randifoord, co. Stirling (son of Sir William and brother of Sir William Menteth, of West Kerse, co. Stirling, and Alva. co. Clackmannan); m. 1501, Janet, widow of Archibald Craw-
[ford, of Brecroft, and had issue.

Menzies.

(——) laird of Wemyss —— *Perthshire* 1625 conv.

Alexander —— *Aberdeen* 1468 (chosen an auditor of complaint), 1482, 1483.

Possibly 3rd son of Sir Robert Menzies, by his wife Margaret, dau. of Sir David Lindsay,
[of Edzell.

Alexander (sir), of that ilk, knt. and bart. —— *Perthshire*, 1693, until his death
[s.b. 16 April 1695.

Cr. a baronet 2 Sept. 1665 (son of Duncan Menzies); m. Agnes, eldest dau. of Sir John
[Campbell, of Glenorchy, bart. (E. BREADALBANE), and had issue.

Andro —— 1458.

Gilbert (Menyheis) —— *Aberdeen,* 1449, 1450.

Gilbert, provost of Aberdeen —— 1513, *Aberdeen* 1526, 1532 (provost), 1535,
[provost.

"Banison Gib" m. Marjory Chalmers, dau. of the laird of Murtle, on Deeside, and had a
[son Thomas, M.P.

Gilbert —— *Aberdeen* 1567, 1578 conv., 1579 (provost), 1581.

[Of Pitfoddels, provost of Aberdeen, Michaelmas 1576; son of Thomas, M.P., 1543-69.

Patrick —— *Aberdeen* 1586 conv.

Paul, of Kynmundie, provost —— *Aberdeen* 1625 conv., 1630 conv., 1633.

Robert —— *Aberdeen* 1597 conv.

Thomas —— *Aberdeen* 1526 (provost).

Thomas, of Pitfoddels —— *Aberdeen* 1543 (provost), 1544, 1567 (provost),
[1569 conv., then provost.

Son of Gilbert, M.P. 1513-35. Marischal depute of Scotland 1538, comptroller of the
royal household 1543, provost of Aberdeen on various occasions before 1547, and continuously
[until his death 1576.

Thomas, appearand of Durne —— *Aberdeen* 1593.

Thomas (sir), provost —— *Aberdeen* 1617 conv. and parlt.

Probably knighted between 7 March and 27 May 1617.

William —— *Aberdeen* 1588 conv.

William, merchant in Edinburgh, burgess of Lochmaben —— *Lochmaben*
[1695-1702.

SCOTCH MEMBERS.   I I

Mercer.

Andro —— *Culross* 1645.

Archibald, merchant burgess —— *Culross* 1639-41, 1644-5.

(Sir James), laird of Aldie —— *Perthshire* 1645-7.

Son of Sir Lawrence, M.P., taken prisoner after the battle of Kilsyth, 1645; genl. usher to Charles II.; m. 1648, Jean, eldest dau. of Sir Thomas Stewart, of Grandtully. and d. 1671,
[leaving issue.

John —— *Perth* 1357.

Of Aldie, provost of Perth, 1374, and member of the parliament assembled at Perth 13 Jan. 1364-5, etc. (son of Thomas Mercer); m. Ada, dau. of—— Murray, laird of Tullibardine,
[and had a son, Sir Andrew.

John —— *Perth* 1648.

(Sir Lawrence), laird of Aldie —— 1609 conv. as a minor baron.

Son of Andrew Mercer, of Meikillour; he m. 1stly, Cecilia, dau. of James, 1st lord Colville,
[of Culross, and 2ndly, Christian Bruce, d. 1645, having had a son, Sir James, M.P., 1645.

Robert —— *Perth* 1456, 1458, 1462.

Of Baleif, co. Kinross (2nd son of Sir Michael Mercer, of Aldie); he d. after 1468; father
[of Robert, next named.

Robert —— *Perth* 1493, 1494, 1504 (then provost).

Provost of Perth, son of Robert, last named; m. Margaret, dau. and co-heir of ——
[Baldwin, of Seres; d. 1504, having had issue.

Robert —— *Anstruther Easter* 1617, 1621.

Of Sawline (2nd son of Laurence Mercer, of Meikillour, by his 2nd wife, Jean Ruthven),
[m. Rebecca Carmichael, and had issue.

Merry.

James, of Belladrum, Inverness-shire —— *Falkirk burghs* 1857 until unseated
[July following, 1859-65, 1865-8, 1868-74.

Of Glasgow, merchant and iron-master, J.P., D.L., co. Inverness, J.P. Lanarkshire (son of James Merry, of Glasgow, by his wife Janet, dau. of William Crealman), d. 3 Feb. 1877, aged 72, having m. 1847, Ann, dau. of James McHardy, of Glenboig, co. Lanark, and had
[issue.

Mewo.

Robert —— *Dysart* 1594 conv.

Middleton.

John (col.), of Seton —— *Aberdeen* (now *Montrose*) *burghs* 1713-15, 1715-22,
[1722-7 (of Seton), 1727-34, 1734 until his death, s.b. 8 June 1739.

Of Seaton, co. Aberdeen, by purchase 1715, also of Fettercairn; brigadier-general 1735, comd. 25th regt. 1725, 13th regt. 1732, governor of Holy Island, deputy-governor of Tynemouth Castle (5th son of George Middleton, D.D., minister of Glamis and principal of King's Coll. Aberdeen, by his wife Jane, dau. of James Gordon, of Seaton, co. Aberdeen); d. 4 April 1739, having m. Elizabeth Cunningham; she bd. at Aberdeen 17 April 1734,
[leaving issue.

Middleton—*continued.*

Robert Tweedie, of Glasgow —— *Glasgow* since 1880. See foot-note.

Mill.

James, merchant burgess, baillie —— *Montrose*, 1615-6.

Millar.

Allan —— *Crail* 1650.

David —— *Annan* 1612, 1621.

Miller.

John, of Leithen, esq. —— *Edinburgh* 1868-74. See foot-note.

Patrick (captain), younger, of Dalswinton —— *Dumfries burghs* 1790-6.

> Of Dalswinton, by purchase, younger brother of Sir Thomas next named (3rd son of [William Miller, W.S.); d. 26 Feb., 1845, having had 3 sons and 2 daus.

Thomas, lord advocate for Scotland —— *Dumfries* 1761 until appointed lord [justice clerk of Scotland, s.b. 28 May 1766.

> Sir Thomas Miller, of Glenlee (2nd son of William Miller, W.S. and grandson of Matthew Miller, of Glenlee, and of Barskimming, Ayrshire), lord president of the court of session in Scotland 1788, advocate 1742, steward depute of Kirkcudbright 1748, joint principal clerk of the City of Glasgow 1748, resigned his office as sheriff on being appointed solr. of excise 1755, solicitor-genL 1759, and lord advocate, lord justice clerk 1766, with title of Lord Barskimming, afterwards changed to Lord Glenlee; cr. a baronet 3 March 1788 ; b. 3 Nov. 1717, d. 27 Sept. 1789, having m. 1st 1752, Margaret, eldest dau. of John Murdoch, provost of Glasgow. IIe m. 2ndly, Anne, dau of John Lockhart, esq., of Castle IIill (Sinclair, bart.) ; she d. s.p. By his 1st wife he had with a dau. an only son, William, [M.P., next named.

William, younger, esq., of Barskimming, advocate —— *Edinburgh* (16 Sept.), [1780, until unseated 23 March 1781.

> Lord Glenlee, of session, 1795, 2nd bart. (on the death of his father, Sir Thomas, M.P.), advocate, 1777 ; b. 12 Aug., 1755, d. 9 May 1846, having m. 5 Nov. 1777, his cousin Grizel, dau. of George Chalmers, esq.; she d. 1817, leaving issue. See Foster's Baronetage.

M IDDLETON, ROBERT TWEEDIE, of Hillfoot, co. Lanark, J.P., J.P. co. Dumbarton, of Glasgow, merchant, M.P. as above (son of James Middleton, of Glasgow, merchant, by his wife Mary Tweedie) ; b. 1831, m. 1864, Rachel Rattray, dau. of Sir James Watson, of Broomknowe Row, Helensburgh, N.B., and has issue.
Hillfoot, New Kilpatrick, Glasgow.
Clubs : Reform, Liberal (Edinburgh), New (Glasgow).

M ILLER, JOHN, of Leithen, co. Peebles, J.P., and of Drumlithie, co. Kincardine, J.P., D.L.; D.L. Edinburgh city, also J.P. cos. Stirling and Linlithgow, F.R.S. Edin., M.I.C.E. London, M.P. as above (son of James Miller, of Spring Vale, Ayrshire); b. 26 July 1805, m. 1 Dec. 1834, Isabella, dau. of Duncan Ogilvie, esq., of Perth.
Leithen Lodge, Inverleithen, N.B.; 2, Melville Crescent, Edinburgh.

Miller—continued.

William, of Manderston, co. Berwick —— *Leith burghs* 1859-65, 1865-8, [*Berwickshire* 1873-4. See foot-note.

Milne. See also Home.

Alexander, merchant provost —— *Linlithgow* 1681-2, 1685-6.

Andrew —— *Linlithgow* 1617, conv. and parlt., then provost.

James —— *Montrose* 1649 (or Andrew Gray).

James, of Balwylloe —— *Forfarshire* 1693-8, did not sign the Association.

John, town clerk —— *Forfar* 1639-40, Queensferry (South) 1641, Queens-
                                                                        [ferry 1645-6.
John —— *Edinburgh* 1662-3.

Patrick, of Croinonmogate (co. Aberdeen) —— *Elgin burghs* 1812-18.

Robert —— *Dundee* 1543.

Robert, merchant provost —— *Linlithgow* 1667 conv. (provost), 1669-74, 1678
                                                                        [conv.
Thomas —— *Elgin* 1622.

Mitchell.

Andrew (sir), of Thainston, K.B. —— *Aberdeenshire* 1747-54, *Elgin burghs* 1755-61, 1761-8, 1768 (then a knt.) until his death, s.b. 20 March 1771.

Bar.-at-law, Middle Temple 1738 (admitted 1733), sec. to Marquis of Tweeddale 1741, under sec. of State Scotland 1742, envoy to Berlin 1756, ambassador-extraordinary and minister-plenipotentiary at the court of Frederick William the Great of Prussia 13 Dec. 1765, until his death 28 Jan. 1771 ; invested knight of the bath 13 Dec. 1765, but never installed (son and heir of rev. William Mitchell, a chaplain to the king in Scotland, etc.) ; b. 1708, m. Barbara, only dau. and heir of Thomas Mitchell, of Thainston, and had a dau. Barbara, died [young.

Charles, writer in Edinburgh —— *Orkney and Zetland Stewartry* 5 Nov. 1700, his commission was returned to him 29th Nov. same year, as his election [could not be sustained.
See pedigree, Douglas' Baronage, page 427.

MILLER, SIR WILLIAM, of Manderston, co. Berwick, J.P., D.L., hon. British vice-consul at St. Petersburg 1838-54, M.P. as above ; created a bart. 24 Mar. 1874 (son of James Miller, of Leith) ; b. 25 Mar. 1809 ; m. 11 Nov. 1858, Mary Anne, dau. of John Farley Leith, of London, Q.C. bencher M.T. late M.P. Aberdeen, and has 2 sons and 2 daus.

(1) James Percy, b. 22 Oct. 1864.　　　　(3) Amy Elizabeth.
(2) John Alexander, b. 27 Sept. 1867.　　　(4) Evelyn Mary.
Seats: Manderston, Berwick, and Barny Hill, Dunbar. Town House : 1, *Park Lane, W*

Mitchell—*continued.*

David, late bailie —— *Culross* 1667 conv.

John —— *Culross* 1650.

William (col.) —— *Sheriffdom of Inverness* 1654-5, *Sheriffdom of Aberdeen* [1656-8 (WILLIS).

Mitchellhill.

James —— *Selkirk* 1612, 1617.

John —— *Selkirk* 1579.

William —— *Selkirk* 1640.

William, bailie —— *Selkirk* 1665 conv. (late bailie), 1667 conv.

Moir.

Gilbert —— *Banff* 1646-7, 1648.

Henry, late bailie —— *Kirkcudbright* 1685 until his death s.b. 20 April 1686.

James, of Stoneywood —— *Aberdeenshire* 1689 conv., 1689-1702, 1702-7.

William, advocate —— *Kintore* 1667 conv., 1669-74.

> Admitted advocate 12 Feb., 1664 ; on 5 July 1672, he was, by order of the parliament, sent to prison in the Tollbooth of Edinburgh during the lord commissioner's pleasure "for some words uttered by him tending to the subversion of the constitution of parliament ;" he was released on the 10th, having craved pardon of the commissioner and the parliament on [his knees.

Mollison.

Francis, bailie —— *Brechin* 1685-6, 1693-1702, 1703-7 (dean of guild).

Moncreiffe.

Andrew —— *Crail* 1645.

George, portioner of Sauchope, bailie —— *Crail* 1678 conv., 1681-2, 1689 conv., [1689-1702, 1702-7.

George, of Reidie —— *Fifeshire* 1690-1702.

James —— *Crail* 1644 conv., 1646-7 (or Andrew Daw) —— *Crail* 1661-3, [bailie.

James, merchant burgess —— *Kirkwall* 1669-74.

Moncreiff.

James —— *Leith burghs* 1851-2 (queen's advocate for Scotland), 1852-7 (lord advocate 1853), 1857-9 (lord advocate); *Edinburgh* 1859-65 (then dean of faculty of advocates, lord advocate 28 June 1859), 1865-8 (lord advocate); *Glasgow* and *Aberdeen* Universities 1868 until app. lord justice clerk in Scot-
[land s.b. 22 Nov. 1869.

Sir James Moncreiff, LL.D., P.C. 1869, baron Moncreiff, of Tullybole, Kinross-shire, so created 9 Jan. 1874, also created a baronet 23 May 1871, advocate, 1833, etc., as above, lord justice clerk of Scotland, and presdt. 2nd divn. court of session 1869, lord rector of Edinburgh University 1868-71, lieut.-col. comd. Edinburgh vols. 1859-73, hon. col. since 1873;
[b. 29 Nov. 1811, m. and has issue. See Foster's Peerage

John (sir) —— *Perthshire* 1605 (as a minor baron); 1605 conv. (laird of Easter Moncreiff, as a minor baron), *Perthshire* 1639-41 (of that ilk, knight and
[baronet).

Created a baronet of Nova Scotia 22 Apl. 1646 (son of William Moncreiff, M.P.); m.
[twice, and died about 1650, having had issue.

Patrick (Mr.), of Reidie, advocate —— *Kinghorn* 1706-7 —— 1707-8, 1st
[parlt. Great Britain.
Admitted advocate 15 Feb. 1701.

Patrick (master), junr., of Reidie —— *Fifeshire* 1708 until his death s.b. Feb. 1710.
A colonel in the army.

(William) laird of Moncreiff —— 1579 conv. as a minor baron.

Son of William Moncreiff and his wife Jean Oliphant; he m. Anne, dau. of Robert
[Murray, of Abercairnie, and had with other issue Sir John, M.P.

Monro.   See Munro.

Monorgund.

William (? Morgan) —— *Dundee* 1472, 1478 bis, 1479, 1488.

Monteith

Henry, of Carstairs —— *Linlithgow burghs*, 1820-6, 1830-1.   See also England
[M.P.

Of Carstairs, co. Lanark, by purchase, thrice lord provost of Glasgow, M.P. Saltash, 1826-30 (son of James Monteith); m. 1st Christina, dau. of J. Cameron, esq., of Over Carntyne, co. Lanark, and 2ndly Miss Fullerton; he d. 14 Dec., 1848, aged 84, leaving
[issue.

James —— *Edinburgh* 1650.

Montgomerie.

Archibald (col.), of Minnock and Gill, brother of the Earl of Eglintoun ——
[*Wigtown burghs and Ayrshire* (elected to sit for the latter) 1761-8.

Archibald, 11th earl of Eglintoun (on the death of his brother Alex., 10th earl, 24 Oct. 1769), lieut.-col. comdt. 77th highlanders, which he raised, equerry to the Queen 1761-9, gov. Dumbarton Castle 1764, deputy ranger Hyde Park and St. James's Park 1766, a representative peer 1776, 1780, 1784, 1790, gov. Edinburgh Castle 1782, gen. in the army 1793; b. 18 May, 1726, d. 30 Oct. 1796, having married 1st, 30 Mar. 1772, Lady Jane Lindsay, eldest dau. of George, 18th Earl of Crawford, she d. s.p. 22 Jan. 1771; he m. 2ndly, 9 Aug. 1783, Frances, only dau. of Sir William Twysden, bart., of Roydon Hall, Kent (she re-m. 29 Nov. 1794, to [Francis, brother of Gen. Sir John Moore, K.B.), and had 2 daus. See Foster's Peerage.

Francis (Mr.), of Giffen —— *Ayrshire* 1690-1702, 1702-7, 1707-8 (1st parlt. [G. B.), 1708-10.

P.C. to K. William and Q. Anne, a lord of the treasury, Scotland 1703-7, a commissioner for the treaty of union 1705 (2nd son of Hugh, 7th Earl of Eglintoun); m. 1st, 1674, Margaret, Countess of Leven, she d. s.p. 6 Nov. same year ; he m. 2ndly Elizabeth, relict of Sir James Primrose, of Barnbougle, knt., dau. of Sir Robert Sinclair, of Longformacus, bart., and had [with other issue a son John, M.P. 1710, etc.

Henry, of Giffen —— *Ayrshire* 1640-1.

Of Giffen, by charter 1736 (2nd son of Alexander, 6th Earl of Eglintoun) ; b. 26 June 1614, d. 3 May 1643, having m. 21 Sept. 1640, Jean, relict of Robert, 1st Viscount Kenmure [(ext.), 3rd dau. of Archibald Campbell, 7th Earl of Argyll. See Foster's Peerage.

Hugh, of Busbie, provost ——*Glasgow* 1702-7, 1707-8, 1st parlt. G. B.

Of Skelmorly, 5th bart. (on the death of his nephew, Sir Robert, Aug. 1731), of Glasgow, merchant, one of the commissioners for the treaty of the Union; m. Lillias, dau. of Peter [Geumill, merchant and bailie of Glasgow; and d. s. p.   1735.

Hugh, of Skelmorlie —— *Ayrshire* 1780 (till unseated 2 April 1781) ; 1784 until appointed inspector of military roads in Scotland, s.b. 3 Aug. 1789; 1796 [(17 June) until he succeeded as Earl of Eglintoun, 30 Oct. same year.

12th earl (on the death of his kinsman Archibald, 11th earl, 30 Oct. 1796), col. of regt. of West Lowland fencibles, which he raised ; inspector of military roads Scotland, raised the "Glasgow regt." reduced in 1795, lieut.-gov. Edinburgh Castle, a representative peer 1798, 1802, created Baron Ardrossan, of Ardrossan, co. Ayr, 21 Feb. 1806, in the peerage of the U.K. ; b. 5 Nov. 1739, d. 14 Dec. 1819, having m. (contract 3 June 1772) his cousin Eleanor, 4th dau. of Robert Hamilton esq., of Bourtreehill, co. Ayr.; she d. 17 Jan. 1817, having had [a son and 2 daus. See Foster's Peerage.

James (sir), of Skelmorlie —— *Ayrshire* 1689 conv. and parlt., until his seat was [declared vacant 28 April 1693, because he had not signed the assurance.

3rd baronet (on the death of his father, Sir Robert Montgomerie, 7th Feb, 1684) ; one of those deputed from the Parliament of Scotland to administer the oath to K. William and Q. Mary 1689; he engaged in the conspiracy against William, and went over to James VII. at St. Germains; he d. Sept. 1694, having m. Margaret, dau. of James Johnston, Earl of Annandale, and had with other issue Sir Robert, 4th bart., who died Aug. 1731, leaving [issue.

Montgomerie—*continued.*

James (lt.-gen.), of Wrighthill, col. 74th regt. —— *Ayrshire* 1818-20, 1820-6, [1826 (then col. 30th regt.) until his death s.b. 13 May 1829.

Lieut.-genl. in the army 1814, major of brigade Jamaica 1780-1, lieut.-col. 64th regt. 1804, brig.-genl. West Indies 1804, gov. of Tobago, of Demerara, etc., 1805-8, of Dominica 1808-9, col. 74th regt. 1813, of 30th regt. 1823 (brother of Hugh, 12th earl of Eglintoun); d. s.p. 13 April 1829, having m. 1810, Harriet Elizabeth, dau. of Thomas Jackson, esq., of [Westbury, co. Gloucester.

John (younger), of Beoch, merchant burgess —— *Irvine* 1678 conv.

John (Mr.), of Wrae —— *Linlithgowshire* 1704-7

John, of Giffen —— *Ayrshire* 1710-13, 1713-15, 1715-22 (an officer of the [crown 1715), 1722-7.

Lt.-col. in the foot guards, master of the mint Scotland 1715, (son of Francis Montgomerie, [M.P.); m. Mary, 2nd dau. of John Carmichael, 1st earl of Hyndford, and had issue

Robert (sir), of Skelmorlie —— *Buteshire* 1644 conv.

Knighted by James VI., and created a baronet by Charles I. 23 Dec. 1628 (son of Robert Montgomerie, of Skelmorlie, and his wife Dorothy, dau. of Robert, 3rd Lord Semple); d. Nov. 1651, having m. Margaret, eldest dau. of Sir William Douglas, of Drumlanrig, she d. [1624, leaving a son Robert, o. v. p. father of Sir Robert 2nd bart.

Robert, of Hazelhead —— *Ayrshire* 1661.

Probably identical with maj.-genl. Robert Montgomerie, brother of Hugh, 7th earl of [Eglintoun.

Roger, advocate, of Annick Lodge, Dreghorn, Ayrshire —— *N. Ayrshire* [1874-80.

J.P. D.L. Ayrshire, advocate 1852, advocate depute 1858, 1866-8, 1874-80, deputy clerk register 1880, capt., Queen's city of Edinburgh R. V. brigade, B.A. St. John's Coll. Cambr. 1851, M.A., 1854, (son of Lt.-col. Wm. Montgomerie, of Annick); b. 22 Oct. 1828, d. unm. [25 Oct. 1880.

Montgomery.

George (sir), of Macbie hill, bart. —— *Peebleshire* (4 March) 1831, (17 May) [1831, until his death s.b. 9 Aug. same year.

2nd bart (on the death of his father, Sir William, 25 Dec. 1788), d. unm. 9 July 1831, [aged 65.

Graham Graham (sir), of Stanhope, bart. —— *Peebles-shire* 1852-7, 1857-9, 1859-65, 1865-8 (a lord of the treasury 1866), *Peebles-shire and Selkirkshire* [1868-74, 1874-80.

3rd baronet (on the death of his father, Sir James, 27 May 1839), a lord of the treasury 1866-8, and 1880, ld.-lieut. Kinross since 1854, lieut. Midlothian yeo. cavy. 1854, a brig.-genl. "royal company of archers," the Queen's body-guard in Scotland; b. 9 July 1823, m. [and has issue. See Foster's Baronetage.

Montgomery—*continued.*

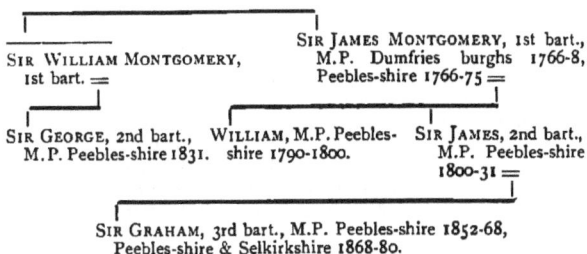

```
          ┌──────────────────────────────┐
  ───────────────          SIR JAMES MONTGOMERY, 1st bart.,
  SIR WILLIAM MONTGOMERY,   M.P. Dumfries burghs 1766-8,
  1st bart. ═               Peebles-shire 1766-75 ═
       │              ┌─────────────────────────────┐
  ┌────┴──────────────────────┬─────────────────────┐
  SIR GEORGE, 2nd bart.,  WILLIAM, M.P. Peebles-  SIR JAMES, 2nd bart.,
  M.P. Peebles-shire 1831.  shire 1790-1800.      M.P. Peebles-shire
                                                   1800-31 ═
                       ┌──────────────────────────────────────┘
  SIR GRAHAM, 3rd bart., M.P. Peebles-shire 1852-68,
  Peebles-shire & Selkirkshire 1868-80.
```

James, of Stanhope, lord advocate for Scotland —— *Dumfries burghs* 1766-8 ; *Peebles-shire* 1768-74, 1774 until chief baron of the exchequer in Scotland [s.b. 17 June 1775.

> Sir James Montgomery, cr. a baronet 16 July 1801, chief baron in Scotland 1775-81, solicitor-genl. Scotland, lord advocate 1766-75 (younger brother of Sir William Montgomery, of Macbie Hill, cr. a baronet 29 Oct. 1774, son of William Montgomery of the same) ; m. Margaret, only dau. and heir of Robert Scot, esq., of Killearn, co. Stirling, and d. 2 April [1803, leaving with other issue 2 sons, William, M.P., and James, M.P.

James (sir),▪of Stanhope —— *Peebles-shire* 1800-2 (advocate, younger), 1802-6 (lord advocate 1804), 1806-7, 1807-12, 1812-18, 1818-20, 1820-6, 1826-30, [1830 until he accepted the Chiltern hundreds s.b. 4 March 1831.

> 2nd baronet (on the death of his father, Sir James, 2 April 1803), B.A. admitted advocate 1787, lord advocate 1804-6, presenter of signatures in the court of exchequer, Scotland ; b. 9 Oct. 1766, d. 27 May, 1839, having m. twice (see Foster's Baronetage), and left with [other issue a son, Sir Graham Graham Montgomery, 3rd baronet, M.P.

William, younger, of Stanhope —— *Peebles-shire* 1790-6 (lieut. 4th regt.), 1796 [until his death s.b. 23 Dec. 1800.

> Eldest son of Sir James, M.P. 1776, etc.; died lieut.-col. 43rd regt. 25 Oct. 1800.

Montrose.

(——), the provost of —— *Montrose* 1568.

Monypenny.

Thomas —— *Perth* 1567, 1569 conv.

Moodie.

James (sir), younger, of Melsitter -—— *Orkney & Shetlandshire* 1715-22.

> Secretary to the commissioners for army accounts (James Moodie, jun.) ; distinguished himself in the relief of the town and castle of Denis when besieged by the French 1707-8, [and for this service had an augmentation in the 1st and 4th quarters of his arms.

Moore.

John, provost —— *Ayr* 1703-7.

John (capt. 82nd regt.) —— *Linlithgow burghs* 1784-90.

The hero of Corunna ; entered the army 1776 ; wounded in storming the Mozello fort at the siege of Calvi, in Corsica, 1794 ; had a principal share in capture of St. Lucia, then brig.-genl. under Sir Ralph Abercrombie ; major-genl. for his services in Ireland during the rebellion 1797 ; wounded in the expedition to Holland 1799 ; shot in the thigh and wounded with a sabre cut at the battle of Alexandria ; knight of the bath, invested 14 Nov. 1804 ; landed in Portugal Oct. 1808 ; fell in the retreat on Corunna 16 Jan. 1809, when he repulsed the French troops (eldest son of John Moore, M.D.) ; b. in Glasgow 13 Nov. 1761.

Morislaw.

(——), the laird of —— *Roxburghshire* 1625 conv.

Morison.

(——), the laird of Preston Grange —— *Peebles-shire* 1646-7, 1648.

John, of Auchintoul —— *Banffshire* 1827-30, 1830-1, 1831-2.

William, of Prestongrange —— *Haddington constabulary* 1690-1702 ; *Peebles-shire* 1702-7 (1707-8, 1st parlt. Great Britain), 1708-10 ; *Sutherlandshire &* [*Peebles-shire* 1713-15 (elected to sit for the latter).

William (major-genl., C.B.) —— *Clackmannanshire & Kinross-shire* 1842-7, [1847 until his death s.b. 9 June 1851.

Lieut.-genl. Sir William Morison, K.C.B 1848, F.R.S. and F.R.A.S., entered Madras military service 1799, sec. to the board of ordnance Madras 1809, commissary-general Mahratta war 1817 and 1818, served in commissariat department 1810-25, resident at Travancore 1825, administered government of Mysore, military member supreme council India 1834-9, C.B. 1821 (2nd son of James Morison, of Greenfield, co. Clackmannan) ; he [d. 15 May 1851.

Morris.

Staats Long (major-genl.) —— *Elgin burghs* 1774-80 (then col.), 1780-4.

Genl. in the army 1796, brigadier-genl. in East Indies 1774, col. 61st foot 1778 ; died gov. of Quebec 2 April 1800 ; m. Catherine (Duchess), relict of Cosmo George, 3rd Duke [of Gordon, K.T., dau. of William, 2nd earl of Aberdeen, she died 10 Dec. 1779.

Morrison.

James, of Fonthill, Wilts, a merchant in London —— *Inverness burghs* 1840-1, [1841-7. See also England M.P.

Senior partner and founder of the celebrated firm of Morrison, Dillon, and Co., of Fore Street, London ; M.P. St. Ives, Cornwall, 1830-1, Ipswich 1832-5 (contested Ipswich 1835), 1835-7, contested Sudbury 1837 (son of James Morrison, of Hampshire) ; d. at his seat, Basildon Park, Berks, 30 Oct. 1857, aged 67 ; m. Mary Anne, dau. of John Todd, of [London, merchant, and left with other issue a son Walter, M.P. Plymouth 1861-74.

Mortimer.

Patrick, bailie —— *Cupar* 1681-2.

Moultrie.

Johne (Multrar) —— *Ayr* 1463, 1469, 1471, 1472, 1474, 1478.

Mudie.

George —— *Dundee* 1594.

James, late bailie —— *Dunfermline* 1661-3.

James, merchant burgess —— *Montrose* 1689 conv., 1698-1702.

Thomas —— *Dundee* 1643 conv.

Muir. See also Mure.

Archibald (sir), of Thornton —— *Cupar* 1693-1702.

John —— *North Berwick* 1628-33.

John, late provost —— *Ayr* 1689 conv., 1689 to 1702.

John, merchant burgess —— *Peebles* 1689 conv., 1689 to 1702.

Muirhead

James, younger of Lachop —— *Dumbartonshire* 1628-33.

> Son of Sir James Muirhead, of Lauchop, knt.; m. Jean, dau. of Robert, Lord Dalzell,
> [afterwards Earl of Carnwath, and had issue.

Munro or Monro

Alexander, of Bearcroft —— *Stirlingshire* 1690-1702.

George, of Tarrell —— *Inverness-shire*, including *Caithness* and *Ross*, 1621.

George (sir), of Culraine and Newmore —— *Ross-shire* 1661-3; *Sutherlandshire* [1669-74; *Ross-shire* 1685-6; 1689 until his death s.b. 11 July 1693.

> Sir George, of Culrain, K.B., Ross-shire, lt.-col., commanded a division at the battle of
> Lutzen, major-genl. of the royal forces in Ireland 1649, commanded a division of the
> Scottish army, and after the battle of Worcester joined Charles II. in Holland, com.-in-chief
> in Scotland at the Restoration (son of Col. John Munro, of Obisdale); m. Margaret, only dau.
> of Sir Frederick Hamilton, and sister of Gustavus, 1st Viscount Boyne, and had issue. See
> [Foster's Baronetage.

George, bailie —— *Irvine*, 1705-7.

Harry (sir), of Foulis, bart. —— *Ross-shire* 1746-7; *Wick burghs* 1747-54, [1754-61.

> 7th bart. (on the death of his father, Sir Robert, M.P., who fell at Falkirk 1746); the
> parly. return erroneously states him to have represented Caithness-shire 1754; m. Anne,
> dau. of Hugh Rose, of Kilravock, co. Nairn, and d. 12 June 1781, having had a son, Sir
> [Hugh, d. 2 May 1848.

Munro or Monro—*continued.*

SIR ROBERT MUNRO, 3rd bart.,   SIR GEORGE MUNRO. M.P. Ross-
M.P. Inverness-shire 1649, Ross-   shire 1661-3, 1685-93, Suther-
shire 1649-50 =   landshire 1669-74.

SIR JOHN, 4th bart., M.P. Ross-shire 1689-97 =

SIR ROBERT, 5th bart., M.P. Ross-shire 1697-1702 =

SIR ROBERT, 6th bart., M.P. Wick burghs 1710-41 =

SIR HARRY, 7th bart., M.P. Ross-shire 1746-7, Wick
burghs 1747-54, 1754-61.

Hector (lt.-genl. sir), of Novar, knight of the bath —— *Inverness burghs* 1768-74,
[1774-80, 1780-4, 1784-90, 1790-6, 1796-1802.

Genl. Sir Hector Munro, of Novar, K.B., invested by the Nabob of Arcot 1778 ; commander of Bengal Army 1764, lt.-col. East Indies 1768, lt.-col. in the army 1774, major-genl.
1782, col. 42nd Highlanders 1787, lt.-genl. 1793, genl. 1798; d. 6 Jan. 1806, married and
[had issue.

John (sir), of Foulis —— *Ross-shire* 1689 until his death s.b. 29 Sept. 1697.

4th bart. (on the death of his father, Sir Robert, M.P. 1668) ; m. Anne, dau. of Sir
[Kenneth Mackenzie, of Coul, and had a son, Sir Robert, M.P. 1697.

John, of Newmore —— *Ross-shire* 1733-4.

Robert —— *Tain* 1617.

Robert, of Obsdaill —— *Inverness-shire* 1649 ; *Ross-shire* 1649-50.

3rd bart. (on the death of his father, Col. John, in 1651) ; m. his cousin Jean, dau. of Sir
[Hector Munro, 1st bart., and d. 1668, having had a son, Sir John, M.P. 1689.

Robert (sir), of Foulis —— *Ross-shire* 1697-1702.

5th bart. (on the death of his father, Sir John, M.P., about 1696), Sheriff of counties Ross
and Cromarty ; m. Jean, dau. of John Forbes, of Culloden, and d. 1729, having had with
[other issue a son, Sir Robert, M.P.

Robert (sir), of Foulis, bart. —— *Wick burghs* 1710-13 ; 1713-15 (captain,
[younger), 1715-22, 1722-7, 1727-34 (col. younger), 1734-41, then a baronet.

6th bart. (on the death of his father, Sir Robert, M.P. 1697), served in Flanders, capt. in
the Earl of Orkney's regt. or royal Scots, governor of the castle of Inverness 1715, a comissr.
for forfeited estates 1716, lt.-col. of the highland regt. at Fontenoy, where he greatly
distinguished himself ; m. Mary, dau. of Henry Seymour, of Woodlands, Dorset, and fell at
[the battle of Falkirk 17 Jan. 1746, aged 62, leaving a son, Sir Harry, M.P.

Murdock.

Patrick, of Camlodden —— *Whithorn* 1689 conv., 1689-1702.

Mure.

David, queen's advocate for Scotland —— *Buteshire* 1859, until app. a judge of [court of session s.b. 6 Feb. 1865.

Lord Mure of session, advocate 1831, sheriff of Perthshire 1853, solicitor-genl. (Scotland) and lord advocate 1858-9, D.L. Buteshire and co. Edinburgh, etc. (3rd son of Col. William Mure, of Caldwell); b. Nov. 1810, m. 1841, Helen, eldest dau. of John Tod, esq., of Kirkhill, [co. Midlothian ; she d. 1849, leaving a daughter·

(James), laird of Caldwell —— *Renfrewshire* 1645-7.

Of Caldwell, on the death of his brother Robert 1644 (sons of Robert Mure and his wife, [Jean, dau. of Uchtred Knox, of Ramphorlie), and d. s.p. 1654·

Richard —— *Stirling* 1468.

Rolland —— *Lanark* 1579.

William (sir), of Rowallan —— *Ayrshire* 1643-4.

Author of a history of his family, of the committee of war in the sheriffdom of Ayr 1644, with the Scots army in England that year (son of Sir William Mure, by his wife, Janet Maxwell); m. 1st, Anna Dundas, of Newliston, and 2ndly, Dame Jane Hamilton, Lady [Duntreath, and d. 1667, aged 63, leaving issue ; grandfather of William, M.P. 1690.

William, of Rowallan —— *Ayrshire* 1690 until his death s.b. 20 Nov. 1700.

Son of the 3rd Sir William Mure, of Rowallan ; m. about 1670, Mary Scott, of Collarny, [co. Fife, and had 3 daus.

William, of Caldwell —— *Renfrewshire,* 1742-7, 1747-52, 1754·61.

A baron of the exchequer (Scotland) 1761, (son of William Mure); m. Katherine, dau. of [James Graham, Lord Easdale of session, and d. 21 March 1776, leaving issue.

William (col.), of Caldwell —— *Renfrewshire* 1846-7, 1847-52, 1852 until he [accepted the *Chiltern hundreds* s.b. 14 May 1855.

"The historian," J.P., D.L., co. Renfrew; vice-lieut. Renfrew, col. Renfrew militia, lord rector of Glasgow university 1847-8 (son of Col. Wm. Mure, vice-lieut. Renfrewshire); b. 9 July 1799, d. 1 April 1860, having m. 7 Feb. 1825, Laura, 2nd dau. of William Markham, esq., [of Becca Hall, Yorks., and had a son, William, M.P.

William (lt.-col.), of Caldwell —— *Renfrewshire* 1874-80, April 1880 until his [death 9 Nov. same year.

J.P., D.L., cos. Ayr and Renfrew, lt.-col. late Scots' guards, served with 60th rifles in Kaffir war 1851-3 (medal), with 79th highlanders in Crimea, at the Alma, Balaklava, and Sebastapol (son of Col. William Mure, M.P. 1846-55); b. 9 May 1830, d. 9 Nov. 1880, having m. 26 April 1859, Hon. Constance Elizabeth Wyndham, yst. dau. of George, 1st [Lord Leconfield (see Foster's Peerage), and had issue.

Murray.

Alexander (sir), of Blackbarony, knt. —— *Peebles-shire* 1639-41.

2nd bart. (on the death of his father, Sir Archibald, M.P.), ordered to be fined by parliament for his services to Chas. I. 1646, high sheriff of Peebles 1667 ; m. 1st, Margaret, dau. of Sir Richard Cockburn, of Clerkington, and had a son, Sir Archibald, M.P., 3rd bart. ; he m. 2ndly, Margaret, dau. of William and sister of Sir David Murray, of Stanhope, and had with [5 daus. a son John. See chart pedigree, next page.

Murray—*continued.*

MURRAY OF BLACKBARONY AND ELIBANK.

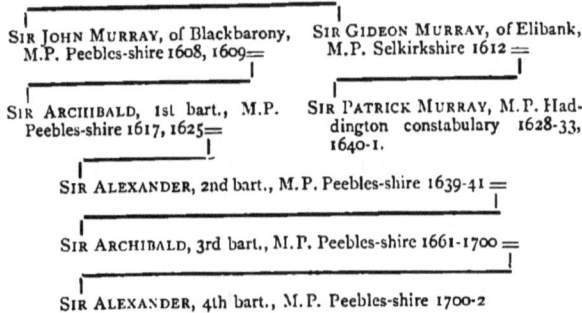

```
┌────────────────────────────────┬────────────────────────────────┐
SIR JOHN MURRAY, of Blackbarony,   SIR GIDEON MURRAY, of Elibank,
M.P. Peebles-shire 1608, 1609=     M.P. Selkirkshire 1612 =
             │                                  │
┌────────────┴──────────┐          ┌────────────┴──────────┐
SIR ARCHIBALD, 1st bart., M.P.     SIR PATRICK MURRAY, M.P. Had-
  Peebles-shire 1617, 1625=          dington constabulary 1628-33,
             │                       1640-1.
   SIR ALEXANDER, 2nd bart., M.P. Peebles-shire 1639-41 =
                                                        │
   SIR ARCHIBALD, 3rd bart., M.P. Peebles-shire 1661-1700 =
                                                         │
   SIR ALEXANDER, 4th bart., M.P. Peebles-shire 1700-2
```

Alexander —— *Cullen* 1649.

Alexander, of Halmyre —— *Peebles-shire* 1693 until his death s.b. 31 Dec. 1700.

> Probably descended from Walter, 2nd son of Sir Archibald Murray, of Blackbarony,
> [1st bart.

Alexander (sir), of Blackbarony —— *Peebles-shire* 1700-2.

> 4th bart. (on the death of his father, Sir Archibald, M.P. 1700), sheriff depute co. Peebles,
> 1732; m. Margaret, dau. of Wm. Wallace, of Helington, who d. s.p. See chart pedigree
> [above.

Alexander (master), of Stanhope —— *Peebles-shire* 1710 until appointed to an
[office of profit s.b. 8 Jan. 1711-12 ; 1734, double return.

> 3rd bart. (on the death of his father, Sir David, M.P. 1681); a commissioner of trade,
> Scotland 1712 ; m. Grizel, dau. of George Baillie, esq., of Jerviswood, and d. s.p. 18 May
> [1743. See chart pedigree, page 267.

Alexander, of Broughton —— *Kirkcudbright stewartry* 1715-22, 1722-7.

> Possibly son of John Murray, M.P. 1702 ; d. at Calley, 1 May 1750, having m. Euphemia,
> dau. of James Stewart, 5th Earl of Galloway; she d. at Ayr 9 Nov. 1760, leaving a son,
> [James. M.P. 1762-74. See chart pedigree, next page.

Alexander, of Cringletie —— *Peebles-shire* 1712-13, 1715-22, 1741-7.

> Sheriff depute of Peebles (son of Alexander Murray, of Cringletie, by his wife Susan, dau.
> of John Douglas, of Mains) ; m. Katharine, dau. of Sir Robert Stewart, of Tillicoultry,
> [a senator of the college of justice, and a lord of justiciary, and had issue.

Alexander, of Murrayfield, solr.-gen. for Scotland —— *Peebles-shire* 1780, until
[apptd. a lord of session s.b. 20 March, 1783.

> Lord Henderland, of session 6 March, 1783, and a commissioner of the court of justiciary,
> advocate 1758, sheriff depute Peebles 1761-95, a commissary of Edinburgh 1765, solr.-gen.
> 1775-83 (son of Archibald Murray, of Murrayfield, advocate); m. 15 April 1773, Katherine,
> dau. of Sir Alexander Lindsay, of Evelisk, co. Perth, bart., and d. 16 March, 1795, having
> [had with other issue a son John Archibald, M.P. 1833, etc.

Murray—*continued.*

MURRAY OF BROUGHTON.

RICHARD MURRAY, M.P. Wigtownshire 1661-3, Kirkcudbright
stewartry 1678 =

.... |

JOHN, M.P. Kirkcudbright stewartry 1702 =

.... |

ALEXANDER, M.P. Kirkcudbright stewartry 1715-22, 1722-7 =

JAMES, M.P. Wigtownshire 1762-8, Kirkcudbright stewartry
1768-74 =

ALEXANDER, M.P. Kirkcudbright stewartry 1838-45.

Alexander, of Blackbarony —— *Peebles-shire* 1783-4.

7th Lord Elibank (on the death of George, 6th Lord, 12 Nov. 1785), lieut. 3rd regt.,
lord-lieut. Peebles-shire, and col. of militia ; b. 24 April, 1747; d. 24 Sept. 1820, leaving
[issue. See Foster's Peerage.

Alexander, of Broughton —— *Kirkcudbright stewartry* 1838-41, 1841 until his
[death s.b. 20 Aug. 1845.

Of Broughton co. Wigtown (natural son of James Murray, M.P. 1762) ; d. s.p. at Killy-
begs, co. Kildare, 15 July, 1845, aged 55, having m. 18 July 1816, Lady Anne Bingham, 3rd
[dau. of Richard, 2nd Earl of Lucan ; she d. 28 Oct. 1850. See chart pedigree above.

(Sir Andrew), laird of Balvaird —— 1599 conv., *Fifeshire,* 1607, 1608, and
[1609 conv., as a minor baron.

Only son of Sir Andrew Murray, of Arngosk ; he m. Catherine, dau. of Sir William Men-
[teth, of Carse ; and d. s.p. 14 Dec. 1624.

Andrew (sir), of Ettilstown —— *Peebles* 1605.

(Sir Archibald), laird of Blackbarony —— *Peebles-shire* 1617 conv. and parlt.,
[1625 conv.

Knighted by James VI., then designated of Darnhall, had a charter of Blackbarony, 1607 ;
cr. a bart. 15 May, 1628 ; m. Margaret Maule, of the Panmure family ; and d. before 1634,
having had with other issue Sir Alexander, M.P., 2nd bart. See chart pedigree, preceding
[page.

Archibald (sir), of Blackbarony —— *sheriffdom of Selkirk and Peebles* 1659-60
(WILLIS); *Peebles-shire* 1661-3, 1665 conv., 1667 conv. (then younger), 1669-74
(then a baronet), 1678 conv., 1681-2, 1685-6, 1689 until his death s.b. 28 May
[1700.

3rd bart. (on the death of his father, Sir Alexander, M.P.), lt.-col. Linlithgow and Peebles-
shire militia, 1669, master of the works, Scotland, 1689 ; m. Mary, widow of Sir James Hope
(E. Hopetown), dau. of William Keith, 7th Earl Marischal, and had with other issue a
[son, Sir Alexander, M.P. See chart pedigree, preceding page.

Murray—*continued.*

Charles —— *Lauder* 1585 —— 1621.

Charles, of Halden —— *Orkney & Zetland stewartry* 1685-6.

David (sir), of Stanhope, knight —— *Peebles-shire* 1639-41, 1644-5 (laird).

Knighted by Charles I., had a charter of the lands of Broughton 1635 (son of William Murray, of Romanno) ; m. Lilias, dau. of John Fleming, Earl of Wigtown ; and had a son, [Sir William, cr. a bart. See chart pedigree, page 267.

David (sir), of Stanhope —— *Peebles-shire* 1681-2, 1689 until his seat was declared vacant, 25 April 1693, because he had not taken the oath of allegiance, and [signed the assurance.

2nd bart. (on the death of his father, Sir William, about 1693) ; m. 1st, Anne, dau. of Alexander Bruce, 2nd Earl of Kincardine ; m. 2ndly, Margaret, widow of Thomas Scot, of Whitside, dau. of Sir John Scott, of Ancrum, bart., and had further issue. See chart [pedigree, page 267.

David, of Hattonknows —— *Peebles-shire* 1784-90. See also England M.P.

Lieut. in Major Listers' corps of light dragoons 1779, M.P. Radnor 1790-4 (brother of Alexander, 7th Lord Elibank) ; b. 10 May 1748, d. 8 May 1794, m. 8 Oct. 1783, Elizabeth, 5th dau. and co.-heir of Hon. Thomas Harley, alderman of London (son of Edward, 3rd Earl [of Oxford, extinct) ; she d. 9 July 1824, leaving issue. See Foster's Baronetage

George (capt. R.N.), of Pitkaithly —— *Perth burghs* 1790, until he accepted the [*Chiltern hundreds* s.b. 4 April, 1796, then rear-adml.

Vice-adml. of the white (brother of John, 3rd Duke of Athole, and James Murray, M.P.) ; d. 17 Oct. 1797, aged 59, having m. 1784, Wilhelmina, dau. of Thomas, 5th Lord King ; she [d. s.p. 28 Dec. 1795. See chart pedigree, page 266.

George (lt.-gen. sir) G.C.B., of Drumlanrig and Bleaton, lieut.-gen. of the ordnance, and col. 42nd regt. of foot —— *Perthshire* 1824-6, 1826-30 ; then commander of the forces in Ireland, etc., (a principal secretary of state, [1828), 1830-1, 1831-2, 1834 (May—Dec.)

Gen. Sir George Murray, P.C., G.C.B. 1813, G.C.H., col. 60th rifles 1813, 72nd foot 1817, 42nd Highlanders 1823, and of 1st foot 1845, gov. of Fort George, knight grand cross of Leopold, St. Alexander Newski and the red eagle of Prussia, a commander of the orders of Maximilian Joseph, and St. Henry of Saxony, 16 Sept. 1825 ; commander of the order of the tower and sword 6 May 1813, a knight of the second class of the Crescent of Turkey, gov. R. Military College, Woolwich 1819, president Royal Geographical Society, D.C.L. 1820, F.R.S. 1824, gov. Edinburgh Castle 1818-19, lt.-gen. of the ordnance 1823, col. 42nd Highlanders 1823-43, commanded the forces in Ireland, sec. of state for the colonies 1828, master-gen. of the ordnance 1834, and col. in chief Royal Art., and corps of Royal Engineers ; contested Perthshire 1834, Westminster 1837, Manchester 1839 and 1841, served in the campaign in Flanders, wounded in the disastrous expedition to the Helder, served in Egypt under Abercromby, served also in peninsula war, etc. (see Gents' Mag. 1846, vol. ii. p. 424), (2nd son of Sir William Murray, of Ochtertyre, bart.) ; b. 6 Feb. 1772, d. 28 July 1846, having m. 1826, Lady Louisa Erskine, widow of Sir James Erskine, of Torrie House, bart., and sister of Henry, Marquis of Anglesey ; she d. 23 Jan. 1842, leaving a dau. See chart pedigree, page 270.

Murray—*continued.*

Gideon (sir), of Elibank, knt —— *Selkirkshire* (*or the forest*) 1612.

Knighted 4 March 1605, treasurer depute 1613, Lord Elibank of session 1613 (son of Andrew Murray, of Blackbarony); m. Margaret Pentland, and died 28 June 1621, leaving a [son, Sir Patrick cr. Lord Elibank ; see Foster's Peerage, and chart pedigree, page 262.

Gideon (captain), merchant burgess —— *Kilrenny* 1669-70.

Homer —— *Annan* 1643 conv.

James, fear of Philiphaugh —— *Selkirkshire* 1628-33.

Knighted by Charles I. (son of Sir John Murray, of Philiphaugh, M.P. 1612) ; m. Anne, dau. of Sir Thomas Craig, of Riccartoun ; o. v.p., leaving a son, Sir John, M.P. 1661 ; see [chart pedigree, page 269.

James (sir), of Skirling —— *Peebles-shire* 1650-1.

Probably descended from, or son of, James, 3rd son of Patrick Murray, of Falahill, and [brother of Sir Patrick M., of Priestfield or Melgum.

James (sir), of Philiphaugh, senator of the College of Justice —— *Selkirkshire* 1678 conv., 1681-2, 1702 until appointed lord clerk register s.b. 11 May [1703.

Lord Philiphaugh of session 1 Nov. 1689, sheriff of Forres, gave evidence against some of the Rye House plotters, lord register 1702-4, 1705-8 (eldest son of Sir John Murray, of Philiphaugh, M.P. 1661, by his first wife, Anne, dau. of Sir Archibald Douglas, of Cavers) ; m. 1st Anne Hepburn, of Blackcastle, and 2ndly Margaret, dau. of Sir Alexander Don, of [Newton, and d. at Inch 1 July 1708, aged 53 ; see chart pedigree, page 269.

James (sir), of Dowally——*Perthshire* 1710, 1710-13 (the laird), 1713-15, a knight.

Lord James Murray, of Dowally (3rd son of John, 1st Marquis of Athole, by his wife Amelia Stanley) ; b. at Knowesley 21 May 1663, m. Anne, dau. of Sir Robert Murray, of [Cockpool, and had 2 daus. ; see chart pedigree, next page.

James (hon.) —— *Dumfries-shire* 1711-13, *Elgin burghs* 1713-15 (elected to an [office of profit by the crown 1714), 1715, until unseated 7 April same year.

Advocate 1710, unduly elected Elgin burghs 1715, a commiss. for settling trade with France (2nd son of David, 5th Viscount of Stormont) ; d. at Avignon Aug. 1770 (brother [of William, Lord Mansfield). See E. MANSFIELD in Foster's Peerage.

James (lord), of Gairth —— *Perthshire* 1715-22, 1722 until he succ. as 2nd [Duke of Athole, 14 Nov. 1724.

2nd Duke of Athole (by act of parlt. on the death of his father, 14 Nov. 1724), and on the death s.p. of James, 10th Earl of Derby, 1 Feb. 1736, he succ. (as heir through his grand-mother) to the barony of Strange and the lordship of Man ; keeper of the great seal of Scotland 1763 ; d. 8 Jan. 1764, leaving an only surviving dau. and heir Charlotte, who m. her coz. John, 3rd Duke of Athole ; See Foster's Peerage, and also chart pedigree, next page.

Murray—*continued.*

MURRAY, DUKE OF ATHOLE.

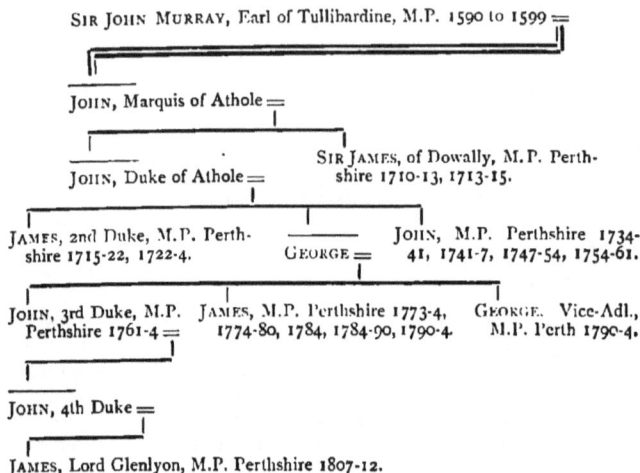

SIR JOHN MURRAY, Earl of Tullibardine, M.P. 1590 to 1599 ═

JOHN, Marquis of Athole ═

JOHN, Duke of Athole ═   SIR JAMES, of Dowally, M.P. Perthshire 1710-13, 1713-15.

JAMES, 2nd Duke, M.P. Perthshire 1715-22, 1722-4.   GEORGE ═   JOHN, M.P. Perthshire 1734-41, 1741-7, 1747-54, 1754-61.

JOHN, 3rd Duke, M.P. Perthshire 1761-4 ═   JAMES, M.P. Perthshire 1773-4, 1774-80, 1784, 1784-90, 1790-4.   GEORGE. Vice-Adl., M.P. Perth 1790-4.

JOHN, 4th Duke ═

JAMES, Lord Glenlyon, M.P. Perthshire 1807-12.

James, of Broughtoun —— *Wigtownshire* 1762-8, *Kirkcudbright stewartry* [1768-74.

Son of Alexander Murray, M.P. 1715, etc., provost of Kirkcudbright 1750; m. 12 April 1752 his coz. Lady Catherine Stewart, dau. of Alexander, 6th Earl of Galloway, and d. at [York 30 April 1799, leaving a dau. ; see chart pedigree, page 263.

James (major-genl.), of Strowan —— *Perthshire* 1773-4 (colonel), 1774-80, 1784, [1784-90, 1790 until his death s.b. 11 April 1794.

Governor of Hull, capt. in foot guards 1774, served under Prince Ferdinand in Germany and wounded, comd. 77th regt. (Athole Highlanders) 1777-83, 72nd Highlanders 1783-94, (brother of John, 3rd Duke of Atholl, and George Murray, M.P.) ; d. unm. 19 March 1794 ; [see chart pedigree, above.

James, of Cairdneys, commonly called Lord James —— *Perthshire* 1807 until [he accepted the Chiltern hundreds, s.b. 19 March 1812.

Major-genl. in the army, lieut.-col. comm. Royal Manx fencibles ; cr. Baron Glenlyon, of Glenlyon, Perthshire, in the peerage of the U.K. 9 July 1821 (son of John, 4th Duke of Athole) ; b. 29 May 1782 ; d. 12 Oct. 1837, having m. 19 May 1810, Lady Emily Frances Percy, dau. of Hugh, 2nd Duke of Northumberland [and aunt of Algernon, 4th Duke, upon whose death, 11 Feb. 1865 s.p., the barony of Percy (cr. by summons to Parliament 1722 of Algernon Seymour, afterwards, 1748, Duke of Somerset, whose dau. and heiress Elizabet wife of Sir Hugh (Smithson) Percy, cr. Duke of Northumberland 1766, was mother of Hugh, 2nd Duke), devolved on her grandson, the 7th Duke of Atholl]; she d. 21 June 1844, having had, with other issue, a son George, who succ. as 6th Duke ; see Foster's [Peerage, and also chart pedigree, above.

Murray—*continued.*

MURRAY OF STANHOPE.

Sir David Murray, M.P. Peebles-shire 1639-41, 1644-5 =

Sir William, 1st bart., M.P. Peebles-shire 1661-3, 1665, 1667 =

Sir David, 2nd bart., M.P. Peebles-shire 1681-2, 1689-93 =

Sir Alexander, 3rd bart., M.P. Peebles-shire 1710-12.

(Sir John), laird of Tullibardine —— 1590 conv., 1592 parlt. [*Perthshire*], 1593, 1593 conv., 1596 and 1597 conv. (bis.), 1598 conv. and 1599 conv. (as [a minor baron).

Earl of Tullibardine, so cr. 10 July 1606, served heir of his father 1583, master of the King's household 1592, P.C. and knighted, cr. Lord Murray of Tullibardine 25th April 1604 (son of Sir William Murray, of Tullibardine); m. Catherine, 4th dau. of David, 2nd Lord Drummond, and had issue. His son William, 2nd earl, resigned the earldom of Tullibardine, and was father of William, who had a confirmation of the earldom of [Athole; see Foster's Peerage, and chart pedigree, preceding page.

(Sir John), laird of Blackbarony —— 1608; *Peebles-shire* 1608 conv., 1609 conv. [as a minor baron.

Knighted at Stirling by James VI.; coroner of Peebles-shire 1595 (son of Sir Andrew Murray, of Blackbarony); m. 1st Margaret, dau. of Sir Alexander Hamilton, of Innerwick, and 2ndly Margaret Wauchope, of Keckmure, and had issue; father of Sir Archibald, M.P. [1617; see chart pedigree, page 262.

(Sir John), laird of Polmaise —— 1609 conv. (as a minor baron) *Stirlingshire* [1625 conv.

Of Polmaise, by charter 8 April 1588, knighted before 1628 (son of William Murray, of Touchadam); m. Jean, dau. of John Cockburn, of Ormiston, and had a son, Sir William, M.P.; [see chart pedigree, next page.

(Sir John), of Fawlayhill —— *Selkirkshire* (or the *forest*) 1612.

Of Philiphaugh, being the first of his family so designated (son of Patrick Murray, of Falahill); m. 1st Janet Scott, of Ardross, and 2ndly Helen, dau. of Sir James Pringle, of Galashiels, and had issue; father of Sir James, M.P. 1628-33; see chart pedigree, page 269.

John (sir), of Eddistoun, knt. —— *Peebles-shire* 1612.

John (sir), of Philiphaugh —— *Selkirkshire* 1661.

Son of James Murray, M.P. 1678; one of the judges for the shires of Roxburgh and Selkirk to try those who had joined Montrose 1646; m. 1st Anne, dau. of Sir Archibald Douglas, of Cavers, and had with other issue Sir James, M.P. 1678, and John, M.P., both senators of the college of justice; he m. 2ndly Margaret, widow of John Trotter, of Charterhall [dau. of Sir John Scot, of Scotstarvet, and d. 1676; see chart pedigree, page 269.

Murray—*continued.*

MURRAY OF POLMAISE.

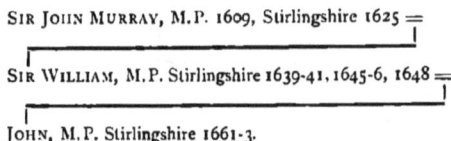

SIR JOHN MURRAY, M.P. 1609, Stirlingshire 1625 =
|
|
SIR WILLIAM, M.P. Stirlingshire 1639-41, 1645-6, 1648 =
|
|
JOHN, M.P. Stirlingshire 1661-3.

John, of Touchadam and Polmaise —— *Stirlingshire,* 1661-3.

> Served heir to his father, Sir William Murray, M.P., Jan. 1655; m. Janet, dau. of Sir John Nisbet, of Dean, lord provost of Edinburgh, and had issue; see chart pedigree, above.

John (sir), of Drumcairne, knt., senator of the college of justice —— *Perthshire* [1685-6

> Ordinary lord of session 1 Nov. 1681, a lord of the articles 29 Apl. 1686, a lord of justiciary 12 July 1687 until the revolution, when he lost these appointments (4th son of Andrew Murray, 1st Lord Balvaird); m. and had an only dau. See EARL OF MANSFIELD, Foster's [Peerage]

John (Mr.), brother-german to James Murray, of Philiphaugh —— *Selkirk* 1689 conv., 1689-1702, 1702-7 (of Bowhill, advocate), 1707 (1st parlt. Great [Britain], of Bowhill.

> Advocate 4 Feb. 1688, a supporter of the Union, lord of session 7 June 1707, a comr. of justiciary 1 June 1709 (2nd son of Sir John Murray, of Philiphaugh, M.P.); died about [1714; see chart pedigree, next page.

John, of Broughton —— *Kirkcudbright stewartry* 1702.

> Possibly son of Richard, M.P. 1661, and father of Alexander, M.P. 1715. See chart pedigree, page 263.

John, of Strowan —— *Perthshire* 1704-7.

> Amelia, his only dau. and heir, m. to James Murray, of Glencarse, and d. at Arnhall 4 [March 1749, leaving an only dau.

John (elder), of Philiphaugh —— *Linlithgow burghs* 1725-27, 1727-34; *Selkirk-shire* 1734-41, 1741-7, 1747 (then styled elder), until his death s.b. 13 Dec. [1753.

> Heritable sheriff co. Selkirk (son of Sir James Murray, M.P. 1678), d. 2 July 1753, having m. 31 Dec. 1711, Eleanora, dau. of Lord Basil Hamilton (son of William, Duke of Hamilton), she d. 27 Dec. 1783, leaving issue—John, M.P. 1754; see chart pedigree, [next page.

John (lord), of Pitnacree, brother of James, Duke of Athole —— *Perthshire* 1734- [41, 1741-7, 1747-54, 1754-61.

> General in the army, entered the service 1727, A.D.C. 1743, comd. 42nd Highlanders 1745-87, major-genl. 1755, lt.-genl. 1758, gen. 1770 (eldest son of John, Duke of Athole, by his 2nd wife); b. 14 Apl. 1711, d. 18 May 1787, being then senior genl.; m. 13 Sept. 1758, Miss Dalton, of Banner Cross, Yorks, she d. 26 May 1765, leaving a dau.; see chart [pedigree, page 266.

Murray—*continued.*

MURRAY OF PHILIPHAUGH.

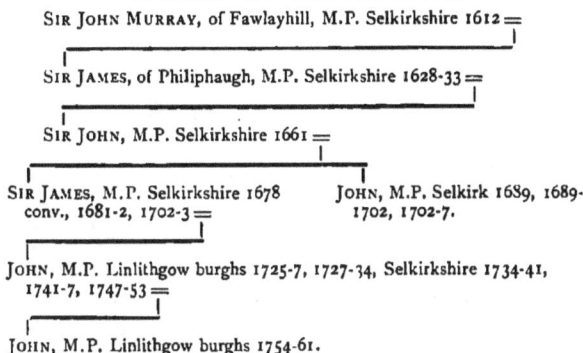

SIR JOHN MURRAY, of Fawlayhill, M.P. Selkirkshire 1612 ═

SIR JAMES, of Philiphaugh, M.P. Selkirkshire 1628-33 ═

SIR JOHN, M.P. Selkirkshire 1661 ═

SIR JAMES, M.P. Selkirkshire 1678 conv., 1681-2, 1702-3 ═   JOHN, M.P. Selkirk 1689, 1689-1702, 1702-7.

JOHN, M.P. Linlithgow burghs 1725-7, 1727-34, Selkirkshire 1734-41, 1741-7, 1747-53 ═

JOHN, M.P. Linlithgow burghs 1754-61.

John, of Philiphaugh —— *Linlithgow burghs* 1754-61.

Son of John Murray, M.P. 1725, last named ; m. — Thomson, and died 1800, leaving [issue ; see chart pedigree, above.

John, of Strowan —— *Perthshire* 1761 until he succ. as 3rd Duke of Athole 8 Jan. [1764.

John, 3rd Duke of Athole (on the death of his uncle James 8 Jan. 1764), but on account of his father's attainder a petition was presented to the king, claiming that title, which petition was referred to the house of lords, and on 7 Feb. 1764 it was resolved "that the petitioner hath a right to the titles, honours, and dignities of Duke of Athole, Marquis of Tullibardine, Earl of Strathtay and Strathardle, Viscount of Balquhiddar, Glenalmond, and Glenlyon, Lord Murray. Balvenie, and Gask, claimed by his said petition," a representative peer of Scotland 1766 and 1768, K.T. 1767 (son of George Murray attainted) ; b. 6 May 1729, d. at Dunkeld 5 Nov. 1774, where he m. 23 Oct. 1753, his cousin, Lady Charlotte Murray, only surviving child of his uncle James, 2nd Duke of Athole, on whose death she succ. to the sovereignty of the Isle of Man, and to the barony of Strange. The sovereignty of the Isle of Man was purchased by the lords of the treasury in 1765. The Duchess d. 13 Oct. 1805, [having had issue ; see Foster's Peerage, and also chart pedigree, page 266.

John Archibald, advocate —— *Leith burghs* 1833-4 (lord advocate 1834), 1835-7 (lord advocate), 1837, until apptd. a judge of the court of sessions s.b. 29 [July 1839.

Lord Murray of session 23 April 1839, advocate 1799, lord advocate 1834, 1835, recorder of the great roll (or clerk of the pipe) in the exchequer court, Scotland, knighted 24 April 1839 (younger son of Alexander Murray, lord Henderland of session, M.P. 1780), d. 7 March 1859, aged 80, having m. 1826, Mary, eldest dau. of William Rigby, of Oldfield Hall, [Cheshire.

Murray—*continued*.

MURRAY OF OCHTERTYRE.

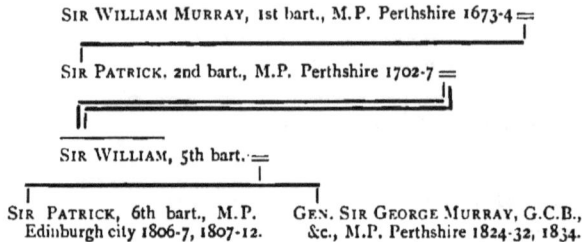

SIR WILLIAM MURRAY, 1st bart., M.P. Perthshire 1673-4 =

SIR PATRICK, 2nd bart., M.P. Perthshire 1702-7 =

SIR WILLIAM, 5th bart. =

| SIR PATRICK, 6th bart., M.P. Edinburgh city 1806-7, 1807-12. | GEN. SIR GEORGE MURRAY, G.C.B., &c., M.P. Perthshire 1824-32, 1834. |

Mungo (sir), of Garth —— *Perthshire* 1661-3, 1669 (then a knight), until his [death s.b. 3 Oct. 1671.

Lieut. K. Charles II.'s guards at the restoration (2nd son of John, 1st Earl of Athole); [d. unm., bd. in St. Giles, Edinburgh.

Patrick —— *Perth* 1567 conv., 1569.

Patrick (sir) —— 1602 conv. as a minor baron.

Patrick (sir), of Lainshaw —— *Selkirkshire* 1617.

Patrick (sir), of Elibank, knt. —— *Haddington Constabulary* 1628-33, 1640-1.

Keeper of Caerlaverock Castle, created a baronet of Nova Scotia 16 May 1628, and advanced to the peerage of Scotland, by the title of Lord Elibank, 18 Mar. 1643, with remainder to his heirs male whatsoever (son of Sir Gideon Murray, M.P.); d. 12 Nov. 1649, having m. 1st, Margaret Hamilton; 2ndly, Elizabeth, dau. of Sir James Dundas (V. Melville, of Arniston); 3rdly, Agnes Nicholson; and 4thly, Helen, dau. of Sir James Lindsay, gent. of the bedchamber; had issue by each wife; see Foster's Peerage, also chart [pedigree, page 262.

Patrick, of Deuchar —— *Selkirkshire* 1665 conv., 1667 conv., 1669-74.

Probably brother of Sir James Murray, of Stirling, M.P. 1650, sons of James, 3rd son of [Patrick Murray, of Falahill.

Patrick —— *Selkirk* 1669-74.

Patrick (sir), their majesties' general receiver —— *Dunfermline* 1685-6, *Stranraer* [1689-1702.

Patrick, of Livingstone —— *Linlithgowshire* 1685-6, 1689 conv., 1689-1702, [1702 until his death s.b. 22 Apl. 1703.

Patrick, of Pennyland —— *Caithness-shire* 1695-1702.

Murray—*continued.*

Patrick (sir), of Ochtertyre —— *Perthshire* 1702-7.

2nd baronet (on the death of his father, Sir William, 18 Feb. 1681); b. 21-24 Jan. 1656, d. 25 Dec. 1735, having m. 15 Feb. 1681, Margaret, eldest dau. of Mungo Haldane, of Gleneagles, N.B., she d. 17 Feb. 1722, leaving issue. See Foster's Baronetage, and also chart [pedigree, preceding page.

Patrick (sir), of Pitdunnes —— *Fifeshire* 1702 until his death s.b. 13 Apl. 1703

Possibly 2nd son of Sir William of Clermont, 1st bart.

Patrick (sir), of Ochtertyre, bart. —— *Edinburgh city* 1806-7, 1807 until he [accepted the Chiltern hundreds, s.b. 26 March 1812.

6th baronet (on the death of his father, Sir William, 6 Dec. 1800), brother of Genl. Sir George Murray, M.P., G.C.B., G.C.H., king's baron of the court of exchequer, Scotland, for life 1799, lieut.-col.-com. of the 1st (or Strathearn) infantry 1803, provincial grandmaster of Perthshire freemasons, lieut.-col. royal Perthshire local militia 1808, secretary to the board of commissioners for Indian affairs 1810; b. 3 Feb. 1771, d. 1 June 1837, having m. 13 Dec. 1794, Lady Mary Ann Hope, youngest dau. of John, 2nd Earl of Hopetoun ; she d. 21 Feb. 1838, having had 5 sons and 4 daus. See Foster's Baronetage, [and also chart pedigree, preceding page.

Richard, of Broughton —— *Wigtownshire* 1661-3; *Kirkcudbright stewartry* 1678, [conv.

Probably son of John Murray, of Broughton ; he m. Anna, only dau. of Alexander Lennox, of Calley, and d. about 1690; possibly father of John, M.P. 1702. See chart pedi- [gree, page 263

Robert, of Spangiedaill —— *Sutherlandshire* 1639-40.

Robert (sir), of Cameron, knt., lord provost —— *Edinburgh* 1661-3.

Walter —— *Dornoch* 1639-41.

William —— *St. Andrews* 1594 conv. ; *Montrose* 1597 conv.

William (sir), of Touchadam and Polmaise —— *Stirlingshire* 1639-41, 1645-6 [(laird of Polmaise), 1648 (laird of Polmaise).

Fined £1,500 (by Oliver Cromwell) for being concerned in the Duke of Hamilton's engagement (son of Sir John Murray, M.P. 1609); m. Elizabeth, dau. of Sir Alexander [Gibson, of Durie, and had a son, John, M.P.; see chart pedigree, page 268.

William (sir), of Stanhope, knt. and bart. —— *Peebles-shire* 1661-3, 1665 conv., [1667 conv.

Fined £2,000 by Oliver Cromwell ; cr. a baronet 13 Feb. 1664 (son of Sir David Murray, M.P.) ; m. Janet, dau. of James Johnston, Earl of Hartfell, and had with other issue a son, [Sir David, M.P. ; see chart pedigree, page 267.

William, of Donypace —— *Stirlingshire* 1665 conv.

Murray—*continued.*

William (sir), of Ochtertyre, knt. bart. —— *Perthshire* 1673-4.

Sir William Murray, of Ochertyre, co. Perth (descended from Patrick Murray, of Ochtertyre, who d. 1476, youngest son of Sir David Murray, of Tullibardine and Gask, ancestor of the Duke of Athole, see Peerage); cr. a baronet 7 June 1673 (patent not recorded); b. 30 Oct. 1615, d. 18 Feb. 1681, having m. 7 June 1649, Isabel, dau. of John Oliphant, of Bachilton ; she d. 6 April 1683, having had issue, father of Sir Patrick, M.P. See Foster's
[Baronetage, and also chart pedigree, page 270.

Muschet.

Alexander —— *Stirling* 1468, 1479.

John —— *Stirling* 1585.

Myrtoun.

John, bailie —— *Pittenweem* 1678 conv.

Thomas (sir), of Cambo —— *Fifeshire* 1633, 1639-41, then a knight

(——) laird of Cambo —— *Fifeshire* 1593 as a minor baron.

N.

Nairne.

Duncan, provost —— *Stirling* 1661-3, 1665 conv.

Robert —— *Stirling* 1456, 1458.

Thomas —— *Forres* 1649.

Napier.

Alexander (sir), of Merchistoun —— *Edinburgh* 1458 (1463), 1464, 1469 (then [provost], 1471, 1473.

Sir Alexander Napier, of Merchistoun (son and heir of Alexander Napare, burgess of Edinburgh, provost 1437), comptroller to James II. 1450, ambassador to England 1451, 1461, provost of Edinburgh 1455, knighted before 7 July 1461, vice-admiral of Scotland 1469, accompanied the lord chancellor who was sent to negotiate the marriage between James III. and the daughter of the king of Denmark 1468, master of the household to James III.; d between 24 Oct. 1473 and the following 15 Feb.; left with other issue a son John, M.P. 1483.

Alexander, of Culcreuch —— *Stirlingshire* 1690 until his seat was declared [vacant 21 May 1700, because he had not signed the Association. Probably descended from Robert, 2nd son of John Napier, the inventor of logarithms.

Francis (Mr.), of Craigannet, "actual trafficker" —— *Stirling* 1697-1702. Probably descended from William, 4th son of John Napier, the inventor of logarithms.

John —— *Edinburgh* 1483, 1484 provost.

Of the household of Mary, dowager of James II., provost of Edinburgh 1470, 1484 (son of Sir Alexander, M.P.); m. Elizabeth, dau. of Murdac de Menteth and sister and co-h. of Patrick de Menteth, of Rusky, and died shortly before 12th July 1488; ancestor of Sir [Archibald Napier, bart., cr. Lord Napier of Merchistoun. See Foster's Peerage.

John, of Kilmahew —— *Dumbartonshire* 1661-3, 1665 conv., 1667 conv., [1669-72.

Son of Robert Napier, by Katherine Haldane; he m. Lillias, dau. of Sir John [Colquhoun, of Luss, and had two daus.

Nasmith.

James, of Posso —— *Peebles-shire* 1628-33, 1630 conv.

Sheriff of Peebles 1627 (son of Thomas Nasmith, falconer to James VI., by his wife Joanna, dau. of William Veitch, of Dawick); m. 1610, Agnes, dau. of William Burnet, of Barns, and had issue; his grandson, Sir James, cr. a baronet 31 July 1712, was father of [Sir James, M.P., next named.

James (sir), of Posso, bart. —— *Peebles-shire* 1732-4, 1734-41.

2nd baronet (on the death of his father, Sir James, July 1720); m. Jean, dau. of Thomas [Keith, esq., and d. 4 Feb. 1779, leaving issue. See Foster's Baronetage.

Newlands.   See also Welands.

David —— *Cupar* 1793 conv.

Nicol.

James Dyce, of Ballogie —— *Kincardineshire* 1865-8, 1868 until his death s.b.
[10 Dec. 1872.

Of Ballogie, co. Aberdeen, J.P., D.L., and Badentoy, co. Kincardine, also J.P., D.L. (son of William Nicol and his wife, Margaret Dyce); b. 13 Aug. 1805, d. 16 Nov. 1872, having m. 14 March 1844, Catherine, dau. of Edward Loyd, of London, banker, uncle of [Lord Overstone (see Foster's Peerage), and had issue.

Nicoll.

James —— *Edinburgh* 1583.

Nicolson.

George —— *Aberdeen* 1617.

George (master) —— *Aberdeen* 1661-2, in absence of William Gray, bailie, late [provost.

Probably identical with Sir George Nicolson, Lord Kemnay of session, so cr. 5 July 1682, admitted advocate 27 July 1661, professor of civil law King's College, Aberdeen, 1673, purchased Kemnay 1682, and sold it to Thos. Burnett in 1688, unduly returned for Aberdeenshire 1685; his 2nd wife, Margaret Halyburton, d. Aug. 1722; his eldest son, [Thomas, was cr. a baronet 15 April 1700, in his father's lifetime.

John (sir) of that ilk, knight baronet —— *Edinburghshire* 1672-4.

(Sir Thomas) —— *Stirlingshire* 1644, laird of Carnock.

Cr. a baronet of Nova Scotia 16 Jan. 1637 (son of John Nicholson, of Lesswade); m. [Isabel, dau. of Walter Henderson, of Granton, and d. 8 Jan. 1646, leaving issue.

Nisbet or Nesbit.

—— (laird of East Nisbet) —— 1609 conv., as a minor baron.

Alexander (sir) —— *Berwickshire* 1625 conv., 1630 conv. (laird of West Nisbet),
[1628-35, Sir Alexander.

Son of Patrick Nisbet of that ilk, principal sheriff of Berwick, espoused the royal cause; m. [Catherine, dau. of —— Swinton of that ilk, and had issue.

Henry —— *Edinburgh* 1579, 1585 conv., 1597 conv., (provost of Edinburgh)
[1598 conv. (bis.), 1604.

Of Edinburgh, mercht., died before 1608, leaving a son, James, next named.

James, bailie —— *Edinburgh* 1612, 1617 conv. and parlt.

Eldest son of Henry, M.P., last named, m. Marion, dau. of Sir John Arnot, of Berwick, lord treasurer depute, and had a son, Sir Henry, knighted by Charles I., father of Sir Patrick, [created a baronet 2 Dec. 1669, &c.

Nisbet or Nesbit—*continued.*

William, of Dirleton —— *Haddington constabulary* 1702-7, 1707-8 (1st parlt.
[Great Britain).

William, younger, of Dirleton —— *Haddingtonshire* 1777-80. See also Eng-
[land M.P.

William Hamilton-Nisbet, of Belhaven and Dirleton, M.P. East Grinstead, 1790-6, New-
port, I.W., 1796-1800 (son of William Nisbet, of Dirleton, by his wife, Mary Hamilton,
heiress of Pencaitland); m. 31 Jan. 1771, Mary, dau. of Genl. Lord Robert Manners, M.P.
[(brother of John, 3rd Duke of Rutland), and d. 22 July 1822.

Noble

William, of Dalnotter —— *Dumbartonshire* 1681-2.

(William Noble, of Ardardans and Ballimenoch, co. Dumbarton, lieut. Dumbs. fencibles,
[and a commissioner of supply.)

Noel.

Ernest, of Lydhurst, Hayward's Heath, Sussex —— *Dumfries burghs* 1874-80,
[and since 1880.

2nd son of Rev. and Hon. Baptist W. Noel, see Foster's Peerage, E. GAINSBOROUGH.

Norie.

David —— *Brechin* 1612.

James —— *Brechin* 1617 conv.

North.

Dudley, of Glemham, Suffolk —— *Haddington burghs* 1818-20. See also
[England M.P.

Dudley Long-North, which latter name he assumed (2nd son of Charles Long, esq., of
Saxmundham, and his wife Mary, dau. of Dudley North, M.P. Thetford); of Glemham by
devise of his maternal aunt, Mrs. Herbert ; M.P. St. Germans 1780-4, Grimsby 1784-90,
1790-6, Banbury 1796-1806, Newtown 1807-8, Banbury 1808-12, Richmond 1812-18, Newtown 1820-21 ; d. s.p. 21 Feb. 1829, having m. 5 Nov. 1802, Hon. Sophia Pelham-Anderson,
[dau. of Charles, Lord Yarborough ; she d. 21 Aug. 1856.

Norton.

William, esq. —— *Wigtown burghs,* 31 Oct. 1774 until unseated 23 March
[following. See also England M.P.

2nd Baron Grantley (on the death of his father, Sir Fletcher, 1 Jan. 1789), admitted to the
Middle Temple 17 April 1755, minister to the Swiss cantons in 1774 ; M.P. Richmond
1768-74, 1775-80, Guildford 1782-4, Surrey 1784-9 ; d. s.p. 12 Nov. 1822, having m. 27 Sept.
1791, Anna Margaretta, elder dau. and co-heir of Jonathan Midgeley, of Beverley, Yorks,
[she d. 23 April 1795. See Foster's Peerage.

Norwell.

William —— *Stirling* 1568 (in the absence of Wm. Darroch, provost), 1569
[conv., 1585 conv., 1586 conv.

O.

Ochterlony.

John —— *Arbroath* 1643-4 conv., 1644-5, 1645-7, 1648 —— 1661-3 (provost).

Ogilvie and Ogilvy.

Alexander (sir), of Forglen, knt. bart. —— *Banff* 1701-2, 1702-7 (councillor).

Created a bart. 24 June 1701, ordered into custody for using improper expressions in parliament 1703, lord Forglen of session 23 July 1706 (2nd son of George, 2nd Lord Banff); d. 30 March 1727, having m. 1st, Mary, eldest dau. of Sir John Allardice, of Allardice, and had issue; he m. 2ndly, 18 Jan. 1702, Mary, relict of Sir Francis Kinloch, of Gilmerton, bart., dau. of David Leslie, 1st Lord Newark; she d. 24 March 1748, aged 93. The baronetcy [expired with William, 8th Lord Banff, who d. unm. 4 June 1803.

David (sir), of Clova, knt. —— *Forfarshire* 1669-72, 1681-2.

Probably 3rd son of James, 1st Earl of Airlie.

David (sir), of Inverquharity, knt. bart. —— *Forfarshire* 1665 conv., 1678 conv., 2nd bart. (on the death of his father, Sir John, cr. a bart. 26 Sept. 1626); m. 1662, [Margaret, dau. of Sir John Erskine, of Dun, and had issue.

Donald, esq. —— *Forfarshire* 3 Oct. 1831 until unseated 31 Jan. following.

Of Clova (brother of David, 6th earl of Airlie); b. May 1788, d. 30 Dec. 1863, leaving [issue, see Foster's Peerage.

(George), laird of Carnousie —— *Banffshire* 1621.

2nd son of Sir George Ogilvie, of Dunlugus, had a charter of the barony of Carnousie, etc., 5 Sept. 1595, and d. 1 Feb. 1625, having had a son, Sir George, cr. a bart. 24 April 1626.

James (Ogilby), —— *Dundee* 1471.

James —— *Cullen* 1617.

Probably James, 1st Earl of Findlater, so cr. 20 Feb. 1638 (son of Sir Walter, Lord Ogilvy, [of Deskford, so cr. 4 Oct. 1616), P.C. 1641; m. twice, and had issue.

James (sir), of Newgrange, knt. —— *Forfarshire* 1661-3.

Ogilvie and Ogilvy—*continued.*

James (sir), second son of James, Earl of Findlater —— *Cullen* 1681-2 (bailie) 1689 conv., 1689, until appointed a principal secretary of state for Scotland [s.b. 1 Sept. 1696.

4th Earl of Findlater, K.T. 1703 (on the death of his father 1711), advocate 16 Jan. 1685, solicitor-genl. Scotland 1693, and knighted, sheriff of Banff, secretary of state, 1695, sat and voted as lord secretary, cr. Viscount of Seafield 28 June 1698, president of the parliament 19 July, lord high commissioner to the general assembly 1700, 1703, 1724, 1727, cr. earl of Seafield 24 June 1701, one of the commissioners of the union 1702 and 1705, lord high chancellor of Scotland 1702-4, 1705-7, high commissioner to the parliament of Scotland 1703. a secretary of state 1704, P.C. England 1707, a representative peer 1707-8, 1708-12, 1712-13, 1715-22, 1723-7, 1727-30, lord chancellor 1727, lord chief baron court of exchequer 1708, keeper of the great seal Scotland ; m. Anne, dau. of Sir Wm. Dunbar, of Durn, bart.; and d. 15 Aug. [1730.

James, younger, of Boyne —— *Banffshire* 1702-7.

Probably son of Sir Patrick Ogilvie of Boyne, M.P. 1669

John —— *Montrose* 1543 (? provost).

John (sir), of Inverquharity —— *Dundee* 1857-9, 1859-65, 1865-8, 1868-74.

9th baronet, (on the death of his father, Sir William, 1823), vice-lieut. Forfarshire 1860-74, convener since 1855, hon. col. Dundee volunteers 1865, major-genl. "royal company of archers," the Queen's body-guard in Scotland; contested Montrose 1855, and Dundee 1874; [m. twice and has issue. See Foster's Baronetage.

(Patrick), laird of Inchmartine —— *Perthshire* 1601, as a lord of the articles.

Of Inchmartine by charter 18 April 1593 (son of William Ogilvie, of Inchmartine); m. 1st Marjory Gray, and 2ndly Margaret, dau. of Sir George Haliburton, of Pitcur, and had a son, [Sir Patrick, next named.

Patrick (sir), of Inchmartyn —— *Perthshire* 1621 (the laird), 1628-33, 1648.

Of Inchmartine by charter 8 Jan. 1611-12 (son of Patrick, M.P., last named); m. Anne, [dau. of Sir Duncan Campbell, of Glenurchy ; and d. 13 March 1651, having had issue.

Patrick (sir), of Boyne, knt. —— *Banffshire* 1669-74, 1678, conv., 1681-2, 1685-6 (then a senator of the college of justice), 1689 conv., 1689 parlt. until 28 April 1693, when his seat was declared vacant because he had not signed the [assurance.

Lord Boyne of session 1 Nov. 1681, and knighted by Charles II. (son of Sir Walter Ogilvie, of Boyne) ; m. 1st Mary, dau. of Sir James Grant of that ilk, he m. 2ndly —— dau. [of —— Douglas, of Whittingham, and had issue.

Patrick (col.), of Loanmay —— *Cullen* 1702-7 (then of Cairnbuilge), 1707-8 (1st parlt. Gr. Britain) ; *Elgin burghs* 1708-10.

3rd son of James, 3rd Earl of Findlater ; he m. his cousin Elizabeth, dau. of Hon. Francis [Montgomerie, of Giffen, and d. at Inchmartin 20 Sept. 1737, aged 72, leaving issue.

Ogilvie and Ogilvy—*continued.*

Thomas (Mr.) —— *Banff* 1587.

Thomas (provost) —— *Banff* 1678 conv.

Walter —— *Banff* 1543.

Probably Sir Walter Ogilvy, of Dunlugus (2nd son of Sir Walter, of Boyne), provost of Banff; d. 29 Nov. 1558, having m. Alison, dau. and co-h. of Sir Patrick Hume, of [Fastcastle ; she d. 25 July 1557, leaving issue.

(Sir Walter), laird of Findlater —— *Banffshire* 1593, 1593, as a minor baron.

Lord Ogilvy, of Deskford, so created 4 Oct. 1616, had a charter of the office of the constabulary of Cullen 1567, a knight in 1594 (son of Alexander Ogilvy); m. twice, and had [with other issue a son James, cr. Earl of Findlater 20 Feb. 1638.

Walter, of Boyne —— *Banffshire* 1644.

Probably Sir Walter Ogilvie, 6th baron of Boyne (son of James, 5th baron of Boyne), [father of Sir Patrick, a senator of the college of justice.

William —— *Cullen* 1649 (or Alexander Murray).

William —— *Forfar burghs* 28 March to 23 April 1831.

Of Logal, Perthshire, comr. R.N. (brother of Donald Ogilvie, M.P. 1831); died unm. [10 April 1871.

Okey.

John (col.) —— *Lithgow* (sic), *Queensferry, &c.* 1654-5 (WILLIS).

Oliphant.

Charles, M.D., burgess of Inverary —— *Ayr burghs,* 1710-13, 1713-15, 1715 [until his death s.b. 9 Jan. 1719-20,

Died 9 Dec. 1719.

Laurence, of Condie —— *Perth,* 1833-4, 1835-7.

Son of Ebenezer Oliphant, of Condie ; b. 22 June 1791, d. 29 May 1862, having m. thrice, [and left issue.

Laurence, of London —— *Stirling burghs* 1865 until he accepted the Chiltern [hundreds s.b. 30 April 1868.

Of Lincoln's Inn, barrister-at-law 30 April 1855, LL.D. Trin. Coll. Dublin, private sec. to late Earl of Elgin's special mission to Washington May 1854, and to China April 1857, civil sec. and superintendent of Indian affairs in Canada, advocate at the Scottish bar 1854, etc. etc., capt. West Middlesex rifle volunteer corps 1860, sec. at legation Japan 3 Jan. 1861, severely wounded at the attack at the British legation at Yeddo 5 July following, resigned [25 Jan. 1862.

Peter —— *Anstruther Wester* 1649 and 1651.

Peter, younger, bailie —— *Anstruther Wester* 1665 conv.

Thomas —— *Edinburgh* 1467, 1468, when chosen an auditor of complaint.

William, of Gask —— *Perthshire* 1702 until his death s.b. 27 April 1704.

3rd and youngest son of Lawrence Oliphant, of Gask ; died unm. 1704.

Ormelie, Earl of. See Campbell.

Osborn.

John (sir), of Chicksands Priory, Beds, bart. —— *Wigtown burghs* 1821 until [apptd. a comissr. of public accounts s.b. 4 March 1824. See also England M.P.

5th bart. (on the death of his father, Sir George, 29 June 1818), D.C.L., M.P. Bedfordshire 1794-1807, 1818-20, Cockermouth 1807-8, Queenborough 1812-18, comissr. for auditing public accounts as above, col. Bedfords. militia; b. 3 Dec. 1772, d. 28 Aug. 1848, having m. 14 Sept. 1809, Frederica Louisa, dau. of Sir Charles Davers, bart.; she d. 23 July 1870, [having had 5 sons and 3 daus. See Foster's Baronetage.

Osborne.

John —— *Ayr* 1617, 1625 conv.

John, provost —— *Ayr* 1639-41, 1644, 1649-50—in the absence of Hew or John [Kennedy.

Oswald.

OSWALD OF DUNNIKIER.

James Oswald, M.P. Kirkcaldy 1702-7, Kirkcaldy burghs 1710-13,1713-15 =
....
|
James, M.P. Kirkcaldy burghs 1741-7, Fifeshire 1747-54, Kirkcaldy burghs 1754-61, 1761-8 =
|
James Townsend Oswald, M.P. Kirkcaldy burghs 1768-74, Fifeshire 1776-9.

Alexander —— *Ayrshire* 1843-7, 1847-52.

Of Auchencruive, Ayrshire; J.P. D.L. for cos. Ayr, Kirkcudbright, and Lanark, contested Weymouth 1852 and Ayrshire 1854, B.A. Ch. Church Oxon 1834, assumed the surname of Haldane before that of Oswald (eldest surviving son of Richard Alexander Oswald esq., of London, who d. 1822); d. 6 Sept. 1868, aged 57, having m. 15 Aug. 1844, Lady Louisa Elizabeth Frederica, widow of Sir George Frederick Johnstone, bart., dau. of William, 1st [Earl Craven; she d. 20 Oct. 1858, leaving issue.

James, of Dunnikier —— *Kirkcaldy*, 1702-7 (dean of guild), *Kirkcaldy burghs* [1710-13 (provost), 1713-15.

Probably father of Right Hon. James Oswald, next named.

James, of Dunnikier, commissioner of the burgh of Dysart —— *Kirkcaldy burghs* 1741-7 (a commissioner of the navy 1745); *Fifeshire* 1747-54 (a commissioner for trade and plantations 1752); *Kirkcaldy burghs* 1754-61 (a lord of the [treasury 1760), 1761-8, vice-treasurer of Ireland 1763.

P.C. 1763, admitted to Lincoln's Inn 13 Dec. 1733 (probably son of the last-named M.P.); [father of James Townsend Oswald, M.P., died 24 March 1769.

Oswald—*continued.*

OSWALD OF AUCHENCRUIVE.

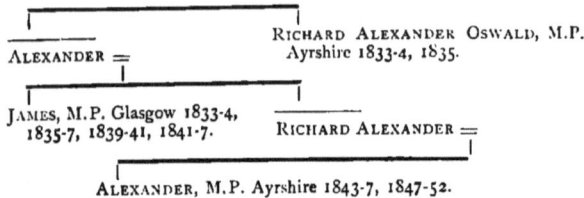

```
        |                        RICHARD ALEXANDER OSWALD, M.P.
ALEXANDER =                      Ayrshire 1833-4, 1835.
        |
   |                                    |
JAMES, M.P. Glasgow 1833-4,       ———————
  1835-7, 1839-41, 1841-7.        RICHARD ALEXANDER =
                                                      |
        |
ALEXANDER, M.P. Ayrshire 1843-7, 1847-52.
```

James, of Shield Hall, Glasgow —— *Glasgow city* 1833-4, 1835 until he accepted the Chiltern hundreds s.b. 27 May 1837, 1839-41 (a merchant in [Glasgow), 1841-7.

Of Auchencruive; first cousin of Richard Alexander Oswald, M.P., and son of Alexander Oswald, of Shield Hall, co. Renfew ; he died unm. 10 June 1853, aged 75, and was succeeded [by his nephew, Alexander, M.P.

James Townsend, of Dunnikier —— *Kirkcaldy burghs* 1768-74 (secretary of the Leeward Islands 1772); *Fifeshire* 1776 until appointed auditor of the [exchequer in Scotland s.b. 2 July 1779.

Son of the Rt. Hon. James Oswald aforesaid ; contested Kirkcaldy 1774 ; d.   1813; having m.   1769, Janet Grey, of Skibo, Sutherlandshire ; she d.   1843, leaving [a son, Genl. Sir John Oswald, G.C.B., G.C.M.G.

Richard Alexander, of Auchencruive —— *Ayrshire* 1833-4, 1835 until he [accepted the Chiltern hundreds s.b. 3 July in that year.

Eldest son of George Oswald, of Scotstoun and Auchencruive; b. 18 Feb. 1771, d. 19 June 1841, having m. 1st   1793, Louisa, dau. of Wynne Johnston, of Hilton-on-the-Merse ; she d.   1797, leaving a son ; he m. 2ndly 21 Aug. 1817, Lady Lilias, widow of Robert Dundas Macqueen, esq., of Braxfield, dau. of Hugh, 12th Earl of [Eglinton ; she d. 10 Sept. 1845.

Otterburne.

Adam (Mr.) —— *Edinburgh* 1524, 1525, a lord of the articles in parlt. 1528, [1531 (then provost), 1535, 1543 (provost), 1546.

Sir Adam Otterburne, of Auldhame and Redhall (son of Thomas Otterburn, merchant burgess of Edinburgh, who fell at Flodden), king's advocate 1525-34, a commissioner to manage Queen Margaret's estate 1518, and to treat of peace with England 1520, then of Auldhame, "unicus consilii nostri," ambassador to England 1524, 1525. 1528, etc., a judge of session 27 May 1532, knighted 1534, provost of Edinburgh 1534-35, 1543 ; d. in 1548.

Oxborow.

Laurence (esq.) —— *Forfar, &c.* 1659-60 (WILLIS).

Laurence Oxborough, alias Hewar of Emneth, Norfolk (son of Thomas and grandson of Thomas Oxborough, of Kings Lynn, Norfolk, by his wife Thomasine, sister and heir of [Thomas Hewer), see pedigree Norfolk visitation, vol. i., p. 15.

P.

Panmure. See also Maule.

William Maule, Earl Panmure in the kingdom of Ireland —— *Forfarshire* 1735-41, 1741-7 (of Panmure), 1747-54 (then earl), 1754-61, 1761-8, 1768-[74, 1774-80, 1780 until his death s.b. 11 Feb. 1782.
See note, page 243.

Parker.

Charles Stewart, M.A., fellow of University College, Oxford —— *Perthshir* 1868-74; *Perth city* 1878-80, and since 1880. See foot-note.

Parkle.

James, of ——. *Linlithgow* 1435, 1439, 1440, 1445, 1449.

Parnell.

Henry (sir), bart. —— *Dundee* 1833-4, 1835-7 (paymaster-general of the land [forces and treasurer of the navy), 1837-41. See also Ireland M.P.

Sir Henry Brooke Parnell, 4th baronet (on the death of his brother, Sir John, 30 July 1812), M.P. Maryborough in last Irish parlt. 1798-1800, Portarlington July to Dec. 1802, Queen's co. 1802, Feb. to Oct. 1806, 1806-7, 1807-12, 1812-18, 1818-20, 1820-6, 1826-30, 1830-1, 1831-2, and as above, lord of the treasury Ireland 1806, secretary-at-war 1831-2, paymaster-genl. of the forces, treasurer of the navy and ordnance 1835-41 ,cr. Baron Congleton, of Congleton, Cheshire, in the peerage of the United Kingdom, 18 Aug. 1841 ; b. 3 July 1776, d. 8 June 1842, having m. 17 Feb. 1801, Lady Caroline Elizabeth Dawson, eldest dau. of John, 1st Earl of Portarlington ; she d. 16 Feb., 1861, having had 3 sons and [2 daus

Paterson.

Andrew, of Kilmeny —— *Cupar* 1662-3, 1665 conv. (bailie), 1667 conv.

David (Peterson) —— *Cupar* 1599.

P ARKER, CHARLES STUART, of Fairlie, Ayrshire, fellow of University College, Oxford, B.A. 1852, M.A. 1856, etc., private secretary, Colonial Office 1864-6, special commissioner Public Schools Act 1868, on royal commissions military education 1869-70, and Endowed Schools, Scotland, 1872-5, contested Perthshire 1874, M.P. as above (son of late Charles Stuart Parker, of Fairlie, Ayrshire, and of Liverpool, merchant) ; b. 1 June 1829.
Club—Athenæum.

N N

Paterson—*continued*.

Duncan —— *Stirling* 1621.

Hugh (sir), of Bannockburn, bart. —— *Stirlingshire* 1708, until unseated Jan. 1709; 1710, 1710-13 (appointed to a crown office of profit 1711), 1713-15.

Commissioner of trade in Scotland, query if son of Sir Hugh Paterson (cr. a baronet 16 March 1686), by his wife Barbara, dau. of Sir Wm. Ruthven, of Dunglas; Sir Hugh was unduly elected for Stirlingshire 1708, was forfeited for having engaged in the rebellion 1715, and d. at Touch 23 March 1777, aged 91, having m. at Twickenham, 21 Feb. 1712, Jean, dau. of Charles Erskine, 10th Earl of Mar; she d. at Bannockburn 16 Nov. 1763, having [had issue.

James —— *Perth* 1596 conv.

John, provost —— *Cupar* 1575 conv.

John (Mr.), of Beuchillis, provost —— *Perth* 1661-3, in his absence either James [Dykes, bailie, or Patrick Threipland, dean of guild.

John (sir), of Eccles, bart. —— *Berwickshire* 1779-80.

Son of Sir John Paterson, of Eccles, bart., by his wife Margaret, eldest dau. of Sir Wm. Seton, 2nd bart., and probably descended from Sir William Paterson, clerk of the council; cr. a baronet 2 July 1687; he d. at Bath 14 Jan. 1782; having m. at Redbraes, 2 Nov. 1755, Anne Hume Campbell, eldest dau. and co-heir of Hugh, 3rd Earl of Marchmont; she d. at Newcastle 27 July 1790, aged 56, leaving an only dau. Anne, m. at Eccles 17 Feb. 1778 to (Sir) Philip Anstruther, of Anstruther, who assumed the name of Paterson.

Patrick, provost —— *Stranraer* 1685-6.

Robert —— *Cupar* 1617, 1621, 1628-33.

Thomas —— *Edinburgh* 1644 conv.

William —— *Dumfries* 1708 (double return), until declared not duly elected [Jan. 1709.

William Paterson, the founder of the Bank of England 1694, and projector of the Darien [expedition, also originated "the Sinking fund;" d. 22 Jan. 1719.

Cochran-Patrick.

Robert William, of Woodside —— *North Ayrshire* since 1880. See foot-note.

COCHRAN-PATRICK, ROBERT WILLIAM, of Woodside, Ayrshire, J.P., D.L., and J.P. co. Renfrew, B.A. Edinburgh 1860, LL.B. Cambridge 1864, Hon. LL.D. Glasgow, assumed the additional name of Cochran, M.P. as above (eldest son of late Wm. Charles Richard Patrick, esq., by Agnes, eldest dau. and co-heir of Wm. Cochran, esq., of Ladyland, Kilbirnie, N.B.); b. 4 Feb. 1842; m. 31 Oct. 1866, Eleanora, youngest dau. of Robert Hunter, of Hunter, West Kilbryde, Ayrshire, and has a son and dau.

(1) William Arthur, b. 1869.   (2) Eleanora Agnes.
Ladyland and Woodside, Beith, Ayrshire; 22, Thurloe Square, S.W.

Pearson.

Alexander —— *Edinburgh* 1602 conv., 1608.
Possibly an ancestor of Alexander Pearson, a lord of session 1649.

David —— *Arbroath* 1579.

David (Mr.) —— *Forfar* 1625 conv., 1628-33.

James —— *Forfar* 1644.

William, bailie —— *Culross* 1665 conv.

Peddie.

John Dick, of Muckerach —— *Kilmarnock burghs* since 1800. See foot-note.

Pedie.

James —— *Montrose* 1645-7, 1648.

Peebles.

Oliver —— *Perth* 1572 conv. —— 1590 conv., 1597 conv.

William, of —— *Peebles* 1468, an auditor of complaint.

Pender.

John, of Minard, Argyllshire —— *Wick burghs* 1872-4, 1874-80, and since 1880.
[See foot-note, next page. See also England M.P.
William —— *Lanark* 1544.

Petrie.

George —— *Montrose* 1579.

Robert (Patrie), of Portlethine, provost —— *Aberdeen* 1665 conv., 1669-74.

Pennycuik.

George —— *Edinburgh* 1466, an auditor of complaint.

PEDDIE, JOHN DICK, of Muckerach House, Inverness-shire, architect 1848-78, an associate Royal Scottish Academy 1868, Academician 1870, M.P. as above (son of James Peddie, writer to the signet, and his wife, Margaret Coventry, dau. of Professor John Dick, D.D., of Glasgow); b. 24 Feb. 1824; m. 21 July 1851, Euphemia Lochart, dau. of James Stephen More, esq., of Edinburgh, and has 6 sons and 3 daus.

(1) John More, b. 21 Aug. 1853.   (2) James, b. 25 Aug. 1857.
(3) William, b. 27 March 1859.   (4) Coventry, b. 2 Dec. 1863.
(5) Walter Lockhart, b. 7 Nov. 1865.   (6) Alexander Louis, b. 10 Sept. 1869.
(7) Margaret, b. 17 June 1852.   (8) Catherine H. Lockhart, b. 31 Jan. 1856.
(9) Euphemia Lockhart Moore, b. 27 April 1859.
Muckerach House, Inverness-shire.
Clubs—University and Scottish Liberal, Edinburgh; Reform, London.

Perth.

—— the alderman of —— *Perth* 1482. See also Haddington.

—— the provost of —— *Perth* 1532 —— 1540 —— 1558.

Philp.

David —— *Cupar* 1583.

Phipill.

Roger —— *Inverkeithing* 1357.

Pigott. See Graham.

Pinkerton.

Andrew —— *Rutherglen* 1612 —— 1649 —— 1667 conv. ; bailie.

John —— *Rutherglen* 1621.

Pitscottie.

Johnne, of —— *Perth* 1367.

Pittendreighe.

Adam, bailie —— *Kintore* 1678 conv.

Playfair.

Lyon, C.B., doctor of philosophy and LL.D. —— *Edinburgh and St. Andrews Universities* 1868-74, (postmaster-general 1873), 1874-80, and since 1880.
[See foot-note.

PENDER, JOHN, of Blackburn House, Linlithgow, F.R.G.S. and F.R.S.E., formerly a merchant, chairman of various public companies, J.P. cos. Kent, Argyll, Linlithgow, Middlesex and Denbigh, J.P. D.L. Lancashire, M.P. Totnes 1865-6 and as above (2nd son of James Pender, of Vale of Leven, Dumbartonshire); b.   1816 ; m. 1st, Marion, dau. of James Ceams, esq. ; 2ndly   1851, Emma, dau. of Henry Denison, esq., of Daybrook, Notts.

Foots Cray Place, Kent ; Blackburn House, Linlithgow. Clubs—Brooks, City, Reform, and Garrick.

PLAYFAIR, RT. HON. LYON, P.C., C.B., F.R.S., LL.D., professor of chemistry at Royal Institution, Manchester 1843, government inspector-general of schools and museums of science and art 1853-8, professor of chemistry, university of Edinburgh 1858-69, special commissioner at the great exhibition 1851, C.B. 25 Oct. 1851, a member of various foreign orders, postmaster-general 1873-4, chairman of ways and means, and deputy-speaker of the House of Commons since April 1880, P.C. 1873, M.P. as above, (nephew of Lt.-Col. Sir Hugh Lyon Playfair, LL.D., and son of George Playfair, inspector-general of hospitals, Bengal, by his wife, Jessie Ross) ; born at Meerut 21 May 1819 ; m. 1st, 28 July 1846, Margaret Eliza, dau. of James Oakes, esq., she d. 13 Aug. 1855, leaving a son and dau. ; he m. 2ndly, 17 Dec. 1857, Jean Ann, dau. of Crowley Millington, of Greenwich, she d. 21 April 1877, leaving a dau., Ethel Mary ; he m. 3rdly, 3 Oct. 1878, Edith, eldest dau. of Samuel H. Russell, esq., of Boston, America ; by his first wife he had a son and dau.

  (1) George James, captain R.A.; b. 31 March 1849; m. 4 Jan. 1876, Lucy Matthews, she d. leaving a daughter.

  (2) Jessie Anne; m. 5 Jan. 1869 to Capt. Edmund Peel, late 14th Hussars.

68, Onslow Gardens, S.W.   Clubs—Athenæum, —— University, Edinburgh.

Plenderleith.

John, provost —— *Peebles* 1669-70.

Pollock.

Robert, of Milburne, provost —— *Renfrew* 1669-74.

Robert (sir) of that ilk, knt. and bart. —— *Renfrewshire* 1700-2, 1702-7, 1707-8 (1st parlt. G.B.), 1710-13, 1713-15, 1715-22 (accepted office of profit of the [crown 1715).

Sir Robert Pollok, cr. a bart. 30 Nov. 1703, "for his predecessor's services to King David and King William, and for his own to King William of eternall happy memory; and for his fixedness to the Reformed Religion the tyme of the Revolution, withstanding superstition and dispotick power, and for suffering nyne months' imprisonment inter the barbarous and inhuman mountaineers when he was carried away by Viscount of Dundie," Governor of Fort William (son of Robert Pollok of that ilk); m. 1st, Annabella, dau. of Sir George Maxwell, of Nether Pollok, and 2ndly, Annabella, dau. of Walter Stewart, of Pardovan; and [died 1736, leaving issue.

Polrassie.

—— the laird of —— *Sutherlandshire* 1641.

Polwarth, Viscount.   See Hume.

Pomfret.

Andro, of —— *Lanark* 1357.

Porterfield.

(? **George**) —— *Renfrewshire* 1648 (the laird).

George —— *Glasgow* 1645-7, 1648-9, 1649-50 (or John Grahame), 1650.

Alexander of that ilk —— *Renfrewshire* 1700-2.

Potter.

Symon —— *Dumbarton* 1357.

Power.

John —— *Ayr* 1600.

Prateris.

William —— *Dunfermline* 1594 conv.

Preston.

Charles (sir), of Valleyfield, bart. —— *Kirkcaldy burghs* 1784-90.

5th bart. (on the death of the father of Sir George, 1779), capt. 26th regt. celebrated in military annals for his gallant defence of fort St. John, against the American general, Montgomery, a commissioner of customs ; d. unm. 23 March 1800.

Henry —— *Edinburgh* 1488, 1493-4.

A younger son of Preston of Craigmiller, a burgess of Edinburgh, father of James, [next named.

James —— *Edinburgh* 1524, 1525, then provost.

Son of Henry, last named ; acquired the lands and barony of Valleyfield, Perthshire, [1544 ; m. Margaret Home, and had issue, ancestor of Sir Charles, M.P.

John (Mr.) —— *Edinburgh* 1567, 1572 conv.

Probably younger son of last-named M.P.

(John), laird of Fentonbarns —— 1597 conv., as a minor baron.

Advocate before 1575, a commissary of Edinburgh 1580-99, and an assessor of the town, an ordinary judge of session 8 March 1595, P.C., collector-general of the king's augmentations, vice-president 1607, president 1609 until his death, 14 June 1616, said to have been [the son of an Edinburgh baker.

John (Mr.), of Pennycuik —— 1608.

John (Mr.), eldest son of capt. Walter Preston, of Drumraik —— *Crail* 1685-6.

Symon (sir), of that ilk, knt. —— *Edinburgh* 1540 bis, (provost) 1543, 1544, [1567 *bis*, then a knight, also provost.

Town-clerk of Edinburgh 1540 for life (a son of George Preston, of Preston) ; m. 1st, Jonet, eldest dau. of John Betoun, of Creich, &c. ; he m. 2ndly, Elizabeth, dau. of Wm. [Menteith ; and had a son, David, ancestor of Richard, Lord Dingwall.

Primrose.

Adam —— *Culross* 1628-33.

Probably a grandson of Gilbert Primrose, principal surgeon to James VI. and Q. Anne, [who d. 8 April 1615, aged 80, leaving issue.

Archibald, of Dalmeny —— *Edinburghshire* 1696, until cr. Viscount of Rose-
[bery, s.b. 1 Oct. 1700.

Gentleman of the bedchamber to Prince George of Denmark, created Viscount of Rosebery, Lord Primrose and Dalmeny, 1 April 1700, with remainder in default of issue male to his female issue, and in default to the heirs entail in the lands of Rosebery, P.C. ; created Earl of Rosebery, Viscount of Inverkeithing, and Lord Dalmeny and Primrose, 10 April 1703, with remainder to his issue male and female successively ; a commissioner for the treaty of Union, a representative peer 1707, 1708, 1710, 1713 (only son of Sir Archibald Primrose, 1st bart, by his 2nd wife) ; b. 18 Dec. 1664, d. 20 Oct. 1723, m. Feb. 1690, Dorothy, only child and heir of Everingham Cressy, of Birkin, Yorks, and had with other issue a son, Sir [James, ancestor of Earl of Rosebery. See Foster's Peerage

Primrose—*continued*.

James (sir), of Carrington —— *Edinburghshire* 1702, until cr. Viscount Primrose
[s.b. 11 July 1702.

3rd baronet (on the death of his father, Sir William, 23 Sept. 1687), created Viscount of Primrose, Lord Primrose and Castlefield, 30 Nov. 1703, in default of issue male, with remainder to the heirs male of Sir William Primrose, his father ; d. 13 July, 1706. His sons, Archibald and Hugh, succeeded to the titles in succession, and on the death of the latter, 8 May 1741, it is said to have been uncertain whether the peerage became extinct or devolved upon [the Earl of Rosebery, who succeeded to the estates and property. See Foster's Peerage.

Francis Ward, of Bixley Hall, Norfolk —— *Stirling burghs* 1819-20.

Bar.-at-law L.I. (son of Neil, 3rd Earl of Rosebery, K.T.) ; b. 13 Feb. 1785, d. 26 May 1860, having m. 10 Nov. 1829, Percy, 3rd dau. of Col. Ralph Gore, of Barrowmount, co. [Kilkenny (E. Arran) ; she d. 30 Aug. 1864, having had issue. See Foster's Peerage.

Pringle.

Alexander, of Whitebank —— *Selkirkshire* 1830-1, 1831-2, 1835-7, 1837-41, 1841 (a lord of the treasury 1841), until appointed a clerk of sasines, s.b.
[12 Jan. 1846.

Vice-lieut. Selkirkshire, J.P. and D.L., lord of the treasury (Scot'and) 1841-5, (eldest son of Alexander Pringle, of Whitbank) ; b. 30 Jan. 1791,d. 2 Sept. 1857, having m. 12 Jan. 1830, Agnes Joanna, 2nd dau. and heir portioner of Sir Wm. Dick, bart., of Prestonfield, and had [issue.

George, laird of Torwoodlee —— *Selkirkshire* 1617, 1621 laird.

Son of William Pringle, of Torwoodlee ; m. twice, and had with other issue, James, M.P., [1641.

George, elder, of Torwoodlee —— *Selkirkshire* 1689 conv., 1689.

An active royalist concerned in the Rye House plot, fled to Holland ; his estates were confiscated, but at the revolution his attainder was removed and his estates restored (son of James, M.P. 1641) ; m. 1654, Janet Brodie, of Lethen, and d. 1689, leaving with two daus. [a son James, M.P. 1693.

James (sir), of Galashiels, knt. —— *Selkirkshire* 1621, 1630 conv.

Knighted by James VI., had a charter of the lands and barony of Galashiels 1629 (son of James, only son of Andrew Hop-Pringle, of Smallholm and Galashiels) ; m. —— dau. of Kerr, [of Linton, and had issue.

James, of Whytbank —— *Selkirkshire* 1628-33.

A great loyalist, and fined by parliament (son of James Pringle, by Christian, dau. of Wm. Lundin of that ilk) ; m. Sophia Schooner, a maid of honour to Anne of Denmark, [and d. May 1667.

James, of Torwoodlee —— *Selkirkshire* 1641, 1645 the laird.

Son of George Pringle, M.P. 1617 ; m. 1st 1620, Jean, dau. of Sir Richard Cockburn, of Clerkington, lord privy seal ; 2ndly, 1628, Janet, dau. of Sir Lewis Craig, of Riccarton, [and d. 1657, leaving with other issue a son George, M.P. 1689.

Pringle—*continued.*

PRINGLE OF TORWOODLEE.

GEORGE PRINGLE, M.P. Selkirkshire 1617, 1621 conv. =

JAMES PRINGLE, M.P. Selkirkshire 1641, 1645 =

GEORGE PRINGLE, M.P. Selkirkshire 1689 conv., 1689 =

JAMES PRINGLE, M.P. Selkirkshire 1693-1702.

James, of Torwoodlee, —— *Selkirkshire* 1693-1702.

Son of George, M.P. 1689 ; m. 1690, Isabel, dau. of Sir John Hall, of Dunglas, and had
[with other issue a son James, a principal clerk of session.

James, younger, of Stichill —— *Berwickshire* 1761, 1761-8, 1768-74, 1774 until
[he accepted the Chiltern hundreds s.b 15 April 1779.

4th baronet (on the death of his father Sir Robert, 14 Dec. 1779) ; lt.-col. 59th regt.
lt.-col. Duke of Buccleuch's fencibles, master of works in Scotland ; d. 7 April 1809, having
m. 11 Sept. 1767, Elizabeth, dau. of Norman Macleod, of Macleod, and had issue. See
[Foster's Baronetage.

John (Mr.), of Hayning —— *Selkirkshire* 1703-7, 1707-8 (1st parlt. G.B.),
1708-10 (then " master John "), 1710-13 (one of the keepers of the signet for
Scotland 1711), 1713-15, 1715-22, 1722-7, 1727 (then advocate) until he
[acc. a crown office of profit, s.b. 13 Feb. 1729-30.

Of Haining, co. Selkirk, by purchase 1702 ; advocate 18 June 1698, commissioner
equivalent, Lord Haining of session 1 July 1729 ; (2nd son of Andrew Pringle, of Clifton,
by his wife Violet, dau. of John Rutherfurd, of Edgerston) ; m. Ann, eldest dau. of Sir
James Murray, of Philiphaugh, and d. 19 Aug. 1754, aged 80, having had with other issue
[John, M.P. 1765.

John, of Haining and of Clifton —— *Selkirkshire* 1765-8, 1768-74, 1774-80,
1780-4 (of Clifton), 1784 until he accepted the Chiltern hundreds s.b. 14
[April 1786.

A merchant in Madeira, succ. to Haining on the death of his brother, Lord Alemore, 1776,
and to Clifton on the death of his cousin, Robert Pringle, 1780 (son of John, M.P. 1703) ;
[d. unm.   1792.

John, of Clifton —— *Linlithgow burghs* 1819-20.

Of Clifton and Haining, cornet 7th hussars, served in the army of occupation in France,
[retired 1819 (son of Mark, M.P., next named) ; died unm. 1831.

Pringle—*continued.*

PRINGLE OF CLIFTON AND HAINING.

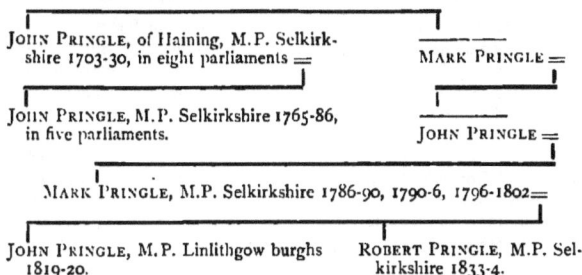

JOHN PRINGLE, of Haining, M.P. Selkirk-shire 1703-30, in eight parliaments ═══   MARK PRINGLE ═

JOHN PRINGLE, M.P. Selkirkshire 1765-86, in five parliaments.   JOHN PRINGLE ═

MARK PRINGLE, M.P. Selkirkshire 1786-90, 1790-6, 1796-1802═

JOHN PRINGLE, M.P. Linlithgow burghs 1819-20.   ROBERT PRINGLE, M.P. Selkirkshire 1833-4.

Mark, of Fairnilee —— *Selkirkshire* 1786-90, 1790-6, 1796-1802, of Clifton.

Of Haining and Clifton on the death, 1792, of John, M.P. 1765, advocate 2 Aug. 1777 (son of John Pringle, of Crichton, by Anne, eldest dau. of Robert Rutherfurd of Fairnilee) ; m. 1795, Ann Elizabeth, dau. of Robert Chalmers, esq., and d. 25 April 1812, aged 58, [leaving with other issue John, M.P. 1819, and Robert, M.P. 1833.

Robert, of Stichill —— *Roxburghshire* 1639-41.

Of Bartingbush, a writer to the signet, purchased lands of Templehall, co. Berwick, and also in 1628 the estate of Stichill, co. Roxburgh, from Sir John Gordon, of Lochinvar (2nd son of George, of Newhall) ; m. Katherine Hamilton, of the Silvertonhill family, and had a [son John, father of Robert, M.P., next named.

Robert, of Stichill —— *Roxburghshire* 1678 conv., 1681-2.

Sir Robert Pringle, of Stichill (grandson of Robert, M.P., last named, descended from William Pringle, of Whittoun, co. Roxburgh, 1492) ; cr. baronet of Nova Scotia, 5 Jan. 1683, m. 1660, Margaret, dau. of Sir John Hope, bart., Lord Craighall of session, and had with other issue Sir John, 2nd bart. (father of Sir Robert, 3rd bart., and Sir John, cr. a bart., but died s.p.), Sir Walter, Lord Newhall of session, Rt. Hon. Robert Pringle, secretary-at-war (see England M.P.), and Thomas, writer to the signet, father of Robert, Lord Edgefield [of session. See Foster's Baronetage

Robert, of Clifton —— *Selkirkshire* 1833-4.

Son of Mark Pringle, M.P., and heir of his brother John, M.P. 1819 ; served in 7th hussars ; [contested Selkirkshire 1835 ; d. unm. Dec. 1842.

William (Hoppringill) —— *Lauder* 1587, 1593, 1600, 1612.

SCOTCH MEMBERS.   O O

Pulteney. See also Johnstone.

William (formerly Johnstone) of Bath House, Westminster —— *Forfar burghs* [and *Cromartyshire*, sat for the latter 1768-74. See also England M.P.

Sir William, 5th baronet (on the death of his brother, Sir James, 4 Sept. 1794), advocate 13 July 1751, one of the assessors for the city of Edinburgh, M.P. Shrewsbury 1775-1805 (3rd son of Sir William Johnstone, 3rd bart.); b. 19 Oct. 1729 ; died one of the richest subjects in Britain 31 May 1805, bur. in Westminster Abbey 11 June, having assumed 1767 the name of Pulteney in addition to his own ; m. 1st, 10 Nov. 1760, Frances, only dau. and heiress of Daniel Pulteney, first cousin of William, Earl of Bath (ext.) ; she d. 1 June 1782, bur. in Westminster Abbey ; he m. 2ndly 5 Jan. 1804, Margaret, widow of Andrew Stewart, of Castlemilk and Torrance, M.P., and dau. of Sir William Stirling, bart., of Ardoch. By his 1st wife he had an only dau., Henrietta Laura, heiress of Pulteney property, cr. Baroness of Bath 21 July 1792, and Countess of Bath 26 Oct. 1803 ; d. s.p. 14 July 1808, having m. 23 July 1794, to her cousin, Gen. Sir James Murray-Pulteney, bart., M.P. (MURRAY) ; he d.
[26 April 1811.

Purves.

George —— *Dunbar* 1621, 1628-33, 1630 conv., 1639-41 (or John).

James —— *Dunbar* 1643 conv., 1644, 1645-6.

Thomas ——*Dunbar* 1649, in absence of William.

Thomas Purves and James Lauder, two of the bailies conjunctly and [severally M.P. —— *Dunbar* 1661-3, but the latter alone appears.

William —— *Dunbar* 1644 conv., 1649, or Thomas Purves in his absence.

Possibly 1st baronet of this name, so created 6 July 1665 ; clerk to the committee of parliament temp. Charles II., solr.-genl. 1660. See HUME-CAMPBELL in Foster's Baronetage

R.

Rae.

Arthur, burgess of Edinburgh —— *Bervie or Inverbervie* 1612.

William (sir), of St. Catherines, bart., lord advocate for Scotland —— *Anstruther Easter* (now *St. Andrews*) *burghs* 1819-20, 1820-6, *Buteshire* 1830-1, 1833-4, 1835-7, 1837-41, 1841 (lord advocate same year) until his death s.b. 1 Dec.
[1842. See England M.P.

3rd baronet (on the death of his brother, Sir David, 22 May 1815), advocate 1791, lord advocate 1827-30, 1834-5, 1841-2, M.P. Harwich 1826-30, Portarlington 1831-2 (younger son of Sir David Rae, lord Eskgrove of session, and lord justice clerk, cr. a bart. 27 June 1804); m. Mary, dau. of Charles Steuart, esq., and d. s.p. 18 Oct. 1842, when the title
[became extinct.

Raitt.

William, of Hallgreen —— *Kincardineshire* 1649.

Ramsay. See also **Maule**.

Adam —— *Perth* 1543, 1544.

Alexander —— *Dundee* 1594.

Alexander (sir), of Balmain, bart. —— *Kincardineshire* 1710-13.

5th baronet (on the death of his brother, Sir David, M.P. 1710); d. unm. 27 Jan. 1754.

Alexander Ramsay-Irvine (sir), of Balmain, bart. —— *Kincardineshire*
[1765-8.

6th baronet (on the death of his uncle, Sir Alexander, 1754, M.P. 1710); d. unm. 11 Feb.
[1806.

Alexander (sir), of Balmain, bart. —— *Kincardineshire* 1820-6.

2nd baronet (on the death of his father, Sir Alexander, 17 May 1810), b. 14 Feb. 1785, d. 26 April 1852, having m. twice, and had with other issue a son, Sir Alexander, 3rd
[bart., M.P. Rochdale 1857-9. See England M.P

Ramsay—*continued*.

Andrew (sir), of Abbotshall, lord provost —— *Edinburgh* 1665 conv., 1667 [conv., 1669-74.

Of Edinburgh, mercht., elected provost 1654-5-6-7, 1662-73, P.C., lord Abbotshall of session 23 Nov. 1671, resigned Nov. 1673, named a commissioner for trade 1685 (son of Andrew Ramsay, a rector in the college of Edinburgh, minister of the Grey Friars' Church); d. at [Abbotshall 17 Jan. 1688, having had a son, Sir Alexander, M.P., next named.

Andrew (sir), knt., bart., eldest son of Sir Andrew R., of Abbotshall —— *North* [*Berwick* 1669-74.

" First knighted by the usurper Cromwell," created a baronet of Nova Scotia 23 Jan. 1669 ; [m. Anne, dau. of Hugh Montgomerie, 7th Earl of Eglinton, and d. s.p. 1709.

(David), laird of Balmain —— 1609 conv.

Son of William Ramsay, of Balmain, and grandson of the outlawed Lord Bothwell : m Katherine, dau. of Sir Robert Carnegie, of Kinnaird (E. SOUTHESK), and d. 1624, leaving [a son, David, M.P. 1625, next named.

(David), laird of Balmain —— *Kincardineshire* 1612 (younger), 1625 conv., 1630 [conv.

Son of David, M.P., last-named ; m. Margaret, dau. of Sir Gilbert Ogilvie of that ilk, and [d. 1636, leaving with other issue Sir Gilbert, M.P. 1639.

David, bailie —— *Arbroath* 1639-41, 1649.

David (sir), of Balmain —— *Kincardineshire* 1705-7, 1707-8 (1st parlt. G. B.), [1708-10.

4th baronet (on the death of his father, Sir Charles, 1695), d. s.p. Sept. 1710.

(George), laird of Dalhousie —— *Edinburghshire* 1617 conv. and parlt.

Sir George Ramsay, of Dalhousie (brother of Sir John, Earl of Holderness, celebrated for defending James VI. against the treasonable attempts of the Earl of Gowrie and his brother Alexander Ruthven, of Perth, both of whom he slew), was on 19 Aug. 1601, served heir to Sir Alexander Ramsay, of Dalhousie (his grandfather's grandfather), who sat in parliament 4 Oct. 1479, as Dominus de Dalwousy, and fell at Flodden 9 Sept. 1513. The barony of Dalhousie and lordship of Melrose were erected into a free barony of Melrose, with a grant to him and his heirs male and successors in the said lordship and barony of Melrose of the title, honour, and dignity of a free baron and lord of parliament, as Lord Ramsay, of Melrose, by charter 25 Aug. 1618 ; this title was altered to that of Lord Ramsay, of Dalhouise, 5 Jan. 1619. He d. 1629, having m. 1st, Margaret, dau. and heir of Sir George Douglas, of Helen-hill, brother of William, Earl of Morton, and Robert, Earl of Buchan, and 2ndly, Margaret [Ker. By his 1st wife he had a son, William, M.P. 1617, cr. Earl of Dalhousie.

Gilbert (sir), of Balmain, knt., bart. —— *Kincardineshire* 1639-41, 1645-6 (laird), [1661-3.

Created a baronet 3 Sept. 1625, a covenanter, a commissioner of excise, etc., etc. (son of David Ramsay, M.P. 1625) ; m. Elizabeth, dau. of George Auchinleck, of Balandro, and had [issue.

Ramsay—*continued*.

James, younger, of Banff —— *Perthshire* 1689 conv., 1689 until his seat was [declared vacant 28 April 1693, because he had not signed the assurance.

2nd baronet (on the death of his father, Sir Gilbert Ramsay) ; m. Christian, dau. and co-heir of Sir William Ogilvie, brother of James, cr. Earl of Airlie, and died 1730, having had [issue. See Foster's Baronetage.

James Andrew, commonly called Lord R. —— *Haddingtonshire* 1837 until he [succ. as Earl of Dalhousie 21 March 1838.

10th Earl of Dalhousie (on the death of his father, George, 9th Earl, 21 March 1838), K.T., P.C., cr. Marquis Dalhousie, of Dalhousie Castle, co. Edinburgh, and of the Punjab, in the Peerage of U.K. 25 Aug. 1849 (ext. on his death, together with the English barony of Dalhousie); contested Edinburgh 1835, constable of Dover castle, lord warden of the cinque ports, lord register of Scotland, major.-gen. of royal archers, the Queen's body-guard of Scotland, gov.-gen. of India 1847-56, assumed the prefix surname of Brown ; b. 22 Apl. 1812, d. 19 Dec. 1860, having m. 21 Jan. 1836, Lady Susan Georgiana Hay, dau. of George. 8th Marquis of Tweeddale, K.T.; she d. 4 May 1853, having had 2 daus. See Foster's Peerage.

John —— *Crail* 1585 conv., 1586 conv.

John, of Kelly —— *Aberdeen* (now *Montrose*) *burghs* 1806-7.

Hon. John Ramsay, lieut.-gen. in the army, and on Indian staff (son of 1st lord Panmure), b. 21 Apl. 1775, d. 28 June 1842, having m. 19 Apl. 1800, Mary, dau. of Philip Delisle, esq., of Calcutta ; she d. 28 Oct. 1843, having had with other issue a son, George, 12th Earl [of Dalhousie. See Foster's Peerage.

John, of Kildalton —— *Stirling burghs* Apl. to Nov. 1868, *Falkirk burghs* 1874- [80, and since 1880. See foot-note.

Robert Balfour, of Whitehill —— *Edinburghshire* 1751-4.

Robert Balfour Ramsay, of Balbirnie and Whitehill; m. Anne, dau. and heir of Sir Andrew Ramsay, 3rd bart., of Whitehill, and had a dau., Elizabeth, m. to Captain William [Wardlaw, ancestor of Wardlaw-Ramsay.

William —— *Montrose* 1617 conv. and parlt. 1621.

William, 2nd lord (on the death of his father, Sir George, M.P. 1617, in 1629), cr. Earl of Dalhousie and Lord Ramsay, of Kerrington, 29 June 1633, high sheriff co. Edinburgh 1646, had a fine of £1,500 imposed on him by Cromwell's act of grace and pardon 12 April 1654 ; m. 1st, Margaret, eldest dau. of David Carnegie, 1st Earl of Southesk, and 2ndly, Jocosa, widow of Lyster, son of Sir Richard Blount, of Mapledurham, Oxon, dau. of Sir Allen Apsley, lieut. of the Tower of London (by his 2nd wife, Anne, dau. and heir of Sir Peter Carew); she d. 28 April, 1663. By his 1st wife he was ancestor of James Andrew, Marquis Dalhousie. [See above and Foster's Peerage.

RAMSAY, John, of Kildalton, Argyllshire, J.P., D.L., and of Glasgow, merchant, J.P. co. Lanark, contested Stirling burghs 1868, M.P. as above (son of Robert Ramsay, by Elizabeth, dau. of Wm. Stirling, of Craigforth, co. Stirling) ; b. 15 Aug. 1814, m. 1st, 29 Sept. 1857, Elizabeth, dau. of late Wm. Shields, esq., of Lanchester, co. Durham, she d. 2 Feb. 1864 ; he m. 2ndly, 16 Nov. 1871, Lucy, dau. of George Martin, esq., of Auchendennan, co. Dumbarton, and has a son and 2 daus.

(1) John, b. 14 Oct. 1878.   (2) Mary Anne.   (3) Elizabeth Lucy.
Kildalton House, Greenock, N.B.; 52, Warwick Sq., S.W.
Clubs—Athenæum, Windham.

Ramsay—*continued.*

William Ramsay, of Barnton —— *Stirlingshire* 1831-2; *Edinburghshire* 1841 [until he accepted the Chiltern hundreds s.b. 25 June 1845.

Only son and heir of George Ramsay, of Barnton, by Hon. Jean Hamilton, 2nd dau. of Robert Lord Belhaven ; b. 29 May 1809, d. 15 March 1850, having m. 4 Aug. 1828, Hon. Mary Sandilands, only dau. of James, 10th lord of Torphichen, and had an only son, Charles [William, died unm. 30 Dec. 1865.

Rany.

Herbert —— *Dumfries,* 1572 conv.

Read.

Thomas (col.), governor of Stirling —— *Linlithgow, Stirling, &c.* 1654-5 (WILLIS).

Reddie.

John, younger, merchant trafficker, bailie —— *Dysart* 1681-2.

Redheugh.

Richard —— 1485.

Reid

Alexander, deacon of the goldsmiths —— *Edinburgh* 1678 conv.

Alexander, of Bairie, burgess of Kintore —— *Elgin burghs* 1710-13.

Of Barra, 2nd bart. (on the death of his father, Sir John Reid, created a baronet 30 Nov. 1703); m. 28 Jan. 1705, Agnes, eldest dau. of Sir Alexander Ogilvie, of Forglen, bart., a senator of the college of justice, and d. 5 Feb. 1750, leaving issue. See Foster's Baronetage.

Andro —— *Inverness* 1439.

James, provost —— *Dunfermline* 1639-41, 1643 conv.

John (*Rid*) —— *Irvine* 1644 conv.

Patrick —— *Rutherglen* 1357.

Robert, of Baldovie —— *Forfarshire* 1689-1702.

Robert, of Iffley, Oxon —— *Kirkcaldy burghs* 1874 until his death s.b. 23 April [1875.

Bar.-at-law Inner Temple 1872, B.A. Worcester Coll., Oxon, 1869, contested Wick burghs Feb. 1872 (son of David Reid, of Dunfermline); b. 1831, m. 1858, Mary, dau. of Wm. [Newby, of Manchester, and died 30 March 1875.

William, bailie —— *Edinburgh* 1641.

Rennald. See Ronnald.

Renton.

(———) laird of Lamberton —— *Berwickshire* 1650-1.

Richardson.

Andrew —— *Anstruther Wester* 1645, 1649 (Peter Thomson in his absence).

(James), laird of Smeton —— *Edinburghshire* 1617 conv. and parlt.

> Possibly Sir James Richardson, of Smeaton, knt., whose son James was father of
> [Sir James, 3rd bart.

(James), laird of Smeaton —— *Edinburghshire* 1630 conv.

> Possibly son of the preceding M.P., and father of Sir James Richardson, 3rd bart., who
> recorded arms in the Lyon office 1673, and d. 1680, leaving a son, Sir James. See "CHAOS"
> [in Foster's Baronetage.

James (Reidsone) —— *Pittenweem* 1641, 1649 (in his absence Alexander Burnet
[or James Cuik), 1650-1.

Robert —— *Anstruther Wester* 1612, 1617, 1621, 1628-33, 1630 conv.

Robert (sir), of Pencaitland —— *Haddington constabulary*, 1630 conv.

> Sir Robert Richardson, of Pencaitland (son of James Richardson, of Smeaton), bart. of
> of Nova Scotia, the patent of creation not recorded. On 13 Nov. 1660 he had seisine of the
> barony of Pencaitland in New Brunswick from Sir William Alexander !!! and according to
> Milne's list had a precept the same day for a baronetcy, with remainder to his heirs male.
> His son, Sir Robert, 2nd bart., sold Pencaitland, N.B., and d. s.p. 1642, and was succeeded
> by his cousin, Sir James. Although there is no record of the limitations of this creation, yet
> Sir James, 3rd bart., recorded his arms at the Lyon office in 1673, presumably as heir male of
> the 1st bart. The 8th bart. so called assumed the title, and the present representative being
> served heir male in 1837 has been acknowledged by the Lyon office. See "CHAOS,"
> [Foster's Baronetage.

Robert (or John), bailie —— *Burntisland* 1643 conv.; *Dumfries* 1649 (in absence
[of Thomes McBirney).

Riddell.

(Andrew) laird of Riddell —— *Roxburghshire* 1617 conv. and parlt., 1621.

> Son of Walter Riddell of that ilk; and by his wife Violet, dau. of William Douglas of
> [Pumpherston, had with other issue Sir John, cr. a baronet 14 May 1628,

Andrew of Hayning, sheriff principal —— *Selkirkshire* (the *forest*) 1639-41.

> Probably son of Walter, 4th son of Andrew, 1st named, and father of John, M.P. 1665.

Riddell—*continued.*

James, bailie after provost —— *Rutherglen* 1669 until 29 June 1671, when he was decerned by the lords of the privy council incapable to bear office for [malversation.

John of Hayning —— *Selkirkshire* 1665 conv., 1678 conv.

Probably son of Andrew, M.P. 1639.

John —— *Rutherglen* 1593.

John (sir), of that ilk —— *Roxburghshire* (or sheriffdom of Teviotdale) 1690, [until his death s.b. 13 May 1700.

3rd baronet (on the death of his father, Sir Walter, M.P. 1628); m. thrice (see Foster's [Baronetage), and left issue.

John Buchanan (sir), of Riddell, bart —— *Linlithgow burghs* 1812-18, 1818 [until his death s.b. 31 May 1819.

9th baronet (on the death of his brother, Sir James, 4 Sept. 1784); he died 26 April 1819, having m. 17 Aug. 1805, Lady Frances Marsham, eldest dau. of Charles, 1st earl of Romney; [she d. 30 June 1868, aged 90, leaving issue. See Foster's Baronetage.

Walter (sir), of that ilk —— *Roxburghshire* 1628-33, 1646-7, (laird) 1650.

2nd baronet (on the death of his father Sir John), knighted in his father's lifetime ; m. [Jane, dau. of Wm. Rigg, of Athenrie, co. Fife, and had a son, Sir John, M.P. 1690.

Rigg.

Hugh —— *Edinburgh* 1544, 1545, 1546 bis.

James (Rige) —— *Dunfermline* 1640.

William, of Athernie —— *Stirlingshire* 1639-41, 1643 conv.

Rind.

William (Rynde) —— *Edinburgh* 1479.

Robertson.

Alexander, of Craig, dean of guild —— *Perth* 1702-7.

David, of Ladykirk —— *Berwickshire* 1859-65, 1865-8, 1868 until cr. Lord [Marjoribanks s.b. 30 June 1873.

Baron Marjoribanks of Ladykirk, co. Berwick, so cr. 12 June 1873. d. 7 days after, assumed the surname and arms of Robertson in lieu of Marjoribanks by R.L. 2 Sept. 1834; lord-lieut. Berwickshire, contested the county 1857, (4th son of Sir John Marjoribanks, 1st bart., and 1st cousin of Sir Dudley Coutts, Lord Tweedmouth) ; b. 2 April 1797, m. 10 Sept. 1834, Marianne, eldest dau. of Sir Thos. Haggerston, bart., and co-heir of her mother Margaret, only child and heir of William Robertson, esq., of Ladykirk, N.B., and had issue. See [Foster's Baronetage.

Robertson—*continued*.

James —— *Irvine* 1585.

James —— *St. Andrews* 1645 (?also 1646-7), 1648, *Kirkcaldy* 1649.

John —— *Edinburgh* 1593, 1594 conv., 1597 conv., 1604, 1605, 1607.

John —— *Crail* 1649 (or Alex. Cunynghame).

Thomas —— *St. Andrews* 1617, conv. and parlt.

Walter, town clerk —— *Aberdeen* 1633.

William (Mr.), of Inchis —— *Inverness-shire* 1665 conv.
Bred to the law, and studied at Leyden, admitted advocate 29 July 1646 (son of John
[Robertson, who acquired Inches 1619), m. twice, and left issue.

Robinson.

James (Robieson) —— *Linlithgow* 1531.

Rodes.

Edward (sir), one of his highness' council in Scotland —— *sheriffdom of Perth*
[1656-8, 1659-60 (WILLIS).
Sir Edward Rodes, of Great Houghton, Yorks, justice of the peace, a colonel of horse
1654, and a privy councillor (eldest son of Sir Godfrey Rodes, of Great Houghton, by his
2nd wife, Anne Lewknor) ; d. 19 Feb. 1666, aged 66 ; he m. May 1629, Margaret, dau.
of Sir Hamond Whichcote, of Harpswell, co. Linc. ; she d. 22 April 1681, aged 72, buried
[with her husband at Darfield, having had with other issue Godfrey, next named.

Godfrey (master), esq. —— *sheriffdom of Linlithgow, Stirling, and Clackmannan*
[1656-8 (WILLIS).
Of Great Houghton (eldest son of Sir Edward Rodes, last named) ; bp. 5 Oct. 1631, d.
[unm. 27 April 1681.

Roger.

Robert, merchant, present provost of Glasgow —— *Glasgow burghs* 1708-10.
Said to be grandson of William Roger of Glasgow 1605, and father of Hugh Roger, also
[lord provost of Glasgow.

William —— *Ayr* 1594 conv.
Son of Thomas Roger, of Ayr, and father of Rev. Ralph Roger, minister of Ardrossan
1647, and of the cathedral church Glasgow 1659, deprived 1662, etc., etc.; and d. 3 Feb.
[1689.

Rolland.

William, —— *Aberdeen* 1526.
Master of the mint at Aberdeen to James V.

Rollo.

(Sir Andrew), laird of Duncrub —— *Perthshire* 1621, 1630 conv., *Clackmannan-*
[*shire* 1650-1.
Sir Andrew Rollo, of Duncrub, Perthshire (descended from William Rollo, of Duncrub, living
1511), knighted by James VI. 1621, sheriff principal, co. Perth 1633, created a peer of Scotland
by Charles II. 10 Jan. 1651, with remainder to his heirs male whatsoever, fined £1,000 by
Cromwell's act of grace and pardon 1654 ; b. at Dunning 12 June 1659, having m. Catherine,
[4th dau. of James Drummond, 1st Lord Maderty, and had issue. See Foster's Peerage.

Rollo—*continued.*

David (Rollok) —— *Dundee* 1479 bis —— —— 1535, 1540 bis, 1543.

James Rollok —— *Dundee* 1304 (prov ost) —— —— 1524.

Robert (Rowok) —— 1461, an auditor of complaint.
Probably of the Duncrub family.

Robert, of Powhouse —— *Stirlingshire* 1702-7.

Ronnald.

John —— *Montrose* 1661.

Robert (Rennald), merchant burgess, provost —— *Montrose* 1681-2.

Rose.

Alexander (Mr.), second son of Hugh Rose, of Clava, late provost —— *Nairn*
[1669-72.

David, merchant trafficker, bailie —— *Nairn* 1678, conv.

(Hugh), laird of Kilravock —— *Nairnshire* 1646-7, 1648, *Nairn* 1649.
Colonel of the Inverness-shire regt. for Duke of Hamilton's engagement 4 May 1648, (son
of Hugh Rose) ; m. Margaret, dau. of Sir John Sinclair, of Dunbeath, and d. March 1649,
[leaving Hugh, M.P. 1685.

Hugh, of Clava —— *Nairnshire* 1665 conv.

Hugh, younger, of Brodley, merchant bailie —— *Nairn* 1681-2.
Brother of John, M.P. 1689.

Hugh, elder, of Kilravock —— *Nairnshire* 1685-6.
Died 1687, son of Hugh Rose, M.P. 1647, and father of Hugh, M.P., next named.

Hugh, of Kilravock —— *Nairnshire* 1700-2, 1702-7, 1707-8 (1st parlt. Great
[Britain.)
Sheriff of Ross ; son of Hugh last named, by his 1st wife, Margaret, dau. of Sir Robert
Innes of that ilk ; he m. thrice, and d. 23 July 1732, leaving a son, Hugh, M.P., next
[named.

Hugh, younger, of Kilravock —— *Ross-shire* 26 June 1708 until unseated
[28 Jan. following ; *Nairnshire* 1708-10 ; *Ross-shire* 1734-41.
Eldest son of Hugh, M.P. 1700, by his 1st wife, Margaret, eldest dau. of Sir Hugh
Campbell, of Calder ; he m. 1st, Elizabeth, dau. of Sir Lewis Grant, of Grant, and 2ndly,
[Jean, eldest dau. of Hugh Rose, of Broadley, and d. 1755, leaving issue.

Hugh, of Kilravock —— *Nairnshire* 1812 until he accepted the Chiltern
[hundreds s.b. 25 June 1813.
Vice-lieut. Nairnshire, col. Nairnshire militia (son of Hugh Rose, by his wife Elizabeth,
dau. of Hugh Rose, of Kilravock) ; m. 1st, Katherine, dau. of John Baillie, of Dunain, co.
[Inverness, and 2ndly, Catherine Mackintosh, of Far, and d. 1828.

John —— *Nairn* 1648 —— 1661 (councillor).

Rose—*continued*.

ROSE OF KILRAVOCK.

Hugh Rose, M.P. Nairnshire 1646-7, 1648, Nairn 1649 =

Hugh Rose, M.P. Nairnshire 1685-6 =

Hugh Rose, M.P. Nairnshire 1700-2, 1702-7, 1707-8 =

Hugh Rose, M.P. Ross-shire 1708, Nairnshire 1708-10, Ross-shire 1734-41.

John, brother-german to Hugh Rose, bailie —— *Nairn* 1689 conv., 1689-1702, [1703-7 (of Newck).

William, provost —— *Nairn* 1665 conv., 1667 conv. (councillor, "appearand [of Clava."

Ross.

Alexander —— *Dornoch* 1670-4.

Andrew —— *Tain* 1628-33 —— 1661-3.

Archibald, merchant burgess —— *Tain* 1612.

Charles (genl.), brother-german of William, Lord Ross —— *Ross-shire* 1709-10, 1710-13, 1713-15 (lieut. of Balnagowan), 1715-22 (colonel), 1727 until his [death s.b. 15 Feb. 1732-3.

Genl. in the army 1712, col. 5th or royal Irish regt. of dragoons 1695-1715, 1729-32, committed to the Tower of London for participation in Sir James Montgomery's plot for the restoration of the Stuarts 1690, a lessee of the poll-tax 1693, deprived of his regt. on the accession of George I., restored by George II., envoy-extraordinary to France (eldest son of George, 11th Lord Ross, by his 2nd wife Jean, eldest dau. of George Ramsay, 2nd Earl of [Dalhousie) ; d. unm. at Bath 5 Aug. 1732 ; bd. at Fearn, Ross-shire.

Charles, of Balnagowan —— *Ross-shire* 1741 until his death s.b. 11 Dec. 1746.

2nd son of George, 13th Lord Ross ; fell at Fontenoy 30 April 1745.

Charles (col.) of Morangie —— *Wick burghs* 1780-4.

Col. 39th foot 1777, a major-general 19 Oct. 1787, lieut.-general 12 Oct. 1793.

Charles (sir), of Balnagowan, bart. —— *Wick burghs* 1786-90 (then captain and younger), 1790-6 (bart.); *Ross-shire* 1796-1802, 1802-6 (major-genl.); *Lin-[lithgow burghs* 1806-7.

7th baronet (on the death of his father, Sir John Lockhart-Ross, M.P. 1761), lt.-genl. in the army 1805, col. 86th regt. ; m. twice, and d. 8 Feb. 1814, leaving issue. See Foster's [Baronetage.

David, of Balnagowan —— *Ross-shire* 1669-74.

Son of David Ross, of Balnagowan, by Margery Fraser, dau. of Hugh, Lord Lovat ; he d. [s.p. 1711, leaving his estate to Charles, M.P. 1709.

Ross—*continued.*

George, of Cromarty —— *Cromartyshire* 1780-4; *Wick burghs* 15 March 1786
[until his death s.b. 30 June same year.
Of Cromarty, by purchase 1772 (son of Andrew Ross of Pitkerrie), died s.p.s. 7 April 1786.

Harie —— *Forres* 1667 conv.

Horatio, of Rossie —— *Aberdeen* (now *Montrose*) *burghs* 1831-2, 1832-4.
Of Netherley, Kincardineshire, J.P., D.L., and for co. Forfar. entered 14th light dragoons 1820, contested Paisley 1835 (son of Hercules Ross, of Rossie Castle, Montrose); m. 1833, [Justine Henriette, dau. of Colin Macrae. esq., of Cornhill, Perthshire, and has issue.

James, of Merkinsche, provost —— *Inverness* 1641.

John —— *Glasgow* 1598 conv.

John —— *Tain* 1650.

John (Mr.) —— *Inverness* 1621.

John, of Balnagowan —— *Linlithgow burghs* 1761-8; (*Linlithgow burghs* and)
[*Lanarkshire* 1768-74.
Sir John Lockhart-Ross, 6th bart. (on the death of his brother, Sir George, 13 Aug. 1778), vice-adm. of the blue, capt. H.M.S. "Tartar," 28 guns, and with it captured in 15 months nine French ships of war; he assumed the additional surname of Ross on succeeding to the estates of his maternal uncle, Genl. Ross; b. 11 Nov. 1721, d. 9 June 1790, having m. 6 Sept. 1762, Elizabeth, dau. of Robert Dundas (V. MELVILLE), of Arniston, lord president of the court of session, and sole heir of her mother, Henrietta, heiress of Lamington (dau. and heir of Sir James Carmichael, bart., by his wife Margaret, dau. and heir of William [Baillie, of Lamington), and had 4 sons. See Foster's Baronetage.

Patrick —— *Perth* 1649, 1650.
(Patrick Ross, sheriff clerk of Perth and of Innernethie by purchase.)

Walter, bailie —— *Tain* 1669-70.

William, eldest son of Alexander Ross, elder, of Easter Ferne, principal bailie
[—— *Tain* 1685 conv.
William, younger, of Easter Ferne —— *Tain* 1689-1702.

Rowan.

Robert —— *Glasgow* 1594 conv.

Rowett or Rowatt.

Robert —— *Glasgow* 1585 conv. and parlt.
Possibly identical with Rowan, last named.

Rule.

John, bailie —— *Queensferry* 1685-6.

Russell.

David (Mr.) —— *St. Andrews* 1579, 1590 conv.

George —— *Pittenweem* 1665 conv. (bailie), 1681-2, councillor.

Robert —— *Stirling* 1678 conv. (provost), 1681-2 " actual trafficker," provost.

Thomas, of Ascog —— *Buteshire* April 1880 until following month, when his [election was declared void.

William (Mr.) —— *St. Andrews* 1586, 1596 conv., 1602 conv., 1604, 1605, 1607, 1608 conv.

Rutherford and Rutherfurd.

(——), laird of Hunthill —— *Roxburghshire* 1630 conv.

Probably father of Sir Thomas Rutherfurd, of Hunthill, who succeeded as 2nd Lord [Rutherfurd.

Alexander —— *Aberdeen* 1583, 1585, 1587, 1597 conv., 1600, 1604, 1605, 1608, [1612 (provost).

Andrew —— *Leith burghs* 1839-41 (advocate for Scotland), 1841-7 (lord advo- [cate 1846), 1847, until apptd. a judge of court of session s.b. 14 April 1851.

Of Crossbill, Lord Rutherfurd of session 1815 and P.C., advocate 27 June 1812, sol.- genl. Scotland 1837, lord advocate 1839-41, 1846-51 ; d. 13 Dec. 1854, having m. Sophia [Frances, dau. of Sir James Stewart, bart., M.P. (see Ireland) ; she d. 10 Oct. 1852.

David (Mr.), *Aberdeen* 1621.

James —— *Elgin* 1617 conv.

James, of Bowland —— *Selkirkshire* 1730-4, apptd. to a crown office of profit [1733.

Commissary Peebles 1733.

John (Mr.) —— *Jedburgh* 1617, 1621.

John (Mr.) —— *Jedburgh* 1639-41 (late provost), 1643 (conv.), 1646-7, 1649-50 [in absence of Mr. John Brown.

John —— *Jedburgh* 1661-3 (bailie), 1665 conv. (provost), 1667 conv. (then [provost), 1669-74.

John, younger, of Rutherfurd —— *Roxburghshire* 1734-41, 1741 until apptd. captain of one of the independent companies in the army before 18 Feb. [following.

Of Edgerston, co. Roxburgh, advocate 20 July 1734, admitted to Lincoln's Inn 20 Feb. 1730-1 (eldest son of Sir John Rutherfurd of that ilk); b. 12 April 1712, accepted an independent command in America, had rank of major, fell at the battle of Ticonderago 1758, having m. Nov. 1737, Ellinor, dau. of Sir Gilbert Elliot, of Minto, lord of session, [and had with other issue John, M.P.

Rutherford and Rutherfurd—*continued.*

John, of Edgerston —— *Selkirkshire* 1802-6 ; *Roxburghshire* 1806-7, 1807-12.

Vice-lieut., co. Roxburgh, col. of militia, admitted to Lincoln's Inn 20 April 1771 (son of John, M.P., last named); d. s.p. 6 May 1834, aged 85, having m. 15 June 1787, Mary [Anne, only dau. of M.-Genl. the Hon. Alexander Leslie (E. LEVEN and MELVILLE).

Richard —— *Jedburgh* 1568 (? then provost).

Robert —— *Jedburgh* 1648.

William —— *Jedburgh* 1583 —— 1612.

Ruthven.

Thomas (sir), of Frieland, knt. —— *Perthshire* 1639-41, 1645-7 (the laird), [1649-51.

Sir Thomas Ruthven, of Freeland, co. Perth (grandson and heir of Alexander, 3rd son of William, 2nd Lord Ruthven, ancestor of the earls of Gowrie), a comissr. for the treaty of Ripon 1641, col. of a regt. sent against the Marquis of Huntly, a comissr. of exchequer 1649, created a peer by Charles II. with the title of Lord Ruthven, of Freeland, between 28 Mar. 1751, and 1 Jan. 1661 ; the patent was burnt with the house of Freeland 14 Mar. 1750, and the limitations are not on record, but as the title was kept on the Union roll it is presumed that the honours were to the heirs general of the patentee's body ; he d. 6 May 1673, having m. Isabel, 3rd dau. of Robert, Lord Balfour, of Burleigh, and had a son and [2 daus. See Foster's Peerage.

William, lord —— *Perth* 1567 (provost), also 1575 conv. (as a baron), [1578 conv.

Earl of Gowrie, so created 23 August 1581 (2nd son of Patrick, 3rd Lord Ruthven and Direlton, the principal assassin of David Rizzio), fled with his father into England after Rizzio's murder ; treasurer for life on the death of the commendator of St. Mary's isle 1571, of the king's privy council 1578, and lieut. of the borders ; the principal actor in "the raid of Ruthven" when James VI. was confined at Ruthven for nearly a year, he was subsequently found guilty of treasonable practices and beheaded 4-28 May 1584 ; he m. at Perth 17 Aug. [1561, Dorothea, 2nd dau. of Henry, Lord Methven, and had issue.

S.

St. Andrews.

(——) the provost of —— *St. Andrews* 1525 —— 1526 —— 1540 —— 1560
[—— 1568.

Salmon.

(——) col. —— *Dumfries, &c.*, 1656-8 (WILLIS).

Saltoun.

William, of —— *Linlithgow* 1357.
(? Sir William Abernethy.)

Sandford.

Daniel Keyte (sir), knt., D.C.L. —— *Paisley* 1834.

Greek Professor University of Glasgow, B.A. Ch. Ch., Oxon, 1820, M.A. 1825 (grand compounder), D.C.L. 1833, knighted 27 Oct. 1830, contested Glasgow 1832 (son of David Sandford, bishop of Edinburgh); b. 3 Feb. 1798, d. 4 Feb. 1838, having m. 2 July 1823, Henrietta, only dau. of Robert Charnock, esq., and had with other issue 2 sons, Sir Francis, [K.C.B., and Sir Herbert Sandford. See Foster's Knightage.

Sandilands.

(Sir William) laird of St. Monanis ——*Fifeshire* 1617.

Son of James Sandilands, and died Oct. 1644, aged 72, and was grandfather of Sir James, [created Lord Abercrombie, 12 Dec. 1647.

William (Mr.), of Hilderstoun —— *Linlithgowshire* 1649.

3rd son of James, 2nd Lord Torphichen. According to Douglas, this family took the [surname and arms of Hamilton of Westport on succeeding to that estate.

Sauser.

William —— *Stirling* 1357.

Scot or Scott.

(——) laird of Abbotshall —— 1593 *bis.*, as a minor baron.

(——) laird of Hartwoodmyres —— *Selkirkshire* 1644-5.

Alexander —— 1473, 1482.

Scot or Scott—*continued.*

Alexander —— *Forfar* 1649, 1650 (or Wm. Luck).

David, of Scotstarvit —— *Crail* (double return 1722); *Fifeshire* 1741-7 (then master); *Aberdeen* (now *Montrose*) *burghs* 1751-4, 1754-61, 1761 until his [death, s.b. 9 Jan. 1767.

> Advocate 19 Jan. 1712 (only son of David Scott, of Scotstarvit) ; m. Lucy, dau. of Sir Robert Gordon, of Gordonstoun, and d. 1 Dec. 1766, having had with other issue a son John, [of Balcomie, M.P. 1754.

David, of Duninald —— *Forfarshire* 1790 until he accepted the Chiltern hundreds s.b. 25 April 1796 ; *Forfar burghs* 1796, 1796-1802, 1802 until his [death s.b. 27 Nov. 1805.

> David Scott (son of Robert, M.P. 1733, and grandson of Patrick Scott, of Duninald, by Margaret, dau. of Sir Archibald Hope, bart., of Rankeilour), M.P. co. Forfar, chairman of the E.I.C. board of directors ; d. 5 Oct. 1805, having m. Louisa (sister of Lady Sibbald), 2nd dau. of William Delagard, esq., and widow of late Benjamin Jervis, esq. ; she d. 23 March 1803, having had with 3 daus. an only son, Sir David Scott, of Duninald, K.C.H., 2nd baronet (on the death of his uncle, Sir James Sibbald), M.P. Great Yarmouth 1806-7. [See Foster's Baronetage.

Francis (sir), of Thirlestane, bart. —— *Selkirkshire* 1669-74, 1685-6, 1693-[1702.

> Sir Francis Scott, of Thirlestane (eldest son of Patrick Scott, M.P. 1648-9) cr. a baronet of Nova Scotia 22 April 1666, to him and the heirs male of his body, master of works 1704 ; b. 11 May 1645, d. 7 March 1712, having m. (contract 27 Nov. 1673) Henrietta, 6th dau. of William Kerr, 3rd Earl of Lothian ; she d. 30 June 1741, aged 90, having had an only [surviving son, Sir William. See NAPIER in Foster's Peerage.

Francis, of Mertoun House —— *Roxburghshire* 1841-7, *Berwickshire* 1847-52, [1852-7, 1857-9.

> Hon. Francis Scott, of Sandhurst Grange, Surrey, J.P., and of Mertoun House, co. Berwick J.P., and J.P. Roxburgh, bar.-at-law of the Middle Temple 1832, contested Roxburghshire 1837 (5th son of Hugh, 4th baron Polwarth, M.P. 1780); b. 31 Jan. 1806, m. and [has issue. See Foster's Peerage.

Gideon, of Highchester —— *Roxburghshire* 1650.

> Knighted 29 Aug. 1660 ; sheriff principal co. Roxburgh (son of Sir William Scott, of Harden) ; m. Margaret, dau. of Thomas Hamilton, of Preston, and d. 1672, leaving with [other issue a son, Walter, cr. Earl of Tarras. See POLWARTH in Foster's Peerage.

Henry Francis (younger), of Harden —— *Roxburghshire* 1826, 1826-30, 1830-1, [1831-2.

> 5th Lord Polwarth (on the death of his father, Hugh, 28 Dec. 1841, see below), a representative peer, lord-lieutenant Selkirkshire, and a lord-in-waiting to the Queen ; b. 1 Jan. [1800, d. 16 Aug. 1867, leaving issue. See Foster's Peerage.

Scott—*continued.*

Henry John Montagu Douglas, commonly called Lord Henry Scott ——
[*Selkirkshire* 1861-5, 1865-8. See also England M.P.

2nd son of Walter Francis, 5th Duke of Buccleuch and 7th Duke of Queensberry, K.G., M.P. (south) Hants since 1868, capt. Midlothian yeo. 1856-76 ; b. 5 Nov. 1832 ; m. and has [issue. See Foster's Peerage.

Hugh —— *Irvine* 1571 conv. —— 1593 —— 1617 conv. and parlt.

Hugh, of Galashiels —— *Selkirk* 1681-2.

Son of James Scott ; he m. Isabella, dau. of Sir Thomas Scott, of Cavers, and had a [son, Sir James, probably M.P. 1698, 1702.

Hugh, younger, of Harden —— *Berwickshire* 1780-4.

Hugh Scott, 5th Baron Polwarth, by virtue of a decision of the House of Lords June 1835, declared unduly elected for Berwickshire 1781, but re-elected, assumed the additional surname and arms of Hepburne on succeeding to the estates of his great-grandmother, the Countess of Tarras (son of Walter Scott, of Harden, M.P.) ; b. 10 Sept. 1758, d. 28 Dec. 1841, having m. 29 Sept. 1795, Henrietta, dau. of Hans Moritz, Count von Bruhl, envoy from the elector of Saxony and the king of Poland at the court of St. James's, knight of the White Eagle, by his wife, Alicia Maria, Countess-Dowager of Egremont (ext.) ; she d. 19 Aug. 1853, having had with other issue (see Foster's Peerage) Henry Francis, M.P. 1826, and Francis, M.P. [1841.

(Sir James), laird of Balwery —— 1593 bis., 1594 as a minor baron.

Knighted by James VI. at Queen Anne's coronation 1590, com. with the Earls of Angus, Errol, etc., at the battle of Glenlivet 1594, for which he obtained a remission 24 Feb. 1595, was one of Bothwell's accomplices (son of Sir Wm. Scott, of Balwery) ; m. Elizabeth. dau. of [Sir Andrew Wardlaw, of Torrie, and had issue.

James —— *Selkirk* 1593.

James —— *Irvine* 1630 conv.

James, of Logie, merchant burgess —— *Montrose* 1640-1.

James Scott, of Logie (son of James Scott, of Logie) ; b. 1593, m. 1st Margaret Ramsay, [of Balmain, and 2ndly Jean Tailyour, of Borrowfield, and had issue.

James, of Logie —— *Forfarshire* 1693-1702.

Grandson of James, M.P., last named ; m. 1670, Agnes, 4th dau. of Sir Alexander [Falconer, bart., of Glenfarquhar, and had a son, James, M.P., next named.

James, of Gala —— *Roxburghshire* (or *sheriffdom of Teviotdale*) 1698-1702.

James, of Logie —— *Montrose* 1702-7 (1707-8, 1st. parlt. G.B.), 1710-11 (unseated) ; *Forfarshire* 1716-22 (younger), 1722-7, 1727 until his death s.b. [1 March 1732-3.

Son of James, M.P., last named (probably son of Hugh, M.P. 1681-2) ; m. Isabella, dau. [of Sir Alexander Bannerman, of Elsick, bart., and d. 17 Jan. 1733, having had issue.

Scott—*continued.*

James (colonel), of Comiestoun —— *Kincardineshire* 1713-15, 1715-22, 1722-7, [1727-34.

Lieut.-genl. in the army 1743, envoy to Poland (2nd son of Hercules Scott, of Brotherton); [m. Margaret Wallace, of Ingliston.

John —— *Rutherglen* 1628-33, 1644.

John, of Langschaw —— *Roxburghshire* 1665 conv.

John, maltman —— *Rutherglen* 1689 conv., 1689 to 1702.

John, of Wooll —— *Roxburghshire* (or *sheriffdom of Teviotdale*) 1693-1702.

Probably youngest son of Sir William Scott, baron of Harden, M.P. 1641 ; he m. Agnes, [only dau. of Robert Scott, of Harwood.

John (major-genl.), of Balcomie —— *Caithness-shire* 1754-61 (captain of the royal regiment commanded by Gen. James St. Clair); *Wick burghs* 1761-8 (col. 3rd regiment of guards); *Fifeshire* 1768-74 (col. 26th regt. of foot), 1774 [(major-genl.) until his death s.b. 24 Jan. 1776.

Major-genl. in the army 1770 (2nd son of David Scott, of Scotstarvet, M.P. 1741) ; m. 2ndly, 5 Nov. 1770, Lady Mary Boyd, only dau. of James, 14th earl of Errol; d. 7 Dec. 1775, leaving by his 1st wife, with other issue, Henrietta, duchess of Portland, and Lucy, countess of Moray, the duke of Portland had royal licence (5 Sept. 1795) to assume the [additional surname of Scott, together with the arms, but the latter were never exemplified.

John Douglas Montagu Douglas, commonly called Lord John Scott —— [*Roxburghshire* 1835-7.

2nd son of Charles, 4th Duke of Buccleuch, K.T., contested Roxburghshire 1832; b. 13 July 1809, d. s.p. 3 Jan. 1860, having m. 16 March 1836, Alicia Anne, elder dau. of John [Spottiswoode, esq., of Spottiswoode, co. Berwick. See Foster's Peerage.

Patrick, of Thirlestane —— *Selkirkshire* 1648-9.

Of Tanlawhill and of Howpaisley by devise of his cousin, Robert Scott, and also of Thirlestane by purchase (son of Walter Scott, by his wife Janet, dau. of Sir Patrick Porteous, of Hackshaw) ; m. Isabel, dau. of Sir John Murray, of Blackbarony, bart., and d. 22 June [1666, leaving with other issue a son, Sir Francis, M.P. 1669.

Patrick (sir), of Ancrum, bart. —— *Roxburghshire* 1685-6 (of Lang Newton), 1689 conv., 1689 until 28th April 1693, when his seat was declared vacant [because he had not signed the assurance.

It is not quite clear whether the above entry refers to the 1st or 2nd bart., as the blue book is evidently in error. Sir Patrick, a lawyer of eminence, and to whom the entry is evidently intended to refer, became 2nd bart. on the death of his father, Sir John, 1712. See Foster's [Baronetage.

Robert —— *Irvine* 1543.

Robert (sir), of Thirlestane —— *Selkirkshire* 1607, as a minor baron.

Son of Robert, of Thirlstane, warden-depute of the West Borders; m. twice, and had issue.

Robert, of Whitslaid —— *Selkirkshire* 1639-41, 1643 conv.

He married Jean, natural sister of Walter, Earl of Buccleuch.

Scott—*continued.*

Robert, bailie —— *Selkirk* 1702-7.

Robert, of Duninald —— *Forfarshire* 1733-4.

Supported the Hanoverian interest in the '45 (son of Patrick Scott, of Rossie); m. Anne Middleton, of Seaton, co. Aberdeen, and d. Dec., 1780, leaving a son, David, M.P. 1790.

Thomas —— *Selkirk* 1568.

Thomas, late bailie —— *Selkirk* 10 Sept. to 17 Nov. 1641, 1643-4 conv., 1645-7, [1649.

Thomas, of Whitslaid —— *Selkirkshire* 1661-3.

(Sir Walter), laird of Buccleuch —— 1597 conv., as a minor baron.

Sir Walter Scott, of Buccleuch (descended—but how is not shown—from Richard le Scot, one of the barons of Scotland who swore fealty to Edward I. of England 1296), acquired the lands of Murthockstoun. now Murdistoun, co. Lanark, by his wife, and the assumed the bend Az. charging it with the crescents and star, the arms of Scot (see also " Scott of Buccleuch," by Wm. Fraser); knighted at the coronation of Anne, queen of James I. 1590, who appointed him warden of the West Marches in 1599. On the accession of James VI. to England he raised a regiment of his followers, with whom he served in the Netherlands under Maurice, Prince of Orange, and was raised to the dignity of a peerage of Scotland as Lord Scott, of Buccleuch, 16 Mar. 1606; he d. 5-25 Dec. 1611, having m. Margaret, dau. of Sir William Ker, of Cessford, sister of Robert, 1st Earl of Roxburgh, and had with 2 daus. an only son, Walter, 2nd Lord Scot, created Earl of Buccleuch, Lord Whytchester and Eskdale, in the peerage of Scotland, by patent, dated at Newmarket 16 Mar. 1619, which was extended by [a subsequent patent or charter to heirs female. See Foster's Peerage.

Walter (col.), of Hartwoodburne —— *Selkirkshire* 1646-7 (laird), 1648-9.

Walter (sir), of Whitslaid —— *Selkirkshire* 1645-6 (laird), 1650, 1651.

Walter, late provost, councillor —— *Jedburgh* 1700-2, 1702-7 (provost).

Walter, of Harden —— *Roxburghshire* 1747-54, 1754-61, 1761 until receiver [and cashier of the excise in Scotland, s.b. 20 June 1765.

Son of Hon. Walter Scott, of Harden and Highchester, son of Walter, Earl of Tarras (see [Foster's Peerage, POLWARTH); d. 25 Jan. 1793, leaving a son Hugh, M.P. 1780.

William —— *Irvine* 1540 —— 1583.

William, bailie —— *Selkirk* 1639, until disabled " by sickness " s.b. 10 Sept. [1641.

William (sir), of Harden, knt. —— *Selkirkshire* 1641, 1643-4 conv., 1644-6 [(laird).

Sir William Scot, baron of Harden (grandson of William, 2nd son of Robert Scot, of Strickshaws, who obtained from his brother Walter, of Synton, a disposition of the lands and barony of Harden), knighted by James VI., a commissioner for the treaty of Ripon 1641, sheriff of Selkirk 1647, fined by Oliver Cromwell £3,000; m. 1st. Agnes, dau. of Sir Gideon Murray, of Elibank, treasurer depute of Scotland, temp. James VI.; he m. 2ndly, Margaret, dau. of William Ker, of Linton, who d. s.p.; he d. 1655, having had with other issue Sir [William, next named, Sir Gideon, M.P. 1660.

Scott—*continued.*

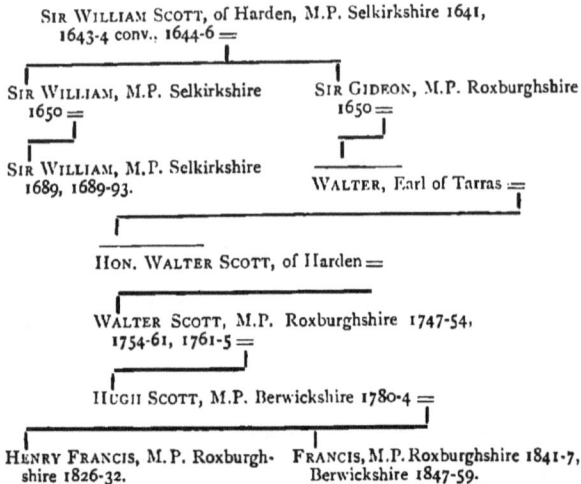

SIR WILLIAM SCOTT, of Harden, M.P. Selkirkshire 1641,
1643-4 conv., 1644-6 =

SIR WILLIAM, M.P. Selkirkshire   SIR GIDEON, M.P. Roxburghshire
1650 =   1650 =

SIR WILLIAM, M.P. Selkirkshire
1689, 1689-93.   WALTER, Earl of Tarras =

HON. WALTER SCOTT, of Harden =

WALTER SCOTT, M.P. Roxburghshire 1747-54,
1754-61, 1761-5 =

HUGH SCOTT, M.P. Berwickshire 1780-4 =

HENRY FRANCIS, M.P. Roxburgh-   FRANCIS, M.P. Roxburghshire 1841-7,
shire 1826-32.   Berwickshire 1847-59.

William (sir), younger, of Harden —— *Selkirkshire* 1650.

Knighted by Charles II. after the restoration (son of Sir William, last named); m.
Christian, 3rd dau. of Robert, 6th Lord Boyd, and had with other issue Sir William, M.P.
[1689.

William (sir), younger, of Harden —— *Selkirkshire* 1689 conv., 1689 until
28 April 1693, when his seat was declared vacant because he had not signed
[the assurance.

Engaged in Argyle's rebellion, but obtained a remission 12 Dec. 1685 (son of Sir William
Scott, M.P. 1650); m. Jean, only dau. of John Nisbet, of Dirleton, he d. s.p. 1707, she
[re-m. to Sir William Scott, of Thirlestane.

William, of Ardross —— *Fifeshire* 1648 (laird) —— 1661-3.

(? Anna, his 2nd dau., m. 11 July 1661 to Sir David Carmichael, of Hyndford, treasurer
[depute to Chas. II.)

William (sir), laird of Clerkingtoun, senator of the college of justice —— *Had-*
[*dington constabulary* 1644-7, 1648 (laird); *Edinburghshire* 1650-1.

Eldest son of Laurence Scott, of Harprig (advocate, clerk of session of the privy counci
and of parliament), ordinary lord 8 June 1649, knighted by Charles I. Nov. 1641 ; m. twice,
[and d. 23 Dec. 1656, leaving issue.

William, of Hartwoodmyres —— *Selkirkshire* 1667 conv.

Scott—*continued.*

William (sir), of Ancrum, Roxburghshire, bart. —— *Roxburghshire* 1859 65, 1865-8, 1868 until he accepted the stewardship of the manor of Northstead, [Yorks, s.b. 2 March 1870, see also England M.P.

6th baronet (on the death of his father, Sir John, 1814); M.P. Carlisle 1829-30 and as above ; b. 26 July 1803, d. 12 Oct. 1871, having m. 1828, Elizabeth, dau. and heir of David Anderson, of Balgay, co. Forfar; she d. 11 April 1878, leaving with other issue a son, Sir [William Monteath Scott. 7th bart See Foster's Baronetage.

Scougall.

James (Mr.), advocate, one of the commissaries of Edinburgh —— *Kintore* [1693-1702.

Advocate 8 June 1687, seven years commissar of Aberdeen, an ordinary lord of session 9 [June 1696 (son of John Scougall, Lord Whytekirk of session); d. 23 Dec. 1702.

Scroger.

Richard —— *Crail* 1357.

Scrogs.

Johnne of —— *Aberdeen* 1445.

Scrope.

Adrian (col.), one of his highness' council —— *sheriffdom of Linlithgow, Stirling,* [*and Clackmannan* 1659-60 (WILLIS).

Of Wormsley, Oxon—one of the council of the lord protector Cromwell,—" the regicide," hanged, drawn, and quartered at Charing Cross, 17 Oct. 1660 (eldest son of Robert Scrope, of Wormsley); baptized at Lewknor 12 Jan. 1600-1, m. at St. Giles' in the Fields 29 Nov. 1624, Mary, dau. of Robert Waller, of Beaconsfield, Bucks, and had issue; ancestor of the Earl of [Westmorland.

Scrymgeour.

(————) constable of St. Andrews —— *Forfarshire* 1594 (as a minor baron), [1608 conv.

Alexander —— *Dundee* 1579, 1583, 1585 conv., 1586 conv.

Burgess of Dundee, named in the entail of the barony of Dudhope, etc., 1565.

James —— *Dundee* 1491, 1492.

Probably of Dudhope, constable of Dundee (son of James Scrimgeour) ; m. Isabella, 3rd [dau. of Andrew, 3rd Lord Gray, and d. 1503, leaving a son James, next named.

(**James**), constable of Dundee —— 1543, 1544 (a lord of the articles).

Son of James, M.P., last named; m. Mariot Stewart, from whom he was divorced before 1544, [and had 2 daus.

James, of Balbewchy —— *Dundee* 1569 conv.

James (sir), of Dudhope —— 1594 conv., 1597 conv. (3), 1598 conv. (bis), 1604 the laird, sat as a minor baron —— *Dundee* 1600, 1605 conv. (as constable of Dundee) ; *Forfarshire* 1605 (Sir James of Dudhope), 1607 (as constable of [Dundee).

Son of John Scrimgeour, of Glaster, after of Dudhope ; m. Margaret, dau of Sir Robert [Carnegie of Kinnaird, and had Sir John, next named.

Scrymgeour—*continued*.

John (sir), of Dudhope, constable of Dundee —— *Forfarshire* 1612, 1617, 1621
[(as constable) ; *Argyllshire* 1628-33 (Sir John).

Viscount of Dudhope, and Lord Scrimgeour. so cr. 15 Nov. 1641. (son of James, last named) ; d. 7 March 1643, having m. Margaret Seton, of Parbroath, co. Fife, and had a son [James. 2nd visct., wounded at Marston Moor, father of John, cr. Earl of Dundee, &c.

Scrymsoure.

John, of Kirktoune, provost —— *Dundee* 1681-2 (bailie), 1702 (provost), 1702-7.

Probably son of John S. of Kirkton ; he m. Magdalene, dau. of Alexander Wedderburn, of Kingcussie, &c., and had a son, Dr. Alexander Scrimgeour. See Douglas' Peerage,
[vol. i. 467.

Selwyn.

George Augustus, of Chesterfield St., Westminster —— *Wigtown burghs* and
[*city of Gloucester*, sat for latter 1768-74, see England M.P.

The celebrated wit, &c., M.P. Ludgershall 1747-54, 1780-91, Gloucester 1754-74 (son of [Col. John Selwyn, of Matson, co. Glouc.) ; d. unm. 25 Jan. 1791, aged 72.

Sempill.

Andrew —— *Renfrew* 1640, 1644 conv.

Andrew —— *Renfrew* 1661.

John —— *Dumbarton* 1628-33, 1630 conv., 1639-41 (provost), 1643-4 conv.,
[1644 (provost), 1646-7, 1649-50 (or James Campbell).

William, of Fowlewood —— *Dumbartonshire* 1617, *Renfrewshire* 1621, the
[laird.

William, of Foulwood —— *Dumbartonshire* 1643 conv., 1645-7 (laird), 1648-9.

Seton.

Alexander (Mr.), of Gargunnock —— *Stirlingshire* 1612.

Sir Alexander Seton, of Kilcreuch, knighted by Charles I. at Holyrood 12 July 1633, had the barony of Gargunnock from his father, was admitted a lord of session 14 Feb. 1626, and resigned 6 June 1637 (son of James Seton, of Touch) ; he m. Marian, dau. of Wm. Maule, of Glaster, and had a son Alexander, father of Sir Walter, M.P. 1665,'cr. a bart. 1663.

Alexander (sir), of Pitmedden, senator of the college of justice —— *Aberdeen*-
[*shire* 1681-2, 1685-6.

Sir Alexander Seton, of Pitmedden, knighted by Charles II. 1664, advocate 10 Dec. 1664, a senator college of justice, as Lord Pitmedden, 13 Nov. 1677, a lord of justiciary 5 July 1682, cr. a bart. of Nova Scotia 15 Jan. 1684 (or 11 Dec. 1683, according to Milne's list), with remainder to his issue male (son of John Seton, of Pitmedden, who was killed at the battle of Dee, June 1639) ; d. in 1719, having m. Margaret, dau. and heir of William Lauder, one of the principal clerks of session, and had with other issue (see Foster's Baronetage)
[a son William, M.P. 1702.

Seton—*continued.*

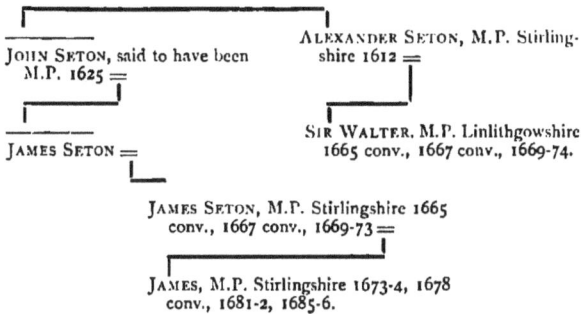

```
┌──────────────────────────────┬──────────────────────────────┐
│ ─────────                    │ ALEXANDER SETON, M.P. Stirling-│
│ JOHN SETON, said to have been│ shire 1612 =                   │
│ M.P. 1625 =                  │                                │
│                              │                                │
│ ┌─────────                  │ ┌──────────────────────────────│
│ │ ─────────                 │ │ SIR WALTER. M.P. Linlithgowshire│
│ │ JAMES SETON =             │ │ 1665 conv., 1667 conv., 1669-74.│
│ └──                         │ └──                             │
```

JAMES SETON, M.P. Stirlingshire 1665
conv., 1667 conv., 1669-73 =

JAMES, M.P. Stirlingshire 1673-4, 1678
conv., 1681-2, 1685-6.

David, merchant burgess —— *Burntisland* 1665 conv., 1667 conv., 1669 until [his death s.b. 25 July 1670.

(George) lord —— *Edinburgh* 1558, provost.

George, Lord Seton, a commissioner to witness the marriage of Q. Mary with the Dauphin of France, on the Queen's return to Scotland was sworn P.C. and constituted master of her household ; after the murder of Lord Darnley the Queen and Bothwell went to Seton, where they passed some days, and where their marriage contract was signed ; was of those who assisted the Queen after her escape from Lochleven, and joined the association on her behalf; after the battle of Langside he retired to Flanders ; in 1570 he was in Scotland actively engaged in the Queen's cause ; ambassador to France 1583 ; d. 8 Jan. 1584-5, bd. at Seton, having m. Isabel, dau. of Sir William Hamilton. of Sanquhar, high treasurer of Scotland ; she d. 12 Nov. 1606, having had with other issue (see EGLINTON, Foster's Peerage) Robert, Lord Seton, cr. Earl of Winton, Sir John, of Barns, an extraordinary lord of session, [Alexander, cr. Earl of Dunfermline, and Sir William of Kyllismore, M.P.

James (elder), of Touch —— *Stirlingshire* 1665 conv., 1667 conv., 1669 until his [death s.b. 15 Nov. 1673.

Son of James Seton, of Touch, and father, by —— dau. of Sir Archibald Stirling, of [Keir, of a son James, M.P., next named.

James, "now of Touch" —— *Stirlingshire* 1673-4, 1678 conv., 1681-2, 1685-6.

Married —— dau. of —— Stirling, and had issue.

John (sir) —— *Haddington constabulary* 1625 conv.

Probably 5th son of Robert, 1st Earl of Winton.

(?John), laird of Touch —— *Dumbartonshire* 1593 and 1596 conv., as a minor [baron.

Died 1622, son of James Seton, of Touch, and father, by Elizabeth, dau. of Sir George [Home, of Wedderburn, of James of Touch, who was father of James, M.P. 1665.

Michael, late bailie —— *Burntisland* 1685-6.

Seton—*continued.*

Walter (sir), of Abercorn, knt. bart. —— *Linlithgowshire* 1665 conv., 1667 conv.,
[1669-74.

Sir Walter Seton, of Northbank (7th in descent from Sir Alexander Seton, eldest son of Alexander, 1st Earl of Huntly), had a charter of the barony of Abercorn, co. Linlithgow, 1662, cr. a baronet of Nova Scotia 3 June 1663; m. Christian, dau. of George Dundas, of
[Dundas. See Foster's Baronetage.

William (sir) —— *Haddington* 1577 (then provost), 1598 conv., 1605 (then of Kylismure); *Haddington constabulary* 1617 conv. and parlt.

Sheriff co. Edinburgh (5th son of George, Lord Seton); m.   , dau. of Stirling, of Glorat, and d. 1634, aged 73, leaving a son, Sir William, postmaster, of
[Scotland.

William, provost —— *Haddington* 1661-3, 1665 conv., 1667 conv.
Of the family of Northrigg.

William, younger, of Pitmedden —— *Aberdeenshire* 1702-7, 1707-8, 1st parlt.
[Great Britain.

2nd baronet (on the death of his father, Sir Alexander, M.P. 1719), a commissioner to treat for the union, etc.; m. Catherine, dau. of Sir Thomas Burnet, of Leys, bart.; he d.
[1744, ancestor of Sir James Lumsden Seton, bart. See Foster's Baronetage.

Shank.

Henry —— *Kinghorn* 1643 conv.

Henry Schank (son of Henry Schank); m. 1609, Janet, dau. of Robert Cuninghame, of
[Woodfield, and had issue.

Sharp.

John, of Collistoun, merchant burgess, councillor —— *Dumfries* 1686.

John, of Hoddom —— *Dumfries* (or *Nithsdale*) *sheriffdom and stewartry of*
[*Annandale* 1702, 1702-7.
Of Hoddam, by purchase 1690.

Matthew (Sharpe), of Hoddam (lieut.-genl.) —— *Dumfries burghs* 1833-4,
[1835-7, 1837-41.

Genl. Sharpe, major 28th dragoons 1796, lt.-col. in the army 1799, col. 1809, major-genl. 1812, lieut.-genl. 1825, genl. 1841; d. 12 Feb. 1845, having m. Jane, younger dau. of Godfrey
[Higgins, esq., F.S.A., of Skellow Grange, Yorkshire.

Thomas (Shairp), of Houston —— *Linlithgowshire* 1699-1702, 1703-7.
Father of Sir Walter Shairp, consul at St. Petersburg.

William, of Houston —— *Linlithgowshire* 1678 conv.

William (sir), of Tullibodie (or Stony Hill) —— *Clackmannanshire* 1681-2.
Sir William Sharp, of Scotscraig, cr. a baronet 21 April 1683.

Shaw.

Alexander (sir), of Sauchie, knt. —— *Clackmannanshire* 1639-40 (to serve in
[the absence of Sir Thomas Hope, of Kerse), 1643 conv., 1644-7 (laird)·
He m. 2ndly, Elizabeth, dau. of Wm. Cunningham, of Glengarnock, and had a son John.

James, of Sauchie —— *Stirling* 1474.

James —— *Stirling* 1572 conv.   ·

John, of Greenock —— *Renfrewshire* 1643-4 conv., 1644 (laird), 1649, 1667
[conv. (elder).

> Only son and heir of James Shaw, who d. 1620, by his wife Margaret, dau. of Hugh
> Montgomery, of Haslehead ; he m. Helen, dau. of John Houston of that ilk, and d. 1679,
> [having had with other issue a son, Sir John, next named.

John (sir), of Greenock —— *Renfrewshire* 1669-74, 1678 conv. (then younger),
[1681-2 (a baronet).

> Sir John Shaw, of Greenock, bart., so cr. 28 June 1687, lt.-col. of regt. of horse commanded
> by the Earl of Dunfermline, in the army of King Charles 1651, knighted at the battle of
> Worcester for his valour and loyalty 3 Sept. (son of John, M.P., last named) ; he m. Jean,
> dau. of Sir William Mure, of Rowallan, and d. 1694, leaving with other issue Sir John,
> [father of Sir John, M.P., next named.

John (sir), knt. bart. of Greenock —— *Renfrewshire* 1708-10 ; *Clackmannanshire*
[1722-7 ; *Renfrewshire* 1727-34.

> 3rd baronet (on the death of his father, Sir John, 1702) ; d. 5 April 1752, having m.
> (contract 1 March 1700) Margaret, dau. of Sir Hugh Dalrymple, of North Berwick ; she d.
> [8 Oct. 1757, and their only surviving child, Marion, m. to Charles, 8th Lord Cathcart.

Sheills.

Archibald, provost —— *Peebles* 1702-7.

Sherar.

John —— *Stirling* 1612.

Sheroun.

Walter —— *Banff* 1667 conv.

Sheves.

Thomas, of Muretoun —— *Inverness* 1643 conv;

Shorte.

John —— *Stirling* 1646-7, 1648 (provost), 1649, 1650, 1651.
SCOTCH MEMBERS.   R R

Sibbald.

Alexander (Mr.) —— *St. Andrews* 1571 conv.

Simpson.

Alexander —— *Dysart* 1628-33.

David (Symsoun) —— *Dysart* 1612, 1617, 1621.

David (Simson), merchant trafficker —— *Dysart* 1639, 1643 conv., 1645, 1645-7 [1650 (or John Gray), 1665 conv. (councillor).

Donald (or Daniel), younger —— *Fortrose* 1692-1702.

George —— *Anstruther Wester* 1617.

George (Simson), bailie —— *Dysart* 1678 conv.

James —— *Dundee* 1640, 1645.

Thomas —— *Kilrenny* 1628-33; *Anstruther Easter* 1639-41 (town clerk).

William (Simson) —— *Pittenweem* 1594 conv.

William —— *Dysart* 1640-1 (in the absence of the commissioner, David Symsone, through sickness), 1644, 1645, 1648-9, 1650-1, 1661-3 (bailie), [1667 conv.

Sinclair and St. Clair.

Archibald (sir 1696-8), advocate —— *Wick* 1690-1702.
    Advocate 4 March 1686, 2nd son of Sir Robert Sinclair, bart., of Longformacus, advocate.

Edward, of Essintoy —— *Orkney and Zetlandshire* 1617.

George (sir), of Clyth —— *Caithness-shire* 1681-2, (of Ulbster, or Bilbster) 1685-6, [1702 until his death s.b. 1 Oct. 1706.
    2nd son of Sir Patrick Sinclair, of Ulbster; he m. 1682, Jean, dau. of William Sinclair, [of Dunbeath, and died s.p.

George (sir), of Ulbster —— *Caithness-shire* 1811-12, 1818-20, 1831-2, 1833-4, [1835-7 (younger), 1837-41 (a baronet).
    2nd baronet (on the death of his father, Sir John, M.P., 21 Dec. 1835); b. 28 Aug. 1790, d. 9 Oct. 1868, having m. 1 May 1816, Lady Catherine Camilla Tollemache, sister of Lionel, 6th Earl of Dysart; she d. 17 March 1863, leaving with other issue a son, Sir John, M.P. [1870.

Hew, of Inglistoune, provost —— *Annan* 1661-3, 1665 conv., 1667 conv.

James (sir), of Murkhill —— *Caithness-shire* 1641, 1646-7 (laird), 1661.
    Son of Sir James Sinclair; m. (contract 18 Oct. 1634), Jean, dau. of William Stewart, of Mains and Burray, brother of the 1st Earl of Galloway, and had a son John, succeeded as [8th Earl of Caithness, etc.

Sinclair—*continued.*

JOHN SINCLAIR, of Ulbster, M.P. Caithness-shire 1678 conv., &c.

SIR JOHN SINCLAIR, of Ulbster, M.P. Caithness-shire 1780-4, 1790-6, 1802-6, 1807-11 ==

SIR GEORGE, 2nd bart., M.P. Caithness-shire 1811-12, 1818-20, 1831-2, 1833-4, 1835-7, 1837-41==

SIR JOHN GEORGE TOLLEMACHE SINCLAIR, 3rd bart., M.P. Caithness-shire since 1869.

James, of Freswick —— *Caithness-shire* probably from 1689 until his death s.b. [17 April 1693.

Son of William Sinclair, of Rattar, by his 2nd wife, Jane Cunnyngham.

James, of Stempster —— *Caithness-shire* 1703-7.

According to the Baronetages, he succeeded as 3rd baronet, but see Foster's Baronetage, "CHAOS" (2nd son of Sir William, M.P. 1661); m. Isabel, dau. of Sir Archibald Muir, [provost of Edinburgh, and d. 1742, leaving issue.

James (St. Clair), lt.-genl. —— *Dysart burghs* 1722-7, 1727-34; *Sutherlandshire* 1736-41 (as of Balblair and a colonel), 1741-7 (of Balblair then brig.-genl.); *Dysart burghs* 1747-54 (then lt.-genl.); *Fifeshire* 1754-61 (of Sinclair, Fife-[shire), 1761-3, until his death s.b. 7 Jan. 1763.

Genl. St. Clair (2nd son of Henry, Lord Sinclair, see Foster's Peerage), col. 1722, major-genl. 1741, lt.-genl. 1745, genl. 1761, commanded 3rd regt. foot guards 1734-7, col. 22nd foot 1734-7, 1st or royal Scots regt. of foot 1737-62, quartermaster-genl. British forces in Flanders 1745, ambassador at Vienna and Turin, governor of Cork, a major-genl. on the staff in Ireland, became entitled to the honour of Lord Sinclair 1750, on the death of his brother John, M.P. 1708; d. s.p. at Dysart 30 Nov. 1762, having m. Janet, widow of Sir John Baird, of Newbyth, yst dau. of Sir David Dalrymple, of Hailes, bart., king's advo-[cate; she d. s.p. 8 Jan. 1766, aged 68.

James, of Braelangwell —— *Caithness-shire* 1826-30.

Lt.-col. Ross and Caithness, &c. militia, D.L. cos. Cromarty and Caithness, major in the army, (3rd son of James, 12th Earl of Caithness); b. 24 Oct. 1797, d. s.p. 18 Jan. 1856, having [m. 9 March 1819, Elizabeth, dau. of George Tritton, esq., of West Hill, Wandsworth.

John, bailie —— *Edinburgh* 1633.

(Sir John St. Clair), laird of Hermestoun or Hirdingstoun —— *Haddington* [*constabulary* 1644-5.

He m. Elizabeth Sinclair, and had a son John, who m. Catherine, sole heir of John, 6th [Lord Sinclair, ancestor of the present peer. See Foster's Peerage.

Sinclair— *continued.*

John (sir), of Dunbeath —— *Caithness-shire* 1649.

Of Dunbeath, etc., co. Caithness, and of Genzies, Ross-shire, a merchant, said to have been created a baronet of Nova Scotia 2 Jan. 1631, by patent (not registered), to the heirs male of his body, which title appears however to have been assumed by the Sinclairs of Mey (nephew of Sir William Sinclair, of Mey, ancestor of the Earls of Caithness); he m. 1st Christian Mouat, dau. of the laird of Bucholly, he m. 2ndly Catherine Fraser, dau. of Hugh, 8th Lord Lovat (she re-m. 1st, to Robert Viscount Arbuthnott, and 2ndly, 1663, to Andrew, 3rd Lord Fraser); by his first wife he had an only child, Margaret, m. to Hugh Rose, of [Kilravock. See "CHAOS," Foster's Baronetage.

John, of Ulbster —— *Caithness-shire* 1678 conv.

Brother of George Sinclair, M.P. 1681, etc.

John, younger, of Stevinston —— *Lanarkshire* 1702-7.

4th bart. (on the death of his father, Sir Robert, M.P., 1689); m. Martha, dau. and heir of Sir John Lockhart, of Castlehill, co. Lanark, Lord Castlehill of session, and d. 1726, leaving [issue. See Foster's Baronetage.

John —— *Dysart burghs* 1708, until declared to be incapable of taking his seat, [being the eldest son of a peer of Scotland, s.b. 16 Jan. 1709-10.

Master of Sinclair, engaged in the rebellion of 1715, pardoned 1726, the title remained dormant from his father's death 1723 until his own decease 2 Nov. 1750, s.p., married twice. [See Foster's Peerage.

John (sir), of Ulbster, bart. —— *Caithness-shire* 1780-4, 1790-6 (then a baronet), 1802-6, 1807 until apptd. receiver of taxes in Scotland s.b. 26 Aug. 1811. [See also England M.P.

Rt. Hon. Sir John Sinclair, of Ulbster, bart., so created 14 Feb. 1786, with remainder to the male issue of his daughters respectively, P.C. 29 Aug. 1810, advocate Edinburgh 1775, admitted to Lincoln's Inn 22 March 1774, bar.-at-law 9 May 1782, M.P. Lostwithiel 1784-90, and Petersfield 1797-1802, etc., as above, LL.D. Glasgow 1788, D.C.L. Oxon, F.R. & A.S., president board of agriculture, director bank of Scotland, captured with his tutor 1802, and taken before Buonaparte as spies, author of various literary works (only surviving son of George Sinclair, of Ulbster, heritable sheriff of Caithness); b. 10 May 1754, d. 21 Dec. 1835, having m. twice, and had with other issue a son, Sir George, M.P. 1811. See Foster's [Baronetage.

John George Tollemache (sir), of Ulbster —— *Caithness-shire* 1869-74, [1874-80, and since 1880.

3rd bart. (on the death, 9 Oct. 1868, of his father, George, M.P. 1811), late Scots guards, [vice-lieut. Caithness-shire since 1876, has issue. See Foster's Baronetage.

Robert (sir), of Longformacus, knt. bart. —— *Berwickshire* 1665 conv., 1667 [conv., 1669-74.

Sir Robert Sinclair, of Longformacus, an advocate of the court of session (son of James Sinclair, of Longformacus), created a baronet of Nova Scotia 10 Dec. 1664, with remainder to his issue males; he m. 1st, Elizabeth Douglas, heiress of Blackerston, he m. 2ndly, Margaret, 2nd dau. of William, Lord Alexander, and d. 1678, having had by his 1st wife, with other issue, Sir Archibald, M.P. 1690; his descendant, Sir John, 6th bart., d. 7 Jan. 1798, having m. Elizabeth, dau. of Charles Allen, esq., and is said to have been succeeded by Sir John [Sinclair, bart., of whom no information can be obtained.

Sinclair—*continued.*

Robert (sir), of Stevenston —— *Haddington constabulary* 1689 conv., 1689-
[1702.

> 3rd bart. (on the death of his brother, Sir John, to whom he was served heir 5 July 1652), sheriff of Haddington 1689, privy councillor 1690, and a lord of the exchequer, nominated but declined to be elected a lord of session, P.C. Queen Anne 1703 ; m. 1st, 10 Sept. 1663, Helen, dau. of John Lindsay, 14th Earl of Crawford, and 2ndly —— relict of Sir Daniel Carmichael ; by his first wife he had with other issue a son, Sir John, M.P. 1702.

Robert (sir), of Longformacus —— *Berwickshire* 1702-7.

> 3rd bart. (on the death of his father, Sir John, 1698) ; m. Christian, dau. of Adam [Cockburn, of Ormiston, lord justice clerk, and d. 1725-6, leaving issue.

(Sir William), laird of Rosslyn —— 1598 conv., as a minor baron.

> Son of Edward Sinclair, of Rosslyn, and father, by Janet Edmonstone, of Sir William [Sinclair.

William, of Dunbeath —— *Caithness-shire* 1661-3.

> 2nd bart., of Lathrone and Dunbeath (on the death of his uncle, Sir John Sinclair, of Dunbeath, M.P., 1649), a zealous loyalist, his house and goods were plundered by the covenanters 1650 ; m. his cousin Elizabeth, dau. of Sir James Sinclair, of Mey, and had [3 sons, of whom Sir James, M.P. 1703-7. See "CHAOS" in Foster's Baronetage.

Skene.

George (sir), of Fintray, provost —— *Aberdeen* 1678 conv., 1681-2 (a knight), [1685-6, or in his absence, David Aldie, bailie.

> Of Rubieslaw, by purchase, son of David Skene, of Potterton ; d. s.p.

(James), laird of Skene —— *Aberdeenshire* 1646-7.

> Heir of his father, Alexander, 1634, "a great loyalist," served also under Gustavus [Adolphus ; m. Elizabeth, dau. of Arthur, 9th Lord Forbes, and had issue.

George Skene —— *Aberdeenshire* 1786-90, *Elgin burghs* 1806-7.

> Son of George Skene ; m. his cousin Mary, dau. of George Forbes of Alfoord ; and d. [1827, having had issue.

Robert (lieut.-genl.), of Hallyards —— *Fifeshire* 2 July 1779 until unseated [7 Feb. 1780, 1780-4, (major-genl.) 1784 until his death s.b. 6 July 1787.

> Lieut.-genl. 20 Nov. 1782, d. May 1787.

Skynner.

John, councillor —— *Brechin city* 1633, 1643 conv., 1649.

Slamannan-Mure.

—— The laird of —— 1596 conv. *bis*, as a minor baron.

Sleigh.

John —— *Haddington* 1644 conv., (Sleich) 1645, 1649, 1650, or John Aston.

John, younger, merchant provost —— *Haddington* 1685-6, 1689 conv., 1689 until [his death s.b. 15 March 1690.

Smith or Smyth.

George, one of the judges in Scotland —— *sheriffdom of Midlothian* 1654-5, [*sheriffdom of Dumfries* 1656-8 (WILLIS).
One of the commonwealth judges, appointed 18 May 1652. A George Smyth, of Morfield, Salop, was admitted to the Inner Temple 1616, but there is no mention of his having been [called to the bar.

George (Smyth), fiar of Giblistoune —— *Pittenweem* 1689 conv., 1689-1702.

George, younger, of Gibliston, councillor —— *Pittenweem* 1702-7.

James (Mr.), heritor —— *Forres* 1685-6.

James, bailie —— *Dunbar* 1685-6, 1689 conv., (then merchant burgess), 1689 until 28 April 1693, when his seat was declared vacant because he had not [signed the assurance.

James, merchant —— *St. Andrews* 1689 conv., 1689-1702.

Sir John (Smythe), of Grottell, knt. —— *Edinburgh* 1639-40, (merchant) [1643-4 conv. (a knight), 1644-6 (provost), 1650-1.

John Benjamin, of Vicar's Field House, Eccles, co. Lancaster —— *Stirling* [*burghs* 1847-52. See also England M.P.
Of King's Ride, Ascott, Berks, and of Manchester, merchant, M.P. Stockport 1852-7, 1857-9, 1859-65, 1865-8, 1868-74, contested Blackburn 1837, and Walsall and Dundee 1841, president of the Anti-Corn Law League and of the Manchester Chamber of Commerce, (son of Benjamin Smith) ; m. 1841, Jemima, dau. of Wm. Dunning, of Liverpool, and d. 15 Sept. [1879, aged 85.

Robert, late bailie —— *Perth* 1689 conv., 1689-1702.

Thomas, "Dean of Guild" of the city of Glasgow —— *Glasgow burghs* 1710-13, [1713-15, 1715 until his death s. b. 24 Feb. 1715-16.
King's proctor, and commissioner army debts, d. 16 Aug. 1715.

Smollett.

Alexander, younger, of Bonhill, lieut.-col. 26th regt. light dragoons —— *Dum-* [*bartonshire* 1797 until his death s.b. 7 Nov. 1799.
Son of Alexander Telfer Smollett, slain at the Helder, unmarried, 27 Aug. 1799.

Alexander, younger, of Bonhill —— *Dumbartonshire* 1841-7, 1847-52, 1852-7, [1857-9.
Eldest son of rear-admiral John Rouett Smollett, and brother of Patrick Boyle Smollett, M.P. advocate 1824, contested Dumbartonshire 1835 and 1837, convener 1847-80; b. 29 Nov. [1801 ; d. unm. 25 Feb. 1881.

James —— *Dumbarton* 1645.

James (sir, 1689) —— *Dumbarton* 1685-6 (provost), 1689 conv. (late provost), [1689-1702, 1702-7 of Bonhill, 1707-8 (1st parlt. G.B.).
Depute clerk of the regality of Lennox 1676, a judge in the commissary court of Edinburgh and knighted, a commissioner for the Union, deputy lieut. Dumbartonshire 1715, (son of John Smollett) ; m. 1st, Jane Macaulay, of Ardincaple, he m. 2ndly, Elizabeth, dau. of William Hamilton of Orbiston, and d. 1731, leaving by his first wife only, with other issue, a son, [Archibald, father of Tobias, the celebrated author.

Smollett—*continued.*

Patrick Boyle —— *Dumbartonshire* 1859-65, 1865-8. See also England M.P.

Of Cameron House, co. Dumbarton, D.L., H.E.I.C.S. Madras 1826-57, gov.-genl's. agent Vizagapatam 1846-57, M.P. Cambridge 1874-80, contested it 1880 (younger son of Rear-
[Admiral John Rouett Smollett) ; b. 1805.

Somerville.

Johnne (Mr.) of —— *Dundee* 1357.

Possibly youngest son of Sir Thomas Somerville of Linton and Carnwath.

John —— *Renfrew* 1643 conv., 1644.

John, skinner —— *Edinburgh* 1665 conv., 1667 conv.

John, of Townhead, provost —— *Renfrew* 1665 conv., 1678 conv.

William —— *Renfrew* 1612, 1617, 1621.

Spalding.

David —— *Dundee* 1456, 1458.

John, of London —— *Wigtown burghs* 1796-1802, 1802 (of Holme, Wigtown),
[until he accepted the Chiltern hundreds s.b. 29 July 1803.

Died 26 Aug. 1815, having m. at Beckenham, 19 Dec. 1807, Mary Anne, eldest dau. of Thomas Eden, deputy auditor of Greenwich Hospital (B. AUCKLAND) ; she d. 12 Jan. 1865,
[having re-m. 1 April 1819, to Henry, Lord Brougham, who d. 7 May 1868.

William —— *Dundee* 1543.

William —— (*Auchterarder?*) 1583.

Speirs.

Alexander Graham, of Culcreuch —— *Paisley* 1835 until he accepted the
[Chiltern hundreds, s.b. 17 March 1836.

Advocate 8 July 1820 (2nd son of Peter Speirs, esq., of Culcreuch), d. 24 Dec. 1847.

Archibald, of Elderslie —— *Renfrewshire* 1810-12, 1812-18.

Son of Alexander Speirs ; d. 2 Nov. 1832, having m. 24 Jan. 1794, Hon. Margaret [Dundas, eldest dau. of Thomas, 1st Lord Dundas ; she d. 8 May 1852, leaving issue.

Archibald Alexander, of Elderslie —— *Renfrewshire* 1865-8, 1868 until his
[death s.b. 25 Jan. 1869.

Capt. Scots fusilier guards (son of Alexander Speirs, and grandson of Archibald, M.P.) ; b. 5 June 1840 ; d. 30 Dec. 1868, having m. 3 Sept. 1867, Lady Anne Pleydell-Bouverie, [eldest dau. of Jacob, 4th Earl of Radnor, and had a posthumous son.

Spens.

David —— *Rutherglen* 1587.

David —— *Rutherglen* 1639-41, 1643 conv., 1645, 1646-7, 1648.

Spens—*continued.*

David —— *Rutherglen* 1661, 1665 conv., 1672-4, 1678 conv.

David (Spence) late bailie of Edinburgh and burgess of this burgh ——
Anstruther Easter 1689 conv., 1689 until 28 April 1693, when his seat was
[declared vacant because he had not signed the assurance.

> Probably 3rd son of Thomas Spens, of Lathallan, of whom Douglas states that he was
> "bred a merchant in Edinburgh, whose arms as matriculated in the lyon office are, or, a lion
> rampant gu, over all on a bend waved sa, a buckle between lozenges arg, with an anchor for his
> crest and motto, etc. This David afterwards went to Ireland, where he settled and acquired
> [a considerable fortune. He had issue 3 sons, who all died unmarried."

George, provost —— *Rutherglen,* etc. 1702-7.

Johnne, of —— *Perth* 1435.

> John de Spens, of Glen Douglas (son of William de Spens, of Lathallan); m. Isabel, dau.
> of Sir John Wemyss, of Rires, and had with other issue Thomas, bishop of Galloway, then
> [of Aberdeen.

Johnne —— *Edinburgh* 1558.

(Mr.) **John** (Spence) —— *Forres* 1643 conv.

Matthew —— *Rothesay* 1628-33, 1639-41 provost.

Spittle.

Alexander, of Lewquhat —— *Inverkeithing* 1689 conv., 1689 until his death
[s.b. 30 March 1696.

Edward (Spittale) —— *Stirling* 1504, 1524, 1525.

James, of Lewquhat (provost), son of late Alexander—— *Inverkeithing* 1696-1702,
[1702-7.

Spreull.

John —— *Renfrew* 1579.

> Probably son of Robert Sprewel, of Glasgow and of Cowden, 1555, made rector of Cambus-
> [lang upon the reformation, and was so designed 1588. Nisbet.

John —— *Renfrew* 1639-41 (late provost), 1645-7, 1649.

> Son of John Sprewel and father of John Sprewel, town clerk of Glasgow and a principal
> [clerk of session.

Stafford.   See also Strathnaver.

George Granville William, marquis of, etc. —— *Sutherlandshire* 1852-7,
[1857-9, 1859 until he succeeded as 3rd Duke of Sutherland 28 Feb. 1861.

> Duke of Sutherland, K.G., lord lieut. Sutherland since 1861 and of Cromarty since 1853,
> hon. col. 20th Middlesex volunteers since 1867, lieut.-col. 1st Sutherland volunteers since
> 1864, grand cross of Greek order of the Saviour, vice-president of the Æronautical Society
> [of Great Britain; b. 19 Dec. 1828, m. and has issue. See Foster's Peerage.

Stafford—*continued.*

(Cromartie) Marquis of, 2nd life guards, of Stafford House, London —— *Suther-[landshire* 1874-80 and since 1880.

Eldest son of Duke of Sutherland last named, lieut. late 2nd life guards, capt. Stafford-[shire yeomanry since 1876, major Sutherland volunteers since 1881 ; b. 21 July 1851.

Steill.

George —— *Brechin* 1646-7, 1648 —— 1661 bailie.

Steven.

Patrick, merchant trafficker, provost —— *Arbroath* 1689 conv., 1689-1702.

Stevenson.

Alexander, merchant burgess —— *Kilrenny* 1693-1702.

James —— *Peebles* 1593.

James —— *Pittenweem* 1628-33.

James —— *Stirling* 1667 conv., 1669-74 provost.

William —— *Pittenweem* 1612, 1617 —— 1643 conv., 1645.

William (Stevenston) —— *Inverurie* 1612.

Stewart, Steuart, and Stuart.

(——) laird of Rossythe —— *Clackmannanshire* 1644 conv.

(——) laird of Kilchattan —— *Buteshire* 1648.

Probably descended from Robert, 2nd son of James Stewart, and Elizabeth Blair, who [was ancestor of Stewart of Kilchattan and Ascog.

Adam —— *Rothesay* 1661.

(Sir Alexander) laird of Garlies —— *Wigtownshire* 1594 and 1596 conv., as a [minor baron.

Sir Alexander Stewart, of Garlies, knighted at the coronation of Queen Anne 1590 (son of Alexander Stewart) ; m. 1st Christian, dau. of Sir William Douglas, of Drumlanrig, and 2ndly Elizabeth, relict of John, 7th Lord Maxwell, 2nd dau. of David Douglas, 7th Earl of Angus. By his 1st wife he was father of Alexander, 1st Earl of Galloway. [See Foster's Peerage.

Stewart, Steuart, and Stuart—*continued*.

STUART, MARQUIS OF BUTE.

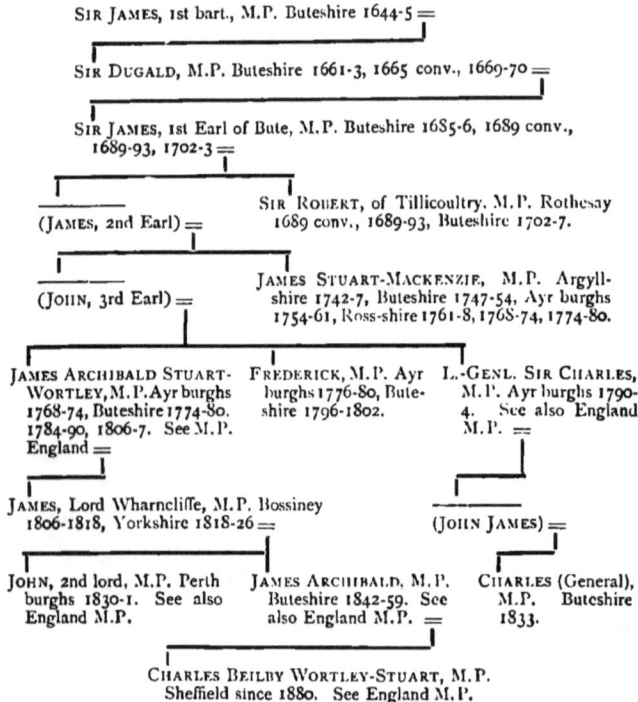

SIR JAMES, 1st bart., M.P. Buteshire 1644-5 =

SIR DUGALD, M.P. Buteshire 1661-3, 1665 conv., 1669-70 =

SIR JAMES, 1st Earl of Bute, M.P. Buteshire 1685-6, 1689 conv., 1689-93, 1702-3 =

———— (JAMES, 2nd Earl) =   SIR ROBERT, of Tillicoultry. M.P. Rothesay 1689 conv., 1689-93, Buteshire 1702-7.

———— (JOHN, 3rd Earl) =   JAMES STUART-MACKENZIE, M.P. Argyllshire 1742-7, Buteshire 1747-54, Ayr burghs 1754-61, Ross-shire 1761-8, 1768-74, 1774-80.

JAMES ARCHIBALD STUART-WORTLEY, M.P. Ayr burghs 1768-74, Buteshire 1774-80. 1784-90, 1806-7. See M.P. England =

FREDERICK, M.P. Ayr burghs 1776-80, Buteshire 1796-1802.

L.-GENL. SIR CHARLES, M.P. Ayr burghs 1790-4. See also England M.P. =

JAMES, Lord Wharncliffe, M.P. Bossiney 1806-1818, Yorkshire 1818-26 =

(JOHN JAMES) =

JOHN, 2nd lord, M.P. Perth burghs 1830-1. See also England M.P.

JAMES ARCHIBALD, M.P. Buteshire 1842-59. See also England M.P. =

CHARLES (General), M.P. Buteshire 1833.

CHARLES BEILBY WORTLEY-STUART, M.P. Sheffield since 1880. See England M.P.

Alexander (major-genl.) —— *Kirkcudbright stewartry* 1786-90 (then col. 3rd [foot], 1790 until his death s.b. 23 March 1795. Col. Queen's royal regt. of foot, comd. 1st brigade infantry in the Peninsular war 1794 ; [d. 17 Dec. 1794.

Andrew, of Craigthorn, esq. —— *Lanarkshire* 1774-80 (keeper of the signet of [Scotland 1770, a commissioner for trade and plantations 1779), 1780-4, see [also England M.P. M.P. Weymouth 1790-6, 1796 till his death 18 May 1801 ; 2nd son of Archibald, who was [7th son of Alexander Stuart, of Torrence.

Archibald —— 1458.

Archibald —— *Edinburgh* 1578 conv.

(Sir Archibald), laird of Castlemilk —— *Renfrewshire* 1617.

Son of Sir Archibald Stewart ; he m. Anne, eldest dau. of Robert, 4th Lord Semple ; and [d. 1643, leaving a son, Sir Archibald, father of Sir Archibald, M.P. 1669. See chart [pedigree, page 326.

Stewart, Steuart, and Stuart—*continued.*

STEWART, EARL OF GALLOWAY.

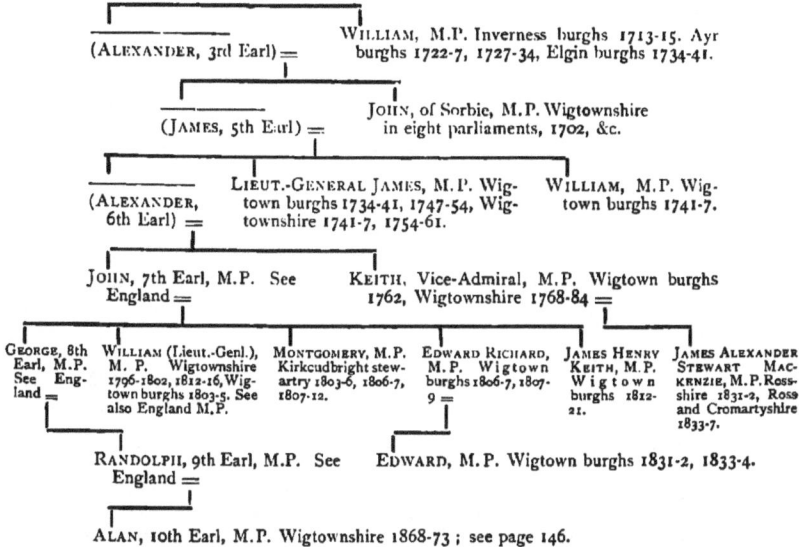

WILLIAM, M.P. Inverness burghs 1713-15. Ayr
(ALEXANDER, 3rd Earl) = burghs 1722-7, 1727-34, Elgin burghs 1734-41.

JOHN, of Sorbie, M.P. Wigtownshire
(JAMES, 5th Earl) = in eight parliaments, 1702, &c.

LIEUT.-GENERAL JAMES, M.P. Wig- WILLIAM, M.P. Wig-
(ALEXANDER, town burghs 1734-41, 1747-54, Wig- town burghs 1741-7.
6th Earl) = townshire 1741-7, 1754-61.

JOHN, 7th Earl, M.P. See   KEITH, Vice-Admiral, M.P. Wigtown burghs
England =   1762, Wigtownshire 1768-84 =

| GEORGE, 8th Earl, M.P. See England = | WILLIAM (Lieut.-Genl.), M.P. Wigtown burghs 1796-1802, 1812-16, Wigtown burghs 1803-5. See also England M.P. | MONTGOMERY, M.P. Kirkcudbright stewartry 1803-6, 1806-7, 1807-12. | EDWARD RICHARD, M.P. Wigtown burghs 1806-7, 1807-9 = | JAMES HENRY KEITH, M.P. Wigtown burghs 1812-21. | JAMES ALEXANDER STEWART MACKRNZIE, M.P. Rossshire 1831-2, Ross and Cromartyshire 1833-7. |

RANDOLPH, 9th Earl, M.P. See   EDWARD, M.P. Wigtown burghs 1831-2, 1833-4.
England =

ALAN, 10th Earl, M.P. Wigtownshire 1868-73 ; see page 146.

Archibald (sir), of Blackhall —— *Renfrewshire* 1628-33.

Sir Archibald Stewart, of Blackhall, which was a royal residence in 1294, and of Ardgowan (descended from John Stewart, of Blackhall and Ardgowan, who in 1508 obtained from James IV. a confirmation of those lands granted by Robert III. by charters dated 1390, 1396, and 1404, to his natural son, Sir John Stewart, the progenitor of this family), infeft in family estates 8 April 1613, served heir of his elder brother in the lands of Gass 26 March same year, knighted between 19 April and 23 Oct. 1637, P.C. Charles II. 1650, imprisoned six months in Edinburgh Castle, together with the Earl (afterward Marquis) of Montrose, Lord Napier, and Sir George Stirling, of Keir; d. 1665, having m. 1st, Margaret, dau. of Bryce Blair of that ilk ; she d. Aug. 1621, having had five sons and two daus, his son John was father of Archibald, M.P., next named ; he m. 2ndly (contract 16 July 1624), Margaret, widow of Hew, Earl of Loudoun, dau. of Sir George Home, of Wedderburn, and had a son David. See Foster's Baronetage, and chart pedigree, [page 325.

Archibald, of Blackhall —— *Renfrewshire,* 1667 conv.

Sir Archibald Stewart (2nd son of John Stewart, by his wife Maria, dau. of Sir James Stirling, of Keir, marriage contract 23 Aug. 1633), cr. a bart. of Nova Scotia, by patent dated at Whitehall, 27 Mar. 1667, to him and his heirs male (not recorded in great seal register) ; m. 1st (contract dated 12 Mar. 1659), Anne, dau. of Sir John Craufurd, bart. of Kilbirnie (Crawford-Pollock) ; he m. 2ndly, Dame Agnes Dalmahoy, she d. s.p. ; he m. 3rdly, Mary, dau. of Sir John Douglas, of Kellhead (M. Queensberry), by whom he had two sons, both d. unm., and 2 daus ; by his first wife he had with other issue a son John, [M.P. 1700. See Foster's Baronetage, and chart pedigree, page 325.

Stewart, Steuart, and Stuart—*continued.*

Archibald (sir), of Castlemilk —— *Renfrewshire* 1669-70.

Created a bart. 28 Feb. 1668 (son of Sir Archibald Stewart, M.P. 1617, by Mary, dau. of John Fleming, Earl of Wigton) ; m. Mary, dau. of William, master of Carmichael, and [had a son. Sir William, M.P. 1696. See chart pedigree, page 326.

Archibald (sir), of Burray —— *Orkney and Zetland stewartry* 1702, 1702-7.

Created a bart. 4 Nov. 1687 (grandson of William Stewart of Mains in Galloway, by his wife Barbara, dau. and heiress of James Stewart of Burray), and d. 13 May 1689 ; according to Douglas, his grandson, Sir James, d. 24 Aug. 1746, in the new gaol, Southwark, a prisoner under suspicion of high treason, and the Earl of Galloway was served heir to Sir [Archibald 24 June 1747.

Archibald, merchant, councillor of the city of Edinburgh —— *Edinburgh city* Died 24 January 1780.   [1741-7.

Charles Stuart (col.), son of the Earl of Bute —— *Ayr burghs* 1790, until he accepted the Chiltern hundreds s.b. 12 June 1794, then a major-genl.   See [also England M.P.

Lieut.-Genl. Sir Charles Stuart, K.B., invested 8 Jan. 1799 or 1800, major 43rd regt. 1775, lt.-col. 26th Cameronians 1777 in the American war, and greatly distinguished himself, col. in the army 1782, major-genl. 1793, col. 68th regt. 1794, and 26th Cameronians 1795-1801, commanded the forces in Portugal with local rank of genl. 1796, lt.-genl. 9 Jan. 1798, landed at Minorca 7 Nov. same year, and by the 18th he had taken it from the Spaniards without the loss of a man, governor 17—, M.P. Bossiney 1776-80, 1780-4, 1784-90, returned for Ayr burghs and Poole, Dorset, 1790, unseated on petition 25 Feb. 1791, Poole 1796 until his death, deputy-ranger of Richmond Park ; b. Jan. 1753; d. 25 May 1801, having m. 19 April 1778, Louisa, 2nd dau. and co-heir (with her sister Albinia, Countess of Buckinghamshire) of Lord Vere Bertie, 3rd son of Robert, 1st Duke of Ancaster and Kesteven (extinct) ; she d. 5 Feb. 1841, having had with other issue a son, Sir Charles Stuart, G.C.B., cr. Baron Stuart [de Rothesay. See Foster's Peerage, and chart pedigree, page 322.

Charles Stuart, capt. and lt. of 1st grenadier regt. of foot guards —— *Buteshire* [1833, until he accepted the Chiltern hundreds s.b. 4 Sept. of that year.

Genl. Stuart, of Hoburne, Hants., J.P., lt. and capt. grenadier guards 26 July 1832, capt. and lt.-col. 15 April 1845, lt.-col. 13th Prince Albert's L.I. 1846, major-genl. 1860, lt.-genl. 1868, genl. 1875, retired list 1880, col. 46th foot since 1870, extra A.D.C. to Lord High Com. Ionian Islands 1837-8, brigade major northern district 1844-5, col. on staff 1855-6, mil. sec. to gov.-gen. of India 1857-9, vice-lieut. Buteshire since 1862, (son of Capt. William Stuart, R.N., and nephew Charles, Lord Rothesay, G.C.B. afsd.) ; b. 16 March 1810, m. 1st, 4 Sept. 1839, (Hon.) Georgiana Stuart (maid of honour to Q. Adelaide), dau. of Vice-Adml. Sir John Gore, K.C.B., K.C.H. (E. Arran) ; she d. 18 July 1877, and he m. 2ndly, 24 Sept. 1878, Louisa Gambier, dau. of John Gordon Murdoch, esq. See Bute in Foster's Peerage, and [chart pedigree, page 322.

Cuthbert —— *Rothesay* 1681-2 (late provost), 1685-6 (provost).

David, merchant burgess, bailie —— *Elgin* 1678 conv., 1685-6.

Dougall (sir), of Kirktone, knt., sheriff —— *Buteshire* 1661-3, 1665 conv., [1669-70.

2nd bart (on the death, 1662, of his father, Sir James, M.P. 1644), bailie of the regality of Glasgow 1671 ; m. Elizabeth, dau. of Sir Thomas Ruthven, and d. 1672, leaving Sir James, [M.P. 1665. See chart pedigree, page 322.

Stewart, Steuart and Stuart—*continued.*

SHAW-STEWART OF BLACKHALL.

SIR ARCHIBALD STEWART, M.P. Renfrewshire 1628-33 =

(JOHN STEWART) =

SIR ARCHIBALD, M.P. Renfrewshire 1667 conv. =

JOHN, M.P. Renfrewshire 1700-2, 1702-4 =

(————) SIR MICHAEL STEWART) =

SIR JOHN SHAW-STEWART, M.P. Renfrewshire 1780-3, 1786-96.

(————) HOUSTON =

(————) SIR MICHAEL SHAW-STEWART =

SIR MICHAEL, 6th bart., M.P. Lanarkshire 1827-30, Renfrewshire 1830-1, 1831-2, 1833-4, 1835-6 =	SIR HOUSTON (Admiral), M.P. Greenwich 1852. See England M.P.	PATRICK MAXWELL, M.P. Lancaster 1831-7, Renfrewshire 1841-6.

SIR MICHAEL ROBERT, 7th bart., M.P. Renfrewshire 1855-65.

Dugald (Mr.) of Blairhall, advocate —— *Rothesay* 1702-7 (Steuart); *Perthshire* 1708 (of Blairhall), and *Buteshire* (of Chapeltoun, brother-german of James, Earl of Bute) 1708 until appointed to a crown office of profit s.b. 28 Feb. [following year.

> Lord Blairhall of session, and also lord of justiciary 7 June 1709, advocate 30 Nov. 1694 ; according to Douglas, a petition was presented against his return to Perth, but he sat for both counties till his elevation to the bench in the room of his uncle, Sir Robert Stewart, Lord Tillicoultry, as above, new writs were ordered 24 Jan. and 22 Feb. 1710, (2nd son of Sir Dugald Stewart, of Bute) ; d. at Blairhall 16 June 1712, having m. 10 March 1700, [Mary, dau. and heir of John Bruce, of Blair Hall, she d. 1759, leaving issue.

Edward, of 7, York Place, Portman Square, London —— *Wigtown burghs* 1831-2 (then a student of Lincoln's Inn), 1832-4.

> Admitted to Lincoln's Inn 17 May 1830, M.A., Oriel Coll., Oxon, 1834, rector of Lainstone 1850, and vicar of Sparsholt 1842 (son of Hon. Edward R. Stewart, M.P., next named); b. 9 Oct. 1808, d. 21 March 1875, leaving issue. See GALLOWAY in Foster's Peerage, and [chart pedigree, page 323.

Stewart, Steuart, and Stuart—*continued.*

STEWART OF CASTLEMILK.

SIR ARCHIBALD, M.P. Renfrewshire 1617 ═
┃
SIR ARCHIBALD, 1st bart., M.P. Renfrewshire 1669-70 ═
┏
SIR WILLIAM, 2nd bart., M.P. Lanarkshire 1696-1702.

Edward Richard, 5th son of the deceased John, Earl of Galloway, capt. 7th regt. dragoon guards ——— *Wigtown burghs* 1806-7, 1807 until appointed a [commissioner for victualling the navy s.b. 27 Feb. 1809.

Deputy chairman of commissioners of customs, resigned 1846, capt. of the dragoon guards 1804, 97th foot 1807, a major of brigade on the North British staff; b. 5 May 1782, d. 27 Aug. 1851, having m. 19 Nov. 1805, Lady Katharine Wemyss (p.p.) dau. of Francis, Baron Elcho (E. Wemyss), she d. 8 Oct. 1863, having had issue. See Foster's Peerage, and chart [pedigree, page 323.

Frederic Stuart, of Kirkton, Buteshire ——— *Ayr burghs* 1776-80; *Buteshire* [1796-1802.

3rd son of John, 3rd Earl of Bute; b. Sept. 1751, d. unm. 17 May 1802. See chart [pedigree, page 322.

Gilbert (sir), of Tullinedes and Poltalk, knt. ——— *Perthshire* 1671 until his death [s.b. 30 Sept. 1673.

James ——— *Glasgow* 1593 ——— 1617.

James (sir), of Kirktoune, sheriff of Bute ——— *Buteshire* 1644-5.

Sir James Stuart, of Bute (seventh in descent from Sir John Stuart, natural son of Robert II. who appointed him hereditary sheriff of Buteshire, together with a small grant of lands), was cr. a bart. of Nova Scotia 28 March 1627, with remainder to his heirs male, espoused the royal cause, garrisoned his castle of Rothesay at his own expense, appointed lieut. over the west of Scotland, and subsequently suffered both by fines and sequestrations ; he d. 1662, having m. Isabella, eldest dau. of Sir Dugald Campbell, of Auchinbreck, bart., [and had with other issue a son, Sir Dugald, M.P. 1665. See chart pedigree, page 322.

James (sir), of Kirkfield, provost ——— *Edinburgh* 1649-50.

Sir James Steuart, of Kirkfield and Coltness by purchase (posthumous son of James Steuart, of Allanton), of Edinburgh, merchant and banker, lord provost of Edinburgh 1649 and 1659, he was dismissed at the restoration as a covenanter, and committed to Edinburgh castle ; d. 31 March 1681, aged 73, having m. 1st, 1630, Anne, dau. of Henry Hope, and niece of Sir Thomas Hope, of Craighall, co. Fife, lord advocate, she d. 1646, and he m. 2ndly, 1648, Marion, widow of Sir John Elliot, advocate, only dau. of David M'Culloch, of Goodtrees, Midlothian, and had with other issue Sir Thomas, M.P. 1689, and Sir Robert, M.P. 1698, both cr. barts., and Sir James, lord advocate of Scotland, father of Sir James, M.P. 1705, [cr. a bart. that year. See chart pedigree, page 329.

Stewart, Steuart, and Stuart—*continued.*

STEWART OF GRANDTULLY.

SIR WILLIAM, of Grandtully, M.P. Perthshire 1612, 1617 conv. and parlt.$=$

SIR THOMAS, of Grandtully; Perthshire
1665 conv., 1667 conv.   (HENRY)$=$

SIR THOMAS, of Balcaskie, bart., M.P. Fifeshire 1685-6.

James (sir), sheriff —— *Buteshire* 1685-6, 1689 conv., 1689 until 25th Apl. 1693, when his place was declared vacant because he had not taken the oath of allegiance and signed the assurance; 1702 (then of Bute) until cr. Earl of Bute [14 Apl. 1703.

Sir James, 3rd bart. (on the death in 1672, of his father, Sir Dugald, M.P. 1661), M.P. Buteshire, and P.C. temp. Queen Anne, cr. Earl of Bute, Viscount Kingarth, Lord Mountstuart, Cumra, and Inchmarnock, by patent dated at St. James' 14 April 1703, with remainder to his heirs male whatsoever; he d. at Bath 4 June 1710, having m. 1st, Agnes, eldest dau. of Sir George Mackenzie, of Rosehaugh, nephew of the 1st and 2nd Earls of Seaforth, and had an only son and dau. He m. 2ndly, Christian, dau. of William Dundas, of Kincavel, advocate, she d. 25 May, 1740, and had issue. See chart pedigree, page 322.

James, merchant, dean of guild —— *Elgin* 1689 conv., 1689-?702.

James (sir), of Goodtrees —— *Queensferry* 1705-7 (then Mr. James, advocate, eldest son of Sir James Stewart, of Goodtrees, her majesty's advocate); [*Edinburgh city* 1713-15 then of Goodtrees, knt.

Sir James Steuart cr. a baronet 22 Dec. 1705 (as "Mr. James Steuart, younger, of Coltnes"), advocate 19 June 1704, solicitor-general Scotland 1709; m. 1705, Anne, dau. of Sir Hugh Dalrymple, of North Berwick, lord-president of the court of session, and d. 1727, [leaving issue.

James (col.) **Stuart,** of Torrence —— *Ayr burghs* 1734-41.

Eldest son of Alexander Stuart, of Torrence, A.D.C. to John, Duke of Argyll 1715, when commanding in Scotland, was at the battle of Sheriffmuir, served in Spain and Flanders, lt.-col. 3rd regt. of foot guards, a gent. usher to George II.; d. unm. 3 April 1743; brother of [Patrick, M.P. 1750.

James (col.), of Bailliewhirr —— *Wigtown burghs* 1734-41 (capt.); *Wigtownshire* 1741-7 (of Barvennan, col.); *Wigtown burghs* 1747-54 (col. 3rd foot [guards); *Wigtownshire* 1754-61 (of Auckland).

Lt.-genl. Stewart (2nd son of James, 5th Earl of Galloway), major 3rd foot guards after battle of Fontenoy 1745, lt.-col. 1748, col. 1752, lt.-genl. 20 Jan. 1758; d. unm. at Calley [27 April 1768; brother of William, M.P. 1741. See chart pedigree, page 323.

James (lt.-col.), of Kerimoran —— *Buteshire* 1761 until his death s.b. 3 June [1762.

Possibly eldest son of Dougal Stewart, of Blairhall, M.P. 1702; died col. 37th regt. of foot [7 Feb. 1762.

Stewart, Steuart, and Stuart—*continued.*

James Stuart, of Ardmaleish, 2nd son of John, Earl of Bute —— *Ayr burghs* 1768-74; *Buteshire* 1774-80, 1784-90, 1806-7, then James Stuart Wortley-[Mackenzie, of Rosehaugh and Ardmaleish. See also England M.P.

Hon. James Archibald Stuart-Wortley-Mackenzie, of Rosehaugh, lt.-col. in the army, M.P. as above, and Plympton 1780-4. Bossiney 1790-6, 1797-1802, 1802-6 (2nd son of John, 3rd Earl of Bute, K.G.), assumed the additional surname and arms of Wortley by royal licence 7 Jan. 1795, on the death of his mother (Mary, Baroness Mountstuart, only dau. of Edward Wortley-Montagu, whose mother was Anne Newcomen, dau. of Sir Francis Wortley, bart.), and on succeeding to the estates of his uncle, Rt. Hon. James Stuart-Mackenzie (see also Bute), in 1803, he assumed the additional arms and designation of Mackenzie, of Rosehaugh, and the surname of Mackenzie was confirmed to him by royal licence 17 June 1826; b. 19 Nov. 1747, d. 1 March 1818, having m. 8 June 1767, Margaret, dau. of Sir David Cuninghame, bart., of Levingstone, co. Linlithgow ; she d. Jan. 1808, having had with other issue a son [James (see M.P. England), cr. Lord Wharncliffe. See chart pedigree, page 322.

James, of Garvoch, merchant and shipowner, co. Renfrew —— *Greenock* 1878-80, [and since 1880. See foot-note.

James (sir) **Steuart-Denham**, of Coltness and Westshields, bart. —— *Lanark-* [*shire* 1784-90, 1790-6, 1796-1802 (a baronet).

3rd baronet (on the death, 1780, of his father, Sir James, who contested Edinburghshire 1744), general in the army, col. 2nd regt. of dragoons ; b. Aug. 1744, m. 1772, Alice, dau. of Wm. Blacker, esq., of Carrick Blacker, co. Armagh, and d. s.p. 12-23 Aug. 1839. [See chart pedigree, page 322.

James Stuart-Mackenzie, of Rosehaugh —— *Argyllshire* 1742-7; *Buteshire* 1747-54; *Ayr burghs* 1754-61; *Ross-shire* 1761-8 (keeper of the privy seal in [Scotland 1763 and 1766), 1768-74, 1774-80.

Rt. Hon. James Stewart-Mackenzie, of Rosehaugh, assumed that designation on succeeding to the estate of his great-grandfather, Sir George Mackenzie ; envoy-extraordinary to the king of Sardinia (at Turin) 1758, P.C. 1763, keeper of the great seal 1763-5, 1766 until his death s.p.s. 6 April 1800, aged 82, having m. 16 Feb. 1749, Lady Elizabeth Campbell, 4th dau. of John, Duke of Argyll and Greenwich ; she d. 16 July 1799, aged 77. See chart pedigree, [page 322.

STEWART, JAMES, of Garvocks, co. Renfrew, J.P., and of St. Fillans, Ayrshire, J.P., D.L., merchant and shipowner, M.P. as above (eldest son of late James Stewart, esq., of Clydebank, Greenock, by Joanna, dau. of Donald Shaw, esq.); b. 14 June 1827, m. 1st, 27 June 1855, Margaret, dau. of Major Duncan Darroch, of Gourock, co. Renfrew ; she d. 3 Oct. 1859, leaving 2 daus., Susan and Margaret ; he m. 2ndly, 5 March 1868, Margaret Sandilands, dau. of late William Stirling, esq., and has 4 sons and a dau.
   (1) James Stirling, b. 10 June 1871.
   (2) William Norman, b. 11 Dec. 1872.
   (3) Ian, b. 2 Nov. 1874.
   (4) Patrick Douglas, b. 11 April 1876.
   (5) Olive Juana.
   Garvock, Greenock ; Routenburn, Largs, Ayrshire.
   Club—Reform.

Stewart, Steuart, and Stuart—*continued.*

STEUART OF COLTNESS, &c.

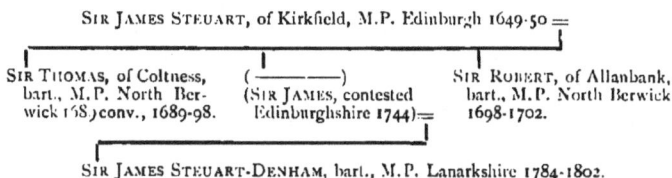

Sir James Steuart, of Kirkfield, M.P. Edinburgh 1649-50 =

Sir Thomas, of Coltness, bart., M.P. North Berwick 1 ?S)conv., 1689-98.	(————) (Sir James, contested Edinburghshire 1744)=	Sir Robert, of Allanbank, bart., M.P. North Berwick 1698-1702.

Sir James Steuart-Denham, bart., M.P. Lanarkshire 1784-1802.

James Alexander Stewart-Mackenzie, of Seaforth —— *Ross-shire* 1831-2 ; *Ross and Cromarty shires* 1833-4, 1835 until appointed governor of Ceylon, [s.b. 18 April 1837.

> Rt. Hon. James Alexander Stewart-Mackenzie, P.C. 1837, commissioner of the India board 1832-4, governor and com.-in-chief in Ceylon 1837-40, lord high commissioner Ionian Islands 1840-3 (son of admiral the Hon. Keith Stewart, M.P.); b. 23 Sept. 1784, d. 24 Sept. 1843; assumed the surname of Stewart-Mackenzie on his marriage, 21 May 1817, with Hon. Mary Elizabeth Frederica Mackenzie, widow of Vice-Adm. Sir Samuel Hood, bart., K.C.B., eldest dau. and co-heir of Francis, Baron Seaforth (ext.); she d. 28 Nov. 1862, having had [2 sons and 3 daus. See Foster's Peerage, E. Galloway, and chart pedigree, page 323.

James Archibald Stuart-Wortley —— *Buteshire* 1842-7 (judge-advocate-genl. 1846), 1847-52, 1852-7 (solicitor-genl. 1857), 1857-9. See also England [M.P.

> Rt. Hon. James Archibald Stuart-Wortley, P.C. 1846, Q.C. 1841, standing counsel to the Bank of England 1844, solicitor-genl. to Queen Adelaide 1845, attorney-genl. to duchy of Lancaster 1845, judge-advocate-genl. 1846-50, recorder of London 1850-6, solicitor-genl. 1856-7, M.P. Halifax 1835-7, contested co. Forfar 1835 and Yorkshire (West Riding) 1835 and 1837, bar.-at-law I.T. 1831, senior bencher (son of James, Lord Wharncliffe—see M.P. England); b. 3 July 1805, d. 22 Aug. 1881, having m. 6 May 1846, Hon. Jane Lawley, only dau. of Paul Beilby, 1st Baron Wenlock, and had with other issue (see [Foster's Peerage] a son Charles, M.P. Sheffield 1880. See chart pedigree, page 322.

James Henry Keith, youngest son of the late John, Earl of Galloway, and major in the army —— *Wigtown burghs* 1812-18, 1818-20, 1821 until he [accepted the Chiltern hundreds, s.b. 21 March of that year.

> Hon. James Henry Keith Stewart, C.B., lt.-col. in the army, assistant secretary treasury; b. 22 Oct. 1783, d. 18 July 1836, having m. 10 Aug. 1819, Henrietta Anne, 2nd dau. of Rev. Spencer Madan, D.D. ; she d. 24 Oct. 1829, having had 2 sons. See Foster's Peerage, [and chart pedigree, page 323.

John —— 1469 —— 1493.

John, of Minto, knt., provost —— *Glasgow* 1569 conv.

> Served heir of his father, Sir Robert Stewart, of Minto, 20 May 1555, took part in the coronation of James VI. 1567, had command of the castle of Glasgow ; m. 1st Joanna Hepburn, and had a son, Sir Matthew Stewart, of Minto, M.P. 1571 ; he m. 2ndly, Margaret, dau. of James Stewart, of Cardonald, and d. Feb. 1583, having had with other [issue a son Walter, ancestor of Lord Blantyre.

Johne (Mr.) —— *Stirling* 1581.

Scotch Members. T T

Stewart, Steuart, and Stuart—*continued.*

(Sir John), laird of Traquair —— *Peebles-shire* 1621, 1625 conv.

Sir John Stewart, Earl of Traquair, served heir of his father (John) 10 May 1606, etc., P.C. and knighted 1621, cr. Lord Stewart, of Traquair, 19 April 1628, high treasurer of Scotland 1630, and cr. Earl of Traquair, Lord Lintoun and Caberstoun 23 June 1633. commissioner to the general assembly at Edinburgh 1639, impeached as an incendiary by the Scots parlt. 1641 ; his son, Lord Lintoun, joined Montrose with a troop of horse shortly before the battle of Philiphaugh 1645, and the Earl raised a regt. of horse for " the engagement" to attempt the rescue of Charles I. in 1648, and was taken prisoner at Preston, and sent to Warwick Castle, where he remained four years ; he m. Catherine, dau. of David, Earl of Southesk,
[and d. Sept. 1659, leaving issue.

John, of Ethok —— *Buteshire* 1628-33.

John (Mr.), of Ascoge, advocate —— *Buteshire* 1651 (as the laird?) —— *Rothesay*
[1669-72.

2nd son of Sir Lewis Stewart, of Kirkhill, advocate, admitted advocate 2 June 1646.
[(John, younger, of Ascough, admitted advocate 25 Jan. 1690.)

John (Mr.), younger, of Blackhall, advocate —— *Renfrewshire* 1700-2, 1702-4.*

Advocate 2 July 1692, infeft in the family estate 18 Nov. 1696 (son of Sir Archibald Stewart, bart., M.P. 1667) ; m. (contract 15 March 1700) Rebecca, dau. of Michael Wallace of Glasgow, physician, and d. v.p. April 1713, leaving with 5 daus., 2 sons, Sir Archibald and Sir Michael, 2nd and 3rd baronets. See Foster's Baronetage, and chart
[pedigree, page 325.

John, of Sorbie (brigadier-genl.) —— *Wigtownshire* 1702, 1702-7 (Mr.), 1707-8 (1st. parlt. G.B.), 1708-10 (brother-german of the Earl of Galloway), 1711-13 (esq.) 1713-15 (brigadier-genl.), 1715-22, 1722-7.

Brigadier-general 10 June 1702; died at Sorbie, 22 April 1748.   See chart pedigree,
[page 323.

John Steuart, of Kinwhinlick —— *Buteshire* 1704-7.

John (col. sir), of Stewartfield, bart. —— *Kirkcudbright stewartry* 1708-10 (then of Livingstone or Stewartfield, lieut.-col.) 1710-13, 1713-15 (colonel and a
[baronet.

(? Of Allanbank), 2nd baronet (on the death of his father, Sir Robert); m. Margaret, dau.
[of John Ker, of Moristoun, and d. 19 May 1753, aged 68,

John, brother to the Earl of Moray —— *Anstruther-Easter* (now *St. Andrews*)
[*burghs* 1741-7.

2nd son of Francis, 6th Earl of Moray.   Douglas states that he got a company in the 54th foot, Lord Loudoun's Highlanders 8 June 1745, taken prisoner at the battle of Preston, lt.-col. of Lord Drumlanrig's regt. in the service of the states of Holland 1747, etc.; d. unm.
[13 Aug. 1796, aged 88.

John, of Castle Stewart —— *Wigtownshire* 1747-54, clerk of the pipe of the
[exchequer in Scotland.
Possibly descended from William, 3rd son of James, 2nd Earl of Galloway.

John (sir), of Fettercairn, bart. —— *Kincardineshire* 1797-1802 (Sir John Wishart
[Belshes), 1802-6 (Sir John Stewart).
See note on page 26.

Stewart, Steuart, and Stuart—*continued.*

John Shaw, of Greenock —— *Renfrewshire* 1780 until he accepted the Chiltern
[hundreds s.b. 21 Aug. 1783, 1786-90, 1790-6.

4th baronet (on the death of his father, Sir Michael, 20 Oct. 1796), assumed the additional surname of Shaw on inheriting the entailed estate of Greenock 1752 ; d. s.p. 7 Aug. 1812, having m. April 1786, Frances, relict of Sir James Maxwell, bart., of Pollock, dau. of [Robert Colquhoun of St. Christopher. See chart pedigree, page 325.

John Stuart-Wortley, younger, of Belmont —— *Perth burghs* 1830 until his
[election was declared void, s.b. 13 Jan. 1831. See also England M.P.

2nd Lord Wharncliffe (on the death of his father, James, 19 Dec. 1845, see M. P. England,) lt.-col. south-west regt. of Yorkshire yeo. cav., col. 1st W. Yorkshire militia, B.A. Ch. Ch. Oxon 1822, M.P. Bossiney 1829-30, 1830-1, contested Forfarshire 1835, and Yorkshire (west riding) in 1835 and 1837, M.P. 1841-5, and as above ; b. 20 April 1801, d. 22 Oct. 1855, [leaving issue. See Foster's Peerage, and chart pedigree, page 322.

Josias Steuart, of Bonytown —— *Ayrshire* 1617 conv. and parlt.

Keith, 2nd son of the Earl of Galloway —— *Wigtown burghs* 19 Feb. 1762 (then
capt. H.M.S. "Lynx") until he accepted the stewardship of the manor of
Old Shoreham, Sussex, s.b. 15 April following; *Wigtownshire* 1768-74 (of
Glasserton), 1774-80, 1780-4, 1 May 1784 until appointed receiver-genl. of
[land tax in Scotland, s.b. 17 Sept. following.

Of Glasserton, vice-admiral R.N. 1794, rear-admiral 1790, had a command in Admiral Keppel's engagement with the French fleet 1778, in the action with the Dutch on the Doggerbank 1781 and with the combined fleets at the relief of Gibraltar 1782 ; d. 5 May 1795, aged 56 ; having m. and left with other issue (see Foster's Peerage) a son James, M.P. [1831. See chart pedigree, page 323.

Mark John, of Ardwell, Wigtownshire —— *Wigtown burghs* (15 June) 1874-80.
[See foot-note.

Matthew, laird of Minto —— *Glasgow* 1571 conv. (then younger), 1572 conv.,
[1581 (laird), 1594.
Son of Sir John Stewart, M.P. 1569 ; m. Janet Stuart, and had issue.

STEWART, MARK JOHN, of Southwick, co. Kirkcudbright, J.P. and D.L., J.P. Wigtownshire, B.A. Ch. Ch. Oxford 1858, M.A. 1860, bar.-at-law Lincoln's Inn 1862, afterwards translated to the Inner Temple, M.P. Wigtown burghs as above, elected Feb. 1874, unseated May following ; contested the same constituency at general election April 1880, but elected on a vacancy the following month, but again unseated on petition ; lt.-col. 1st Ayr and Galloway art. vols. since 1879 (son of Mark Sprot Stewart, esq., of Southwick, co. Kirkcudbright, J.P. D.L.) ; b. 1834, m. 26 July 1668, Marianne, Susanna, only child of John Orde Ommaney, esq., and granddau. of Sir John McTaggart, bart., M.P., and has a dau.

Ardwell, Stranraer, Wigtownshire, Southwick, Dumfries.
Clubs—Carlton, Athenæum ; New Club, Edinburgh.

Stewart, Steuart and Stuart—*continued*.

Michael Shaw (sir), of Greenock and Blackhall, bart. —— *Lanarkshire* 1827-30, *Renfrewshire* 1830-1, 1831-2, 1833-4, 1835 until his death s.b. 30 Jan. 1837.

6th baronet (on the death of his father, Sir Michael, 1825), D.L. co.s. Lanark and Renfrew; d. 19 Dec. 1836, aged 48; he is said to have m. twice, 1st Eliza Mary, 2nd dau. of J. Murdoch, and 2ndly, as Michael Shaw Nicolson, esq., of Carnock, 16 Sept. 1819, Eliza Mary, only child of Robert Farquhar, of Newark, co. Renfrew, and of London; she d. 25 Jan. 1851, leaving a son, Sir Michael, 7th bart., next named. See chart pedigree, page 325.

Michael Robert Shaw (sir), of Greenock and Blackhall —— *Renfrewshire* [1855-7, 1857-9, 1859-65.

7th baronet (on the death of his father, Sir Michael, last named), lord lieut. Renfrewshire since 1869, vice-lieut. 1860-9. D.L., lieut.-col. 1st Renfrew vols. since 1860, grand master mason of Scotland since 1863, M.A. Oxon, late 2nd life guards ; contested Renfrewshire 1865; b. 25 Nov. 1826, m. 28 Dec. 1852. Lady Octavia Grosvenor, sister of Hugh, Duke [of Westminster, K.G. See Foster's Baronetage, and chart pedigree, page 325.

Montgomerie Granville John, of Grennan —— *Kirkcudbright stewartry* [1803-6, 1806-7, 1807-12.

4th son of John, 7th Earl of Galloway, and brother of Hon. Edward R. Stewart, M.P. 1806-7 ; b. 15 April 1780, and d. 10 Jan. 1860, leaving issue. See Foster's Peerage, and [chart pedigree, page 323.

Patrick, town clerk —— *Banff* 1661, 1663.

Patrick, bailie —— *Wigtown* 1678 conv.

Patrick Stuart, of Torrence —— *Lanarkshire* 1750-4.

Capt. in the royal regiment, served in Flanders and Germany, severely wounded, retired 1740 (brother of Col. James Stuart, M.P. 1734, and son of Alexander Stuart) ; d. unm. [1760.

Patrick James Herbert Crichton Stuart, of Rosemount, commonly called Lord James Stuart —— *Buteshire* 1820-6 ; *Ayr burghs* March to Dec. 1834, 1835-7, 1837-41, 1841-7, 1847-52 ; *Ayrshire* 1857-9, 1859 (3 May) until his [death s.b. 31 Oct. same year. See also England M.P.

Only brother of John, 2nd Marquis of Bute, and son of John, Lord Mountstuart (see M.P. England), lord lieut. Buteshire, M.P. Cardiff 1818-20, 1826-32, and as above ; assumed the addl. surname and arms of Crichton by royal licence 21 March 1817, and had patent of precedency as the son of a marquis 28 May 1817 ; b. (posthumous) 23 Aug. 1794, d. 7 Sept. 1859, having m. 13 July 1818, Hannah, dau. of Wm. Tighe, esq., of Woodstock, co. [Kilkenny, M.P.; she d. 5 June 1872, leaving issue. See Foster's Peerage.

Patrick Maxwell, merchant, London. *Renfrewshire* 1841 until his death s.b. [9 Dec. 1846. See also England M.P.

4th son of Sir Michael Shaw-Stewart, bart., M.P. Lancaster 1831-2, 1832-7, which he also contested 1837, chairman Oriental Steam Navigation Company and of the London & [Westminster Bank ; d. unm. 30 Oct. 1846, aged 55. See chart pedigree, page 325.

Robert Steuart —— *Linlithgow* 1602 conv.

Robert (sir), of Schillinglaw, knt. —— *Peebles-shire* 1612, 1617 conv. and parlt. [1621

Stewart, Steuart, and Stuart—*continued*.

Robert, provost —— *Linlithgow* 1665 conv.

Robert —— *Rothesay* 1678 conv.

Robert (Mr.), of Tillicoultrie, one of the senators of the college of justice —— *Rothesay* 1689 conv. (advocate, uncle of the sheriff, Sir James), 1689 until 25 April 1693 (when his seat was declared vacant because he had not taken the oath of allegiance and signed the assurance); *Dingwall* 1698-1702; (one of the comissars of Edinburgh, and burgess of Dingwall); *Buteshire* 1702-7, [sheriff principal of Clackmannan.

> Advocate 15 Nov. 1681, a comissioner for the treaty of the union, a commmissary of Edinburgh 1696, lord of session 25 July 1701, a commissioner of justiciary 18 March 1707, created a baronet 29 April following (son of Sir James Stewart, M.P., who was created a baronet 80 years before his son!!); m. Cecil, dau. of Robert Hamilton, of Presmennan, a lord [of session, and had issue. See chart pedigree, page 322.

Robert, of Lochlie, writer in Edinburgh —— *Rothesay* 1693-1702.

Robert (sir), of Allanbank —— *North Berwick* 1698-1702.

> Sir Robert Stuart, of Allanbank, bart., so created 15 Aug. 1687 (youngest son of Sir James Stuart, M.P. 1649); d. 1707, having m. 1st, Jean, dau. of Sir John Gilmour. of Craigmiller, bart., lord president of the court of session; he m. 2ndly, Helen, dau. of Sir Archibald [Cockburn, of Langton, and had issue. See chart pedigree, page 329.

Robert Steuart, of Alderston —— *Haddington burghs* 14 June 1831 until unseated August following; 1833-4, 1835-7 (a lord of the treasury), 1837-41, also a [lord of the treasury.

> A comissioner of supply for Haddingtonshire (son of Robert Steuart of Alderston), vice-president of Highland Society, London, lord of the treasury 1835-40, chargé d'affaires and consul-genl. at Santa Fè da Bogota, Spain, where he died 15 July 1843; he m. 1827, Maria, [3rd dau. of Col. Samuel Dalrymple, C.B., and had a son and 2 daus.

Thomas —— *Wigtown* 1648 —— 1661, provost.

Thomas (sir), of Grandtully, knt. —— *Perthshire* 1665 conv., 1667 conv.

> Son of Sir William Stewart, M.P. 1612, and his wife, Agnes Moncrieff. He was knighted by Charles I.; m. Grizel, dau. of Sir Alexander Menzies, of Wemyss, and d. 10 Aug. 1688, aged 80, having had a son John, who d. 1720, and 7 daughters. See chart pedigree, page 327.

Thomas (sir), of Balcaskie, senator of the college of justice —— *Fifeshire* [1685-6.

> Created a bart. 2 June 1683, a lord of session 7 Nov. 1683 as Lord Balcaskie, a lord of justiciary 28 July 1688, deprived of both offices at the revolution, a comissr. for the plantation of kirks (eldest son of Henry Stewart, 4th son of Sir William, M.P. 1612); m. Jean, dau. of George Mackenzie, Earl of Cromarty, and had issue. See Stewart, of Grandtully, [Foster's Baronetage, and chart pedigree, page 327.

Stewart, Steuart, and Stuart—*continued.*

Thomas (sir, 1689), of Coltness —— *North Berwick* 1689 conv., 1689 until his
[death s.b. 7 May 1698.

Sir Thomas Stewart, of Coltness, bart., so created 29 Jan. 1698, withdrew to Holland and his estates were forfeited, knighted by the Earl of Melville, lord high comissr. 1689 (eldest son of·Sir James Stewart, M.P. 1649); m.   dau. of Sir John Elliot, advocate,
[and d. 1698, leaving issue. See chart pedigree, page 329.

Walter (alderman) —— *Stirling* 1469, 1471, 1472.

Walter (sir), of Minto —— *Lanarkshire* 1639-41.

Walter (Steuart), provost —— *Banff* 1685-6, 1689 conv. (merchant), 1689 until
[his death s.b. 1 Nov. 1701.

Walter, of Pardovin —— *Linlithgow* 1700-2 (late provost), 1702-7 (provost).

William —— *Ayr* 1586 conv.

(**Sir William**), laird of Traquair —— *Peebles-shire* (as a minor baron) 1593, 1594 conv., 1596 conv. *bis.*, 1597, conv. (3), 1598 conv. (3), 1599 conv., 1602
[conv., 1604 parlt.

Gent. of the bedchamber to James VI., and governor of Dumbarton castle 1582 (3rd son
[of William Stewart, of Traquair); d. unm. 20 May 1605.

William (sir), of Grandtully, knt. —— *Perthshire* 1612, 1617 conv. and parlt.

Gent. of the bedchamber, knighted by James VI. (son of William Stuart, said to have been a member of the convention 1560); bd. 19 March 1672, having m. Agnes, dau. of Sir John Moncreiff, of Kinmonth, and had a son, Sir Thomas, M.P. 1665. See chart
[pedigree, page 327.

William, of Kilchattan —— *Buteshire* 1621 —— 1648 laird.

Probably descended from Robert, 2nd son of James Stewart and Elizabeth Blair, whom
[Douglas states to be ancestors of Stewart of Kilchattan and Ascog.

William (col.), of Castle Stewart —— *Wigtownshire* 1650.

William, of Castle Stewart —— *Wigtownshire* 1685, 1700-2, 1702-7.

William (Mr.), of Ambrismore —— *Buteshire* 1693-1702.

William (sir), of Castlemilk, bart. —— *Lanarkshire* 1696-1702.

2nd bart. (according to Douglas, on the death of his father, Sir Archibald, M.P. 1669); m. Margaret, dau. and sole heir of John Crawfurd, of Milton, and died Nov. 1715, leaving
[issue. See chart pedigree, page 326.

William—— *Inverness burghs* 1713-15 (remembrancer of the exchequer), 1715-22, *Ayr burghs* 1722-7 (sec. to the Prince of Wales), 1727-34 (elected also for the *Elgin burghs*), appointed to a crown office of profit 1731; *Elgin burghs*
[1734-41.

Of Castle Stewart, king's remembrancer of exchequer, and paymaster of annual bounties 1727 (3rd son of James, 2nd Earl of Galloway); m. Elizabeth, dau. and heir of John Gordon,
[of Cardoness, and had issue, probably ancestor of William, M.P. 1770.

Stewart, Steuart, and Stuart—*continued*.

William (capt.), provost of Whithorn —— *Wigtown burghs* 1741-7.

> Capt. 12th regt. of dragoons, brother of James, M.P. 1734, sons of James, 5th Earl of
> [Galloway. See chart pedigree, page 323.

William, of Castle Stewart —— *Wigtown burghs* 1770-4, *Kirkcudbright stewartry*
[1774-80.
> Of Lord Galloway's family, of the same branch as William, M.P. 1713.

William (lt.-genl., K.B.), of Over and Nether Clackans of Kirkcum, second lawful son of the deceased John, Earl of Galloway —— *Wigtownshire* 1796-1802,
Wigtown burghs 1803, until he accepted the Chiltern hundreds, s.b. 9 Aug.
1805 (then col.), *Wigtownshire* 1812 until he accepted the Chiltern hundreds,
[s.b. 2 Aug. 1816. See also England M.P.

> Lieut.-genl. the hon. Sir William Stewart, G.C.B., nominated 11 Sept. 1813, installed
> 1821, K.T.S., col. of the rifle brigade, on a diplomatic mission to Vienna 1792, commd.
> the Grenadier company under lieut.-genl. Sir Charles Grey in the West Indies 1793, and in
> the Leeward Islands 1794, lieut.-col. and assist. adjt.-genl., head-quarters 1795, and subse-
> quently to Major-genl. Doyle's army employed in France, commanded the 67th regt. at St.
> Domingo 1796, commandant at Mole St. Nicholas 1797, served with the allied armies under
> Archduke Charles, etc., in Suabia, Switzerland, and Italy. He formed the rifle corps (after-
> wards 95th regt.) in 1800, and appointed lieut.-col. of that regt. 1801, commanded the troops
> on board the British fleet in the Baltic, col. 2 April, after the action of Copenhagen, brigadier
> genl. 1804, commd. volunteer district of Cambridge, &c., and on staff in Sicily 1806, in Egypt
> 1807, commanded at Syracuse and Faro, Sicily 1808, major-genl., commanded the light
> brigade in the Walcheren expedition 1809, commanded at Cadiz 1810, and also commanded
> the 2nd division of the allied army in Portugal, on the staff of the eastern district 1812, and
> rejoined the allied army in his former command, until the termination of the campaign,
> including the actions of Busaco, Albuera, Vittoria, Pyrenees, Nivelle, Nive, Bayonne,
> Orthes, and Toulouse, he is said to have served in seventeen foreign campaigns, and was
> several times wounded, he received the thanks of the house of commons 1st for his great
> exertions at the battle of Vittoria 21 June 1813, 2ndly for the successful repulse of Marshal
> Soult between 25 July and 1 Aug., and lastly for the operations which concluded with the entire
> defeat of the enemy at Orthes, and the occupation of Bordeaux by the allied forces ; M.P
> Saltash 1795-6 and as above ; b. 10 Jan. 1772, d. 7 Jan. 1827, having m. 21 April 1804,
> Frances, dau. of hon. John Douglas (E. MORTON), she d. 6 Aug. 1833, leaving issue. See
> [Foster's Peerage, and chart pedigree, page 323.

Stirling.

—— the provost of —— *Stirling* 1524 —— 1531 —— 1532 —— 1543 ——
[1567.

(Sir Archibald), laird of Keir —— 1609 conv. (as a minor baron), *Stirlingshire*
[1617 conv. and parlt., 1621, 1625 conv.

> Knighted by James VI. before 1592 (son of Sir James Stirling, of Keir, who d. 1588) ; m.
> 1st, Mary, youngest dau. of David, 2nd Lord Drummond, and had a son, Sir James, of Keir,
> knighted 1607, o. v. p. 1614, he m. 2ndly (cont. 18 March 1589) Grizel, dau. of James, Lord
> [Ross, and died 1630, leaving with other issue a son, Sir John, of Garden, M.P. 1640-1.

Stirling—*continued*.

STIRLING OF GARDEN.

SIR ARCHIBALD, M.P. Stirlingshire 1617 conv., 1621, 1625 conv. =

SIR JOHN, M.P. Linlithgowshire 1640-1 =

SIR ARCHIBALD, M.P. Linlithgowshire 1646-7, 1648. 1661-3. 1667 conv.=

SIR JOHN, of Keir, M.P. Stirlingshire 1667-72, 1674, 1678 conv.

Archibald (sir), of Garden, knight, senator of the college of justice —— *Linlith-* [*gowshire* 1646-7, 1648, 1661-3, 1667 conv.

> Of Garden (on the death. 1643, of his father, Sir John, M.P. 1641) ; a member of various committees of war 1643, etc., commanded a troop of horse after the battle of Preston, fined £1,500 in 1654 by Oliver Cromwell's act of grace and pardon, a senator of the college of [justice 1 June 1661 ; d. 1667-8, leaving a son, Sir John, M.P. 1669.

George (Mr.) —— *Montrose* 1504.

George (sir), of Keir, knt. —— *Stirlingshire* 1639-41.

> Knighted at Holyrood House 2 June 1632 (son of Sir James Stirling, knt.), succeeded to Keir and Garden on the death, 1630, of his grandfather, Sir Archibald, M.P. 1617 ; was a [zealous supporter of the royal cause ; m. four times, and d. s.p. June 1667.

George, late deacon of the chirurgeon —— *Edinburgh* 1689 conv., 1689 until [his death s.b. 8 May 1695.

(Henry), of Ardoch —— *Dumbartonshire* 1621.

> Son of William Stirling, of Ardoch ; he d. Feb. 1628, having m. Helen, dau. of Sir John [Haldane, of Gleneagles, knt., she d. before 12 June 1622.

(Sir John), laird of Keir —— *Stirling* 1524.

> Sheriff of Perth 1515, one of the guardians of James V. (son of Sir Wm. Stirling, of Keir, who d. 1503) ; m. 1513, Margaret, dau. of Sir Walter Forrester, of Torwood, and d. 1539, [leaving issue.

John (sir), of Garden, knight —— *Linlithgowshire* 1640-1.

> Son of Sir Archibald Stirling, M.P. 1609, etc. ; m. twice, and d. 1643, leaving with other [issue a son, Sir Archibald, M.P. 1646.

John (sir), of Keir —— *Stirlingshire* 1669-72, 1674 (of Garden), 1678 conv.

> Eldest son of Sir Archibald Stirling, M.P. 1646, by his 1st wife, Elizabeth, dau. of Patrick Murray, 1st Lord Elibank ; Sir John b. at Ochiltree 13 April 1638 ; m. twice, and [d. March 1684, leaving issue.

Stirling—*continued.*

Sir William Stirling-Maxwell, of Keir House, Perthshire, bart.——*Perthshire* 1852-7, 1857-9, 1859-65, 1865-8 (William S. of Keir), 1874 until his [death s.b. 4 Feb. 1878, then a baronet.

Sir William Stirling-Maxwell, 9th baronet (as heir of entail in the estate of Pollok on the death of his maternal uncle Sir John in 1865), K.T. lord rector of Edinburgh university 1872-4, chancellor Glasgow university 1875-8, D.L. Perth, Lanark, and Renfrew, member of senate London university 1874-8, trustee of the British museum, assumed the additional name of Maxwell ; contested Perthshire 1868 ; b. 8 March 1818 ; d. 15 Jan. 1878, having m. 1st, 26 April 1865, Lady Anne Maria Leslie, 3rd dau. of David, Earl of Leven and Melville, she d. 8 Dec. 1874 ; he m. 2ndly, 1 Feb. 1877, Caroline Elizabeth Sarah, widow of Hon. George Chapple Norton (B. GRANTLEY), and dau. of Thomas Sheridan, esq., she d. 15 June following ; by his 1st wife he had 2 sons, (1) John Maxwell, and (2) Archibald, b. 1867. By the will of the late baronet, Sir William Stirling-Maxwell, his elder son, is, upon attaining his majority, to elect between the estates of Pollok and Keir, the baronetcy having originally been limited o the heirs of entail of the former, to which accordingly, as stated in the said will, it properly [belongs.

Stoddart.

Thomas —— *Lanark* 1678 conv.

Stone.

William (Stane), esq. —— *sheriffdom of Dumbarton, Argyle & Bute* 1659-60 [(WILLIS).

Stopford.

James George, commonly called Lord Viscount S. —— *Linlithgow burghs* [1796-1802, *Dumfries burghs* 1803-6. See also England M.P.

3rd Earl of Courtoun (on the death of his father, James, 2nd earl, 30 March 1810) ; K.T. 1821, P.C. 1793, a governor of the county Wexford, ensign in foot guards, lieut.-col. in Villier's fencible cavalry, treasurer of the household, 1793-1806, 1806-12, capt. of the band of gentlemen pensioners 1812, M.P. Gt. Bedwin, Wilts, 1790-6,1806-7, Marlborough 1807-10, [and as above ; b. 15 Aug. 1768, d. 15 June 1835, leaving issue. See Foster's Peerage.

Stormont.

William David Murray, commonly called Viscount S. —— *Perthshire* 1837 until he succ. as Earl of Mansfield 18 Feb. 1840. See also England M.P.

4th Earl of Mansfield K.T., hereditary keeper of Scone palace, a lord of the treasury 1834-5, M.P. Aldborough 1830-1, Woodstock 1831-2, Norwich 1832-7 and as above, lord high commissioner to general assembly of the Kirk of Scotland 1852, 1858, 1859, lieut.-col. Stirlingshire militia 1828-55, lord lieut. of Clackmannan since 1852, succeeded his father as 4th earl 18 Feb. 1840 as above, and succ. his grandmother as 3rd earl 11 July 1843 ; b. 21 [Feb. 1806 ; m. and has issue. See Foster's Peerage.

Strachan.

(Sir Alexander) laird of Thornton —— *Kincardineshire* 1617 conv. and parlt., [1630 conv.

Sir Alexander Strachan, of Thornton, cr. a baronet 28 May 1625, a commissioner of exchequer 1630 (son of Robert Strachan) ; m. Sarah, dau. of William Douglas, 9th Earl of [Angus, and d. about 1646, leaving Sir Alexander, next named.

Strachan—*continued.*

(Sir Alexander), laird of Thornton —— *Kincardineshire* 1650.

> 2nd baronet (on the death of his father, Sir Alexander, last named, 1646), joined the parliamentary forces, was forfeited and his estates confiscated; he m. twice, and d. s.p. at
> [Bruges 1659.

(Alexander ?) laird of Glenkindie —— *Aberdeenshire* 1650, 1651.

James —— *Brechin* 1669-72.

> Commissary of Brechin (son of David, bishop of Brechin); m. his cousin Barbara Hender-
> [son, and d. April 1685, leaving issue.

William —— 1450.

Straiton.

(——) laird of Lauriston —— 1604 and 1605 conv., as a minor baron.

Alexander (Stratoune) of that ilk, and of Lowriestoun —— *Kincardineshire*
[1661-3.

Strange.

Nicholas —— *Pittenweem* 1593.

Strong.

Alexander (Strang) —— *Forfar* 1645, 1645-6, 1648.

Sutherland.   See also Dunbar.

(Alexander), laird of Duffus —— *Sutherlandshire* 1646-7, *Elgin and Forres-shire*
[1650.

> One of the colonels for arming the kingdom 1649, cr. Lord Duffus 8 Dec. 1650, governor of Perth 1651, when he was compelled to surrender to Cromwell, fined £1500 by Cromwell's act of grace and pardon 1654 (son of William Sutherland, of Duffus); m. 1st, Margaret, relict of John, master of Berriedale, dau. of Colin Mackenzie, 1st Earl of Seaforth; he m. 2ndly, dau. of Sir Robert Innes, of Innes, bart.; and lastly, Margaret, 2nd dau. of James
> [Stewart, 5th Earl of Moray, by whom he had issue.

David, younger, of Kinnauld —— *Sutherlandshire* 1702-4.

William (Mr.), son of James, Lord Duffus, merchant burgess —— *Elgin* 1702-7.

> Hon. William Sutherland, of Roscommon (brother of James Dunbar, M.P. 1706), engaged in the rebellion of 1715, and was forfeited by act of parliament; he m. Helen Duff, sister of
> [the 1st Earl Fife, and died s.p.

Strathnaver.

William Sutherland, commonly called Lord Strathnaver —— *Wick burghs* May 1708 until s.b. 5 May 1709, because rendered incapable of taking his [seat being the eldest son of a peer of Scotland.

Only son of John, 15th Earl of Sutherland, was actively engaged with his father against the rebels in 1715, had the command of a regiment, distinguished himself at the battle of Glenshiel against the Spaniards and the rebels 1719 ; d. before his father, 19 July 1720, having m. (contract 9 Oct. 1705) Catherine, dau. of Wm. Morison, of Prestongrange, M.P., a commissioner for the union ; she d. 21 March 1765, having had with other issue a son [William, M.P., next named.

William Sutherland, commonly called Lord Strathnaver —— *Sutherlandshire* [1727 until he succeeded as 16th Earl of Sutherland 27 June 1733.

16th Earl of Sutherland (on the death of his grandfather, John, 15th Earl 27 June 1733), F.R.S. 1732, a representative peer 1734, 1741, first lord of police 1744, (son of William, M.P., last named) ; d. 7 Dec. 1750, aged 43, having m. 2 April 1734, Lady Elizabeth [Wemyss, eldest dau. of David, Earl of Wemyss ; she d. 20 Feb. 1747, leaving issue.

Suttie.

George, merchant burgess —— *Edinburgh* 1641.

George (sir), of Balgone, bart. —— *Haddingtonshire* 1768-74, 1774 until he ac-[cepted the manor of East Hendred s.b. 29 May 1777.

3rd bart. (on the death of his father, Sir George), lt.-col. of foot 1751 ; b. 11 Oct. 1715, d. 25 Nov. 1783, having m. 7 June 1757, Anne Grant, 2nd dau of William, Lord Preston-grange of session ; she d. 25 April 1809, having had with other issue a son, Sir James, M.P. [1816.

James —— *Forfar* 1617.

James Grant (sir), of Prestongrange and Balgone, bart. —— *Haddingtonshire* [1816-18, 1818-20, 1820-6.

Sir James Grant-Suttie, 4th bart. (on the death 1783 of his father, Sir George, M.P. 1768), succ. to the Prestongrange estates on the death of his aunt, Janet Grant, Countess of Hynd-ford 1818, lt.-col. in the army, admitted to Lincoln's Inn 4 April 1777 ; b. 10 May 1759, d.   1836, having m. 18 April 1792, Katherine Isabella, 2nd dau. of James Hamilton, esq. of Bangour, N.B. ; she d.   having had with two daus. a son, viz., Sir George, [5th bart. See Foster's Baronetage.

Swinton.

(Sir Alexander), laird of Swinton —— *Berwickshire* 1644-5.

Sheriff of Berwick 1640 (son of Robert Swinton, M.P.) ; m. 1620, Margaret, dau. of James Home, of Framspath and St. Bothans, and d. about 1652, having had with other issue John, M.P., Alexander, Lord Mersington of session, and Robert, who fell at the battle [of Worcester.

Archibald, merchant trafficker, bailie —— *Dysart* 1695-1702.

Swinton—*continued.*

ROBERT SWINTON, M.P. Berwickshire 1612, 1621 =

SIR ALEXANDER SWINTON, M.P. Berwickshire 1644-5 =

JOHN SWINTON, M.P. Berwickshire 1649, 1650, 1653 =

SIR JOHN SWINTON, M.P. Berwickshire 1690-1702, 1702-7, 1707-8.

John of that ilk —— *Berwickshire* 1649 (younger), 1650 (1653, *sheriffdom of [Merse* 1654-5, 1656-8, 1659-60, WILLIS).

One of the colonels for Berwickshire for putting the kingdom into a posture of defence 1649, and (according to Douglas) he was taken prisoner to England by Oliver Cromwell, and was in that capacity at the battle of Worcester, forfeited in his absence 1651. Oliver made him a lord of the privy council, and a comissr. for the administration of justice to the people of Scotland, his forfeiture was confirmed on the restoration; m. 1st, 1645, Margaret, dau. of William Stewart, Lord Blantyre. and 2ndly, Frances Hancock, widow of Aront Sommans, of [Jersey, and d. 1639, leaving by his first wife a son, Sir John, next named.

John (sir 1695-6), of that ilk —— *Berwickshire* 1690-1702, 1702-7, 1707-8 (1st [parlt. G.B.)

A merchant in Holland, where he resided until 1690, when his father's forfeiture was rescinded (son of John, M.P., last named); m. 1st, Sarah, dau. of William Welsh, of London, merchant, and 2ndly, Anne, dau. of Sir Robert Sinclair, of Longformacus, bart., and d. 1724, having [had issue.

Mark —— *Inverkeithing* 1540.

Robert of that ilk —— *Berwickshire* 1612 (the laird), 1621.

Sheriff of Berwickshire (son of Sir John Swinton of that ilk, who d. 1584); m. 1st, Katherine, dau. of William Hay, Lord Yester; he m. 2ndly, 1597, Jean, sister of Patrick [Hepburn, of Whitecastle, by whom he had a son, Sir Alexander, M.P. 1644.

Thomas —— *Pittenweem* 1662-3.

Walter (Mr.) —— *Dornoch* 1650.

Sword.

James —— *St. Andrews* 1641, 1649-51 (*St. Andrews, Dysart, &c.* 1654-5, then a [burgess of St. Andrews, WILLIS.

Sydserf.

Archibald, merchant burgess —— *Edinburgh* 1648, 1651.

Sykes.

William Henry (colonel) —— *Aberdeen* 1857-9, 1859-65, 1866-8, 1868 until [his death s.b. 29 June 1872.

East India director and chairman 1856-7, lord rector of Marischal College, Aberdeen, 1854-5, entered the Bombay army 1804, statistical reporter to the Government at Bombay and retired with rank of colonel 1838; contested Aberdeen 1847 (son of Samuel Sykes, of Friezing Hall, Yorkshire); d. 16 June 1872, aged 82, having m. 1824, Elizabeth, [youngest dau. of Wm. Hay, esq., of Renistoun, N.B., and had issue.

Symmer.

George, of Balzeordie —— *Forfarshire* 1649.

T.

Tailyour.

Robert —— *St. Andrews* 1617, 1625 conv., 1628-33, 1643-4 conv. ; *Montrose,*
[1645.

Robert, merchant burgess —— *Montrose* 1665 conv. (provost), 1667 conv.,
[1669-74, 1678 conv. (late bailie).

Tait.

William —— *Stirling burghs* 1797 until his death s.b. 24 Feb. 1800.

Died 7 Jan. 1800. [Mem. William Tait, esq., 2nd son of Alexander Tait, clerk of the
[sasines at Edinburgh, esq., admitted to Lincoln's Inn 4 June 1777.

Temple.

Arthur, of Ravelrig, chirurgeon —— *Edinburgh* 1669.

Tenent.

Alexander —— *Lanark* 1644 conv. ; *Lanarkshire* 1649, or Gideon Jak.

Tennant.

Charles, of Glasgow, merchant of the Glen, Peebles-shire —— *Glasgow* 1879-80;
[*Selkirkshire* and *Peebles-shire* since 1880. See foot-note

Terbrax.

George (esq.) —— *Lanark, Glasgow, &c.* 1656-8. WILLIS.

Teviotdale.

(——), the sheriff of —— *Roxburghshire* 1645.

Sir William Douglas or Sir Thomas Ker. See note in official return.

TENNANT, CHARLES, of the Glen, Peebles-shire, D.L., and St. Rollox, co. Lanark, D.L., and of
Glasgow, merchant and manufacturer, M.P. as above (son of John Tennant, of St. Rollox);
b. 4 Nov. 1823, m. 2 Aug. 1849, Emma, dau. of Richard Winsloe, of Mount Nebo, Somerset, and has
3 sons and 5 daus.

(1) Edward Priaulx, b. 30 Nov. 1859.

(2) Francis John, b. 20 Oct. 1861.   · (3) Harold John, b. 18 Nov. 1865.

.(4) Pauline, m. 2 Feb. 1875 to Thomas Gordon-Duff, jun., of Drummuir and Park, co. Banff. See
page 107.

(5) Charlotte, m. 7 April 1877 to Thomas, 4th Lord Ribblesdale.

(6) Lucy, m. 30 April 1879 to Thomas Graham Smith, esq., of Easton Grey, Wilts.

(7) Laura.   (8) Margaret.

The Glen, Peebles ; St. Rollox, Glasgow.

Clubs—Brooks and Reform.

Thane.

James —— *Brechin* 1585.

Thomson.

Alexander, hammerman and present deacon convener —— *Edinburgh* 1695-
[1702.

Gawen, provost —— *Peebles* 1678 conv.

George (Thompson), jun., merchant and shipowner, Aberdeen —— *Aberdeen*
[1852-7.

Of Pittmedden House, Dyce, near Aberdeen, provost of Aberdeen 1847-50, J.P. Aberdeenshire (son of A. Thompson, esq., of Madras, by Anne, dau. of G. Stephens, esq.) ; b.
[1804, m.   1830, Christian Little, dau. of Rev. Dr. Kidd ; she d. 1874.

John, auditor-genl. for the revenues of Scotland —— *Peebles-shire and Selkirk*
[*sheriffdom* 1654-5 (English parlt.). *Edinburgh* 1656-8, 1659-60. (WILLIS.)

Patrick —— *Peebles* 1640.   •

Patrick, treasurer of the burgh of Edinburgh and merchant burgess of Stirling
[—— *Stirling* 1696 until his death s.b. 7 Dec. 1697.

Peter —— *Anstruther Wester* 1649 (in absence of Andro Richardson).

Thomas, bailie —— *Inverkeithing* 1661-3.

Walter —— *Inverness* 1458.   •

William —— *Forfar* 1583.   .

William Thompson, (Mr.) burgess of Haddington —— *Haddington burghs*
[1654-5 (in English parlt.)

Threipland.

Patrick, dean of guild —— *Perth* 1661-3 (in absence of Mr. John Paterson of
Benchillis, provost), 1665 conv. (merchant trafficker, provost), 1667 conv.,
1669-74.

Sir Patrick Threipland, treasurer of the burgh of Perth 1657, bailie 1659-62, provost 1664,
1669, and in 1670 was succeeded by his brother George Threipland, but resumed that office
1671, when he is for the first time styled " Threipland of Fingask," knighted by Charles II.
1674, provost 1687, cr. a bart. of Nova Scotia, with remainder to his heirs male, 10 Nov.
1687 ; m. 13 Mar. 1665, Euphemia, dau. of John Conqueror, esq., of Frierton ; he d. 1689,
[leaving issue. See Foster's Peerage.

Tindal.

Nicolas Conyngham, of London —— *Wigtown burghs* 1824-6. See also
[England M.P.

Sir Nicolas Conyngham Tindal, chief justice of the common pleas, Hon. D.C.L., B.A. (8th wrangler) Trin. Coll. Camb. 1799, M.A. 1802 and fellow, called to the bar of Lincoln's Inn 20 June 1809, one of the counsel for Queen Caroline 1820, solicitor-genl. and knighted 20 Sept. 1826, M.P. Harwich 1826-7, Cambridge University 1827, chief justice common pleas 9 June 1829 until his death 6 July 1846 (son of Robert Tindal, of Coval Hall, Chelmsford, attorney-at-law, by his wife Sarah, only dau. of John Pocock, of Greenwich Hospital) ; b. at Coval 12 Dec. 1776, m. 2 Sept. 1809, Merelina, dau. of Thomas Symonds, capt. R.N., and sister of Admiral Sir Wm. Symonds, C.B., surveyor of the navy; she d.
[22 Feb. 1818, leaving issue.

Tod.

Robert —— 1479 *bis.*

Thomas —— *Edinburgh* 1485.

Tolhurst.

Jeremy (esq.) burgess of Dumfries —— *Dumfries, &c.* 1654-5, 1659-60. (WILLIS.)

Tore.

Adam —— *Edinburgh* 1357.

Touris.

—— (the laird of) —— *Edinburgh* 1605 (a minor baron).

George, of —— *Edinburgh* 1504.

John, of Inverleith —— 1597.

Townsend.

Chauncy —— *Wigtown burghs* 1768 until his death s.b. 7 May 1770. See also
[England M.P.

Of Austin Friars, London, M.P. Westbury 1748, 1754-61, 1761-68 ; died 28 March 1770, father of James Townsend, admitted to Lincoln's Inn 19 Jan. 1756, Lord Mayor of London
[1773.

Traill.

George, of Quendall, provost —— *Kirkwall* 1689 conv., 1689-98.

Provost of Kirkwall 1690, fined for absence 10 July 1689 and 25 April 1693, but took the oath and signed the assurance 2 May 1693 (son of James Traill, of Westore), ancestor of
[George Traill, M.P. 1830; m. Anne Blaikie.

George, of Hobbister —— *Orkney and Shetlandshire* 1830-1, 1831-2 (younger), 1833-4, *Caithness-shire* 1841-7 (of Ratter), 1847-52, 1852-7, 1857-9, 1859-65, 1865-8, 1868 until he accepted the stewardship of the manor of Northstead,
[Yorkshire, s. b. 26 Aug. 1869.

Of Castle Hill, Caithness, and Tretness and Gramont, isle of Orkney, N.B., J.P. D.L., advocate 1811, vice-lieut. Caithness-shire ; contested Orkney 1835, Caithness 1837 (son of
[James Traill, of Ratter, N.B.) ; d. unm. 29 Sept. 1871, aged 83.

John —— *Forfar* 1579, 1587, 1597 conv.

John —— *Forfar* 1612.

Tran.
Patrick —— *Irvine* 1594 conv.

Tranent.
William, of —— *Haddington* 1367.

Trevelyan.
George Otto, of London —— *Hawick* (or *Border*) *burghs* 1868-74 (a lord of the
[admiralty 1869), 1874-80, and since 1880. See also M.P. England.
Chief secretary Ireland May 1882, lord of the admiralty 1869-70, sec. to the admiralty
1880-2, M.P. Tynemouth 1865-80 as above ; b. 20 July 1838, m. and has issue. See
[Foster's Baronetage.

Trotter.
George —— *North Berwick* 1665 conv.
Of Charter Hall, son of Robert Trotter, and d. s.p.

Tulloch.
John —— *Nairn* 1639-41, 1649 (or Hugh Ross).
Patrick, of Boigtoun, provost —— *Forres* 1669-72, 1678 conv.
Thomas (younger), of Tannachies —— *Forres* 1689 conv., 1689 until 25 April
1693, when his seat was declared vacant because he had not taken the oath of
[allegiance and signed the assurance.

Tullonis.
John, town clerk ——*Anstruther Wester* 1639-40.

Turing.
Alexander —— *Edinburgh* 1479.

Turnbull.
George, bailie —— *Cupar* 1661 until his death s. b. 23 April 1662.

Turnoure.
John —— *Wigtown* 1612 (*alias* Curroure), 1617, 1621.

Tweeddale.
John, Earl of —— *Sheriffdom of East Lothian* 1656-8, 1659-60 (WILLIS).
2nd Earl (on the death of his father John 1654), joined the standard of Charles I. at
Nottingham, had the command of a regt. at Marston Moor against the royal army 1644, had
the command of the East Lothian regt. at the battle of Preston, etc. 1648, when the Scots
were totally routed, assisted at the coronation of Charles II. at Scone, P.C. Charles II., a
commissioner of the treasury, extra lord of session 1664, high chancellor of Scotland 5 Jan.
1692, created Marquis of Tweeddale, Earl of Gifford, Viscount of Walden, and Lord Hay, of
Yester, with remainder to his heirs male whatsoever, 17 Dec. 1694 ; d. 11 Aug, 1697, aged
71, having m. Jean, dau. of Walter Scott, 1st Earl of Buccleuch, and had with other issue 3
[sons. See Foster's Peerage.

Tweedie.
Gilbert —— *Peebles* 1579.
(James) laird of Drummelzier —— 1605 conv. (as a minor baron) *Peebles-shire*
[1608 conv.

U.

Udny.

John —— (? *Brechin* 1625 conv.), *Aberdeenshire* 1645 (laird of Udnie), 1648.

4th son of William Udny of that ilk; served in the army of Charles I. in England, but on his return to Scotland he was compelled to subscribe the covenant; m. Isobel Fraser, and was [dead in 1665, leaving issue.

John, merchant trafficker, bailie —— *Kintore* 1681-2, 1685-6, then of Culter-
Probably 3rd son of the last named M.P.   [cullone, bailie.

John of that ilk —— *Aberdeenshire* 1702-7.

Son of Alexander Udny of that ilk and Anna Renton; he m. March 1701, Martha, dau. [of George Gordon, Earl of Aberdeen, lord high chancellor of Scotland, and had issue·

Udwart.

Nicholas —— *Edinburgh* 1585.

Urquhart.

Adam, of Meldrum —— *Aberdeenshire* 1665 conv., 1667 conv., 1669-74, 1678
[conv.

Lieut. of the independent troop of horse guards commanded by his uncle, the Earl of Airly, upon whose resignation he was made captain, etc. (2nd son of Patrick Urquhart, of Lethinty); d. 10 Nov. 1684, having m. 1667, Mary, dau. of Lewis Gordon, Marquis of Huntly, and had a son, John, M.P. 1703; she re-m. to James, Earl of Perth, lord high chancellor of Scotland, [and d. at St. Germans March 1726, aged 80.

Alexander (sir), of Cromartie, knt. bart. —— *Banffshire* 1667 conv.

Probably 2nd son of Sir Thomas Urquhart, of Cromarty, M.P. 1600, and only a knight; [he m. ——, dau. of Lord Elphinstone, and Douglas adds that he died in 1661.

Alexander, of Newhall —— *Cromartyshire* 1715-22 (capt.); *Ross-shire* 1722-7
[(lt.-col.)

Duncan, provost of Forres —— *Inverness burghs* 1737-41.
Served in the foot guards; d. 11 Jan. 1741-2.

John (sir), of Cromartie, knt. —— *Inverness-shire* 1661-3.

Son of John Urquhart, of Leathers, etc., knighted by Charles II.; m. ——, dau. of George [Mackenzie, 2nd Earl of Seaforth, and had issue.

John, of Craighouse —— *Cromartyshire* 1693.

SCOTCH MEMBERS.   x x

Urquhart—*continued.*

John, of Meldrum —— *Dornoch* 1703-7.

Master of the works in Scotland (son of Adam Urquhart, M.P. 1665) ; m. Jean, dau. of Sir
[Hugh Campbell, of Calder, and d. 1726, aged 59, leaving issue.

Robert, jun., of Burdsyeards —— *Elginshire* 1708-10.

[Mem.   Robert, only son of lieut.-col. Duncan Urquhart, of Birdsyards, co. Elgin, was
[admitted to Lincoln's Inn 4 Feb. 1786.

(Sir Thomas), of Cromartie —— *Cromartyshire* 1600 (a lord of the articles),
1605 (as a minor baron), 1608 conv. (tutor of Cromartie), 1617 (Thomas, of
Cromartie) ; *Inverness-shire* 1625 conv. (sheriff of Cromartie) ; *Cromartyshire*
[1628-33 (then a knight).

Knighted by James VI. 1617 (son of Henry Urquhart) ; m. Christian, dau. of Alexander,
Lord Elphinstone, and had with 3 daus. 2 sons, viz., Sir Thomas, knighted 7 April 1641, and
[Sir Alexander, M.P. 1667.

Thomas —— *Forres* 1681-2.

Thomas —— *Cromarty* 1669-70.

Walter, of Crombie —— *Banffshire* 1639-40, went "furth of the realme."

V.

Vans (or Vaus).

(**Sir John**), laird of Barnbarroch —— *Wigtownshire* 1617.

Of Longcastle, Wigtownshire, of the privy chamber to James VI.; up to the beginning of the 18th century this name was written Waus or Vaus, Wauss or Vauss (son of Sir Patrick, next named); m. Margaret, dau. of Uchtred McDouall, of Garthland, and d. 1642, having [had issue.

(**Sir Patrick**), laird of Barnbarroch (as a minor baron) —— 1590 conv. and 1592 [parlt.; *Wigtownshire* 1593 (bis), 1594.

Sir Patrick Vans, of Barnbarroch, nominated one of the privy council, and a senator of the college of justice 1576, in 1587 he was one of an embassy to Denmark (2nd son of John Vans, of Barnbarroch); m. Katherine Kennedy, dau. of the Earl of Cassilis; he d. [22 July 1597, having had a son, Sir John.

Patrick, of Barnbarroch, —— *Wigtownshire* 10 Nov. 1710 until unseated 3 [March following (col.); *Wigtown burghs* 1715-22.

Son of Alexander Vans, of Barnbarroch; he m. 1st Jean, dau. of Sir James Campbell, of Lawers, and had a son and dau.; he m. 2ndly, 28 Feb. 1715, Barbara, dau. of Patrick [McDouall, of Freugh, and d. 27 Jan. 1733, having had 2 sons and 3 daus.

Vans-Agnew.

Robert, of Barnbarroch and Wigtownshire —— *Wigtownshire* 1873-4, 1874-80. [See foot-note.

Veitch.

James, of Elliock, advocate —— *Dumfries-shire* 1755-60.

Son of William Veitch, of Elliock, W.S., admitted advocate 15 Feb. 1738, sheriff depu [of Peebles-shire 1747, a lord of session 6 March 1761; d. at Edinburgh July 1793.

VANS-AGNEW, ROBERT, of Barnbarroch and Sheuchan, co. Wigtown, J.P., D.L., M.P. as above, served in rifle brigade 1835-42 (son of Patrick Vans-Agnew); b. 4 March 1817, m. 22 April 1852, Mary Elizabeth, 2nd dau. of Sir David Hunter-Blair, bart., of Blairquhan, co. Ayr; she d. 1 August 1870, having had 3 sons and 3 daus.

(1) Patrick Alexander, b. 20 Oct. 1856.

(2) James David, b. 4 April 1858.   (3) John, b. 23 Aug. 1859.

(4) Elizabeth, m. 10 June 1880 to Edward Salvin Bowlby, esq.

(5) Catherine; m. 20 Jan. 1875, to Erasmus, only son of Robert Frederick Gower, esq., of Castle Malgwin, co. Cardigan.

(6) Mary.

Barnbarroch, near Wigtown, and Park House, Stranraer, N.B.

Clubs—Carlton and Conservative; New Club, Edinburgh.

Veitch—*continued.*

John (sir), of Dawick —— *Peebles-shire* 1630 (the laird), 1643-4 conv., 1644-5, [1648 (the laird).

He m. about 1643 Christian, dau. of James Nasmyth, M.P., and had issue.

John, of Dawick —— *Peebles-shire* 1669-74, 1678 conv.

Vere. See also Weir.

Daniel Weir, of Stonebyres —— *Linlithgow burghs* 1722 until his death s.b. [16 April 1725.

Died 21 May 1724.

James Vere, of Stonebyres —— *Lanarkshire* 1754 until his death s.b. 17 Jan. [1760

Died 4 Dec. 1759.

Villiers.

John Charles, a privy councillor —— *Wick burghs* 1802 until he accepted the Chiltern hundreds, s.b. 26 June 1805, prothonotary of common pleas co. [pal. Lanc. 1804. See also England M.P.

3rd Earl of Clarendon (on the death of his brother Thomas, 7 March 1824), P.C. 1787, chief justice in Eyre north of Trent 1790, prothonotary co. pal. Lanc. 1804, M.A. St. John's Coll. 1776, barrister-at-law Lincoln's Inn 22 June 1779, M.P. Old Sarum 1783-4 (then joint king's counsel in the duchy court of Lancaster), 1784-90, Dartmouth 1790-6, 1796-1802, Queenborough 1807-12, 1820-4, and as above (son of Thomas, 1st earl); b. 14 Nov. 1757, [d. s.p.s. 22 Dec. 1838. See Foster's Peerage.

Vinththropegesse.

Stephen (col.), of Aberdeen —— *Banff and Aberdeen* 1656-8 (WILLIS).

W.

Wade.

David (Wald) —— *Anstruther Easter* 1593, 1594 conv.

Waghorn.

Peter —— *Dumbarton* 1357.

Walker.

George Gustavus, of Crawfordton —— *Dumfries-shire* 1865-8, 1869-74 (major).
[See foot-note.

Peter —— *Dunfermline* 1648, 1649 (or William Walker), 1650, 1665 conv. (pro-
[vost), 1667 conv. (late provost), 1669-74 (provost).

William —— *Dunfermline* 1644 conv., 1644-5, 1645-7, 1649 (or Peter Walker),
[1650-1.

Wallace.

(——), laird of Carnell —— 1604 (as a minor baron); *Ayrshire* 1605, 1609 conv.,
[—— 1621.

Adam —— *Ayr* 1526.

Edward —— *Ayr* 1579.

Hugh, of Inglistoun, "heritor of the barony of Larg and others in the stewartry,"
his Majesty's cash keeper —— *Kirkcudbright stewartry* 1685-6 ; *Kintore* 1689
conv. (then writer to the signet at Edinburgh), 1689 parlt. until 28 April
1693, when his seat was declared vacant because he had not signed the
[assurance.

Matthew —— 1494.

Patrick, bailie —— *Kinghorn* 1689 conv., 1689-1702.

WALKER, GEORGE GUSTAVUS, of Crawfordton, co. Dumfries, J.P. and for co. Kirkcudbright, D.L.
Inverness-shire, B.A. Balliol Coll., Oxford, 1851, M.A. 1855, lt.-col.-comdt. Scottish borderers
militia, M.P. as above (eldest son of John Walker, of Crawfordton) ; b. 1831, m.   1856, Anne
Murray, dau. of late Adml. George Gustavus Lennock, and has with other issue a son.
    (1) George Laurie, b. 1871.
    Crawfordton, Thornhill, and Loch Treig, Kingussie, N.B.
    Club—Carlton, S.W.

Wallace—continued.

Robert, of Kelly——*Greenock* 1833-4, 1835-7; 1837-41, 1841 until he accepted
[the Chiltern hundreds s.b. 18 April 1845.

Son of John Wallace and brother of Col. Sir James Maxwell Wallace, K.H.; he m.
[Margaret, 2nd dau. of Sir Wm. Forbes, bart., of Craigievar, and d. s.p. 1 April 1855.

Thomas (sir), of Craigie, knt. —— *Ayrshire* 1665 conv., 1667 conv.

"Sir Thomas Wallace, of Craigie. He seems to have a former patent disponed to him by
the last Sir Hewgh Wallace, which is ratified 8th of March 1670, bot maketh him not to
take place conforme to date of the said patent.   A.M.B."—Milne's list of Nova Scotia
baronets, see Foster's Baronetage.   (Son of William Wallace, of Failford), advocate before
the Restoration, re-admitted 4 July 1661, a lord of session 8 June 1671, justice clerk 9 July
[1675 ; d. 26 March 1680.

Wallch.

Thomas —— *St. Andrews* 1572 conv.

Waller.

Thomas, of Gray's Inn —— *Linlithgow, Queensferry, Perth, Culross, and Stirling*
[1659-60 (WILLIS).

Thomas Waller of Bentley, Yorkshire, cornet to Sir Francis Cobb, knt., under Prince
Rupert, capt. of foot in the regiment of Sir John Hotham, bart., admitted to Gray's Inn
4 May 1638 (son of Nicholas Waller, of Beverley) ; m. Hannah, dau. and co-h. of Gervase
Hamerton, of Aukeburgh, co. Linc., and had with other issue a son Thomas, admitted to
[Gray's Inn 6 Nov. 1651.

Wardlaw.

Henry (sir), of Pitreavie —— *Fifeshire* 1661-3.

Query, cr. a baronet 5 March 1631. See Foster's Baronetage.

Patrick (Mr.), of Torry —— *Fifeshire* 1625 conv., *Kinghorn* 1630 conv.

Thomas (Mr.) —— *Dunfermline* 1612, 1617, 1621.

Of Logie (brother of Sir Henry, of Pitreavie, father of the 1st baronet) ; m. 1601,
[Catherine Alison, and had 4 sons and 6 daus.

Warrand.

Thomas —— *Forres* 1649.

Warrender.

George, of Lochend, lord provost of Edinburgh —— *Edinburgh city* 1715 until
[his death, as a baronet, s.b. 18 March 1721.

Sir George Warrender, of Edinburgh, merchant (son of George Warrender, of Lochend,
and his wife Margaret, dau. of Sir David Cuninghame, bart., of Milncraig), lord provost of
Edinburgh at the time of the union and the accession of George I., cr. a baronet 2 June
1715 ; d. in London, March 1720-1, having married twice, and had issue.   See Foster's
[Baronetage.

George (sir), of Lochend, bart —— *Haddington burghs* 1807-12. See England M.P.

4th baronet (on the death of his father, Sir Patrick, next named M.P.), P.C. 1822, F.R.S.,
lieut.-col. Berwickshire mil., M.P. Truro 1812-18, Sandwich 1818-26, Westbury 1826-30,
Honiton 1830-2 ; d. s.p. 21 Feb. 1849, aged 68, having m. 3 Oct. 1810, Hon. Anne Boscawen,
[dau. of George Evelyn, 3rd Viscount Falmouth ; she d. 5 March 1871.

Warrender—*continued.*

SIR GEORGE WARRENDER, Bart., M.P. Edinburgh city 1715-21 =⌐

SIR PATRICK, 3rd bart., M.P. Haddington burghs 1768-74 =⌐

SIR GEORGE, 4th bart., M.P. Haddington burghs 1807-12, etc.

Patrick, younger, of Lochend (lieut.-col.) —— *Haddington burghs* 1768-74, [remembrancer of the exchequer in Scotland 1771.

3rd baronet (on the death of his father, Sir John, Jan. 1773); lieut.-col. of dragoons, served in the cavalry at Minden; b. 7 March 1731; d. 14 June 1799, having m. 1780, H. Blair; she d. 8 May, 1838, leaving with other issue Sir George, 4th baronet, M.P. 1807.

Waterlow.

Sydney Hedley (sir), of Highgate, London, knt. —— *Dumfries-shire* 1868 (23 Nov.) until declared incapable of sitting in parlt. under statute 22 Geo. III., [c. 45, s.b. 31 March 1869. See also England M.P. See foot-note.

Watson.

Alexander, of Æthernie —— *St. Andrews* 1702-7.

Andrew —— *Burntisland* 1628-33.

David —— *St. Andrews* 1593, 1597 conv. (bis.), 1598 conv. (bis.)

James —— *St. Andrews* 1630 conv.

John —— *Selkirk* 1587.

Robert, provost —— *Dumbarton* 1672, 1678 conv.

Thomas, councillor —— *Anstruther Wester* 1661.

Walter, provost —— *Dumbarton* 1661-3, 1669-70.

WATERLOW, ALDERMAN SIR SYDNEY HEDLEY, of Fairseat, Kent, baronet, so cr. 4 Aug. 1873, J.P. Middlesex, Kent, and Londonderry, one of H.M.'s lieutenants for the city of London and Middlesex 1866-7, lord mayor 1872-3, knight of the Medjidie, knight of the Lion and Sun of Persia, knight of the Iron Crown of Italy, officer of the Legion of Honour of the French republic, hon. treasurer of St. Bartholomew's hospital, governor of the Irish society, deputy-chairman of the London, Chatham and Dover railway company, M.P. Maidstone 1874-80, Gravesend since 1880, and as above (4th son of late James Waterlow, of Peckham, Surrey); b. 1 Nov. 1822; m. 1st, 7 May 1845, Anna Maria, youngest dau. of William Hickson, of Fairseat, Kent; she d. 21 Jan. 1880; he m. 2ndly, 28 March 1882, Margaret, 2nd dau. of late William Hamilton, of Napa, California, U.S. By his 1st wife he has with other issue (see Foster's Baronetage) a son.

(1) Philip Hickson; b. 30 Oct. 1847; m. and has issue.

Fairseat House, Highgate, N.; Addington Park, near Malling, Kent.

Clubs—Reform, City Liberal.

Watson—*continued.*

William —— *Pittenweem* 1640, 1645, (26 Nov.) till 27 Jan. following; 1648.

William —— *Edinburgh* 1685-6.

William, LL.D. of the University of Edinburgh, Queen's advocate for Scotland, and dean of the faculty of advocates —— *Glasgow and Aberdeen* universities [1876-80.

Baron Watson, of Thankerton, so created 28 April, 1880, under the "appellate jurisdiction act," P.C. 1878, LL.D. Edin. 1876, advocate 1851, dean of the faculty 1875-6, lord advocate for Scotland 1876-80, solicitor-genl. 1874-6 (son of Rev. Thomas Watson, minister of Covington, Lanarks.) ; b. 1828, m. 1868, Margaret, youngest dau. of Dugald John Banna-[tyne, esq.　See Foster's Peerage.

Watt.

John —— *Edinburgh* 1597 conv.

John *Inverness* 1651.

Wauchope.

Henry, of Kildavannan —— *Buteshire* 1762-8.

John (sir), of Niddrie, knt. marischal —— *Edinburghshire* 1639-41, 1644 (laird), [1649-50, 1650-1.

Knighted by Charles I. in 1638 (son of Francis Wauchope, of Niddrie) ; m. twice and had [issue.

Waugh.

William —— *Forres* 1579.

William, merchant trafficker, bailie —— *Selkirk* 1678 conv., 1685-6.

Webster.

John, LL.D., of Edgehill, Aberdeen —— *Aberdeen* since 1880.　See foot-note.

Wedderburn.　See also Halkett.

Alexander —— *Dundee* 1585, 1594 conv., 1597 conv., 1604, 1605 parlt. and [conv., 1607, 1608, 1609 conv.

Son of David Wedderburn; according to Douglas, he accompanied James VI. to England, and received a ring from the king ; he m. Helen, dau. of John Ramsay, of Brachmont, co. [Fife, and died (it is said) in 1618, leaving with other issue a son Alexander, next named.

Alexander (Mr.), town clerk —— *Dundee* 1612, 1618, 1621, 1628-33.

Of Kingennie, a commissioner for regulating weights and measures, Scotland 1618 (son of Alexander, last named) ; m. Magdalene, dau. of John Scrimgeour, of Kirkton, and had [Alexander, M.P. 1661.

WEBSTER, JOHN, of Edgehill, Aberdeen, advocate 1831, LL.D. Aberdeen, lord provost of Aberdeen 1856-9, vice-president British association, Aberdeen, 1859, &c. (son of Alexander Webster, of Aberdeen, advocate); b. 1810, m. 1839, Margaret, dau. of Mr. David Chalmers, of Westburn, Aberdeen. *Edgehill, Aberdeen.*

Wedderburn—*continued.*

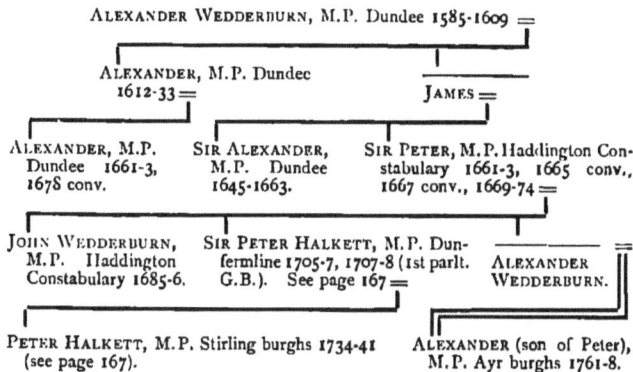

ALEXANDER WEDDERBURN, M.P. Dundee 1585-1609 =

ALEXANDER, M.P. Dundee
1612-33 =

JAMES =

ALEXANDER, M.P. Dundee 1661-3, 1678 conv.

SIR ALEXANDER, M.P. Dundee 1645-1663.

SIR PETER, M.P. Haddington Constabulary 1661-3, 1665 conv., 1667 conv., 1669-74 =

JOHN WEDDERBURN, M.P. Haddington Constabulary 1685-6.

SIR PETER HALKETT, M.P. Dunfermline 1705-7, 1707-8 (1st parlt. G.B.). See page 167 =

ALEXANDER WEDDERBURN.

PETER HALKETT, M.P. Stirling burghs 1734-41 (see page 167).

ALEXANDER (son of Peter), M.P. Ayr burghs 1761-8.

Alexander (sir), town clerk —— *Dundee* 1645-7, 1646-7 (or Robert Davidson), 1648, 1651, (*Forfar, Dundee, &c.* 1654-5, 1656-8, WILLIS); *Dundee* 1661-3 [(or Alexander, of Kingennie).

Sir Alexander Wedderburn, of Blackness, co. Forfar (brother of Sir Peter Wedderburn, of Gosford, M.P. Haddington), town clerk of Dundee, one of the committee of parliament 1640, a commissioner to the treaty of Ripon 1641, knighted 1642, a commissioner for regulating weights and measures of Scotland 1661, had an annual pension of £100 for his services under the great seal, by grant dated at Whitehall 10 Feb. 1664 ; m. Matilda, dau. of Sir Andrew Fletcher, of Innerpeffer, a lord of session, he d. 18 Nov. 1676, having had with 6 daus. [5 sons, of whom the eldest, Sir John, cr. a bart. See Foster's Baronetage.

Alexander, of Kingany (provost) —— *Dundee* 1661-3 (or Sir Alexander, of Blackness, knt.), 1678 conv.

Son of Alexander, M.P. 1621 ; m. twice, and had with other issue a dau. Magdalene, m. [to John Scrimgeour, of Kirkton, and had issue.

Alexander, councillor-at-law —— *Ayr burghs* 1761-8. See also England, M.P.

Earl of Rosslyn, sergeant-at-law and solicitor-gen. 1771, attorney-gen. 1778, lord chief justice common pleas 1780, advocate 29 June 1754, admitted to Lincoln's Inn 12 May 1763, elected for Castle Rising, Norfolk, and Okehampton, Devon, in 1774, sat for the latter, M.P. Richmond, Yorks. 1768-9, Bishops Castle, Salop 1770, until created Baron Loughborough, of Loughborough, co. Leic. 14 June 1780, lord privy seal 1783, lord high chancellor of Great Britain 1793-1801, created by 2nd patent 31 Oct. 1795, Baron Loughborough, of Loughborough, Surrey, and 21 April 1801, Earl of Rosslyn, co. Midlothian, both creations in default of male issue, with remainder severally and successively to his nephews, Sir James St. Clair Erskine, bart., and John Erskine. He (son of Peter Wedderburn, of Chester Hall, Haddington), b. 13 Feb. 1733, d. s.p. 3 Jan. 1805, having m. 1st, 31 Dec. 1767, Betty Ann, dau. of John Dawson, of Morley, Yorks; she died s.p. 15 Feb. 1781 ; he m. 2ndly, 12 Sept. 1782, Hon. Charlotte Courtenay, dau. of William, 1st Viscount Courtenay (E. DEVON). [See Earl of Rosslyn, Foster's Peerage.

Wedderburn—*continued.*

David (sir), of Ballindean, bart. —— *Perth burghs* 1805-6, 1806-7, 1807-12, [1812-18.

Sir David Wedderburn, of Ballindean, co. Perth, postmaster-gen. Scotland 1823-31, cr. a baronet of the United Kingdom 10 Oct. 1803, with remainder in default of male issue to the heirs male of the body of his great-grandfather, Sir Alexander, 4th bart. aforesaid (son of John Wedderburn); b. 10 March 1775, d. s.p.s. 7 April, 1858, having m. 2 Sept. 1800, Margaret, 2nd dau. of George Brown, of Elliston, co. Roxburgh, a commissioner of excise [she d. 14 Feb. 1845. See Foster's Baronetage.

David (sir), of Ballindean, bart. —— *So. Ayrshire* 1868-74, *Haddington burghs* [1879-80, and since 1880.

3rd bart. (on the death of his father, Sir John, 1862), advocate 1861, capt. so. Glouc. [mil. since 1870; b. 20 Dec. 1835. See Foster's Baronetage.

James —— *Dundee* 1549.
Ancestor of Alexander, M.P.

John, of Gosford —— *Haddington constabulary* 1685-6.

Eldest son of Sir Peter Wedderburn, next named, P.C. before he was 20 years of age, engaged to furnish the king of Denmark with a regiment of his own countrymen, consisting of twelve companies of 100 men each, etc.; shipwrecked off Calais, 26 May 1688; bd. at [Aberlody v.p. s.p.

Peter (sir), of Gosford, knight, senator of the college of justice —— *Haddington constabulary* 1661-3 (advocate), 1665 conv., 1667 conv., 1669-74 (a senator).

Sir Peter Wedderburn, of Gosford, co. Haddington, which he acquired from Sir Alexander Auchmuty, knt., of Gosford, 3 Jan. 1658-9 (brother of Sir Alexander, of Blackness, co. Forfar, sons of James Wedderburn, of Blackness, co. Forfar, and of Dundee, merchant, youngest son of Alexander Wedderburn, of Kingennie, co. Forfar), advocate 1642, knighted by King Charles II. shortly after the Restoration, clerk of privy council, Scotland, July 1661, keeper of the signet for life, with power to appoint his own deputy or deputies, 28 Aug. 1660, a lord of session 17 June 1668; d. 11 Nov. 1679, having m. Agnes, dau. of John Dickson, of Hartree, a judge of the court of session, and had three sons, John, M.P., last named, Sir Peter, cr. a bart. (see Halkett, M.P.), and Alexander, grandfather of Alexander, [Earl of Rosslyn, M.P. 1761.

Weir. See also Vere.

James, merchant burgess —— *Lanark* 1685, 1686 (then designed James Hair?)

Thomas, —— *Edinburgh* 1625 conv.

Welands. See also Newlands.

David —— *Cupar* 1593 (bis) conv., 1594 conv.

William —— *Edinburgh* 1609 conv.

Welch.

(——) —— *Dumfries* 1472.

Welwood.

Thomas Walwood —— *St. Andrews* 1578 conv.

Wemyss. See also Lord Elcho.

WEMYSS OF BOGIE.

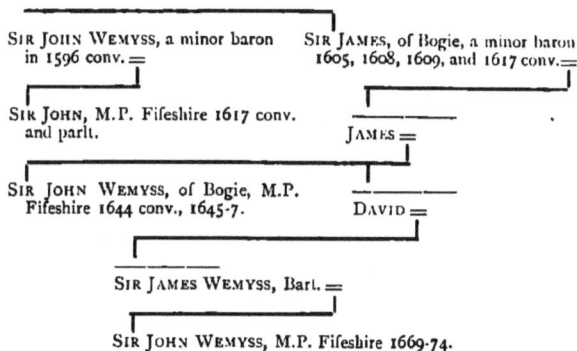

SIR JOHN WEMYSS, a minor baron in 1596 conv. =   SIR JAMES, of Bogie, a minor baron 1605, 1608, 1609, and 1617 conv. =

SIR JOHN, M.P. Fifeshire 1617 conv. and parlt.   JAMES =

SIR JOHN WEMYSS, of Bogie, M.P. Fifeshire 1644 conv., 1645-7.   DAVID =

SIR JAMES WEMYSS, Bart. =

SIR JOHN WEMYSS, M.P. Fifeshire 1669-74.

David, of Fingask —— *Fifeshire* 1650.

Probably descended from David, 3rd son of Sir David Wemyss, of Wemyss.

James (sir), of Bogie, knt. —— 1605 conv., 1608 and 1609 conv. (laird of Bogie, [as a minor baron) —— *Fifeshire* 1617 conv.

Vice-adml. of Scotland 1591, knighted by James VI. (2nd son of Sir David Wemyss, of Wemyss) ; m. 1st, Margaret, dau. of John Melville, of Raith, and 2ndly, Margaret Durie ; [he d. 1640, leaving issue.

James, of Wemyss —— *Fifeshire* 1763-8, *Sutherlandshire* 1768-74, 1774-80, [1780-4.

3rd son of James, 5th Earl of Wemyss, lieut. R.N. ; d. 10 May 1786, aged 60, leaving issue, [a son William, M.P. See Foster's Peerage.

James (capt.), of Wemyss —— *Fifeshire* 1820-6 (younger), 1826-30, 1830-1, [1833-4, 1835-7, 1837-41, (James Erskine-Wemyss) 1841-7.

Of Wemyss Castle and Torrie House, co. Fife, lord-lieut. of the county 1840, rear-adml., R.N. 1850 (son of lt.-gen. William Wemyss, and grandson of James Wemyss, M.P. 1763, last named) ; b. July 1789, d. 3 April 1854, leaving an only son, James, M.P., next named.

James Hay-Erskine, of Wemyss and Torrie —— *Fifeshire* 1859 until his death [s.b. 19 April 1864

Only son of Adml. Erskine-Wemyss, M.P., last named, lieut. and sheriff-principal Fifeshire [1864 ; b. 29 Aug. 1829, and d. 29 March 1864, leaving issue. See Foster's Peerage.

(? Sir John), the laird of Wester Wemyss —— 1596 conv., as a minor baron.

Sir John Wemyss (eldest son of Sir David Wemyss), m. 1st, 1574, Margaret, eldest dau. of William, Earl of Morton ; 2ndly, 1581, Anne Stewart, sister of James, Earl of Moray, [and had a son, Sir John, cr. Earl of Wemyss, next named.

Wemyss—*continued.*

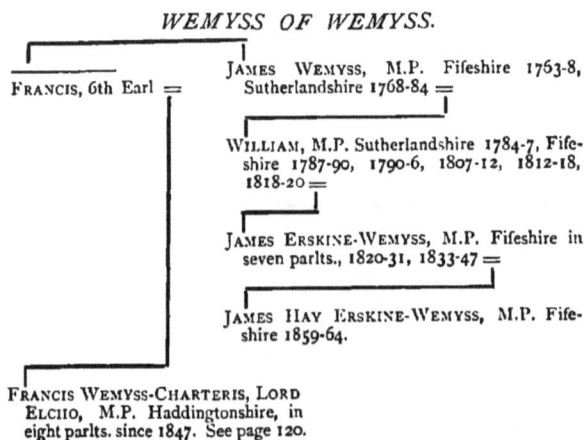

WEMYSS OF WEMYSS.

```
┌─────────────────────────────────────────┐
│                                           JAMES WEMYSS, M.P.  Fifeshire 1763-8,
FRANCIS, 6th Earl ═                          Sutherlandshire 1768-84 ═
                                                │
                                           WILLIAM, M.P. Sutherlandshire 1784-7, Fife-
                                           shire 1787-90, 1790-6, 1807-12, 1812-18,
                                           1818-20 ═
                                                │
                                           JAMES ERSKINE-WEMYSS, M.P. Fifeshire in
                                           seven parlts., 1820-31, 1833-47 ═
                                                │
                                           JAMES HAY ERSKINE-WEMYSS, M.P. Fife-
                                           shire 1859-64.
        │
    FRANCIS WEMYSS-CHARTERIS, LORD
    ELCHO, M.P. Haddingtonshire, in
    eight parlts. since 1847.  See page 120.
```

(Sir John), laird of Wemyss —— *Fifeshire* 1617 conv. and parlt.

> Sir John Wemyss, of Wemyss, cr. a bart. 29 May 1625, Lord Wemyss of Elcno 1 April 1628, and Earl of Wemyss, Lord Elcho and Methel 25 June 1633, high commissioner to the general assembly 23 July 1641, P.C., one of the committee of estates, 1644 (son of Sir John, last named); d. 22 Nov. 1649, having m. 1610, Jean, eldest dau. of Patrick, 7th Lord Gray;
> [she d. 17 Aug. 1640, leaving issue.

John (sir), of Bogie —— *Fifeshire* 1644 conv., (laird) 1645-7, (*Fife and Kinross* [1656-8, WILLIS.)

> Son of James Wemyss, of Bogie, knighted by Charles I.; m. 1st, Margaret, dau. of Sir John Ayton of that ilk, and 2ndly,   dau. of Archibald Johnston, of Warriston, and
> [d. s.p.

John (sir), of Bogie —— *Fifeshire* 1669-74.

> 2nd bart. (on the death of his father, Sir James, so created 12 Oct. 1704); m. Anne, dau. of Sir Wm. Lockart, advocate, and had a son, Sir James, on whose death the baronetcy became
> [dormant. See "CHAOS" in Foster's Baronetage.

William (Mr.) —— 1597 conv.

Willam (lt.-genl.), of Wemyss —— *Sutherlandshire* 1784 (then late colonel Sutherland fencibles) until he accepted the Chiltern hundreds s.b. 1 Aug. 1787; *Fifeshire* 1787-90, 1790-6, 1807-12 (then lt.-genl.), 1812-18, 1818-20.

> Lt.-genl. in the army 1805, raised the Sutherland fencible regt. of 1,000 rank and file, D.A.G. to the forces in North Britain 1786, raised the Sutherland fencibles 1793, and in 1798 commanded at Drogheda during the Irish rebellion, defeated the rebels near Ardee 14 July, and was placed on the Irish staff; he raised the 93rd regt. and was appointed its col. 1800 (son of James Wemyss, M.P. 1763); b. 9 April 1760; d. Feb. 1822, having m. 16 Sept. 1788, Frances, eldest dau. of Sir William Erskine, bart., of Torrie; she d. 1 Feb. 1798,
> [having had with other issue a son James, M.P. 1820.

Whalley.

Henry, judge advocate of the armies in England and Scotland —— *Sheriffdom [of Selkirk and Peebles* 1656-8 (WILLIS).
Said to have been an alderman of London, 3rd son of Richard Whalley, M.P. Borough-
[bridge, and brother of maj.-gen. Edward Whalley, one of King Charles' judges.

Whetham.

Nathan (col.), one of his highness' council —— *St. Andrews, Dysart, Kirkcaldy, [Cupar, Anstruther East, &c.* 1656-8, 1659-60 (WILLIS).
Colonel in the parliamentary army, governor of Portsmouth, was of the council to the lord
protector Oliver Cromwell; born in London about 1603, died at Chard, Somerset, 1668; m.
[twice, and left issue.

White.

John, of Collistoun, merchant trafficker, provost —— *Kirkcaldy* 1669-74.

Robert, of Purim —— *Kirkcaldy* 1645-7, 1650, 1665 conv., provost.

Whitefoord.

John (Quhytefurde) —— *Irvine* 1586 conv.
Son of John Whitefoord of that ilk; he m. 1st, Elizabeth Lindsay, and 2ndly, Elizabeth
[Houston, of that ilk, and d. s.p. 1606.

Whitelaw.

Alexander, of Gartsherrie House, Coatbridge, Lanarkshire —— *Glasgow* 1874
[until his death s.b. 16 July 1879.
J.P. D.L., cos. Dumbarton and Lanark (eldest son of Alexander Whitelaw, of Drumpark,
co. Lanark, by Janet Baird); m. 1859, Barbara Forbes, dau. of Robert Lockhart, esq.,
of Castle Hill, co. Lanark (see SINCLAIR, of STEVENSTON, Foster's Baronetage); d. 1 July
[1879, leaving issue.

Patrick (Mr.) —— *Perth* 1581, 1586 conv.

Wilk.

John (Mr.), of Bromhouse —— *Lanark, Glasgow, &c.* 1654-5 (WILLIS).

Wilkie.

Gawin —— *Selkirk* 1583.
Harie (Mr.), merchant burgess —— *Pittenweem* 1669-74.
John —— *Haddington* 1587 —— 1602 conv.
William —— *Lanark* 1593.
William, commissar, bailie —— *Lanark* 1681-2.

Wilkin.

William —— *Lanark* 1581.

Wilkinson.

Alexander —— *Lauder* 1628-33.

Alexander —— *Lauder* 1639-40 (younger), 1643-4 conv., 1644-6, 1648.

Williamson.

Alexander —— *Peebles* 1661-3 (late provost, now councillor), 1665 conv., 1667 [conv. (provost), 1672-4.

James, of Aikerfield —— *Peeebles* 1621, 1628-33, 1630 conv., 1639-41, 1643 [conv., 1646-7, 1649 (or William Lowis).

Johnne —— *Peebles* 1357.

John —— *Stirling* 1600, 1604, 1605, 1612 (town clerk), 1617 conv. and parlt.

John —— *Kirkcaldy* 1628-33, 1630 conv., 1639-41, 1643-4 (conv.), 1648-9, [1661-3, elder, late bailie.

John, bailie —— *Sanquhar* 1661-3 ; *Kirkcaldy* 1681-2 (elder), late bailie.

Leonard —— *St. Andrews* 1568, in the absence of the provost.

Stephen, of Copley, Cheshire —— *St. Andrews burghs* since 1880. See foot-note.

Thomas —— *Cupar* 1586 conv.

William, town clerk ——*Peebles* 1681-2.

Wilson.

Andrew —— *Burntisland* 1593, 1594 conv.

Archibald, bailie —— *Queensferry* 1661-3, 1665 conv., 1667 conv., 1669-74, [merchant burgess, 1678 conv.

David —— *Anstruther Wester* 1645, 1650.

George, dean of guild —— *Culross* 1681-2.

Samuel —— *Queensferry* 1650, or Robert Hall, elder.

Winrahame.

George (Mr.), of Libbertoun, senator of the college of justice —— *Edinburghshire* [1643-4 conv., 1645 laird, 1649.

Advocate 20 Dec. 1626, colonel of one of the regiments for Edinburghshire for the defence of the country 1649, employed with others to conclude the treaty of Breda, etc., ordinary lord of session 22 June 1649 (son of James Winram, of Libbertoun), mortally wounded at the [battle of Dunbar 3 Sept. 1650, and d. 8 days after.

WILLIAMSON, STEPHEN, of Copley, Cheshire, J.P., and of Liverpool, merchant and ship-owner, vice-president of Liverpool chamber of commerce (eldest son of late Archibald Williamson, esq., of Anstruther, co. Fife) ; b. 1827, m. 1859, Annie, dau. of late Rev. Thomas Guthrie, D.D., of Edinburgh.

Copley, Neston, Cheshire ; Queen Anne Mansions, S.W.

Winrahame—*continued.*

James, of Wistone —— *Lanarkshire* 1640-1.

Wishart.

(——) laird of Pitarrow —— 1592, 1596 conv. and 1597 conv. as a minor baron.

James (Mr.) —— *Montrose* 1593.

Wood.

(——) laird of Largo —— as a minor baron, 1590 conv., 1594 (bis) conv., 1594, [1596 conv., 1599 conv.

George —— *Forfar* 1651.

Harie (sir), of Bonytown —— *Forfarshire* 1628-33.

James, of Ballbigno —— *Kincardineshire* 1649.

James, merchant burgess —— *Kinghorn* 1667 conv., 1669-70.

Ninian —— *Crail* 1583.

Thomas, bailie —— *Lauder* 1661, 1665 conv., 1670-2.

Wooseley.

Robert (master), commissary of Ayrshire —— *Dornoch, Tain, Inverness, &c.* [1656-8 (WILLIS).

Wortley. See Stewart.

Wotherspoon.

Robert or William (Wedderspune) —— *Linlithgow* 1543, 1546.

Y.

Yeaman.

George —— *Perth burghs* 1710-13, 1713-15, then styled master.

James, merchant, of Craigie Cliff, Dundee —— *Dundee* 1873-4, 1874-80.

Of Dundee, ship-owner, provost 1869-72, formerly J.P. co. Forfar (youngest son of late James Yeaman, of Rattray, co. Perth); b. 1816, m. 1843, Jane, youngest dau. of Henry [Tullo, esq., of Dundee.

Young.

Andrew —— *Elgin* 1665 conv.

George, solicitor-genl. for Scotland —— *Wigtown burghs* 1865, 1865-8 (solicitor-genl.), 1868-74, (Q.C., advocate, solicitor-genl. 1869), 1874 (28 May on petition) until appointed a judge of court of session s.b. 15 June following. [See foot-note.

Oliver —— *Perth* 1593, 1594.

Patrick —— *Haddington* 1644 conv., 1646-7 (or Richard Chaipland).

Walter —— *Edinburgh* 1468, an auditor of complaint; 1469, 1471, 1472.

Yuill.

John, provost —— *Inverary* 1661.

YOUNG, RT. HON. GEORGE, P.C., of Silverknowe Cramond, a judge of the court of session since Feb. 1874, advocate 1840, bar.-at-law Middle Temple 1869, sheriff of Inverness-shire 1853-60, of cos. Haddington and Berwick 1860-9, sol.-genl. Scotland 1862-6, 1868-9, lord advocate 1869-74, (eldest son of Alexander Young, of Rosefield, co. Kirkcudbright); b   1819, m.   1846, Janet, dau. of G. Graham Bell, of Crurie, Dumfries, and has with other issue a son,

(1) Alexander, bar.-at-law M.T. 1874, admitted to Lincoln's Inn 6 April 1876.
Silverknowe Cramond, Edinburgh, and 28, *Moray Place.*
Clubs—Brooks', Reform; New, and University (Edinburgh).

www.ingramcontent.com/pod-product-compliance
Lightning Source LLC
Chambersburg PA
CBHW030907270326
41929CB00008B/608